The Data Warehouse Toolkit

The Data Warehouse Toolkit

The Definitive Guide to Dimensional Modeling

Third Edition

Ralph Kimball
Margy Ross

WILEY

The Data Warehouse Toolkit: The Definitive Guide to Dimensional Modeling, Third Edition

Published by
John Wiley & Sons, Inc.
10475 Crosspoint Boulevard
Indianapolis, IN 46256
www.wiley.com

Copyright © 2013 by Ralph Kimball and Margy Ross

Published by John Wiley & Sons, Inc., Indianapolis, Indiana

Published simultaneously in Canada

ISBN: 978-1-118-53080-1
ISBN: 978-1-118-53077-1 (ebk)
ISBN: 978-1-118-73228-1 (ebk)
ISBN: 978-1-118-73219-9 (ebk)

Printed and bound by CPI Group (UK) Ltd, Croydon, CR0 4YY

C9781118530801_260724

About the Authors

Ralph Kimball founded the Kimball Group. Since the mid-1980s, he has been the data warehouse and business intelligence industry's thought leader on the dimensional approach. He has educated tens of thousands of IT professionals. The Toolkit books written by Ralph and his colleagues have been the industry's best sellers since 1996. Prior to working at Metaphor and founding Red Brick Systems, Ralph coinvented the Star workstation, the first commercial product with windows, icons, and a mouse, at Xerox's Palo Alto Research Center (PARC). Ralph has a PhD in electrical engineering from Stanford University.

Margy Ross is president of the Kimball Group. She has focused exclusively on data warehousing and business intelligence since 1982 with an emphasis on business requirements and dimensional modeling. Like Ralph, Margy has taught the dimensional best practices to thousands of students; she also coauthored five Toolkit books with Ralph. Margy previously worked at Metaphor and cofounded DecisionWorks Consulting. She graduated with a BS in industrial engineering from Northwestern University.

Credits

Executive Editor
Robert Elliott

Project Editor
Maureen Spears

Senior Production Editor
Kathleen Wisor

Copy Editor
Apostrophe Editing Services

Editorial Manager
Mary Beth Wakefield

Freelancer Editorial Manager
Rosemarie Graham

Associate Director of Marketing
David Mayhew

Marketing Manager
Ashley Zurcher

Business Manager
Amy Knies

Production Manager
Tim Tate

Vice President and Executive Group Publisher
Richard Swadley

Vice President and Executive Publisher
Neil Edde

Associate Publisher
Jim Minatel

Project Coordinator, Cover
Katie Crocker

Proofreader
Word One, New York

Indexer
Johnna VanHoose Dinse

Cover Image
iStockphoto.com / teekid

Cover Designer
Ryan Sneed

Acknowledgments

First, thanks to the hundreds of thousands who have read our Toolkit books, attended our courses, and engaged us in consulting projects. We have learned as much from you as we have taught. Collectively, you have had a profoundly positive impact on the data warehousing and business intelligence industry. Congratulations!

Our Kimball Group colleagues, Bob Becker, Joy Mundy, and Warren Thornthwaite, have worked with us to apply the techniques described in this book literally thousands of times, over nearly 30 years of working together. Every technique in this book has been thoroughly vetted by practice in the real world. We appreciate their input and feedback on this book—and more important, the years we have shared as business partners, along with Julie Kimball.

Bob Elliott, our executive editor at John Wiley & Sons, project editor Maureen Spears, and the rest of the Wiley team have supported this project with skill and enthusiasm. As always, it has been a pleasure to work with them.

To our families, thank you for your unconditional support throughout our careers. Spouses Julie Kimball and Scott Ross and children Sara Hayden Smith, Brian Kimball, and Katie Ross all contributed in countless ways to this book.

Contents

Introduction

The data warehousing and business intelligence (DW/BI) industry certainly has matured since Ralph Kimball published the first edition of *The Data Warehouse Toolkit* (Wiley) in 1996. Although large corporate early adopters paved the way, DW/BI has since been embraced by organizations of all sizes. The industry has built thousands of DW/BI systems. The volume of data continues to grow as warehouses are populated with increasingly atomic data and updated with greater frequency. Over the course of our careers, we have seen databases grow from megabytes to gigabytes to terabytes to petabytes, yet the basic challenge of DW/BI systems has remained remarkably constant. Our job is to marshal an organization's data and bring it to business users for their decision making. Collectively, you've delivered on this objective; business professionals everywhere are making better decisions and generating payback on their DW/BI investments.

Since the first edition of *The Data Warehouse Toolkit* was published, dimensional modeling has been broadly accepted as the dominant technique for DW/BI presentation. Practitioners and pundits alike have recognized that the presentation of data must be grounded in simplicity if it is to stand any chance of success. Simplicity is the fundamental key that allows users to easily understand databases and software to efficiently navigate databases. In many ways, dimensional modeling amounts to holding the fort against assaults on simplicity. By consistently returning to a business-driven perspective and by refusing to compromise on the goals of user understandability and query performance, you establish a coherent design that serves the organization's analytic needs. This dimensionally modeled framework becomes the *platform for BI*. Based on our experience and the overwhelming feedback from numerous practitioners from companies like your own, we believe that dimensional modeling is absolutely critical to a successful DW/BI initiative.

Dimensional modeling also has emerged as the leading architecture for building integrated DW/BI systems. When you use the conformed dimensions and conformed facts of a set of dimensional models, you have a practical and predictable framework for incrementally building complex DW/BI systems that are inherently distributed.

For all that has changed in our industry, the core dimensional modeling techniques that Ralph Kimball published 17 years ago have withstood the test of time. Concepts such as conformed dimensions, slowly changing dimensions, heterogeneous products, factless fact tables, and the enterprise data warehouse bus matrix continue to be discussed in design workshops around the globe. The original concepts have been embellished and enhanced by new and complementary techniques. We decided to publish this third edition of Kimball's seminal work because we felt that it would be useful to summarize our collective dimensional modeling experience under a single cover. We have each focused exclusively on decision support, data warehousing, and business intelligence for more than three decades. We want to share the dimensional modeling patterns that have emerged repeatedly during the course of our careers. This book is loaded with specific, practical design recommendations based on real-world scenarios.

The goal of this book is to provide a one-stop shop for dimensional modeling techniques. True to its title, it is a toolkit of dimensional design principles and techniques. We address the needs of those just starting in dimensional DW/BI and we describe advanced concepts for those of you who have been at this a while. We believe that this book stands alone in its depth of coverage on the topic of dimensional modeling. It's the definitive guide.

Intended Audience

This book is intended for data warehouse and business intelligence designers, implementers, and managers. In addition, business analysts and data stewards who are active participants in a DW/BI initiative will find the content useful.

Even if you're not directly responsible for the dimensional model, we believe it is important for all members of a project team to be comfortable with dimensional modeling concepts. The dimensional model has an impact on most aspects of a DW/BI implementation, beginning with the translation of business requirements, through the extract, transformation and load (ETL) processes, and finally, to the unveiling of a data warehouse through business intelligence applications. Due to the broad implications, you need to be conversant in dimensional modeling regardless of whether you are responsible primarily for project management, business analysis, data architecture, database design, ETL, BI applications, or education and support. We've written this book so it is accessible to a broad audience.

For those of you who have read the earlier editions of this book, some of the familiar case studies will reappear in this edition; however, they have been updated significantly and fleshed out with richer content, including sample enterprise data warehouse bus matrices for nearly every case study. We have developed vignettes for new subject areas, including big data analytics.

The content in this book is somewhat technical. We primarily discuss dimensional modeling in the context of a relational database with nuances for online analytical processing (OLAP) cubes noted where appropriate. We presume you have basic knowledge of relational database concepts such as tables, rows, keys, and joins. Given we will be discussing dimensional models in a nondenominational manner, we won't dive into specific physical design and tuning guidance for any given database management systems.

Chapter Preview

The book is organized around a series of business vignettes or case studies. We believe developing the design techniques by example is an extremely effective approach because it allows us to share very tangible guidance and the benefits of real world experience. Although not intended to be full-scale application or industry solutions, these examples serve as a framework to discuss the patterns that emerge in dimensional modeling. In our experience, it is often easier to grasp the main elements of a design technique by stepping away from the all-too-familiar complexities of one's own business. Readers of the earlier editions have responded very favorably to this approach.

Be forewarned that we deviate from the case study approach in Chapter 2: Kimball Dimensional Modeling Techniques Overview. Given the broad industry acceptance of the dimensional modeling techniques invented by the Kimball Group, we have consolidated the official listing of our techniques, along with concise descriptions and pointers to more detailed coverage and illustrations of these techniques in subsequent chapters. Although not intended to be read from start to finish like the other chapters, we feel this technique-centric chapter is a useful reference and can even serve as a professional checklist for DW/BI designers.

With the exception of Chapter 2, the other chapters of this book build on one another. We start with basic concepts and introduce more advanced content as the book unfolds. The chapters should be read in order by every reader. For example, it might be difficult to comprehend Chapter 16: Insurance, unless you have read the preceding chapters on retailing, procurement, order management, and customer relationship management.

Those of you who have read the last edition may be tempted to skip the first few chapters. Although some of the early fact and dimension grounding may be familiar turf, we don't want you to sprint too far ahead. You'll miss out on updates to fundamental concepts if you skip ahead too quickly.

NOTE This book is laced with tips (like this note), key concept listings, and chapter pointers to make it more useful and easily referenced in the future.

Chapter 1: Data Warehousing, Business Intelligence, and Dimensional Modeling Primer

The book begins with a primer on data warehousing, business intelligence, and dimensional modeling. We explore the components of the overall DW/BI architecture and establish the core vocabulary used during the remainder of the book. Some of the myths and misconceptions about dimensional modeling are dispelled.

Chapter 2: Kimball Dimensional Modeling Techniques Overview

This chapter describes more than 75 dimensional modeling techniques and patterns. This official listing of the Kimball techniques includes forward pointers to subsequent chapters where the techniques are brought to life in case study vignettes.

Chapter 3: Retail Sales

Retailing is the classic example used to illustrate dimensional modeling. We start with the classic because it is one that we all understand. Hopefully, you won't need to think very hard about the industry because we want you to focus on core dimensional modeling concepts instead. We begin by discussing the four-step process for designing dimensional models. We explore dimension tables in depth, including the date dimension that will be reused repeatedly throughout the book. We also discuss degenerate dimensions, snowflaking, and surrogate keys. Even if you're not a retailer, this chapter is required reading because it is chock full of fundamentals.

Chapter 4: Inventory

We remain within the retail industry for the second case study but turn your attention to another business process. This chapter introduces the enterprise data warehouse bus architecture and the bus matrix with conformed dimensions. These concepts are critical to anyone looking to construct a DW/BI architecture that is integrated and extensible. We also compare the three fundamental types of fact tables: transaction, periodic snapshot, and accumulating snapshot.

Chapter 5: Procurement

This chapter reinforces the importance of looking at your organization's value chain as you plot your DW/BI environment. We also explore a series of basic and advanced techniques for handling slowly changing dimension attributes; we've built on the long-standing foundation of type 1 (overwrite), type 2 (add a row), and type 3 (add a column) as we introduce readers to type 0 and types 4 through 7.

Chapter 6: Order Management

In this case study, we look at the business processes that are often the first to be implemented in DW/BI systems as they supply core business performance metrics—what are we selling to which customers at what price? We discuss dimensions that play multiple roles within a schema. We also explore the common challenges modelers face when dealing with order management information, such as header/ line item considerations, multiple currencies or units of measure, and junk dimensions with miscellaneous transaction indicators.

Chapter 7: Accounting

We discuss the modeling of general ledger information for the data warehouse in this chapter. We describe the appropriate handling of year-to-date facts and multiple fiscal calendars, as well as consolidated fact tables that combine data from multiple business processes. We also provide detailed guidance on dimension attribute hierarchies, from simple denormalized fixed depth hierarchies to bridge tables for navigating more complex ragged, variable depth hierarchies.

Chapter 8: Customer Relationship Management

Numerous DW/BI systems have been built on the premise that you need to better understand and service your customers. This chapter discusses the customer dimension, including address standardization and bridge tables for multivalued dimension attributes. We also describe complex customer behavior modeling patterns, as well as the consolidation of customer data from multiple sources.

Chapter 9: Human Resources Management

This chapter explores several unique aspects of human resources dimensional models, including the situation in which a dimension table begins to behave like a fact table. We discuss packaged analytic solutions, the handling of recursive management hierarchies, and survey questionnaires. Several techniques for handling multivalued skill keyword attributes are compared.

Chapter 10: Financial Services

The banking case study explores the concept of supertype and subtype schemas for heterogeneous products in which each line of business has unique descriptive attributes and performance metrics. Obviously, the need to handle heterogeneous products is not unique to financial services. We also discuss the complicated relationships among accounts, customers, and households.

Chapter 11: Telecommunications

This chapter is structured somewhat differently to encourage you to think critically when performing a dimensional model design review. We start with a dimensional design that looks plausible at first glance. Can you find the problems? In addition, we explore the idiosyncrasies of geographic location dimensions.

Chapter 12: Transportation

In this case study we look at related fact tables at different levels of granularity while pointing out the unique characteristics of fact tables describing segments in a journey or network. We take a closer look at date and time dimensions, covering country-specific calendars and synchronization across multiple time zones.

Chapter 13: Education

We look at several factless fact tables in this chapter. In addition, we explore accumulating snapshot fact tables to handle the student application and research grant proposal pipelines. This chapter gives you an appreciation for the diversity of business processes in an educational institution.

Chapter 14: Healthcare

Some of the most complex models that we have ever worked with are from the healthcare industry. This chapter illustrates the handling of such complexities, including the use of a bridge table to model the multiple diagnoses and providers associated with patient treatment events.

Chapter 15: Electronic Commerce

This chapter focuses on the nuances of clickstream web data, including its unique dimensionality. We also introduce the step dimension that's used to better understand any process that consists of sequential steps.

Chapter 16: Insurance

The final case study reinforces many of the patterns we discussed earlier in the book in a single set of interrelated schemas. It can be viewed as a pulling-it-all-together chapter because the modeling techniques are layered on top of one another.

Chapter 17: Kimball Lifecycle Overview

Now that you are comfortable designing dimensional models, we provide a high-level overview of the activities encountered during the life of a typical DW/BI project. This chapter is a lightning tour of *The Data Warehouse Lifecycle Toolkit*, *Second Edition* (Wiley, 2008) that we coauthored with Bob Becker, Joy Mundy, and Warren Thornthwaite.

Chapter 18: Dimensional Modeling Process and Tasks

This chapter outlines specific recommendations for tackling the dimensional modeling tasks within the Kimball Lifecycle. The first 16 chapters of this book cover dimensional modeling techniques and design patterns; this chapter describes responsibilities, how-tos, and deliverables for the dimensional modeling design activity.

Chapter 19: ETL Subsystems and Techniques

The extract, transformation, and load system consumes a disproportionate share of the time and effort required to build a DW/BI environment. Careful consideration of best practices has revealed 34 subsystems found in almost every dimensional data warehouse back room. This chapter starts with the requirements and constraints that must be considered before designing the ETL system and then describes the 34 extraction, cleaning, conforming, delivery, and management subsystems.

Chapter 20: ETL System Design and Development Process and Tasks

This chapter delves into specific, tactical dos and don'ts surrounding the ETL design and development activities. It is required reading for anyone tasked with ETL responsibilities.

Chapter 21: Big Data Analytics

We focus on the popular topic of big data in the final chapter. Our perspective is that big data is a natural extension of your DW/BI responsibilities. We begin with an overview of several architectural alternatives, including MapReduce and

Hadoop, and describe how these alternatives can coexist with your current DW/BI architecture. We then explore the management, architecture, data modeling, and data governance best practices for big data.

Website Resources

The Kimball Group's website is loaded with complementary dimensional modeling content and resources:

- Register for *Kimball Design Tips* to receive practical guidance about dimensional modeling and DW/BI topics.
- Access the archive of more than 300 *Design Tips* and articles.
- Learn about public and onsite Kimball University classes for quality, vendor-independent education consistent with our experiences and writings.
- Learn about the Kimball Group's consulting services to leverage our decades of DW/BI expertise.
- Pose questions to other dimensionally aware participants on the Kimball Forum.

Summary

The goal of this book is to communicate the official dimensional design and development techniques based on the authors' more than 60 years of experience and hard won lessons in real business environments. DW/BI systems must be driven from the needs of business users, and therefore are designed and presented from a simple dimensional perspective. We are confident you will be one giant step closer to DW/BI success if you buy into this premise.

Now that you know where you are headed, it is time to dive into the details. We'll begin with a primer on DW/BI and dimensional modeling in Chapter 1 to ensure that everyone is on the same page regarding key terminology and architectural concepts.

1

Data Warehousing, Business Intelligence, and Dimensional Modeling Primer

This first chapter lays the groundwork for the following chapters. We begin by considering *data warehousing and business intelligence (DW/BI)* systems from a high-level perspective. You may be disappointed to learn that we don't start with technology and tools—first and foremost, the DW/BI system must consider the needs of the business. With the business needs firmly in hand, we work backwards through the logical and then physical designs, along with decisions about technology and tools.

We drive stakes in the ground regarding the goals of data warehousing and business intelligence in this chapter, while observing the uncanny similarities between the responsibilities of a DW/BI manager and those of a publisher.

With this big picture perspective, we explore dimensional modeling core concepts and establish fundamental vocabulary. From there, this chapter discusses the major components of the Kimball DW/BI architecture, along with a comparison of alternative architectural approaches; fortunately, there's a role for dimensional modeling regardless of your architectural persuasion. Finally, we review common dimensional modeling myths. By the end of this chapter, you'll have an appreciation for the need to be one-half DBA (database administrator) and one-half MBA (business analyst) as you tackle your DW/BI project.

Chapter 1 discusses the following concepts:

- Business-driven goals of data warehousing and business intelligence
- Publishing metaphor for DW/BI systems
- Dimensional modeling core concepts and vocabulary, including fact and dimension tables
- Kimball DW/BI architecture's components and tenets
- Comparison of alternative DW/BI architectures, and the role of dimensional modeling within each
- Misunderstandings about dimensional modeling

Different Worlds of Data Capture and Data Analysis

One of the most important assets of any organization is its information. This asset is almost always used for two purposes: operational record keeping and analytical decision making. Simply speaking, the operational systems are where you put the data in, and the DW/BI system is where you get the data out.

Users of an operational system turn the wheels of the organization. They take orders, sign up new customers, monitor the status of operational activities, and log complaints. The operational systems are optimized to process transactions quickly. These systems almost always deal with one transaction record at a time. They predictably perform the same operational tasks over and over, executing the organization's business processes. Given this execution focus, operational systems typically do not maintain history, but rather update data to reflect the most current state.

Users of a DW/BI system, on the other hand, watch the wheels of the organization turn to evaluate performance. They count the new orders and compare them with last week's orders, and ask why the new customers signed up, and what the customers complained about. They worry about whether operational processes are working correctly. Although they need detailed data to support their constantly changing questions, DW/BI users almost never deal with one transaction at a time. These systems are optimized for high-performance queries as users' questions often require that hundreds or hundreds of thousands of transactions be searched and compressed into an answer set. To further complicate matters, users of a DW/BI system typically demand that historical context be preserved to accurately evaluate the organization's performance over time.

In the first edition of *The Data Warehouse Toolkit* (Wiley, 1996), Ralph Kimball devoted an entire chapter to describe the dichotomy between the worlds of operational processing and data warehousing. At this time, it is widely recognized that the DW/BI system has profoundly different needs, clients, structures, and rhythms than the operational systems of record. Unfortunately, we still encounter supposed DW/BI systems that are mere copies of the operational systems of record stored on a separate hardware platform. Although these environments may address the need to isolate the operational and analytical environments for performance reasons, they do nothing to address the other inherent differences between the two types of systems. Business users are underwhelmed by the usability and performance provided by these pseudo data warehouses; these imposters do a disservice to DW/BI because they don't acknowledge their users have drastically different needs than operational system users.

Goals of Data Warehousing and Business Intelligence

Before we delve into the details of dimensional modeling, it is helpful to focus on the fundamental goals of data warehousing and business intelligence. The goals can be readily developed by walking through the halls of any organization and listening to business management. These recurring themes have existed for more than three decades:

- "We collect tons of data, but we can't access it."
- "We need to slice and dice the data every which way."
- "Business people need to get at the data easily."
- "Just show me what is important."
- "We spend entire meetings arguing about who has the right numbers rather than making decisions."
- "We want people to use information to support more fact-based decision making."

Based on our experience, these concerns are still so universal that they drive the bedrock requirements for the DW/BI system. Now turn these business management quotations into requirements.

- **The DW/BI system must make information easily accessible.** The contents of the DW/BI system must be understandable. The data must be intuitive and obvious to the business user, not merely the developer. The data's structures and labels should mimic the business users' thought processes and vocabulary. Business users want to separate and combine analytic data in endless combinations. The business intelligence tools and applications that access the data must be simple and easy to use. They also must return query results to the user with minimal wait times. We can summarize this requirement by simply saying *simple* and *fast*.
- **The DW/BI system must present information consistently.** The data in the DW/BI system must be credible. Data must be carefully assembled from a variety of sources, cleansed, quality assured, and released only when it is fit for user consumption. Consistency also implies common labels and definitions for the DW/BI system's contents are used across data sources. If two performance measures have the same name, they must mean the same thing. Conversely, if two measures don't mean the same thing, they should be labeled differently.

- **The DW/BI system must adapt to change.** User needs, business conditions, data, and technology are all subject to change. The DW/BI system must be designed to handle this inevitable change gracefully so that it doesn't invalidate existing data or applications. Existing data and applications should not be changed or disrupted when the business community asks new questions or new data is added to the warehouse. Finally, if descriptive data in the DW/BI system must be modified, you must appropriately account for the changes and make these changes transparent to the users.

- **The DW/BI system must present information in a timely way.** As the DW/BI system is used more intensively for operational decisions, raw data may need to be converted into actionable information within hours, minutes, or even seconds. The DW/BI team and business users need to have realistic expectations for what it means to deliver data when there is little time to clean or validate it.

- **The DW/BI system must be a secure bastion that protects the information assets.** An organization's informational crown jewels are stored in the data warehouse. At a minimum, the warehouse likely contains information about what you're selling to whom at what price—potentially harmful details in the hands of the wrong people. The DW/BI system must effectively control access to the organization's confidential information.

- **The DW/BI system must serve as the authoritative and trustworthy foundation for improved decision making.** The data warehouse must have the right data to support decision making. The most important outputs from a DW/BI system are the decisions that are made based on the analytic evidence presented; these decisions deliver the business impact and value attributable to the DW/BI system. The original label that predates DW/BI is still the best description of what you are designing: a decision support system.

- **The business community must accept the DW/BI system to deem it successful.** It doesn't matter that you built an elegant solution using best-of-breed products and platforms. If the business community does not embrace the DW/BI environment and actively use it, you have failed the acceptance test. Unlike an operational system implementation where business users have no choice but to use the new system, DW/BI usage is sometimes optional. Business users will embrace the DW/BI system if it is the "simple and fast" source for actionable information.

Although each requirement on this list is important, the final two are the most critical, and unfortunately, often the most overlooked. Successful data warehousing and business intelligence demands more than being a stellar architect, technician, modeler, or database administrator. With a DW/BI initiative, you have one foot in your information technology (IT) comfort zone while your other foot is on the unfamiliar turf of business users. You must straddle the two, modifying some tried-and-true skills to adapt to the unique demands of DW/BI. Clearly, you need to bring a spectrum of skills to the party to behave like you're a hybrid DBA/MBA.

Publishing Metaphor for DW/BI Managers

With the goals of DW/BI as a backdrop, let's compare the responsibilities of DW/BI managers with those of a publishing editor-in-chief. As the editor of a high-quality magazine, you would have broad latitude to manage the magazine's content, style, and delivery. Anyone with this job title would likely tackle the following activities:

- Understand the readers:
    - Identify their demographic characteristics.
    - Find out what readers want in this kind of magazine.
    - Identify the "best" readers who will renew their subscriptions and buy products from the magazine's advertisers.
    - Find potential new readers and make them aware of the magazine.
- Ensure the magazine appeals to the readers:
    - Choose interesting and compelling magazine content.
    - Make layout and rendering decisions that maximize the readers' pleasure.
    - Uphold high-quality writing and editing standards while adopting a consistent presentation style.
    - Continuously monitor the accuracy of the articles and advertisers' claims.
    - Adapt to changing reader profiles and the availability of new input from a network of writers and contributors.
- Sustain the publication:
    - Attract advertisers and run the magazine profitably.
    - Publish the magazine on a regular basis.
    - Maintain the readers' trust.
    - Keep the business owners happy.

You also can identify items that should be non-goals for the magazine's editor-in-chief, such as building the magazine around a particular printing technology or exclusively putting management's energy into operational efficiencies, such as imposing a technical writing style that readers don't easily understand, or creating an intricate and crowded layout that is difficult to read.

By building the publishing business on a foundation of serving the readers effectively, the magazine is likely to be successful. Conversely, go through the list and imagine what happens if you omit any single item; ultimately, the magazine would have serious problems.

There are strong parallels that can be drawn between being a conventional publisher and being a DW/BI manager. Driven by the needs of the business, DW/BI managers must publish data that has been collected from a variety of sources and edited for quality and consistency. The main responsibility is to serve the readers, otherwise known as business users. The publishing metaphor underscores the need to focus outward on your customers rather than merely focusing inward on products and processes. Although you use technology to deliver the DW/BI system, the technology is at best a means to an end. As such, the technology and techniques used to build the system should not appear directly in your top job responsibilities.

Now recast the magazine publisher's responsibilities as DW/BI manager responsibilities:

- Understand the business users:
    - Understand their job responsibilities, goals, and objectives.
    - Determine the decisions that the business users want to make with the help of the DW/BI system.
    - Identify the "best" users who make effective, high-impact decisions.
    - Find potential new users and make them aware of the DW/BI system's capabilities.
- Deliver high-quality, relevant, and accessible information and analytics to the business users:
    - Choose the most robust, actionable data to present in the DW/BI system, carefully selected from the vast universe of possible data sources in your organization.
    - Make the user interfaces and applications simple and template-driven, explicitly matched to the users' cognitive processing profiles.
    - Make sure the data is accurate and can be trusted, labeling it consistently across the enterprise.
    - Continuously monitor the accuracy of the data and analyses.
    - Adapt to changing user profiles, requirements, and business priorities, along with the availability of new data sources.
- Sustain the DW/BI environment:
    - Take a portion of the credit for the business decisions made using the DW/BI system, and use these successes to justify staffing and ongoing expenditures.
    - Update the DW/BI system on a regular basis.
    - Maintain the business users' trust.
    - Keep the business users, executive sponsors, and IT management happy.

If you do a good job with all these responsibilities, you will be a great DW/BI manager! Conversely, go through the list and imagine what happens if you omit any single item. Ultimately, the environment would have serious problems. Now contrast this view of a DW/BI manager's job with your own job description. Chances are the preceding list is more oriented toward user and business issues and may not even sound like a job in IT. In our opinion, this is what makes data warehousing and business intelligence interesting.

Dimensional Modeling Introduction

Now that you understand the DW/BI system's goals, let's consider the basics of dimensional modeling. *Dimensional modeling* is widely accepted as the preferred technique for presenting analytic data because it addresses two simultaneous requirements:

- Deliver data that's understandable to the business users.
- Deliver fast query performance.

Dimensional modeling is a longstanding technique for making databases simple. In case after case, for more than five decades, IT organizations, consultants, and business users have naturally gravitated to a simple dimensional structure to match the fundamental human need for simplicity. Simplicity is critical because it ensures that users can easily understand the data, as well as allows software to navigate and deliver results quickly and efficiently.

Imagine an executive who describes her business as, "We sell products in various markets and measure our performance over time." Dimensional designers listen carefully to the emphasis on product, market, and time. Most people find it intuitive to think of such a business as a cube of data, with the edges labeled product, market, and time. Imagine slicing and dicing along each of these dimensions. Points inside the cube are where the measurements, such as sales volume or profit, for that combination of product, market, and time are stored. The ability to visualize something as abstract as a set of data in a concrete and tangible way is the secret of understandability. If this perspective seems too simple, good! A data model that starts simple has a chance of remaining simple at the end of the design. A model that starts complicated surely will be overly complicated at the end, resulting in slow query performance and business user rejection. Albert Einstein captured the basic philosophy driving dimensional design when he said, "Make everything as simple as possible, but not simpler."

Although dimensional models are often instantiated in relational database management systems, they are quite different from *third normal form (3NF) models* which seek to remove data redundancies. Normalized 3NF structures divide data into many discrete entities, each of which becomes a relational table. A database of sales orders might start with a record for each order line but turn into a complex spider web diagram as a 3NF model, perhaps consisting of hundreds of normalized tables.

The industry sometimes refers to 3NF models as entity-relationship (ER) models. *Entity-relationship diagrams* (*ER diagrams or ERDs*) are drawings that communicate the relationships between tables. Both 3NF and dimensional models can be represented in ERDs because both consist of joined relational tables; the key difference between 3NF and dimensional models is the degree of normalization. Because both model types can be presented as ERDs, we refrain from referring to 3NF models as ER models; instead, we call them normalized models to minimize confusion.

Normalized 3NF structures are immensely useful in operational processing because an update or insert transaction touches the database in only one place. Normalized models, however, are too complicated for BI queries. Users can't understand, navigate, or remember normalized models that resemble a map of the Los Angeles freeway system. Likewise, most relational database management systems can't efficiently query a normalized model; the complexity of users' unpredictable queries overwhelms the database optimizers, resulting in disastrous query performance. The use of normalized modeling in the DW/BI presentation area defeats the intuitive and high-performance retrieval of data. Fortunately, dimensional modeling addresses the problem of overly complex schemas in the presentation area.

NOTE A dimensional model contains the same information as a normalized model, but packages the data in a format that delivers user understandability, query performance, and resilience to change.

Star Schemas Versus OLAP Cubes

Dimensional models implemented in relational database management systems are referred to as *star schemas* because of their resemblance to a star-like structure. Dimensional models implemented in multidimensional database environments are referred to as *online analytical processing (OLAP) cubes*, as illustrated in Figure 1-1.

If your DW/BI environment includes either star schemas or OLAP cubes, it leverages dimensional concepts. Both stars and cubes have a common logical design with recognizable dimensions; however, the physical implementation differs.

When data is loaded into an OLAP cube, it is stored and indexed using formats and techniques that are designed for dimensional data. Performance aggregations or precalculated summary tables are often created and managed by the OLAP cube engine. Consequently, cubes deliver superior query performance because of the precalculations, indexing strategies, and other optimizations. Business users can drill down or up by adding or removing attributes from their analyses with excellent performance without issuing new queries. OLAP cubes also provide more analytically robust functions that exceed those available with SQL. The downside is that you pay a load performance price for these capabilities, especially with large data sets.

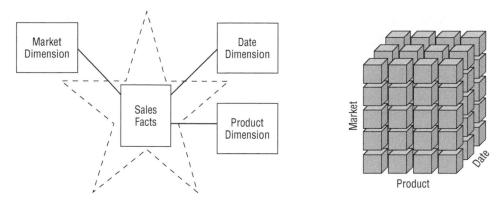

Figure 1-1: Star schema versus OLAP cube.

Fortunately, most of the recommendations in this book pertain regardless of the relational versus multidimensional database platform. Although the capabilities of OLAP technology are continuously improving, we generally recommend that detailed, atomic information be loaded into a star schema; optional OLAP cubes are then populated from the star schema. For this reason, most dimensional modeling techniques in this book are couched in terms of a relational star schema.

OLAP Deployment Considerations

Here are some things to keep in mind if you deploy data into OLAP cubes:

■ A star schema hosted in a relational database is a good physical foundation for building an OLAP cube, and is generally regarded as a more stable basis for backup and recovery.

■ OLAP cubes have traditionally been noted for extreme performance advantages over RDBMSs, but that distinction has become less important with advances in computer hardware, such as appliances and in-memory databases, and RDBMS software, such as columnar databases.

■ OLAP cube data structures are more variable across different vendors than relational DBMSs, thus the final deployment details often depend on which OLAP vendor is chosen. It is typically more difficult to port BI applications between different OLAP tools than to port BI applications across different relational databases.

- OLAP cubes typically offer more sophisticated security options than RDBMSs, such as limiting access to detailed data but providing more open access to summary data.
- OLAP cubes offer significantly richer analysis capabilities than RDBMSs, which are saddled by the constraints of SQL. This may be the main justification for using an OLAP product.
- OLAP cubes gracefully support slowly changing dimension type 2 changes (which are discussed in Chapter 5: Procurement), but cubes often need to be reprocessed partially or totally whenever data is overwritten using alternative slowly changing dimension techniques.
- OLAP cubes gracefully support transaction and periodic snapshot fact tables, but do not handle accumulating snapshot fact tables because of the limitations on overwriting data described in the previous point.
- OLAP cubes typically support complex ragged hierarchies of indeterminate depth, such as organization charts or bills of material, using native query syntax that is superior to the approaches required for RDBMSs.
- OLAP cubes may impose detailed constraints on the structure of dimension keys that implement drill-down hierarchies compared to relational databases.
- Some OLAP products do not enable dimensional roles or aliases, thus requiring separate physical dimensions to be defined.

We'll return to the world of dimensional modeling in a relational platform as we consider the two key components of a star schema.

Fact Tables for Measurements

The *fact table* in a dimensional model stores the performance measurements resulting from an organization's business process events. You should strive to store the low-level measurement data resulting from a business process in a single dimensional model. Because measurement data is overwhelmingly the largest set of data, it should not be replicated in multiple places for multiple organizational functions around the enterprise. Allowing business users from multiple organizations to access a single centralized repository for each set of measurement data ensures the use of consistent data throughout the enterprise.

The term *fact* represents a business measure. Imagine standing in the marketplace watching products being sold and writing down the unit quantity and dollar sales amount for each product in each sales transaction. These measurements are captured as products are scanned at the register, as illustrated in Figure 1-2.

Each row in a fact table corresponds to a measurement event. The data on each row is at a specific level of detail, referred to as the *grain*, such as one row per product sold on a sales transaction. One of the core tenets of dimensional modeling is that all the measurement rows in a fact table must be at the same grain. Having the discipline to create fact tables with a single level of detail ensures that measurements aren't inappropriately double-counted.

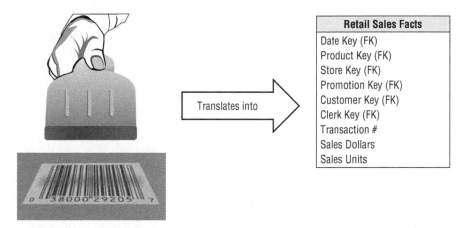

Translates into

Retail Sales Facts
Date Key (FK)
Product Key (FK)
Store Key (FK)
Promotion Key (FK)
Customer Key (FK)
Clerk Key (FK)
Transaction #
Sales Dollars
Sales Units

Figure 1-2: Business process measurement events translate into fact tables.

NOTE   The idea that a measurement event in the physical world has a one-to-one relationship to a single row in the corresponding fact table is a bedrock principle for dimensional modeling. Everything else builds from this foundation.

The most useful facts are numeric and additive, such as dollar sales amount. Throughout this book we will use dollars as the standard currency to make the case study examples more tangible—you can substitute your own local currency if it isn't dollars.

Additivity is crucial because BI applications rarely retrieve a single fact table row. Rather, they bring back hundreds, thousands, or even millions of fact rows at a time, and the most useful thing to do with so many rows is to add them up. No matter how the user slices the data in Figure 1-2, the sales units and dollars sum to a valid total. You will see that facts are sometimes semi-additive or even non-additive. Semi-additive facts, such as account balances, cannot be summed across the time dimension. Non-additive facts, such as unit prices, can never be added. You are forced to use counts and averages or are reduced to printing out the fact rows one at a time—an impractical exercise with a billion-row fact table.

Facts are often described as continuously valued to help sort out what is a fact versus a dimension attribute. The dollar sales amount fact is continuously valued in this example because it can take on virtually any value within a broad range. As an observer, you must stand out in the marketplace and wait for the measurement before you have any idea what the value will be.

It is theoretically possible for a measured fact to be textual; however, the condition rarely arises. In most cases, a textual measurement is a description of something and is drawn from a discrete list of values. The designer should make every effort to put textual data into dimensions where they can be correlated more effectively with the other textual dimension attributes and consume much less space. You should not store redundant textual information in fact tables. Unless the text is unique for every row in the fact table, it belongs in the dimension table. A true text fact is rare because the unpredictable content of a text fact, like a freeform text comment, makes it nearly impossible to analyze.

Referring to the sample fact table in Figure 1-2, if there is no sales activity for a given product, you don't put any rows in the table. It is important that you do not try to fill the fact table with zeros representing no activity because these zeros would overwhelm most fact tables. By including only true activity, fact tables tend to be quite sparse. Despite their sparsity, fact tables usually make up 90 percent or more of the total space consumed by a dimensional model. Fact tables tend to be deep in terms of the number of rows, but narrow in terms of the number of columns. Given their size, you should be judicious about fact table space utilization.

As examples are developed throughout this book, you will see that all fact table grains fall into one of three categories: transaction, periodic snapshot, and accumulating snapshot. Transaction grain fact tables are the most common. We will introduce transaction fact tables in Chapter 3: Retail Sales, and both periodic and accumulating snapshots in Chapter 4: Inventory.

All fact tables have two or more foreign keys (refer to the FK notation in Figure 1-2) that connect to the dimension tables' primary keys. For example, the product key in the fact table always matches a specific product key in the product dimension table. When all the keys in the fact table correctly match their respective primary keys in the corresponding dimension tables, the tables satisfy *referential integrity*. You access the fact table via the dimension tables joined to it.

The fact table generally has its own primary key composed of a subset of the foreign keys. This key is often called a *composite key*. Every table that has a composite key is a fact table. Fact tables express many-to-many relationships. All others are dimension tables.

There are usually a handful of dimensions that together uniquely identify each fact table row. After this subset of the overall dimension list has been identified, the rest of the dimensions take on a single value in the context of the fact table row's primary key. In other words, they go along for the ride.

Dimension Tables for Descriptive Context

Dimension tables are integral companions to a fact table. The dimension tables contain the textual context associated with a business process measurement event. They describe the "who, what, where, when, how, and why" associated with the event.

As illustrated in Figure 1-3, dimension tables often have many columns or attributes. It is not uncommon for a dimension table to have 50 to 100 attributes; although, some dimension tables naturally have only a handful of attributes. Dimension tables tend to have fewer rows than fact tables, but can be wide with many large text columns. Each dimension is defined by a single primary key (refer to the PK notation in Figure 1-3), which serves as the basis for referential integrity with any given fact table to which it is joined.

Product Dimension
Product Key (PK)
SKU Number (Natural Key)
Product Description
Brand Name
Category Name
Department Name
Package Type
Package Size
Abrasive Indicator
Weight
Weight Unit of Measure
Storage Type
Shelf Life Type
Shelf Width
Shelf Height
Shelf Depth
...

Figure 1-3: Dimension tables contain descriptive characteristics of business process nouns.

Dimension attributes serve as the primary source of query constraints, groupings, and report labels. In a query or report request, attributes are identified as the *by* words. For example, when a user wants to see dollar sales by brand, brand must be available as a dimension attribute.

Dimension table attributes play a vital role in the DW/BI system. Because they are the source of virtually all constraints and report labels, dimension attributes are critical to making the DW/BI system usable and understandable. Attributes should consist of real words rather than cryptic abbreviations. You should strive to minimize the use of codes in dimension tables by replacing them with more verbose textual attributes. You may have already trained the business users to memorize operational codes, but going forward, minimize their reliance on miniature notes attached to their monitor for code translations. You should make standard decodes for the operational codes available as dimension attributes to provide consistent labeling on queries, reports, and BI applications. The decode values should never be buried in the reporting applications where inconsistency is inevitable.

Sometimes operational codes or identifiers have legitimate business significance to users or are required to communicate back to the operational world. In these cases, the codes should appear as explicit dimension attributes, in addition to the corresponding user-friendly textual descriptors. Operational codes sometimes have intelligence embedded in them. For example, the first two digits may identify the line of business, whereas the next two digits may identify the global region. Rather than forcing users to interrogate or filter on substrings within the operational codes, pull out the embedded meanings and present them to users as separate dimension attributes that can easily be filtered, grouped, or reported.

In many ways, the data warehouse is only as good as the dimension attributes; the analytic power of the DW/BI environment is directly proportional to the quality and depth of the dimension attributes. The more time spent providing attributes with verbose business terminology, the better. The more time spent populating the domain values in an attribute column, the better. The more time spent ensuring the quality of the values in an attribute column, the better. Robust dimension attributes deliver robust analytic slicing-and-dicing capabilities.

NOTE Dimensions provide the entry points to the data, and the final labels and groupings on all DW/BI analyses.

When triaging operational source data, it is sometimes unclear whether a numeric data element is a fact or dimension attribute. You often make the decision by asking whether the column is a measurement that takes on lots of values and participates in calculations (making it a fact) or is a discretely valued description that is more or less constant and participates in constraints and row labels (making it a dimensional attribute). For example, the standard cost for a product seems like a constant attribute of the product but may be changed so often that you decide it is more like a measured fact. Occasionally, you can't be certain of the classification; it is possible to model the data element either way (or both ways) as a matter of the designer's prerogative.

NOTE The designer's dilemma of whether a numeric quantity is a fact or a dimension attribute is rarely a difficult decision. Continuously valued numeric observations are almost always facts; discrete numeric observations drawn from a small list are almost always dimension attributes.

Figure 1-4 shows that dimension tables often represent hierarchical relationships. For example, products roll up into brands and then into categories. For each row in the product dimension, you should store the associated brand and category description. The hierarchical descriptive information is stored redundantly in the spirit of ease of use and query performance. You should resist the perhaps habitual urge to normalize data by storing only the brand code in the product dimension and creating a separate brand lookup table, and likewise for the category description in a separate category lookup table. This normalization is called *snowflaking*. Instead of third normal form, dimension tables typically are highly denormalized with flattened many-to-one relationships within a single dimension table. Because dimension tables typically are geometrically smaller than fact tables, improving storage efficiency by normalizing or snowflaking has virtually no impact on the overall database size. You should almost always trade off dimension table space for simplicity and accessibility.

Product Key	Product Description	Brand Name	Category Name
1	PowerAll 20 oz	PowerClean	All Purpose Cleaner
2	PowerAll 32 oz	PowerClean	All Purpose Cleaner
3	PowerAll 48 oz	PowerClean	All Purpose Cleaner
4	PowerAll 64 oz	PowerClean	All Purpose Cleaner
5	ZipAll 20 oz	Zippy	All Purpose Cleaner
6	ZipAll 32 oz	Zippy	All Purpose Cleaner
7	ZipAll 48 oz	Zippy	All Purpose Cleaner
8	Shiny 20 oz	Clean Fast	Glass Cleaner
9	Shiny 32 oz	Clean Fast	Glass Cleaner
10	ZipGlass 20 oz	Zippy	Glass Cleaner
11	ZipGlass 32 oz	Zippy	Glass Cleaner

Figure 1-4: Sample rows from a dimension table with denormalized hierarchies.

Contrary to popular folklore, Ralph Kimball didn't invent the terms fact and dimension. As best as can be determined, the dimension and fact terminology originated from a joint research project conducted by General Mills and Dartmouth University in the 1960s. In the 1970s, both AC Nielsen and IRI used the terms consistently to describe their syndicated data offerings and gravitated to dimensional models for simplifying the presentation of their analytic information. They understood that their data wouldn't be used unless it was packaged simply. It is probably accurate to say that no single person invented the dimensional approach. It is an irresistible force in designing databases that always results when the designer places understandability and performance as the highest goals.

Facts and Dimensions Joined in a Star Schema

Now that you understand fact and dimension tables, it's time to bring the building blocks together in a dimensional model, as shown in Figure 1-5. Each business process is represented by a dimensional model that consists of a fact table containing the event's numeric measurements surrounded by a halo of dimension tables that contain the textual context that was true at the moment the event occurred. This characteristic star-like structure is often called a *star join*, a term dating back to the earliest days of relational databases.

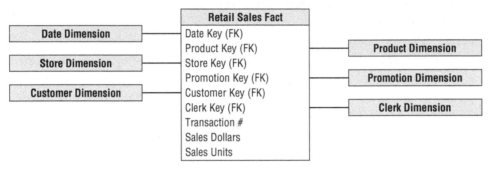

Figure 1-5: Fact and dimension tables in a dimensional model.

The first thing to notice about the dimensional schema is its simplicity and symmetry. Obviously, business users benefit from the simplicity because the data is easier to understand and navigate. The charm of the design in Figure 1-5 is that it is highly recognizable to business users. We have observed literally hundreds of instances in which users immediately agree that the dimensional model is their business. Furthermore, the reduced number of tables and use of meaningful business descriptors make it easy to navigate and less likely that mistakes will occur.

The simplicity of a dimensional model also has performance benefits. Database optimizers process these simple schemas with fewer joins more efficiently. A database engine can make strong assumptions about first constraining the heavily indexed dimension tables, and then attacking the fact table all at once with the Cartesian product of the dimension table keys satisfying the user's constraints. Amazingly, using this approach, the optimizer can evaluate arbitrary n-way joins to a fact table in a single pass through the fact table's index.

Finally, dimensional models are gracefully extensible to accommodate change. The predictable framework of a dimensional model withstands unexpected changes in user behavior. Every dimension is equivalent; all dimensions are symmetrically-equal entry points into the fact table. The dimensional model has no built-in bias regarding expected query patterns. There are no preferences for the business questions asked this month versus the questions asked next month. You certainly don't want to adjust schemas if business users suggest new ways to analyze their business.

This book illustrates repeatedly that the most granular or atomic data has the most dimensionality. Atomic data that has not been aggregated is the most expressive data; this atomic data should be the foundation for every fact table design to withstand business users' ad hoc attacks in which they pose unexpected queries. With dimensional models, you can add completely new dimensions to the schema as long as a single value of that dimension is defined for each existing fact row. Likewise, you can add new facts to the fact table, assuming that the level of detail is consistent with the existing fact table. You can supplement preexisting dimension tables with new, unanticipated attributes. In each case, existing tables can be changed in place either by simply adding new data rows in the table or by executing an SQL ALTER TABLE command. Data would not need to be reloaded, and existing BI applications would continue to run without yielding different results. We examine this graceful extensibility of dimensional models more fully in Chapter 3.

Another way to think about the complementary nature of fact and dimension tables is to see them translated into a report. As illustrated in Figure 1-6, dimension attributes supply the report filters and labeling, whereas the fact tables supply the report's numeric values.

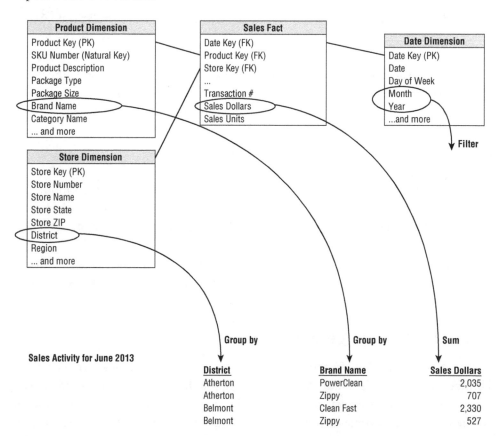

Figure 1-6: Dimensional attributes and facts form a simple report.

You can easily envision the SQL that's written (or more likely generated by a BI tool) to create this report:

```
SELECT
    store.district_name,
    product.brand,
    sum(sales_facts.sales_dollars) AS "Sales Dollars"
FROM
    store,
    product,
    date,
    sales_facts
WHERE
    date.month_name="January" AND
    date.year=2013 AND
    store.store_key = sales_facts.store_key AND
    product.product_key = sales_facts.product_key AND
    date.date_key = sales_facts.date_key
GROUP BY
    store.district_name,
    product.brand
```

If you study this code snippet line-by-line, the first two lines under the SELECT statement identify the dimension attributes in the report, followed by the aggregated metric from the fact table. The FROM clause identifies all the tables involved in the query. The first two lines in the WHERE clause declare the report's filter, and the remainder declare the joins between the dimension and fact tables. Finally, the GROUP BY clause establishes the aggregation within the report.

Kimball's DW/BI Architecture

Let's build on your understanding of DW/BI systems and dimensional modeling fundamentals by investigating the components of a DW/BI environment based on the Kimball architecture. You need to learn the strategic significance of each component to avoid confusing their role and function.

As illustrated in Figure 1-7, there are four separate and distinct components to consider in the DW/BI environment: operational source systems, ETL system, data presentation area, and business intelligence applications.

Operational Source Systems

These are the operational systems of record that capture the business's transactions. Think of the source systems as outside the data warehouse because presumably you have little or no control over the content and format of the data in these operational systems. The main priorities of the source systems are processing performance and availability. Operational queries against source systems are narrow, one-record-at-a-time queries that are part of the normal transaction flow and severely restricted in their demands on the operational system. It is safe to assume that source systems are not queried in the broad and unexpected ways that DW/BI systems typically are queried. Source systems maintain little historical data; a good data warehouse can relieve the source systems of much of the responsibility for representing the past. In many cases, the source systems are special purpose applications without any commitment to sharing common data such as product, customer, geography, or calendar with other operational systems in the organization. Of course, a broadly adopted cross-application enterprise resource planning (ERP) system or operational master data management system could help address these shortcomings.

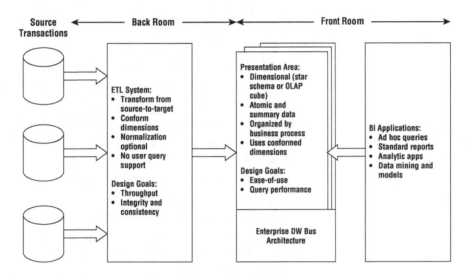

Figure 1-7: Core elements of the Kimball DW/BI architecture.

Extract, Transformation, and Load System

The *extract, transformation, and load (ETL) system* of the DW/BI environment consists of a work area, instantiated data structures, and a set of processes. The ETL system is everything between the operational source systems and the DW/BI presentation area. We elaborate on the architecture of ETL systems and associated techniques in Chapter 19: ETL Subsystems and Techniques, but we want to introduce this fundamental piece of the overall DW/BI system puzzle.

Extraction is the first step in the process of getting data into the data warehouse environment. *Extracting* means reading and understanding the source data and copying the data needed into the ETL system for further manipulation. At this point, the data belongs to the data warehouse.

After the data is extracted to the ETL system, there are numerous potential transformations, such as cleansing the data (correcting misspellings, resolving domain conflicts, dealing with missing elements, or parsing into standard formats), combining data from multiple sources, and de-duplicating data. The ETL system adds value to the data with these cleansing and conforming tasks by changing the data and enhancing it. In addition, these activities can be architected to create diagnostic metadata, eventually leading to business process reengineering to improve data quality in the source systems over time.

The final step of the ETL process is the physical structuring and loading of data into the presentation area's target dimensional models. Because the primary mission of the ETL system is to hand off the dimension and fact tables in the delivery step, these subsystems are critical. Many of these defined subsystems focus on dimension table processing, such as surrogate key assignments, code lookups to provide appropriate descriptions, splitting, or combining columns to present the appropriate data values, or joining underlying third normal form table structures into flattened denormalized dimensions. In contrast, fact tables are typically large and time consuming to load, but preparing them for the presentation area is typically straightforward. When the dimension and fact tables in a dimensional model have been updated, indexed, supplied with appropriate aggregates, and further quality assured, the business community is notified that the new data has been published.

There remains industry consternation about whether the data in the ETL system should be repurposed into physical normalized structures prior to loading into the presentation area's dimensional structures for querying and reporting. The ETL system is typically dominated by the simple activities of sorting and sequential processing. In many cases, the ETL system is not based on relational technology but instead may rely on a system of flat files. After validating the data for conformance with the defined one-to-one and many-to-one business rules, it may be pointless to take the final step of building a 3NF physical database, just before transforming the data once again into denormalized structures for the BI presentation area.

However, there are cases in which the data arrives at the doorstep of the ETL system in a 3NF relational format. In these situations, the ETL system developers may be more comfortable performing the cleansing and transformation tasks using normalized structures. Although a normalized database for ETL processing is acceptable, we have some reservations about this approach. The creation of both normalized structures for the ETL and dimensional structures for presentation means that the data is potentially extracted, transformed, and loaded twice—once into the normalized database and then again when you load the dimensional model. Obviously, this two-step process requires more time and investment for the development, more time for the periodic loading or updating of data, and more capacity to store the multiple copies of the data. At the bottom line, this typically translates into the need for larger development, ongoing support, and hardware platform budgets.

Unfortunately, some DW/BI initiatives have failed miserably because they focused all their energy and resources on constructing the normalized structures rather than allocating time to developing a dimensional presentation area that supports improved business decision making. Although enterprise-wide data consistency is a fundamental goal of the DW/BI environment, there may be effective and less costly approaches than physically creating normalized tables in the ETL system, if these structures don't already exist.

> **NOTE** It is acceptable to create a normalized database to support the ETL processes; however, this is not the end goal. The normalized structures must be off-limits to user queries because they defeat the twin goals of understandability and performance.

Presentation Area to Support Business Intelligence

The DW/BI *presentation area* is where data is organized, stored, and made available for direct querying by users, report writers, and other analytical BI applications. Because the back room ETL system is off-limits, the presentation area is the DW/BI environment as far as the business community is concerned; it is all the business sees and touches via their access tools and BI applications. The original pre-release working title for the first edition of *The Data Warehouse Toolkit* was *Getting the Data Out*. This is what the presentation area with its dimensional models is all about.

We have several strong opinions about the presentation area. First of all, we insist that the data be presented, stored, and accessed in dimensional schemas, either relational star schemas or OLAP cubes. Fortunately, the industry has matured to the point where we're no longer debating this approach; it has concluded that dimensional modeling is the most viable technique for delivering data to DW/BI users.

Our second stake in the ground about the presentation area is that it must contain detailed, atomic data. Atomic data is required to withstand assaults from unpredictable ad hoc user queries. Although the presentation area also may contain performance-enhancing aggregated data, it is not sufficient to deliver these summaries without the underlying granular data in a dimensional form. In other words, it is completely unacceptable to store only summary data in dimensional models while the atomic data is locked up in normalized models. It is impractical to expect a user to drill down through dimensional data almost to the most granular level and then lose the benefits of a dimensional presentation at the final step. Although DW/BI users and applications may look infrequently at a single line item on an order, they may be very interested in last week's orders for products of a given size (or flavor, package type, or manufacturer) for customers who first purchased within the last 6 months (or reside in a given state or have certain credit terms). The most finely grained data must be available in the presentation area so that users can ask the most precise questions possible. Because users' requirements are unpredictable and constantly changing, you must provide access to the exquisite details so they can roll up to address the questions of the moment.

The presentation data area should be structured around business process measurement events. This approach naturally aligns with the operational source data capture systems. Dimensional models should correspond to physical data capture events; they should not be designed to deliver the report-of-the-day. An enterprise's business processes cross the boundaries of organizational departments and functions. In other words, you should construct a single fact table for atomic sales metrics rather than populating separate similar, but slightly different, databases containing sales metrics for the sales, marketing, logistics, and finance teams.

All the dimensional structures must be built using common, conformed dimensions. This is the basis of the *enterprise data warehouse bus architecture* described in Chapter 4. Adherence to the bus architecture is the final stake in the ground for the presentation area. Without shared, conformed dimensions, a dimensional model becomes a standalone application. Isolated stovepipe data sets that cannot be tied together are the bane of the DW/BI movement as they perpetuate incompatible views of the enterprise. If you have any hope of building a robust and integrated DW/BI environment, you must commit to the enterprise bus architecture. When dimensional models have been designed with conformed dimensions, they can be readily combined and used together. The presentation area in a large enterprise DW/BI solution ultimately consists of dozens of dimensional models with many of the associated dimension tables shared across fact tables.

Using the bus architecture is the secret to building distributed DW/BI systems. When the bus architecture is used as a framework, you can develop the enterprise data warehouse in an agile, decentralized, realistically scoped, iterative manner.

NOTE   Data in the queryable presentation area of the DW/BI system must be dimensional, atomic (complemented by performance-enhancing aggregates), business process-centric, and adhere to the enterprise data warehouse bus architecture. The data must not be structured according to individual departments' interpretation of the data.

Business Intelligence Applications

The final major component of the Kimball DW/BI architecture is the *business intelligence (BI) application*. The term BI application loosely refers to the range of capabilities provided to business users to leverage the presentation area for analytic decision making.

By definition, all BI applications query the data in the DW/BI presentation area. Querying, obviously, is the whole point of using data for improved decision making.

A BI application can be as simple as an ad hoc query tool or as complex as a sophisticated data mining or modeling application. Ad hoc query tools, as powerful as they are, can be understood and used effectively by only a small percentage of the potential DW/BI business user population. Most business users will likely access the data via prebuilt parameter-driven applications and templates that do not require users to construct queries directly. Some of the more sophisticated applications, such as modeling or forecasting tools, may upload results back into the operational source systems, ETL system, or presentation area.

Restaurant Metaphor for the Kimball Architecture

One of our favorite metaphors reinforces the importance of separating the overall DW/BI environment into distinct components. In this case, we'll consider the similarities between a restaurant and the DW/BI environment.

ETL in the Back Room Kitchen

The ETL system is analogous to the kitchen of a restaurant. The restaurant's kitchen is a world unto itself. Talented chefs take raw materials and transform them into appetizing, delicious meals for the restaurant's diners. But long before a commercial kitchen swings into operation, a significant amount of planning goes into designing the workspace layout and components.

The kitchen is organized with several design goals in mind. First, the layout must be highly efficient. Restaurant managers want high kitchen throughput. When the restaurant is packed and everyone is hungry, there is no time for wasted movement. Delivering consistent quality from the restaurant's kitchen is the second important goal. The establishment is doomed if the plates coming out of the kitchen repeatedly fail to meet expectations. To achieve consistency, chefs create their special sauces once in the kitchen, rather than sending ingredients out to the table where variations will inevitably occur. Finally, the kitchen's output, the meals delivered to restaurant customers, must also be of high integrity. You wouldn't want someone to get food poisoning from dining at your restaurant. Consequently, kitchens are designed with integrity in mind; salad preparation doesn't happen on the same surfaces where raw chicken is handled.

Just as quality, consistency, and integrity are major considerations when designing the restaurant's kitchen, they are also ongoing concerns for everyday management of the restaurant. Chefs strive to obtain the best raw materials possible. Procured products must meet quality standards and are rejected if they don't meet minimum standards. Most fine restaurants modify their menus based on the availability of quality ingredients.

The restaurant staffs its kitchen with skilled professionals wielding the tools of their trade. Cooks manipulate razor-sharp knives with incredible confidence and ease. They operate powerful equipment and work around extremely hot surfaces without incident.

Given the dangerous surroundings, the back room kitchen is off limits to restaurant patrons. Things happen in the kitchen that customers just shouldn't see. It simply isn't safe. Professional cooks handling sharp knives shouldn't be distracted by diners' inquiries. You also wouldn't want patrons entering the kitchen to dip their fingers into a sauce to see whether they want to order an entree. To prevent these intrusions, most restaurants have a closed door that separates the kitchen from the area where diners are served. Even restaurants that boast an open kitchen format typically have a barrier, such as a partial wall of glass, separating the two environments. Diners are invited to watch but can't wander into the kitchen. Although part of the kitchen may be visible, there are always out-of-view back rooms where the less visually desirable preparation occurs.

The data warehouse's ETL system resembles the restaurant's kitchen. Source data is magically transformed into meaningful, presentable information. The back room ETL system must be laid out and architected long before any data is extracted from the source. Like the kitchen, the ETL system is designed to ensure throughput. It must transform raw source data into the target model efficiently, minimizing unnecessary movement.

Obviously, the ETL system is also highly concerned about data quality, integrity, and consistency. Incoming data is checked for reasonable quality as it enters. Conditions are continually monitored to ensure ETL outputs are of high integrity. Business rules to consistently derive value-add metrics and attributes are applied once by skilled professionals in the ETL system rather than relying on each patron to develop them independently. Yes, that puts extra burden on the ETL team, but it's done to deliver a better, more consistent product to the DW/BI patrons.

NOTE A properly designed DW/BI environment trades off work in the front room BI applications in favor of work in the back room ETL system. Front room work must be done over and over by business users, whereas back room work is done once by the ETL staff.

Finally, ETL system should be off limits to the business users and BI application developers. Just as you don't want restaurant patrons wandering into the kitchen and potentially consuming semi-cooked food, you don't want busy ETL professionals distracted by unpredictable inquiries from BI users. The consequences might be highly unpleasant if users dip their fingers into interim staging pots while data preparation is still in process. As with the restaurant kitchen, activities occur in the ETL system that the DW/BI patrons shouldn't see. When the data is ready and quality checked for user consumption, it's brought through the doorway into the DW/BI presentation area.

Data Presentation and BI in the Front Dining Room

Now turn your attention to the restaurant's dining room. What are the key factors that differentiate restaurants? According to the popular restaurant ratings and reviews, restaurants are typically scored on four distinct qualities:

- Food (quality, taste, and presentation)
- Decor (appealing, comfortable surroundings for the patrons)
- Service (prompt food delivery, attentive support staff, and food received as ordered)
- Cost

Most patrons focus initially on the food score when they're evaluating dining options. First and foremost, does the restaurant serve good food? That's the restaurant's primary deliverable. However, the decor, service, and cost factors also affect the patrons' overall dining experience and are considerations when evaluating whether to eat at a restaurant.

Of course, the primary deliverable from the DW/BI kitchen is the data in the presentation area. What data is available? Like the restaurant, the DW/BI system provides "menus" to describe what's available via metadata, published reports, and parameterized analytic applications. The DW/BI patrons expect consistency and high quality. The presentation area's data must be properly prepared and safe to consume.

The presentation area's decor should be organized for the patrons' comfort. It must be designed based on the preferences of the BI diners, not the development staff. Service is also critical in the DW/BI system. Data must be delivered, as ordered, promptly in a form that is appealing to the business user or BI application developer.

Finally, cost is a factor for the DW/BI system. The kitchen staff may be dreaming up elaborate, expensive meals, but if there's no market at that price point, the restaurant won't survive.

If restaurant patrons like their dining experience, then everything is rosy for the restaurant manager. The dining room is always busy; sometimes there's even a waiting list. The restaurant manager's performance metrics are all promising: high numbers of diners, table turnovers, and nightly revenue and profit, while staff turnover is low. Things look so good that the restaurant's owner is considering an expansion site to handle the traffic. On the other hand, if the restaurant's diners aren't happy, things go downhill in a hurry. With a limited number of patrons, the restaurant isn't making enough money to cover its expenses, and the staff isn't making any tips. In a relatively short time, the restaurant closes.

Restaurant managers often proactively check on their diners' satisfaction with the food and dining experience. If a patron is unhappy, they take immediate action to rectify the situation. Similarly, DW/BI managers should proactively monitor satisfaction. You can't afford to wait to hear complaints. Often, people will abandon a restaurant without even voicing their concerns. Over time, managers notice that diner counts have dropped but may not even know why.

Inevitably, the prior DW/BI patrons will locate another "restaurant" that better suits their needs and preferences, wasting the millions of dollars invested to design, build, and staff the DW/BI system. Of course, you can prevent this unhappy ending by managing the restaurant proactively; make sure the kitchen is properly organized and utilized to deliver as needed to the presentation area's food, decor, service, and cost.

Alternative DW/BI Architectures

Having just described the Kimball architecture, let's discuss several other DW/BI architectural approaches. We'll quickly review the two dominant alternatives to the Kimball architecture, highlighting the similarities and differences. We'll then close this section by focusing on a hybrid approach that combines alternatives.

Fortunately, over the past few decades, the differences between the Kimball architecture and the alternatives have softened. Even more fortunate, there's a role for dimensional modeling regardless of your architectural predisposition.

We acknowledge that organizations have successfully constructed DW/BI systems based on the approaches advocated by others. We strongly believe that rather than encouraging more consternation over our philosophical differences, the industry would be far better off devoting energy to ensure that our DW/BI deliverables are broadly accepted by the business to make better, more informed decisions. The architecture should merely be a means to this objective.

Independent Data Mart Architecture

With this approach, analytic data is deployed on a departmental basis without concern to sharing and integrating information across the enterprise, as illustrated in Figure 1-8. Typically, a single department identifies requirements for data from an operational source system. The department works with IT staff or outside consultants to construct a database that satisfies their departmental needs, reflecting their business rules and preferred labeling. Working in isolation, this departmental data mart addresses the department's analytic requirements.

Meanwhile, another department is interested in the same source data. It's extremely common for multiple departments to be interested in the same performance metrics resulting from an organization's core business process events. But because this department doesn't have access to the data mart initially constructed by the other department, it proceeds down a similar path on its own, obtaining resources and building a departmental solution that contains similar, but slightly different data. When business users from these two departments discuss organizational performance based on reports from their respective repositories, not surprisingly, none of the numbers match because of the differences in business rules and labeling.

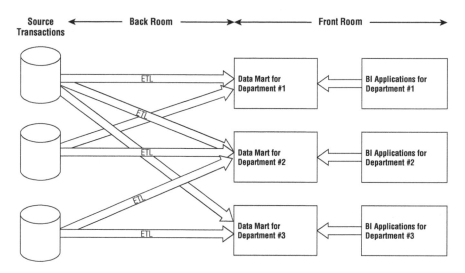

Figure 1-8: Simplified illustration of the independent data mart "architecture."

These standalone analytic silos represent a DW/BI "architecture" that's essentially un-architected. Although no industry leaders advocate these independent data marts, this approach is prevalent, especially in large organizations. It mirrors the way many organizations fund IT projects, plus it requires zero cross-organizational data governance and coordination. It's the path of least resistance for fast development at relatively low cost, at least in the short run. Of course, multiple uncoordinated extracts from the same operational sources and redundant storage of analytic data are inefficient and wasteful in the long run. Without any enterprise perspective, this independent approach results in myriad standalone point solutions that perpetuate incompatible views of the organization's performance, resulting in unnecessary organizational debate and reconciliation.

We strongly discourage the independent data mart approach. However, often these independent data marts have embraced dimensional modeling because they're interested in delivering data that's easy for the business to understand and highly responsive to queries. So our concepts of dimensional modeling are often applied in this architecture, despite the complete disregard for some of our core tenets, such as focusing on atomic details, building by business process instead of department, and leveraging conformed dimensions for enterprise consistency and integration.

Hub-and-Spoke Corporate Information Factory Inmon Architecture

The hub-and-spoke Corporate Information Factory (CIF) approach is advocated by Bill Inmon and others in the industry. Figure 1-9 illustrates a simplified version of the CIF, focusing on the core elements and concepts that warrant discussion.

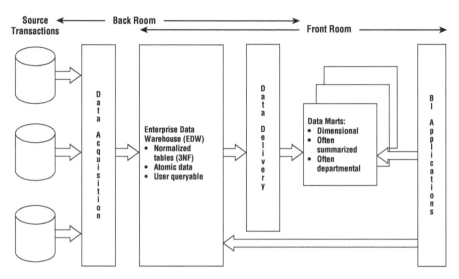

Figure 1-9: Simplified illustration of the hub-and-spoke Corporate Information Factory architecture.

With the CIF, data is extracted from the operational source systems and processed through an ETL system sometimes referred to as data acquisition. The atomic data that results from this processing lands in a 3NF database; this normalized, atomic repository is referred to as the Enterprise Data Warehouse (EDW) within the CIF architecture. Although the Kimball architecture enables optional normalization to support ETL processing, the normalized EDW is a mandatory construct in the CIF. Like the Kimball approach, the CIF advocates enterprise data coordination and integration. The CIF says the normalized EDW fills this role, whereas the Kimball architecture stresses the importance of an enterprise bus with conformed dimensions.

NOTE   The process of normalization does not technically speak to integration. Normalization simply creates physical tables that implement many-to-one relationships. Integration, on the other hand, requires that inconsistencies arising from separate sources be resolved. Separate incompatible database sources can be normalized to the hilt without addressing integration. The Kimball architecture based on conformed dimensions reverses this logic and focuses on resolving data inconsistencies without explicitly requiring normalization.

Organizations who have adopted the CIF approach often have business users accessing the EDW repository due to its level of detail or data availability timeliness. However, subsequent ETL data delivery processes also populate downstream reporting and analytic environments to support business users. Although often dimensionally structured, the resultant analytic databases typically differ from structures in the Kimball architecture's presentation area in that they're frequently departmentally-centric (rather than organized around business processes) and populated with aggregated data (rather than atomic details). If the data delivery ETL processes apply business rules beyond basic summarization, such as departmental renaming of columns or alternative calculations, it may be difficult to tie these analytic databases to the EDW's atomic repository.

NOTE   The most extreme form of a pure CIF architecture is unworkable as a data warehouse, in our opinion. Such an architecture locks the atomic data in difficult-to-query normalized structures, while delivering departmentally incompatible data marts to different groups of business users. But before being too depressed by this view, stay tuned for the next section.

Hybrid Hub-and-Spoke and Kimball Architecture

The final architecture warranting discussion is the marriage of the Kimball and Inmon CIF architectures. As illustrated in Figure 1-10, this architecture populates a CIF-centric EDW that is completely off-limits to business users for analysis and reporting. It's merely the source to populate a Kimball-esque presentation area in which the data is dimensional, atomic (complemented by aggregates), process-centric, and conforms to the enterprise data warehouse bus architecture.

Some proponents of this blended approach claim it's the best of both worlds. Yes, it blends the two enterprise-oriented approaches. It may leverage a preexisting investment in an integrated repository, while addressing the performance and usability issues associated with the 3NF EDW by offloading queries to the dimensional presentation area. And because the end deliverable to the business users and BI applications is constructed based on Kimball tenets, who can argue with the approach?

If you've already invested in the creation of a 3NF EDW, but it's not delivering on the users' expectations of fast and flexible reporting and analysis, this hybrid approach might be appropriate for your organization. If you're starting with a blank sheet of paper, the hybrid approach will likely cost more time and money, both during development and ongoing operation, given the multiple movements of data and redundant storage of atomic details. If you have the appetite, the perceived need, and perhaps most important, the budget and organizational patience to fully normalize and instantiate your data before loading it into dimensional structures that are well designed according to the Kimball methods, go for it.

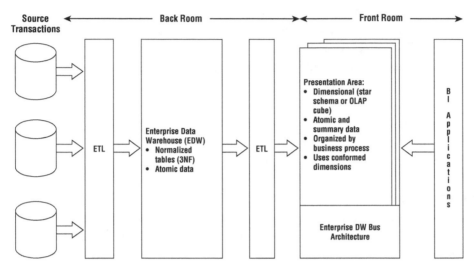

Figure 1-10: Hybrid architecture with 3NF structures and dimensional Kimball presentation area.

Dimensional Modeling Myths

Despite the widespread acceptance of dimensional modeling, some misperceptions persist in the industry. These false assertions are a distraction, especially when you want to align your team around common best practices. If folks in your organization continually lob criticisms about dimensional modeling, this section should be on their recommended reading list; their perceptions may be clouded by these common misunderstandings.

Myth 1: Dimensional Models are Only for Summary Data

This first myth is frequently the root cause of ill-designed dimensional models. Because you can't possibly predict all the questions asked by business users, you need to provide them with queryable access to the most detailed data so they can roll it up based on the business question. Data at the lowest level of detail is practically impervious to surprises or changes. Summary data should complement the granular detail solely to provide improved performance for common queries, but not replace the details.

A related corollary to this first myth is that only a limited amount of historical data should be stored in dimensional structures. Nothing about a dimensional model prohibits storing substantial history. The amount of history available in dimensional models must only be driven by the business's requirements.

Myth 2: Dimensional Models are Departmental, Not Enterprise

Rather than drawing boundaries based on organizational departments, dimensional models should be organized around business processes, such as orders, invoices, and service calls. Multiple business functions often want to analyze the same metrics resulting from a single business process. Multiple extracts of the same source data that create multiple, inconsistent analytic databases should be avoided.

Myth 3: Dimensional Models are Not Scalable

Dimensional models are extremely scalable. Fact tables frequently have billions of rows; fact tables containing 2 trillion rows have been reported. The database vendors have wholeheartedly embraced DW/BI and continue to incorporate capabilities into their products to optimize dimensional models' scalability and performance.

Both normalized and dimensional models contain the same information and data relationships; the logical content is identical. Every data relationship expressed in one model can be accurately expressed in the other. Both normalized and dimensional models can answer exactly the same questions, albeit with varying difficulty.

Myth 4: Dimensional Models are Only for Predictable Usage

Dimensional models should not be designed by focusing on predefined reports or analyses; the design should center on measurement processes. Obviously, it's important to consider the BI application's filtering and labeling requirements. But you shouldn't design for a top ten list of reports in a vacuum because this list is bound to change, making the dimensional model a moving target. The key is to focus on the organization's measurement events that are typically stable, unlike analyses that are constantly evolving.

A related corollary is that dimensional models aren't responsive to changing business needs. On the contrary, because of their symmetry, dimensional structures are extremely flexible and adaptive to change. The secret to query flexibility is building fact tables at the most granular level. Dimensional models that deliver only summary data are bound to be problematic; users run into analytic brick walls when they try to drill down into details not available in the summary tables. Developers also run into brick walls because they can't easily accommodate new dimensions, attributes, or facts with these prematurely summarized tables. The correct starting point for your dimensional models is to express data at the lowest detail possible for maximum flexibility and extensibility. Remember, when you pre-suppose the business question, you'll likely pre-summarize the data, which can be fatal in the long run.

As the architect Mies van der Rohe is credited with saying, "God is in the details." Delivering dimensional models populated with the most detailed data possible ensures maximum flexibility and extensibility. Delivering anything less in your dimensional models undermines the foundation necessary for robust business intelligence.

Myth 5: Dimensional Models Can't Be Integrated

Dimensional models most certainly can be integrated if they conform to the enterprise data warehouse bus architecture. Conformed dimensions are built and maintained as centralized, persistent master data in the ETL system and then reused across dimensional models to enable data integration and ensure semantic consistency. Data integration depends on standardized labels, values, and definitions. It is hard work to reach organizational consensus and then implement the corresponding ETL rules, but you can't dodge the effort, regardless of whether you're populating normalized or dimensional models.

Presentation area databases that don't adhere to the bus architecture with shared conformed dimensions lead to standalone solutions. You can't hold dimensional modeling responsible for organizations' failure to embrace one of its fundamental tenets.

More Reasons to Think Dimensionally

The majority of this book focuses on dimensional modeling for designing databases in the DW/BI presentation area. But dimensional modeling concepts go beyond the design of simple and fast data structures. You should think dimensionally at other critical junctures of a DW/BI project.

When gathering requirements for a DW/BI initiative, you need to listen for and then synthesize the findings around business processes. Sometimes teams get lulled into focusing on a set of required reports or dashboard gauges. Instead you should constantly ask yourself about the business process measurement events producing the report or dashboard metrics. When specifying the project's scope, you must stand firm to focus on a single business process per project and not sign up to deploy a dashboard that covers a handful of them in a single iteration.

Although it's critical that the DW/BI team concentrates on business processes, it's equally important to get IT and business management on the same wavelength. Due to historical IT funding policies, the business may be more familiar with departmental data deployments. You need to shift their mindset about the DW/BI rollout to a process perspective. When prioritizing opportunities and developing the DW/BI roadmap, business processes are the unit of work. Fortunately, business management typically embraces this approach because it mirrors their thinking about key performance indicators. Plus, they've lived with the inconsistencies, incessant debates, and never ending reconciliations caused by the departmental approach, so they're ready for a fresh tactic. Working with business leadership partners, rank each business process on business value and feasibility, then tackle processes with the highest impact and feasibility scores first. Although prioritization is a joint activity with the business, your underlying understanding of the organization's business processes is essential to its effectiveness and subsequent actionability.

If tasked with drafting the DW/BI system's data architecture, you need to wrap your head around the organization's processes, along with the associated master descriptive dimension data. The prime deliverable for this activity, the enterprise data warehouse bus matrix, will be fully vetted in Chapter 4. The matrix also serves as a useful tool for touting the potential benefits of a more rigorous master data management platform.

Data stewardship or governance programs should focus first on the major dimensions. Depending on the industry, the list might include date, customer, product, employee, facility, provider, student, faculty, account, and so on. Thinking about the central nouns used to describe the business translates into a list of data governance efforts to be led by subject matter experts from the business community. Establishing data governance responsibilities for these nouns is the key to eventually deploying dimensions that deliver consistency and address the business's needs for analytic filtering, grouping, and labeling. Robust dimensions translate into robust DW/BI systems.

As you can see, the fundamental motivation for dimensional modeling is front and center long before you design star schemas or OLAP cubes. Likewise, the dimensional model will remain in the forefront during the subsequent ETL system and BI application designs. Dimensional modeling concepts link the business and technical communities together as they jointly design the DW/BI deliverables. We'll elaborate on these ideas in Chapter 17: Kimball DW/BI Lifecycle Overview and Chapter 18: Dimensional Modeling Process and Tasks, but wanted to plant the seeds early so they have time to germinate.

Agile Considerations

Currently, there's significant interest within the DW/BI industry on *agile development* practices. At the risk of oversimplification, agile methodologies focus on manageably sized increments of work that can be completed within reasonable timeframes measured in weeks, rather than tackling a much larger scoped (and hence riskier) project with deliverables promised in months or years. Sounds good, doesn't it?

Many of the core tenets of agile methodologies align with Kimball best practices, including

- Focus on delivering business value. This has been the Kimball mantra for decades.
- Value collaboration between the development team and business stakeholders. Like the agile camp, we strongly encourage a close partnership with the business.
- Stress ongoing face-to-face communication, feedback, and prioritization with the business stakeholders.
- Adapt quickly to inevitably evolving requirements.
- Tackle development in an iterative, incremental manner.

Although this list is compelling, a common criticism of the agile approaches is the lack of planning and architecture, coupled with ongoing governance challenges. The enterprise data warehouse bus matrix is a powerful tool to address these shortcomings. The bus matrix provides a framework and master plan for agile development, plus identifies the reusable common descriptive dimensions that provide both data consistency and reduced time-to-market delivery. With the right collaborative mix of business and IT stakeholders in a room, the enterprise data warehouse bus matrix can be produced in relatively short order. Incremental development work can produce components of the framework until sufficient functionality is available and then released to the business community.

Some clients and students lament that although they want to deliver consistently defined conformed dimensions in their DW/BI environments, it's "just not feasible." They explain that they would if they could, but with the focus on agile development techniques, it's "impossible" to take the time to get organizational agreement on conformed dimensions. We argue that conformed dimensions enable agile DW/BI development, along with agile decision making. As you flesh out the portfolio of master conformed dimensions, the development crank starts turning faster and faster. The time-to-market for a new business process data source shrinks as developers reuse existing conformed dimensions. Ultimately, new ETL development focuses almost exclusively on delivering more fact tables because the associated dimension tables are already sitting on the shelf ready to go.

Without a framework like the enterprise data warehouse bus matrix, some DW/BI teams have fallen into the trap of using agile techniques to create analytic or reporting solutions in a vacuum. In most situations, the team worked with a small set of users to extract a limited set of source data and make it available to solve their unique problems. The outcome is often a standalone data stovepipe that others can't leverage, or worse yet, delivers data that doesn't tie to the organization's other analytic information. We encourage agility, when appropriate, however building isolated data sets should be avoided. As with most things in life, moderation and balance between extremes is almost always prudent.

Summary

In this chapter we discussed the overriding goals for DW/BI systems and the fundamental concepts of dimensional modeling. The Kimball DW/BI architecture and several alternatives were compared. We closed out the chapter by identifying common misunderstandings that some still hold about dimensional modeling, despite its widespread acceptance across the industry, and challenged you to think dimensionally beyond data modeling. In the next chapter, you get a turbocharged tour of dimensional modeling patterns and techniques, and then begin putting these concepts into action in your first case study in Chapter 3.

2

Kimball Dimensional Modeling Techniques Overview

Starting with the first edition of *The Data Warehouse Toolkit* (Wiley, 1996), the Kimball Group has defined the complete set of techniques for modeling data in a dimensional way. In the first two editions of this book, we felt the techniques needed to be introduced through familiar use cases drawn from various industries. Although we still feel business use cases are an essential pedagogical approach, the techniques have become so standardized that some dimensional modelers reverse the logic by starting with the technique and then proceeding to the use case for context. All of this is good news!

The Kimball techniques have been accepted as industry best practices. As evidence, some former Kimball University students have published their own dimensional modeling books. These books usually explain the Kimball techniques accurately, but it is a sign of our techniques' resilience that alternative books have not extended the library of techniques in significant ways or offered conflicting guidance.

This chapter is the "official" list of Kimball Dimensional Modeling Techniques from the inventors of these design patterns. We don't expect you to read this chapter from beginning to end at first. But we intend the chapter to be a reference for our techniques. With each technique, we've included pointers to subsequent chapters for further explanation and illustrations based on the motivating use cases.

Fundamental Concepts

The techniques in this section must be considered during every dimensional design. Nearly every chapter in the book references or illustrates the concepts in this section.

Gather Business Requirements and Data Realities

Before launching a dimensional modeling effort, the team needs to understand the needs of the business, as well as the realities of the underlying source data. You uncover the requirements via sessions with business representatives to understand their objectives based on key performance indicators, compelling business issues, decision-making processes, and supporting analytic needs. At the same time, data realities are uncovered by meeting with source system experts and doing high-level data profiling to assess data feasibilities.

Collaborative Dimensional Modeling Workshops

Dimensional models should be designed in collaboration with subject matter experts and data governance representatives from the business. The data modeler is in charge, but the model should unfold via a series of highly interactive workshops with business representatives. These workshops provide another opportunity to flesh out the requirements with the business. Dimensional models should not be designed in isolation by folks who don't fully understand the business and their needs; collaboration is critical!

Four-Step Dimensional Design Process

The four key decisions made during the design of a dimensional model include:

1. Select the business process.
2. Declare the grain.
3. Identify the dimensions.
4. Identify the facts.

The answers to these questions are determined by considering the needs of the business along with the realities of the underlying source data during the collaborative modeling sessions. Following the business process, grain, dimension, and fact declarations, the design team determines the table and column names, sample domain values, and business rules. Business data governance representatives must participate in this detailed design activity to ensure business buy-in.

Business Processes

Business processes are the operational activities performed by your organization, such as taking an order, processing an insurance claim, registering students for a class, or snapshotting every account each month. Business process events generate or capture performance metrics that translate into facts in a fact table. Most fact tables focus on the results of a single business process. Choosing the process is important because it defines a specific design target and allows the grain, dimensions, and facts to be declared. Each business process corresponds to a row in the enterprise data warehouse bus matrix.

Grain

Declaring the grain is the pivotal step in a dimensional design. The *grain* establishes exactly what a single fact table row represents. The grain declaration becomes a binding contract on the design. The grain must be declared before choosing dimensions or facts because every candidate dimension or fact must be consistent with the grain. This consistency enforces a uniformity on all dimensional designs that is critical to BI application performance and ease of use. *Atomic grain* refers to the lowest level at which data is captured by a given business process. We strongly encourage you to start by focusing on atomic-grained data because it withstands the assault of unpredictable user queries; rolled-up summary grains are important for performance tuning, but they pre-suppose the business's common questions. Each proposed fact table grain results in a separate physical table; different grains must not be mixed in the same fact table.

Dimensions for Descriptive Context

Dimensions provide the "who, what, where, when, why, and how" context surrounding a business process event. Dimension tables contain the descriptive attributes used by BI applications for filtering and grouping the facts. With the grain of a fact table firmly in mind, all the possible dimensions can be identified. Whenever possible, a dimension should be single valued when associated with a given fact row.

Dimension tables are sometimes called the "soul" of the data warehouse because they contain the entry points and descriptive labels that enable the DW/BI system to be leveraged for business analysis. A disproportionate amount of effort is put into the data governance and development of dimension tables because they are the drivers of the user's BI experience.

Facts for Measurements

Facts are the measurements that result from a business process event and are almost always numeric. A single fact table row has a one-to-one relationship to a measurement event as described by the fact table's grain. Thus a fact table corresponds to a physical observable event, and not to the demands of a particular report. Within a fact table, only facts consistent with the declared grain are allowed. For example, in a retail sales transaction, the quantity of a product sold and its extended price are good facts, whereas the store manager's salary is disallowed.

Star Schemas and OLAP Cubes

Star schemas are dimensional structures deployed in a relational database management system (RDBMS). They characteristically consist of fact tables linked to associated dimension tables via primary/foreign key relationships. An *online analytical processing (OLAP) cube* is a dimensional structure implemented in a multidimensional database; it can be equivalent in content to, or more often derived from, a relational star schema. An OLAP cube contains dimensional attributes and facts, but it is accessed through languages with more analytic capabilities than SQL, such as XMLA and MDX. OLAP cubes are included in this list of basic techniques because an OLAP cube is often the final step in the deployment of a dimensional DW/BI system, or may exist as an aggregate structure based on a more atomic relational star schema.

Graceful Extensions to Dimensional Models

Dimensional models are resilient when data relationships change. All the following changes can be implemented without altering any existing BI query or application, and without any change in query results.

- Facts consistent with the grain of an existing fact table can be added by creating new columns.
- Dimensions can be added to an existing fact table by creating new foreign key columns, presuming they don't alter the fact table's grain.
- Attributes can be added to an existing dimension table by creating new columns.
- The grain of a fact table can be made more atomic by adding attributes to an existing dimension table, and then restating the fact table at the lower grain, being careful to preserve the existing column names in the fact and dimension tables.

Basic Fact Table Techniques

The techniques in this section apply to all fact tables. There are illustrations of fact tables in nearly every chapter.

Fact Table Structure

A *fact table* contains the numeric measures produced by an operational measurement event in the real world. At the lowest grain, a fact table row corresponds to a measurement event and vice versa. Thus the fundamental design of a fact table is entirely based on a physical activity and is not influenced by the eventual reports that may be produced. In addition to numeric measures, a fact table always contains foreign keys for each of its associated dimensions, as well as optional degenerate dimension keys and date/time stamps. Fact tables are the primary target of computations and dynamic aggregations arising from queries.

Additive, Semi-Additive, Non-Additive Facts

The numeric measures in a fact table fall into three categories. The most flexible and useful facts are *fully additive*; additive measures can be summed across any of the dimensions associated with the fact table. *Semi-additive* measures can be summed across some dimensions, but not all; balance amounts are common semi-additive facts because they are additive across all dimensions except time. Finally, some measures are completely *non-additive*, such as ratios. A good approach for non-additive facts is, where possible, to store the fully additive components of the non-additive measure and sum these components into the final answer set before calculating the final non-additive fact. This final calculation is often done in the BI layer or OLAP cube.

Nulls in Fact Tables

Null-valued measurements behave gracefully in fact tables. The aggregate functions (SUM, COUNT, MIN, MAX, and AVG) all do the "right thing" with null facts. However, nulls must be avoided in the fact table's foreign keys because these nulls would automatically cause a referential integrity violation. Rather than a null foreign key, the associated dimension table must have a default row (and surrogate key) representing the unknown or not applicable condition.

Conformed Facts

If the same measurement appears in separate fact tables, care must be taken to make sure the technical definitions of the facts are identical if they are to be compared or computed together. If the separate fact definitions are consistent, the *conformed facts* should be identically named; but if they are incompatible, they should be differently named to alert the business users and BI applications.

Transaction Fact Tables

A row in a *transaction fact table* corresponds to a measurement event at a point in space and time. Atomic transaction grain fact tables are the most dimensional and expressive fact tables; this robust dimensionality enables the maximum slicing and dicing of transaction data. Transaction fact tables may be dense or sparse because rows exist only if measurements take place. These fact tables always contain a foreign key for each associated dimension, and optionally contain precise time stamps and degenerate dimension keys. The measured numeric facts must be consistent with the transaction grain.

Periodic Snapshot Fact Tables

A row in a *periodic snapshot fact table* summarizes many measurement events occurring over a standard period, such as a day, a week, or a month. The grain is the period, not the individual transaction. Periodic snapshot fact tables often contain many facts because any measurement event consistent with the fact table grain is permissible. These fact tables are uniformly dense in their foreign keys because even if no activity takes place during the period, a row is typically inserted in the fact table containing a zero or null for each fact.

Accumulating Snapshot Fact Tables

A row in an *accumulating snapshot fact table* summarizes the measurement events occurring at predictable steps between the beginning and the end of a process. Pipeline or workflow processes, such as order fulfillment or claim processing, that have a defined start point, standard intermediate steps, and defined end point can be modeled with this type of fact table. There is a date foreign key in the fact table for each critical milestone in the process. An individual row in an accumulating snapshot fact table, corresponding for instance to a line on an order, is initially inserted when the order line is created. As pipeline progress occurs, the accumulating fact table row is revisited and updated. This consistent updating of accumulating snapshot fact rows is unique among the three types of fact tables. In addition to the date foreign keys associated with each critical process step, accumulating snapshot fact tables contain foreign keys for other dimensions and optionally contain degenerate dimensions. They often include numeric lag measurements consistent with the grain, along with milestone completion counters.

Factless Fact Tables

Although most measurement events capture numerical results, it is possible that the event merely records a set of dimensional entities coming together at a moment in time. For example, an event of a student attending a class on a given day may not have a recorded numeric fact, but a fact row with foreign keys for calendar day, student, teacher, location, and class is well-defined. Likewise, customer communications are events, but there may be no associated metrics. *Factless fact tables* can also be used to analyze what didn't happen. These queries always have two parts: a factless coverage table that contains all the possibilities of events that might happen and an activity table that contains the events that did happen. When the activity is subtracted from the coverage, the result is the set of events that did not happen.

Aggregate Fact Tables or OLAP Cubes

Aggregate fact tables are simple numeric rollups of atomic fact table data built solely to accelerate query performance. These aggregate fact tables should be available to the BI layer at the same time as the atomic fact tables so that BI tools smoothly choose the appropriate aggregate level at query time. This process, known as *aggregate navigation*, must be *open* so that every report writer, query tool, and BI application harvests the same performance benefits. A properly designed set of aggregates should behave like database indexes, which accelerate query performance but are not encountered directly by the BI applications or business users. Aggregate fact tables contain foreign keys to shrunken conformed dimensions, as well as aggregated facts created by summing measures from more atomic fact tables. Finally, *aggregate OLAP cubes* with summarized measures are frequently built in the same way as relational aggregates, but the OLAP cubes are meant to be accessed directly by the business users.

Consolidated Fact Tables

It is often convenient to combine facts from multiple processes together into a single *consolidated fact table* if they can be expressed at the same grain. For example, sales actuals can be consolidated with sales forecasts in a single fact table to make the task of analyzing actuals versus forecasts simple and fast, as compared to assembling a drill-across application using separate fact tables. Consolidated fact tables add burden to the ETL processing, but ease the analytic burden on the BI applications. They should be considered for cross-process metrics that are frequently analyzed together.

Basic Dimension Table Techniques

The techniques in this section apply to all dimension tables. Dimension tables are discussed and illustrated in every chapter.

Dimension Table Structure

Every dimension table has a single primary key column. This primary key is embedded as a foreign key in any associated fact table where the dimension row's descriptive context is exactly correct for that fact table row. Dimension tables are usually wide, flat denormalized tables with many low-cardinality text attributes. While operational codes and indicators can be treated as attributes, the most powerful dimension attributes are populated with verbose descriptions. Dimension table attributes are the primary target of constraints and grouping specifications from queries and BI applications. The descriptive labels on reports are typically dimension attribute domain values.

Dimension Surrogate Keys

A dimension table is designed with one column serving as a unique primary key. This primary key cannot be the operational system's natural key because there will be multiple dimension rows for that natural key when changes are tracked over time. In addition, natural keys for a dimension may be created by more than one source system, and these natural keys may be incompatible or poorly administered. The DW/BI system needs to claim control of the primary keys of all dimensions; rather than using explicit natural keys or natural keys with appended dates, you should create anonymous integer primary keys for every dimension. These *dimension surrogate keys* are simple integers, assigned in sequence, starting with the value 1, every time a new key is needed. The date dimension is exempt from the surrogate key rule; this highly predictable and stable dimension can use a more meaningful primary key. See the section "Calendar Date Dimensions."

Natural, Durable, and Supernatural Keys

Natural keys created by operational source systems are subject to business rules outside the control of the DW/BI system. For instance, an employee number (natural key) may be changed if the employee resigns and then is rehired. When the data warehouse wants to have a single key for that employee, a new *durable key* must be created that is persistent and does not change in this situation. This key is sometimes referred to as a *durable supernatural key*. The best durable keys have a format that is independent of the original business process and thus should be simple integers assigned in sequence beginning with 1. While multiple surrogate keys may be associated with an employee over time as their profile changes, the durable key never changes.

Drilling Down

Drilling down is the most fundamental way data is analyzed by business users. Drilling down simply means adding a row header to an existing query; the new row header is a dimension attribute appended to the GROUP BY expression in an SQL query. The attribute can come from any dimension attached to the fact table in the query. Drilling down does not require the definition of predetermined hierarchies or drill-down paths. See the section "Drilling Across."

Degenerate Dimensions

Sometimes a dimension is defined that has no content except for its primary key. For example, when an invoice has multiple line items, the line item fact rows inherit all the descriptive dimension foreign keys of the invoice, and the invoice is left with no unique content. But the invoice number remains a valid dimension key for fact tables at the line item level. This *degenerate dimension* is placed in the fact table with the explicit acknowledgment that there is no associated dimension table. Degenerate dimensions are most common with transaction and accumulating snapshot fact tables.

Denormalized Flattened Dimensions

In general, dimensional designers must resist the normalization urges caused by years of operational database designs and instead denormalize the many-to-one fixed depth hierarchies into separate attributes on a flattened dimension row. Dimension denormalization supports dimensional modeling's twin objectives of simplicity and speed.

Chapter 1   DW/BI and Dimensional Modeling Primer, p 13
Chapter 3   Retail Sales, p 84

Multiple Hierarchies in Dimensions

Many dimensions contain more than one natural hierarchy. For example, calendar date dimensions may have a day to week to fiscal period hierarchy, as well as a day to month to year hierarchy. Location intensive dimensions may have multiple geographic hierarchies. In all of these cases, the separate hierarchies can gracefully coexist in the same dimension table.

Chapter 3   Retail Sales, p 88
Chapter 19   ETL Subsystems and Techniques, p 470

Flags and Indicators as Textual Attributes

Cryptic abbreviations, true/false flags, and operational indicators should be supplemented in dimension tables with full text words that have meaning when independently viewed. Operational codes with embedded meaning within the code value should be broken down with each part of the code expanded into its own separate descriptive dimension attribute.

Chapter 3   Retail Sales, p 82
Chapter 11   Telecommunications, p 301
Chapter 16   Insurance, p 383

Null Attributes in Dimensions

Null-valued dimension attributes result when a given dimension row has not been fully populated, or when there are attributes that are not applicable to all the dimension's rows. In both cases, we recommend substituting a descriptive string, such as Unknown or Not Applicable in place of the null value. Nulls in dimension attributes should be avoided because different databases handle grouping and constraining on nulls inconsistently.

Chapter 3   Retail Sales, p 92

Calendar Date Dimensions

Calendar date dimensions are attached to virtually every fact table to allow navigation of the fact table through familiar dates, months, fiscal periods, and special days on the calendar. You would never want to compute Easter in SQL, but rather want to look it up in the calendar date dimension. The calendar date dimension typically has many attributes describing characteristics such as week number, month name, fiscal period, and national holiday indicator. To facilitate partitioning, the primary key of a date dimension can be more meaningful, such as an integer representing YYYYMMDD, instead of a sequentially-assigned surrogate key. However, the date dimension table needs a special row to represent unknown or to-be-determined dates. When further precision is needed, a separate date/time stamp can be added to the fact table. The date/time stamp is not a foreign key to a dimension table, but rather is a standalone column. If business users constrain or group on time-of-day attributes, such as day part grouping or shift number, then you would add a separate time-of-day dimension foreign key to the fact table.

Role-Playing Dimensions

A single physical dimension can be referenced multiple times in a fact table, with each reference linking to a logically distinct role for the dimension. For instance, a fact table can have several dates, each of which is represented by a foreign key to the date dimension. It is essential that each foreign key refers to a separate view of the date dimension so that the references are independent. These separate dimension views (with unique attribute column names) are called *roles*.

Junk Dimensions

Transactional business processes typically produce a number of miscellaneous, low-cardinality flags and indicators. Rather than making separate dimensions for each flag and attribute, you can create a single *junk dimension* combining them together. This dimension, frequently labeled as a *transaction profile dimension* in a schema, does not need to be the Cartesian product of all the attributes' possible values, but should only contain the combination of values that actually occur in the source data.

Snowflaked Dimensions

When a hierarchical relationship in a dimension table is normalized, low-cardinality attributes appear as secondary tables connected to the base dimension table by an attribute key. When this process is repeated with all the dimension table's hierarchies, a characteristic multilevel structure is created that is called a *snowflake*. Although the snowflake represents hierarchical data accurately, you should avoid snowflakes because it is difficult for business users to understand and navigate snowflakes. They can also negatively impact query performance. A flattened denormalized dimension table contains exactly the same information as a snowflaked dimension.

Outrigger Dimensions

A dimension can contain a reference to another dimension table. For instance, a bank account dimension can reference a separate dimension representing the date the account was opened. These secondary dimension references are called *outrigger dimensions*. Outrigger dimensions are permissible, but should be used sparingly. In most cases, the correlations between dimensions should be demoted to a fact table, where both dimensions are represented as separate foreign keys.

Integration via Conformed Dimensions

One of the marquee successes of the dimensional modeling approach has been to define a simple but powerful recipe for integrating data from different business processes.

Conformed Dimensions

Dimension tables *conform* when attributes in separate dimension tables have the same column names and domain contents. Information from separate fact tables can be combined in a single report by using conformed dimension attributes that are associated with each fact table. When a conformed attribute is used as the row header (that is, the grouping column in the SQL query), the results from the separate fact tables can be aligned on the same rows in a drill-across report. This is the essence of integration in an enterprise DW/BI system. *Conformed dimensions*, defined once in collaboration with the business's data governance representatives, are reused across fact tables; they deliver both analytic consistency and reduced future development costs because the wheel is not repeatedly re-created.

Shrunken Dimensions

Shrunken dimensions are conformed dimensions that are a *subset* of rows and/or columns of a base dimension. *Shrunken rollup* dimensions are required when constructing aggregate fact tables. They are also necessary for business processes that naturally capture data at a higher level of granularity, such as a forecast by month and brand (instead of the more atomic date and product associated with sales data). Another case of conformed dimension subsetting occurs when two dimensions are at the same level of detail, but one represents only a subset of rows.

Drilling Across

Drilling across simply means making separate queries against two or more fact tables where the row headers of each query consist of identical conformed attributes. The answer sets from the two queries are aligned by performing a sort-merge operation on the common dimension attribute row headers. BI tool vendors refer to this functionality by various names, including stitch and multipass query.

Value Chain

A *value chain* identifies the natural flow of an organization's primary business processes. For example, a retailer's value chain may consist of purchasing to warehousing to retail sales. A general ledger value chain may consist of budgeting to commitments to payments. Operational source systems typically produce transactions or snapshots at each step of the value chain. Because each process produces unique metrics at unique time intervals with unique granularity and dimensionality, each process typically spawns at least one atomic fact table.

Enterprise Data Warehouse Bus Architecture

The *enterprise data warehouse bus architecture* provides an incremental approach to building the enterprise DW/BI system. This architecture decomposes the DW/BI planning process into manageable pieces by focusing on business processes, while delivering integration via standardized conformed dimensions that are reused across processes. It provides an architectural framework, while also decomposing the program to encourage manageable agile implementations corresponding to the rows on the enterprise data warehouse bus matrix. The bus architecture is technology and database platform independent; both relational and OLAP dimensional structures can participate.

Enterprise Data Warehouse Bus Matrix

The *enterprise data warehouse bus matrix* is the essential tool for designing and communicating the enterprise data warehouse bus architecture. The rows of the matrix are business processes and the columns are dimensions. The shaded cells of the matrix indicate whether a dimension is associated with a given business process. The design team scans each row to test whether a candidate dimension is well-defined for the business process and also scans each column to see where a dimension should be conformed across multiple business processes. Besides the technical design considerations, the bus matrix is used as input to prioritize DW/BI projects with business management as teams should implement one row of the matrix at a time.

Detailed Implementation Bus Matrix

The *detailed implementation bus matrix* is a more granular bus matrix where each business process row has been expanded to show specific fact tables or OLAP cubes. At this level of detail, the precise grain statement and list of facts can be documented.

Opportunity/Stakeholder Matrix

After the enterprise data warehouse bus matrix rows have been identified, you can draft a different matrix by replacing the dimension columns with business functions, such as marketing, sales, and finance, and then shading the matrix cells to indicate which business functions are interested in which business process rows. The *opportunity/stakeholder matrix* helps identify which business groups should be invited to the collaborative design sessions for each process-centric row.

Dealing with Slowly Changing Dimension Attributes

The following section describes the fundamental approaches for dealing with slowly changing dimension (SCD) attributes. It is quite common to have attributes in the same dimension table that are handled with different change tracking techniques.

Type 0: Retain Original

With *type 0*, the dimension attribute value never changes, so facts are always grouped by this original value. Type 0 is appropriate for any attribute labeled "original," such as a customer's original credit score or a durable identifier. It also applies to most attributes in a date dimension.

Type 1: Overwrite

With *type 1*, the old attribute value in the dimension row is overwritten with the new value; type 1 attributes always reflects the most recent assignment, and therefore this technique destroys history. Although this approach is easy to implement and does not create additional dimension rows, you must be careful that aggregate fact tables and OLAP cubes affected by this change are recomputed.

Type 2: Add New Row

Type 2 changes add a new row in the dimension with the updated attribute values. This requires generalizing the primary key of the dimension beyond the natural or durable key because there will potentially be multiple rows describing each member. When a new row is created for a dimension member, a new primary surrogate key is assigned and used as a foreign key in all fact tables from the moment of the update until a subsequent change creates a new dimension key and updated dimension row.

A minimum of three additional columns should be added to the dimension row with type 2 changes: 1) row effective date or date/time stamp; 2) row expiration date or date/time stamp; and 3) current row indicator.

Type 3: Add New Attribute

Type 3 changes add a new attribute in the dimension to preserve the old attribute value; the new value overwrites the main attribute as in a type 1 change. This kind of type 3 change is sometimes called an *alternate reality*. A business user can group and filter fact data by either the current value or alternate reality. This slowly changing dimension technique is used relatively infrequently.

Type 4: Add Mini-Dimension

The *type 4* technique is used when a group of attributes in a dimension rapidly changes and is split off to a *mini-dimension*. This situation is sometimes called a *rapidly changing monster dimension*. Frequently used attributes in multimillion-row dimension tables are mini-dimension design candidates, even if they don't frequently change. The type 4 mini-dimension requires its own unique primary key; the primary keys of both the base dimension and mini-dimension are captured in the associated fact tables.

Type 5: Add Mini-Dimension and Type 1 Outrigger

The *type 5* technique is used to accurately preserve historical attribute values, plus report historical facts according to current attribute values. Type 5 builds on the type 4 mini-dimension by also embedding a current type 1 reference to the mini-dimension in the base dimension. This enables the currently-assigned mini-dimension attributes to be accessed along with the others in the base dimension without linking through a fact table. Logically, you'd represent the base dimension and mini-dimension outrigger as a single table in the presentation area. The ETL team must overwrite this type 1 mini-dimension reference whenever the current mini-dimension assignment changes.

Type 6: Add Type 1 Attributes to Type 2 Dimension

Like type 5, *type 6* also delivers both historical and current dimension attribute values. Type 6 builds on the type 2 technique by also embedding current type 1 versions of the same attributes in the dimension row so that fact rows can be filtered or grouped by either the type 2 attribute value in effect when the measurement occurred or the attribute's current value. In this case, the type 1 attribute is systematically overwritten on all rows associated with a particular durable key whenever the attribute is updated.

| Chapter 5 | Procurement, p 160 |
| Chapter 19 | ETL Subsystems and Techniques, p 468 |

Type 7: Dual Type 1 and Type 2 Dimensions

Type 7 is the final hybrid technique used to support both as-was and as-is reporting. A fact table can be accessed through a dimension modeled both as a type 1 dimension showing only the most current attribute values, or as a type 2 dimension showing correct contemporary historical profiles. The same dimension table enables both perspectives. Both the durable key and primary surrogate key of the dimension are placed in the fact table. For the type 1 perspective, the current flag in the dimension is constrained to be current, and the fact table is joined via the durable key. For the type 2 perspective, the current flag is not constrained, and the fact table is joined via the surrogate primary key. These two perspectives would be deployed as separate views to the BI applications.

| Chapter 5 | Procurement, p 162 |
| Chapter 19 | ETL Subsystems and Techniques, p 468 |

Dealing with Dimension Hierarchies

Dimensional hierarchies are commonplace. This section describes approaches for dealing with hierarchies, starting with the most basic.

Fixed Depth Positional Hierarchies

A *fixed depth hierarchy* is a series of many-to-one relationships, such as product to brand to category to department. When a fixed depth hierarchy is defined and the hierarchy levels have agreed upon names, the hierarchy levels should appear as separate positional attributes in a dimension table. A fixed depth hierarchy is by far the easiest to understand and navigate as long as the above criteria are met. It also delivers predictable and fast query performance. When the hierarchy is not a series of many-to-one relationships or the number of levels varies such that the levels do not have agreed upon names, a ragged hierarchy technique, described below, must be used.

Slightly Ragged/Variable Depth Hierarchies

Slightly ragged hierarchies don't have a fixed number of levels, but the range in depth is small. Geographic hierarchies often range in depth from perhaps three levels to six levels. Rather than using the complex machinery for unpredictably variable hierarchies, you can force-fit slightly ragged hierarchies into a fixed depth positional design with separate dimension attributes for the maximum number of levels, and then populate the attribute value based on rules from the business.

Ragged/Variable Depth Hierarchies with Hierarchy Bridge Tables

Ragged hierarchies of indeterminate depth are difficult to model and query in a relational database. Although SQL extensions and OLAP access languages provide some support for recursive parent/child relationships, these approaches have limitations. With SQL extensions, alternative ragged hierarchies cannot be substituted at query time, shared ownership structures are not supported, and time varying ragged hierarchies are not supported. All these objections can be overcome in relational databases by modeling a ragged hierarchy with a specially constructed *bridge table*. This bridge table contains a row for every possible path in the ragged hierarchy and enables all forms of hierarchy traversal to be accomplished with standard SQL rather than using special language extensions.

Ragged/Variable Depth Hierarchies with Pathstring Attributes

The use of a bridge table for ragged variable depth hierarchies can be avoided by implementing a *pathstring attribute* in the dimension. For each row in the dimension, the pathstring attribute contains a specially encoded text string containing the complete path description from the supreme node of a hierarchy down to the node described by the particular dimension row. Many of the standard hierarchy analysis requests can then be handled by standard SQL, without resorting to SQL language extensions. However, the pathstring approach does not enable rapid substitution of alternative hierarchies or shared ownership hierarchies. The pathstring approach may also be vulnerable to structure changes in the ragged hierarchy that could force the entire hierarchy to be relabeled.

Advanced Fact Table Techniques

The techniques in this section refer to less common fact table patterns.

Fact Table Surrogate Keys

Surrogate keys are used to implement the primary keys of almost all dimension tables. In addition, single column surrogate fact keys can be useful, albeit not required. *Fact table surrogate keys*, which are not associated with any dimension, are assigned sequentially during the ETL load process and are used 1) as the single column primary key of the fact table; 2) to serve as an immediate identifier of a fact table row without navigating multiple dimensions for ETL purposes; 3) to allow an interrupted load process to either back out or resume; 4) to allow fact table update operations to be decomposed into less risky inserts plus deletes.

Centipede Fact Tables

Some designers create separate normalized dimensions for each level of a many-to-one hierarchy, such as a date dimension, month dimension, quarter dimension, and year dimension, and then include all these foreign keys in a fact table. This results in a *centipede fact table* with dozens of hierarchically related dimensions. Centipede fact tables should be avoided. All these fixed depth, many-to-one hierarchically related dimensions should be collapsed back to their unique lowest grains, such as the date for the example mentioned. Centipede fact tables also result when designers embed numerous foreign keys to individual low-cardinality dimension tables rather than creating a junk dimension.

Numeric Values as Attributes or Facts

Designers sometimes encounter numeric values that don't clearly fall into either the fact or dimension attribute categories. A classic example is a product's standard list price. If the numeric value is used primarily for calculation purposes, it likely belongs in the fact table. If a stable numeric value is used predominantly for filtering and grouping, it should be treated as a dimension attribute; the discrete numeric values can be supplemented with value band attributes (such as $0-50). In some cases, it is useful to model the numeric value as both a fact and dimension attribute, such as a quantitative on-time delivery metric and qualitative textual descriptor.

Lag/Duration Facts

Accumulating snapshot fact tables capture multiple process milestones, each with a date foreign key and possibly a date/time stamp. Business users often want to analyze the lags or durations between these milestones; sometimes these lags are just the differences between dates, but other times the lags are based on more complicated business rules. If there are dozens of steps in a pipeline, there could be hundreds of possible lags. Rather than forcing the user's query to calculate each possible lag from the date/time stamps or date dimension foreign keys, just one time lag can be stored for each step measured against the process's start point. Then every possible lag between two steps can be calculated as a simple subtraction between the two lags stored in the fact table.

Header/Line Fact Tables

Operational transaction systems often consist of a transaction header row that's associated with multiple transaction lines. With *header/line* schemas (also known as *parent/child* schemas), all the header-level dimension foreign keys and degenerate dimensions should be included on the line-level fact table.

Allocated Facts

It is quite common in header/line transaction data to encounter facts of differing granularity, such as a header freight charge. You should strive to *allocate* the header facts down to the line level based on rules provided by the business, so the allocated facts can be sliced and rolled up by all the dimensions. In many cases, you can avoid creating a header-level fact table, unless this aggregation delivers query performance advantages.

Chapter 6   Order Management, p 184

Profit and Loss Fact Tables Using Allocations

Fact tables that expose the full equation of *profit* are among the most powerful deliverables of an enterprise DW/BI system. The equation of profit is (revenue) – (costs) = (profit). Fact tables ideally implement the profit equation at the grain of the atomic revenue transaction and contain many components of cost. Because these tables are at the atomic grain, numerous rollups are possible, including customer profitability, product profitability, promotion profitability, channel profitability, and others. However, these fact tables are difficult to build because the cost components must be allocated from their original sources to the fact table's grain. This allocation step is often a major ETL subsystem and is a politically charged step that requires high-level executive support. For these reasons, profit and loss fact tables are typically not tackled during the early implementation phases of a DW/BI program.

Chapter 6   Order Management, p 189
Chapter 15   Electronic Commerce, p 370

Multiple Currency Facts

Fact tables that record financial transactions in multiple currencies should contain a pair of columns for every financial fact in the row. One column contains the fact expressed in the true currency of the transaction, and the other contains the same fact expressed in a single standard currency that is used throughout the fact table. The standard currency value is created in an ETL process according to an approved business rule for currency conversion. This fact table also must have a currency dimension to identify the transaction's true currency.

Chapter 6   Order Management, p 182
Chapter 7   Accounting, p 206

Multiple Units of Measure Facts

Some business processes require facts to be stated simultaneously in several units of measure. For example, depending on the perspective of the business user, a supply chain may need to report the same facts as pallets, ship cases, retail cases, or individual scan units. If the fact table contains a large number of facts, each of which must be expressed in all units of measure, a convenient technique is to store the facts once in the table at an agreed standard unit of measure, but also simultaneously store conversion factors between the standard measure and all the others. This fact table could be deployed through views to each user constituency, using an appropriate selected conversion factor. The conversion factors must reside in the underlying fact table row to ensure the view calculation is simple and correct, while minimizing query complexity.

> Chapter 6   Order Management, p 197

Year-to-Date Facts

Business users often request year-to-date (YTD) values in a fact table. It is hard to argue against a single request, but YTD requests can easily morph into "YTD at the close of the fiscal period" or "fiscal period to date." A more reliable, extensible way to handle these assorted requests is to calculate the YTD metrics in the BI applications or OLAP cube rather than storing YTD facts in the fact table.

> Chapter 7   Accounting, p 206

Multipass SQL to Avoid Fact-to-Fact Table Joins

A BI application must never issue SQL that joins two fact tables together across the fact table's foreign keys. It is impossible to control the cardinality of the answer set of such a join in a relational database, and incorrect results will be returned to the BI tool. For instance, if two fact tables contain customer's product shipments and returns, these two fact tables must not be joined directly across the customer and product foreign keys. Instead, the technique of drilling across two fact tables should be used, where the answer sets from shipments and returns are separately created, and the results sort-merged on the common row header attribute values to produce the correct result.

> Chapter 4   Inventory, p 130
> Chapter 8   Customer Relationship Management, p 259

Timespan Tracking in Fact Tables

There are three basic fact table grains: transaction, periodic snapshot, and accumulating snapshot. In isolated cases, it is useful to add a row effective date, row expiration date, and current row indicator to the fact table, much like you do with type 2 slowly changing dimensions, to capture a *timespan* when the fact row was effective. Although an unusual pattern, this pattern addresses scenarios such as slowly changing inventory balances where a frequent periodic snapshot would load identical rows with each snapshot.

Late Arriving Facts

A fact row is *late arriving* if the most current dimensional context for new fact rows does not match the incoming row. This happens when the fact row is delayed. In this case, the relevant dimensions must be searched to find the dimension keys that were effective when the late arriving measurement event occurred.

Advanced Dimension Techniques

The techniques in this section refer to more advanced dimension table patterns.

Dimension-to-Dimension Table Joins

Dimensions can contain references to other dimensions. Although these relationships can be modeled with outrigger dimensions, in some cases, the existence of a foreign key to the outrigger dimension in the base dimension can result in explosive growth of the base dimension because type 2 changes in the outrigger force corresponding type 2 processing in the base dimension. This explosive growth can often be avoided if you demote the correlation between dimensions by placing the foreign key of the outrigger in the fact table rather than in the base dimension. This means the correlation between the dimensions can be discovered only by traversing the fact table, but this may be acceptable, especially if the fact table is a periodic snapshot where all the keys for all the dimensions are guaranteed to be present for each reporting period.

Multivalued Dimensions and Bridge Tables

In a classic dimensional schema, each dimension attached to a fact table has a single value consistent with the fact table's grain. But there are a number of situations in which a dimension is legitimately *multivalued*. For example, a patient receiving a healthcare treatment may have multiple simultaneous diagnoses. In these cases, the multivalued dimension must be attached to the fact table through a group dimension key to a bridge table with one row for each simultaneous diagnosis in a group.

Time Varying Multivalued Bridge Tables

A *multivalued bridge table* may need to be based on a type 2 slowly changing dimension. For example, the bridge table that implements the many-to-many relationship between bank accounts and individual customers usually must be based on type 2 account and customer dimensions. In this case, to prevent incorrect linkages between accounts and customers, the bridge table must include effective and expiration date/time stamps, and the requesting application must constrain the bridge table to a specific moment in time to produce a consistent snapshot.

Behavior Tag Time Series

Almost all text in a data warehouse is descriptive text in dimension tables. Data mining customer cluster analyses typically results in textual *behavior tags*, often identified on a periodic basis. In this case, the customers' behavior measurements over time become a sequence of these behavior tags; this time series should be stored as positional attributes in the customer dimension, along with an optional text string for the complete sequence of tags. The behavior tags are modeled in a positional design because the behavior tags are the target of complex simultaneous queries rather than numeric computations.

Behavior Study Groups

Complex customer behavior can sometimes be discovered only by running lengthy iterative analyses. In these cases, it is impractical to embed the behavior analyses inside every BI application that wants to constrain all the members of the customer dimension who exhibit the complex behavior. The results of the complex behavior analyses, however, can be captured in a simple table, called a *study group*, consisting only of the customers' durable keys. This static table can then be used as a kind of filter on any dimensional schema with a customer dimension by constraining the study group column to the customer dimension's durable key in the target schema at query time. Multiple study groups can be defined and derivative study groups can be created with intersections, unions, and set differences.

> Chapter 8   Customer Relationship Management, p 249

Aggregated Facts as Dimension Attributes

Business users are often interested in constraining the customer dimension based on aggregated performance metrics, such as filtering on all customers who spent over a certain dollar amount during last year or perhaps over the customer's lifetime. Selected *aggregated facts* can be placed in a dimension as targets for constraining and as row labels for reporting. The metrics are often presented as banded ranges in the dimension table. Dimension attributes representing aggregated performance metrics add burden to the ETL processing, but ease the analytic burden in the BI layer.

> Chapter 8   Customer Relationship Management, p 239

Dynamic Value Bands

A *dynamic value banding report* is organized as a series of report row headers that define a progressive set of varying-sized ranges of a target numeric fact. For instance, a common value banding report in a bank has many rows with labels such as "Balance from 0 to $10," "Balance from $10.01 to $25," and so on. This kind of report is dynamic because the specific row headers are defined at query time, not during the ETL processing. The row definitions can be implemented in a small value banding dimension table that is joined via greater-than/less-than joins to the fact table, or the definitions can exist only in an SQL CASE statement. The value banding dimension approach is probably higher performing, especially in a columnar database, because the CASE statement approach involves an almost unconstrained relation scan of the fact table.

> Chapter 10   Financial Services, p 291

Text Comments Dimension

Rather than treating freeform comments as textual metrics in a fact table, they should be stored outside the fact table in a separate comments dimension (or as attributes in a dimension with one row per transaction if the comments' cardinality matches the number of unique transactions) with a corresponding foreign key in the fact table.

Multiple Time Zones

To capture both universal standard time, as well as local times in *multi-time zone* applications, dual foreign keys should be placed in the affected fact tables that join to two role-playing date (and potentially time-of-day) dimension tables.

Measure Type Dimensions

Sometimes when a fact table has a long list of facts that is sparsely populated in any individual row, it is tempting to create a *measure type dimension* that collapses the fact table row down to a single generic fact identified by the measure type dimension. We generally do not recommend this approach. Although it removes all the empty fact columns, it multiplies the size of the fact table by the average number of occupied columns in each row, and it makes intra-column computations much more difficult. This technique is acceptable when the number of potential facts is extreme (in the hundreds), but less than a handful would be applicable to any given fact table row.

Step Dimensions

Sequential processes, such as web page events, normally have a separate row in a transaction fact table for each step in a process. To tell where the individual step fits into the overall session, a *step dimension* is used that shows what step number is represented by the current step and how many more steps were required to complete the session.

Hot Swappable Dimensions

Hot swappable dimensions are used when the same fact table is alternatively paired with different copies of the same dimension. For example, a single fact table containing stock ticker quotes could be simultaneously exposed to multiple separate investors, each of whom has unique and proprietary attributes assigned to different stocks.

Abstract Generic Dimensions

Some modelers are attracted to abstract generic dimensions. For example, their schemas include a single generic location dimension rather than embedded geographic attributes in the store, warehouse, and customer dimensions. Similarly, their person dimension includes rows for employees, customers, and vendor contacts because they are all human beings, regardless that significantly different attributes are collected for each type. Abstract generic dimensions should be avoided in dimensional models. The attribute sets associated with each type often differ. If the attributes are common, such as a geographic state, then they should be uniquely labeled to distinguish a store's state from a customer's. Finally, dumping all varieties of locations, people, or products into a single dimension invariably results in a larger dimension table. Data abstraction may be appropriate in the operational source system or ETL processing, but it negatively impacts query performance and legibility in the dimensional model.

Audit Dimensions

When a fact table row is created in the ETL back room, it is helpful to create an *audit dimension* containing the ETL processing metadata known at the time. A simple audit dimension row could contain one or more basic indicators of data quality, perhaps derived from examining an error event schema that records data quality violations encountered while processing the data. Other useful audit dimension attributes could include environment variables describing the versions of ETL code used to create the fact rows or the ETL process execution time stamps.

These environment variables are especially useful for compliance and auditing purposes because they enable BI tools to drill down to determine which rows were created with what versions of the ETL software.

Late Arriving Dimensions

Sometimes the facts from an operational business process arrive minutes, hours, days, or weeks before the associated dimension context. For example, in a real-time data delivery situation, an inventory depletion row may arrive showing the natural key of a customer committing to purchase a particular product. In a real-time ETL system, this row must be posted to the BI layer, even if the identity of the customer or product cannot be immediately determined. In these cases, special dimension rows are created with the unresolved natural keys as attributes. Of course, these dimension rows must contain generic unknown values for most of the descriptive columns; presumably the proper dimensional context will follow from the source at a later time. When this dimensional context is eventually supplied, the placeholder dimension rows are updated with type 1 overwrites. Late arriving dimension data also occurs when retroactive changes are made to type 2 dimension attributes. In this case, a new row needs to be inserted in the dimension table, and then the associated fact rows must be restated.

Special Purpose Schemas

The following design patterns are needed for specific use cases.

Supertype and Subtype Schemas for Heterogeneous Products

Financial services and other businesses frequently offer a wide variety of products in disparate lines of business. For example, a retail bank may offer dozens of types of accounts ranging from checking accounts to mortgages to business loans, but all are examples of an account. Attempts to build a single, consolidated fact table with the union of all possible facts, linked to dimension tables with all possible attributes of these divergent products, will fail because there can be hundreds of incompatible facts and attributes. The solution is to build a single *supertype fact table* that has the intersection of the facts from all the account types (along with a supertype dimension table containing the common attributes), and then systematically build separate fact tables (and associated dimension tables) for each of the subtypes. *Supertype* and *subtype* fact tables are also called *core* and *custom fact tables*.

Real-Time Fact Tables

Real-time fact tables need to be updated more frequently than the more traditional nightly batch process. There are many techniques for supporting this requirement, depending on the capabilities of the DBMS or OLAP cube used for final deployment to the BI reporting layer. For example, a "hot partition" can be defined on a fact table that is pinned in physical memory. Aggregations and indexes are deliberately not built on this partition. Other DBMSs or OLAP cubes may support deferred updating that allows existing queries to run to completion but then perform the updates.

Error Event Schemas

Managing data quality in a data warehouse requires a comprehensive system of data quality screens or filters that test the data as it flows from the source systems to the BI platform. When a data quality screen detects an error, this event is recorded in a special dimensional schema that is available only in the ETL back room. This schema consists of an error event fact table whose grain is the individual error event and an associated error event detail fact table whose grain is each column in each table that participates in an error event.

3 Retail Sales

The best way to understand the principles of dimensional modeling is to work through a series of tangible examples. By visualizing real cases, you hold the particular design challenges and solutions in your mind more effectively than if they are presented abstractly. This book uses case studies from a range of businesses to help move past the idiosyncrasies of your own environment and reinforce dimensional modeling best practices.

To learn dimensional modeling, please read all the chapters in this book, even if you don't manage a retail store or work for a telecommunications company. The chapters are not intended to be full-scale solutions for a given industry or business function. Each chapter covers a set of dimensional modeling patterns that comes up in nearly every kind of business. Universities, insurance companies, banks, and airlines alike surely need the techniques developed in this retail chapter. Besides, thinking about someone else's business is refreshing. It is too easy to let historical complexities derail you when dealing with data from your company. By stepping outside your organization and then returning with a well-understood design principle (or two), it is easier to remember the spirit of the design principles as you descend into the intricate details of your business.

Chapter 3 discusses the following concepts:

- Four-step process for designing dimensional models
- Fact table granularity
- Transaction fact tables
- Additive, non-additive, and derived facts
- Dimension attributes, including indicators, numeric descriptors, and multiple hierarchies
- Calendar date dimensions, plus time-of-day
- Causal dimensions, such as promotion
- Degenerate dimensions, such as the transaction receipt number

- Nulls in a dimensional model
- Extensibility of dimension models
- Factless fact tables
- Surrogate, natural, and durable keys
- Snowflaked dimension attributes
- Centipede fact tables with "too many dimensions"

Four-Step Dimensional Design Process

Throughout this book, we will approach the design of a dimensional model by consistently considering four steps, as the following sections discuss in more detail.

Step 1: Select the Business Process

A *business process* is a low-level activity performed by an organization, such as taking orders, invoicing, receiving payments, handling service calls, registering students, performing a medical procedure, or processing claims. To identify your organization's business processes, it's helpful to understand several common characteristics:

- Business processes are frequently expressed as action verbs because they represent activities that the business performs. The companion dimensions describe descriptive context associated with each business process event.
- Business processes are typically supported by an operational system, such as the billing or purchasing system.
- Business processes generate or capture key performance metrics. Sometimes the metrics are a direct result of the business process; the measurements are derivations at other times. Analysts invariably want to scrutinize and evaluate these metrics by a seemingly limitless combination of filters and constraints.
- Business processes are usually triggered by an input and result in output metrics. In many organizations, there's a series of processes in which the outputs from one process become the inputs to the next. In the parlance of a dimensional modeler, this series of processes results in a series of fact tables.

You need to listen carefully to the business to identify the organization's business processes because business users can't readily answer the question, "What business process are you interested in?" The performance measurements users want to analyze in the DW/BI system result from business process events.

Sometimes business users talk about strategic business initiatives instead of business processes. These initiatives are typically broad enterprise plans championed by executive leadership to deliver competitive advantage. In order to tie a business initiative to a business process representing a project-sized unit of work for the

DW/BI team, you need to decompose the business initiative into the underlying processes. This means digging a bit deeper to understand the data and operational systems that support the initiative's analytic requirements.

It's also worth noting what a business process is not. Organizational business departments or functions do not equate to business processes. By focusing on processes, rather than on functional departments, consistent information is delivered more economically throughout the organization. If you design departmentally bound dimensional models, you inevitably duplicate data with different labels and data values. The best way to ensure consistency is to publish the data once.

Step 2: Declare the Grain

Declaring the *grain* means specifying exactly what an individual fact table row represents. The grain conveys the level of detail associated with the fact table measurements. It provides the answer to the question, "How do you describe a single row in the fact table?" The grain is determined by the physical realities of the operational system that captures the business process's events.

Example grain declarations include:

- One row per scan of an individual product on a customer's sales transaction
- One row per line item on a bill from a doctor
- One row per individual boarding pass scanned at an airport gate
- One row per daily snapshot of the inventory levels for each item in a warehouse
- One row per bank account each month

These grain declarations are expressed in business terms. Perhaps you were expecting the grain to be a traditional declaration of the fact table's primary key. Although the grain ultimately is equivalent to the primary key, it's a mistake to list a set of dimensions and then assume this list is the grain declaration. Whenever possible, you should express the grain in business terms.

Dimensional modelers sometimes try to bypass this seemingly unnecessary step of the four-step design process. Please don't! Declaring the grain is a critical step that can't be taken lightly. In debugging thousands of dimensional designs over the years, the most frequent error is not declaring the grain of the fact table at the beginning of the design process. If the grain isn't clearly defined, the whole design rests on quicksand; discussions about candidate dimensions go around in circles, and rogue facts sneak into the design. An inappropriate grain haunts a DW/BI implementation! It is extremely important that everyone on the design team reaches agreement on the fact table's granularity. Having said this, you may discover in steps 3 or 4 of the design process that the grain statement is wrong. This is okay, but then you must return to step 2, restate the grain correctly, and revisit steps 3 and 4 again.

Step 3: Identify the Dimensions

Dimensions fall out of the question, "How do business people describe the data resulting from the business process measurement events?" You need to decorate fact tables with a robust set of dimensions representing all possible descriptions that take on single values in the context of each measurement. If you are clear about the grain, the dimensions typically can easily be identified as they represent the "who, what, where, when, why, and how" associated with the event. Examples of common dimensions include date, product, customer, employee, and facility. With the choice of each dimension, you then list all the discrete, text-like attributes that flesh out each dimension table.

Step 4: Identify the Facts

Facts are determined by answering the question, "What is the process measuring?" Business users are keenly interested in analyzing these performance metrics. All candidate facts in a design must be true to the grain defined in step 2. Facts that clearly belong to a different grain must be in a separate fact table. Typical facts are numeric additive figures, such as quantity ordered or dollar cost amount.

You need to consider both your business users' requirements and the realities of your source data in tandem to make decisions regarding the four steps, as illustrated in Figure 3-1. We strongly encourage you to resist the temptation to model the data by looking at source data alone. It may be less intimidating to dive into the data rather than interview a business person; however, the data is no substitute for business user input. Unfortunately, many organizations have attempted this path-of-least-resistance data-driven approach but without much success.

Figure 3-1: Key input to the four-step dimensional design process.

Retail Case Study

Let's start with a brief description of the retail business used in this case study. We begin with this industry simply because it is one we are all familiar with. But the patterns discussed in the context of this case study are relevant to virtually every dimensional model regardless of the industry.

Imagine you work in the headquarters of a large grocery chain. The business has 100 grocery stores spread across five states. Each store has a full complement of departments, including grocery, frozen foods, dairy, meat, produce, bakery, floral, and health/beauty aids. Each store has approximately 60,000 individual products, called *stock keeping units (SKUs)*, on its shelves.

Data is collected at several interesting places in a grocery store. Some of the most useful data is collected at the cash registers as customers purchase products. The *point-of-sale (POS)* system scans product barcodes at the cash register, measuring consumer takeaway at the front door of the grocery store, as illustrated in Figure 3-2's cash register receipt. Other data is captured at the store's back door where vendors make deliveries.

Figure 3-2: Sample cash register receipt.

At the grocery store, management is concerned with the logistics of ordering, stocking, and selling products while maximizing profit. The profit ultimately comes from charging as much as possible for each product, lowering costs for product acquisition and overhead, and at the same time attracting as many customers as possible in a highly competitive environment. Some of the most significant management decisions have to do with pricing and promotions. Both store management and headquarters marketing spend a great deal of time tinkering with pricing and promotions. Promotions in a grocery store include temporary price reductions, ads in newspapers and newspaper inserts, displays in the grocery store, and coupons. The most direct and effective way to create a surge in the volume of product sold is to lower the price dramatically. A 50-cent reduction in the price of paper towels, especially when coupled with an ad and display, can cause the sale of the paper towels to jump by a factor of 10. Unfortunately, such a big price reduction usually is not sustainable because the towels probably are being sold at a loss. As a result of these issues, the visibility of all forms of promotion is an important part of analyzing the operations of a grocery store.

Now that we have described our business case study, we'll begin to design the dimensional model.

Step 1: Select the Business Process

The first step in the design is to decide what business process to model by combining an understanding of the business requirements with an understanding of the available source data.

> **NOTE**   The first DW/BI project should focus on the business process that is both the most critical to the business users, as well as the most feasible. Feasibility covers a range of considerations, including data availability and quality, as well as organizational readiness.

In our retail case study, management wants to better understand customer purchases as captured by the POS system. Thus the business process you're modeling is POS retail sales transactions. This data enables the business users to analyze which products are selling in which stores on which days under what promotional conditions in which transactions.

Step 2: Declare the Grain

After the business process has been identified, the design team faces a serious decision about the granularity. What level of data detail should be made available in the dimensional model?

Tackling data at its lowest atomic grain makes sense for many reasons. Atomic data is highly dimensional. The more detailed and atomic the fact measurement, the more things you know for sure. All those things you know for sure translate into dimensions. In this regard, atomic data is a perfect match for the dimensional approach.

Atomic data provides maximum analytic flexibility because it can be constrained and rolled up in every way possible. Detailed data in a dimensional model is poised and ready for the ad hoc attack by business users.

> **NOTE**   You should develop dimensional models representing the most detailed, atomic information captured by a business process.

Of course, you could declare a more summarized granularity representing an aggregation of the atomic data. However, as soon as you select a higher level grain, you limit yourself to fewer and/or potentially less detailed dimensions. The less granular model is immediately vulnerable to unexpected user requests to drill down into the details. Users inevitably run into an analytic wall when not given access to the atomic data. Although aggregated data plays an important role for performance tuning, it is not a substitute for giving users access to the lowest level details; users can easily summarize atomic data, but it's impossible to create details from summary data. Unfortunately, some industry pundits remain confused about this point. They claim dimensional models are only appropriate for summarized data and then criticize the dimensional modeling approach for its supposed need to anticipate the business question. This misunderstanding goes away when detailed, atomic data is made available in a dimensional model.

In our case study, the most granular data is an individual product on a POS transaction, assuming the POS system rolls up all sales for a given product within a shopping cart into a single line item. Although users probably are not interested in analyzing single items associated with a specific POS transaction, you can't predict all the ways they'll want to cull through that data. For example, they may want to understand the difference in sales on Monday versus Sunday. Or they may want to assess whether it's worthwhile to stock so many individual sizes of certain brands. Or they may want to understand how many shoppers took advantage of the 50-cents-off promotion on shampoo. Or they may want to determine the impact of decreased sales when a competitive diet soda product was promoted heavily. Although none of these queries calls for data from one specific transaction, they are broad questions that require detailed data sliced in precise ways. None of them could have been answered if you elected to provide access only to summarized data.

> **NOTE**   A DW/BI system almost always demands data expressed at the lowest possible grain, not because queries want to see individual rows but because queries need to cut through the details in very precise ways.

Step 3: Identify the Dimensions

After the grain of the fact table has been chosen, the choice of dimensions is straight-forward. The product and transaction fall out immediately. Within the framework of the primary dimensions, you can ask whether other dimensions can be attributed to the POS measurements, such as the date of the sale, the store where the sale occurred, the promotion under which the product is sold, the cashier who handled the sale, and potentially the method of payment. We express this as another design principle.

> **NOTE** A careful grain statement determines the primary dimensionality of the fact table. You then add more dimensions to the fact table if these additional dimensions naturally take on only one value under each combination of the primary dimensions. If the additional dimension violates the grain by causing additional fact rows to be generated, the dimension needs to be disqualified or the grain statement needs to be revisited.

The following descriptive dimensions apply to the case: date, product, store, promotion, cashier, and method of payment. In addition, the POS transaction ticket number is included as a special dimension, as described in the section "Degenerate Dimensions for Transaction Numbers" later in this chapter.

Before fleshing out the dimension tables with descriptive attributes, let's complete the final step of the four-step process. You don't want to lose sight of the forest for the trees at this stage of the design.

Step 4: Identify the Facts

The fourth and final step in the design is to make a careful determination of which facts will appear in the fact table. Again, the grain declaration helps anchor your thinking. Simply put, the facts must be true to the grain: the individual product line item on the POS transaction in this case. When considering potential facts, you may again discover adjustments need to be made to either your earlier grain assumptions or choice of dimensions.

The facts collected by the POS system include the sales quantity (for example, the number of cans of chicken noodle soup), per unit regular, discount, and net paid prices, and extended discount and sales dollar amounts. The extended sales dollar amount equals the sales quantity multiplied by the net unit price. Likewise, the extended discount dollar amount is the sales quantity multiplied by the unit discount amount. Some sophisticated POS systems also provide a standard dollar cost for the product as delivered to the store by the vendor. Presuming this cost fact is readily available and doesn't require a heroic activity-based costing initiative, you can include the extended cost amount in the fact table. The fact table begins to take shape in Figure 3-3.

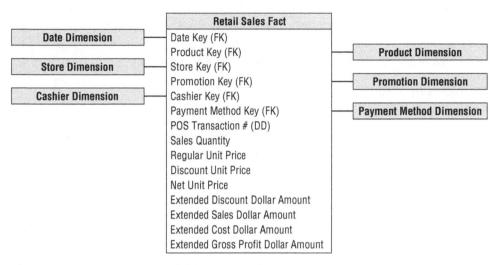

Figure 3-3: Measured facts in retail sales schema.

Four of the facts, sales quantity and the extended discount, sales, and cost dollar amounts, are beautifully additive across all the dimensions. You can slice and dice the fact table by the dimension attributes with impunity, and every sum of these four facts is valid and correct.

Derived Facts

You can compute the gross profit by subtracting the extended cost dollar amount from the extended sales dollar amount, or revenue. Although computed, gross profit is also perfectly additive across all the dimensions; you can calculate the gross profit of any combination of products sold in any set of stores on any set of days. Dimensional modelers sometimes question whether a calculated derived fact should be stored in the database. We generally recommend it be stored physically. In this case study, the gross profit calculation is straightforward, but storing it means it's computed consistently in the ETL process, eliminating the possibility of user calculation errors. The cost of a user incorrectly representing gross profit overwhelms the minor incremental storage cost. Storing it also ensures all users and BI reporting applications refer to gross profit consistently. Because gross profit can be calculated from adjacent data within a single fact table row, some would argue that you should perform the calculation in a view that is indistinguishable from the table. This is a reasonable approach if all users access the data via the view and no users with ad hoc query tools can sneak around the view to get at the physical table. Views are a reasonable way to minimize user error while saving on storage, but the DBA must allow no exceptions to accessing the data through the view. Likewise, some organizations want to perform the calculation in the BI tool. Again, this works if all users access the data using a common tool, which is seldom the case in our experience. However, sometimes non-additive metrics on a report such as percentages or ratios must be computed in the BI application because the calculation cannot be precalculated and stored in a fact table. OLAP cubes excel in these situations.

Non-Additive Facts

Gross margin can be calculated by dividing the gross profit by the extended sales dollar revenue. Gross margin is a *non-additive fact* because it can't be summarized along any dimension. You can calculate the gross margin of any set of products, stores, or days by remembering to sum the revenues and costs respectively before dividing.

> **NOTE** Percentages and ratios, such as gross margin, are non-additive. The numerator and denominator should be stored in the fact table. The ratio can then be calculated in a BI tool for any slice of the fact table by remembering to calculate the ratio of the sums, not the sum of the ratios.

Unit price is another non-additive fact. Unlike the extended amounts in the fact table, summing unit price across any of the dimensions results in a meaningless, nonsensical number. Consider this simple example: You sold one widget at a unit price of $1.00 and four widgets at a unit price of 50 cents each. You could sum the sales quantity to determine that five widgets were sold. Likewise, you could sum the sales dollar amounts ($1.00 and $2.00) to arrive at a total sales amount of $3.00. However, you can't sum the unit prices ($1.00 and 50 cents) and declare that the total unit price is $1.50. Similarly, you shouldn't announce that the average unit price is 75 cents. The properly weighted average unit price should be calculated by taking the total sales amount ($3.00) and dividing by the total quantity (five widgets) to arrive at a 60 cent average unit price. You'd never arrive at this conclusion by looking at the unit price for each transaction line in isolation. To analyze the average price, you must add up the sales dollars and sales quantities before dividing the total dollars by the total quantity sold. Fortunately, many BI tools perform this function correctly. Some question whether non-additive facts should be physically stored in a fact table. This is a legitimate question given their limited analytic value, aside from printing individual values on a report or applying a filter directly on the fact, which are both atypical. In some situations, a fundamentally non-additive fact such as a temperature is supplied by the source system. These non-additive facts may be averaged carefully over many records, if the business analysts agree that this makes sense.

Transaction Fact Tables

Transactional business processes are the most common. The fact tables representing these processes share several characteristics:

- The grain of atomic transaction fact tables can be succinctly expressed in the context of the transaction, such as one row per transaction or one row per transaction line.
- Because these fact tables record a transactional event, they are often sparsely populated. In our case study, we certainly wouldn't sell every product in every shopping cart.
- Even though transaction fact tables are unpredictably and sparsely populated, they can be truly enormous. Most billion and trillion row tables in a data warehouse are transaction fact tables.
- Transaction fact tables tend to be highly dimensional.
- The metrics resulting from transactional events are typically additive as long as they have been extended by the quantity amount, rather than capturing per unit metrics.

At this early stage of the design, it is often helpful to estimate the number of rows in your largest table, the fact table. In this case study, it simply may be a matter of talking with a source system expert to understand how many POS transaction line items are generated on a periodic basis. Retail traffic fluctuates significantly from day to day, so you need to understand the transaction activity over a reasonable period of time. Alternatively, you could estimate the number of rows added to the fact table annually by dividing the chain's annual gross revenue by the average item selling price. Assuming that gross revenues are $4 billion per year and that the average price of an item on a customer ticket is $2.00, you can calculate that there are approximately 2 billion transaction line items per year. This is a typical engineer's estimate that gets you surprisingly close to sizing a design directly from your armchair. As designers, you always should be triangulating to determine whether your calculations are reasonable.

Dimension Table Details

Now that we've walked through the four-step process, let's return to the dimension tables and focus on populating them with robust attributes.

Date Dimension

The date dimension is a special dimension because it is the one dimension nearly guaranteed to be in every dimensional model since virtually every business process captures a time series of performance metrics. In fact, date is usually the first dimension in the underlying partitioning scheme of the database so that the successive time interval data loads are placed into virgin territory on the disk.

For readers of the first edition of *The Data Warehouse Toolkit* (Wiley, 1996), this dimension was referred to as the time dimension. However, for more than a decade, we've used the "date dimension" to mean a daily grained dimension table. This helps distinguish between date and time-of-day dimensions.

Unlike most of the other dimensions, you can build the date dimension table in advance. You may put 10 or 20 years of rows representing individual days in the table, so you can cover the history you have stored, as well as several years in the future. Even 20 years' worth of days is only approximately 7,300 rows, which is a relatively small dimension table. For a daily date dimension table in a retail environment, we recommend the partial list of columns shown in Figure 3-4.

Date Dimension
Date Key (PK)
Date
Full Date Description
Day of Week
Day Number in Calendar Month
Day Number in Calendar Year
Day Number in Fiscal Month
Day Number in Fiscal Year
Last Day in Month Indicator
Calendar Week Ending Date
Calendar Week Number in Year
Calendar Month Name
Calendar Month Number in Year
Calendar Year-Month (YYYY-MM)
Calendar Quarter
Calendar Year-Quarter
Calendar Year
Fiscal Week
Fiscal Week Number in Year
Fiscal Month
Fiscal Month Number in Year
Fiscal Year-Month
Fiscal Quarter
Fiscal Year-Quarter
Fiscal Half Year
Fiscal Year
Holiday Indicator
Weekday Indicator
SQL Date Stamp
...

Figure 3-4: Date dimension table.

Each column in the date dimension table is defined by the particular day that the row represents. The day-of-week column contains the day's name, such as Monday. This column would be used to create reports comparing Monday business with Sunday business. The day number in calendar month column starts with 1 at the beginning of each month and runs to 28, 29, 30, or 31 depending on the month. This column is useful for comparing the same day each month. Similarly, you could have a month number in year (1, . . ., 12). All these integers support simple date arithmetic across year and month boundaries.

For reporting, you should include both long and abbreviated labels. For example, you would want a month name attribute with values such as January. In addition, a year-month (YYYY-MM) column is useful as a report column header. You likely also want a quarter number (Q1, . . ., Q4), as well as a year-quarter, such as 2013-Q1. You would include similar columns for the fiscal periods if they differ from calendar periods. Sample rows containing several date dimension columns are illustrated in Figure 3-5.

Date Key	Date	Full Date Description	Day of Week	Calendar Month	Calendar Quarter	Calendar Year	Fiscal Year-Month	Holiday Indicator	Weekday Indicator
20130101	01/01/2013	January 1, 2013	Tuesday	January	Q1	2013	F2013-01	Holiday	Weekday
20130102	01/02/2013	January 2, 2013	Wednesday	January	Q1	2013	F2013-01	Non-Holiday	Weekday
20130103	01/03/2013	January 3, 2013	Thursday	January	Q1	2013	F2013-01	Non-Holiday	Weekday
20130104	01/04/2013	January 4, 2013	Friday	January	Q1	2013	F2013-01	Non-Holiday	Weekday
20130105	01/05/2013	January 5, 2013	Saturday	January	Q1	2013	F2013-01	Non-Holiday	Weekday
20130106	01/06/2013	January 6, 2013	Sunday	January	Q1	2013	F2013-01	Non-Holiday	Weekday
20130107	01/07/2013	January 7, 2013	Monday	January	Q1	2013	F2013-01	Non-Holiday	Weekday
20130108	01/08/2013	January 8, 2013	Tuesday	January	Q1	2013	F2013-01	Non-Holiday	Weekday

Figure 3-5: Date dimension sample rows.

NOTE A sample date dimension is available at www.kimballgroup.com under the Tools and Utilities tab for this book title.

Some designers pause at this point to ask why an explicit date dimension table is needed. They reason that if the date key in the fact table is a date type column, then any SQL query can directly constrain on the fact table date key and use natural SQL date semantics to filter on month or year while avoiding a supposedly expensive join. This reasoning falls apart for several reasons. First, if your relational database can't handle an efficient join to the date dimension table, you're in deep trouble. Most database optimizers are quite efficient at resolving dimensional queries; it is not necessary to avoid joins like the plague.

Since the average business user is not versed in SQL date semantics, he would be unable to request typical calendar groupings. SQL date functions do not support filtering by attributes such as weekdays versus weekends, holidays, fiscal periods, or seasons. Presuming the business needs to slice data by these nonstandard date attributes, then an explicit date dimension table is essential. Calendar logic belongs in a dimension table, not in the application code.

NOTE Dimensional models always need an explicit date dimension table. There are many date attributes not supported by the SQL date function, including week numbers, fiscal periods, seasons, holidays, and weekends. Rather than attempting to determine these nonstandard calendar calculations in a query, you should look them up in a date dimension table.

Flags and Indicators as Textual Attributes

Like many operational flags and indicators, the date dimension's holiday indicator is a simple indicator with two potential values. Because dimension table attributes serve as report labels and values in pull-down query filter lists, this indicator should be populated with meaningful values such as Holiday or Non-holiday instead of the cryptic Y/N, 1/0, or True/False. As illustrated in Figure 3-6, imagine a report comparing holiday versus non-holiday sales for a product. More meaningful domain values for this indicator translate into a more meaningful, self-explanatory report. Rather than decoding flags into understandable labels in the BI application, we prefer that decoded values be stored in the database so they're consistently available to all users regardless of their BI reporting environment or tools.

Monthly Sales

Period:	June 2013
Product	Baked Well Sourdough

Holiday Indicator	Extended Sales Dollar Amount
N	1,009
Y	6,298

OR

Monthly Sales

Period:	June 2013
Product	Baked Well Sourdough

Holiday Indicator	Extended Sales Dollar Amount
Holiday	6,298
Non-holiday	1,009

Figure 3-6: Sample reports with cryptic versus textual indicators.

A similar argument holds true for the weekday indicator that would have a value of Weekday or Weekend. Saturdays and Sundays obviously would be assigned the weekend value. Of course, multiple date table attributes can be jointly constrained, so you can easily compare weekday holidays with weekend holidays.

Current and Relative Date Attributes

Most date dimension attributes are not subject to updates. June 1, 2013 will always roll up to June, Calendar Q2, and 2013. However, there are attributes you can add to the basic date dimension that will change over time, including IsCurrentDay, IsCurrentMonth, IsPrior60Days, and so on. IsCurrentDay obviously must be updated each day; the attribute is useful for generating reports that always run for today. A nuance to consider is the day that IsCurrentDay refers to. Most data warehouses load data daily, so IsCurrentDay would refer to yesterday (or more accurately, the most recent day loaded). You might also add attributes to the date dimension that are unique to your corporate calendar, such as IsFiscalMonthEnd.

Some date dimensions include updated lag attributes. The lag day column would take the value 0 for today, −1 for yesterday, +1 for tomorrow, and so on. This attribute could easily be a computed column rather than physically stored. It might be useful to set up similar structures for month, quarter, and year. Many BI tools include functionality to do prior period calculations, so these lag columns may be unnecessary.

Time-of-Day as a Dimension or Fact

Although date and time are comingled in an operational date/time stamp, time-of-day is typically separated from the date dimension to avoid a row count explosion in the date dimension. As noted earlier, a date dimension with 20 years of history contains approximately 7,300 rows. If you changed the grain of this dimension to one row per minute in a day, you'd end up with over 10 million rows to accommodate the 1,440 minutes per day. If you tracked time to the second, you'd have more than 31 million rows per year! Because the date dimension is likely the most frequently constrained dimension in a schema, it should be kept as small and manageable as possible.

If you want to filter or roll up time periods based on summarized day part groupings, such as activity during 15-minute intervals, hours, shifts, lunch hour, or prime time, time-of-day would be treated as a full-fledged dimension table with one row per discrete time period, such as one row per minute within a 24-hour period resulting in a dimension with 1,440 rows.

If there's no need to roll up or filter on time-of-day groupings, time-of-day should be handled as a simple date/time fact in the fact table. By the way, business users are often more interested in time lags, such as the transaction's duration, rather than discreet start and stop times. Time lags can easily be computed by taking the difference between date/time stamps. These date/time stamps also allow an application to determine the time gap between two transactions of interest, even if these transactions exist in different days, months, or years.

Product Dimension

The product dimension describes every SKU in the grocery store. Although a typical store may stock 60,000 SKUs, when you account for different merchandising schemes and historical products that are no longer available, the product dimension may have 300,000 or more rows. The product dimension is almost always sourced from the operational product master file. Most retailers administer their product master file at headquarters and download a subset to each store's POS system at frequent intervals. It is headquarters' responsibility to define the appropriate product master record (and unique SKU number) for each new product.

Flatten Many-to-One Hierarchies

The product dimension represents the many descriptive attributes of each SKU. The merchandise hierarchy is an important group of attributes. Typically, individual SKUs roll up to brands, brands roll up to categories, and categories roll up to departments. Each of these is a many-to-one relationship. This merchandise hierarchy and additional attributes are shown for a subset of products in Figure 3-7.

Product Key	Product Description	Brand Description	Subcategory Description	Category Description	Department Description	Fat Content
1	Baked Well Light Sourdough Fresh Bread	Baked Well	Fresh	Bread	Bakery	Reduced Fat
2	Fluffy Sliced Whole Wheat	Fluffy	Pre-Packaged	Bread	Bakery	Regular Fat
3	Fluffy Light Sliced Whole Wheat	Fluffy	Pre-Packaged	Bread	Bakery	Reduced Fat
4	Light Mini Cinnamon Rolls	Light	Pre-Packaged	Sweeten Bread	Bakery	Non-Fat
5	Diet Lovers Vanilla 2 Gallon	Coldpack	Ice Cream	Frozen Desserts	Frozen Foods	Non-Fat
6	Light and Creamy Butter Pecan 1 Pint	Freshlike	Ice Cream	Frozen Desserts	Frozen Foods	Reduced Fat
7	Chocolate Lovers 1/2 Gallon	Frigid	Ice Cream	Frozen Desserts	Frozen Foods	Regular Fat
8	Strawberry Ice Creamy 1 Pint	Icy	Ice Cream	Frozen Desserts	Frozen Foods	Regular Fat
9	Icy Ice Cream Sandwiches	Icy	Novelties	Frozen Desserts	Frozen Foods	Regular Fat

Figure 3-7: Product dimension sample rows.

For each SKU, all levels of the merchandise hierarchy are well defined. Some attributes, such as the SKU description, are unique. In this case, there are 300,000 different values in the SKU description column. At the other extreme, there are only perhaps 50 distinct values of the department attribute. Thus, on average, there are 6,000 repetitions of each unique value in the department attribute. This is perfectly acceptable! You do not need to separate these repeated values into a second normalized table to save space. Remember dimension table space requirements pale in comparison with fact table space considerations.

NOTE   Keeping the repeated low cardinality values in the primary dimension table is a fundamental dimensional modeling technique. Normalizing these values into separate tables defeats the primary goals of simplicity and performance, as discussed in "Resisting Normalization Urges" later in this chapter.

Many of the attributes in the product dimension table are not part of the merchandise hierarchy. The package type attribute might have values such as Bottle, Bag, Box, or Can. Any SKU in any department could have one of these values.

It often makes sense to combine a constraint on this attribute with a constraint on a merchandise hierarchy attribute. For example, you could look at all the SKUs in the Cereal category packaged in Bags. Put another way, you can browse among dimension attributes regardless of whether they belong to the merchandise hierarchy. Product dimension tables typically have more than one explicit hierarchy.

A recommended partial product dimension for a retail grocery dimensional model is shown in Figure 3-8.

Product Dimension
Product Key (PK)
SKU Number (NK)
Product Description
Brand Description
Subcategory Description
Category Description
Department Number
Department Description
Package Type Description
Package Size
Fat Content
Diet Type
Weight
Weight Unit of Measure
Storage Type
Shelf Life Type
Shelf Width
Shelf Height
Shelf Depth
...

Figure 3-8: Product dimension table.

Attributes with Embedded Meaning

Often operational product codes, identified in the dimension table by the NK notation for natural key, have embedded meaning with different parts of the code representing significant characteristics of the product. In this case, the multipart attribute should be both preserved in its entirety within the dimension table, as well as broken down into its component parts, which are handled as separate attributes. For example, if the fifth through ninth characters in the operational code identify the manufacturer, the manufacturer's name should also be included as a dimension table attribute.

Numeric Values as Attributes or Facts

You will sometimes encounter numeric values that don't clearly fall into either the fact or dimension attribute categories. A classic example is the standard list price for a product. It's definitely a numeric value, so the initial instinct is to place it in the fact table. But typically the standard price changes infrequently, unlike most facts that are often differently valued on every measurement event.

If the numeric value is used primarily for calculation purposes, it likely belongs in the fact table. Because standard price is non-additive, you might multiply it by the quantity for an extended amount which would be additive. Alternatively, if the standard price is used primarily for price variance analysis, perhaps the variance metric should be stored in the fact table instead. If the stable numeric value is used predominantly for filtering and grouping, it should be treated as a product dimension attribute.

Sometimes numeric values serve both calculation and filtering/grouping functions. In these cases, you should store the value in both the fact and dimension tables. Perhaps the standard price in the fact table represents the valuation at the time of the sales transaction, whereas the dimension attribute is labeled to indicate it's the current standard price.

NOTE   Data elements that are used both for fact calculations and dimension constraining, grouping, and labeling should be stored in both locations, even though a clever programmer could write applications that access these data elements from a single location. It is important that dimensional models be as consistent as possible and application development be predictably simple. Data involved in calculations should be in fact tables and data involved in constraints, groups and labels should be in dimension tables.

Drilling Down on Dimension Attributes

A reasonable product dimension table can have 50 or more descriptive attributes. Each attribute is a rich source for constraining and constructing row header labels. *Drilling down* is nothing more than asking for a row header from a dimension that provides more information.

Let's say you have a simple report summarizing the sales dollar amount by department. As illustrated in Figure 3-9, if you want to drill down, you can drag any other attribute, such as brand, from the product dimension into the report next to department, and you can automatically drill down to this next level of detail. You could drill down by the fat content attribute, even though it isn't in the merchandise hierarchy rollup.

NOTE   Drilling down in a dimensional model is nothing more than adding row header attributes from the dimension tables. *Drilling up* is removing row headers. You can drill down or up on attributes from more than one explicit hierarchy and with attributes that are part of no hierarchy.

Department Name	Sales Dollar Amount
Bakery	12,331
Frozen Foods	31,776

Drill down by brand name:

Department Name	Brand Name	Sales Dollar Amount
Bakery	Baked Well	3,009
Bakery	Fluffy	3,024
Bakery	Light	6,298
Frozen Foods	Coldpack	5,321
Frozen Foods	Freshlike	10,476
Frozen Foods	Frigid	7,328
Frozen Foods	Icy	2,184
Frozen Foods	QuickFreeze	6,467

Or drill down by fat content:

Department Name	Fat Content	Sales Dollar Amount
Bakery	Nonfat	6,298
Bakery	Reduced fat	5,027
Bakery	Regular fat	1,006
Frozen Foods	Nonfat	5,321
Frozen Foods	Reduced fat	10,476
Frozen Foods	Regular fat	15,979

Figure 3-9: Drilling down on dimension attributes.

The product dimension is a common dimension in many dimensional models. Great care should be taken to fill this dimension with as many descriptive attributes as possible. A robust and complete set of dimension attributes translates into robust and complete analysis capabilities for the business users. We'll further explore the product dimension in Chapter 5: Procurement where we'll also discuss the handling of product attribute changes.

Store Dimension

The store dimension describes every store in the grocery chain. Unlike the product master file that is almost guaranteed to be available in every large grocery business, there may not be a comprehensive store master file. POS systems may simply supply a store number on the transaction records. In these cases, project teams must assemble the necessary components of the store dimension from multiple operational sources. Often there will be a store real estate department at headquarters who will help define a detailed store master file.

Multiple Hierarchies in Dimension Tables

The store dimension is the case study's primary geographic dimension. Each store can be thought of as a location. You can roll stores up to any geographic attribute, such as ZIP code, county, and state in the United States. Contrary to popular belief, cities and states within the United States are not a hierarchy. Since many states have identically named cities, you'll want to include a City-State attribute in the store dimension.

Stores likely also roll up an internal organization hierarchy consisting of store districts and regions. These two different store hierarchies are both easily represented in the dimension because both the geographic and organizational hierarchies are well defined for a single store row.

> **NOTE**   It is not uncommon to represent multiple hierarchies in a dimension table. The attribute names and values should be unique across the multiple hierarchies.

A recommended retail store dimension table is shown in Figure 3-10.

Store Dimension
Store Key (PK)
Store Number (NK)
Store Name
Store Street Address
Store City
Store County
Store City-State
Store State
Store Zip Code
Store Manager
Store District
Store Region
Floor Plan Type
Photo Processing Type
Financial Service Type
Selling Square Footage
Total Square Footage
First Open Date
Last Remodel Date
...

Figure 3-10: Store dimension table.

The floor plan type, photo processing type, and finance services type are all short text descriptors that describe the particular store. These should not be one-character codes but rather should be 10- to 20-character descriptors that make sense when viewed in a pull-down filter list or used as a report label.

The column describing selling square footage is numeric and theoretically additive across stores. You might be tempted to place it in the fact table. However, it is clearly a constant attribute of a store and is used as a constraint or label more often than it is used as an additive element in a summation. For these reasons, selling square footage belongs in the store dimension table.

Dates Within Dimension Tables

The first open date and last remodel date in the store dimension could be date type columns. However, if users want to group and constrain on nonstandard calendar attributes (like the open date's fiscal period), then they are typically join keys to copies of the date dimension table. These date dimension copies are declared in SQL by the view construct and are semantically distinct from the primary date dimension. The view declaration would look like the following:

```
create view first_open_date (first_open_day_number, first_open_month,
...)
    as select day_number, month, ...
    from date
```

Now the system acts as if there is another physical copy of the date dimension table called FIRST_OPEN_DATE. Constraints on this new date table have nothing to do with constraints on the primary date dimension joined to the fact table. The first open date view is a permissible *outrigger* to the store dimension; outriggers will be described in more detail later in this chapter. Notice we have carefully relabeled all the columns in the view so they cannot be confused with columns from the primary date dimension. These distinct logical views on a single physical date dimension are an example of dimension *role playing*, which we'll discuss more fully in Chapter 6: Order Management.

Promotion Dimension

The promotion dimension is potentially the most interesting dimension in the retail sales schema. The promotion dimension describes the promotion conditions under which a product is sold. Promotion conditions include temporary price reductions, end aisle displays, newspaper ads, and coupons. This dimension is often called a *causal dimension* because it describes factors thought to cause a change in product sales.

Business analysts at both headquarters and the stores are interested in determining whether a promotion is effective. Promotions are judged on one or more of the following factors:

- Whether the products under promotion experienced a gain in sales, called *lift*, during the promotional period. The lift can be measured only if the store can agree on what the baseline sales of the promoted products would have been without the promotion. Baseline values can be estimated from prior sales history and, in some cases, with the help of sophisticated models.

- Whether the products under promotion showed a drop in sales just prior to or after the promotion, canceling the gain in sales during the promotion (*time shifting*). In other words, did you transfer sales from regularly priced products to temporarily reduced priced products?

- Whether the products under promotion showed a gain in sales but other products nearby on the shelf showed a corresponding sales decrease (*cannibalization*).

- Whether all the products in the promoted category of products experienced a net overall gain in sales taking into account the time periods before, during, and after the promotion (*market growth*).

- Whether the promotion was profitable. Usually the profit of a promotion is taken to be the incremental gain in profit of the promoted category over the baseline sales taking into account time shifting and cannibalization, as well as the costs of the promotion.

The causal conditions potentially affecting a sale are not necessarily tracked directly by the POS system. The transaction system keeps track of price reductions and markdowns. The presence of coupons also typically is captured with the transaction because the customer either presents coupons at the time of sale or does not. Ads and in-store display conditions may need to be linked from other sources.

The various possible causal conditions are highly correlated. A temporary price reduction usually is associated with an ad and perhaps an end aisle display. For this reason, it makes sense to create one row in the promotion dimension for each combination of promotion conditions that occurs. Over the course of a year, there may be 1,000 ads, 5,000 temporary price reductions, and 1,000 end aisle displays, but there may be only 10,000 combinations of these three conditions affecting any particular product. For example, in a given promotion, most of the stores would run all three promotion mechanisms simultaneously, but a few of the stores may not deploy the end aisle displays. In this case, two separate promotion condition rows would be needed, one for the normal price reduction plus ad plus display and one for the price reduction plus ad only. A recommended promotion dimension table is shown in Figure 3-11.

From a purely logical point of view, you could record similar information about the promotions by separating the four causal mechanisms (price reductions, ads, displays, and coupons) into separate dimensions rather than combining them into one dimension. Ultimately, this choice is the designer's prerogative. The trade-offs in favor of keeping the four dimensions together include the following:

- If the four causal mechanisms are highly correlated, the combined single dimension is not much larger than any one of the separated dimensions would be.
- The combined single dimension can be browsed efficiently to see how the various price reductions, ads, displays, and coupons are used together. However, this browsing only shows the possible promotion combinations. Browsing in the dimension table does not reveal which stores or products were affected by the promotion; this information is found in the fact table.

Promotion Dimension
Promotion Key (PK)
Promotion Code
Promotion Name
Price Reduction Type
Promotion Media Type
Ad Type
Display Type
Coupon Type
Ad Media Name
Display Provider
Promotion Cost
Promotion Begin Date
Promotion End Date
...

Figure 3-11: Promotion dimension table.

The trade-offs in favor of separating the causal mechanisms into four distinct dimension tables include the following:

- The separated dimensions may be more understandable to the business community if users think of these mechanisms separately. This would be revealed during the business requirement interviews.
- Administration of the separate dimensions may be more straightforward than administering a combined dimension.

Keep in mind there is no difference in the content between these two choices.

NOTE   The inclusion of promotion cost attribute in the promotion dimension should be done with careful thought. This attribute can be used for constraining and grouping. However, this cost should not appear in the POS transaction fact table representing individual product sales because it is at the wrong grain; this cost would have to reside in a fact table whose grain is the overall promotion.

Null Foreign Keys, Attributes, and Facts

Typically, many sales transactions include products that are not being promoted. Hopefully, consumers aren't just filling their shopping cart with promoted products; you want them paying full price for some products in their cart! The promotion dimension must include a row, with a unique key such as 0 or –1, to identify this no promotion condition and avoid a null promotion key in the fact table. Referential integrity is violated if you put a null in a fact table column declared as a foreign key to a dimension table. In addition to the referential integrity alarms, null keys are the source of great confusion to users because they can't join on null keys.

WARNING   You must avoid null keys in the fact table. A proper design includes a row in the corresponding dimension table to identify that the dimension is not applicable to the measurement.

We sometimes encounter nulls as dimension attribute values. These usually result when a given dimension row has not been fully populated, or when there are attributes that are not applicable to all the dimension's rows. In either case, we recommend substituting a descriptive string, such as Unknown or Not Applicable, in place of the null value. Null values essentially disappear in pull-down menus of possible attribute values or in report groupings; special syntax is required to identify them. If users sum up facts by grouping on a fully populated dimension attribute, and then alternatively, sum by grouping on a dimension attribute with null values, they'll get different query results. And you'll get a phone call because the data doesn't appear to be consistent. Rather than leaving the attribute null, or substituting a blank space or a period, it's best to label the condition; users can then purposely decide to exclude the Unknown or Not Applicable from their query. It's worth noting that some OLAP products prohibit null attribute values, so this is one more reason to avoid them.

Finally, we can also encounter nulls as metrics in the fact table. We generally leave these null so that they're properly handled in aggregate functions such as SUM, MIN, MAX, COUNT, and AVG which do the "right thing" with nulls. Substituting a zero instead would improperly skew these aggregated calculations.

Data mining tools may use different techniques for tracking nulls. You may need to do some additional transformation work beyond the above recommendations if creating an observation set for data mining.

Other Retail Sales Dimensions

Any descriptive attribute that takes on a single value in the presence of a fact table measurement event is a good candidate to be added to an existing dimension or be its own dimension. The decision whether a dimension should be associated with a fact table should be a binary yes/no based on the fact table's declared grain. For example, there's probably a cashier identified for each transaction. The corresponding cashier dimension would likely contain a small subset of non-private employee attributes. Like the promotion dimension, the cashier dimension will likely have a No Cashier row for transactions that are processed through self-service registers.

A trickier situation unfolds for the payment method. Perhaps the store has rigid rules and only accepts one payment method per transaction. This would make your life as a dimensional modeler easier because you'd attach a simple payment method dimension to the sales schema that would likely include a payment method description, along with perhaps a grouping of payment methods into either cash equivalent or credit payment types.

In real life, payment methods often present a more complicated scenario. If multiple payment methods are accepted on a single POS transaction, the payment method does not take on a single value at the declared grain. Rather than altering the declared grain to be something unnatural such as one row per payment method per product on a POS transaction, you would likely capture the payment method in a separate fact table with a granularity of either one row per transaction (then the various payment method options would appear as separate facts) or one row per payment method per transaction (which would require a separate payment method dimension to associate with each row).

Degenerate Dimensions for Transaction Numbers

The retail sales fact table includes the POS transaction number on every line item row. In an operational parent/child database, the POS transaction number would be the key to the transaction header record, containing all the information valid for the transaction as a whole, such as the transaction date and store identifier. However, in the dimensional model, you have already extracted this interesting header information into other dimensions. The POS transaction number is still useful because it serves as the grouping key for pulling together all the products purchased in a single market basket transaction. It also potentially enables you to link back to the operational system.

Although the POS transaction number looks like a dimension key in the fact table, the descriptive items that might otherwise fall in a POS transaction dimension have been stripped off. Because the resulting dimension is empty, we refer to the POS transaction number as a *degenerate dimension* (identified by the DD notation in this book's figures). The natural operational ticket number, such as the POS transaction number, sits by itself in the fact table without joining to a dimension table. Degenerate dimensions are very common when the grain of a fact table represents a single transaction or transaction line because the degenerate dimension represents the unique identifier of the parent. Order numbers, invoice numbers, and bill-of-lading numbers almost always appear as degenerate dimensions in a dimensional model.

Degenerate dimensions often play an integral role in the fact table's primary key. In our case study, the primary key of the retail sales fact table consists of the degenerate POS transaction number and product key, assuming scans of identical products in the market basket are grouped together as a single line item.

NOTE   Operational transaction control numbers such as order numbers, invoice numbers, and bill-of-lading numbers usually give rise to empty dimensions and are represented as degenerate dimensions in transaction fact tables. The degenerate dimension is a dimension key without a corresponding dimension table.

If, for some reason, one or more attributes are legitimately left over after all the other dimensions have been created and seem to belong to this header entity, you would simply create a normal dimension row with a normal join. However, you would no longer have a degenerate dimension.

Retail Schema in Action

With our retail POS schema designed, let's illustrate how it would be put to use in a query environment. A business user might be interested in better understanding weekly sales dollar volume by promotion for the snacks category during January 2013 for stores in the Boston district. As illustrated in Figure 3-12, you would place query constraints on month and year in the date dimension, district in the store dimension, and category in the product dimension.

If the query tool summed the sales dollar amount grouped by week ending date and promotion, the SQL query results would look similar to those below in Figure 3-13. You can plainly see the relationship between the dimensional model and the associated query. High-quality dimension attributes are crucial because they are the source of query constraints and report labels. If you use a BI tool with more functionality, the results would likely appear as a cross-tabular "pivoted" report, which may be more appealing to business users than the columnar data resulting from an SQL statement.

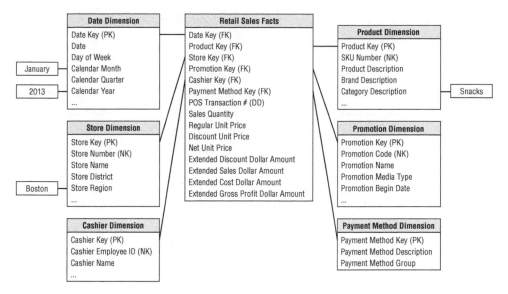

Figure 3-12: Querying the retail sales schema.

Calendar Week Ending Date	Promotion Name	Extended Sales Dollar Amount
January 6, 2013	No Promotion	2,647
January 13, 2013	No Promotion	4,851
January 20, 2013	Super Bowl Promotion	7,248
January 27, 2013	Super Bowl Promotion	13,798

Department Name	No Promotion Extended Sales Dollar Amount	Super Bowl Promotion Extended Sales Dollar Amount
January 6, 2013	2,647	0
January 13, 2013	4,851	0
January 20, 2013	0	7,248
January 27, 2013	0	13,798

Figure 3-13: Query results and cross-tabular report.

Retail Schema Extensibility

Let's turn our attention to extending the initial dimensional design. Several years after the rollout of the retail sales schema, the retailer implements a frequent shopper program. Rather than knowing an unidentified shopper purchased 26 items on a cash register receipt, you can now identify the specific shopper. Just imagine the business users' interest in analyzing shopping patterns by a multitude of geographic, demographic, behavioral, and other differentiating shopper characteristics.

The handling of this new frequent shopper information is relatively straightforward. You'd create a frequent shopper dimension table and add another foreign key in the fact table. Because you can't ask shoppers to bring in all their old cash register receipts to tag their historical sales transactions with their new frequent shopper number, you'd substitute a default shopper dimension surrogate key, corresponding to a Prior to Frequent Shopper Program dimension row, on the historical fact table rows. Likewise, not everyone who shops at the grocery store will have a frequent shopper card, so you'd also want to include a Frequent Shopper Not Identified row in the shopper dimension. As we discussed earlier with the promotion dimension, you can't have a null frequent shopper key in the fact table.

Our original schema gracefully extends to accommodate this new dimension largely because the POS transaction data was initially modeled at its most granular level. The addition of dimensions applicable at that granularity did not alter the existing dimension keys or facts; all existing BI applications continue to run without any changes. If the grain was originally declared as daily retail sales (transactions summarized by day, store, product, and promotion) rather than the transaction line detail, you would not have been able to incorporate the frequent shopper dimension. Premature summarization or aggregation inherently limits your ability to add supplemental dimensions because the additional dimensions often don't apply at the higher grain.

The predictable symmetry of dimensional models enable them to absorb some rather significant changes in source data and/or modeling assumptions without invalidating existing BI applications, including:

- **New dimension attributes.** If you discover new textual descriptors of a dimension, you can add these attributes as new columns. All existing applications will be oblivious to the new attributes and continue to function. If the new attributes are available only after a specific point in time, then Not Available or its equivalent should be populated in the old dimension rows. Be forewarned that this scenario is more complicated if the business users want to track historical changes to this newly identified attribute. If this is the case, pay close attention to the slowly changing dimension coverage in Chapter 5.
- **New dimensions.** As we just discussed, you can add a dimension to an existing fact table by adding a new foreign key column and populating it correctly with values of the primary key from the new dimension.

■ **New measured facts.** If new measured facts become available, you can add them gracefully to the fact table. The simplest case is when the new facts are available in the same measurement event and at the same grain as the existing facts. In this case, the fact table is altered to add the new columns, and the values are populated into the table. If the new facts are only available from a point in time forward, null values need to be placed in the older fact rows. A more complex situation arises when new measured facts occur naturally at a different grain. If the new facts cannot be allocated or assigned to the original grain of the fact table, the new facts belong in their own fact table because it's a mistake to mix grains in the same fact table.

Factless Fact Tables

There is one important question that cannot be answered by the previous retail sales schema: What products were on promotion but did not sell? The sales fact table records only the SKUs actually sold. There are no fact table rows with zero facts for SKUs that didn't sell because doing so would enlarge the fact table enormously.

In the relational world, a promotion coverage or event fact table is needed to answer the question concerning what didn't happen. The promotion coverage fact table keys would be date, product, store, and promotion in this case study. This obviously looks similar to the sales fact table you just designed; however, the grain would be significantly different. In the case of the promotion coverage fact table, you'd load one row for each product on promotion in a store each day (or week, if retail promotions are a week in duration) regardless of whether the product sold. This fact table enables you to see the relationship between the keys as defined by a promotion, independent of other events, such as actual product sales. We refer to it as a *factless fact table* because it has no measurement metrics; it merely captures the relationship between the involved keys, as illustrated in Figure 3-14. To facilitate counting, you can include a dummy fact, such as promotion count in this example, which always contains the constant value of 1; this is a cosmetic enhancement that enables the BI application to avoid counting one of the foreign keys.

To determine what products were on promotion but didn't sell requires a two-step process. First, you'd query the promotion factless fact table to determine the universe of products that were on promotion on a given day. You'd then determine what products sold from the POS sales fact table. The answer to our original question is the *set difference* between these two lists of products. If you work with data in an OLAP cube, it is often easier to answer the "what didn't happen" question because the cube typically contains explicit cells for nonbehavior.

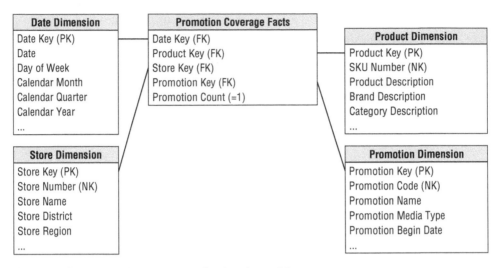

Figure 3-14: Promotion coverage factless fact table.

Dimension and Fact Table Keys

Now that the schemas have been designed, we'll focus on the dimension and fact tables' primary keys, along with other row identifiers.

Dimension Table Surrogate Keys

The unique primary key of a dimension table should be a *surrogate key* rather than relying on the operational system identifier, known as the *natural key*. Surrogate keys go by many other aliases: meaningless keys, integer keys, non-natural keys, artificial keys, and synthetic keys. Surrogate keys are simply integers that are assigned sequentially as needed to populate a dimension. The first product row is assigned a product surrogate key with the value of 1; the next product row is assigned product key 2; and so forth. The actual surrogate key value has no business significance. The surrogate keys merely serve to join the dimension tables to the fact table. Throughout this book, column names with a Key suffix, identified as a primary key (PK) or foreign key (FK), imply a surrogate.

Modelers sometimes are reluctant to relinquish the natural keys because they want to navigate the fact table based on the operational code while avoiding a join to the dimension table. They also don't want to lose the embedded intelligence that's often part of a natural multipart key. However, you should avoid relying on intelligent dimension keys because any assumptions you make eventually may be invalidated. Likewise, queries and data access applications should not have any built-in dependency on the keys because the logic also would be vulnerable to invalidation. Even if the natural keys appear to be stable and devoid of meaning, don't be tempted to use them as the dimension table's primary key.

NOTE Every join between dimension and fact tables in the data warehouse should be based on meaningless integer surrogate keys. You should avoid using a natural key as the dimension table's primary key.

Initially, it may be faster to implement a dimensional model using operational natural keys, but surrogate keys pay off in the long run. We sometimes think of them as being similar to a flu shot for the data warehouse—like an immunization, there's a small amount of pain to initiate and administer surrogate keys, but the long run benefits are substantial, especially considering the reduced risk of substantial rework. Here are several advantages:

- **Buffer the data warehouse from operational changes.** Surrogate keys enable the warehouse team to maintain control of the DW/BI environment rather than being whipsawed by operational rules for generating, updating, deleting, recycling, and reusing production codes. In many organizations, historical operational codes, such as inactive account numbers or obsolete product codes, get reassigned after a period of dormancy. If account numbers get recycled following 12 months of inactivity, the operational systems don't miss a beat because their business rules prohibit data from hanging around for that long. But the DW/BI system may retain data for years. Surrogate keys provide the warehouse with a mechanism to differentiate these two separate instances of the same operational account number. If you rely solely on operational codes, you might also be vulnerable to key overlaps in the case of an acquisition or consolidation of data.
- **Integrate multiple source systems.** Surrogate keys enable the data warehouse team to integrate data from multiple operational source systems, even if they lack consistent source keys by using a back room cross-reference mapping table to link the multiple natural keys to a common surrogate.
- **Improve performance.** The surrogate key is as small an integer as possible while ensuring it will comfortably accommodate the future anticipated cardinality (number of rows in the dimension). Often the operational code is a bulky alphanumeric character string or even a group of fields. The smaller surrogate key translates into smaller fact tables, smaller fact table indexes, and more fact table rows per block input-output operation. Typically, a 4-byte

integer is sufficient to handle most dimensions. A 4-byte integer is a single integer, not four decimal digits. It has 32 bits and therefore can handle approximately 2 billion positive values (2^{32}) or 4 billion total positive and negative values (-2^{32} to $+2^{32}$). This is more than enough for just about any dimension. Remember, if you have a large fact table with 1 billion rows of data, every byte in each fact table row translates into another gigabyte of storage.

■ **Handle null or unknown conditions.** As mentioned earlier, special surrogate key values are used to record dimension conditions that may not have an operational code, such as the No Promotion condition or the anonymous customer. You can assign a surrogate key to identify these despite the lack of operational coding. Similarly, fact tables sometimes have dates that are yet to be determined. There is no SQL date type value for Date to Be Determined or Date Not Applicable.

■ **Support dimension attribute change tracking.** One of the primary techniques for handling changes to dimension attributes relies on surrogate keys to handle the multiple profiles for a single natural key. This is actually one of the most important reasons to use surrogate keys, which we'll describe in Chapter 5. A pseudo surrogate key created by simply gluing together the natural key with a time stamp is perilous. You need to avoid multiple joins between the dimension and fact tables, sometimes referred to as double-barreled joins, due to their adverse impact on performance and ease of use.

Of course, some effort is required to assign and administer surrogate keys, but it's not nearly as intimidating as many people imagine. You need to establish and maintain a cross-reference table in the ETL system that will be used to substitute the appropriate surrogate key on each fact and dimension table row. We lay out a process for administering surrogate keys in Chapter 19: ETL Subsystems and Techniques.

Dimension Natural and Durable Supernatural Keys

Like surrogate keys, the *natural keys* assigned and used by operational source systems go by other names, such as business keys, production keys, and operational keys. They are identified with the NK notation in the book's figures. The natural key is often modeled as an attribute in the dimension table. If the natural key comes from multiple sources, you might use a character data type that prepends a source code, such as SAP|43251 or CRM|6539152. If the same entity is represented in both operational source systems, then you'd likely have two natural key attributes in the dimension corresponding to both sources. Operational natural keys are often composed of meaningful constituent parts, such as the product's line of business or country of origin; these components should be split apart and made available as separate attributes.

In a dimension table with attribute change tracking, it's important to have an identifier that uniquely and reliably identifies the dimension entity across its attribute changes. Although the operational natural key may seem to fit this bill, sometimes the natural key changes due to unexpected business rules (like an organizational merger) or to handle either duplicate entries or data integration from multiple sources. If the dimension's natural keys are not absolutely protected and preserved over time, the ETL system needs to assign permanent durable identifiers, also known as *supernatural keys*. A persistent *durable supernatural key* is controlled by the DW/BI system and remains immutable for the life of the system. Like the dimension surrogate key, it's a simple integer sequentially assigned. And like the natural keys discussed earlier, the durable supernatural key is handled as a dimension attribute; it's not a replacement for the dimension table's surrogate primary key. Chapter 19 also discusses the ETL system's responsibility for these durable identifiers.

Degenerate Dimension Surrogate Keys

Although surrogate keys aren't typically assigned to degenerate dimensions, each situation needs to be evaluated to determine if one is required. A surrogate key is necessary if the transaction control numbers are not unique across locations or get reused. For example, the retailer's POS system may not assign unique transaction numbers across stores. The system may wrap back to zero and reuse previous control numbers when its maximum has been reached. Also, the transaction control number may be a bulky 24-byte alphanumeric column. Finally, depending on the capabilities of the BI tool, you may need to assign a surrogate key (and create an associated dimension table) to drill across on the transaction number. Obviously, control number dimensions modeled in this way with corresponding dimension tables are no longer degenerate.

Date Dimension Smart Keys

As we've noted, the date dimension has unique characteristics and requirements. Calendar dates are fixed and predetermined; you never need to worry about deleting dates or handling new, unexpected dates on the calendar. Because of its predictability, you can use a more intelligent key for the date dimension.

If a sequential integer serves as the primary key of the date dimension, it should be chronologically assigned. In other words, January 1 of the first year would be assigned surrogate key value 1, January 2 would be assigned surrogate key 2, February 1 would be assigned surrogate key 32, and so on.

More commonly, the primary key of the date dimension is a meaningful integer formatted as yyyymmdd. The yyyymmdd key is not intended to provide business users and their BI applications with an intelligent key so they can bypass the date dimension and directly query the fact table. Filtering on the fact table's yyyymmdd key would have a detrimental impact on usability and performance. Filtering and grouping on calendar attributes should occur in a dimension table, not in the BI application's code.

However, the yyyymmdd key is useful for partitioning fact tables. Partitioning enables a table to be segmented into smaller tables under the covers. Partitioning a large fact table on the basis of date is effective because it allows old data to be removed gracefully and new data to be loaded and indexed in the current partition without disturbing the rest of the fact table. It reduces the time required for loads, backups, archiving, and query response. Programmatically updating and maintaining partitions is straightforward if the date key is an ordered integer: year increments by 1 up to the number of years wanted, month increments by 1 up to 12, and so on. Using a smart yyyymmdd key provides the benefits of a surrogate, plus the advantages of easier partition management.

Although the yyyymmdd integer is the most common approach for date dimension keys, some relational database optimizers prefer a true date type column for partitioning. In these cases, the optimizer knows there are 31 values between March 1 and April 1, as opposed to the apparent 100 values between 20130301 and 20130401. Likewise, it understands there are 31 values between December 1 and January 1, as opposed to the 8,900 integer values between 20121201 and 20130101. This intelligence can impact the query strategy chosen by the optimizer and further reduce query times. If the optimizer incorporates date type intelligence, it should be considered for the date key. If the only rationale for a date type key is simplified administration for the DBA, then you can feel less compelled.

With more intelligent date keys, whether chronologically assigned or a more meaningful yyyymmdd integer or date type column, you need to reserve a special date key value for the situation in which the date is unknown when the fact row is initially loaded.

Fact Table Surrogate Keys

Although we're adamant about using surrogate keys for dimension tables, we're less demanding about a surrogate key for fact tables. Fact table surrogate keys typically only make sense for back room ETL processing. As we mentioned, the primary key of a fact table typically consists of a subset of the table's foreign keys and/or degenerate dimension. However, single column surrogate keys for fact tables have some interesting back room benefits.

Like its dimensional counterpart, a fact table surrogate key is a simple integer, devoid of any business content, that is assigned in sequence as fact table rows are generated. Although the fact table surrogate key is unlikely to deliver query performance advantages, it does have the following benefits:

- **Immediate unique identification.** A single fact table row is immediately identified by the key. During ETL processing, a specific row can be identified without navigating multiple dimensions.

- **Backing out or resuming a bulk load.** If a large number of rows are being loaded with sequentially assigned surrogate keys, and the process halts before completion, the DBA can determine exactly where the process stopped by finding the maximum key in the table. The DBA could back out the complete load by specifying the range of keys just loaded or perhaps could resume the load from exactly the correct point.

- **Replacing updates with inserts plus deletes.** The fact table surrogate key becomes the true physical key of the fact table. No longer is the key of the fact table determined by a set of dimensional foreign keys, at least as far as the RDBMS is concerned. Thus it becomes possible to replace a fact table update operation with an insert followed by a delete. The first step is to place the new row into the database with all the same business foreign keys as the row it is to replace. This is now possible because the key enforcement depends only on the surrogate key, and the replacement row has a new surrogate key. Then the second step deletes the original row, thereby accomplishing the update. For a large set of updates, this sequence is more efficient than a set of true update operations. The insertions can be processed with the ability to back out or resume the insertions as described in the previous bullet. These insertions do not need to be protected with full transaction machinery. Then the final deletion step can be performed safely because the insertions have run to completion.

- **Using the fact table surrogate key as a parent in a parent/child schema.** In those cases in which one fact table contains rows that are parents of those in a lower grain fact table, the fact table surrogate key in the parent table is also exposed in the child table. The argument of using the fact table surrogate key in this case rather than a natural parent key is similar to the argument for using surrogate keys in dimension tables. Natural keys are messy and unpredictable, whereas surrogate keys are clean integers and are assigned by the ETL system, not the source system. Of course, in addition to including the parent fact table's surrogate key, the lower grained fact table should also include the parent's dimension foreign keys so the child facts can be sliced and diced without traversing the parent fact table's surrogate key. And as we'll discuss in Chapter 4: Inventory, you should never join fact tables directly to other fact tables.

Resisting Normalization Urges

In this section, let's directly confront several of the natural urges that tempt modelers coming from a more normalized background. We've been consciously breaking some traditional modeling rules because we're focused on delivering value through ease of use and performance, not on transaction processing efficiencies.

Snowflake Schemas with Normalized Dimensions

The flattened, denormalized dimension tables with repeating textual values make data modelers from the operational world uncomfortable. Let's revisit the case study product dimension table. The 300,000 products roll up into 50 distinct departments. Rather than redundantly storing the 20-byte department description in the product dimension table, modelers with a normalized upbringing want to store a 2-byte department code and then create a new department dimension for the department decodes. In fact, they would feel more comfortable if all the descriptors in the original design were normalized into separate dimension tables. They argue this design saves space because the 300,000-row dimension table only contains codes, not lengthy descriptors.

In addition, some modelers contend that more normalized dimension tables are easier to maintain. If a department description changes, they'd need to update only the one occurrence in the department dimension rather than the 6,000 repetitions in the original product dimension. Maintenance often is addressed by normalization disciplines, but all this happens back in the ETL system long before the data is loaded into a presentation area's dimensional schema.

Dimension table normalization is referred to as *snowflaking*. Redundant attributes are removed from the flat, denormalized dimension table and placed in separate normalized dimension tables. Figure 3-15 illustrates the partial snowflaking of the product dimension into third normal form. The contrast between Figure 3-15 and Figure 3-8 is startling. The plethora of snowflaked tables (even in our simplistic example) is overwhelming. Imagine the impact on Figure 3-12 if all the schema's hierarchies were normalized.

Snowflaking is a legal extension of the dimensional model, however, we encourage you to resist the urge to snowflake given the two primary design drivers: ease of use and performance.

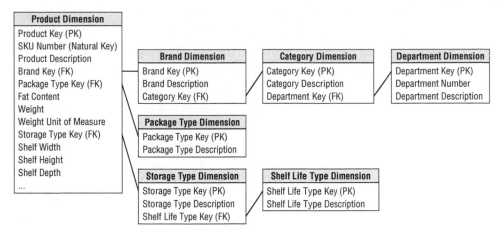

Figure 3-15: Snowflaked product dimension.

- The multitude of snowflaked tables makes for a much more complex presentation. Business users inevitably will struggle with the complexity; simplicity is one of the primary objectives of a dimensional model.
- Most database optimizers also struggle with the snowflaked schema's complexity. Numerous tables and joins usually translate into slower query performance. The complexities of the resulting join specifications increase the chances that the optimizer will get sidetracked and choose a poor strategy.
- The minor disk space savings associated with snowflaked dimension tables are insignificant. If you replace the 20-byte department description in the 300,000 row product dimension table with a 2-byte code, you'd save a whopping 5.4 MB (300,000 x 18 bytes); meanwhile, you may have a 10 GB fact table! Dimension tables are almost always geometrically smaller than fact tables. Efforts to normalize dimension tables to save disk space are usually a waste of time.
- Snowflaking negatively impacts the users' ability to browse within a dimension. Browsing often involves constraining one or more dimension attributes and looking at the distinct values of another attribute in the presence of these constraints. Browsing allows users to understand the relationship between dimension attribute values.

- Obviously, a snowflaked product dimension table responds well if you just want a list of the category descriptions. However, if you want to see all the brands within a category, you need to traverse the brand and category dimensions. If you want to also list the package types for each brand in a category, you'd be traversing even more tables. The SQL needed to perform these seemingly simple queries is complex, and you haven't touched the other dimensions or fact table.

- Finally, snowflaking defeats the use of bitmap indexes. Bitmap indexes are useful when indexing low-cardinality columns, such as the category and department attributes in the product dimension table. They greatly speed the performance of a query or constraint on the single column in question. Snowflaking inevitably would interfere with your ability to leverage this performance tuning technique.

NOTE Fixed depth hierarchies should be flattened in dimension tables. Normalized, snowflaked dimension tables penalize cross-attribute browsing and prohibit the use of bitmapped indexes. Disk space savings gained by normalizing the dimension tables typically are less than 1 percent of the total disk space needed for the overall schema. You should knowingly sacrifice this dimension table space in the spirit of performance and ease of use advantages.

Some database vendors argue their platform has the horsepower to query a fully normalized dimensional model without performance penalties. If you can achieve satisfactory performance without physically denormalizing the dimension tables, that's fine. However, you'll still want to implement a logical dimensional model with denormalized dimensions to present an easily understood schema to the business users and their BI applications.

In the past, some BI tools indicated a preference for snowflake schemas; snowflaking to address the idiosyncratic requirements of a BI tool is acceptable. Likewise, if all the data is delivered to business users via an OLAP cube (where the snowflaked dimensions are used to populate the cube but are never visible to the users), then snowflaking is acceptable. However, in these situations, you need to consider the impact on users of alternative BI tools and the flexibility to migrate to alternatives in the future.

Outriggers

Although we generally do not recommend snowflaking, there are situations in which it is permissible to build an *outrigger dimension* that attaches to a dimension within the fact table's immediate halo, as illustrated in Figure 3-16. In this example, the "once removed" outrigger is a date dimension snowflaked off a primary dimension. The outrigger date attributes are descriptively and uniquely labeled to distinguish them from the other dates associated with the business process. It only makes sense to outrigger a primary dimension table's date attribute if the business wants to filter and group this date by nonstandard calendar attributes, such as the fiscal period, business day indicator, or holiday period. Otherwise, you could just treat the date attribute as a standard date type column in the product dimension. If a date outrigger is used, be careful that the outrigger dates fall within the range stored in the standard date dimension table.

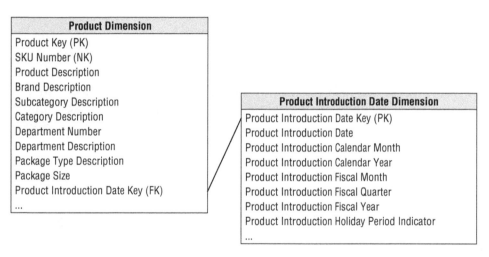

Figure 3-16: Example of a permissible outrigger.

You'll encounter more outrigger examples later in the book, such as the handling of customers' county-level demographic attributes in Chapter 8: Customer Relationship Management.

Although outriggers may save space and ensure the same attributes are referenced consistently, there are downsides. Outriggers introduce more joins, which can negatively impact performance. More important, outriggers can negatively impact the legibility for business users and hamper their ability to browse among attributes within a single dimension.

WARNING Though outriggers are permissible, a dimensional model should not be littered with outriggers given the potentially negative impact. Outriggers should be the exception rather than the rule.

Centipede Fact Tables with Too Many Dimensions

The fact table in a dimensional schema is naturally highly normalized and compact. There is no way to further normalize the extremely complex many-to-many relationships among the keys in the fact table because the dimensions are not correlated with each other. Every store is open every day. Sooner or later, almost every product is sold on promotion in most or all of our stores.

Interestingly, while uncomfortable with denormalized dimension tables, some modelers are tempted to denormalize the fact table. They have an uncontrollable urge to normalize dimension hierarchies but know snowflaking is highly discouraged, so the normalized tables end up joined to the fact table instead. Rather than having a single product foreign key on the fact table, they include foreign keys for the frequently analyzed elements on the product hierarchy, such as brand, category, and department. Likewise, the date key suddenly turns into a series of keys joining to separate week, month, quarter, and year dimension tables. Before you know it, your compact fact table has turned into an unruly monster that joins to literally dozens of dimension tables. We affectionately refer to these designs as *centipede fact tables* because they appear to have nearly 100 legs, as shown in Figure 3-17.

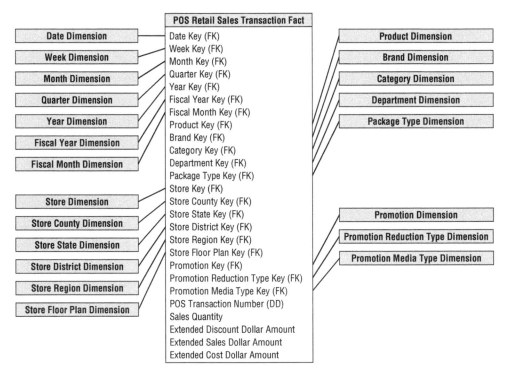

Figure 3-17: Centipede fact table with too many normalized dimensions.

Even with its tight format, the fact table is the behemoth in a dimensional model. Designing a fact table with too many dimensions leads to significantly increased fact table disk space requirements. Although denormalized dimension tables consume extra space, fact table space consumption is a concern because it is your largest table by orders of magnitude. There is no way to index the enormous multipart key effectively in the centipede example. The numerous joins are an issue for both usability and query performance.

Most business processes can be represented with less than 20 dimensions in the fact table. If a design has 25 or more dimensions, you should look for ways to combine correlated dimensions into a single dimension. Perfectly correlated attributes, such as the levels of a hierarchy, as well as attributes with a reasonable statistical correlation, should be part of the same dimension. It's a good decision to combine dimensions when the resulting new single dimension is noticeably smaller than the Cartesian product of the separate dimensions.

> **NOTE**   A very large number of dimensions typically are a sign that several dimensions are not completely independent and should be combined into a single dimension. It is a dimensional modeling mistake to represent elements of a single hierarchy as separate dimensions in the fact table.

Developments with columnar databases may reduce the query and storage penalties associated with wide centipede fact table designs. Rather than storing each table row, a columnar database stores each table column as a contiguous object that is heavily indexed for access. Even though the underlying physical storage is columnar, at the query level, the table appears to be made up of familiar rows. But when queried, only the named columns are actually retrieved from the disk, rather than the entire row in a more conventional row-oriented relational database. Columnar databases are much more tolerant of the centipede fact tables just described; however, the ability to browse across hierarchically related dimension attributes may be compromised.

Summary

This chapter was your first exposure to designing a dimensional model. Regardless of the industry, we strongly encourage the four-step process for tackling dimensional model designs. Remember it is especially important to clearly state the grain associated with a dimensional schema. Loading the fact table with atomic data provides the greatest flexibility because the data can be summarized "every which way." As soon as the fact table is restricted to more aggregated information, you run into walls when the summarization assumptions prove to be invalid. Also it is vitally important to populate your dimension tables with verbose, robust descriptive attributes for analytic filtering and labeling.

In the next chapter we'll remain within the retail industry to discuss techniques for tackling a second business process within the organization, ensuring your earlier efforts are leveraged while avoiding stovepipes.

4   Inventory

In Chapter 3: Retail Sales, we developed a dimensional model for the sales transactions in a large grocery chain. We remain within the same industry in this chapter but move up the value chain to tackle the inventory process. The designs developed in this chapter apply to a broad set of inventory pipelines both inside and outside the retail industry.

More important, this chapter provides a thorough discussion of the enterprise data warehouse bus architecture. The bus architecture is essential to creating an integrated DW/BI system. It provides a framework for planning the overall environment, even though it will be built incrementally. We will underscore the importance of using common conformed dimensions and facts across dimensional models, and will close by encouraging the adoption of an enterprise data governance program.

Chapter 4 discusses the following concepts:

- Representing organizational value chains via a series of dimensional models
- Semi-additive facts
- Three fact table types: periodic snapshots, transaction, and accumulating snapshots
- Enterprise data warehouse bus architecture and bus matrix
- Opportunity/stakeholder matrix
- Conformed dimensions and facts, and their impact on agile methods
- Importance of data governance

Value Chain Introduction

Most organizations have an underlying *value chain* of key business processes. The value chain identifies the natural, logical flow of an organization's primary activities. For example, a retailer issues purchase orders to product manufacturers. The products are delivered to the retailer's warehouse, where they are held in inventory. A delivery is then made to an individual store, where again the products sit in inventory until a consumer makes a purchase. Figure 4-1 illustrates this subset of a retailer's value chain. Obviously, products sourced from manufacturers that deliver directly to the retail store would bypass the warehousing processes.

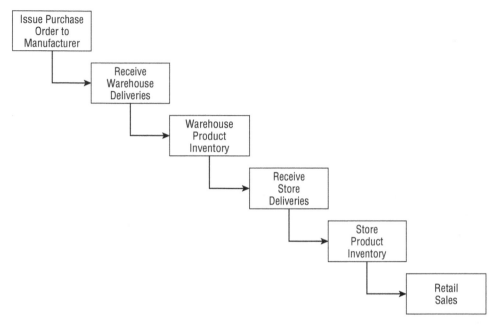

Figure 4-1: Subset of a retailer's value chain.

Operational source systems typically produce transactions or snapshots at each step of the value chain. The primary objective of most analytic DW/BI systems is to monitor the performance results of these key processes. Because each process produces unique metrics at unique time intervals with unique granularity and dimensionality, each process typically spawns one or more fact tables. To this end, the value chain provides high-level insight into the overall data architecture for an enterprise DW/BI environment. We'll devote more time to this topic in the "Value Chain Integration" section later in this chapter.

Inventory Models

In the meantime, we'll discuss several complementary inventory models. The first is the inventory *periodic snapshot* where product inventory levels are measured at regular intervals and placed as separate rows in a fact table. These periodic snapshot rows appear over time as a series of data layers in the dimensional model, much like geologic layers represent the accumulation of sediment over long periods of time. We'll then discuss a second inventory model where every transaction that impacts inventory levels as products move through the warehouse is recorded. Finally, in the third model, we'll describe the inventory accumulating snapshot where a fact table row is inserted for each product delivery and then the row is updated as the product moves through the warehouse. Each model tells a different story. For some analytic requirements, two or even all three models may be appropriate simultaneously.

Inventory Periodic Snapshot

Let's return to our retail case study. Optimized inventory levels in the stores can have a major impact on chain profitability. Making sure the right product is in the right store at the right time minimizes out-of-stocks (where the product isn't available on the shelf to be sold) and reduces overall inventory carrying costs. The retailer wants to analyze daily quantity-on-hand inventory levels by product and store.

It is time to put the four-step dimensional design process to work again. The business process we're interested in analyzing is the periodic snapshotting of retail store inventory. The most atomic level of detail provided by the operational inventory system is a daily inventory for each product in each store. The dimensions immediately fall out of this grain declaration: date, product, and store. This often happens with periodic snapshot fact tables where you cannot express the granularity in the context of a transaction, so a list of dimensions is needed instead. In this case study, there are no additional descriptive dimensions at this granularity. For example, promotion dimensions are typically associated with product movement, such as when the product is ordered, received, or sold, but not with inventory.

The simplest view of inventory involves only a single fact: quantity on hand. This leads to an exceptionally clean dimensional design, as shown in Figure 4-2.

Figure 4-2: Store inventory periodic snapshot schema.

The date dimension table in this case study is identical to the table developed in Chapter 3 for retail store sales. The product and store dimensions may be decorated with additional attributes that would be useful for inventory analysis. For example, the product dimension could be enhanced with columns such as the minimum reorder quantity or the storage requirement, assuming they are constant and discrete descriptors of each product. If the minimum reorder quantity varies for a product by store, it couldn't be included as a product dimension attribute. In the store dimension, you might include attributes to identify the frozen and refrigerated storage square footages.

Even a schema as simple as Figure 4-2 can be very useful. Numerous insights can be derived if inventory levels are measured frequently for many products in many locations. However, this periodic snapshot fact table faces a serious challenge that Chapter 3's sales transaction fact table did not. The sales fact table was reasonably sparse because you don't sell every product in every shopping cart. Inventory, on the other hand, generates dense snapshot tables. Because the retailer strives to avoid out-of-stock situations in which the product is not available, there may be a row in the fact table for every product in every store every day. In that case you would include the zero out-of-stock measurements as explicit rows. For the grocery retailer with 60,000 products stocked in 100 stores, approximately 6 million rows (60,000 products x 100 stores) would be inserted with each nightly fact table load. However, because the row width is just 14 bytes, the fact table would grow by only 84 MB with each load.

Although the data volumes in this case are manageable, the denseness of some periodic snapshots may mandate compromises. Perhaps the most obvious is to reduce the snapshot frequencies over time. It may be acceptable to keep the last 60 days of inventory at the daily level and then revert to less granular weekly snapshots for historical data. In this way, instead of retaining 1,095 snapshots during a 3-year period, the number could be reduced to 208 total snapshots; the 60 daily and 148 weekly snapshots should be stored in two separate fact tables given their unique periodicity.

Semi-Additive Facts

We stressed the importance of fact additivity in Chapter 3. In the inventory snapshot schema, the quantity on hand can be summarized across products or stores and result in a valid total. Inventory levels, however, are not additive across dates because they represent snapshots of a level or balance at one point in time. Because inventory levels (and all forms of financial account balances) are additive across some dimensions but not all, we refer to them as *semi-additive facts*.

The semi-additive nature of inventory balance facts is even more understandable if you think about your checking account balances. On Monday, presume that you have $50 in your account. On Tuesday, the balance remains unchanged. On Wednesday, you deposit another $50 so the balance is now $100. The account has no further activity through the end of the week. On Friday, you can't merely add up the daily balances during the week and declare that the ending balance is $400 (based on $50 + $50 + $100 + $100 + $100). The most useful way to combine account balances and inventory levels across dates is to average them (resulting in an $80 average balance in the checking example). You are probably familiar with your bank referring to the average daily balance on a monthly account summary.

> **NOTE** All measures that record a static level (inventory levels, financial account balances, and measures of intensity such as room temperatures) are inherently non-additive across the date dimension and possibly other dimensions. In these cases, the measure may be aggregated across dates by averaging over the number of time periods.

Unfortunately, you cannot use the SQL AVG function to calculate the average over time. This function averages over all the rows received by the query, not just the number of dates. For example, if a query requested the average inventory for a cluster of three products in four stores across seven dates (e.g., the average daily inventory of a brand in a geographic region during a week), the SQL AVG function would divide the summed inventory value by 84 (3 products × 4 stores × 7 dates). Obviously, the correct answer is to divide the summed inventory value by 7, which is the number of daily time periods.

OLAP products provide the capability to define aggregation rules within the cube, so semi-additive measures like balances are less problematic if the data is deployed via OLAP cubes.

Enhanced Inventory Facts

The simplistic view in the periodic inventory snapshot fact table enables you to see a time series of inventory levels. For most inventory analysis, quantity on hand isn't enough. Quantity on hand needs to be used in conjunction with additional facts to measure the velocity of inventory movement and develop other interesting metrics such as the number of turns and number of days' supply.

If quantity sold (or equivalently, quantity shipped for a warehouse location) was added to each fact row, you could calculate the number of turns and days' supply. For daily inventory snapshots, the number of turns measured each day is calculated as the quantity sold divided by the quantity on hand. For an extended time span, such as a year, the number of turns is the total quantity sold divided by the daily average quantity on hand. The number of days' supply is a similar calculation. Over a time span, the number of days' supply is the final quantity on hand divided by the average quantity sold.

In addition to the quantity sold, inventory analysts are also interested in the extended value of the inventory at cost, as well as the value at the latest selling price. The initial periodic snapshot is embellished in Figure 4-3.

Figure 4-3: Enhanced inventory periodic snapshot.

Notice that quantity on hand is semi-additive, but the other measures in the enhanced periodic snapshot are all fully additive. The quantity sold amount has been rolled up to the snapshot's daily granularity. The valuation columns are extended, additive amounts. In some periodic snapshot inventory schemas, it is useful to store the beginning balance, the inventory change or delta, along with the ending balance. In this scenario, the balances are again semi-additive, whereas the deltas are fully additive across all the dimensions.

The periodic snapshot is the most common inventory schema. We'll briefly discuss two alternative perspectives that complement the inventory snapshot just designed. For a change of pace, rather than describing these models in the context of the retail store inventory, we'll move up the value chain to discuss the inventory located in the warehouses.

Inventory Transactions

A second way to model an inventory business process is to record every transaction that affects inventory. Inventory transactions at the warehouse might include the following:

- Receive product.
- Place product into inspection hold.
- Release product from inspection hold.
- Return product to vendor due to inspection failure.
- Place product in bin.
- Pick product from bin.
- Package product for shipment.
- Ship product to customer.
- Receive product from customer.
- Return product to inventory from customer return.
- Remove product from inventory.

Each inventory transaction identifies the date, product, warehouse, vendor, transaction type, and in most cases, a single amount representing the inventory quantity impact caused by the transaction. Assuming the granularity of the fact table is one row per inventory transaction, the resulting schema is illustrated in Figure 4-4.

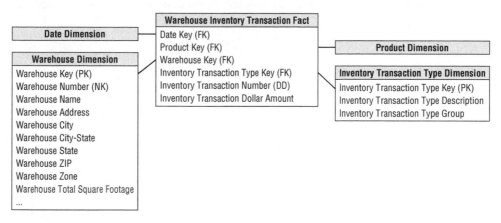

Figure 4-4: Warehouse inventory transaction model.

Even though the transaction fact table is simple, it contains detailed information that mirrors individual inventory manipulations. The transaction fact table is useful for measuring the frequency and timing of specific transaction types to answer questions that couldn't be answered by the less granular periodic snapshot.

Even so, it is impractical to use the transaction fact table as the sole basis for analyzing inventory performance. Although it is theoretically possible to reconstruct the exact inventory position at any moment in time by rolling all possible transactions forward from a known inventory position, it is too cumbersome and impractical for broad analytic questions that span dates, products, warehouses, or vendors.

NOTE Remember there's more to life than transactions alone. Some form of a snapshot table to give a more cumulative view of a process often complements a transaction fact table.

Before leaving the transaction fact table, our example presumes each type of transaction impacting inventory levels positively or negatively has consistent dimensionality: date, product, warehouse, vendor, and transaction type. We recognize some transaction types may have varied dimensionality in the real world. For example, a shipper may be associated with the warehouse receipts and shipments; customer information is likely associated with shipments and customer returns. If the transactions' dimensionality varies by event, then a series of related fact tables should be designed rather than capturing all inventory transactions in a single fact table.

NOTE If performance measurements have different natural granularity or dimensionality, they likely result from separate processes that should be modeled as separate fact tables.

Inventory Accumulating Snapshot

The final inventory model is the *accumulating snapshot*. Accumulating snapshot fact tables are used for processes that have a definite beginning, definite end, and identifiable milestones in between. In this inventory model, one row is placed in the fact table when a particular product is received at the warehouse. The disposition of the product is tracked on this single fact row until it leaves the warehouse. In this example, the accumulating snapshot model is only possible if you can reliably distinguish products received in one shipment from those received at a later time; it is also appropriate if you track product movement by product serial number or lot number.

Now assume that inventory levels for a product lot captured a series of well-defined events or milestones as it moves through the warehouse, such as receiving, inspection, bin placement, and shipping. As illustrated in Figure 4-5, the inventory accumulating snapshot fact table with its multitude of dates and facts looks quite different from the transaction or periodic snapshot schemas.

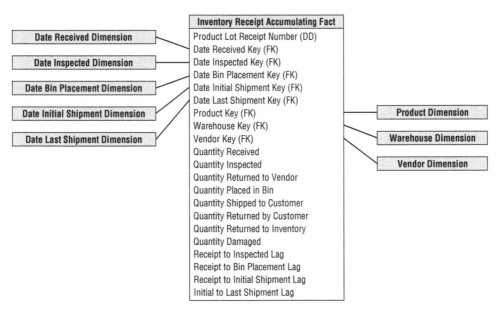

Figure 4-5: Warehouse inventory accumulating snapshot.

The accumulating snapshot fact table provides an updated status of the lot as it moves through standard milestones represented by multiple date-valued foreign keys. Each accumulating snapshot fact table row is updated repeatedly until the products received in a lot are completely depleted from the warehouse, as shown in Figure 4-6.

Fact row inserted when lot received:

Lot Receipt Number	Date Received Key	Date Inspected Key	Date Bin Placement Key	Product Key	Quantity Received	Receipt to Inspected Lag	Receipt to Bin Placement Lag
101	20130101	0	0	1	100		

Fact row updated when lot inspected:

Lot Receipt Number	Date Received Key	Date Inspected Key	Date Bin Placement Key	Product Key	Quantity Received	Receipt to Inspected Lag	Receipt to Bin Placement Lag
101	20130101	20130103	0	1	100	2	

Fact row updated when lot placed in bin:

Lot Receipt Number	Date Received Key	Date Inspected Key	Date Bin Placement Key	Product Key	Quantity Received	Receipt to Inspected Lag	Receipt to Bin Placement Lag
101	20130101	20130103	20130104	1	100	2	3

Figure 4-6: Evolution of an accumulating snapshot fact row.

Fact Table Types

There are just three fundamental types of fact tables: transaction, periodic snapshot, and accumulating snapshot. Amazingly, this simple pattern holds true regardless of the industry. All three types serve a useful purpose; you often need two complementary fact tables to get a complete picture of the business, yet the administration and rhythm of the three fact tables are quite different. Figure 4-7 compares and contrasts the variations.

	Transaction	Periodic Snapshot	Accumulating Snapshot
Periodicity	Discrete transaction point in time	Recurring snapshots at regular, predictable intervals	Indeterminate time span for evolving pipeline/workflow
Grain	1 row per transaction or transaction line	1 row per snapshot period plus other dimensions	1 row per pipeline occurrence
Date dimension(s)	Transaction date	Snapshot date	Multiple dates for pipeline's key milestones
Facts	Transaction performance	Cumulative performance for time interval	Performance for pipeline occurrence
Fact table sparsity	Sparse or dense, depending on activity	Predictably dense	Sparse or dense, depending on pipeline occurrence
Fact table updates	No updates, unless error correction	No updates, unless error correction	Updated whenever pipeline activity occurs

Figure 4-7: Fact table type comparisons.

Transaction Fact Tables

The most fundamental view of the business's operations is at the individual transaction or transaction line level. These fact tables represent an event that occurred at an instantaneous point in time. A row exists in the fact table for a given customer or product only if a transaction event occurred. Conversely, a given customer or product likely is linked to multiple rows in the fact table because hopefully the customer or product is involved in more than one transaction.

Transaction data fits easily into a dimensional framework. Atomic transaction data is the most naturally dimensional data, enabling you to analyze behavior in extreme detail. After a transaction has been posted in the fact table, you typically don't revisit it.

Having made a solid case for the charm of transaction detail, you may be thinking that all you need is a big, fast server to handle the gory transaction minutiae, and your job is over. Unfortunately, even with transaction level data, there are business questions that are impractical to answer using only these details. As indicated earlier, you cannot survive on transactions alone.

Periodic Snapshot Fact Tables

Periodic snapshots are needed to see the cumulative performance of the business at regular, predictable time intervals. Unlike the transaction fact table where a row is loaded for each event occurrence, with the periodic snapshot, you take a picture (hence the snapshot terminology) of the activity at the end of a day, week, or month, then another picture at the end of the next period, and so on. The periodic snapshots are stacked consecutively into the fact table. The periodic snapshot fact table often is the only place to easily retrieve a regular, predictable view of longitudinal performance trends.

When transactions equate to little pieces of revenue, you can move easily from individual transactions to a daily snapshot merely by adding up the transactions. In this situation, the periodic snapshot represents an aggregation of the transactional activity that occurred during a time period; you would build the snapshot only if needed for performance reasons. The design of the snapshot table is closely related to the design of its companion transaction table in this case. The fact tables share many dimension tables; the snapshot usually has fewer dimensions overall. Conversely, there are usually more facts in a summarized periodic snapshot table than in a transactional table because any activity that happens during the period is fair game for a metric in a periodic snapshot.

In many businesses, however, transaction details are not easily summarized to present management performance metrics. As you saw in this inventory case study, crawling through the transactions would be extremely time-consuming, plus the logic required to interpret the effect of different kinds of transactions on inventory levels could be horrendously complicated, presuming you even have access to the required historical data. The periodic snapshot again comes to the rescue to provide management with a quick, flexible view of inventory levels. Hopefully, the data for this snapshot schema is sourced directly from an operational system that handles these complex calculations. If not, the ETL system must also implement this complex logic to correctly interpret the impact of each transaction type.

Accumulating Snapshot Fact Tables

Last, but not least, the third type of fact table is the accumulating snapshot. Although perhaps not as common as the other two fact table types, accumulating snapshots can be very insightful. Accumulating snapshots represent processes that have a definite beginning and definite end together with a standard set of intermediate process steps. Accumulating snapshots are most appropriate when business users want to perform workflow or pipeline analysis.

Accumulating snapshots always have multiple date foreign keys, representing the predictable major events or process milestones; sometimes there's an additional date column that indicates when the snapshot row was last updated. As we'll discuss in Chapter 6: Order Management, these dates are each handled by a role-playing date dimension. Because most of these dates are not known when the fact row is first loaded, a default surrogate date key is used for the undefined dates.

Lags Between Milestones and Milestone Counts

Because accumulating snapshots often represent the efficiency and elapsed time of a workflow or pipeline, the fact table typically contains metrics representing the durations or lags between key milestones. It would be difficult to answer duration questions using a transaction fact table because you would need to correlate rows to calculate time lapses. Sometimes the lag metrics are simply the raw difference between the milestone dates or date/time stamps. In other situations, the lag calculation is made more complicated by taking workdays and holidays into consideration.

Accumulating snapshot fact tables sometimes include milestone completion counters, valued as either 0 or 1. Finally, accumulating snapshots often have a foreign key to a status dimension, which is updated to reflect the pipeline's latest status.

Accumulating Snapshot Updates and OLAP Cubes

In sharp contrast to the other fact table types, you purposely revisit accumulating snapshot fact table rows to update them. Unlike the periodic snapshot where the prior snapshots are preserved, the accumulating snapshot merely reflects the most current status and metrics. Accumulating snapshots do not attempt to accommodate complex scenarios that occur infrequently. The analysis of these outliers can always be done with the transaction fact table.

It is worth noting that accumulating snapshots are typically problematic for OLAP cubes. Because updates to an accumulating snapshot force both facts and dimension foreign keys to change, much of the cube would need to be reprocessed with updates to these snapshots, unless the fact row is only loaded once the pipeline occurrence is complete.

Complementary Fact Table Types

Sometimes accumulating and periodic snapshots work in conjunction with one another, such as when you incrementally build the monthly snapshot by adding the effect of each day's transactions to a rolling accumulating snapshot while also storing 36 months of historical data in a periodic snapshot. Ideally, when the last day of the month has been reached, the accumulating snapshot simply becomes the new regular month in the time series, and a new accumulating snapshot is started the next day.

Transactions and snapshots are the yin and yang of dimensional designs. Used together, companion transaction and snapshot fact tables provide a complete view of the business. Both are needed because there is often no simple way to combine these two contrasting perspectives in a single fact table. Although there is some theoretical data redundancy between transaction and snapshot tables, you don't object to such redundancy because as DW/BI publishers, your mission is to publish data so that the organization can effectively analyze it. These separate types of fact tables each provide different vantage points on the same story. Amazingly, these three types of fact tables turn out to be all the fact table types needed for the use cases described in this book.

Value Chain Integration

Now that we've completed the design of three inventory models, let's revisit our earlier discussion about the retailer's value chain. Both business and IT organizations are typically interested in value chain integration. Business management needs to look across the business's processes to better evaluate performance. For example, numerous DW/BI projects have focused on better understanding customer behavior from an end-to-end perspective. Obviously, this requires the ability to consistently look at customer information across processes, such as quotes, orders, invoicing, payments, and customer service. Similarly, organizations want to analyze their products across processes, or their employees, students, vendors, and so on.

IT managers recognize integration is needed to deliver on the promises of data warehousing and business intelligence. Many consider it their fiduciary responsibility to manage the organization's information assets. They know they're not fulfilling their responsibilities if they allow standalone, nonintegrated databases to proliferate. In addition to addressing the business's needs, IT also benefits from integration because it allows the organization to better leverage scarce resources and gain efficiencies through the use of reusable components.

Fortunately, the senior managers who typically are most interested in integration also have the necessary organizational influence and economic willpower to make it happen. If they don't place a high value on integration, you face a much more serious organizational challenge, or put more bluntly, your integration project will probably fail. It shouldn't be the sole responsibility of the DW/BI manager to garner organizational consensus for integration across the value chain. The political support of senior management is important; it takes the DW/BI manager off the hook and places the burden on senior leadership's shoulders where it belongs.

In Chapters 3 and 4, we modeled data from several processes of the retailer's value chain. Although separate fact tables in separate dimensional schemas represent the data from each process, the models share several common business dimensions: date, product, and store. We've logically represented this dimension sharing in Figure 4-8. Using shared, common dimensions is absolutely critical to designing dimensional models that can be integrated.

Figure 4-8: Sharing dimensions among business processes.

Enterprise Data Warehouse Bus Architecture

Obviously, building the enterprise's DW/BI system in one galactic effort is too daunting, yet building it as isolated pieces defeats the overriding goal of consistency. For long-term DW/BI success, you need to use an architected, incremental approach to build the enterprise's warehouse. The approach we advocate is the *enterprise data warehouse bus architecture.*

Understanding the Bus Architecture

Contrary to popular belief, the word *bus* is not shorthand for business; it's an old term from the electrical power industry that is now used in the computer industry. A bus is a common structure to which everything connects and from which everything derives power. The bus in a computer is a standard interface specification that enables you to plug in a disk drive, DVD, or any number of other specialized cards or devices. Because of the computer's bus standard, these peripheral devices work together and usefully coexist, even though they were manufactured at different times by different vendors.

NOTE   By defining a standard bus interface for the DW/BI environment, separate dimensional models can be implemented by different groups at different times. The separate business process subject areas plug together and usefully coexist if they adhere to the standard.

If you refer back to the value chain diagram in Figure 4-1, you can envision many business processes plugging into the enterprise data warehouse bus, as illustrated in Figure 4-9. Ultimately, all the processes of an organization's value chain create a family of dimensional models that share a comprehensive set of common, conformed dimensions.

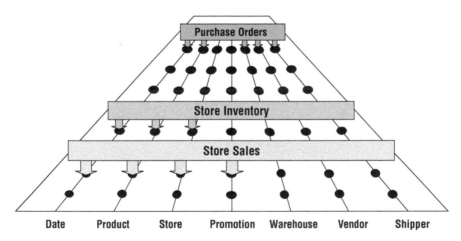

Figure 4-9: Enterprise data warehouse bus with shared dimensions.

The enterprise data warehouse bus architecture provides a rational approach to decomposing the enterprise DW/BI planning task. The master suite of standardized dimensions and facts has a uniform interpretation across the enterprise. This establishes the data architecture framework. You can then tackle the implementation of separate process-centric dimensional models, with each implementation closely adhering to the architecture. As the separate dimensional models become available, they fit together like the pieces of a puzzle. At some point, enough dimensional models exist to make good on the promise of an integrated enterprise DW/BI environment.

The bus architecture enables DW/BI managers to get the best of both worlds. They have an architectural framework guiding the overall design, but the problem has been divided into bite-sized business process chunks that can be implemented in realistic time frames. Separate development teams follow the architecture while working fairly independently and asynchronously.

The bus architecture is independent of technology and database platforms. All flavors of relational and OLAP-based dimensional models can be full participants in the enterprise data warehouse bus if they are designed around conformed dimensions and facts. DW/BI systems inevitably consist of separate machines with different operating systems and database management systems. Designed coherently, they share a common architecture of conformed dimensions and facts, allowing them to be fused into an integrated whole.

Enterprise Data Warehouse Bus Matrix

We recommend using an *enterprise data warehouse bus matrix* to document and communicate the bus architecture, as illustrated in Figure 4-10. Others have renamed the bus matrix, such as the conformance or event matrix, but these are merely synonyms for this fundamental Kimball concept first introduced in the 1990s.

COMMON DIMENSIONS

BUSINESS PROCESSES	Date	Product	Warehouse	Store	Promotion	Customer	Employee
Issue Purchase Orders	X	X	X				
Receive Warehouse Deliveries	X	X	X				X
Warehouse Inventory	X	X	X				
Receive Store Deliveries	X	X	X	X			X
Store Inventory	X	X		X			
Retail Sales	X	X		X	X	X	X
Retail Sales Forecast	X	X		X			
Retail Promotion Tracking	X	X		X	X		
Customer Returns	X	X		X	X	X	X
Returns to Vendor	X	X		X			X
Frequent Shopper Sign-Ups	X			X		X	X

Figure 4-10: Sample enterprise data warehouse bus matrix for a retailer.

Working in a tabular fashion, the organization's business processes are represented as matrix rows. It is important to remember you are identifying business processes, not the organization's business departments. The matrix rows translate into dimensional models representing the organization's primary activities and events, which are often recognizable by their operational source. When it's time to tackle a DW/BI development project, start with a single business process matrix row because that minimizes the risk of signing up for an overly ambitious implementation. Most implementation risk comes from biting off too much ETL system design and development. Focusing on the results of a single process, often captured by a single underlying source system, reduces the ETL development risk.

After individual business processes are enumerated, you sometimes identify more complex consolidated processes. Although dimensional models that cross processes can be immensely beneficial in terms of both query performance and ease of use, they are typically more difficult to implement because the ETL effort grows with each additional major source integrated into a single dimensional model. It is prudent to focus on the individual processes as building blocks before tackling the task of consolidating. Profitability is a classic example of a consolidated process in which separate revenue and cost factors are combined from different processes to provide a complete view of profitability. Although a granular profitability dimensional model is exciting, it is definitely not the first dimensional model you should attempt to implement; you could easily drown while trying to wrangle all the revenue and cost components.

The columns of the bus matrix represent the common dimensions used across the enterprise. It is often helpful to create a list of core dimensions before filling in the matrix to assess whether a given dimension should be associated with a business process. The number of bus matrix rows and columns varies by organization. For many, the matrix is surprisingly square with approximately 25 to 50 rows and a comparable number of columns. In other industries, like insurance, there tend to be more columns than rows.

After the core processes and dimensions are identified, you shade or "X" the matrix cells to indicate which columns are related to each row. Presto! You can immediately see the logical relationships and interplay between the organization's conformed dimensions and key business processes.

Multiple Matrix Uses

Creating the enterprise data warehouse bus matrix is one of the most important DW/BI implementation deliverables. It is a hybrid resource that serves multiple purposes, including architecture planning, database design, data governance coordination, project estimating, and organizational communication.

Although it is relatively straightforward to lay out the rows and columns, the enterprise bus matrix defines the overall data architecture for the DW/BI system. The matrix delivers the big picture perspective, regardless of database or technology preferences.

The matrix's columns address the demands of master data management and data integration head-on. As core dimensions participating in multiple dimensional models are defined by folks with data governance responsibilities and built by the DW/BI team, you can envision their use across processes rather than designing in a vacuum based on the needs of a single process, or even worse, a single department. Shared dimensions supply potent integration glue, allowing the business to drill across processes.

Each business process-centric implementation project incrementally builds out the overall architecture. Multiple development teams can work on components of the matrix independently and asynchronously, with confidence they'll fit together. Project managers can look across the process rows to see the dimensionality of each dimensional model at a glance. This vantage point is useful as they're gauging the magnitude of the project's effort. A project focused on a business process with fewer dimensions usually requires less effort, especially if the politically charged dimensions are already sitting on the shelf.

The matrix enables you to communicate effectively within and across data governance and DW/BI teams. Even more important, you can use the matrix to communicate upward and outward throughout the organization. The matrix is a succinct deliverable that visually conveys the master plan. IT management needs to understand this perspective to coordinate across project teams and resist the organizational urge to deploy more departmental solutions quickly. IT management must also ensure that distributed DW/BI development teams are committed to the bus architecture. Business management needs to also appreciate the holistic plan; you want them to understand the staging of the DW/BI rollout by business process. In addition, the matrix illustrates the importance of identifying experts from the business to serve as data governance leaders for the common dimensions. It is a tribute to its simplicity that the matrix can be used effectively to communicate with developers, architects, modelers, and project managers, as well as senior IT and business management.

Opportunity/Stakeholder Matrix

You can draft a different matrix that leverages the same business process rows, but replaces the dimension columns with business functions, such as merchandising, marketing, store operations, and finance. Based on each function's requirements, the matrix cells are shaded to indicate which business functions are interested in which business processes (and projects), as illustrated in Figure 4-11's *opportunity/ stakeholder matrix* variation. It also identifies which groups need to be invited to the detailed requirements, dimensional modeling, and BI application specification parties after a process-centric row is queued up as a project.

BUSINESS PROCESSES	Merchandising	Marketing	Store Operations	Logistics	Finance
Issue Purchase Orders	X		X	X	X
Receive Warehouse Deliveries	X		X	X	X
Warehouse Inventory	X		X	X	X
Receive Store Deliveries	X		X	X	X
Store Inventory	X	X	X	X	X
Retail Sales	X	X	X	X	X
Retail Sales Forecast	X	X	X	X	X
Retail Promotion Tracking	X	X	X	X	X
Customer Returns	X		X	X	X
Returns to Vendor	X		X	X	X
Frequent Shopper Sign-Ups		X	X		X

Figure 4-11: Opportunity/stakeholder matrix.

Common Bus Matrix Mistakes

When drafting a bus matrix, people sometimes struggle with the level of detail expressed by each row, resulting in the following missteps:

- **Departmental or overly encompassing rows.** The matrix rows shouldn't correspond to the boxes on a corporate organization chart representing functional groups. Some departments may be responsible or acutely interested in a single business process, but the matrix rows shouldn't look like a list of the CEO's direct reports.

- **Report-centric or too narrowly defined rows.** At the opposite extreme, the bus matrix shouldn't resemble a laundry list of requested reports. A single business process supports numerous analyses; the matrix row should reference the business process, not the derivative reports or analytics.

When defining the matrix columns, architects naturally fall into the similar traps of defining columns that are either too broad or too narrow:

- **Overly generalized columns.** A "person" column on the bus matrix may refer to a wide variety of people, from internal employees to external suppliers and customer contacts. Because there's virtually zero overlap between these populations, it adds confusion to lump them into a single, generic dimension. Similarly, it's not beneficial to put internal and external addresses referring to corporate facilities, employee addresses, and customer sites into a generic location column in the matrix.
- **Separate columns for each level of a hierarchy.** The columns of the bus matrix should refer to dimensions at their most granular level. Some business process rows may require an aggregated version of the detailed dimension, such as inventory snapshot metrics at the weekly level. Rather than creating separate matrix columns for each level of the calendar hierarchy, use a single column for dates. To express levels of detail above a daily grain, you can denote the granularity within the matrix cell; alternatively, you can subdivide the date column to indicate the hierarchical level associated with each business process row. It's important to retain the overarching identification of common dimensions deployed at different levels of granularity. Some industry pundits advocate matrices that treat every dimension table attribute as a separate, independent column; this defeats the concept of dimensions and results in a completely unruly matrix.

Retrofitting Existing Models to a Bus Matrix

It is unacceptable to build separate dimensional models that ignore a framework tying them together. Isolated, independent dimensional models are worse than simply a lost opportunity for analysis. They deliver access to irreconcilable views of the organization and further enshrine the reports that cannot be compared with one another. Independent dimensional models become legacy implementations in their own right; by their existence, they block the development of a coherent DW/BI environment.

So what happens if you're not starting with a blank slate? Perhaps several dimensional models have been constructed without regard to an architecture using conformed dimensions. Can you rescue your stovepipes and convert them to the bus architecture? To answer this question, you should start first with an honest appraisal of your existing non-integrated dimensional structures. This typically entails meetings with the separate teams (including the clandestine pseudo IT teams within business organizations) to determine the gap between the current environment and the organization's architected goal. When the gap is understood, you need to develop an incremental plan to convert the standalone dimensional models to the enterprise architecture. The plan needs to be internally sold. Senior IT and business management must understand the current state of data chaos, the risks of doing nothing, and the benefits of moving forward according to your game plan. Management also needs to appreciate that the conversion will require a significant commitment of support, resources, and funding.

If an existing dimensional model is based on a sound dimensional design, perhaps you can map an existing dimension to a standardized version. The original dimension table would be rebuilt using a cross-reference map. Likewise, the fact table would need to be reprocessed to replace the original dimension keys with the conformed dimension keys. Of course, if the original and conformed dimension tables contain different attributes, rework of the preexisting BI applications and queries is inevitable.

More typically, existing dimensional models are riddled with dimensional modeling errors beyond the lack of adherence to standardized dimensions. In some cases, the stovepipe dimensional model has outlived its useful life. Isolated dimensional models often are built for a specific functional area. When others try to leverage the data, they typically discover that the dimensional model was implemented at an inappropriate level of granularity and is missing key dimensionality. The effort required to retrofit these dimensional models into the enterprise DW/BI architecture may exceed the effort to start over from scratch. As difficult as it is to admit, stovepipe dimensional models often have to be shut down and rebuilt in the proper bus architecture framework.

Conformed Dimensions

Now that you understand the importance of the enterprise bus architecture, let's further explore the standardized conformed dimensions that serve as the cornerstone of the bus because they're shared across business process fact tables. Conformed dimensions go by many other aliases: common dimensions, master dimensions, reference dimensions, and shared dimensions. Conformed dimensions should be built once in the ETL system and then replicated either logically or physically throughout the enterprise DW/BI environment. When built, it's extremely important that the DW/BI development teams take the pledge to use these dimensions. It's a policy decision that is critical to making the enterprise DW/BI system function; their usage should be mandated by the organization's CIO.

Drilling Across Fact Tables

In addition to consistency and reusability, conformed dimensions enable you to combine performance measurements from different business processes in a single report, as illustrated in Figure 4-12. You can use multipass SQL to query each dimensional model separately and then outer-join the query results based on a common dimension attribute, such as Figure 4-12's product name. The full outer-join ensures all rows are included in the combined report, even if they only appear in one set of query results. This linkage, often referred to as *drill across*, is straightforward if the dimension table attribute values are identical.

Product Description	Open Orders Qty	Inventory Qty	Sales Qty
Baked Well Sourdough	1,201	935	1,042
Fluffy Light Sliced White	1,472	801	922
Fluffy Sliced Whole Wheat	846	513	368

Figure 4-12: Drilling across fact tables with conformed dimension attributes.

Drilling across is supported by many BI products and platforms. Their implementations differ on whether the results are joined in temporary tables, the application server, or the report. The vendors also use different terms to describe this technique, including multipass, multi-select, multi-fact, or stitch queries. Because metrics from different fact tables are brought together with a drill-across query, often any cross-fact calculations must be done in the BI application after the separate conformed results have been returned.

Conformed dimensions come in several different flavors, as described in the following sections.

Identical Conformed Dimensions

At the most basic level, conformed dimensions mean the same thing with every possible fact table to which they are joined. The date dimension table connected to the sales facts is identical to the date dimension table connected to the inventory facts. Identical conformed dimensions have consistent dimension keys, attribute column names, attribute definitions, and attribute values (which translate into consistent report labels and groupings). Dimension attributes don't conform if they're called Month in one dimension and Month Name in another; likewise, they don't conform if the attribute value is "July" in one dimension and "JULY" in another. Identical conformed dimensions in two dimensional models may be the same physical table within the database. However, given the typical complexity of the DW/BI system's technical environment with multiple database platforms, it is more likely that the dimension is built once in the ETL system and then duplicated synchronously outward to each dimensional model. In either case, the conformed date dimensions in both dimensional models have the same number of rows, same key values, same attribute labels, same attribute data definitions, and same attribute values. Attribute column names should be uniquely labeled across dimensions.

Most conformed dimensions are defined naturally at the most granular level possible. The product dimension's grain will be the individual product; the date dimension's grain will be the individual day. However, sometimes dimensions at the same level of granularity do not fully conform. For example, there might be product and store attributes needed for inventory analysis, but they aren't appropriate for analyzing retail sales data. The dimension tables still conform if the keys and common columns are identical, but the supplemental attributes used by the inventory schema are not conformed. It is physically impossible to drill across processes using these add-on attributes.

Shrunken Rollup Conformed Dimension with Attribute Subset

Dimensions also conform when they contain a subset of attributes from a more granular dimension. Shrunken rollup dimensions are required when a fact table captures performance metrics at a higher level of granularity than the atomic base dimension. This would be the case if you had a weekly inventory snapshot in addition to the daily snapshot. In other situations, facts are generated by another business process at a higher level of granularity. For example, the retail sales process captures data at the atomic product level, whereas forecasting generates data at the brand level. You couldn't share a single product dimension table across the two business process schemas because the granularity is different. The product and brand dimensions still conform if the brand table attributes are a strict subset of the atomic product table's attributes. Attributes that are common to both the detailed and rolled-up dimension tables, such as the brand and category descriptions, should be labeled, defined, and identically valued in both tables, as illustrated in Figure 4-13. However, the primary keys of the detailed and rollup dimension tables are separate.

NOTE Shrunken rollup dimensions conform to the base atomic dimension if the attributes are a strict subset of the atomic dimension's attributes.

Shrunken Conformed Dimension with Row Subset

Another case of conformed dimension subsetting occurs when two dimensions are at the same level of detail, but one represents only a subset of rows. For example, a corporate product dimension contains rows for the full portfolio of products across multiple disparate lines of business, as illustrated in Figure 4-14. Analysts in the separate businesses may want to view only their subset of the corporate dimension, restricted to the product rows for their business. By using a subset of rows, they aren't encumbered with the corporation's entire product set. Of course, the fact table joined to this subsetted dimension must be limited to the same subset of products. If a user attempts to use a shrunken subset dimension while accessing a fact table consisting of the complete product set, they may encounter unexpected query results because referential integrity would be violated. You need to be cognizant of the potential opportunity for user confusion or error with dimension row subsetting. We will further elaborate on dimension subsets when we discuss supertype and subtype dimensions in Chapter 10: Financial Services.

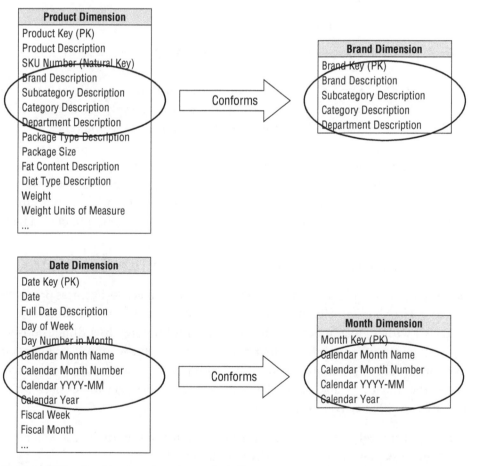

Figure 4-13: Conforming shrunken rollup dimensions.

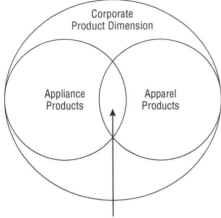

Drilling across requires common conformed attributes.

Figure 4-14: Conforming dimension subsets at the same granularity.

Conformed date and month dimensions are a unique example of both row and column dimension subsetting. Obviously, you can't simply use the same date dimension table for daily and monthly fact tables because of the difference in rollup granularity. However, the month dimension may consist of the month-end daily date table rows with the exclusion of all columns that don't apply at the monthly granularity, such as the weekday/weekend indicator, week ending date, holiday indicator, day number within year, and others. Sometimes a month-end indicator on the daily date dimension is used to facilitate creation of this month dimension table.

Shrunken Conformed Dimensions on the Bus Matrix

The bus matrix identifies the reuse of common dimensions across business processes. Typically, the shaded cells of the matrix indicate that the atomic dimension is associated with a given process. When shrunken rollup or subset dimensions are involved, you want to reinforce their conformance with the atomic dimensions. Therefore, you don't want to create a new, unrelated column on the bus matrix. Instead, there are two viable approaches to represent the shrunken dimensions within the matrix, as illustrated in Figure 4-15:

- Mark the cell for the atomic dimension, but then textually document the rollup or row subset granularity within the cell.
- Subdivide the dimension column to indicate the common rollup or subset granularities, such as day and month if processes collect data at both of these grains.

	Date			Date	
				Day	Month
Issue Purchase Orders	X			X	
Receive Deliveries	X	**OR**		X	
Inventory	X			X	
Retail Sales	X			X	
Retail Sales Forecast	X Month				X

Figure 4-15: Alternatives for identifying shrunken dimensions on the bus matrix.

Limited Conformity

Now that we've preached about the importance of conformed dimensions, we'll discuss the situation in which it may not be realistic or necessary to establish conformed dimensions for the organization. If a conglomerate has subsidiaries spanning widely varied industries, there may be little point in trying to integrate. If each line of business has unique customers and unique products and there's no interest in cross-selling across lines, it may not make sense to attempt an enterprise architecture because there likely isn't much perceived business value. The willingness to seek a common definition for product, customer, or other core dimensions is a major litmus test for an organization theoretically intent on building an enterprise DW/BI system. If the organization is unwilling to agree on common definitions, the organization shouldn't attempt to build an enterprise DW/BI environment. It would be better to build separate, self-contained data warehouses for each subsidiary. But then don't complain when someone asks for "enterprise performance" without going through this logic.

Although organizations may find it difficult to combine data across disparate lines of business, some degree of integration is typically an ultimate goal. Rather than throwing your hands in the air and declaring it can't possibly be done, you should start down the path toward conformity. Perhaps there are a handful of attributes that can be conformed across lines of business. Even if it is merely a product description, category, and line of business attribute that is common to all businesses, this least-common-denominator approach is still a step in the right direction. You don't need to get everyone to agree on everything related to a dimension before proceeding.

Importance of Data Governance and Stewardship

We've touted the importance of conformed dimensions, but we also need to acknowledge a key challenge: reaching enterprise consensus on dimension attribute names and contents (and the handling of content changes which we'll discuss in Chapter 5: Procurement). In many organizations, business rules and data definitions have traditionally been established departmentally. The consequences of this commonly encountered lack of data governance and control are the ubiquitous departmental data silos that perpetuate similar but slightly different versions of the truth. Business and IT management need to recognize the importance of addressing this shortfall if you stand any chance of bringing order to the chaos; if management is reluctant to drive change, the project will never achieve its goals.

Once the data governance issues and opportunities are acknowledged by senior leadership, resources need to be identified to spearhead the effort. IT is often tempted to try leading the charge. They are frustrated by the isolated projects re-creating data around the organization, consuming countless IT and outside resources while delivering inconsistent solutions that ultimately just increase the complexity of the organization's data architecture at significant cost. Although IT can facilitate the definition of conformed dimensions, it is seldom successful as the sole driver, even if it's a temporary assignment. IT simply lacks the organizational authority to make things happen.

Business-Driven Governance

To boost the likelihood of business acceptance, subject matter experts from the business need to lead the initiative. Leading a cross-organizational governance program is not for the faint of heart. The governance resources identified by business leadership should have the following characteristics:

- Respect from the organization
- Broad knowledge of the enterprise's operations
- Ability to balance organizational needs against departmental requirements
- Gravitas and authority to challenge the status quo and enforce policies
- Strong communication skills
- Politically savvy negotiation and consensus building skills

Clearly, not everyone is cut out for the job! Typically those tapped to spearhead the governance program are highly valued and in demand. It takes the right skills, experience, and confidence to rationalize diverse business perspectives and drive the design of common reference data, together with the necessary organizational compromises. Over the years, some have criticized conformed dimensions as being too hard. Yes, it's difficult to get people in different corners of the business to agree on common attribute names, definitions, and values, but that's the crux of unified, integrated data. If everyone demands their own labels and business rules, there's no chance of delivering on the promises made to establish a single version of the truth. The data governance program is critical in facilitating a culture shift away from the typical siloed environment in which each department retains control of their data and analytics to one where information is shared and leveraged across the organization.

Governance Objectives

One of the key objectives of the data governance function is to reach agreement on data definitions, labels, and domain values so that everyone is speaking the same language. Otherwise, the same words may describe different things; different words may describe the same thing; and the same value may have different meaning. Establishing common master data is often a politically charged issue; the challenges are cultural and geopolitical rather than technical. Defining a foundation of master descriptive conformed dimensions requires effort. But after it's agreed upon, subsequent DW/BI efforts can leverage the work, both ensuring consistency and reducing the implementation's delivery cycle time.

In addition to tackling data definitions and contents, the data governance function also establishes policies and responsibilities for data quality and accuracy, as well as data security and access controls.

Historically, DW/BI teams created the "recipes" for conformed dimensions and managed the data cleansing and integration mapping in the ETL system; the operational systems focused on accurately capturing performance metrics, but there was often little effort to ensure consistent common reference data. Enterprise resource planning (ERP) systems promised to fill the void, but many organizations still rely on separate best-of-breed point solutions for niche requirements. Recently, operational *master data management (MDM)* solutions have addressed the need for centralized master data at the source where the transactions are captured. Although technology can encourage data integration, it doesn't fix the problem. A strong data governance function is a necessary prerequisite for conforming information regardless of technical approach.

Conformed Dimensions and the Agile Movement

Some lament that although they want to deliver and share consistently defined master conformed dimensions in their DW/BI environments, it's "just not feasible." They explain they would if they could, but with senior management focused on using agile development techniques, it's "impossible" to take the time to get organizational agreement on conformed dimensions. You can turn this argument upside down by challenging that conformed dimensions enable agile DW/BI development, along with agile decision making.

Conformed dimensions allow a dimension table to be built and maintained once rather than re-creating slightly different versions during each development cycle. Reusing conformed dimensions across projects is where you get the leverage for more agile DW/BI development. As you flesh out the portfolio of master conformed dimensions, the development crank starts turning faster and faster. The time-to-market for a new business process data source shrinks as developers reuse existing conformed dimensions. Ultimately, new ETL development focuses almost exclusively on delivering more fact tables because the associated dimension tables are already sitting on the shelf ready to go.

Defining a conformed dimension requires organizational consensus and commitment to data stewardship. But you don't need to get everyone to agree on every attribute in every dimension table. At a minimum, you should identify a subset of attributes that have significance across the enterprise. These commonly referenced descriptive characteristics become the starter set of conformed attributes, enabling drill-across integration. Even just a single attribute, such as enterprise product category, is a viable starting point for the integration effort. Over time, you can iteratively expand from this minimalist starting point by adding attributes. These dimensions could be tackled during architectural agile *sprints*. When a series of sprint deliverables combine to deliver sufficient value, they constitute a release to the business users.

If you fail to focus on conformed dimensions because you're under pressure to deliver something yesterday, the departmental analytic data silos will likely have inconsistent categorizations and labels. Even more troubling, data sets may look like they can be compared and integrated due to similar labels, but the underlying business rules may be slightly different. Business users waste inordinate amounts of time trying to reconcile and resolve these data inconsistencies, which negatively impact their ability to be agile decision makers.

The senior IT managers who are demanding agile systems development practices should be exerting even greater organizational pressure, in conjunction with their peers in the business, on the development of consistent conformed dimensions if they're interested in both long-term development efficiencies and long-term decision-making effectiveness across the enterprise.

Conformed Facts

Thus far we have considered the central task of setting up conformed dimensions to tie dimensional models together. This is 95 percent or more of the data architecture effort. The remaining 5 percent of the effort goes into establishing conformed fact definitions.

Revenue, profit, standard prices and costs, measures of quality and customer satisfaction, and other *key performance indicators (KPIs)* are facts that must also conform. If facts live in more than one dimensional model, the underlying definitions and equations for these facts must be the same if they are to be called the same thing. If they are labeled identically, they need to be defined in the same dimensional context and with the same units of measure from dimensional model to dimensional model. For example, if several business processes report revenue, then these separate revenue metrics can be added and compared only if they have the same financial definitions. If there are definitional differences, then it is essential that the revenue facts be labeled uniquely.

NOTE You must be disciplined in your data naming practices. If it is impossible to conform a fact exactly, you should give different names to the different interpretations so that business users do not combine these incompatible facts in calculations.

Sometimes a fact has a natural unit of measure in one fact table and another natural unit of measure in another fact table. For example, the flow of product down the retail value chain may best be measured in shipping cases at the warehouse but in scanned units at the store. Even if all the dimensional considerations have been correctly taken into account, it would be difficult to use these two incompatible units of measure in one drill-across report. The usual solution to this kind of problem is to refer the user to a conversion factor buried in the product dimension table and hope that the user can find the conversion factor and correctly use it. This is unacceptable for both overhead and vulnerability to error. The correct solution is to carry the fact in both units of measure, so a report can easily glide down the value chain, picking off comparable facts. Chapter 6: Order Management talks more about multiple units of measure.

Summary

In this chapter we developed dimensional models for the three complementary views of inventory. The periodic snapshot is a good choice for long-running, continuously replenished inventory scenarios. The accumulating snapshot is a good choice for finite inventory pipeline situations with a definite beginning and end. Finally, most inventory analysis will require a transactional schema to augment these snapshot models.

We introduced key concepts surrounding the enterprise data warehouse bus architecture and matrix. Each business process of the value chain, supported by a primary source system, translates into a row in the bus matrix, and eventually, a dimensional model. The matrix rows share a surprising number of standardized, conformed dimensions. Developing and adhering to the enterprise bus architecture is an absolute must if you intend to build a DW/BI system composed of an integrated set of dimensional models.

5   Procurement

We explore procurement processes in this chapter. This subject area has obvious cross-industry appeal because it is applicable to any organization that acquires products or services for either use or resale.

In addition to developing several purchasing models, this chapter provides in-depth coverage of the techniques for handling dimension table attribute value changes. Although descriptive attributes in dimension tables are relatively static, they are subject to change over time. Product lines are restructured, causing product hierarchies to change. Customers move, causing their geographic information to change. We'll describe several approaches to deal with these inevitable dimension table changes. Followers of the Kimball methods will recognize the type 1, 2, and 3 techniques. Continuing in this tradition, we've expanded the slowly changing dimension technique line-up with types 0, 4, 5, 6, and 7.

Chapter 5 discusses the following concepts:

- Bus matrix snippet for procurement processes
- Blended versus separate transaction schemas
- Slowly changing dimension technique types 0 through 7, covering both basic and advanced hybrid scenarios

Procurement Case Study

Thus far we have studied downstream sales and inventory processes in the retailer's value chain. We explained the importance of mapping out the enterprise data warehouse bus architecture where conformed dimensions are used across process-centric fact tables. In this chapter we'll extend these concepts as we work our way further up the value chain to the procurement processes.

For many companies, procurement is a critical business activity. Effective procurement of products at the right price for resale is obviously important to retailers and distributors. Procurement also has strong bottom line implications for any organization that buys products as raw materials for manufacturing. Significant cost savings opportunities are associated with reducing the number of suppliers and negotiating agreements with preferred suppliers.

Demand planning drives efficient materials management. After demand is forecasted, procurement's goal is to source the appropriate materials or products in the most economical manner. Procurement involves a wide range of activities from negotiating contracts to issuing purchase requisitions and purchase orders (POs) to tracking receipts and authorizing payments. The following list gives you a better sense of a procurement organization's common analytic requirements:

- Which materials or products are most frequently purchased? How many vendors supply these products? At what prices? Looking at demand across the enterprise (rather than at a single physical location), are there opportunities to negotiate favorable pricing by consolidating suppliers, single sourcing, or making guaranteed buys?
- Are your employees purchasing from the preferred vendors or skirting the negotiated vendor agreements with maverick spending?
- Are you receiving the negotiated pricing from your vendors or is there vendor contract purchase price variance?
- How are your vendors performing? What is the vendor's fill rate? On-time delivery performance? Late deliveries outstanding? Percent back ordered? Rejection rate based on receipt inspection?

Procurement Transactions and Bus Matrix

As you begin working through the four-step dimensional design process, you determine that procurement is the business process to be modeled. In studying the process, you observe a flurry of procurement transactions, such as purchase requisitions, purchase orders, shipping notifications, receipts, and payments. Similar to the approach taken in Chapter 4: Inventory, you could initially design a fact table with the grain of one row per procurement transaction with transaction date, product, vendor, contract terms, and procurement transaction type as key dimensions. The procurement transaction quantity and dollar amount are the facts. The resulting design is shown in Figure 5-1.

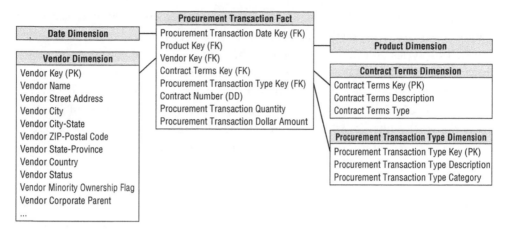

Figure 5-1: Procurement fact table with multiple transaction types.

If you work for the same grocery retailer from the earlier case studies, the transaction date and product dimensions are the same conformed dimensions developed originally in Chapter 3: Retail Sales. If you work with manufacturing procurement, the raw materials products likely are located in a separate raw materials dimension table rather than included in the product dimension for salable products. The vendor, contract terms, and procurement transaction type dimensions are new to this schema. The vendor dimension contains one row for each vendor, along with interesting descriptive attributes to support a variety of vendor analyses. The contract terms dimension contains one row for each generalized set of negotiated terms, similar to the promotion dimension in Chapter 3. The procurement transaction type dimension enables grouping or filtering on transaction types, such as purchase orders. The contract number is a degenerate dimension; it could be used to determine the volume of business conducted under each negotiated contract.

Single Versus Multiple Transaction Fact Tables

As you review the initial procurement schema design with business users, you learn several new details. First, the business users describe the various procurement transactions differently. To the business, purchase orders, shipping notices, warehouse receipts, and vendor payments are all viewed as separate and unique processes.

Several of the procurement transactions come from different source systems. There is a purchasing system that provides purchase requisitions and purchase orders, a warehousing system that provides shipping notices and warehouse receipts, and an accounts payable system that deals with vendor payments.

You further discover that several transaction types have different dimensionality. For example, discounts taken are applicable to vendor payments but not to the other transaction types. Similarly, the name of the employee who received the goods at the warehouse applies to receipts but doesn't make sense elsewhere.

There are also a variety of interesting control numbers, such as purchase order and payment check numbers, created at various steps in the procurement pipeline. These control numbers are perfect candidates for degenerate dimensions. For certain transaction types, more than one control number may apply.

As you sort through these new details, you are faced with a design decision. Should you build a blended transaction fact table with a transaction type dimension to view all procurement transactions together, or do you build separate fact tables for each transaction type? This is a common design quandary that surfaces in many transactional situations, not just procurement.

As dimensional modelers, you need to make design decisions based on a thorough understanding of the business requirements weighed against the realities of the underlying source data. There is no simple formula to make the definite determination of whether to use a single fact table or multiple fact tables. A single fact table may be the most appropriate solution in some situations, whereas multiple fact tables are most appropriate in others. When faced with this design decision, the following considerations help sort out the options:

- **What are the users' analytic requirements?** The goal is to reduce complexity by presenting the data in the most effective form for business users. How will the business users most commonly analyze this data? Which approach most naturally aligns with their business-centric perspective?

- **Are there really multiple unique business processes?** In the procurement example, it seems buying products (purchase orders) is distinctly different from receiving products (receipts). The existence of separate control numbers for each step in the process is a clue that you are dealing with separate processes. Given this situation, you would lean toward separate fact tables. By contrast, in Chapter 4's inventory example, the varied inventory transactions were part of a single inventory process resulting in a single fact table design.

- **Are multiple source systems capturing metrics with unique granularities?** There are three separate source systems in this case study: purchasing, warehousing, and accounts payable. This would suggest separate fact tables.

- **What is the dimensionality of the facts?** In this procurement example, several dimensions are applicable to some transaction types but not to others. This would again lead you to separate fact tables.

A simple way to consider these trade-offs is to draft a bus matrix. As illustrated in Figure 5-2, you can include two additional columns identifying the atomic granularity and metrics for each row. These matrix embellishments cause it to more closely resemble the detailed implementation bus matrix, which we'll more thoroughly discuss in Chapter 16: Insurance.

Business Processes	Atomic Granularity	Metrics	Date	Product	Vendor	Contract Terms	Employee	Warehouse	Carrier
Purchase Requisitions	1 row per requisition line	Requisition Quantity & Dollars	X	X	X	X	X		
Purchase Orders	1 row per PO line	PO Quantity & Dollars	X	X	X	X	X	X	X
Shipping Notifications	1 row per shipping notice line	Shipped Quantity	X	X	X		X	X	X
Warehouse Receipts	1 row per receipt line	Received Quantity	X	X	X		X	X	X
Vendor Invoices	1 row per invoice line	Invoice Quantity & Dollars	X	X	X	X	X	X	
Vendor Payments	1 row per payment	Invoice, Discount & Net Payment Dollars	X	X	X	X		X	

Figure 5-2: Sample bus matrix rows for procurement processes.

Based on the bus matrix for this hypothetical case study, multiple transaction fact tables would be implemented, as illustrated in Figure 5-3. In this example, there are separate fact tables for purchase requisitions, purchase orders, shipping notices, warehouse receipts, and vendor payments. This decision was reached because users view these activities as separate and distinct business processes, the data comes from different source systems, and there is unique dimensionality for the various transaction types. Multiple fact tables enable richer, more descriptive dimensions and attributes. The single fact table approach would have required generalized labeling for some dimensions. For example, purchase order date and receipt date would likely have been generalized to simply transaction date. Likewise, purchasing agent and receiving clerk would become employee. This generalization reduces the legibility of the resulting dimensional model. Also, with separate fact tables as you progress from purchase requisitions to payments, the fact tables inherit dimensions from the previous steps.

Multiple fact tables may require more time to manage and administer because there are more tables to load, index, and aggregate. Some would argue this approach increases the complexity of the ETL processes. Actually, it may simplify the ETL activities. Loading the operational data from separate source systems into separate fact tables likely requires less complex ETL processing than attempting to integrate data from the multiple sources into a single fact table.

Date Dimension

Vendor Dimension

Employee Dimension

Carrier Dimension

Purchase Requisition Fact
Purchase Requisition Date Key (FK)
Product Key (FK)
Vendor Key (FK)
Contract Terms Key (FK)
Employee Requested By Key (FK)
Contract Number (DD)
Purchase Requisition Number (DD)
Purchase Requisition Quantity
Purchase Requisition Dollar Amount

Purchase Order Fact
Purchase Order Date Key (FK)
Requested By Date Key (FK)
Product Key (FK)
Vendor Key (FK)
Contract Terms Key (FK)
Warehouse Key (FK)
Carrier Key (FK)
Employee Ordered By Key (FK)
Employee Purchase Agent Key (FK)
Contract Number (DD)
Purchase Requisition Number (DD)
Purchase Order Number (DD)
Purchase Order Quantity
Purchase Order Dollar Amount

Shipping Notices Fact
Shipping Notification Date Key (FK)
Estimated Arrival Date Key (FK)
Requested By Date Key (FK)
Product Key (FK)
Vendor Key (FK)
Warehouse Key (FK)
Carrier Key (FK)
Employee Ordered By Key (FK)
Purchase Order Number (DD)
Shipping Notification Number (DD)
Shipped Quantity

Warehouse Receipts Fact
Warehouse Receipt Date Key (FK)
Requested By Date Key (FK)
Product Key (FK)
Vendor Key (FK)
Warehouse Key (FK)
Carrier Key (FK)
Employee Ordered By Key (FK)
Employee Received By Key (FK)
Purchase Order Number (DD)
Shipping Notification Number (DD)
Warehouse Receipt Number (DD)
Received Quantity

Vendor Payment Fact
Vendor Payment Date Key (FK)
Product Key (FK)
Vendor Key (FK)
Warehouse Key (FK)
Contract Terms Key (FK)
Contract Number (DD)
Payment Check Number (DD)
Vendor Invoice Dollar Amount
Vendor Discount Dollar Amount
Vendor Net Payment Dollar Amount

Product Dimension

Contract Terms Dimension

Warehouse Dimension

Figure 5-3: Multiple fact tables for procurement processes.

Complementary Procurement Snapshot

Apart from the decision regarding multiple procurement transaction fact tables, you may also need to develop a snapshot fact table to fully address the business's needs. As suggested in Chapter 4, an accumulating snapshot such as Figure 5-4 that crosses processes would be extremely useful if the business is interested in monitoring product movement as it proceeds through the procurement pipeline (including the duration of each stage). Remember that an accumulating snapshot is meant to model processes with well-defined milestones. If the process is a continuous flow that never really ends, it is not a good candidate for an accumulating snapshot.

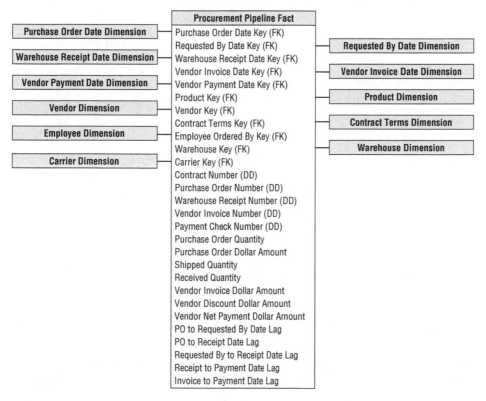

Figure 5-4: Procurement pipeline accumulating snapshot schema.

Slowly Changing Dimension Basics

To this point, we have pretended dimensions are independent of time. Unfortunately, this is not the case in the real world. Although dimension table attributes are relatively static, they aren't fixed forever; attribute values change, albeit rather slowly, over time.

Dimensional designers must proactively work with the business's data governance representatives to determine the appropriate change-handling strategy. You shouldn't simply jump to the conclusion that the business doesn't care about dimension changes just because they weren't mentioned during the requirements gathering. Although IT may assume accurate change tracking is unnecessary, business users may assume the DW/BI system will allow them to see the impact of every attribute value change. It is obviously better to get on the same page sooner rather than later.

NOTE   The business's data governance and stewardship representatives must be actively involved in decisions regarding the handling of slowly changing dimension attributes; IT shouldn't make determinations on its own.

When change tracking is needed, it might be tempting to put every changing attribute into the fact table on the assumption that dimension tables are static. This is unacceptable and unrealistic. Instead you need strategies to deal with slowly changing attributes within dimension tables. Since Ralph Kimball first introduced the notion of *slowly changing dimensions* in 1995, some IT professionals in a never-ending quest to speak in acronym-ese termed them *SCDs*. The acronym stuck.

For each dimension table attribute, you must specify a strategy to handle change. In other words, when an attribute value changes in the operational world, how will you respond to the change in the dimensional model? In the following sections, we describe several basic techniques for dealing with attribute changes, followed by more advanced options. You may need to employ a combination of these techniques within a single dimension table.

Kimball method followers are likely already familiar with SCD types 1, 2, and 3. Because legibility is part of our mantra, we sometimes wish we had given these techniques more descriptive names in the first place, such as "overwrite." But after nearly two decades, the "type numbers" are squarely part of the DW/BI vernacular. As you'll see in the following sections, we've decided to expand the theme by assigning new SCD type numbers to techniques that have been described, but less precisely labeled, in the past; our hope is that assigning specific numbers facilitates clearer communication among team members.

Type 0: Retain Original

This technique hasn't been given a type number in the past, but it's been around since the beginning of SCDs. With type 0, the dimension attribute value never changes, so facts are always grouped by this original value. Type 0 is appropriate for any attribute labeled "original," such as customer original credit score. It also applies to most attributes in a date dimension.

As we staunchly advocated in Chapter 3, the dimension table's primary key is a surrogate key rather than relying on the natural operational key. Although we demoted the natural key to being an ordinary dimension attribute, it still has special significance. Presuming it's durable, it would remain inviolate. Persistent durable keys are always type 0 attributes. Unless otherwise noted, throughout this chapter's SCD discussion, the durable supernatural key is assumed to remain constant, as described in Chapter 3.

Type 1: Overwrite

With the slowly changing dimension type 1 response, you overwrite the old attribute value in the dimension row, replacing it with the current value; the attribute always reflects the most recent assignment.

Assume you work for an electronics retailer where products roll up into the retail store's departments. One of the products is IntelliKidz software. The existing row in the product dimension table for IntelliKidz looks like the top half of Figure 5-5. Of course, there would be additional descriptive attributes in the product dimension, but we've abbreviated the attribute listing for clarity.

Original row in Product dimension:

Product Key	SKU (NK)	Product Description	Department Name
12345	ABC922-Z	IntelliKidz	Education

Updated row in Product dimension:

Product Key	SKU (NK)	Product Description	Department Name
12345	ABC922-Z	IntelliKidz	Strategy

Figure 5-5: SCD type 1 sample rows.

Suppose a new merchandising person decides IntelliKidz software should be moved from the Education department to the Strategy department on February 1, 2013 to boost sales. With a type 1 response, you'd simply update the existing row in the dimension table with the new department description, as illustrated in the updated row of Figure 5-5.

In this case, no dimension or fact table keys were modified when IntelliKidz's department changed. The fact table rows still reference product key 12345, regardless of IntelliKidz's departmental location. When sales take off following the move to the Strategy department, you have no information to explain the performance improvement because the historical and more recent facts both appear as if IntelliKidz always rolled up into Strategy.

The type 1 response is the simplest approach for dimension attribute changes. In the dimension table, you merely overwrite the preexisting value with the current assignment. The fact table is untouched. The problem with a type 1 response is that you lose all history of attribute changes. Because overwriting obliterates historical attribute values, you're left solely with the attribute values as they exist today. A type 1 response is appropriate if the attribute change is an insignificant correction. It also may be appropriate if there is no value in keeping the old description. However, too often DW/BI teams use a type 1 response as the default for dealing with slowly changing dimensions and end up totally missing the mark if the business needs to track historical changes accurately. After you implement a type 1, it's difficult to change course in the future.

NOTE   The type 1 response is easy to implement, but it does not maintain any history of prior attribute values.

Before we leave the topic of type 1 changes, be forewarned that the same BI applications can produce different results before versus after the type 1 attribute change. When the dimension attribute's type 1 overwrite occurs, the fact rows are associated with the new descriptive context. Business users who rolled up sales by department on January 31 will get different department totals when they run the same report on February 1 following the type 1 overwrite.

There's another easily overlooked catch to be aware of. With a type 1 response to deal with the relocation of IntelliKidz, any preexisting aggregations based on the department value need to be rebuilt. The aggregated summary data must continue to tie to the detailed atomic data, where it now appears that IntelliKidz has always rolled up into the Strategy department.

Finally, if a dimensional model is deployed via an OLAP cube and the type 1 attribute is a hierarchical rollup attribute, like the product's department in our example, the cube likely needs to be reprocessed when the type 1 attribute changes. At a minimum, similar to the relational environment, the cube's performance aggregations need to be recalculated.

WARNING   Even though type 1 changes appear the easiest to implement, remember they invalidate relational tables and OLAP cubes that have aggregated data over the affected attribute.

Type 2: Add New Row

In Chapter 1: Data Warehousing, Business Intelligence, and Dimensional Modeling Primer, we stated one of the DW/BI system's goals was to correctly represent history.

A type 2 response is the predominant technique for supporting this requirement when it comes to slowly changing dimension attributes.

Using the type 2 approach, when IntelliKidz's department changed on February 1, 2013, a new product dimension row for IntelliKidz is inserted to reflect the new department attribute value. There are two product dimension rows for IntelliKidz, as illustrated in Figure 5-6. Each row contains a version of IntelliKidz's attribute profile that was true for a span of time.

Original row in Product dimension:

Product Key	SKU (NK)	Product Description	Department Name	...	Row Effective Date	Row Expiration Date	Current Row Indicator
12345	ABC922-Z	IntelliKidz	Education	...	2012-01-01	9999-12-31	Current

Rows in Product dimension following department reassignment:

Product Key	SKU (NK)	Product Description	Department Name	...	Row Effective Date	Row Expiration Date	Current Row Indicator
12345	ABC922-Z	IntelliKidz	Education	...	2012-01-01	2013-01-31	Expired
25984	ABC922-Z	IntelliKidz	Strategy	...	2013-02-01	9999-12-31	Current

Figure 5-6: SCD type 2 sample rows.

With type 2 changes, the fact table is again untouched; you don't go back to the historical fact table rows to modify the product key. In the fact table, rows for IntelliKidz prior to February 1, 2013, would reference product key 12345 when the product rolled up to the Education department. After February 1, new IntelliKidz fact rows would have product key 25984 to reflect the move to the Strategy department. This is why we say type 2 responses perfectly partition or segment history to account for the change. Reports summarizing pre-February 1 facts look identical whether the report is generated before or after the type 2 change.

We want to reinforce that reported results may differ depending on whether attribute changes are handled as a type 1 or type 2. Let's presume the electronic retailer sells $500 of IntelliKidz software during January 2013, followed by a $100 sale in February 2013. If the department attribute is a type 1, the results from a query reporting January and February sales would indicate $600 under Strategy. Conversely, if the department name attribute is a type 2, the sales would be reported as $500 for the Education department and $100 for the Strategy department.

Unlike the type 1 approach, there is no need to revisit preexisting aggregation tables when using the type 2 technique. Likewise, OLAP cubes do not need to be reprocessed if hierarchical attributes are handled as type 2.

If you constrain on the department attribute, the two product profiles are differentiated. If you constrain on the product description, the query automatically fetches both IntelliKidz product dimension rows and automatically joins to the fact table for the complete product history. If you need to count the number of products correctly, then you would just use the SKU natural key attribute as the basis of the distinct count rather than the surrogate key; the natural key column becomes the glue that holds the separate type 2 rows for a single product together.

> **NOTE** The type 2 response is the primary workhorse technique for accurately tracking slowly changing dimension attributes. It is extremely powerful because the new dimension row automatically partitions history in the fact table.

Type 2 is the safest response if the business is not absolutely certain about the SCD business rules for an attribute. As we'll discuss in the "Type 6: Add Type 1 Attributes to Type 2 Dimension" and "Type 7: Dual Type 1 and Type 2 Dimensions" sections later in the chapter, you can provide the illusion of a type 1 overwrite when an attribute has been handled with the type 2 response. The converse is not true. If you treat an attribute as type 1, reverting to type 2 retroactively requires significant effort to create new dimension rows and then appropriately rekey the fact table.

Type 2 Effective and Expiration Dates

When a dimension table includes type 2 attributes, you should include several administrative columns on each row, as shown in Figure 5-6. The effective and expiration dates refer to the moment when the row's attribute values become valid or invalid. Effective and expiration dates or date/time stamps are necessary in the ETL system because it needs to know which surrogate key is valid when loading historical fact rows. The effective and expiration dates support precise time slicing of the dimension; however, there is no need to constrain on these dates in the dimension table to get the right answer from the fact table. The row effective date is the first date the descriptive profile is valid. When a new product is first loaded in the dimension table, the expiration date is set to December 31, 9999. By avoiding a null in the expiration date, you can reliably use a BETWEEN command to find the dimension rows that were in effect on a certain date.

When a new profile row is added to the dimension to capture a type 2 attribute change, the previous row is expired. We typically suggest the end date on the old row should be just prior to the effective date of the new row leaving no gaps between these effective and expiration dates. The definition of "just prior" depends on the grain of the changes being tracked. Typically, the effective and expiration dates represent changes that occur during a day; if you're tracking more granular changes, you'd use a date/time stamp instead. In this case, you may elect to apply different business rules, such as setting the row expiration date exactly equal to the effective date of the next row. This would require logic such as ">= effective date and < expiration date" constraints, invalidating the use of BETWEEN.

Some argue that a single effective date is adequate, but this makes for more complicated searches to locate the dimension row with the latest effective date that is less than or equal to a date filter. Storing an explicit second date simplifies the query processing. Likewise, a current row indicator is another useful administrative dimension attribute to quickly constrain queries to only the current profiles.

The type 2 response to slowly changing dimensions requires the use of surrogate keys, but you're already using them anyhow, right? You certainly can't use the operational natural key because there are multiple profile versions for the same natural key. It is not sufficient to use the natural key with two or three version digits because you'd be vulnerable to the entire list of potential operational issues discussed in Chapter 3. Likewise, it is inadvisable to append an effective date to the otherwise primary key of the dimension table to uniquely identify each version. With the type 2 response, you create a new dimension row with a new single-column primary key to uniquely identify the new product profile. This single-column primary key establishes the linkage between the fact and dimension tables for a given set of product characteristics. There's no need to create a confusing secondary join based on the dimension row's effective or expiration dates.

We recognize some of you may be concerned about the administration of surrogate keys to support type 2 changes. In Chapter 19: ETL Subsystems and Techniques and Chapter 20: ETL System Design and Development Process and Tasks, we'll discuss a workflow for managing surrogate keys and accommodating type 2 changes in more detail.

Type 1 Attributes in Type 2 Dimensions

It is not uncommon to mix multiple slowly changing dimension techniques within the same dimension. When type 1 and type 2 are both used in a dimension, sometimes a type 1 attribute change necessitates updating multiple dimension rows. Let's presume the dimension table includes a product introduction date. If this attribute is corrected using type 1 logic after a type 2 change to another attribute occurs, the introduction date should probably be updated on both versions of IntelliKidz's profile, as illustrated in Figure 5-7.

The data stewards need to be involved in defining the ETL business rules in scenarios like this. Although the DW/BI team can facilitate discussion regarding proper update handling, the business's data stewards should make the final determination, not the DW/BI team.

Original row in Product dimension:

Product Key	SKU (NK)	Product Description	Department Name	Introduction Date	...	Row Effective Date	Row Expiration Date	Current Row Indicator
12345	ABC922-Z	IntelliKidz	Education	2012-12-15	...	2012-01-01	9999-12-31	Current

Rows in Product dimension following type 2 change to Department Name and type 1 change to Introduction Date:

Product Key	SKU (NK)	Product Description	Department Name	Introduction Date	...	Row Effective Date	Row Expiration Date	Current Row Indicator
12345	ABC922-Z	IntelliKidz	Education	2012-01-01	...	2012-01-01	2013-01-31	Expired
25984	ABC922-Z	IntelliKidz	Strategy	2012-01-01	...	2013-02-01	9999-12-31	Current

Figure 5-7: Type 1 updates in a dimension with type 2 attributes sample rows.

Type 3: Add New Attribute

Although the type 2 response partitions history, it does not enable you to associate the new attribute value with old fact history or vice versa. With the type 2 response, when you constrain the department attribute to Strategy, you see only IntelliKidz facts from after February 1, 2013. In most cases, this is exactly what you want.

However, sometimes you want to see fact data as if the change never occurred. This happens most frequently with sales force reorganizations. District boundaries may be redrawn, but some users still want the ability to roll up recent sales for the prior districts just to see how they would have done under the old organizational structure. For a few transitional months, there may be a need to track history for the new districts and conversely to track new fact data in terms of old district boundaries. A type 2 response won't support this requirement, but type 3 comes to the rescue.

In our software example, let's assume there is a legitimate business need to track both the new and prior values of the department attribute for a period of time around the February 1 change. With a type 3 response, you do not issue a new dimension row, but rather add a new column to capture the attribute change, as illustrated in Figure 5-8. You would alter the product dimension table to add a prior department attribute, and populate this new column with the existing department value (Education). The original department attribute is treated as a type 1 where you overwrite to reflect the current value (Strategy). All existing reports and queries immediately switch over to the new department description, but you can still report on the old department value by querying on the prior department attribute.

Original row in Product dimension:

Product Key	SKU (NK)	Product Description	Department Name
12345	ABC922-Z	IntelliKidz	Education

Updated row in Product dimension:

Product Key	SKU (NK)	Product Description	Department Name	Prior Department Name
12345	ABC922-Z	IntelliKidz	Strategy	Education

Figure 5-8: SCD type 3 sample rows.

Don't be fooled into thinking the higher type number associated with type 3 indicates it is the preferred approach; the techniques have not been presented in good, better, and best practice sequence. Frankly, type 3 is infrequently used. It is appropriate when there's a strong need to support two views of the world simultaneously. Type 3 is distinguished from type 2 because the pair of current and prior attribute values are regarded as true at the same time.

NOTE The type 3 slowly changing dimension technique enables you to see new and historical fact data by either the new or prior attribute values, sometimes called *alternate realities*.

Type 3 is not useful for attributes that change unpredictably, such as a customer's home state. There would be no benefit in reporting facts based on a prior home state attribute that reflects a change from 10 days ago for some customers or 10 years ago for others. These unpredictable changes are typically handled best with type 2 instead.

Type 3 is most appropriate when there's a significant change impacting many rows in the dimension table, such as a product line or sales force reorganization. These en masse changes are prime candidates because business users often want the ability to analyze performance metrics using either the pre- or post-hierarchy reorganization for a period of time. With type 3 changes, the prior column is labeled to distinctly represent the prechanged grouping, such as 2012 department or pre-merger department. These column names provide clarity, but there may be unwanted ripples in the BI layer.

Finally, if the type 3 attribute represents a hierarchical rollup level within the dimension, then as discussed with type 1, the type 3 update and additional column would likely cause OLAP cubes to be reprocessed.

Multiple Type 3 Attributes

If a dimension attribute changes with a predictable rhythm, sometimes the business wants to summarize performance metrics based on any of the historic attribute values. Imagine the product line is recategorized at the start of every year and the business wants to look at multiple years of historic facts based on the department assignment for the current year or any prior year.

In this case, we take advantage of the regular, predictable nature of these changes by generalizing the type 3 approach to a series of type 3 dimension attributes, as illustrated in Figure 5-9. On every dimension row, there is a current department attribute that is overwritten, plus attributes for each annual designation, such as 2012 department. Business users can roll up the facts with any of the department assignments. If a product were introduced in 2013, the department attributes for 2012 and 2011 would contain Not Applicable values.

Updated row in Product dimension:

Product Key	SKU (NK)	Product Description	Current Department Name	2012 Department Name	2011 Department Name
12345	ABC922-Z	IntelliKidz	Strategy	Education	Not Applicable

Figure 5-9: Dimension table with multiple SCD type 3 attributes.

The most recent assignment column should be identified as the current department. This attribute will be used most frequently; you don't want to modify existing queries and reports to accommodate next year's change. When the departments are reassigned in January 2014, you'd alter the table to add a 2013 department attribute, populate this column with the current department values, and then overwrite the current attribute with the 2014 department assignment.

Type 4: Add Mini-Dimension

Thus far we've focused on slow evolutionary changes to dimension tables. What happens when the rate of change speeds up, especially within a large multimillion-row dimension table? Large dimensions present two challenges that warrant special treatment. The size of these dimensions can negatively impact browsing and query filtering performance. Plus our tried-and-true type 2 technique for change tracking is unappealing because we don't want to add more rows to a dimension that already has millions of rows, particularly if changes happen frequently.

Fortunately, a single technique comes to the rescue to address both the browsing performance and change tracking challenges. The solution is to break off frequently analyzed or frequently changing attributes into a separate dimension, referred to as a *mini-dimension*. For example, you could create a mini-dimension for a group of more volatile customer demographic attributes, such as age, purchase frequency score, and income level, presuming these columns are used extensively and changes to these attributes are important to the business. There would be one row in the mini-dimension for each unique combination of age, purchase frequency score, and income level encountered in the data, not one row per customer. With this approach, the mini-dimension becomes a set of demographic profiles. Although the number of rows in the customer dimension may be in the millions, the number of mini-dimension rows should be a significantly smaller. You leave behind the more constant attributes in the original multimillion-row customer table.

Sample rows for a demographic mini-dimension are illustrated in Figure 5-10. When creating the mini-dimension, continuously variable attributes, such as income, are converted to banded ranges. In other words, the attributes in the mini-dimension are typically forced to take on a relatively small number of discrete values. Although this restricts use to a set of predefined bands, it drastically reduces the number of combinations in the mini-dimension. If you stored income at a specific dollar and cents value in the mini-dimension, when combined with the other demographic attributes, you could end up with as many rows in the mini-dimension as in the customer dimension itself. The use of band ranges is probably the most significant compromise associated with the mini-dimension technique. Although grouping facts from multiple band values is viable, changing to more discreet bands (such as $30,000-34,999) at a later time is difficult. If users insist on access to a specific raw data value, such as a credit bureau score that is updated monthly, it should be included in the fact table, in addition to being value banded in the demographic mini-dimension. In Chapter 10: Financial Services, we'll discuss dynamic value banding of facts; however, such queries are much less efficient than constraining the value band in a mini-dimension table.

Demographics Key	Age Band	Purchase Frequency Score	Income Level
1	21-25	Low	<$30,000
2	21-25	Medium	<$30,000
3	21-25	High	<$30,000
4	21-25	Low	$30,000-39,999
5	21-25	Medium	$30,000-39,999
6	21-25	High	$30,000-39,999
...	...	...	...
142	26-30	Low	<$30,000
143	26-30	Medium	<$30,000
144	26-30	High	<$30,000
...	...	...	...

Figure 5-10: SCD type 4 mini-dimension sample rows.

Every time a fact table row is built, two foreign keys related to the customer would be included: the customer dimension key and the mini-dimension demographics key in effect at the time of the event, as shown in Figure 5-11. The mini-dimension delivers performance benefits by providing a smaller point of entry to the facts. Queries can avoid the huge customer dimension table unless attributes from that table are constrained or used as report labels.

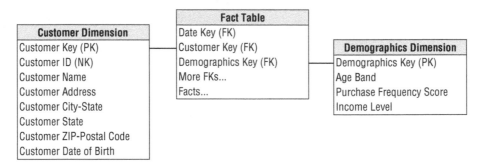

Figure 5-11: Type 4 mini-dimension with customer dimension.

When the mini-dimension key participates as a foreign key in the fact table, another benefit is that the fact table captures the demographic profile changes. Let's presume we are loading data into a periodic snapshot fact table on a monthly basis. Referring back to our sample demographic mini-dimension sample rows in Figure 5-10, if one of our customers, John Smith, were 25 years old with a low purchase frequency score and an income of $25,000, you'd begin by assigning demographics key 1 when loading the fact table. If John has a birthday several weeks later and turns 26 years old, you'd assign demographics key 142 when the fact table was next loaded; the demographics key on John's earlier fact table rows would not be changed. In this manner, the fact table tracks the age change. You'd continue to assign demographics key 142 when the fact table is loaded until there's another change in John's demographic profile. If John receives a raise to $32,000 several months later, a new demographics key would be reflected in the next fact table load. Again, the earlier rows would be unchanged. OLAP cubes also readily accommodate type 4 mini-dimensions.

Customer dimensions are somewhat unique in that customer attributes frequently are queried independently from the fact table. For example, users may want to know how many customers live in Dade County by age bracket for segmentation and profiling. Rather than forcing any analysis that combines customer and demographic data to link through the fact table, the most recent value of the demographics key also can exist as a foreign key on the customer dimension table. We'll further describe this customer demographic outrigger as an SCD type 5 in the next section.

The demographic dimension cannot be allowed to grow too large. If you have five demographic attributes, each with 10 possible values, then the demographics dimension could have 100,000 (10^5) rows. This is a reasonable upper limit for the number of rows in a mini-dimension if you build out all the possible combinations in advance. An alternate ETL approach is to build only the mini-dimension rows that actually occur in the data. However, there are certainly cases where even this approach doesn't help and you need to support more than five demographic attributes with 10 values each. We'll discuss the use of multiple mini-dimensions associated with a single fact table in Chapter 10.

Demographic profile changes sometimes occur outside a business event, such as when a customer's profile is updated in the absence of a sales transaction. If the business requires accurate point-in-time profiling, a supplemental factless fact table with effective and expiration dates can capture every relationship change between the customer and demographics dimensions.

Hybrid Slowly Changing Dimension Techniques

In this final section, we'll discuss hybrid approaches that combine the basic SCD techniques. Designers sometimes become enamored with these hybrids because they seem to provide the best of all worlds. However, the price paid for greater analytic flexibility is often greater complexity. Although IT professionals may be impressed by elegant flexibility, business users may be just as easily turned off by complexity. You should not pursue these options unless the business agrees they are needed to address their requirements.

These final approaches are most relevant if you've been asked to preserve the historically accurate dimension attribute associated with a fact event, while supporting the option to report historical facts according to the current attribute values. The basic slowly changing dimension techniques do not enable this requirement easily on their own.

We'll start by considering a technique that combines type 4 with a type 1 outrigger; because 4 + 1 = 5, we're calling this type 5. Next, we'll describe type 6, which combines types 1 through 3 for a single dimension attribute; it's aptly named type 6 because 2 + 3 + 1 or 2 × 3 × 1 both equal 6. Finally, we'll finish up with type 7, which just happens to be the next available sequence number; there is no underlying mathematical significance to this label.

Type 5: Mini-Dimension and Type 1 Outrigger

Let's return to the type 4 mini-dimension. An embellishment to this technique is to add a current mini-dimension key as an attribute in the primary dimension. This mini-dimension key reference is a type 1 attribute, overwritten with every profile change. You wouldn't want to track this attribute as a type 2 because then you'd be capturing volatile changes within the large multimillion-row dimension and avoiding this explosive growth was one of the original motivations for type 4.

The type 5 technique is useful if you want a current profile count in the absence of fact table metrics or want to roll up historical facts based on the customer's current profile. You'd logically represent the primary dimension and mini-dimension outrigger as a single table in the presentation area, as shown in Figure 5-12. To minimize user confusion and potential error, the current attributes in this role-playing dimension should have distinct column names distinguishing them, such as current age band. Even with unique labeling, be aware that presenting users with two avenues for accessing demographic data, through either the mini-dimension or outrigger, can deliver more functionality and complexity than some can handle.

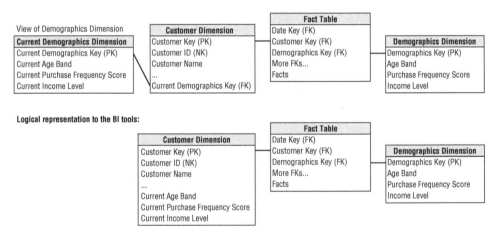

Figure 5-12: Type 4 mini-dimension with type 1 outrigger in customer dimension.

> **NOTE**   The type 4 mini-dimension terminology refers to when the demographics key is part of the fact table composite key. If the demographics key is a foreign key in the customer dimension, it is referred to as an outrigger.

Type 6: Add Type 1 Attributes to Type 2 Dimension

Let's return to the electronics retailer's product dimension. With type 6, you would have two department attributes on each row. The current department column represents the current assignment; the historic department column is a type 2 attribute representing the historically accurate department value.

When IntelliKidz software is introduced, the product dimension row would look like the first scenario in Figure 5-13.

Original row in Product dimension:

Product Key	SKU (NK)	Product Description	Historic Department Name	Current Department Name	...	Row Effective Date	Row Expiration Date	Current Row Indicator
12345	ABC922-Z	IntelliKidz	Education	Education	...	2012-01-01	9999-12-31	Current

Rows in Product dimension following first department reassignment:

Product Key	SKU (NK)	Product Description	Historic Department Name	Current Department Name	...	Row Effective Date	Row Expiration Date	Current Row Indicator
12345	ABC922-Z	IntelliKidz	Education	Strategy	...	2012-01-01	2013-01-31	Expired
25984	ABC922-Z	IntelliKidz	Strategy	Strategy	...	2013-02-01	9999-12-31	Current

Rows in Product dimension following second department reassignment:

Product Key	SKU (NK)	Product Description	Historic Department Name	Current Department Name	...	Row Effective Date	Row Expiration Date	Current Row Indicator
12345	ABC922-Z	IntelliKidz	Education	Critical Thinking	...	2012-01-01	2013-01-31	Expired
25984	ABC922-Z	IntelliKidz	Strategy	Critical Thinking	...	2013-02-01	2013-06-30	Expired
31726	ABC922-Z	IntelliKidz	Critical Thinking	Critical Thinking	...	2013-07-01	9999-12-31	Current

Figure 5-13: SCD type 6 sample rows.

When the departments are restructured and IntelliKidz is moved to the Strategy department, you'd use a type 2 response to capture the attribute change by issuing a new row. In this new IntelliKidz dimension row, the current department will be identical to the historical department. For all previous instances of IntelliKidz dimension rows, the current department attribute will be overwritten to reflect the current structure. Both IntelliKidz rows would identify the Strategy department as the current department (refer to the second scenario in Figure 5-13).

In this manner you can use the historic attribute to group facts based on the attribute value that was in effect when the facts occurred. Meanwhile, the current attribute rolls up all the historical fact data for both product keys 12345 and 25984 into the current department assignment. If IntelliKidz were then moved into the Critical Thinking software department, the product table would look like Figure 5-13's final set of rows. The current column groups all facts by the current assignment, while the historic column preserves the historic assignments accurately and segments the facts accordingly.

With this hybrid approach, you issue a new row to capture the change (type 2) and add a new column to track the current assignment (type 3), where subsequent changes are handled as a type 1 response. An engineer at a technology company suggested we refer to this combo approach as type 6 because both the sum and product of 1, 2, and 3 equals 6.

Again, although this technique may be naturally appealing to some, it is important to always consider the business users' perspective as you strive to arrive at a reasonable balance between flexibility and complexity. You may want to limit which columns are exposed to some users so they're not overwhelmed by choices.

Type 7: Dual Type 1 and Type 2 Dimensions

When we first described type 6, someone asked if the technique would be appropriate for supporting both current and historic perspectives for 150 attributes in a large dimension table. That question sent us back to the drawing board.

In this final hybrid technique, the dimension natural key (assuming it's durable) is included as a fact table foreign key, in addition to the surrogate key for type 2 tracking, as illustrated in Figure 5-14. If the natural key is unwieldy or ever reassigned, you should use a separate durable supernatural key instead. The type 2 dimension contains historically accurate attributes for filtering and grouping based on the effective values when the fact event occurred. The durable key joins to a dimension with just the current type 1 values. Again, the column labels in this table should be prefaced with "current" to reduce the risk of user confusion. You can use these dimension attributes to summarize or filter facts based on the current profile, regardless of the attribute values in effect when the fact event occurred.

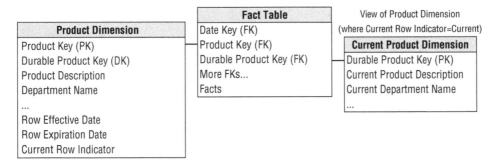

Figure 5-14: Type 7 with dual foreign keys for dual type 1 and type 2 dimension tables.

This approach delivers the same functionality as type 6. Although the type 6 response spawns more attribute columns in a single dimension table, this approach relies on two foreign keys in the fact table. Type 7 invariably requires less ETL effort because the current type 1 attribute table could easily be delivered via a view of the type 2 dimension table, limited to the most current rows. The incremental cost of this final technique is the additional column carried in the fact table; however, queries based on current attribute values would be filtering on a smaller dimension table than previously described with type 6.

Of course, you could avoid storing the durable key in the fact table by joining the type 1 view containing current attributes to the durable key in the type 2 dimension table itself. In this case, however, queries that are only interested in current rollups would need to traverse from the type 1 outrigger through the more voluminous type 2 dimension before finally reaching the facts, which would likely negatively impact query performance for current reporting.

A variation of this dual type 1 and type 2 dimension table approach again relies on a view to deliver current type 1 attributes. However, in this case, the view associates the current attribute values with all the durable key's type 2 rows, as illustrated in Figure 5-15.

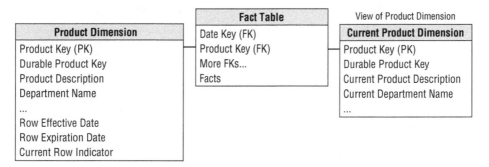

Figure 5-15: Type 7 variation with single surrogate key for dual type 1 and type 2 dimension tables.

Both dimension tables in Figure 5-15 have the same number of rows, but the contents of the tables are different, as shown in Figure 5-16.

Rows in Product dimension:

Product Key	SKU (NK)	Durable Product Key	Product Description	Department Name	...	Row Effective Date	Row Expiration Date	Current Row Indicator
12345	ABC922-Z	12345	IntelliKidz	Education	...	2012-01-01	2013-01-31	Expired
25984	ABC922-Z	12345	IntelliKidz	Strategy	...	2013-02-01	2013-06-30	Expired
31726	ABC922-Z	12345	IntelliKidz	Critical Thinking	...	2013-07-01	9999-12-31	Current

Rows in Product dimension's current view:

Product Key	SKU (NK)	Durable Product Key	Current Product Description	Current Department Name	...
12345	ABC922-Z	12345	IntelliKidz	Critical Thinking	...
25984	ABC922-Z	12345	IntelliKidz	Critical Thinking	...
31726	ABC922-Z	12345	IntelliKidz	Critical Thinking	...

Figure 5-16: SCD type 7 variation sample rows.

Type 7 for Random "As Of" Reporting

Finally, although it's uncommon, you might be asked to roll up historical facts based on any specific point-in-time profile, in addition to reporting by the attribute values in effect when the fact event occurred or by the attribute's current values. For example, perhaps the business wants to report three years of historical metrics based on the hierarchy in effect on December 1 of last year. In this case, you can use the dual dimension keys in the fact table to your advantage. First filter on the type 2 dimension row effective and expiration dates to locate the rows in effect on December 1 of last year. With this constraint, a single row for each durable key in the type 2 dimension is identified. Then join this filtered set to the durable key in the fact table to roll up any facts based on the point-in-time attribute values. It's as if you're defining the meaning of "current" on-the-fly. Obviously, you must filter on the row effective and expiration dates, or you'll have multiple type 2 rows for each durable key. Finally, only unveil this capability to a limited, highly analytic audience; this embellishment is not for the timid.

Slowly Changing Dimension Recap

We've summarized the techniques for tracking dimension attribute changes in Figure 5-17. This chart highlights the implications of each slowly changing dimension technique on the analysis of performance metrics in the fact table.

SCD Type	Dimension Table Action	Impact on Fact Analysis
Type 0	No change to attribute value.	Facts associated with attribute's original value.
Type 1	Overwrite attribute value.	Facts associated with attribute's current value.
Type 2	Add new dimension row for profile with new attribute value.	Facts associated with attribute value in effect when fact occured.
Type 3	Add new column to preserve attribute's current and prior values.	Facts associated with both current and prior attribute alternative values.
Type 4	Add mini-dimension table containing rapidly changing attributes.	Facts associated with rapidly changing attributes in effect when fact occured.
Type 5	Add type 4 mini-dimension, along with overwritten type 1 mini-dimension key in base dimension.	Facts associated with rapidly changing attributes in effect when fact occurred, plus current rapidly changing attribute values.
Type 6	Add type 1 overwritten attributes to type 2 dimension row, and overwrite all prior dimension rows.	Facts associated with attribute value in effect when fact occurred, plus current values.
Type 7	Add type 2 dimension row with new attribute value, plus view limited to current rows and/or attribute values.	Facts associated with attribute value in effect when fact occurred, plus current values.

Figure 5-17: Slowly changing dimension techniques summary.

Summary

In this chapter we discussed several approaches to handling procurement data. Effectively managing procurement performance can have a major impact on an organization's bottom line.

We also introduced techniques to deal with changes to dimension attribute values. The slowly changing responses range from doing nothing (type 0) to overwriting the value (type 1) to complicated hybrid approaches (such as types 5 through 7) which combine techniques to support requirements for both historic attribute preservation and current attribute reporting. You'll undoubtedly need to re-read this section as you consider slowly changing dimension attribute strategies for your DW/BI system.

6 Order Management

Order management consists of several critical business processes, including order, shipment, and invoice processing. These processes spawn metrics, such as sales volume and invoice revenue, that are key performance indicators for any organization that sells products or services to others. In fact, these foundation metrics are so crucial that DW/BI teams frequently tackle one of the order management processes for their initial implementation. Clearly, the topics in this case study transcend industry boundaries.

In this chapter we'll explore several different order management transactions, including the common characteristics and complications encountered when dimensionally modeling these transactions. We'll further develop the concept of an accumulating snapshot to analyze the order fulfillment pipeline from initial order to invoicing.

Chapter 6 discusses the following concepts:

- Bus matrix snippet for order management processes
- Orders transaction schema
- Fact table normalization considerations
- Role-playing dimensions
- Ship-to/bill-to customer dimension considerations
- Factors to determine if single or multiple dimensions
- Junk dimensions for miscellaneous flags and indicators versus alternative designs
- More on degenerate dimensions
- Multiple currencies and units of measure
- Handling of facts with different granularity
- Patterns to avoid with header and line item transactions
- Invoicing transaction schema with profit and loss facts
- Audit dimension

- Quantitative measures and qualitative descriptors of service level performance
- Order fulfillment pipeline as accumulating snapshot schema
- Lag calculations

Order Management Bus Matrix

The order management function is composed of a series of business processes. In its most simplistic form, you can envision a subset of the enterprise data warehouse bus matrix that resembles Figure 6-1.

	Date	Customer	Product	Sales Rep	Deal	Warehouse	Shipper
Quoting	X	X	X	X	X		
Ordering	X	X	X	X	X		
Shipping to Customer	X	X	X	X	X	X	X
Shipment Invoicing	X	X	X	X	X	X	X
Receiving Payments	X	X		X			
Customer Returns	X	X	X	X	X	X	X

Figure 6-1: Bus matrix rows for order management processes.

As described in earlier chapters, the bus matrix closely corresponds to the organization's value chain. In this chapter we'll focus on the order and invoice rows of the matrix. We'll also describe an accumulating snapshot fact table to evaluate performance across multiple stages of the overall order fulfillment process.

Order Transactions

The natural granularity for an order transaction fact table is one row for each line item on an order. The dimensions associated with the orders business process are order date, requested ship date, product, customer, sales rep, and deal. The facts include the order quantity and extended order line gross, discount, and net (equal to the gross amount less discount) dollar amounts. The resulting schema would look similar to Figure 6-2.

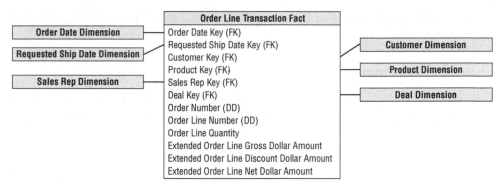

Figure 6-2: Order transaction fact table.

Fact Normalization

Rather than storing the list of facts in Figure 6-2, some designers want to further normalize the fact table so there's a single, generic fact amount along with a dimension that identifies the type of measurement. In this scenario, the fact table granularity is one row per measurement per order line, instead of the more natural one row per order line event. The measurement type dimension would indicate whether the fact is the gross order amount, order discount amount, or some other measure. This technique may make sense when the set of facts is extremely lengthy, but sparsely populated for a given fact row, and no computations are made between facts. You could use this technique to deal with manufacturing quality test data where the facts vary widely depending on the test conducted.

However, you should generally resist the urge to normalize the fact table in this way. Facts usually are not sparsely populated within a row. In the order transaction schema, if you were to normalize the facts, you'd be multiplying the number of rows in the fact table by the number of fact types. For example, assume you started with 10 million order line fact table rows, each with six keys and four facts. If the fact rows were normalized, you'd end up with 40 million fact rows, each with seven keys and one fact. In addition, if any arithmetic function is performed between the facts (such as discount amount as a percentage of gross order amount), it is far easier if the facts are in the same row in a relational star schema because SQL makes it difficult to perform a ratio or difference between facts in different rows. In Chapter 14: Healthcare, we'll explore a situation where a measurement type dimension makes more sense. This pattern is also more appropriate if the primary platform supporting BI applications is an OLAP cube; the cube enables computations that cut the cube along any dimension, regardless if it's a date, product, customer, or measurement type.

Dimension Role Playing

By now you know to expect a date dimension in every fact table because you're always looking at performance over time. In a transaction fact table, the primary date column is the transaction date, such as the order date. Sometimes you discover other dates associated with each transaction, such as the requested ship date for the order.

Each of the dates should be a foreign key in the fact table, as shown in Figure 6-3. However, you cannot simply join these two foreign keys to the same date dimension table. SQL would interpret this two-way simultaneous join as requiring both the dates to be identical, which isn't very likely.

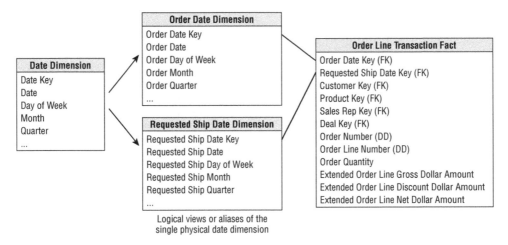

Figure 6-3: Role-playing date dimensions.

Even though you cannot literally join to a single date dimension table, you can build and administer a single physical date dimension table. You then create the illusion of two independent date dimensions by using views or aliases. Be careful to uniquely label the columns in each of the views or aliases. For example, the order month attribute should be uniquely labeled to distinguish it from the requested ship month. If you don't establish unique column names, you wouldn't be able to tell the columns apart when both are dragged into a report.

As we briefly described in Chapter 3: Retail Sales, we would define the order date and requested order date views as follows:

```
create view order_date
  (order_date_key, order_day_of_week, order_month, ...)
  as select date_key, day_of_week, month, ... from date
```

and

```
create view req_ship_date
  (req_ship_date_key, req_ship_day_of_week, req_ship_month, ...)
  as select date_key, day_of_week, month, ... from date
```

Alternatively, SQL supports the concept of aliasing. Many BI tools also enable aliasing within their semantic layer. However, we caution against this approach if multiple BI tools, along with direct SQL-based access, are used within the organization.

Regardless of the implementation approach, you now have two unique logical date dimensions that can be used as if they were independent with completely unrelated constraints. This is referred to as *role playing* because the date dimension simultaneously serves different roles in a single fact table. You'll see additional examples of dimension role playing sprinkled throughout this book.

NOTE Role playing in a dimensional model occurs when a single dimension simultaneously appears several times in the same fact table. The underlying dimension may exist as a single physical table, but each of the roles should be presented to the BI tools as a separately labeled view.

It's worth noting that some OLAP products do not support multiple roles of the same dimension; in this scenario, you'd need to create two separate dimensions for the two roles. In addition, some OLAP products that enable multiple roles do not enable attribute renaming for each role. In the end, OLAP environments may be littered with a plethora of separate dimensions, which are treated simply as roles in the relational star schema.

To handle the multiple dates, some designers are tempted to create a single date table with a key for each unique order date and requested ship date combination. This approach falls apart on several fronts. First, the clean and simple daily date table with approximately 365 rows per year would balloon in size if it needed to handle all the date combinations. Second, a combination date table would no longer conform to the other frequently used daily, weekly, and monthly date dimensions.

Role Playing and the Bus Matrix

The most common technique to document role playing on the bus matrix is to indicate the multiple roles within a single cell, as illustrated in Figure 6-4. We used a similar approach in Chapter 4: Inventory for documenting shrunken conformed dimensions. This method is especially appropriate for the date dimension on the bus matrix given its numerous logical roles. Alternatively, if the number of roles is limited and frequently reused across processes, you can create subcolumns within a single conformed dimension column on the matrix.

	Date
Quoting	Quote Date
Ordering	Order Date Requested Ship Date
Shipping to Customer	Shipment Date
Shipment Invoicing	Invoice Date
Receiving Payments	Payment Receipt Date
Customer Returns	Return Date

Figure 6-4: Communicating role-playing dimensions on the bus matrix.

Product Dimension Revisited

Each of the case study vignettes presented so far has included a product dimension. The product dimension is one of the most common and most important dimension tables. It describes the complete portfolio of products sold by a company. In many cases, the number of products in the portfolio turns out to be surprisingly large, at least from an outsider's perspective. For example, a prominent U.S. manufacturer of dog and cat food tracks more than 25,000 manufacturing variations of its products, including retail products everyone (or every dog and cat) is familiar with, as well as numerous specialized products sold through commercial and veterinary channels. Some durable goods manufacturers, such as window companies, sell millions of unique product configurations.

Most product dimension tables share the following characteristics:

- **Numerous verbose, descriptive columns**. For manufacturers, it's not unusual to maintain 100 or more descriptors about the products they sell. Dimension table attributes naturally describe the dimension row, do not vary because of the influence of another dimension, and are virtually constant over time, although some attributes do change slowly over time.
- **One or more attribute hierarchies, plus non-hierarchical attributes**. Products typically roll up according to multiple defined hierarchies. The many-to-one fixed depth hierarchical data should be presented in a single flattened, denormalized product dimension table. You should resist creating normalized snowflaked sub-tables; the costs of a more complicated presentation and slower intra-dimension browsing performance outweigh the minimal storage savings benefits. Product dimension tables can have thousands of entries. With so many

rows, it is not too useful to request a pull-down list of the product descriptions. It is essential to have the ability to constrain on one attribute, such as flavor, and then another attribute, such as package type, before attempting to display the product descriptions. Any attributes, regardless of whether they belong to a single hierarchy, should be used freely for browsing and drilling up or down. Many product dimension attributes are standalone low-cardinality attributes, not part of explicit hierarchies.

The existence of an operational product master helps create and maintain the product dimension, but a number of transformations and administrative steps must occur to convert the operational master file into the dimension table, including the following:

- **Remap the operational product code to a surrogate key.** As we discussed in Chapter 3, this meaningless surrogate primary key is needed to avoid havoc caused by duplicate use of an operational product code over time. It also might be necessary to integrate product information sourced from different operational systems. Finally, as you just learned in Chapter 5: Procurement, the surrogate key is needed to track type 2 product attribute changes.
- **Add descriptive attribute values to augment or replace operational codes.** You shouldn't accept the excuse that the business users are familiar with the operational codes. The only reason business users are familiar with codes is that they have been forced to use them! The columns in a product dimension are the sole source of query constraints and report labels, so the contents must be legible. Cryptic abbreviations are as bad as outright numeric codes; they also should be augmented or replaced with readable text. Multiple abbreviated codes in a single column should be expanded and separated into distinct attributes.
- **Quality check the attribute values to ensure no misspellings, impossible values, or multiple variations.** BI applications and reports rely on the precise contents of the dimension attributes. SQL will produce another line in a report if the attribute value varies in any way based on trivial punctuation or spelling differences. You should ensure that the attribute values are completely populated because missing values easily cause misinterpretations. Incomplete or poorly administered textual dimension attributes lead to incomplete or poorly produced reports.
- **Document the attribute definitions, interpretations, and origins in the metadata.** Remember that the metadata is analogous to the DW/BI encyclopedia. You must be vigilant about populating and maintaining the metadata repository.

Customer Dimension

The customer dimension contains one row for each discrete location to which you ship a product. Customer dimension tables can range from moderately sized (thousands of rows) to extremely large (millions of rows) depending on the nature of the business. A typical customer dimension is shown in Figure 6-5.

Customer Dimension
Customer Key (PK)
Customer ID (Natural Key)
Customer Name
Customer Ship To Address
Customer Ship To City
Customer Ship To County
Customer Ship To City-State
Customer Ship To State
Customer Ship To ZIP
Customer Ship To ZIP Region
Customer Ship To ZIP Sectional Center
Customer Bill To Name
Customer Bill To Address
Customer Organization Name
Customer Corporate Parent Name
Customer Credit Rating

Figure 6-5: Sample customer dimension.

Several independent hierarchies typically coexist in a customer dimension. The natural geographic hierarchy is clearly defined by the ship-to location. Because the ship-to location is a point in space, any number of geographic hierarchies may be defined by nesting more expansive geographic entities around the point. In the United States, the usual geographic hierarchy is city, county, and state. It is often useful to include a city-state attribute because the same city name exists in multiple states. The ZIP code identifies a secondary geographic breakdown. The first digit of the ZIP code identifies a geographic region of the United States (for example, 0 for the Northeast and 9 for certain western states), whereas the first three digits of the ZIP code identify a mailing sectional center.

Although these geographic characteristics may be captured and managed in a single master data management system, you should embed the attributes within the respective dimensions rather than relying on an abstract, generic geography/location dimension that includes one row for every point in space independent of the dimensions. We'll talk more about this in Chapter 11: Telecommunications.

Another common hierarchy is the customer's organizational hierarchy, assuming the customer is a corporate entity. For each customer ship-to address, you might have a customer bill-to and customer parent corporation. For every row in the customer dimension, both the physical geographies and organizational affiliation are well defined, even though the hierarchies roll up differently.

> **NOTE** It is natural and common, especially for customer-oriented dimensions, for a dimension to simultaneously support multiple independent hierarchies. The hierarchies may have different numbers of levels. Drilling up and drilling down within each of these hierarchies must be supported in a dimensional model.

The alert reader may have a concern with the implied assumption that multiple ship-tos roll up to a single bill-to in a many-to-one relationship. The real world may not be quite this clean and simple. There are always a few exceptions involving ship-to addresses that are associated with more than one bill-to. Obviously, this breaks the simple hierarchical relationship assumed in Figure 6-5. If this is a rare occurrence, it would be reasonable to generalize the customer dimension so that the grain of the dimension is each unique ship-to/bill-to combination. In this scenario, if there are two sets of bill-to information associated with a given ship-to location, then there would be two rows in the dimension, one for each combination. On the other hand, if many of the ship-tos are associated with many bill-tos in a robust many-to-many relationship, then the ship-to and bill-to customers probably need to be handled as separate dimensions that are linked together by the fact table. With either approach, exactly the same information is preserved. We'll spend more time on organizational hierarchies, including the handling of variable depth recursive relationships, in Chapter 7: Accounting.

Single Versus Multiple Dimension Tables

Another potential hierarchy in the customer dimension might be the manufacturer's sales organization. Designers sometimes question whether sales organization attributes should be modeled as a separate dimension or added to the customer dimension. If sales reps are highly correlated with customers in a one-to-one or many-to-one relationship, combining the sales organization attributes with the customer attributes in a single dimension is a viable approach. The resulting dimension is only as big as the larger of the two dimensions. The relationships between sales teams and customers can be browsed efficiently in the single dimension without traversing the fact table.

However, sometimes the relationship between sales organization and customer is more complicated. The following factors must be taken into consideration:

- **Is the one-to-one or many-to-one relationship actually a many-to-many?** As we discussed earlier, if the many-to-many relationship is an exceptional condition, then you may still be tempted to combine the sales rep attributes into the customer dimension, knowing multiple surrogate keys are needed to handle these rare many-to-many occurrences. However, if the many-to-many relationship is the norm, you should handle the sales rep and customer as separate dimensions.

- **Does the sales rep and customer relationship vary over time or under the influence of another dimension?** If so, you'd likely create separate dimensions for the rep and customer.

- **Is the customer dimension extremely large?** If there are millions of customer rows, you'd be more likely to treat the sales rep as a separate dimension rather than forcing all sales rep analysis through a voluminous customer dimension.

- **Do the sales rep and customer dimensions participate independently in other fact tables?** Again, you'd likely keep the dimensions separate. Creating a single customer dimension with sales rep attributes exclusively around order data may cause users to be confused when they're analyzing other processes involving sales reps.

- **Does the business think about the sales rep and customer as separate things?** This factor may be tough to discern and impossible to quantify. But there's no sense forcing two critical dimensions into a single blended dimension if this runs counter to the business's perspectives.

When entities have a fixed, time-invariant, strongly correlated relationship, they should be modeled as a single dimension. In most other cases, the design likely will be simpler and more manageable when the entities are separated into two dimensions (while remembering the general guidelines concerning too many dimensions). If you've already identified 25 dimensions in your schema, you should consider combining dimensions, if possible.

When the dimensions are separate, some designers want to create a little table with just the two dimension keys to show the correlation without using the order fact table. In many scenarios, this two-dimension table is unnecessary. There is no reason to avoid the fact table to respond to this relationship inquiry. Fact tables are incredibly efficient because they contain only dimension keys and measurements, along with the occasional degenerate dimension. The fact table is created specifically to represent the correlations and many-to-many relationships between dimensions.

As we discussed in Chapter 5, you could capture the customer's currently assigned sales rep by including the relevant descriptors as type 1 attributes. Alternatively, you could use the slowly changing dimension (SCD) type 5 technique by embedding a type 1 foreign key to a sales rep dimension outrigger within the customer dimension; the current values could be presented as if they're included on the customer dimension via a view declaration.

Factless Fact Table for Customer/Rep Assignments

Before we leave the topic of sales rep assignments to customers, users sometimes want the ability to analyze the complex assignment of sales reps to customers over time, even if no order activity has occurred. In this case, you could construct a factless fact table, as illustrated in Figure 6-6, to capture the sales rep coverage. The coverage table would provide a complete map of the historical assignments of sales reps to customers, even if some of the assignments never resulted in a sale. This factless fact table contains dual date keys for the effective and expiration dates of each assignment. The expiration date on the current rep assignment row would reference a special date dimension row that identifies a future, undetermined date.

Figure 6-6: Factless fact table for sales rep assignments to customers.

You may want to compare the assignments fact table with the order transactions fact table to identify rep assignments that have not yet resulted in order activity. You would do so by leveraging SQL's capabilities to perform set operations (for example, selecting all the reps in the coverage table and subtracting all the reps in the orders table) or by writing a correlated subquery.

Deal Dimension

The deal dimension is similar to the promotion dimension from Chapter 3. The deal dimension describes the incentives offered to customers that theoretically affect the customers' desire to purchase products. This dimension is also sometimes referred to as the contract. As shown in Figure 6-7, the deal dimension describes the full combination of terms, allowances, and incentives that pertain to the particular order line item.

Deal Dimension
Deal Key (PK)
Deal ID (NK)
Deal Description
Deal Terms Description
Deal Terms Type Description
Allowance Description
Allowance Type Description
Special Incentive Description
Special Incentive Type Description
Local Budget Indicator

Figure 6-7: Sample deal dimension.

The same issues you faced in the retail promotion dimension also arise with this deal dimension. If the terms, allowances, and incentives are usefully correlated, it makes sense to package them into a single deal dimension. If the terms, allowances, and incentives are quite uncorrelated and you end up generating the Cartesian product of these factors in the dimension, it probably makes sense to split the deal dimension into its separate components. Again, this is not an issue of gaining or losing information because the schema contains the same information in both cases. The issues of user convenience and administrative complexity determine whether to represent these deal factors as multiple dimensions. In a very large fact table, with hundreds of millions or billions of rows, the desire to reduce the number of keys in the fact table composite key favors treating the deal attributes as a single dimension, assuming this meshes with the business users' perspectives. Certainly any deal dimension smaller than 100,000 rows would be tractable in this design.

Degenerate Dimension for Order Number

Each line item row in the order fact table includes the order number as a degenerate dimension. Unlike an operational header/line or parent/child database, the order number in a dimensional model is typically not tied to an order header table. You can triage all the interesting details from the order header into separate dimensions such as the order date and customer ship-to. The order number is still useful for several reasons. It enables you to group the separate line items on the order and answer questions such as "What is the average number of line items on an order?" The order number is occasionally used to link the data warehouse back to the operational world. It may also play a role in the fact table's primary key. Because the order number sits in the fact table without joining to a dimension table, it is a degenerate dimension.

> **NOTE** *Degenerate dimensions* typically are reserved for operational transaction identifiers. They should not be used as an excuse to stick cryptic codes in the fact table without joining to dimension tables for descriptive decodes.

Although there is likely no analytic purpose for the order transaction line number, it may be included in the fact table as a second degenerate dimension given its potential role in the primary key, along with the linkage to the operational system of record. In this case, the primary key for the line item grain fact table would be the order number and line number.

Sometimes data elements belong to the order itself and do not naturally fall into other dimension tables. In this situation, the order number is no longer a degenerate dimension but is a standard dimension with its own surrogate key and attributes.

However, designers with a strong operational background should resist the urge to simply dump the traditional order header information into an order dimension. In almost all cases, the header information belongs in other analytic dimensions that can be associated with the line item grain fact table rather than merely being cast off into a dimension that closely resembles the operational order header record.

Junk Dimensions

When modeling complex transactional source data, you often encounter a number of miscellaneous indicators and flags that are populated with a small range of discrete values. You have several rather unappealing options for handling these low cardinality flags and indicators, including:

- **Ignore the flags and indicators.** You can ask the obligatory question about eliminating these miscellaneous flags because they seem rather insignificant, but this notion is often vetoed quickly because someone occasionally needs them. If the indicators are incomprehensible or inconsistently populated, perhaps they should be left out.
- **Leave the flags and indicators unchanged on the fact row.** You don't want to store illegible cryptic indicators in the fact table. Likewise, you don't want to store bulky descriptors on the fact row, which would cause the table to swell alarmingly. It would be a shame to leave a handful of textual indicators on the row.
- **Make each flag and indicator into its own dimension.** Adding separate foreign keys to the fact table is acceptable if the resulting number of foreign keys is still reasonable (no more than 20 or so). However, if the list of foreign keys is already lengthy, you should avoid adding more clutter to the fact table.
- **Store the flags and indicators in an order header dimension.** Rather than treating the order number as a degenerate dimension, you could make it a regular dimension with the low cardinality flags and indicators as attributes. Although this approach accurately represents the data relationships, it is ill-advised, as described below.

An appropriate alternative approach for tackling these flags and indicators is to study them carefully and then pack them into one or more *junk dimensions*. A junk dimension is akin to the junk drawer in your kitchen. The kitchen junk drawer is a dumping ground for miscellaneous household items, such as rubber bands, paper clips, batteries, and tape. Although it may be easier to locate the rubber bands if a separate kitchen drawer is dedicated to them, you don't have adequate storage capacity to do so. Besides, you don't have enough stray rubber bands, nor do you need them frequently, to warrant the allocation of a single-purpose storage space.

The junk drawer provides you with satisfactory access while still retaining storage space for the more critical and frequently accessed dishes and silverware. In the dimensional modeling world, the junk dimension nomenclature is reserved for DW/BI professionals. We typically refer to the junk dimension as a *transaction indicator* or *transaction profile dimension* when talking with the business users.

> **NOTE** A junk dimension is a grouping of low-cardinality flags and indicators. By creating a junk dimension, you remove the flags from the fact table and place them into a useful dimensional framework.

If a single junk dimension has 10 two-value indicators, such as cash versus credit payment type, there would be a maximum of 1,024 (2^{10}) rows. It probably isn't interesting to browse among these flags within the dimension because every flag may occur with every other flag. However, the junk dimension is a useful holding place for constraining or reporting on these flags. The fact table would have a single, small surrogate key for the junk dimension.

On the other hand, if you have highly uncorrelated attributes that take on more numerous values, it may not make sense to lump them together into a single junk dimension. Unfortunately, the decision is not entirely formulaic. If you have five indicators that each take on only three values, a single junk dimension is the best route for these attributes because the dimension has only 243 (3^5) possible rows. However, if the five uncorrelated indicators each have 100 possible values, we'd suggest creating separate dimensions because there are now 100 million (100^5) possible combinations.

Figure 6-8 illustrates sample rows from an order indicator dimension. A subtle issue regarding junk dimensions is whether you should create rows for the full Cartesian product of all the combinations beforehand or create junk dimension rows for the combinations as you encounter them in the data. The answer depends on how many possible combinations you expect and what the maximum number could be. Generally, when the number of theoretical combinations is high and you don't expect to encounter them all, you build a junk dimension row at extract time whenever you encounter a new combination of flags or indicators.

Now that junk dimensions have been explained, contrast them to the handling of the flags and indicators as attributes in an order header dimension. If you want to analyze order facts where the order type is Inbound (refer to Figure 6-8's junk dimension rows), the fact table would be constrained to order indicator key equals 1, 2, 5, 6, 9, 10, and probably a few others. On the other hand, if these attributes were stored in an order header dimension, the constraint on the fact table would be an enormous list of all order numbers with an inbound order type.

Order Indicator Key	Payment Type Description	Payment Type Group	Order Type	Commission Credit Indicator
1	Cash	Cash	Inbound	Commissionable
2	Cash	Cash	Inbound	Non-Commissionable
3	Cash	Cash	Outbound	Commissionable
4	Cash	Cash	Outbound	Non-Commissionable
5	Visa	Credit	Inbound	Commissionable
6	Visa	Credit	Inbound	Non-Commissionable
7	Visa	Credit	Outbound	Commissionable
8	Visa	Credit	Outbound	Non-Commissionable
9	MasterCard	Credit	Inbound	Commissionable
10	MasterCard	Credit	Inbound	Non-Commissionable
11	MasterCard	Credit	Outbound	Non-Commissionable
12	MasterCard	Credit	Outbound	Commissionable

Figure 6-8: Sample rows of order indicator junk dimension.

Header/Line Pattern to Avoid

There are two common design mistakes to avoid when you model header/line data dimensionally. Unfortunately, both of these patterns still accurately represent the data relationships, so they don't stick out like a sore thumb. Perhaps equally unfortunate is that both patterns often feel more comfortable to data modelers and ETL team members with significant transaction processing experience than the patterns we advocate. We'll discuss the first common mistake here; the other is covered in the section "Another Header/Line Pattern to Avoid."

Figure 6-9 illustrates a header/line modeling pattern we frequently observe when conducting design reviews. In this example, the operational order header is virtually replicated in the dimensional model as a dimension. The header dimension contains all the data from its operational equivalent. The natural key for this dimension is the order number. The grain of the fact table is one row per order line item, but there's not much dimensionality associated with it because most descriptive context is embedded in the order header dimension.

Although this design accurately represents the header/line relationship, there are obvious flaws. The order header dimension is likely very large, especially relative to the fact table itself. If there are typically five line items per order, the dimension is 20 percent as large as the fact table; there should be orders of magnitude differences between the size of a fact table and its associated dimensions. Also, dimension tables don't normally grow at nearly the same rate as the fact table. With this design, you would add one row to the dimension table and an average of five rows to the fact table for every new order. Any analysis of the order's interesting characteristics, such as the customer, sales rep, or deal involved, would need to traverse this large dimension table.

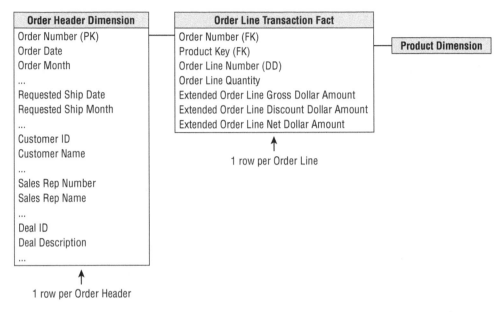

Figure 6-9: Pattern to avoid: treating transaction header as a dimension.

Multiple Currencies

Suppose you track the orders of a large multinational U.S.-based company with sales offices around the world. You may be capturing order transactions in more than 15 different currencies. You certainly wouldn't want to include columns in the fact table for each currency.

The most common analytic requirement is that order transactions be expressed in both the local transaction currency and the standardized corporate currency, such as U.S. dollars in this example. To satisfy this need, each order fact would be replaced with a pair of facts, one for the applicable local currency and another for the equivalent standard corporate currency, as illustrated in Figure 6-10. The conversion rate used to construct each fact row with the dual metrics would depend on the business's requirements. It might be the rate at the moment the order was captured, an end of day rate, or some other rate based on defined business rules. This technique would preserve the transactional metrics, plus allow all transactions to easily roll up to the corporate currency without complicated reporting application coding. The metrics in standard currency would be fully additive. The local currency metrics would be additive only for a single specified currency; otherwise, you'd be trying to sum Japanese yen, Thai bhat, and British pounds. You'd also supplement the fact table with a currency dimension to identify the currency type associated with the local currency facts; a currency dimension is needed even if the location of the transaction is otherwise known because the location does not necessarily guarantee which currency was used.

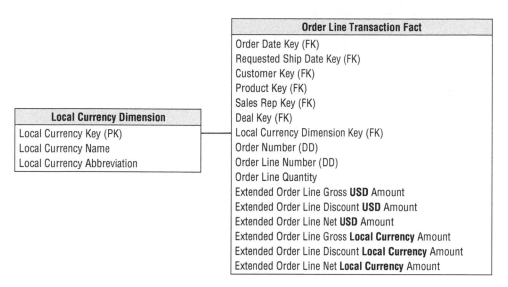

Figure 6-10: Metrics in multiple currencies within the fact table.

This technique can be expanded to support other relatively common examples. If the business's sales offices roll up into a handful of regional centers, you could supplement the fact table with a third set of metrics representing the transactional amounts converted into the appropriate regional currency. Likewise, the fact table columns could represent currencies for the customer ship-to and customer bill-to, or the currencies as quoted and shipped.

In each of the scenarios, the fact table could physically contain a full set of metrics in one currency, along with the appropriate currency conversion rate(s) for that row. Rather than burdening the business users with appropriately multiplying or dividing by the stored rate, the intra-row extrapolation should be done in a view behind the scenes; all reporting applications would access the facts via this logical layer.

Sometimes the multi-currency support requirements are more complicated than just described. You may need to allow a manager in any country to see order volume in any currency. In this case, you can embellish the initial design with an additional currency conversion fact table, as shown in Figure 6-11. The dimensions in this fact table represent currencies, not countries, because the relationship between currencies and countries is not one-to-one. The more common needs of the local sales rep and sales management in headquarters would be met simply by querying the orders fact table, but those with less predictable requirements would use the currency conversion table in a specially crafted query. Navigating the currency conversion table is obviously more complicated than using the converted metrics on the orders fact table.

Currency Conversion Fact
Conversion Date Key (FK)
Source Currency Key (FK)
Destination Currency Key (FK)
Source-Destination Exchange Rate
Destination-Source Exchange Rate

Figure 6-11: Tracking multiple currencies with daily currency exchange fact table.

Within each currency conversion fact table row, the amount expressed in local currency is absolutely accurate because the sale occurred in that currency on that day. The equivalent U.S. dollar value would be based on a conversion rate to U.S. dollars for that day. The conversion rate table contains the combinations of relevant currency exchange rates going in both directions because the symmetric rates between two currencies are not equal. It is unlikely this conversion fact table needs to include the full Cartesian product of all possible currency combinations. Although there are approximately 100 unique currencies globally, there wouldn't need to be 10,000 daily rows in this currency fact table as there's not a meaningful market for every possible pair; likewise, all theoretical combinations are probably overkill for the business users.

The use of a currency conversion table may also be required to support the business's need for multiple rates, such as an end of month or end of quarter close rate, which may not be defined until long after the transactions have been loaded into the orders fact table.

Transaction Facts at Different Granularity

It is quite common in header/line operational data to encounter facts of differing granularity. On an order, there may be a shipping charge that applies to the entire order. The designer's first response should be to try to force all the facts down to the lowest level, as illustrated in Figure 6-12. This procedure is broadly referred to as *allocating*. Allocating the parent order facts to the child line item level is critical if you want the ability to slice and dice and roll up all order facts by all dimensions, including product.

Unfortunately, allocating header-level facts down to the line item level may entail a political wrestling match. It is wonderful if the entire allocation issue is handled by the finance department, not by the DW/BI team. Getting organizational agreement on allocation rules is often a controversial and complicated process. The DW/BI team shouldn't be distracted and delayed by the inevitable organizational negotiation. Fortunately, in many companies, the need to rationally allocate costs has already been recognized. A task force, independent of the DW/BI project, already may have established *activity-based costing measures*. This is just another name for allocating.

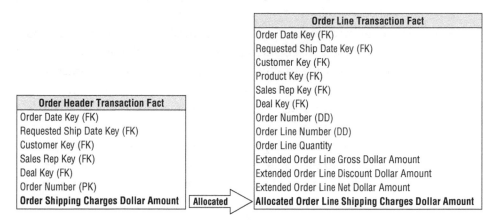

Figure 6-12: Allocating header facts to line items.

If the shipping charges and other header-level facts cannot be successfully allocated, they must be presented in an aggregate table for the overall order. We clearly prefer the allocation approach, if possible, because the separate higher-level fact table has some inherent usability issues. Without allocations, you cannot explore header facts by product because the product isn't identified in a header-grain fact table. If you are successful in allocating facts down to the lowest level, the problem goes away.

WARNING You shouldn't mix fact granularities such as order header and order line facts within a single fact table. Instead, either allocate the higher-level facts to a more detailed level or create two separate fact tables to handle the differently grained facts. Allocation is the preferred approach.

Optimally, the business data stewards obtain enterprise consensus on the allocation rules. But sometimes organizations refuse to agree. For example, the finance department may want to allocate the header freight charged based on the extended gross order amount on each line; meanwhile, the logistics group wants the freight charge to be allocated based on the weight of the line's products. In this case, you would have two allocated freight charges on every order line fact table row; the uniquely calculated metrics would also be uniquely labeled. Obviously, agreeing on a single, standard allocation scheme is preferable.

Design teams sometimes attempt to devise alternative techniques for handling header/line facts at different granularity, including the following:

- **Repeat the unallocated header fact on every line.** This approach is fraught with peril given the risk of overstating the header amount when it's summed on every line.
- **Store the unallocated amount on the transaction's first or last line.** This tactic eliminates the risk of overcounting, but if the first or last lines are excluded from the query results due to a filter constraint on the product dimension, it appears there were no header facts associated with this transaction.
- **Set up a special product key for the header fact.** Teams who adopt this approach sometimes recycle an existing line fact column. For example, if product key = 99999, then the gross order metric is a header fact, like the freight charge. Dimensional models should be straightforward and legible. You don't want to embed complexities requiring a business user to wear a special decoder ring to navigate the dimensional model successfully.

Another Header/Line Pattern to Avoid

The second header/line pattern to avoid is illustrated in Figure 6-13. In this example, the order header is no longer treated as a monolithic dimension but as a fact table instead. The header's associated descriptive information is grouped into dimensions surrounding the order fact. The line item fact table (identical in structure and granularity as the first diagram) joins to the header fact based on the order number.

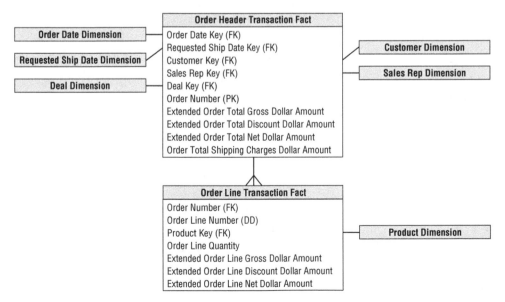

Figure 6-13: Pattern to avoid: not inheriting header dimensionality in line facts.

Again, this design accurately represents the parent/child relationship of the order header and line items, but there are still flaws. Every time the user wants to slice and dice the line facts by any of the header attributes, a large header fact table needs to be associated with an even larger line fact table.

Invoice Transactions

In a manufacturing company, invoicing typically occurs when products are shipped from your facility to the customer. Visualize shipments at the loading dock as boxes of product are placed into a truck destined for a particular customer address. The invoice associated with the shipment is created at this time. The invoice has multiple line items, each corresponding to a particular product being shipped. Various prices, discounts, and allowances are associated with each line item. The extended net amount for each line item is also available.

Although you don't show it on the invoice to the customer, a number of other interesting facts are potentially known about each product at the time of shipment. You certainly know list prices; manufacturing and distribution costs may be available as well. Thus you know a lot about the state of your business at the moment of customer invoicing.

In the invoice fact table, you can see all the company's products, customers, contracts and deals, off-invoice discounts and allowances, revenue generated by customers, variable and fixed costs associated with manufacturing and delivering products (if available), money left over after delivery of product (profit contribution), and customer satisfaction metrics such as on-time shipment.

> **NOTE** For any company that ships products to customers or bills customers for services rendered, the optimal place to start a DW/BI project typically is with invoices. We often refer to invoicing as the most powerful data because it combines the company's customers, products, and components of profitability.

You should choose the grain of the invoice fact table to be the individual invoice line item. A sample invoice fact table associated with manufacturer shipments is illustrated in Figure 6-14.

As expected, the invoice fact table contains a number of dimensions from earlier in this chapter. The conformed date dimension table again would play multiple roles in the fact table. The customer, product, and deal dimensions also would conform, so you can drill across fact tables using common attributes. If a single order number is associated with each invoice line item, it would be included as a second degenerate dimension.

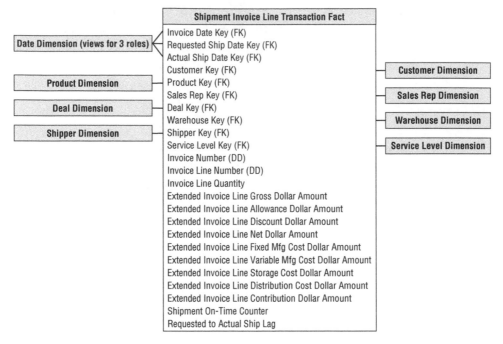

Figure 6-14: Shipment invoice fact table.

The shipment invoice fact table also contains some interesting new dimensions. The warehouse dimension contains one row for each manufacturer warehouse location. This is a relatively simple dimension with name, address, contact person, and storage facility type. The attributes are somewhat reminiscent of the store dimension from Chapter 3. The shipper dimension describes the method and carrier by which the product was shipped from the manufacturer to the customer.

Service Level Performance as Facts, Dimensions, or Both

The fact table in Figure 6-14 includes several critical dates intended to capture shipment service levels. All these dates are known when the operational invoicing process occurs. Delivering the multiple event dates in the invoicing fact table with corresponding role-playing date dimensions allows business users to filter, group, and trend on any of these dates. But sometimes the business requirements are more demanding.

You could include an additional on-time counter in the fact table that's set to an additive zero or one depending on whether the line shipped on time. Likewise, you could include lag metrics representing the number of days, positive or negative, between the requested and actual ship dates. As described later in this chapter, the lag calculation may be more sophisticated than the simple difference between dates.

In addition to the quantitative service metrics, you could also include a qualitative assessment of performance by adding either a new dimension or adding more columns to the junk dimension. Either way, the attribute values might look similar to those shown in Figure 6-15.

Service Level Key	Service Level Description	Service Level Group
1	On-time	On-time
2	1 day early	Early
3	2 days early	Early
4	3 days early	Early
5	> 3 days early	Too early
6	1 day late	Late
7	2 days late	Late
8	3 days late	Late
9	> 3 days late	Too late

Figure 6-15: Sample qualitative service level descriptors.

If service level performance at the invoice line is closely watched by business users, you may embrace all the patterns just described, since quantitative metrics with qualitative text provide different perspectives on the same performance.

Profit and Loss Facts

If your organization has tackled activity-based costing or implemented a robust enterprise resource planning (ERP) system, you might be in a position to identify many of the incremental revenues and costs associated with shipping finished products to the customer. It is traditional to arrange these revenues and costs in sequence from the top line, which represents the undiscounted value of the products shipped to the customer, down to the bottom line, which represents the money left over after discounts, allowances, and costs. This list of revenues and costs is referred to as a *profit and loss (P&L) statement*. You typically don't attempt to carry it all the way to a complete view of company profit including general and administrative costs. For this reason, the bottom line in the P&L statement is referred to as *contribution*.

Keeping in mind that each row in the invoice fact table represents a single line item on the invoice, the elements of the P&L statement shown in Figure 6-14 have the following interpretations:

- **Quantity shipped:** Number of cases of the particular line item's product. The use of multiple equivalent quantities with different units of measure is discussed in the section "Multiple Units of Measure."
- **Extended gross amount:** Also known as *extended list price* because it is the quantity shipped multiplied by the list unit price. This and all subsequent

dollar values are *extended amounts* or, in other words, unit rates multiplied by the quantity shipped. This insistence on additive values simplifies most access and reporting applications. It is relatively rare for a business user to ask for the unit price from a single fact table row. When the user wants an average price drawn from many rows, the extended prices are first added, and then the result is divided by the sum of the quantities.

- **Extended allowance amount:** Amount subtracted from the invoice line gross amount for deal-related allowances. The allowances are described in the adjoined deal dimension. The allowance amount is often called an *off-invoice allowance*. The actual invoice may have several allowances for a given line item; the allowances are combined together in this simplified example. If the allowances need to be tracked separately and there are potentially many simultaneous allowances on a given line item, an allowance detail fact table could augment the invoice line fact table, serving as a drill-down for details on the allowance total in the invoice line fact table.

- **Extended discount amount:** Amount subtracted for volume or payment term discounts. The discount descriptions are found in the deal dimension. As discussed earlier regarding the deal dimension, the decision to describe the allowances and discount types together is the designer's prerogative. It makes sense to do this if allowances and discounts are correlated and business users want to browse within the deal dimension to study the relationships between allowances and discounts.

  All allowances and discounts in this fact table are represented at the line item level. As discussed earlier, some allowances and discounts may be calculated operationally at the invoice level, not at the line item level. An effort should be made to allocate them down to the line item. An invoice P&L statement that does not include the product dimension poses a serious limitation on your ability to present meaningful contribution slices of the business.

- **Extended net amount:** Amount the customer is expected to pay for this line item before tax. It is equal to the gross invoice amount less the allowances and discounts.

The facts described so far likely would be displayed to the customer on the invoice document. The following cost amounts, leading to a bottom line contribution, are for internal consumption only.

- **Extended fixed manufacturing cost:** Amount identified by manufacturing as the pro rata fixed manufacturing cost of the invoice line's product.

- **Extended variable manufacturing cost:** Amount identified by manufacturing as the variable manufacturing cost of the product on the invoice line. This amount may be more or less activity-based, reflecting the actual location and time of the manufacturing run that produced the product being shipped to the customer. Conversely, this number may be a standard value set by a committee. If the manufacturing costs or any of the other storage and distribution costs are averages of averages, the detailed P&Ls may become meaningless. The DW/BI system may illuminate this problem and accelerate the adoption of activity-based costing methods.

- **Extended storage cost:** Cost charged to the invoice line for storage prior to being shipped to the customer.
- **Extended distribution cost:** Cost charged to the invoice line for transportation from the point of manufacture to the point of shipment. This cost is notorious for not being activity-based. The distribution cost possibly can include freight to the customer if the company pays the freight, or the freight cost can be presented as a separate line item in the P&L.
- **Contribution amount:** Extended net invoice less all the costs just discussed. This is not the true bottom line of the overall company because general and administrative expenses and other financial adjustments have not been made, but it is important nonetheless. This column sometimes has alternative labels, such as *margin*, depending on the company culture.

You should step back and admire the robust dimensional model you just built. You constructed a detailed P&L view of your business, showing all the activity-based elements of revenue and costs. You have a full equation of profitability. However, what makes this design so compelling is that the P&L view sits inside a rich dimensional framework of dates, customers, products, and causal factors. Do you want to see customer profitability? Just constrain and group on the customer dimension and bring the components of the P&L into the report. Do you want to see product profitability? Do you want to see deal profitability? All these analyses are equally easy and take the same analytic form in the BI applications. Somewhat tongue in cheek, we recommend you not deliver this dimensional model too early in your career because you will get promoted and won't be able to work directly on any more DW/BI systems!

Profitability Words of Warning

We must balance the last paragraph with a more sober note and pass along some cautionary words of warning. It goes without saying that most of the business users probably are very interested in granular P&L data that can be rolled up to analyze customer and product profitability. The reality is that delivering these detailed P&L statements often is easier said than done. The problems arise with the cost facts. Even with advanced ERP implementations, it is fairly common to be unable to capture the cost facts at this atomic level of granularity. You will face a complex process of mapping or allocating the original cost data down to the invoice line level. Furthermore, each type of cost may require a separate extraction from a source system. Ten cost facts may mean 10 different extract and transformation programs. Before signing up for mission impossible, be certain to perform a detailed assessment of what is available and feasible from the source systems. You certainly don't want the DW/BI team saddled with driving the organization to consensus on activity-based costing as a side project, on top of managing a number of parallel extract implementations. If time and organization patience permits, profitability is often tackled as a consolidated dimensional model after the components of revenue and cost have been sourced and delivered separately to business users in the DW/BI environment.

Audit Dimension

As mentioned, Figure 6-14's invoice line item design is one of the most powerful because it provides a detailed look at customers, products, revenues, costs, and bottom line profit in one schema. During the building of rows for this fact table, a wealth of interesting back room metadata is generated, including data quality indicators, unusual processing requirements, and environment version numbers that identify how the data was processed during the ETL. Although this metadata is frequently of interest to ETL developers and IT management, there are times when it can be interesting to the business users, too. For instance, business users might want to ask the following:

- What is my confidence in these reported numbers?
- Were there any anomalous values encountered while processing this source data?
- What version of the cost allocation logic was used when calculating the costs?
- What version of the foreign currency conversion rules was used when calculating the revenues?

These kinds of questions are often hard to answer because the metadata required is not readily available. However, if you anticipate these kinds of questions, you can include an *audit dimension* with any fact table to expose the metadata context that was true when the fact table rows were built. Figure 6-16 illustrates an example audit dimension.

The audit dimension is added to the fact table by including an audit dimension foreign key. The audit dimension itself contains the metadata conditions encountered when processing fact table rows. It is best to start with a modest audit dimension design, such as shown in Figure 6-16, both to keep the ETL processing from getting too complicated and to limit the number of possible audit dimension rows. The first three attributes (quality indicator, out of bounds indicator, and amount adjusted flag) are all sourced from a special ETL processing table called the error event table, which is discussed in Chapter 19: ETL Subsystems and Techniques. The cost allocation and foreign currency versions are environmental variables that should be available in an ETL back room status table.

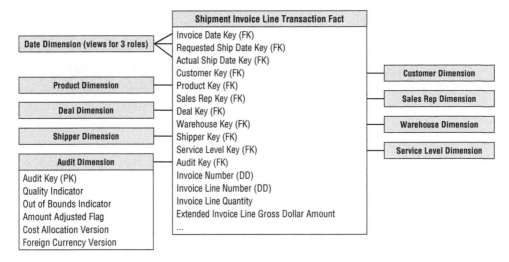

Figure 6-16: Sample audit dimension included on invoice fact table.

Armed with the audit dimension, some powerful queries can be performed. You might want to take this morning's invoice report and ask if any of the reported numbers were based on out-of-bounds measures. Because the audit dimension is now just an ordinary dimension, you can just add the out-of-bounds indicator to your standard report. In the resulting "instrumented" report shown in Figure 6-17, you see multiple rows showing normal and abnormal out-of-bounds results.

Standard Report:

Product	Warehouse	Invoice Line Quantity	Extended Invoice Line Gross Amount
Axon	East	1,438	235,000
Axon	West	2,249	480,000

Instrumented Reported (with Out of Bounds Indicator added):

Product	Warehouse	Out of Bounds Indicator	Invoice Line Quantity	Extended Invoice Line Gross Amount
Axon	East	Abnormal	14	2,350
Axon	East	Normal	1,424	232,650
Axon	West	Abnormal	675	144,000
Axon	West	Normal	1,574	336,000

Figure 6-17: Audit dimension attribute included on standard report.

Accumulating Snapshot for Order Fulfillment Pipeline

The order management process can be thought of as a pipeline, especially in a build-to-order manufacturing business, as illustrated in Figure 6-18. Customers place an order that goes into the backlog until it is released to manufacturing to be built. The manufactured products are placed in finished goods inventory and then shipped to the customers and invoiced. Unique transactions are generated at each spigot of the pipeline. Thus far we've considered each of these pipeline activities as a separate transaction fact table. Doing so allows you to decorate the detailed facts generated by each process with the greatest number of detailed dimensions. It also allows you to isolate analysis to the performance of a single business process, which is often precisely what the business users want.

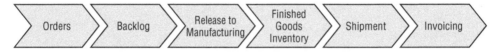

Figure 6-18: Order fulfillment pipeline diagram.

However, there are times when business users want to analyze the entire order fulfillment pipeline. They want to better understand product velocity, or how quickly products move through the pipeline. The accumulating snapshot fact table provides this perspective of the business, as illustrated in Figure 6-19. It enables you to see an updated status and ultimately the final disposition of each order.

The accumulating snapshot complements alternative schemas' perspectives of the pipeline. If you're interested in understanding the amount of product flowing through the pipeline, such as the quantity ordered, produced, or shipped, transaction schemas monitor each of the pipeline's major events. Periodic snapshots would provide insight into the amount of product sitting in the pipeline, such as the backorder or finished goods inventories, or the amount of product flowing through a pipeline spigot during a predefined interval. The accumulating snapshot helps you better understand the current state of an order, as well as product movement velocities to identify pipeline bottlenecks and inefficiencies. If you only captured performance in transaction event fact tables, it would be wildly difficult to calculate the average number of days to move between milestones.

The accumulating snapshot looks different from the transaction fact tables designed thus far in this chapter. The reuse of conformed dimensions is to be expected, but the number of date and fact columns is larger. Each date represents a major milestone of the fulfillment pipeline. The dates are handled as dimension roles by creating either physically distinct tables or logically distinct views. The date dimension needs to have a row for Unknown or To Be Determined because many of these fact table dates are unknown when a pipeline row is initially loaded. Obviously, you don't need to declare all the date columns in the fact table's primary key.

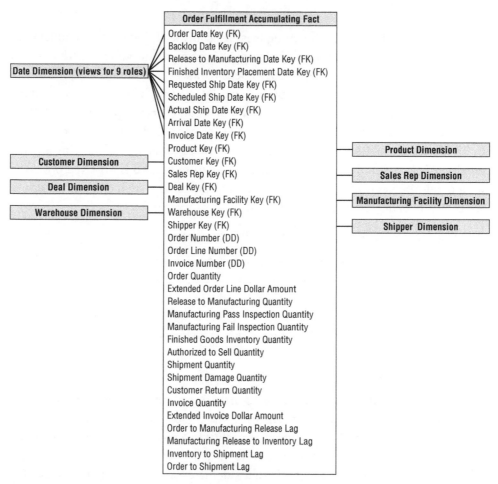

Figure 6-19: Order fulfillment accumulating snapshot fact table.

The fundamental difference between accumulating snapshots and other fact tables is that you can revisit and update existing fact table rows as more information becomes available. The grain of an accumulating snapshot fact table in Figure 6-19 is one row per order line item. However, unlike the order transaction fact table illustrated in Figure 6-2 with the same granularity, accumulating snapshot fact rows are modified while the order moves through the pipeline as more information is collected from every stage of the cycle.

NOTE   Accumulating snapshot fact tables typically have multiple dates representing the major milestones of the process. However, just because a fact table has several dates doesn't dictate that it is an accumulating snapshot. The primary differentiator of an accumulating snapshot is that you revisit the fact rows as activity occurs.

The accumulating snapshot technique is especially useful when the product moving through the pipeline is uniquely identified, such as an automobile with a vehicle identification number, electronics equipment with a serial number, lab specimens with an identification number, or process manufacturing batches with a lot number. The accumulating snapshot helps you understand throughput and yield. If the granularity of an accumulating snapshot is at the serial or lot number, you can see the disposition of a discrete product as it moves through the manufacturing and test pipeline. The accumulating snapshot fits most naturally with short-lived processes with a definite beginning and end. Long-lived processes, such as bank accounts, are typically better modeled with periodic snapshot fact tables.

Accumulating Snapshots and Type 2 Dimensions

Accumulating snapshots present the latest state of a workflow or pipeline. If the dimensions associated with an accumulating snapshot contain type 2 attributes, the fact table should be updated to reference the most current surrogate dimension key for active pipelines. When a single fact table pipeline row is complete, the row is typically not revisited to reflect future type 2 changes.

Lag Calculations

The lengthy list of date columns captures the spans of time over which the order is processed through the fulfillment pipeline. The numerical difference between any two of these dates is a number that can be usefully averaged over all the dimensions. These date lag calculations represent basic measures of fulfillment efficiency. You could build a view on this fact table that calculated a large number of these date differences and presented them as if they were stored in the underlying table. These view columns could include metrics such as orders to manufacturing release lag, manufacturing release to finished goods lag, and order to shipment lag, depending on the date spans monitored by the organization.

Rather than calculating a simple difference between two dates via a view, the ETL system may calculate elapsed times that incorporate more intelligence, such as workday lags that account for weekends and holidays rather than just the raw number of days between milestone dates. The lag metrics may also be calculated by the ETL system at a lower level of granularity (such as the number of hours or minutes between milestone events based on operational timestamps) for short-lived and closely monitored processes.

Multiple Units of Measure

Sometimes, different functional organizations within the business want to see the same performance metrics expressed in different units of measure. For instance, manufacturing managers may want to see the product flow in terms of pallets or shipping cases. Sales and marketing managers, on the other hand, may want to see the quantities in retail cases, scan units (sales packs), or equivalized consumer units (such as individual cans of soda).

Designers are tempted to bury the unit-of-measure conversion factors, such as ship case factor, in the product dimension. Business users are then required to appropriately multiply (or was it divide?) the order quantity by the conversion factor. Obviously, this approach places a burden on users, in addition to being susceptible to calculation errors. The situation is further complicated because the conversion factors may change over time, so users would also need to determine which factor is applicable at a specific point in time.

Rather than risk miscalculating the equivalent quantities by placing conversion factors in a dimension table, they should be stored in the fact table instead. In the orders pipeline fact table, assume you have 10 basic fundamental quantity facts, in addition to five units of measure. If you physically store all the facts expressed in the different units of measure, you end up with 50 (10 × 5) facts in each fact row. Instead, you can compromise by building an underlying physical row with 10 quantity facts and 4 unit-of-measure conversion factors. You need only four conversion factors rather than five because the base facts are already expressed in one of the units of measure. The physical design now has 14 quantity-related facts (10 + 4), as shown in Figure 6-20. With this design, you can see performance across the value chain based on different units of measure.

Of course, you would deliver this fact table to the business users through one or more views. The extra computation involved in multiplying quantities by conversion factors is negligible; intra-row computations are very efficient. The most comprehensive view could show all 50 facts expressed in every unit of measure, but the view could be simplified to deliver only a subset of the quantities in units of measure relevant to a user. Obviously, each unit of measures' metrics should be uniquely labeled.

NOTE Packaging all the facts and conversion factors together in the same fact table row provides the safest guarantee that these factors will be used correctly. The converted facts are presented in a view(s) to the users.

Order Fulfillment Accumulating Fact
Date Keys (FKs)
Product Key (FK)
More FKs...
Order Quantity Shipping Cases
Release to Manufacturing Quantity Shipping Cases
Manufacturing Pass Inspection Quantity Shipping Cases
Manufacturing Fail Inspection Quantity Shipping Cases
Finished Goods Inventory Quantity Shipping Cases
Authorized to Sell Quantity Shipping Cases
Shipment Quantity Shipping Cases
Shipment Damage Quantity Shipping Cases
Customer Return Quantity Shipping Cases
Invoice Quantity Shipping Cases
Pallet Conversion Factor
Retail Cases Conversion Factor
Scan Units Conversion Factor
Equivalized Consumer Units Conversion Factor

Figure 6-20: Physical fact table supporting multiple units of measure with conversion factors.

Finally, another side benefit of storing these factors in the fact table is it reduces the pressure on the product dimension table to issue new product rows to reflect minor conversion factor modifications. These factors, especially if they evolve routinely over time, behave more like facts than dimension attributes.

Beyond the Rearview Mirror

Much of what we've discussed in this chapter focuses on effective ways to analyze historical product movement performance. People sometimes refer to these as *rearview mirror* metrics because they enable you to look backward and see where you've been. As the brokerage industry reminds people, past performance is no guarantee of future results. Many organizations want to supplement these historical performance metrics with facts from other processes to help project what lies ahead. For example, rather than focusing on the pipeline at the time an order is received, organizations are analyzing the key drivers impacting the creation of an order. In a sales organization, drivers such as prospecting or quoting activity can be extrapolated to provide visibility to the expected order activity volume. Many organizations do a better job collecting the rearview mirror information than they do the early indicators. As these front window leading indicators are captured, they can be added gracefully to the DW/BI environment. They're just more rows on the enterprise data warehouse bus matrix sharing common dimensions.

Summary

This chapter covered a lengthy laundry list of topics in the context of the order management process. *Multiples* were discussed on several fronts: multiple references to the same dimension in a fact table (role-playing dimensions), multiple equivalent units of measure, and multiple currencies. We explored several of the common challenges encountered when modeling header/line transaction data, including facts at different levels of granularity and junk dimensions, plus design patterns to avoid. We also explored the rich set of facts associated with invoice transactions. Finally, the order fulfillment pipeline illustrated the power of accumulating snapshot fact tables where you can see the updated status of a specific product or order as it moves through a finite pipeline.

7

Accounting

Financial analysis spans a variety of accounting applications, including the general ledger, as well as detailed subledgers for purchasing and accounts payable, invoicing and accounts receivable, and fixed assets. Because we've already touched upon purchase orders and invoices earlier in this book, we'll focus on the general ledger in this chapter. Given the need for accurate handling of a company's financial records, general ledgers were one of the first applications to be computerized decades ago. Perhaps some of you are still running your business on a 20-year-old ledger system. In this chapter, we'll discuss the data collected by the general ledger, both in terms of journal entry transactions and snapshots at the close of an accounting period. We'll also talk about the budgeting process.

Chapter 7 discusses the following concepts:

- Bus matrix snippet for accounting processes
- General ledger periodic snapshots and journal transactions
- Chart of accounts
- Period close
- Year-to-date facts
- Multiple fiscal accounting calendars
- Drilling down through a multi-ledger hierarchy
- Budgeting chain and associated processes
- Fixed depth position hierarchies
- Slightly ragged, variable depth hierarchies
- Totally ragged hierarchies of indeterminate depth using a bridge table and alternative modeling techniques
- Shared ownership in a ragged hierarchy
- Time varying ragged hierarchies
- Consolidated fact tables that combine metrics from multiple business processes
- Role of OLAP and packaged analytic financial solutions

Accounting Case Study and Bus Matrix

Because finance was an early adopter of technology, it comes as no surprise that early decision support solutions focused on the analysis of financial data. Financial analysts are some of the most data-literate and spreadsheet-savvy individuals. Often their analysis is disseminated or leveraged by many others in the organization. Managers at all levels need timely access to key financial metrics. In addition to receiving standard reports, they need the ability to analyze performance trends, variances, and anomalies with relative speed and minimal effort. Like many operational source systems, the data in the general ledger is likely scattered among hundreds of tables. Gaining access to financial data and/or creating ad hoc reports may require a decoder ring to navigate through the maze of screens. This runs counter to many organizations' objective to push fiscal responsibility and accountability to the line managers.

The DW/BI system can provide a single source of usable, understandable financial information, ensuring everyone is working off the same data with common definitions and common tools. The audience for financial data is quite diverse in many organizations, ranging from analysts to operational managers to executives. For each group, you need to determine which subset of corporate financial data is needed, in which format, and with what frequency. Analysts and managers want to view information at a high level and then drill to the journal entries for more detail. For executives, financial data from the DW/BI system often feeds their dashboard or scorecard of key performance indicators. Armed with direct access to information, managers can obtain answers to questions more readily than when forced to work through a middleman. Meanwhile, finance can turn their attention to information dissemination and value-added analysis, rather than focusing on report creation.

Improved access to accounting data allows you to focus on opportunities to better manage risk, streamline operations, and identify potential cost savings. Although it has cross-organization impact, many businesses focus their initial DW/BI implementation on strategic, revenue-generating opportunities. Consequently, accounting data is often not the first subject area tackled by the DW/BI team. Given its proficiency with technology, the finance department has often already performed magic with spreadsheets and desktop databases to create workaround analytic solutions, perhaps to its short-term detriment, as these imperfect interim fixes are likely stressed to their limits.

Figure 7-1 illustrates an accounting-focused excerpt from an organization's bus matrix. The dimensions associated with accounting processes, such as the general ledger account or organizational cost center, are frequently used solely by these processes, unlike the core customer, product, and employee dimensions which are used repeatedly across many diverse business processes.

	Date	Ledger	Account	Organization	Budget Line	Commitment Profile	Payment Profile
General Ledger Transactions	X	X	X	X			
General Ledger Snapshot	X	X	X	X			
Budget	X	X	X	X	X		
Commitment	X	X	X	X	X	X	
Payments	X	X	X	X	X	X	X
Actual-Budget Variance	X	X	X	X			

Figure 7-1: Bus matrix rows for accounting processes.

General Ledger Data

The *general ledger* (*G/L*) is a core foundation financial system that ties together the detailed information collected by subledgers or separate systems for purchasing, payables (what you owe to others), and receivables (what others owe you). As we work through a basic design for G/L data, you'll discover the need for two complementary schemas with periodic snapshot and transaction fact tables.

General Ledger Periodic Snapshot

We'll begin by delving into a snapshot of the general ledger accounts at the end of each fiscal period (or month if the fiscal accounting periods align with calendar months). Referring back to our four-step process for designing dimensional models (see Chapter 3: Retail Sales), the business process is the general ledger. The grain of this periodic snapshot is one row per accounting period for the most granular level in the general ledger's chart of accounts.

Chart of Accounts

The cornerstone of the general ledger is the chart of accounts. The ledger's *chart of accounts* is the epitome of an intelligent key because it usually consists of a series of identifiers. For example, the first set of digits may identify the account, account type (for example, asset, liability, equity, income, or expense), and other account rollups. Sometimes intelligence is embedded in the account numbering scheme. For example, account numbers from 1,000 through 1,999 might be asset accounts, whereas account numbers ranging from 2,000 to 2,999 may identify liabilities. Obviously, in the data warehouse, you'd include the account type as a dimension attribute rather than forcing users to filter on the first digit of the account number.

The chart of accounts likely associates the organization cost center with the account. Typically, the organization attributes provide a complete rollup from cost center to department to division, for example. If the corporate general ledger combines data across multiple business units, the chart of accounts would also indicate the business unit or subsidiary company.

Obviously, charts of accounts vary from organization to organization. They're often extremely complicated, with hundreds or even thousands of cost centers in large organizations. In this case study vignette, the chart of accounts naturally decomposes into two dimensions. One dimension represents accounts in the general ledger, whereas the other represents the organization rollup.

The organization rollup may be a fixed depth hierarchy, which would be handled as separate hierarchical attributes in the cost center dimension. If the organization hierarchy is ragged with an unbalanced rollup structure, you need the more powerful variable depth hierarchy techniques described in the section "Ragged Variable Depth Hierarchies."

If you are tasked with building a comprehensive general ledger spanning multiple organizations in the DW/BI system, you should try to conform the chart of accounts so the account types mean the same thing across organizations. At the data level, this means the master conformed account dimension contains carefully defined account names. Capital Expenditures and Office Supplies need to have the same financial meaning across organizations. Of course, this kind of conformed dimension has an old and familiar name in financial circles: the *uniform chart of accounts*.

The G/L sometimes tracks financial results for multiple sets of books or subledgers to support different requirements, such as taxation or regulatory agency reporting. You can treat this as a separate dimension because it's such a fundamental filter, but we alert you to carefully read the cautionary note in the next section.

Period Close

At the end of each accounting period, the finance organization is responsible for finalizing the financial results so that they can be officially reported internally and externally. It typically takes several days at the end of each period to reconcile and balance the books before they can be closed with finance's official stamp of approval. From there, finance's focus turns to reporting and interpreting the results. It often produces countless reports and responds to countless variations on the same questions each month.

Financial analysts are constantly looking to streamline the processes for period-end closing, reconciliation, and reporting of general ledger results. Although operational general ledger systems often support these requisite capabilities, they may be cumbersome, especially if you're not dealing with a modern G/L. This chapter focuses on easily analyzing the closed financial results, rather than facilitating the close. However, in many organizations, general ledger trial balances are loaded into the DW/BI system leveraging the capabilities of the DW/BI presentation area to find the needles in the general ledger haystack, and then making the appropriate operational adjustments before the period ends.

The sample schema in Figure 7-2 shows general ledger account balances at the end of each accounting period which would be very useful for many kinds of financial analyses, such as account rankings, trending patterns, and period-to-period comparisons.

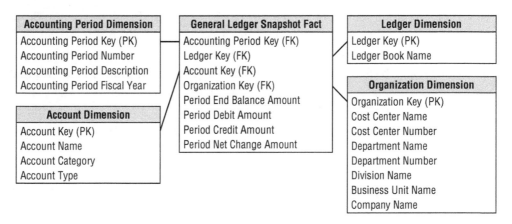

Figure 7-2: General ledger periodic snapshot.

For the moment, we're just representing actual ledger facts in the Figure 7-2 schema; we'll expand our view to cover budget data in the section "Budgeting Process." In this table, the balance amount is a semi-additive fact. Although the balance doesn't represent G/L activity, we include the fact in the design because it is so useful. Otherwise, you would need to go back to the beginning of time to calculate an accurate end-of-period balance.

WARNING The ledger dimension is a convenient and intuitive dimension that enables multiple ledgers to be stored in the same fact table. However, every query that accesses this fact table must constrain the ledger dimension to a single value (for example, Final Approved Domestic Ledger) or the queries will double count values from the various ledgers in this table. The best way to deploy this schema is to release separate views to the business users with the ledger dimension pre-constrained to a single value.

The two most important dimensions in the proposed general ledger design are account and organization. The account dimension is carefully derived from the uniform chart of accounts in the enterprise. The organization dimension describes the financial reporting entities in the enterprise. Unfortunately, these two crucial dimensions almost never conform to operational dimensions such as customer, product, service, or facility. This leads to a characteristic but unavoidable business user frustration that the "GL doesn't tie to my operational reports." It is best to gently explain this to the business users in the interview process, rather than promising to fix it because this is a deep seated issue in the underlying data.

Year-to-Date Facts

Designers are often tempted to store "to-date" columns in fact tables. They think it would be helpful to store quarter-to-date or year-to-date additive totals on each fact row so they don't need to calculate them. Remember that numeric facts must be consistent with the grain. To-date facts are not true to the grain and are fraught with peril. When fact rows are queried and summarized in arbitrary ways, these untrue-to-the-grain facts produce nonsensical, overstated results. They should be left out of the relational schema design and calculated in the BI reporting application instead. It's worth noting that OLAP cubes handle to-date metrics more gracefully.

NOTE In general, "to-date" totals should be calculated, not stored in the fact table.

Multiple Currencies Revisited

If the general ledger consolidates data that has been captured in multiple currencies, you would handle it much as we discussed in Chapter 6: Order Management. With financial data, you typically want to represent the facts both in terms of the local currency, as well as a standardized corporate currency. In this case, each fact table row would represent one set of fact amounts expressed in local currency and a separate set of fact amounts on the same row expressed in the equivalent corporate currency. Doing so allows you to easily summarize the facts in a common corporate currency without jumping through hoops in the BI applications. Of course, you'd also add a currency dimension as a foreign key in the fact table to identify the local currency type.

General Ledger Journal Transactions

While the end-of-period snapshot addresses a multitude of financial analyses, many users need to dive into the underlying details. If an anomaly is identified at the summary level, analysts want to look at the detailed transactions to sort through the issue. Others need access to the details because the summarized monthly balances may obscure large disparities at the granular transaction level. Again, you can complement the periodic snapshot with a detailed journal entry transaction schema. Of course, the accounts payable and receivable subledgers may contain transactions at progressively lower levels of detail, which would be captured in separate fact tables with additional dimensionality.

The grain of the fact table is now one row for every general ledger journal entry transaction. The journal entry transaction identifies the G/L account and the applicable debit or credit amount. As illustrated in Figure 7-3, several dimensions from the last schema are reused, including the account and organization. If the ledger tracks multiple sets of books, you'd also include the ledger/book dimension. You would normally capture journal entry transactions by transaction posting date, so use a daily-grained date table in this schema. Depending on the business rules associated with the source data, you may need a second role-playing date dimension to distinguish the posting date from the effective accounting date.

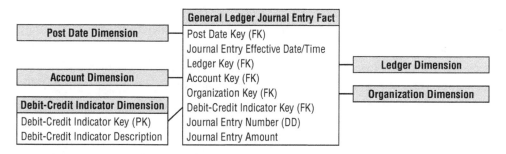

Figure 7-3: General ledger journal entry transactions.

The journal entry number is likely a degenerate dimension with no linkage to an associated dimension table. If the journal entry numbers from the source are ordered, then this degenerate dimension can be used to order the journal entries because the calendar date dimension on this fact table is too coarse to provide this sorting. If the journal entry numbers do not easily support the sort, then an effective date/time stamp must be added to the fact table. Depending on the source data, you may have a journal entry transaction type and even a description. In this situation, you would create a separate journal entry transaction profile dimension (not shown). Assuming the descriptions are not just freeform text, this dimension would have significantly fewer rows than the fact table, which would have one row per journal entry line. The specific journal entry number would still be treated as degenerate.

Each row in the journal entry fact table is identified as either a credit or a debit. The debit/credit indicator takes on two, and only two, values.

Multiple Fiscal Accounting Calendars

In Figure 7-3, the data is captured by posting date, but users may also want to summarize the data by fiscal account period. Unfortunately, fiscal accounting periods often do not align with standard Gregorian calendar months. For example, a company may have 13 4-week accounting periods in a fiscal year that begins on September 1 rather than 12 monthly periods beginning on January 1. If you deal with a single fiscal calendar, then each day in a year corresponds to a single calendar month, as well as a single accounting period. Given these relationships, the calendar and accounting periods are merely hierarchical attributes on the daily date dimension. The daily date dimension table would simultaneously conform to a calendar month dimension table, as well as to a fiscal accounting period dimension table.

In other situations, you may deal with multiple fiscal accounting calendars that vary by subsidiary or line of business. If the number of unique fiscal calendars is a fixed, low number, then you can include each set of uniquely labeled fiscal calendar attributes on a single date dimension. A given row in the daily date dimension would be identified as belonging to accounting period 1 for subsidiary A but accounting period 7 for subsidiary B.

In a more complex situation with a large number of different fiscal calendars, you could identify the official corporate fiscal calendar in the date dimension. You then have several options to address the subsidiary-specific fiscal calendars. The most common approach is to create a date dimension outrigger with a multipart key consisting of the date and subsidiary keys. There would be one row in this table for each day for each subsidiary. The attributes in this outrigger would consist of fiscal groupings (such as fiscal week end date and fiscal period end date). You would need a mechanism for filtering on a specific subsidiary in the outrigger. Doing so through a view would then allow the outrigger to be presented as if it were logically part of the date dimension table.

A second approach for tackling the subsidiary-specific calendars would be to create separate physical date dimensions for each subsidiary calendar, using a common set of surrogate date keys. This option would likely be used if the fact data were decentralized by subsidiary. Depending on the BI tool's capabilities, it may be easier to either filter on the subsidiary outrigger as described in option 1 or ensure usage of the appropriate subsidiary-specific physical date dimension table (option 2). Finally, you could allocate another foreign key in the fact table to a subsidiary fiscal period dimension table. The number of rows in this table would be the number of fiscal periods (approximately 36 for 3 years) times the number of unique calendars. This approach simplifies user access but puts additional strain on the ETL system because it must insert the appropriate fiscal period key during the transformation process.

Drilling Down Through a Multilevel Hierarchy

Very large enterprises or government agencies may have multiple ledgers arranged in an ascending hierarchy, perhaps by enterprise, division, and department. At the lowest level, department ledger entries may be consolidated to roll up to a single division ledger entry. Then the division ledger entries may be consolidated to the enterprise level. This would be particularly common for the periodic snapshot grain of these ledgers. One way to model this hierarchy is by introducing the parent snapshot's fact table surrogate key in the fact table, as shown in Figure 7-4. In this case, because you define a parent/child relationship between rows, you add an explicit fact table surrogate key, a single column numeric identifier incremented as you add rows to the fact table.

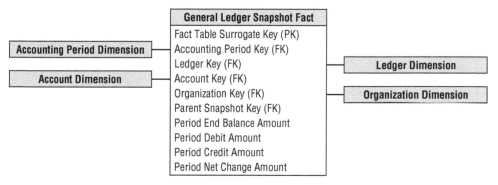

Figure 7-4: Design for drilling down through multiple ledgers.

You can use the parent snapshot surrogate key to drill down in your multilayer general ledger. Suppose that you detect a large travel amount at the top level of the ledger. You grab the surrogate key for that high-level entry and then fetch all the entries whose parent snapshot key equals that key. This exposes the entries at the next lower level that contribute to the original high-level record of interest. The SQL would look something like this:

```
Select * from GL_Fact where Parent_Snapshot_key =
    (select fact_table_surrogate_key from GL_Fact f, Account a
    where <joins> and a.Account = 'Travel' and f.Amount > 1000)
```

Financial Statements

One of the primary functions of a general ledger system is to produce the organization's official financial reports, such as the balance sheet and income statement. The operational system typically handles the production of these reports. You wouldn't want the DW/BI system to attempt to replace the reports published by the operational financial systems.

However, DW/BI teams sometimes create complementary aggregated data that provides simplified access to report information that can be more widely disseminated throughout the organization. Dimensions in the financial statement schema would include the accounting period and cost center. Rather than looking at general ledger account level data, the fact data would be aggregated and tagged with the appropriate financial statement line number and label. In this manner, managers could easily look at performance trends for a given line in the financial statement over time for their organization. Similarly, key performance indicators and financial ratios may be made available at the same level of detail.

Budgeting Process

Most modern general ledger systems include the capability to integrate budget data into the general ledger. However, if the G/L either lacks this capability or it has not been implemented, you need to provide an alternative mechanism for supporting the budgeting process and variance comparisons.

Within most organizations, the budgeting process can be viewed as a series of events. Prior to the start of a fiscal year, each cost center manager typically creates a budget, broken down by budget line items, which is then approved. In reality, budgeting is seldom simply a once-per-year event. Budgets are becoming more dynamic because there are budget adjustments as the year progresses, reflecting changes in business conditions or the realities of actual spending versus the original budget. Managers want to see the current budget's status, as well as how the budget has been altered since the first approved version. As the year unfolds, commitments to spend the budgeted monies are made. Finally, payments are processed.

As a dimensional modeler, you can view the budgeting chain as a series of fact tables, as shown in Figure 7-5. This chain consists of a budget fact table, commitments fact table, and payments fact table, where there is a logical flow that starts with a budget being established for each organization and each account. Then during the operational period, commitments are made against the budgets, and finally payments are made against those commitments.

We'll begin with the budget fact table. For an expense budget line item, each row identifies what an organization in the company is allowed to spend for what purpose during a given time frame. Similarly, if the line item reflects an income forecast, which is just another variation of a budget, it would identify what an organization intends to earn from what source during a time frame.

You could further identify the grain to be a snapshot of the current status of each line item in each budget each month. Although this grain has a familiar ring to it (because it feels like a management report), it is a poor choice as the fact table grain. The facts in such a "status report" are all semi-additive balances, rather than fully additive facts. Also, this grain makes it difficult to determine how much has changed since the previous month or quarter because you must obtain the rows from several time periods and then subtract them from each other. Finally, this grain choice would require the fact table to contain many duplicated rows when nothing changes in successive months for a given line item.

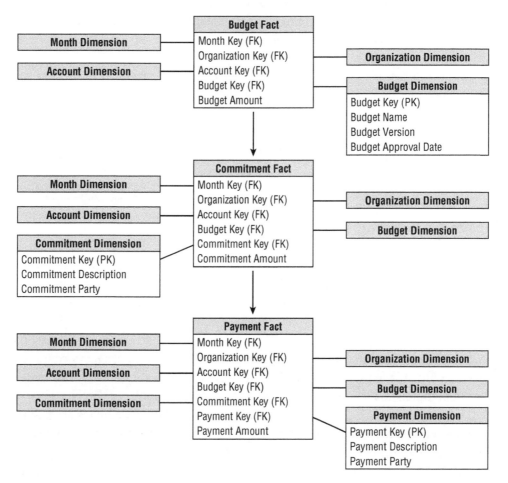

Figure 7-5: Chain of budget processes.

Instead, the grain you're interested in is the net change of the budget line item in an organizational cost center that occurred during the month. Although this suffices for budget reporting purposes, the accountants eventually need to tie the budget line item back to a specific general ledger account that's affected, so you'll also go down to the G/L account level.

Given the grain, the associated budget dimensions would include effective month, organization cost center, budget line item, and G/L account, as illustrated in Figure 7-6. The organization is identical to the dimension used earlier with the general ledger data. The account dimension is also a reused dimension. The only complication regarding the account dimension is that sometimes a single budget line item impacts more than one G/L account. In that case, you would need to allocate the budget line to the individual G/L accounts. Because the grain of the budget fact table is by G/L account, a single budget line for a cost center may be represented as several rows in the fact table.

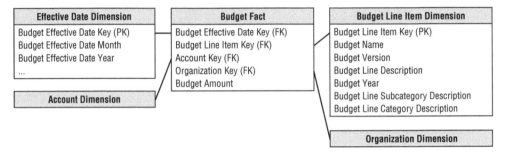

Figure 7-6: Budget schema.

The budget line item identifies the purpose of the proposed spending, such as employee wages or office supplies. There are typically several levels of summarization categories associated with a budget line item. All the budget line items may not have the same number of levels in their summarization hierarchy, such as when some only have a category rollup, but not a subcategory. In this case, you may populate the dimension attributes by replicating the category name in the subcategory column to avoid having line items roll up to a Not Applicable subcategory bucket. The budget line item dimension would also identify the budget year and/or budget version.

The effective month is the month during which the budget changes are posted. The first entries for a given budget year would show the effective month when the budget is first approved. If the budget is updated or modified as the budget year gets underway, the effective months would occur during the budget year. If you don't adjust a budget throughout the year, then the only entries would be the first ones when the budget is initially approved. This is what is meant when the grain is specified to be the net change. It's critical that you understand this point, or you won't understand what is in this budget fact table or how it's used.

Sometimes budgets are created as annual spending plans; other times, they're broken down by month or quarter. Figure 7-6 assumes the budget is an annual amount, with the budget year identified in the budget line item dimension. If you need to express the budget data by spending month, you would need to include a second month dimension table that plays the role of spending month.

The budget fact table has a single budget amount fact that is fully additive. If you budget for a multinational organization, the budget amount may be tagged with the expected currency conversion factor for planning purposes. If the budget amount for a given budget line and account is modified during the year, an additional row is added to the budget fact table representing the net change. For example, if the original budget were $200,000, you might have another row in June for a $40,000 increase and then another in October for a negative $25,000 as you tighten your belt going into year-end.

When the budget year begins, managers make commitments to spend the budget through purchase orders, work orders, or other forms of contracts. Managers are keenly interested in monitoring their commitments and comparing them to the annual budget to manage their spending. We can envision a second fact table for the commitments (refer to Figure 7-5) that shares the same dimensions, in addition to dimensions identifying the specific commitment document (purchase order, work order, or contract) and commitment party. In this case, the fact would be the committed amount.

Finally, payments are made as monies are transferred to the party named in the commitment. From a practical point of view, the money is no longer available in the budget when the commitment is made. But the finance department is interested in the relationship between commitments and payments because it manages the company's cash. The dimensions associated with the payments fact table would include the commitment fact table dimensions, plus a payment dimension to identify the type of payment, as well as the payee to whom the payment was actually made. Referring the budgeting chain shown in Figure 7-5, the list of dimensions expands as you move from the budget to commitments to payments.

With this design, you can create a number of interesting analyses. To look at the current budgeted amount by department and line item, you can constrain on all dates up to the present, adding the amounts by department and line item. Because the grain is the net change of the line items, adding up all the entries over time does exactly the right thing. You end up with the current approved budget amount, and you get exactly those line items in the given departments that have a budget.

To ask for all the changes to the budget for various line items, simply constrain on a single month. You'll report only those line items that experienced a change during the month.

To compare current commitments to the current budget, separately sum the commitment amounts and budget amounts from the beginning of time to the current date (or any date of interest). Then combine the two answer sets on the row headers. This is a standard drill-across application using multipass SQL. Similarly, you could drill across commitments and payments.

Dimension Attribute Hierarchies

Although the budget chain use case described in this chapter is reasonably simple, it contains a number of hierarchies, along with a number of choices for the designer. Remember a hierarchy is defined by a series of many-to-one relationships. You likely have at least four hierarchies: calendar levels, account levels, geographic levels, and organization levels.

Fixed Depth Positional Hierarchies

In the budget chain, the calendar levels are familiar fixed depth position hierarchies. As the name suggests, a fixed position hierarchy has a fixed set of levels, all with meaningful labels. Think of these levels as rollups. One calendar hierarchy may be day ⇨ fiscal period ⇨ year. Another could be day ⇨ month ⇨ year. These two hierarchies may be different if there is no simple relationship between fiscal periods and months. For example, some organizations have 5-4-4 fiscal periods, consisting of a 5-week span followed by two 4-week spans. A single calendar date dimension can comfortably represent these two hierarchies at the same time in sets of parallel attributes since the grain of the date dimension is the individual day.

The account dimension may also have a fixed many-to-one hierarchy such as executive level, director level, and manager level accounts. The grain of the dimension is the manager level account, but the detailed accounts at the lowest grain roll up to the director and executive levels.

In a fixed position hierarchy, it is important that each level have a specific name. That way the business user knows how to constrain and interpret each level.

WARNING Avoid fixed position hierarchies with abstract names such as Level-1, Level-2, and so on. This is a cheap way to avoid correctly modeling a ragged hierarchy. When the levels have abstract names, the business user has no way of knowing where to place a constraint, or what the attribute values in a level mean in a report. If a ragged hierarchy attempts to hide within a fixed position hierarchy with abstract names, the individual levels are essentially meaningless.

Slightly Ragged Variable Depth Hierarchies

Geographic hierarchies present an interesting challenge. Figure 7-7 shows three possibilities. The simple location has four levels: address, city, state, and country. The medium complex location adds a zone level, and the complex location adds both district and zone levels. If you need to represent all three types of locations in a single geographic hierarchy, you have a slightly variable hierarchy. You can combine all three types if you are willing to make a compromise. For the medium location that has no concept of district, you can propagate the city name down into the district attribute. For the simple location that has no concept of either district or zone, you can propagate the city name down into both these attributes. The business data governance representatives may instead decide to propagate labels upward or even populate the empty levels with Not Applicable. The business representatives need to visualize the appropriate row label values on a report if the attribute is grouped on. Regardless of the business rules applied, you have the advantage of a clean positional design with attribute names that make reasonable sense across all three geographies. The key to this compromise is the narrow range of geographic hierarchies, ranging from four levels to only six levels. If the data ranged from four levels to eight or ten or even more, this design compromise would not work. Remember the attribute names need to make sense.

Simple Loc		Medium Loc		Complex Loc
Loc Key (PK)		Loc Key (PK)		Loc Key (PK)
Address+		Address+		Address+
City		City		City
City		City		District
City		Zone		Zone
State		State		State
Country		Country		Country
...		...		...

Figure 7-7: Sample data values exist simultaneously in a single location dimension containing simple, intermediate, and complex hierarchies.

Ragged Variable Depth Hierarchies

In the budget use case, the organization structure is an excellent example of a ragged hierarchy of indeterminate depth. In this chapter, we often refer to the hierarchical structure as a "tree" and the individual organizations in that tree as "nodes." Imagine your enterprise consists of 13 organizations with the rollup structure shown in Figure 7-8. Each of these organizations has its own budget, commitments, and payments.

For a single organization, you can request a specific budget for an account with a simple join from the organization dimension to the fact table, as shown in Figure 7-9. But you also want to roll up the budget across portions of the tree or even all the tree. Figure 7-9 contains no information about the organizational rollup.

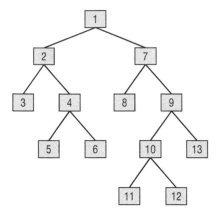

Figure 7-8: Organization rollup structure.

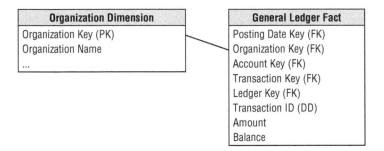

Figure 7-9: Organization dimension joined to fact table.

The classic way to represent a parent/child tree structure is by placing recursive pointers in the organization dimension from each row to its parent, as shown in Figure 7-10. The original definition of SQL did not provide a way to evaluate these recursive pointers. Oracle implemented a CONNECT BY function that traversed these pointers in a downward fashion starting at a high-level parent in the tree and progressively enumerated all the child nodes in lower levels until the tree was exhausted. But the problem with Oracle CONNECT BY and other more general approaches, such as SQL Server's recursive common table expressions, is that the representation of the tree is entangled with the organization dimension because these approaches depend on the recursive pointer embedded in the data. It is impractical to switch from one rollup structure to another because many of the recursive pointers would have to be destructively modified. It is also impractical to maintain organizations as type 2 slowly changing dimension attributes because changing the key for a high-level node would ripple key changes down to the bottom of the tree.

The solution to the problem of representing arbitrary rollup structures is to build a special kind of bridge table that is independent from the primary dimension table and contains all the information about the rollup. The grain of this bridge table is each path in the tree from a parent to all the children below that parent, as shown in Figure 7-11. The first column in the map table is the primary key of the parent, and the second column is the primary key of the child. A row must be constructed from each possible parent to each possible child, including a row that connects the parent to itself.

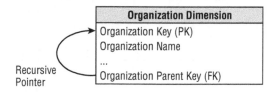

Figure 7-10: Classic parent/child recursive design.

The example tree depicted in Figure 7-8 results in 43 rows in Figure 7-11. There are 13 paths from node number 1, 5 paths from node number 2, one path from node number 3 to itself, as so on.

The highest parent flag in the map table means the particular path comes from the highest parent in the tree. The lowest child flag means the particular path ends in a "leaf node" of the tree.

If you constrain the organization dimension table to a single row, you can join the dimension table to the map table to the fact table, as shown in Figure 7-12. For example, if you constrain the organization table to node number 1 and simply fetch an additive fact from the fact table, you get 13 hits on the fact table, which traverses the entire tree in a single query. If you perform the same query except constrain the map table lowest child flag to true, then you fetch only the additive fact from the six leaf nodes, numbers 3, 5, 6, 8, 10, and 11. Again, this answer was computed without traversing the tree at query time!

NOTE The article "Building Hierarchy Bridge Tables" (available at www .kimballgroup.com under the Tools and Utilities tab for this book title) provides a code example for building the hierarchy bridge table described in this section.

You must be careful when using the map bridge table to constrain the organization dimension to a single row, or else you risk overcounting the children and grandchildren in the tree. For example, if instead of a constraint such as "Node Organization Number = 1" you constrain on "Node Organization Location = California", you would have this problem. In this case you need to craft a custom query, rather than a simple join, with the following constraint:

```
GLfact.orgkey in (select distinct bridge.childkey
            from innerorgdim, bridge
            where innerorgdim.state = 'California' and
            innerorgdim.orgkey = bridge.parentkey)
```

Sample Organization Map bridge table rows for Figure 7-8:

Organization Map Bridge
Parent Organization Key (FK)
Child Organization Key (FK)
Depth from Parent
Highest Parent Flag
Lowest Child Flag

Parent Organization Key	Child Organization Key	Depth from Parent	Highest Parent Flag	Lowest Child Flag
1	1	0	TRUE	FALSE
1	2	1	TRUE	FALSE
1	3	2	TRUE	TRUE
1	4	2	TRUE	FALSE
1	5	3	TRUE	TRUE
1	6	3	TRUE	TRUE
1	7	1	TRUE	FALSE
1	8	2	TRUE	TRUE
1	9	2	TRUE	FALSE
1	10	3	TRUE	FALSE
1	11	4	TRUE	TRUE
1	12	4	TRUE	TRUE
1	13	3	TRUE	TRUE
2	2	0	FALSE	FALSE
2	3	1	FALSE	TRUE
2	4	1	FALSE	FALSE
2	5	2	FALSE	TRUE
2	6	2	FALSE	TRUE
3	3	0	FALSE	TRUE
4	4	0	FALSE	FALSE
4	5	1	FALSE	TRUE
4	6	1	FALSE	TRUE
5	5	0	FALSE	TRUE
6	6	0	FALSE	TRUE
7	7	0	FALSE	FALSE
7	8	1	FALSE	TRUE
7	9	1	FALSE	FALSE
7	10	2	FALSE	FALSE
7	11	3	FALSE	TRUE
7	12	3	FALSE	TRUE
7	13	2	FALSE	TRUE
8	8	0	FALSE	TRUE
9	9	0	FALSE	FALSE
9	10	1	FALSE	FALSE
9	11	2	FALSE	TRUE
9	12	2	FALSE	TRUE
9	13	1	FALSE	TRUE
10	10	0	FALSE	FALSE
10	11	1	FALSE	TRUE
10	12	1	FALSE	TRUE
11	11	0	FALSE	TRUE
12	12	0	FALSE	TRUE
13	13	0	FALSE	TRUE

Figure 7-11: Organization map bridge table sample rows.

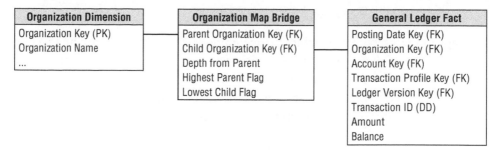

FIGURE 7-12: Joining organization map bridge table to fact table.

Shared Ownership in a Ragged Hierarchy

The map table can represent partial or shared ownership, as shown in Figure 7-13. For instance, suppose node 10 is 50 percent owned by node 6 and 50 percent owned by node 11. In this case, any budget or commitment or payment attributed to node 10 flows upward through node 6 with a 50 percent weighting and also upward through node 11 with a 50 percent weighting. You now need to add extra path rows to the original 43 rows to accommodate the connection of node 10 up to node 6 and its parents. All the relevant path rows ending in node 10 now need a 50 percent weighting in the ownership percentage column in the map table. Other path rows not ending in node 10 do not have their ownership percentage column changed.

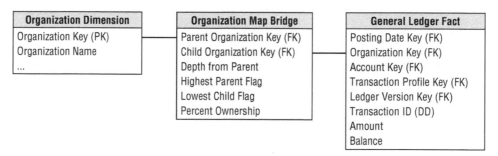

FIGURE 7-13: Bridge table for ragged hierarchy with shared ownership.

Time Varying Ragged Hierarchies

The ragged hierarchy bridge table can accommodate slowly changing hierarchies with the addition of two date/time stamps, as shown in Figure 7-14. When a given node no longer is a child of another node, the end effective date/time of the old relationship must be set to the date/time of the change, and new path rows inserted into the bridge table with the correct begin effective date/time.

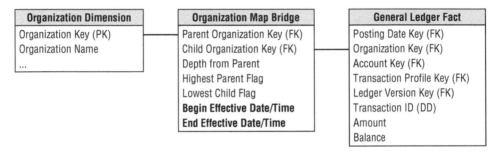

Figure 7-14: Bridge table for time varying ragged hierarchies.

> **WARNING**   When using the bridge table in Figure 7-14, the query must always constrain to a single date/time to "freeze" the bridge table to a single consistent view of the hierarchy. Failing to constrain in this way otherwise would result in multiple paths being fetched that could not exist at the same time.

Modifying Ragged Hierarchies

The organization map bridge table can easily be modified. Suppose you want to move nodes 4, 5, and 6 from their original location reporting up to node 2 to a new location reporting up to node 9, as shown in Figure 7-15.

In the static case in which the bridge table only reflects the current rollup structure, you merely delete the higher level paths in the tree pointing into the group of nodes 4, 5, and 6. Then you attach nodes 4, 5, and 6 into the parents 1, 7, and 9. Here is the static SQL:

```
Delete from Org_Map where child_org in (4, 5,6) and
  parent_org not in (4,5,6)
Insert into Org_Map (parent_org, child_org)
  select parent_org, 4 from Org_Map where parent_org in (1, 7, 9)
Insert into Org_Map (parent_org, child_org)
  select parent_org, 5 from Org_Map where parent_org in (1, 7, 9)
Insert into Org_Map (parent_org, child_org)
  select parent_org, 6 from Org_Map where parent_org in (1, 7, 9)
```

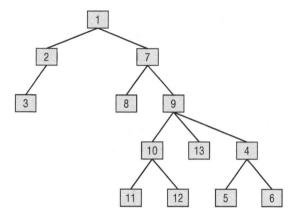

Figure 7-15: Changes to Figure 7-8's organization structure.

In the time varying case in which the bridge table has the pair of date/time stamps, the logic is similar. You can find the higher level paths in the tree pointing into the group of nodes 4, 5, and 6 and set their end effective date/times to the moment of the change. Then you attach nodes 4, 5, and 6 into the parents 1, 7, and 9 with the appropriate date/times. Here is the time varying SQL:

```
Update Org_Map set end_eff_date = #December 31, 2012#
   where child_org in (4, 5,6) and parent_org not in (4,5,6)
   and #Jan 1, 2013# between begin_eff_date and end_eff_date
Insert into Org_Map
   (parent_org, child_org, begin_eff_date, end_eff_date)
   values (1, 4, #Jan 1, 2013#, #Dec 31, 9999#)
Insert into Org_Map
   (parent_org, child_org, begin_eff_date, end_eff_date)
   values (7, 4, #Jan 1, 2013#, #Dec 31, 9999#)
Insert into Org_Map
   (parent_org, child_org, begin_eff_date, end_eff_date)
   values (9, 4, #Jan 1, 2013#, #Dec 31, 9999#)
Identical insert statements for nodes 5 and 6 …
```

This simple recipe for changing the bridge table avoids nightmarish scenarios when changing other types of hierarchical models. In the bridge table, only the paths directly involved in the change are affected. All other paths are untouched. In most other schemes with clever node labels, a change in the tree structure can affect many or even all the nodes in the tree, as shown in the next section.

Alternative Ragged Hierarchy Modeling Approaches

In addition to using recursive pointers in the organization dimension, there are at least two other ways to model a ragged hierarchy, both involving clever columns placed in the organization dimension. There are two disadvantages to these schemes compared to the bridge table approach. First, the definition of the hierarchy is locked into the dimension and cannot easily be replaced. Second, both of these schemes are vulnerable to a relabeling disaster in which a large part of the tree must be relabeled due to a single small change. Textbooks (like this one!) usually show a tiny example, but you need to tread cautiously if there are thousands of nodes in your tree.

One scheme adds a pathstring attribute to the organization dimension table, as shown in Figure 7-16. The values of the pathstring attribute are shown within each node. In this scenario, there is no bridge table. At each level, the pathstring starts with the full pathstring of the parent and then adds the letters A, B, C, and so on, from left to right under that parent. The final character is a "+" if the node has children and is a period if the node has no children. The tree can be navigated by using wild cards in constraints against the pathstring, for example,

- A* retrieves the whole tree where the asterisk is a variable length wild card.
- *. retrieves only the leaf nodes.
- ?+ retrieves the topmost node where the question mark is a single character wild card.

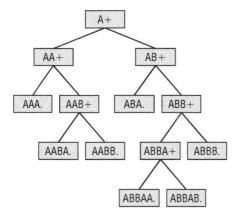

Figure 7-16: Alternate ragged hierarchy design using pathstring attribute.

The pathstring approach is fairly sensitive to relabeling ripples caused by organization changes; if a new node is inserted somewhere in the tree, all the nodes to the right of that node under the same parent must be relabeled.

Another similar scheme, known to computer scientists as the modified preordered tree traversal approach, numbers the tree as shown in Figure 7-17. Every node has a pair of numbers that identifies all the nodes below that point. The whole tree can be enumerated by using the node numbers in the topmost node. If the values in each node have the names Left and Right, then all the nodes in the example tree can be found with the constraint "Left between 1 and 26." Leaf nodes can be found where Left and Right differ by 1, meaning there aren't any children. This approach is even more vulnerable to the relabeling disaster than the pathstring approach because the entire tree must be carefully numbered in sequence, top to bottom and left to right. Any change to the tree causes the entire rest of the tree to the right to be relabeled.

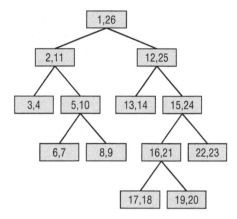

Figure 7-17: Alternative ragged hierarchy design using the modified preordered tree traversal approach.

Advantages of the Bridge Table Approach for Ragged Hierarchies

Although the bridge table requires more ETL work to set up and more work when querying, it offers exceptional flexibility for analyzing ragged hierarchies of indeterminate depth. In particular, the bridge table allows

- Alternative rollup structures to be selected at query time
- Shared ownership rollups
- Time varying ragged hierarchies
- Limited impact when nodes undergo slowly changing dimension (SCD) type 2 changes
- Limited impact when the tree structure is changed

You can use the organization hierarchy bridge table to fetch a fact across all three fact tables in the budget chain. Figure 7-18 shows how an organization map table can connect to the three budget chain fact tables. This would allow a drill-across report such as finding all the travel budgets, commitments, and payments made by all the lowest leaf nodes in a complex organizational structure.

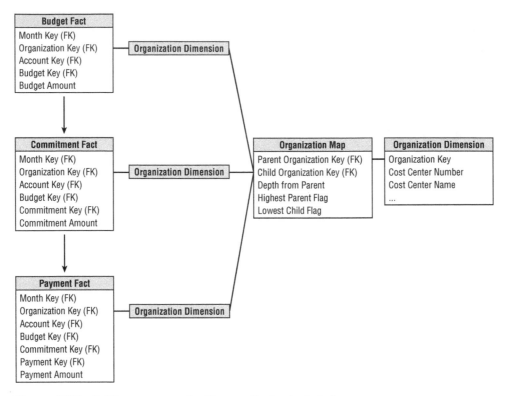

Figure 7-18: Drilling across and rolling up the budget chain.

Consolidated Fact Tables

In the last section, we discussed comparing metrics generated by separate business processes by drilling across fact tables, such as budget and commitments. If this type of drill-across analysis is extremely common in the user community, it likely makes sense to create a single fact table that combines the metrics once rather than relying on business users or their BI reporting applications to stitch together result sets, especially given the inherent issues of complexity, accuracy, tool capabilities, and performance.

Most typically, business managers are interested in comparing actual to budget variances. At this point, you can presume the annual budgets and/or forecasts have been broken down by accounting period. Figure 7-19 shows the actual and budget amounts, as well as the variance (which is a calculated difference) by the common dimensions.

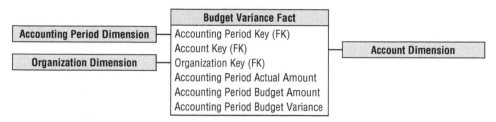

Figure 7-19: Actual versus budget consolidated fact table.

Again, in a multinational organization, you would likely see the actual amounts in both local and the equivalent standard currency, based on the effective conversion rate. In addition, you may convert the actual results based on the planned currency conversion factor. Given the unpredictable nature of currency fluctuations, it is useful to monitor performance based on both the effective and planned conversion rates. In this manner, remote managers aren't penalized for currency rate changes outside their control. Likewise, finance can better understand the big picture impact of unexpected currency conversion fluctuations on the organization's annual plan.

Fact tables that combine metrics from multiple business processes at a common granularity are referred to as *consolidated fact tables*. Although consolidated fact tables can be useful, both in terms of performance and usability, they often represent a dimensionality compromise as they consolidate facts at the "least common denominator" of dimensionality. One potential risk associated with consolidated fact tables is that project teams sometimes base designs solely on the granularity of the consolidated table, while failing to meet user requirements that demand the ability to dive into more granular data. These schemas run into serious problems if project teams attempt to force a one-to-one correspondence to combine data with different granularity or dimensionality.

NOTE   When facts from multiple business processes are combined in a consolidated fact table, they must live at the same level of granularity and dimensionality. Because the separate facts seldom naturally live at a common grain, you are forced to eliminate or aggregate some dimensions to support the one-to-one correspondence, while retaining the atomic data in separate fact tables. Project teams should not create artificial facts or dimensions in an attempt to force-fit the consolidation of differently grained fact data.

Role of OLAP and Packaged Analytic Solutions

While discussing financial dimensional models in the context of relational databases, it is worth noting that multidimensional OLAP vendors have long played a role in this arena. OLAP products have been used extensively for financial reporting, budgeting, and consolidation applications. Relational dimensional models often feed financial OLAP cubes. OLAP cubes can deliver fast query performance that is critical for executive usage. The data volumes, especially for general ledger balances or financial statement aggregates, do not typically overwhelm the practical size constraints of a multidimensional product. OLAP is well suited to handle complicated organizational rollups, as well as complex calculations, including inter-row manipulations. Most OLAP vendors provide finance-specific capabilities, such as financial functions (for example, net present value or compound growth), the appropriate handling of financial statement data (in the expected sequential order such as income before expenses), and the proper treatment of debits and credits depending on the account type, as well as more advanced functions such as financial consolidation. OLAP cubes often also readily support complex security models, such as limiting access to detailed data while providing more open access to summary metrics.

Given the standard nature of general ledger processing, purchasing a general ledger package rather than attempting to build one from scratch has been a popular route for years. Nearly all the operational packages also offer a complementary analytic solution, sometimes in partnership with an OLAP vendor. In many cases, precanned solutions based on the vendor's cumulative experience are a sound way to jump start a financial DW/BI implementation with potentially reduced cost and risk. The analytic solutions often have tools to assist with the extraction and staging of the operational data, as well as tools to assist with analysis and interpretation. However, when leveraging packaged solutions, you need to be cautious in order to avoid stovepipe applications. You could easily end up with separate financial, CRM, human resources, and ERP packaged analytic solutions from as many different vendors, none of which integrate with other internal data. You need to conform dimensions across the entire DW/BI environment, regardless of whether you build a solution or implement packages. Packaged analytic solutions can turbocharge a DW/BI implementation; however, they do not alleviate the need for conformance. Most organizations inevitably rely on a combination of building, buying, and integrating for a complete solution.

Summary

In this chapter, we focused primarily on financial data in the general ledger, both in terms of periodic snapshots as well as journal entry transactions. We discussed the handling of common G/L data challenges, including multiple currencies, multiple fiscal years, unbalanced organizational trees, and the urge to create to-date totals.

We used the familiar organization rollup structure to show how to model complex ragged hierarchies of indeterminate depth. We introduced a special bridge table for these hierarchies, and compared this approach to others.

We explored the series of events in a budgeting process chain. We described the use of "net change" granularity in this situation rather than creating snapshots of the budget data totals. We also discussed the concept of consolidated fact tables that combine the results of separate business processes when they are frequently analyzed together.

Finally, we discussed the natural fit of OLAP products for financial analysis. We also stressed the importance of integrating analytic packages into the overall DW/ BI environment through the use of conformed dimensions.

Customer Relationship Management

Long before the *customer relationship management (CRM)* buzzword existed, organizations were designing and developing customer-centric dimensional models to better understand their customers' behavior. For decades, these models were used to respond to management's inquiries about which customers were solicited, who responded, and what was the magnitude of their response. The business value of understanding the full spectrum of customers' interactions and transactions has propelled CRM to the top of the charts. CRM not only includes familiar residential and commercial customers, but also citizens, patients, students, and many other categories of people and organizations whose behavior and preferences are important. CRM is a mission-critical business strategy that many view as essential to an organization's survival.

In this chapter we start with a CRM overview, including its operational and analytic roles. We then introduce the basic design of the customer dimension, including common attributes such as dates, segmentation attributes, repeated contact roles, and aggregated facts. We discuss customer name and address parsing, along with international considerations. We remind you of the challenges of modeling complex hierarchies when we describe various kinds of customer hierarchies.

Chapter 8 discusses the following concepts:

- CRM overview
- Customer name and address parsing, including international considerations
- Handling of dates, aggregated facts, and segmentation behavior attributes and scores in a customer dimension
- Outriggers for low cardinality attributes
- Bridge tables for sparse attributes, along with trade-offs of bridge tables versus a positional design
- Bridge tables for multiple customer contacts
- Behavior study groups to capture customer cohort groups

- Step dimensions to analyze sequential customer behavior
- Timespan fact tables with effective and expiration dates
- Embellishing fact tables with dimensions for satisfaction or abnormal scenarios
- Integrating customer data via master data management or partial conformity during the downstream ETL processing
- Warnings about fact-to-fact table joins
- Reality check on real time, low latency requirements

Because this chapter's customer-centric modeling issues and patterns are relevant across industries and functional areas, we have not included a bus matrix.

CRM Overview

Regardless of the industry, organizations have flocked to the concept of CRM. They've jumped on the bandwagon in an attempt to migrate from a product-centric orientation to one that is driven by customer needs. Although all-encompassing terms such as customer relationship management sometimes seem ambiguous and/ or overly ambitious, the premise behind CRM is far from rocket science. It's based on the simple notion that the better you know your customers, the better you can maintain long-lasting, valuable relationships with them. The goal of CRM is to maximize relationships with your customers over their lifetime. It entails focusing all aspects of the business, from marketing, sales, operations, and service, on establishing and sustaining mutually beneficial customer relations. To do so, the organization must develop a single, integrated view of each customer.

CRM promises significant returns for organizations that embrace it, both for increased revenue and operational efficiencies. Switching to a customer-driven perspective can lead to increased sales effectiveness and closure rates, revenue growth, enhanced sales productivity at reduced cost, improved customer profitability margins, higher customer satisfaction, and increased customer retention. Ultimately, every organization wants more loyal, more profitable customers. As it often requires a sizeable investment to attract new customers, you can't afford to have the profitable ones leave.

In many organizations, the view of the customer varies depending on the product line business unit, business function, and/or geographic location. Each group may use different customer data in different ways with different results. The evolution from the existing silos to a more integrated perspective obviously requires organizational commitment. CRM is like a stick of dynamite that knocks down the silo walls. It requires the right integration of business processes, people resources, and application technology to be effective.

Over the past decade, the explosive growth of social media, location tracking technology, network usage monitoring, multimedia applications, and sensor networks has provided an ocean of customer behavioral data that even Main Street enterprises recognize as providing actionable insights. Although much of this data lies outside the comfort zone of relational databases, the new "big data" techniques can bring this data back into the DW/BI fold. Chapter 21: Big Data Analytics discusses the best practices for bringing this new kind of big data into the DW/BI environment. But setting aside the purely technological challenges, the real message is the need for profound integration. You must step up to the challenge of integrating as many as 100 customer-facing data sources, most of which are external. These data sources are at different grains, have incompatible customer attributes, and are not under your control. Any questions?

Because it is human nature to resist change, it comes as no surprise that people-related issues often challenge CRM implementations. CRM involves brand new ways of interacting with customers and often entails radical changes to the sales channels. CRM requires new information flows based on the complete acquisition and dissemination of customer "touch point" data. Often organization structures and incentive systems are dramatically altered.

In Chapter 17: Kimball DW/BI Lifecycle Overview, we'll stress the importance of having support from both senior business and IT management for a DW/BI initiative. This advice also applies to a CRM implementation because of its cross-functional focus. CRM requires a clear business vision. Without business strategy, buy-in, and authorization to change, CRM becomes an exercise in futility. Neither IT nor the business community can successfully implement CRM on its own; CRM demands a joint commitment of support.

Operational and Analytic CRM

It could be said that CRM suffers from a split personality syndrome because it needs to address both operational and analytic requirements. Effective CRM relies on the collection of data at every interaction you have with a customer and then leveraging that breadth of data through analysis.

On the operational front, CRM calls for the synchronization of customer-facing processes. Often operational systems must either be updated or supplemented to coordinate across sales, marketing, operations, and service. Think about all the customer interactions that occur during the purchase and usage of a product or service, from the initial prospect contact, quote generation, purchase transaction, fulfillment, payment transaction, and on-going customer service. Rather than thinking about these processes as independent silos (or multiple silos varying by product line), the CRM mindset is to integrate these customer activities. Key customer metrics and characteristics are collected at each touch point and made available to the others.

As data is created on the operational side of the CRM equation, you obviously need to store and analyze the historical metrics resulting from the customer interaction and transaction systems. Sounds familiar, doesn't it? The DW/BI system sits at the core of CRM. It serves as the repository to collect and integrate the breadth of customer information found in the operational systems, as well as from external sources. The data warehouse is the foundation that supports the panoramic 360-degree view of your customers.

Analytic CRM is enabled via accurate, integrated, and accessible customer data in the DW/BI system. You can measure the effectiveness of decisions made in the past to optimize future interactions. Customer data can be leveraged to better identify up-sell and cross-sell opportunities, pinpoint inefficiencies, generate demand, and improve retention. In addition, the historical, integrated data can be leveraged to generate models or scores that close the loop back to the operational world. Recalling the major components of a DW/BI environment from Chapter 1: Data Warehousing, Business Intelligence, and Dimensional Modeling Primer, you can envision the model results pushed back to where the relationship is operationally managed (such as the rep, call center, or website), as illustrated in Figure 8-1. The model output can translate into specific proactive or reactive tactics recommended for the next point of customer contact, such as the appropriate next product offer or anti-attrition response. The model results are also retained in the DW/BI environment for subsequent analysis.

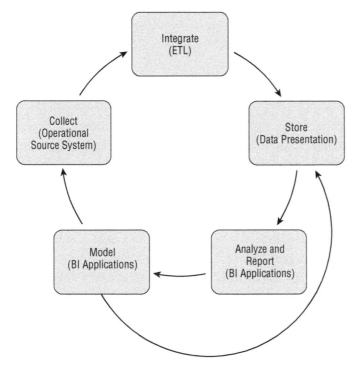

Figure 8-1: Closed loop analytic CRM.

In other situations, information must feed back to the operational website or call center systems on a more real-time basis. In this case, the closed loop is much tighter than Figure 8-1 because it's a matter of collection and storage, and then feedback to the collection system. Today's operational processes must combine the current view with a historical view, so a decision maker can decide, for example, whether to grant credit to a customer in real time, while considering the customer's lifetime history. But generally, the integration requirements for operational CRM are not as far reaching as for analytic CRM.

Obviously, as the organization becomes more centered on the customer, so must the DW/BI system. CRM will inevitably drive change in the data warehouse. DW/BI environments will grow even more rapidly as you collect more and more information about your customers. ETL processes will grow more complicated as you match and integrate data from multiple sources. Most important, the need for a conformed customer dimension becomes even more paramount.

Customer Dimension Attributes

The conformed customer dimension is a critical element for effective CRM. A well-maintained, well-deployed conformed customer dimension is the cornerstone of sound CRM analysis.

The customer dimension is typically the most challenging dimension for any DW/BI system. In a large organization, the customer dimension can be extremely deep (with many millions of rows), extremely wide (with dozens or even hundreds of attributes), and sometimes subject to rapid change. The biggest retailers, credit card companies, and government agencies have monster customer dimensions whose size exceeds 100 million rows. To further complicate matters, the customer dimension often represents an amalgamation of data from multiple internal and external source systems.

In this next section, we focus on numerous customer dimension design considerations. We'll begin with name/address parsing and other common customer attributes, including coverage of dimension outriggers, and then move on to other interesting customer attributes. Of course, the list of customer attributes is typically quite lengthy. The more descriptive information you capture about your customers, the more robust the customer dimension, and the more interesting the analyses.

Name and Address Parsing

Regardless of whether you deal with individual human beings or commercial entities, customers' name and address attributes are typically captured. The operational handling of name and address information is usually too simplistic to be very useful in the DW/BI system. Many designers feel a liberal design of general purpose columns for names and addresses, such as Name-1 through Name-3 and Address-1 through Address-6, can handle any situation. Unfortunately, these catchall columns are virtually worthless when it comes to better understanding and segmenting the customer base. Designing the name and location columns in a generic way can actually contribute to data quality problems. Consider the sample design in Figure 8-2 with general purpose columns.

Column	Sample Data Value
Name	Ms. R. Jane Smith, Atty
Address 1	123 Main Rd, North West, Ste 100A
Address 2	PO Box 2348
City	Kensington
State	Ark.
ZIP Code	88887-2348
Phone Number	888-555-3333 x776 main, 555-4444 fax

Figure 8-2: Sample customer name/address data in overly general columns.

In this design, the name column is far too limited. There is no consistent mechanism for handling salutations, titles, or suffixes. You can't identify what the person's first name is, or how she should be addressed in a personalized greeting. If you look at additional sample data from this operational system, you would potentially find multiple customers listed in a single name attribute. You might also find additional descriptive information in the name column, such as Confidential, Trustee, or UGMA (Uniform Gift to Minors Act).

In the sample address attributes, inconsistent abbreviations are used in various places. The address columns may contain enough room for any address, but there is no discipline imposed by the columns that can guarantee conformance with postal authority regulations or support address matching and latitude/longitude identification.

Instead of using a few, general purpose columns, the name and location attributes should be broken down into as many elemental parts as possible. The extract process needs to perform significant parsing on the original dirty names and addresses. After the attributes have been parsed, they can be standardized. For example, Rd would become Road and Ste would become Suite. The attributes can also be verified, such as verifying the ZIP code and associated state combination is correct. Fortunately, there are name and address data cleansing and scrubbing tools available in the market to assist with parsing, standardization, and verification.

A sample set of name and location attributes for individuals in the United States is shown in Figure 8-3. Every attribute is filled in with sample data to make the design clearer, but no single real instance would look like this. Of course, the business data governance representatives should be involved in determining the analytic value of these parsed data elements in the customer dimension.

Column	Sample Data Value
Salutation	Ms.
Informal Greeting Name	Jane
Formal Greeting Name	Ms. Smith
First and Middle Names	R. Jane
Surname	Smith
Suffix	Jr.
Ethnicity	English
Title	Attorney
Street Number	123
Street Name	Main
Street Type	Road
Street Direction	North West
City	Kensington
District	Cornwall
Second District	Berkeleyshire
State	Arkansas
Region	South
Country	United States
Continent	North America
Primary Postal Code	88887
Secondary Postal Code	2348
Postal Code Type	United States
Office Telephone Country Code	1
Office Telephone Area Code	888
Office Telephone Number	5553333
Office Extension	776
Mobile Telephone Country Code	1
Mobile Telephone Area Code	509
Mobile Telephone Number	5554444
E-mail	RJSmith@ABCGenIntl.com
Web Site	www.ABCGenIntl.com
Public Key Authentication	X.509
Certificate Authority	Verisign
Unique Individual Identifier	7346531

Figure 8-3: Sample customer name/address data with parsed name and address elements.

Commercial customers typically have multiple addresses, such as physical and shipping addresses; each of these addresses would follow much the same logic as the address structure shown in Figure 8-3.

International Name and Address Considerations

International display and printing typically requires representing foreign characters, including not just the accented characters from western European alphabets, but also Cyrillic, Arabic, Japanese, Chinese, and dozens of other less familiar writing systems. It is important to understand this is not a font problem. This is a character set problem. A font is simply an artist's rendering of a set of characters. There are hundreds of fonts available for standard English, but standard English has a relatively small character set that is enough for anyone's use unless you are a professional typographer. This small character set is usually encoded in *American Standard Code for Information Interchange (ASCII)*, which is an 8-bit encoding that has a maximum of 255 possible characters. Only approximately 100 of these 255 characters have a standard interpretation that can be invoked from a normal English keyboard, but this is usually enough for English speaking computer users. It should be clear that ASCII is woefully inadequate for representing the thousands of characters needed for non-English writing systems.

An international body of system architects, the Unicode Consortium, defined a standard known as Unicode for representing characters and alphabets in almost all the world's languages and cultures. Their work can be accessed on the web at www. unicode.org. The Unicode Standard, version 6.2.0 has defined specific interpretations for 110,182 possible characters and now covers the principal written languages of the Americas, Europe, the Middle East, Africa, India, Asia, and Pacifica. Unicode is the foundation you must use for addressing international character sets.

But it is important to understand that implementing Unicode solutions is done in the foundation layers of your systems. First, the operating system must be Unicode-compliant. Fortunately, the most current releases of all the major operating systems are Unicode-compliant.

Above the operating system, all the devices that capture, store, transmit, and print characters must be Unicode-compliant. Data warehouse back room tools must be Unicode-compliant, including sort packages, programming languages, and automated ETL packages. Finally, the DW/BI applications, including database engines, BI application servers and their report writers and query tools, web servers, and browsers must all be Unicode-compliant. The DW/BI architect should not only talk to the vendors of each package in the data pipeline, but also should conduct various end-to-end tests. Capture some names and addresses with Unicode characters at the data capture screens of one of the legacy applications, and send them through the system. Get them to print out of a final report or a final browser window from the DW/BI system and see if the special characters are still there. That simple test will cut through a lot of the confusion. Note that even when you do this, the same character, such as an a-umlaut, sorts differently in different countries such as Norway and Germany. Even though you can't solve all the variations in international collating sequences, at least both the Norwegians and the Germans will agree that the character is an a-umlaut.

Customer geographic attributes become more complicated if you deal with customers from multiple countries. Even if you don't have international customers, you may need to contend with international names and addresses somewhere in the DW/BI system for international suppliers and human resources personnel records.

NOTE Customer dimensions sometimes include a full address block attribute. This is a specially crafted column that assembles a postally-valid address for the customer including mail stop, ZIP code, and other attributes needed to satisfy postal authorities. This attribute is useful for international locations where addresses have local idiosyncrasies.

International DW/BI Goals

After committing to a Unicode foundation, you need to keep the following goals in mind, in addition to the name and address parsing requirements discussed earlier:

- **Universal and consistent.** As they say, in for a penny, in for a pound. If you are going to design a system for international use, you want it to work around the world. You need to think carefully if BI tools are to produce translated versions of reports in many languages. It may be tempting to provide translated versions of dimensions for each language, but translated dimensions give rise to some subtle problems.

  - Sorting sequences will be different, so either the reports will be sorted differently or all reports except those in the "root" language will appear to be unsorted.
  - If the attribute cardinalities are not faithfully preserved across languages, then either group totals will not be the same across reports, or some groups in various languages will contain duplicated row headers that look like mistakes. To avoid the worst of these problems, you should translate dimensions after the report is run; the report first needs to be produced in a single root language, and then the report face needs to be translated into the intended target languages.
  - All the BI tool messages and prompts need to be translated for the benefit of the business user. This process is known as *localization* and is further discussed in Chapter 12: Transportation.

■ **End-to-end data quality and downstream compatibility.** The data warehouse cannot be the only step in the data pipeline that worries about the integrity of international names and addresses. A proper design requires support from the first step of capturing the name and the address, through the data cleaning and storage steps, to the final steps of performing geographic and demographic analysis and printing reports.

■ **Cultural correctness.** In many cases, foreign customers and partners will see the results from your DW/BI system in some form. If we don't understand which name is a first name and which is a last name, and if you don't understand how to refer to a person, you run the risk of insulting these individuals, or at the very least, looking stupid. When outputs are punctuated improperly, or misspelled, your foreign customers and partners will wish they were doing business with a local company, rather than you.

■ **Real-time customer response.** DW/BI systems can play an operational role by supporting real-time customer response systems. A customer service representative may answer the telephone and may have 5 seconds or less to wait for a greeting to appear on the screen that the data warehouse recommends using with the customer. The greeting may include a proper salutation and a proper use of the customer's title and name. This greeting represents an excellent use of a *hot response cache* that contains precalculated responses for each customer.

■ **Other kinds of addresses.** We are in the midst of a revolution in communication and networking. If you are designing a system for identifying international names and addresses, you must anticipate the need to store electronic names, security tokens, and internet addresses.

Similar to international addresses, telephone numbers must be presented differently depending on where the phone call originates. You need to provide attributes to represent the complete foreign dialing sequence, complete domestic dialing sequence, and local dialing sequence. Unfortunately, complete foreign dialing sequences vary by origin country.

Customer-Centric Dates

Customer dimensions often contains dates, such as the date of the first purchase, date of last purchase, and date of birth. Although these dates initially may be SQL date type columns, if you want to summarize these dates by your unique calendar attributes, such as seasons, quarters, and fiscal periods, the dates should be changed to foreign key references to the date dimension. You need to be careful that all such dates fall within the span of the corporate date dimension. These date dimension roles are declared as semantically distinct views, such as a First Purchase

Date dimension table with unique column labels. The system behaves as if there is another physical date table. Constraints on any of these tables have nothing to do with constraints on the primary date dimension table. This design, as shown in Figure 8-4, is an example of a dimension outrigger, which is discussed in the section "Outrigger for Low Cardinality Attribute Set."

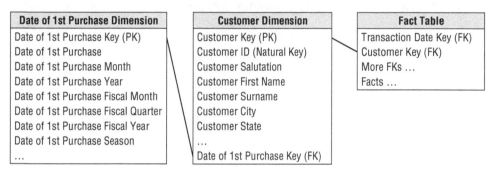

Figure 8-4: Date dimension outrigger.

Aggregated Facts as Dimension Attributes

Business users are often interested in constraining the customer dimension based on aggregated performance metrics, such as filtering on all customers who spent more than a certain dollar amount during last year. Or to make matters worse, perhaps they want to constrain based on how much the customer has purchased in a lifetime. Providing aggregated facts as dimension attributes is sure to be a crowd-pleaser with the business users. They could issue a query to identify all customers who satisfied the spending criteria and then issue another fact query to analyze the behavior for that customer dimension subset. But rather than all that, you can instead store an aggregated fact as a dimension attribute. This allows business users to simply constrain on the spending attribute just like they might on a geographic attribute. These attributes are meant to be used for constraining and labeling; they're not to be used in numeric calculations. Although there are query usability and performance advantages of storing these attributes, the main burden falls on the back room ETL processes to ensure the attributes are accurate, up-to-date, and consistent with the actual fact rows. These attributes can require significant care and feeding. If you opt to include some aggregated facts as dimension attributes, be certain to focus on those that will be frequently used. Also strive to minimize the frequency with which these attributes need to be updated. For example, an attribute for last year's spending would require much less maintenance than one providing year-to-date behavior. Rather than storing attributes down to the specific dollar value, they are sometimes replaced (or supplemented) with more meaningful descriptive values, such as High Spender as discussed in the next section. These descriptive values minimize your vulnerability that the numeric attributes might not tie back to the appropriate fact tables. In addition, they ensure that all users have a consistent definition for high spenders, for example, rather than resorting to their own individual business rules.

Segmentation Attributes and Scores

Some of the most powerful attributes in a customer dimension are segmentation classifications. These attributes obviously vary greatly by business context. For an individual customer, they may include:

- Gender
- Ethnicity
- Age or other life stage classifications
- Income or other lifestyle classifications
- Status (such as new, active, inactive, and closed)
- Referring source
- Business-specific market segment (such as a preferred customer identifier)

Similarly, many organizations score their customers to characterize them. Statistical segmentation models typically generate these scores which cluster customers in a variety of ways, such as based on their purchase behavior, payment behavior, propensity to churn, or probability to default. Each customer is tagged with a resultant score.

Behavior Tag Time Series

One popular approach for scoring and profiling customers looks at the recency (R), frequency (F), and intensity (I) of the customer's behavior. These are known as the *RFI measures*; sometimes intensity is replaced with monetary (M), so it's also known as RFM. Recency is how many days has it been since the customer last ordered or visited your site. Frequency is how many times the customer has ordered or visited, typically in the past year. And intensity is how much money the customer has spent over the same time period. When dealing with a large customer base, every customer's behavior can be modeled as a point in an RFI cube, as depicted in Figure 8-5. In this figure, the scales along each axis are quintiles, from 1 to 5, which spread the actual values into even groups.

If you have millions of points in the cube, it becomes difficult to see meaningful clusters of these points. This is a good time to ask a data mining professional where the meaningful clusters are. The data mining professional may come back with a list of behavior tags like the following, which is drawn from a slightly more complicated scenario that includes credit behavior and returns:

A: High volume repeat customer, good credit, few product returns
B: High volume repeat customer, good credit, many product returns
C: Recent new customer, no established credit pattern
D: Occasional customer, good credit
E: Occasional customer, poor credit
F: Former good customer, not seen recently
G: Frequent window shopper, mostly unproductive
H: Other

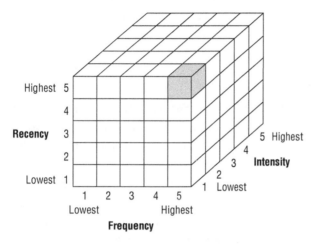

Figure 8-5: Recency, frequency, intensity (RFI) cube.

Now you can look at the customers' time series data and associate each customer in each reporting period with the nearest cluster. The data miner can help do this. Thus, the last 10 observations of a customer named John Doe could look like:

John Doe: C C C D D A A A B B

This time series of behavior tags is unusual because although it comes from a regular periodic measurement process, the observed "values" are textual. The behavior tags are not numeric and cannot be computed or averaged, but they can be queried. For example, you may want to find all the customers who were an A sometime in the fifth, fourth, or third prior period and were a B in the second or first prior period. Perhaps you are concerned by progressions like this and fear losing a valuable customer because of the increasing number of returns.

Behavior tags should not be stored as regular facts. The main use of behavior tags is formulating complex query patterns like the example in the previous paragraph. If the behavior tags were stored in separate fact rows, such querying would be extremely difficult, requiring a cascade of correlated subqueries. The recommended way to handle behavior tags is to build an explicit time series of attributes in the customer dimension. This is another example of a positional design. BI interfaces are simple because the columns are in the same table, and performance is good because you can build bitmapped indexes on them.

In addition to the separate columns for each behavior tag time period, it would be a good idea to create a single attribute with all the behavior tags concatenated together, such as CCCDDAAABB. This column would support wild card searches for exotic patterns, such as "D followed by a B."

> **NOTE** In addition to the customer dimension's time series of behavior tags, it would be reasonable to include the contemporary behavior tag value in a mini-dimension to analyze facts by the behavior tag in effect when the fact row was loaded.

Relationship Between Data Mining and DW/BI System

The data mining team can be a great client of the data warehouse, and especially great users of customer behavior data. However, there can be a mismatch between the velocity that the data warehouse can deliver data and the velocity that the data miners can consume data. For example, a decision tree tool can process hundreds of records per second, but a big drill-across report that produces "customer observations" can never deliver data at such speeds. Consider the following seven-way drill across a report that might produce millions of customer observations from census, demographic, external credit, internal credit, purchases, returns, and website data:

```
SELECT Customer Identifier, Census Tract, City, County, State,
   Postal Code, Demographic Cluster, Age, Sex, Marital Status,
   Years of Residency, Number of Dependents, Employment Profile,
   Education Profile, Sports Magazine Reader Flag,
   Personal Computer Owner Flag, Cellular Telephone Owner Flag,
   Current Credit Rating, Worst Historical Credit Rating,
   Best Historical Credit Rating, Date First Purchase,
   Date Last Purchase, Number Purchases Last Year,
   Change in Number Purchases vs. Previous Year,
   Total Number Purchases Lifetime, Total Value Purchases Lifetime,
   Number Returned Purchases Lifetime, Maximum Debt,
   Average Age Customer's Debt Lifetime, Number Late Payments,
   Number Fully Paid, Times Visited Web Site,
   Change in Frequency of Web Site Access,
   Number of Pages Visited Per Session,
   Average Dwell Time Per Session, Number Web Product Orders,
   Value Web Product Orders, Number Web Site Visits to Partner Web
   Sites, Change in Partner Web Site Visits
FROM *** WHERE *** ORDER BY *** GROUP BY ***
```

Data mining teams would love this data! For example a big file of millions of these observations could be analyzed by a decision tree tool where the tool is "aimed" at the Total Value Purchases Lifetime column, which is highlighted above. In this analysis, the decision tree tool would determine which of the other columns "predict the variance" of the target field. Maybe the answer is Best Historical Credit Rating and Number of Dependents. Armed with this answer, the enterprise now has a simple way to predict who is going to be a good lifetime customer, without needing to know all the other data content.

But the data mining team wants to use these observations over and over for different kinds of analyses perhaps with neural networks or case-based reasoning tools. Rather than producing this answer set on demand as a big, expensive query, this answer set should be written to a file and given to the data mining team to analyze on its servers.

Counts with Type 2 Dimension Changes

Businesses frequently want to count customers based on their attributes without joining to a fact table. If you used type 2 to track customer dimension changes, you need to be careful to avoid overcounting because you may have multiple rows in the customer dimension for the same individual. Doing a COUNT DISTINCT on a unique customer identifier is a possibility, assuming the attribute is indeed unique and durable. A current row indicator in the customer dimension is also helpful to do counts based on the most up-to-date descriptive values for a customer.

Things get more complicated if you need to do a customer count at a given historical point in time using effective and expiration dates in the customer dimension. For example, if you need to know the number of customers you had at the beginning of 2013, you could constrain the row effective date <= '1/1/2013' and row expiration date >= '1/1/2013' to restrict the result set to only those rows that were valid on 1/1/2013. Note the comparison operators are dependent on the business rules used to set the row effective/expiration dates. In this example, the row expiration date on the no longer valid customer row is 1 day less than the effective date on the new row.

Outrigger for Low Cardinality Attribute Set

In Chapter 3: Retail Sales, we encouraged designers to avoid snowflaking where low cardinality columns in the dimension are removed to separate normalized tables, which then link back into the original dimension table. Generally, snowflaking is not recommended in a DW/BI environment because it almost always makes the user presentation more complex, in addition to negatively impacting browsing performance. In spite of this prohibition against snowflaking, there are some special situations in which it is permissible to build a dimension outrigger that begins to look like a snowflaked table.

In Figure 8-6, the dimension outrigger is a set of data from an external data provider consisting of 150 demographic and socio-economic attributes regarding the customers' county of residence. The data for all customers residing in a given county is identical. Rather than repeating this large block of data for every customer within a county, opt to model it as an outrigger. There are several reasons for bending the "no snowflake" rule. First, the demographic data is available at a significantly different grain than the primary dimension data and it's not as analytically valuable. It is loaded at different times than the rest of the data in the customer dimension. Also, you do save significant space in this case if the underlying customer dimension is large. If you have a query tool that insists on a classic star schema with no snowflakes, the outrigger can be hidden under a view declaration.

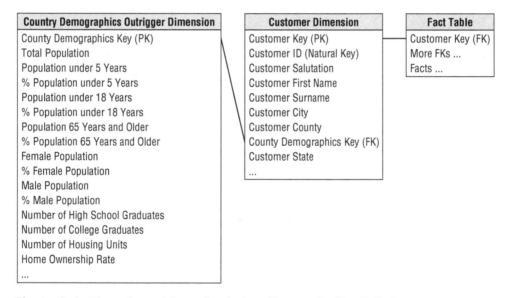

Figure 8-6: Dimension outrigger for cluster of low cardinality attributes.

> **WARNING** Dimension outriggers are permissible, but they should be the exception rather than the rule. A red warning flag should go up if your design is riddled with outriggers; you may have succumbed to the temptation to overly normalize the design.

Customer Hierarchy Considerations

One of the most challenging aspects of dealing with commercial customers is modeling their internal organizational hierarchy. Commercial customers often have a nested hierarchy of entities ranging from individual locations or organizations up through regional offices, business unit headquarters, and ultimate parent companies. These hierarchical relationships may change frequently as customers reorganize themselves internally or are involved in acquisitions and divestitures.

> **NOTE** In Chapter 7: Accounting, we described how to handle fixed hierarchies, slightly variable hierarchies, and ragged hierarchies of indeterminate depth. Chapter 7 focuses on financial cost center rollups, but the techniques are exactly transferrable to customer hierarchies. If you skipped Chapter 7, you need to backtrack to read that chapter to make sense of the following recommendations.

Although relatively uncommon, the lucky ones amongst us sometimes are confronted with a customer hierarchy that has a highly predictable fixed number of levels. Suppose you track a maximum of three rollup levels, such as the ultimate corporate parent, business unit headquarters, and regional headquarters. In this case, you have three distinct attributes in the customer dimension corresponding to these three levels. For commercial customers with complicated organizational hierarchies, you'd populate all three levels to appropriately represent the three different entities involved at each rollup level. This is the fixed depth hierarchy approach from Chapter 7.

By contrast, if another customer had a mixture of one, two, and three level organizations, you'd duplicate the lower-level value to populate the higher-level attributes. In this way, all regional headquarters would sum to the sum of all business unit headquarters, which would sum to the sum of all ultimate corporate parents. You can report by any level of the hierarchy and see the complete customer base represented. This is the slightly variable hierarchy approach.

But in many cases, complex commercial customer hierarchies are ragged hierarchies with an indeterminate depth, so you must use a ragged hierarchy modeling technique, as described in Chapter 7. For example, if a utility company is devising a custom rate plan for all the utility consumers that are part of a huge customer with many levels of offices, branch locations, manufacturing locations, and sales locations, you cannot use a fixed hierarchy. As pointed out in Chapter 7, the worst design is a set of generic levels named such as Level-1, Level-2, and so on. This makes for an unusable customer dimension because you don't know how to constrain against these levels when you have a ragged hierarchy of indeterminate depth.

Bridge Tables for Multivalued Dimensions

A fundamental tenet of dimensional modeling is to decide on the grain of the fact table, and then carefully add dimensions and facts to the design that are true to the grain. For example, if you record customer purchase transactions, the grain of the individual purchase is natural and physically compelling. You do not want to change that grain. Thus you normally require any dimension attached to this fact table to take on a single value because then there's a clean single foreign key in the fact table that identifies a single member of the dimension. Dimensions such as the customer, location, product or service, and time are always single valued. But you may have some "problem" dimensions that take on multiple values at the grain of the individual transaction. Common examples of these multivalued dimensions include:

- Demographic descriptors drawn from a multiplicity of sources
- Contact addresses for a commercial customer
- Professional skills of a job applicant
- Hobbies of an individual
- Diagnoses or symptoms of a patient
- Optional features for an automobile or truck
- Joint account holders in a bank account
- Tenants in a rental property

When faced with a multivalued dimension, there are two basic choices: a positional design or bridge table design. Positional designs are very attractive because the multivalued dimension is spread out into named columns that are easy to query. For example, if modeling the hobbies of an individual as previously mentioned, you could have a hobby dimension with named columns for all the hobbies gathered from your customers, including stamp collecting, coin collecting, astronomy, photography, and many others! Immediately you can see the problem. The positional design approach isn't very scalable. You can easily run out of columns in your database, and it is awkward to add new columns. Also if you have a column for every possible hobby, then any single individual's hobby dimension row will contain mostly null values.

The bridge table approach to multivalued dimensions is powerful but comes with a big compromise. The bridge table removes the scalability and null value objections because rows in the bridge table exist only if they are actually needed, and you can add hundreds or even thousands of hobbies in the previous example. But the resulting table design requires a complex query that must be hidden from direct view by the business users.

WARNING   Be aware that complex queries using bridge tables may require SQL that is beyond the normal reach of BI tools.

In the next two sections, we illustrate multivalued bridge table designs that fit with the customer-centric topics of this chapter. We will revisit multivalued bridges in Chapter 9: Human Resources Management, Chapter 10: Financial Services, Chapter 13: Education, Chapter 14: Healthcare, and Chapter 16: Insurance. We'll then describe how to build these bridges in Chapter 19: ETL Subsystems and Techniques.

Bridge Table for Sparse Attributes

Organizations are increasingly collecting demographics and status information about their customers, but the traditional fixed column modeling approach for handling these attributes becomes difficult to scale with hundreds of attributes.

Positional designs have a named column for each attribute. BI tool interfaces are easy to construct for positional attributes because the named columns are easily presented in the tool. Because many columns contain low cardinality contents, the query performance using these attributes can be very good if bitmapped indexes are placed on each column. Positional designs can be scaled up to perhaps 100 or so columns before the databases and user interfaces become awkward or hard to maintain. Columnar databases are well suited to these kinds of designs because new columns can be easily added with minimal disruption to the internal storage of the data, and the low-cardinality columns containing only a few discrete values are dramatically compressed.

When the number of different attributes grows beyond your comfort zone, and if new attributes are added frequently, a bridge table is recommended. Ultimately, when you have a very large and expanding set of demographics indicators, using outriggers or mini-dimensions simply does not gracefully scale. For example, you may collect loan application information as a set of open ended name-value pairs, as shown in Figure 8-7. Name-value pair data is interesting because the values can be numeric, textual, a file pointer, a URL, or even a recursive reference to enclosed name-value pair data.

Over a period of time, you could collect hundreds or even thousands of different loan application variables. For a true name-value pair data source, the value field itself can be stored as a text string to handle the open-ended modality of the values, which is interpreted by the analysis application. In these situations whenever the number of variables is open-ended and unpredictable, a bridge table design is appropriate, as shown in Figure 8-8.

Loan Application Name-Value Pair Data
Photograph: <image>
Primary Income: $72345
Other Taxable Income: $2345
Tax-Free Income: $3456
Long Term Gains: $2367
Garnished Wages: $789
Pending Judgment Potential: $555
Alimony: $666
Jointly Owned Real Estate Appraised Value: $123456
Jointly Owned Real Estate Image: <image>
Jointly Owned Real Estate MLS Listing: <URL>
Percentage Ownership Real Estate: 50
Number Dependents: 4
Pre-existing Medical Disability: Back Injury
Number of Weeks Lost to Disability: 6
Employer Disability Support Statement: <document archive>
Previous Bankruptcy Declaration Type: 11
Years Since Bankruptcy: 8
Spouse Financial Disclosure: <name-value pair>
... 100 more name-value pairs...

Figure 8-7: Loan application name-value pair data.

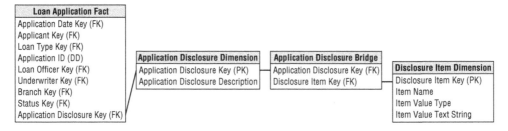

Figure 8-8: Bridge table for wide and sparse name-value pair data set.

Bridge Table for Multiple Customer Contacts

Large commercial customers have many points of contact, including decision makers, purchasing agents, department heads, and user liaisons; each point of contact is associated with a specific role. Because the number of contacts is unpredictable but possibly large, a bridge table design is a convenient way to handle this situation, as shown in Figure 8-9. Some care should be taken not to overdo the contact dimension and make it a dumping ground for every employee or citizen or salesperson or human being the organization interacts with. Restrict the dimension for this use case of contacts as part of the customer relationship.

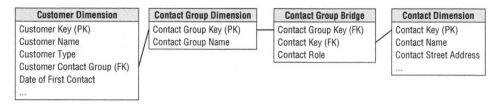

Figure 8-9: Bridge table design for multiple contacts.

Complex Customer Behavior

Customer behavior can be very complex. In this section, we'll discuss the handling of customer cohort groups and capturing sequential behavior. We'll also cover precise timespan fact tables and tagging fact events with indicators of customer satisfaction or abnormal scenarios.

Behavior Study Groups for Cohorts

With customer analysis, simple queries such as how much was sold to customers in this geographic area in the past year rapidly evolve to much more complex inquiries, such as how many customers bought more this past month than their average monthly purchase amount from last year. The latter question is too complex for business users to express in a single SQL request. Some BI tool vendors allow embedded subqueries, whereas others have implemented drill-across capabilities in which complex requests are broken into multiple select statements and then combined in a subsequent pass.

In other situations, you may want to capture the set of customers from a query or exception report, such as the top 100 customers from last year, customers who spent more than $1,000 last month, or customers who received a specific test solicitation, and then use that group of customers, called a *behavior study group*, for subsequent analyses without reprocessing to identify the initial condition. To create a behavior study group, run a query (or series of queries) to identify the set of customers you want to further analyze, and then capture the customer durable keys of the identified set as an actual physical table consisting of a single customer key column. By leveraging the customers' durable keys, the study group dimension is impervious to type 2 changes to the customer dimension which may occur after the study group members are identified.

> **NOTE** The secret to building complex behavioral study group queries is to capture the keys of the customers or products whose behavior you are tracking. You then use the captured keys to subsequently constrain other fact tables without having to rerun the original behavior analysis.

You can now use this special behavior study group dimension table of customer keys whenever you want to constrain any analysis on any table to that set of specially defined customers. The only requirement is that the fact table contains a customer key reference. The use of the behavior study group dimension is shown in Figure 8-10.

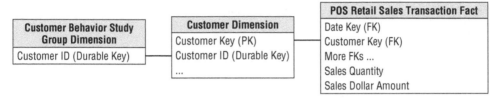

Figure 8-10: Behavior study group dimension joined to customer dimension's durable key.

The behavior study group dimension is attached with an equijoin to the customer dimension's durable key (refer to Customer ID in Figure 8-10). This can even be done in a view that hides the explicit join to the behavior dimension. In this way, the resulting dimensional model looks and behaves like an uncomplicated star. If the special dimension table is hidden under a view, it should be labeled to uniquely identify it as being associated with the top 100 customers, for example. Virtually any BI tool can now analyze this specially restricted schema without paying syntax or user-interface penalties for the complex processing that defined the original subset of customers.

NOTE   The exceptional simplicity of study group tables allows them to be combined with union, intersection, and set difference operations. For example, a set of problem customers this month can be intersected with the set of problem customers from last month to identify customers who were problems for two consecutive months.

Study groups can be made even more powerful by including an occurrence date as a second column correlated with each durable key. For example, a panel study of consumer purchases can be conducted where consumers enter the study when they exhibit some behavior such as switching brands of peanut butter. Then further purchases can be tracked after the event to see if they switched brands again. To get this right, these purchase events must be tracked with the right time stamps to get the behavior in the right sequence.

Like many design decisions, this one represents certain compromises. First, this approach requires a user interface for capturing, creating, and administering real physical behavior study group tables in the data warehouse. After a complex exception report has been defined, you need the ability to capture the resulting keys into an applet to create the special behavior study group dimension. These study group tables must live in the same space as the primary fact table because they are going to be joined directly to the customer dimension table. This obviously affects the DBA's responsibilities.

Step Dimension for Sequential Behavior

Most DW/BI systems do not have good examples of sequential processes. Usually measurements are taken at a particular place watching the stream of customers or products going by. Sequential measurements, by contrast, need to follow a customer or a product through a series of steps, often measured by different data capture systems. Perhaps the most familiar example of a sequential process comes from web events where a session is constructed by collecting individual page events on multiple web servers tied together via a customer's cookie. Understanding where an individual step fits in the overall sequence is a major challenge when analyzing sequential processes.

By introducing a step dimension, you can place an individual step into the context of an overall session, as shown in Figure 8-11.

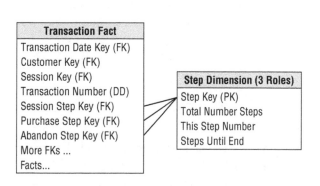

	Sample Step Dimension Rows:		
Step Key	Total Number Steps	This Step Number	Steps Until End
1	1	1	0
2	2	1	1
3	2	2	0
4	3	1	2
5	3	2	1
6	3	3	0
7	4	1	3
8	4	2	2
9	4	3	1
10	4	4	0

Figure 8-11: Step dimension to capture sequential activities.

The step dimension is an abstract dimension defined in advance. The first row in the dimension is used only for one-step sessions, where the current step is the first step and there are no more steps remaining. The next two rows in the step dimension are used for two-step sessions. The first row (Step Key = 2) is for step number 1 where there is one more step to go, and the next row (Step Key = 3) is for step number 2 where there are no more steps. The step dimension can be prebuilt to accommodate sessions of at least 100 steps. In Figure 8-11 you see the step dimension can be associated with a transaction fact table whose grain is the individual page event. In this example, the step dimension has three roles. The first role is the overall session. The second role is a successful purchase subsession, where a sequence of page events leads to a confirmed purchase. The third role is the abandoned shopping cart, where the sequence of page events is terminated without a purchase.

Using the step dimension, a specific page can immediately be placed into one or more understandable contexts (overall session, successful purchase, and abandoned shopping cart). But even more interestingly, a query can constrain exclusively only to the first page of successful purchases. This is a classic web event query, where the "attractant" page of successful sessions is identified. Conversely, a query could constrain exclusively to the last page of abandoned shopping carts, where the customer is about to decide to go elsewhere.

Another approach for modeling sequential behavior takes advantage of specific fixed codes for each possible step. If you track customer product purchases in a retail environment, and if each product can be encoded, for instance, as a 5 digit number, then you can create a single wide text column for each customer with the sequence of product codes. You separate the codes with a unique non-numeric character. Such a sequence might look like

11254|45882|53340|74934|21399|93636|36217|87952|…etc.

Now using wild cards you can search for specific products bought sequentially, or bought with other products intervening, or situations in which one product was bought but another was never bought. Modern relational DBMSs can store and process wide text fields of 64,000 characters or more with wild card searches.

Timespan Fact Tables

In more operational applications, you may want to retrieve the exact status of a customer at some arbitrary instant in the past. Was the customer on fraud alert when denied an extension of credit? How long had he been on fraud alert? How many times in the past two years has he been on fraud alert? How many customers were on fraud alert at some point in the past two years? All these questions can be addressed if you carefully manage the transaction fact table containing all customer events. The key modeling step is to include a pair of date/time stamps, as shown in Figure 8-12. The first date/time stamp is the precise moment of the transaction, and the second date/time stamp is the exact moment of the next transaction. If this is done correctly, then the time history of customer transactions maintains an unbroken sequence of date/time stamps with no gaps. Each actual transaction enables you to associate both demographics and status with the customer. Dense transaction fact tables are interesting because you potentially can change the demographics and especially the status each time a transaction occurs.

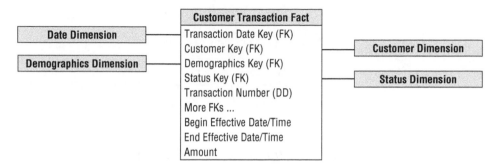

Figure 8-12: Twin date/time stamps in a timespan fact table.

The critical insight is that the pair of date/time stamps on a given transaction defines a span of time in which the demographics and the status are constant. Queries can take advantage of this "quiet" span of time. Thus if you want to know what the status of the customer "Jane Smith" was on July 18, 2013 at 6:33 am, you can issue the following query:

```
Select Customer.Customer_Name, Status
From Transaction_Fact, Customer_dim, Status_dim
Where Transaction_Fact_Customer_Key = Customer_dim.Customer_key
    And Transaction_Fact.Status_key = Status_dim.Status_key
    And Customer_dim.Customer_Name = 'Jane Smith'
    And #July 18, 2013 6:33:00# >= Transaction_Fact.Begin_Eff_
DateTime
    And #July 18, 2013 6:33:00# < Transaction_Fact.End_Eff_DateTime
```

These date/time stamps can be used to perform tricky queries on your customer base. If you want to find all the customers who were on fraud alert sometime in the year 2013, issue the following query:

```
Select Customer.Customer_Name
From Transaction_Fact, Customer_dim, Status_dim
Where <joins>
    And Status_dim Status_Description = 'Fraud Alert'
    And Transaction_Fact.Begin_Eff_DateTime <= 12/31/2013:23:59:59
    And Transaction_Fact.End_Eff_DateTime >= 1/1/2013:0:0:0
```

Amazingly, this one query handles all the possible cases of begin and end effective date/times straddling the beginning or end of 2013, being entirely contained with 2013, or completely straddling 2013.

You can even count the number of days each customer was on fraud alert in 2013:

```
Select Customer.Customer_Name,
    sum( least(12/31/2013:23:59:59, Transaction_Fact.End_Eff_
DateTime)
        - greatest(1/1/2013:0:0:0, Transaction_Fact.Begin_Eff_
DateTime))
From Transaction_Fact, Customer_dim, Status_dim
Where <joins>
    And Status_dim Status_Description = 'Fraud Alert'
    And Transaction_Fact.Begin_Eff_DateTime <= 12/31/2013:23:59:59
    And Transaction_Fact.End_Eff_DateTime >= 1/1/2013:0:0:0
Group By Customer.Customer_Name
```

Back Room Administration of Dual Date/Time Stamps

For a given customer, the date/time stamps on the sequence of transactions must form a perfect unbroken sequence with no gaps. It is tempting to make the end effective date/time stamp be one "tick" less than the beginning effective date/time stamp of the next transaction, so the query SQL can use the BETWEEN syntax rather than the uglier constraints shown above. However, in many situations the little gap defined by that tick could be significant if a transaction could fall within the gap. By making the end effective date/time exactly equal to the begin date time of the next transaction, you eliminate this risk.

Using the pair of date/time stamps requires a two-step process whenever a new transaction row is entered. In the first step, the end effective date/time stamp of the most current transaction must be set to a fictitious date/time far in the future. Although it would be semantically correct to insert NULL for this date/time, nulls become a headache when you encounter them in constraints because they can cause a database error when you ask if the field is equal to a specific value. By using a fictitious date/time far in the future, this problem is avoided.

In the second step, after the new transaction is entered into the database, the ETL process must retrieve the previous transaction and set its end effective date/time to the date/time of the newly entered transaction. Although this two-step process is a noticeable cost of this twin date/time approach, it is a classic and desirable trade-off between extra ETL overhead in the back room and reduced query complexity in the front room.

Tagging Fact Tables with Satisfaction Indicators

Although profitability might be the most important key performance indicator in many organizations, customer satisfaction is a close second. And in organizations without profit metrics, such as government agencies, satisfaction is (or should be) number one.

Satisfaction, like profitability, requires integration across many sources. Virtually every customer facing process is a potential source of satisfaction information, whether the source is sales, returns, customer support, billing, website activity, social media, or even geopositioning data.

Satisfaction data can be either numeric or textual. In the Chapter 6: Order Management, you saw how classic measures of customer satisfaction could be modeled both ways simultaneously. The on-time measures could be both additive numeric facts as well as textual attributes in a service level dimension. Other purely numeric measures of satisfaction include numbers of product returns, numbers of lost customers, numbers of support calls, and product attitude metrics from social media.

Figure 8-13 illustrates a frequent flyer satisfaction dimension that could be added to the flight activity fact tables described in Chapter 12. Textual satisfaction data is generally modeled in two ways, depending on the number of satisfaction attributes and the sparsity of the incoming data. When the list of satisfaction attributes is bounded and reasonably stable, a positional design is very effective, as shown in Figure 8-13.

Satisfaction Dimension
Satisfaction Key (PK)
Delayed Arrival Indicator
Diversion to Other Airport Indicator
Lost Luggage Indicator
Failure to Get Upgrade Indicator
Middle Seat Indicator
Personnel Problem Indicator

Figure 8-13: Positional satisfaction dimension for airline frequent flyers.

Tagging Fact Tables with Abnormal Scenario Indicators

Accumulating snapshot fact tables depend on a series of dates that implement the "standard scenario" for the pipeline process. For order fulfillment, you may have the steps of order created, order shipped, order delivered, order paid, and order returned as standard steps in the order scenario. This kind of design is successful when 90 percent or more of the orders progress through these steps (hopefully without the return) without any unusual exceptions.

But if an occasional situation deviates from the standard scenario, you don't have a good way to reveal what happened. For example, maybe when the order was shipped, the delivery truck had a flat tire. A decision was made to unload the delivery to another truck, but unfortunately it began to rain and the shipment was water damaged. Then it was refused by the customer, and ultimately there was a lawsuit. None of these unusual steps are modeled in the standard scenario in the accumulating snapshot. Nor should they be!

The way to describe unusual departures from the standard scenario is to add a delivery status dimension to the accumulating snapshot fact table. For the case of the weird delivery scenario, you tag this order fulfillment row with the status Weird. Then if the analyst wants to see the complete story, the analyst can join to a companion transaction fact table through the order number and line number that has every step of the story. The transaction fact table joins to a transaction dimension, which indeed has Flat Tire, Damaged Shipment, and Lawsuit as transactions. Even though this transaction dimension will grow over time with unusual entries, it is well bounded and stable.

Customer Data Integration Approaches

In typical environments with many customer facing processes, you need to choose between two approaches: a single customer dimension derived from all the versions of customer source system records or multiple customer dimensions tied together by conformed attributes.

Master Data Management Creating a Single Customer Dimension

In some cases, you can build a single customer dimension that is the "best of breed" choice among a number of available customer data sources. It is likely that such a conformed customer dimension is a distillation of data from several operational systems within your organization. But it would be typical for a unique customer to have multiple identifiers in multiple touch point systems. To make matters worse, data entry systems often don't incorporate adequate validation rules. Obviously, an operational CRM objective is to create a unique customer identifier and restrict the creation of unnecessary identifiers. In the meantime, the DW/BI team will likely be responsible for sorting out and integrating the disparate sources of customer information.

Some organizations are lucky enough to have a centralized *master data management (MDM)* system that takes responsibility for creating and controlling the single enterprise-wide customer entity. But such centralization is rare in the real world. More frequently, the data warehouse extracts multiple incompatible customer data files and builds a "downstream" MDM system. These two styles of MDM are illustrated in Figure 8-14.

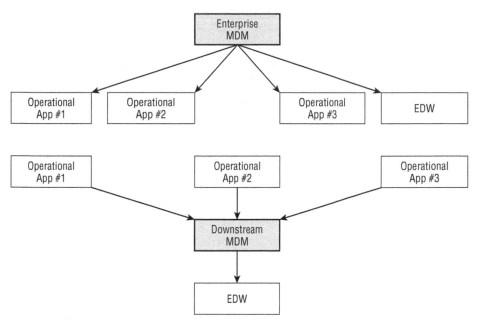

Figure 8-14: Two styles of master data management.

Unfortunately, there's no secret weapon for tackling this data consolidation. The attributes in the customer dimension should represent the "best" source available in the enterprise. A *national change of address (NCOA)* process should be integrated to ensure address changes are captured. Much of the heavy lifting associated with customer data consolidation demands customer matching or deduplicating logic. Removing duplicates or invalid addresses from large customer lists is critical to eliminate the costs associated with redundant, misdirected, or undeliverable communication, avoid misleading customer counts, and improve customer satisfaction through higher quality communication.

The science of customer matching is more sophisticated than it might first appear. It involves fuzzy logic, address parsing algorithms, and enormous look-up directories to validate address elements and postal codes, which vary significantly by country. There are specialized, commercially available software and service offerings that perform individual customer or commercial entity matching with remarkable accuracy. Often these products match the address components to standardized census codes, such as state codes, country codes, census tracts, block groups, metropolitan statistical areas (MSAs), and latitude/longitude, which facilitate the merging of external data. As discussed in Chapter 10, there are also householding capabilities to group or link customers sharing similar name and/or address information. Rather than merely performing intrafile matching, some services maintain an enormous external reference file of everyone in the United States to match against. Although these products and services are expensive and/or complex, it's worthwhile to make the investment if customer matching is strategic to the organization. In the end, effective consolidation of customer data depends on a balance of capturing the data as accurately as possible in the source systems, coupled with powerful data cleansing/merging tools in the ETL process.

Partial Conformity of Multiple Customer Dimensions

Enterprises today build customer knowledge stores that collect all the internal and external customer-facing data sources they can find. A large organization could have as many as 20 internal data sources and 50 or more external data sources, all of which relate in some way to the customer. These sources can vary wildly in granularity and consistency. Of course, there is no guaranteed high-quality customer key defined across all these data sources and no consistent attributes. You don't have any control over these sources. It seems like a hopeless mess.

In Chapter 4: Inventory, we laid the groundwork for conformed dimensions, which are the required glue for achieving integration across separate data sources. In the ideal case, you examine all the data sources and define a single comprehensive dimension which you attach to all the data sources, either simultaneously within a single tablespace or by replicating across multiple tablespaces. Such a single comprehensive conformed dimension becomes a wonderful driver for creating integrated queries, analyses, and reports by making consistent row labels available for drill-across queries.

But in the extreme integration world with dozens of customer-related dimensions of different granularity and different quality, such a single comprehensive customer dimension is impossible to build. Fortunately, you can implement a lighter weight kind of conformed customer dimension. Remember the essential requirement for two dimensions to be conformed is they share one or more specially administered attributes that have the same column names and data values. Instead of requiring dozens of customer-related dimensions to be identical, you only require they share the specially administered conformed attributes.

Not only have you taken the pressure off the data warehouse by relaxing the requirement that all the customer dimensions in your environment be equal from top to bottom, but in addition you can proceed in an incremental and agile way to plant the specially administered conformed attributes in each of the customer-related dimensions. For example, suppose you start by defining a fairly high-level categorization of customers called customer category. You can proceed methodically across all the customer-related dimensions, planting this attribute in each dimension without changing the grain of any target dimension and without invalidating any existing applications that depend on those dimensions. Over a period of time, you gradually increase the scope of integration as you add the special attributes to the separate customer dimensions attached to different sources. At any point in time, you can stop and perform drill-across reports using the dimensions where you have inserted the customer category attribute.

When the customer category attribute has been inserted into as many of the customer-related dimensions as possible, you can then define more conformed attributes. Geographic attributes such as city, county, state, and country should be even easier than the customer category. Over a period of time, the scope and power of the conformed customer dimensions let you do increasingly sophisticated analyses. This incremental development with its closely spaced deliverables fits an agile approach.

Avoiding Fact-to-Fact Table Joins

DW/BI systems should be built process-by-process, not department-by-department, on a foundation of conformed dimensions to support integration. You can imagine querying the sales or support fact tables to better understand a customers' purchase or service history.

Because the sales and support tables both contain a customer foreign key, you can further imagine joining both fact tables to a common customer dimension to simultaneously summarize sales facts along with support facts for a given customer. Unfortunately, the many-to-one-to-many join will return the wrong answer in a relational environment due to the differences in fact table cardinality, even when the relational database is working perfectly. There is no combination of inner, outer, left, or right joins that produces the desired answer when the two fact tables have incompatible cardinalities.

Consider the case in which you have a fact table of customer solicitations, and another fact table with the customer responses to solicitations, as shown in Figure 8-15. There is a one-to-many relationship between customer and solicitation, and another one-to-many relationship between customer and response. The solicitation and response fact tables have different cardinalities; in other words, not every solicitation results in a response (unfortunately for the marketing department) and some responses are received for which there is no solicitation. Simultaneously joining the solicitations fact table to the customer dimension, which is, in turn, joined to the responses fact table, does not return the correct answer in a relational DBMS due to the cardinality differences. Fortunately, this problem is easily avoided. You simply issue the drill-across technique explained in Chapter 4 to query the solicitations table and responses table in separate queries and then outer join the two answer sets. The drill-across approach has additional benefits for better controlling performance parameters, in addition to supporting queries that combine data from fact tables in different physical locations.

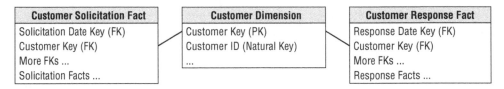

Figure 8-15: Many-to-one-to-many joined tables should *not* be queried with a single SELECT statement.

> **WARNING**   Be very careful when simultaneously joining a single dimension table to two fact tables of different cardinality. In many cases, relational engines return the "wrong" answer.

If business users are frequently combining data from multiple business processes, a final approach is to define an additional fact table that combines the data once into a consolidated fact table rather than relying on users to consistently and accurately combine the data on their own, as described in Chapter 7. Merely using SQL to drill across fact tables to combine the results makes more sense when the underlying processes are less closely correlated. Of course, when constructing the consolidated fact table, you still need to establish business rules to deal with the differing cardinality. For example, does the consolidated fact table include all the solicitations and responses or only those where both a solicitation and response occurred?

Low Latency Reality Check

The behavior of a customer in the last few hours or minutes can be extremely interesting. You may even want to make decisions while dealing with the customer in real time. But you need to be thoughtful in recognizing the costs and limitations of low latency data. Generally, data quality suffers as the data is delivered closer to real time.

Business users may automatically think that the faster the information arrives in the DW/BI system, the better. But decreasing the latency increases the data quality problems. Figure 20-6 summarizes the issues that arise as data is delivered faster. In the conventional batch world, perhaps downloading a batch file once each 24 hours, you typically get complete transaction sets. For example, if a commercial customer places an order, they may have to pass a credit check and verify the final commitment. The batch download includes orders only where all these steps have taken place. In addition, because the batch download is processed just once each 24 hours, the ETL team has the time to run the full spectrum of data quality checks, as we'll describe in Chapter 19: ETL Subsystems and Techniques.

If the data is extracted many times per day, then the guarantee of complete transaction sets may have to be relinquished. The customer may have placed the order but has not passed the credit check. Thus there is the possibility that results may have to be adjusted after the fact. You also may not run the full spectrum of data quality checks because you don't have time for extensive multitable lookups. Finally, you may have to post data into the data warehouse when all the keys have not been resolved. In this case, temporary dimensional entries may need to be used while waiting for additional data feeds.

Finally, if you deliver data instantaneously, you may be getting only transaction fragments, and you may not have time to perform any data quality checks or other processing of the data.

Low latency data delivery can be very valuable, but the business users need to be informed about these trade-offs. An interesting hybrid approach is to provide low latency intraday delivery but then revert to a batch extract at night, thereby correcting various data problems that could not be addressed during the day. We discuss the impact of low latency requirements on the ETL system in Chapter 20: ETL System Design and Development Process and Tasks.

Summary

In this chapter, we focused exclusively on the customer, beginning with an overview of customer relationship management (CRM) basics. We then delved into design issues surrounding the customer dimension table. We discussed name and address parsing where operational fields are decomposed to their basic elements so that they can be standardized and validated. We explored several other types of common customer dimension attributes, such as dates, segmentation attributes, and aggregated facts. Dimension outriggers that contain a large block of relatively low-cardinality attributes were described.

This chapter introduced the use of bridge tables to handle unpredictable, sparsely populated dimension attributes, as well as multivalued dimension attributes.

We also explored several complex customer behavior scenarios, including sequential activities, timespan fact tables, and tagging fact events with indicators to identify abnormal situations.

We closed the chapter by discussing alternative approaches for consistently identifying customers and consolidating a rich set of characteristics from the source data, either via operational master data management or downstream processing in the ETL back room with potentially partial conformity. Finally, we touched on the challenges of low latency data requirements.

9

Human Resources Management

This chapter, which focuses on *human resources* (*HR*) data, is the last in the series dealing with cross-industry business applications. Similar to the accounting and finance data described in Chapter 7: Accounting, HR information is disseminated broadly throughout the organization. Organizations want to better understand their employees' demographics, skills, earnings, and performance to maximize their impact. In this chapter we'll explore several dimensional modeling techniques in the context of HR data.

Chapter 9 discusses the following concepts:

- Dimension tables to track employee profile changes
- Periodic headcount snapshots
- Bus matrix for a snippet of HR-centric processes
- Pros and cons of packaged DW/BI solutions or data models
- Recursive employee hierarchies
- Multivalued skill keyword attributes handled via dimension attributes, outriggers, or bridges
- Survey questionnaire data
- Text comments

Employee Profile Tracking

Thus far the dimensional models we have designed closely resemble each other; the fact tables contain key performance metrics that typically can be added across all the dimensions. It is easy for dimensional modelers to get lulled into a kind of additive complacency. In most cases, this is exactly how it is supposed to work. However, with HR employee data, a robust employee dimension supports numerous metrics required by the business on its own.

To frame the problem with a business vignette, let's assume you work in the HR department of a large enterprise. Each employee has a detailed HR profile with at least 100 attributes, including hire date, job grade, salary, review dates, review outcomes, vacation entitlement, organization, education, address, insurance plan, and many others. Employees are constantly hired, transferred, and promoted, as well as adjusting their profiles in a variety of ways.

A high-priority business requirement is to accurately track and analyze employee profile changes. You might immediately visualize a schema in which each employee profile change event is captured in a transaction-grained fact table, as depicted in Figure 9-1. The granularity of this somewhat generalized fact table would be one row per employee profile transaction. Because no numeric metrics are associated with changes made to employee profiles, such as a new address or job grade promotion, the fact table is factless.

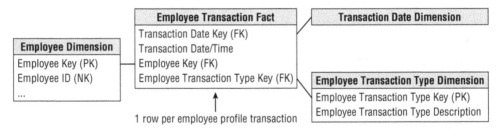

Figure 9-1: Initial draft schema for tracking employees' profile changes.

In this draft schema, the dimensions include the transaction date, transaction type, and employee. The transaction type dimension refers to the reason code that caused the creation of this particular row, such as a promotion or address change. The employee dimension is extremely wide with many attribute columns.

We envision using the type 2 slowly changing dimension technique for tracking changed profile attributes within the employee dimension. Consequently, with every employee profile transaction in the Figure 9-1 fact table, you would also create a new type 2 row in the employee dimension that represents the employee's profile as a result of the profile change event. This new row continues to accurately describe the employee until the next employee transaction occurs at some indeterminate time in the future. The alert reader is quick to point out that the employee profile transaction fact table and type 2 employee dimension table have the same number of rows; plus they are almost always joined to one another. At this point dimensional modeling alarms should be going off. You certainly don't want to have as many rows in a fact table as you do in a related dimension table.

Instead of using the initial schema, you can simplify the design by embellishing the employee dimension table to make it more powerful and thereby doing away with the profile transaction event fact table. As depicted in Figure 9-2, the employee dimension contains a snapshot of the employee profile characteristics following the employee's profile change. The transaction type description becomes a change reason attribute in the employee dimension to track the cause for the profile change. In some cases, the affected characteristics are numeric. If the numeric attributes are summarized rather than simply constrained upon, they belong in a fact table instead.

Employee Dimension
Employee Key (PK)
Employee ID (NK)
Employee Name ...
Employee Address ...
Job Grade ...
Salary ...
Education ...
Original Hire Date (FK)
Last Review Date (FK)
Appraisal Rating ...
Health Insurance Plan ...
Vacation Plan ...
Change Reason Code
Change Reason Description
Row Effective Date/Time
Row Expiration Date/Time
Current Row Indicator

Figure 9-2: Employee dimension with profile characteristics.

As you'd expect, the surrogate employee key is the primary key of the dimension table; the durable natural employee ID used in the HR operational system to persistently identify an employee is included as a dimension attribute.

Precise Effective and Expiration Timespans

As discussed in Chapter 5: Procurement with the coverage of slowly changing dimension techniques, you should include two columns on the employee dimension to capture when a specific row is effective and then expired. These columns define a precise timespan during which the employee's profile is accurate. Historically, when daily data latency was the norm, the effective and expiration columns were dates. However, if you load data from any business process on a more frequent basis, the columns should be date/time stamps so that you can associate the appropriate employee profile row, which may differ between 9 a.m. and 9 p.m. on the same day, to operational events.

The expiration attribute for the current row is set to a future date. When the row needs to be expired because the ETL system has detected a new profile of attributes, the expiration attribute is typically set to "just before" the new row's effective stamp, meaning either the prior day, minute, or second.

If the employee's profile is accurately changed for a period of time, then the employee reverts back to an earlier set of characteristics, a new employee dimension row is inserted. You should resist the urge to simply revisit the earlier profile row and modify the expiration date because multiple dimension rows would be effective at the same time.

The current row indicator enables the most recent status of any employee to be retrieved quickly. If a new profile row occurs for this employee, the indicator in the former profile row needs to be updated to indicate it is no longer the current profile.

On its own, a date/time stamped type 2 employee dimension answers a number of interesting HR inquiries. You can choose an exact historical point in time and ask how many employees you have and what their detailed profiles were at that specific moment by constraining the date/time to be equal to or greater than the effective date/time and strictly less than the expiration date/time. The query can perform counts and constraints against all the rows returned from these constraints.

Dimension Change Reason Tracking

When a dimension row contains type 2 attributes, you can embellish it with a change reason. In this way, some ETL-centric metadata is embedded with the actual data. The change reason attribute could contain a two-character abbreviation for each changed attribute on a dimension row. For example, the change reason attribute value for a last name change could be LN or a more legible value, such as Last Name, depending on the intended usage and audience. If someone asks how many people changed ZIP codes last year, the `SELECT` statement would include a `LIKE` operator and wild cards, such as `"WHERE ChangeReason LIKE '%ZIP%'"`.

Because multiple dimension attributes may change concurrently and be represented by a single new row in the dimension, the change reason would be multivalued. As we'll explore later in the chapter when discussing employee skills, the multiple reason codes could be handled as a single text string attribute, such as "|Last Name|ZIP|" or via a multivalued bridge table.

NOTE The effective and expiration date/time stamps, along with a reason code description, on each row of a type 2 slowly changing dimension allows very precise time slicing of the dimension by itself.

Finally, employee profile changes may be captured in the underlying source system by a set of micro-transactions corresponding to each individual employee attribute change. In the DW/BI system, you may want to encapsulate the series of micro-transactions from the source system and treat them as a super transaction, such as an employee promotion because it would be silly to treat these artificial micro-transactions as separate type 2 changes. The new type 2 employee dimension row would reflect all the relevant changed attributes in one step. Identifying these super transactions may be tricky. Obviously the best way to identify them is to ensure the HR operational application captures the higher level action.

Profile Changes as Type 2 Attributes or Fact Events

We just described the handling of employee attribute changes as slowly changing dimension type 2 attributes with profile effective and expiration dates within the employee dimension. Designers sometimes wholeheartedly embrace this pattern and try to leverage it to capture every employee-centric change. This results in a dimension table with potentially hundreds of attributes and millions of rows for a 100,000-employee organization given the attributes' volatility.

Tracking changes within the employee dimension table enables you to easily associate the employee's accurate profile with multiple business processes. You simply load these fact tables with the employee key in effect when the fact event occurred, and filter and group based on the full spectrum of employee attributes.

But the pendulum can swing too far. You probably shouldn't use the employee dimension to track every employee review event, every benefit participation event, or every professional development event. As illustrated in Figure 9-4's bus matrix in the next section, many of these events involve other dimensions, like an event date, organization, benefit description, reviewer, approver, exit interviewer, separation reasons, and the list goes on. Consequently, most of them should be handled as separate process-centric fact tables. Although many human resources events are factless, capturing them within a fact table enables business users to easily count or trend by time periods and all the other associated dimensions.

It's certainly common to include the outcome of these HR events, like the job grade resulting from a promotion, as an attribute on the employee dimension. But designers sometimes err by including lots of foreign keys to outriggers for the reviewer, benefit, separation reason and other dimensions within the employee dimension, resulting in an overloaded dimension that's difficult to navigate.

Headcount Periodic Snapshot

In addition to profiling employees in HR, you also want to report statuses of the employees on a regular basis. Business managers are interested in counts, statistics, and totals, including number of employees, salary paid, vacation days taken, vacation days accrued, number of new hires, and number of promotions. They want to analyze the data by all possible slices, including time and organization, plus employee characteristics.

As shown in Figure 9-3, the employee headcount periodic snapshot consists of an ordinary looking fact table with three dimensions: month, employee, and organization. The month dimension table contains the usual descriptors for the corporate calendar at the month grain. The employee key corresponds to the employee dimension row in effect at the end of the last day of the given reporting month to guarantee the month-end report is a correct depiction of the employees' profiles. The organization dimension contains a description of the organization to which the employee belongs at the close of the relevant month.

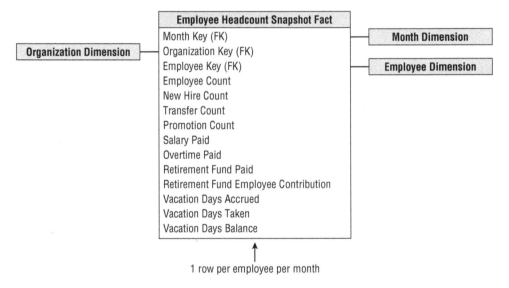

Figure 9-3: Employee headcount periodic snapshot.

The facts in this headcount snapshot consist of monthly numeric metrics and counts that may be difficult to calculate from the employee dimension table alone. These monthly counts and metrics are additive across all the dimensions or dimension attributes, except for any facts labeled as balances. These balances, like all balances, are semi-additive and must be averaged across the month dimension after adding across the other dimensions.

Bus Matrix for HR Processes

Although an employee dimension with precise type 2 slowly changing dimension tracking coupled with a monthly periodic snapshot of core HR performance metrics is a good start, they just scratch the surface when it comes to tracking HR data.

Figure 9-4 illustrates other processes that HR professionals and functional managers are likely keen to analyze. We've embellished this preliminary bus matrix with the type of fact table that might be used for each process; however, your source data realities and business requirements may warrant a different or complementary treatment.

	Fact Type	Date	Position	Employee	Organization	Benefit
Hiring Processes						
Employee Position Snapshot	Periodic	X	X	Empl Mgr	X	
Employee Requisition Pipeline	Accumulating	X	X	Empl Mgr	X	
Employee Hiring	Transaction	X	X	Empl Mgr	X	
Employee "On Board" Pipeline	Accumulating	X	X	Empl Mgr	X	
Benefits Processes						
Employee Benefits Eligibility	Periodic	X		X	X	X
Employee Benefits Application	Accumulating	X		X	X	X
Employee Benefit Participation	Periodic	X		X	X	X
Employee Management Processes						
Employee Headcount Snapshot	Periodic	X		X	X	X
Employee Compensation	Transaction	X		X	X	X
Employee Benefit Accruals	Transaction	X		X	X	X
Employee Performance Review Pipeline	Accumulating	X		Empl Mgr	X	X
Employee Performance Review	Transaction	X		Empl Mgr	X	X
Employee Prof Dev Completed Courses	Transaction	X		X	X	
Employee Disciplinary Action Pipeline	Accumulating	X		Empl Mgr	X	
Employee Separations	Transaction	X		Empl Mgr	X	

Figure 9-4: Bus matrix rows for HR processes.

Some of these business processes capture performance metrics, but many result in factless fact tables, such as benefit eligibility or participation.

Packaged Analytic Solutions and Data Models

Many organizations purchase a vendor solution to address their operational HR application needs. Most of these products offer an add-on DW/BI solution. In addition, other vendors sell standard data models, potentially with prebuilt data loaders for the popular HR application products.

Vendors and proponents argue these standard, prebuilt solutions and models allow for more rapid, less risky implementations by reducing the scope of the data modeling and ETL development effort. After all, every HR department hires employees, signs them up for benefits, compensates them, reviews them, and eventually processes employee separations. Why bother re-creating the wheel by designing custom data models and solutions to support these common business processes when you can buy a standard data model or complete solution instead?

Although there are undoubtedly common functions, especially within the HR space, businesses typically have unique peculiarities. To handle these nuances, most application software vendors introduce abstractions in their products, which enable them to be more easily "customized."

These abstractions, like the party table and associated apparatus to describe each role or generic attribute column names rather than more meaningful labels, provide flexibility to adapt to a variety of business situations. Although implementation adaptability is a win for vendors who want their products to address a broad range of potential customers' business scenarios, the downside is the associated complexity.

HR professionals who live with the vendor's product 24x7 are often willing to adjust their vocabulary to accommodate the abstractions. But these abstractions can feel like a foreign language for less-immersed functional managers. Delivering data to the business via a packaged DW/BI solution or industry-standard data model may bypass the necessary translations into the business's vernacular.

Besides the reliance on the vendor's terminology instead of incorporating the business's vocabulary in the DW/BI solution, another potential sharp corner is the integration of source data from other domains. Can you readily conform the dimensions in the vendor solution or industry model with other internally available master data? If not, the packaged model is destined to become another isolated stovepipe data set. Clearly, this outcome is unappealing; although it may be less of an obstacle if all your operational systems are supported by the same ERP vendor, or you're a small organization without an IT shop doing independent development.

What can you realistically expect to gain from a packaged model? Prebuilt generic models can help identify core business processes and associate common dimensions. That provides some comfort for DW/BI teams feeling initially overwhelmed by the design task. After a few days or weeks studying the standard model, most teams gain enough confidence to want to customize the schema for their data.

However, is this knowledge worth the price tag associated with the packaged solution or data model? You could likely gain the same insight by spending a few weeks with the business users. You'd not only improve your understanding of the business's needs, but also begin bonding business users to the DW/BI initiative.

It's also worth mentioning that just because a packaged model or solution costs thousands of dollars doesn't mean it exhibits generally accepted dimensional modeling best practices. Unfortunately, some standard models embody common dimensional modeling design flaws; this isn't surprising if the model's designers focused more on best practices for source system data capture rather than those required for BI reporting and analytics. It's difficult to design a predefined generic model, even if the vendor owns the data capture source code.

Recursive Employee Hierarchies

A common employee characteristic is the name of the employee's manager. You could simply embed this attribute along with the other attributes in the employee dimension. But if the business users want more than the manager's name, more complex structures are necessary.

One approach is to include the manager's employee key as another foreign key in the fact table, as shown in Figure 9-5. This manager employee key joins to a role-playing employee dimension where every attribute name refers to "manager" to differentiate the manager's profile from the employee's. This approach associates the employee and their manager whenever a row is inserted into a fact table. BI analyses can easily filter and group by either employee or manager attributes with virtually identical query performance because both dimensions provide symmetrical access to the fact table. The downside of this approach is these dual foreign keys must be embedded in every fact table to support managerial reporting.

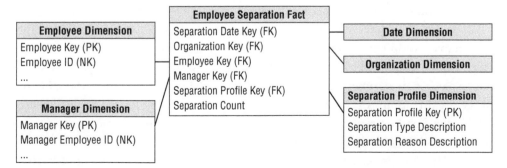

Figure 9-5: Dual role-playing employee and manager dimensions.

Another option is to include the manager's employee key as an attribute on the employee's dimension row. The manager key would join to an outrigger consisting of a role play on the employee dimension where all the attributes reference "manager" to differentiate them from the employee's characteristics, as shown in Figure 9-6.

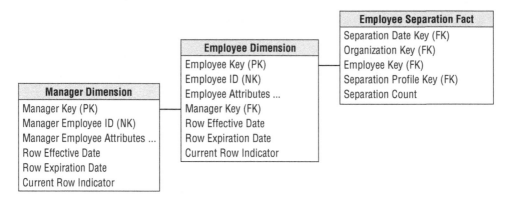

Figure 9-6: Manager role-playing dimension as an outrigger.

If the manager's foreign key in the employee dimension is designated as a type 2 attribute, then new employee rows would be generated with each manager change. However, we encourage you to think carefully about the underlying ETL business rules.

Change Tracking on Embedded Manager Key

Let's walk through an example. Abby is Hayden's manager. With the outrigger approach just described, Hayden's employee dimension row would include an attribute linking to Abby's row in the manager role-play employee dimension. If Hayden's manager changes, and assuming the business wants to track these historical changes, then treating the manager foreign key as a type 2 and creating a new row for Hayden to capture his new profile with a new manager would be appropriate.

However, think about the desired outcome if Abby were still Hayden's manager, but her employee profile changes, perhaps caused by something as innocuous as a home address change. If the home address is designated as a type 2 attribute, this move would spawn a new employee dimension row for Abby. If the manager key is also designated as a type 2 attribute, then Abby's new employee key would also spawn a new dimension row for Hayden. Now imagine Abby is the CEO of a large organization. A type 2 change in her profile would ripple through the entire table; you'd end up replicating a new profile row for every employee due to a single type 2 attribute change on the CEO's profile.

Does the business want to capture these manager profile changes? If not, perhaps the manager key on the employee's row should be the manager's durable natural key linked to a role-playing dimension limited to just the current row for each manager's durable natural key in the dimension.

If you designate the manager's key in the employee dimension to be a type 1 attribute, it would always associate an employee with her current manager. Although this simplistic approach obliterates history, it may completely satisfy the business user's needs.

Drilling Up and Down Management Hierarchies

Adding an attribute, either a textual label or a foreign key to a role-playing dimension, to an employee dimension row is appropriate for handling the fixed depth, many-to-one employee-to-manager relationship. However, more complex approaches might be required if the business wants to navigate a deeper recursive hierarchy, such as identifying an employee's entire management chain or drilling down to identify the activity for all employees who directly or indirectly work for a given manager.

If you use an OLAP tool to query employee data, the embedded manager key on every employee dimension row may suffice. Popular OLAP products contain a parent/child hierarchy structure that works smoothly with variable depth recursive hierarchies. In fact, this is one of the strengths of OLAP products.

However, if you want to query the recursive employee/manager relationship in the relational environment, you must use Oracle's nonstandard `CONNECT BY` syntax or SQL's recursive common table extension (CTE) syntax. Both approaches are virtually unworkable for business users armed with a BI reporting tool.

So you're left with the options described in Chapter 7 for dealing with variable depth customer hierarchies. In Figure 9-7, the employee dimension from Figure 9-6 relates to the fact table through a bridge table. The bridge table has one row for each manager and each employee who is directly or indirectly in their management chain, plus an additional row for the manager to himself. The bridge joins shown in Figure 9-7 enable you to drill down within a manager's chain of command.

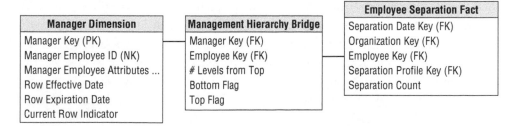

Figure 9-7: Bridge table to drill down into a manager's reporting structure.

As previously described, there are several disadvantages to this approach. The bridge table is somewhat challenging to build, plus it contains many rows, so query performance can suffer. The BI user experience is complicated for ad hoc queries, although we've seen analysts effectively use it. Finally, if users want to aggregate information up rather than down a management chain, the join paths must be reversed.

Once again, the situation is further complicated if you want to track employee profile changes in conjunction with the bridge table. If the manager and employee reflect employee profiles with type 2 changes, the bridge table will experience rapid growth, especially when senior management profile changes cause new keys to ripple across the organization.

You could use durable natural keys in the bridge table, instead of the employee keys which capture type 2 profile changes. Limiting the relationship to the management hierarchy's current profiles is one thing. However, if the business wants to retain a history of employee/manager rollups, you need to embellish the bridge table with effective and expiration dates that capture the effective timespan for each employee/manager relationship.

The propagation of new rows in this bridge table using durable keys is substantially reduced compared to the Figure 9-7 bridge because new rows are added when reporting relationships change, not when any type 2 employee attribute is modified. A bridge table built on durable keys is easier to manage, but quite challenging to navigate, especially given the need to associate the relevant organizational structures with the event dates in the fact table. Given the complexities, the bridge table should be buried within a canned BI application for all but a small subset of power BI users.

The alternative approaches discussed in Chapter 7 for handling recursive hierarchies, like the pathstring attribute, are also relevant to the management hierarchy conundrum. Unfortunately, there's no silver bullet solution for handling these complex structures in a simple and fast way.

Multivalued Skill Keyword Attributes

Let's assume the IT department wants to supplement the employee dimension with technical skillset proficiency information. You could consider these technical skills, such as programming languages, operating systems, or database platforms, to be keywords describing employees. Each employee is tagged with a number of skill keywords. You want to search the IT employee population by their descriptive skills.

If the technical skills of interest were a finite number, you could include them as individual attributes in the employee dimension. The advantage of using positional dimension attributes, such as a Linux attribute with domain values such as

Linux Skills and No Linux Skills, is they're easy to query and deliver fast query performance. This approach works well to a point but falls apart when the number of potential skills expands.

Skill Keyword Bridge

More realistically, each employee will have a variable, unpredictable number of skills. In this case, the skill keyword attribute is a prime candidate to be a multi-valued dimension. Skill keywords, by their nature, are open-ended; new skills are added regularly as domain values. We'll show two logically equivalent modeling schemes for handling open-ended sets of skills.

Figure 9-8 shows a multivalued dimension design for handling the skills as an outrigger bridge table to the employee dimension table. As you'll see in Chapter 14: Healthcare, sometimes the multivalued bridge table is joined directly to a fact table.

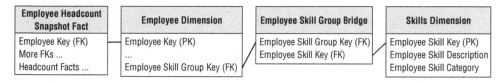

Figure 9-8: Skills group keyword bridge table.

The skills group bridge identifies a given set of skill keywords. IT employees who are proficient in Oracle, Unix, and SQL would be assigned the same skills group key. In the skills group bridge table, there would be three rows for this particular group, one for each of the associated skill keywords (Oracle, Unix, and SQL).

AND/OR Query Dilemma

Assuming you built the schema shown in Figure 9-8, you are still left with a serious query problem. Query requests against the skill keywords fall into two categories. The OR queries (for example, Unix or Linux experience) can be satisfied by a simple OR constraint on the skills description attribute in the skills dimension table. However, AND queries (for example, Unix and Linux experience) are difficult because the AND constraint is a constraint across two rows in the skills dimension. SQL is notoriously poor at handling constraints across rows. The answer is to create SQL code using unions and intersections, probably in a custom interface that hides the complex logic from the business user. The SQL code would look like this:

```
(SELECT employee_ID, employee_name
FROM Employee, SkillBridge, Skills
WHERE Employee.SkillGroupKey = SkillBridge.SkillGroupKey AND
  SkillGroup.SkillKey = Skill.SkillKey AND
```

```
    Skill.Skill = "UNIX")
UNION / INTERSECTION
 (SELECT employee_ID, employee_name
  FROM Employee, SkillBridge, Skills
  WHERE Employee.SkillGroupKey = SkillBridge.SkillGroupKey AND
    SkillGroup.SkillKey = Skill.SkillKey AND
    Skill.Skill = "LINUX")
```

Using the UNION lists employees with Unix or Linux experience, whereas using INTERSECTION identifies employees with Unix and Linux experience.

Skill Keyword Text String

You can remove the many-to-many bridge and the need for union/intersection SQL by simplifying the design. One approach would be to add a skills list outrigger to the employee dimension containing one long text string concatenating all the skill keywords for that list key. You would need a special delimiter such as a backslash or vertical bar at the beginning of the skills text string and after each skill in the list. Thus the skills string containing Unix and C++ would look like |Unix|C++|. This outrigger approach presumes a number of employees share a common list of skills. If the lists are not reused frequently, you could collapse the skills list outrigger by simply including the skills list text string as an employee dimension attribute, as shown in Figure 9-9.

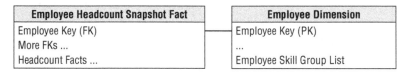

Figure 9-9: Delimited skills list string.

Text string searches can be challenging because of the ambiguity caused by searching on uppercase or lowercase. Is it UNIX or Unix or unix? You can resolve this by coercing the skills list to upper case with the UCase function in most SQL environments.

With the design in Figure 9-9, the AND/OR dilemma can be addressed in a single SELECT statement. The OR constraint looks like this:

```
UCase(skill_list) like '%|UNIX|% OR UCase(skill_list) like '%|LINUX|%'
```

Meanwhile, the AND constraint has exactly the same structure:

```
UCase(skill_list) like '%|UNIX|' AND UCase(skill_list) like '%|LINUX|%'
```

The % symbol is a wild card pattern-matching character defined in SQL that matches zero or more characters. The vertical bar delimiter is used explicitly in the constraints to exactly match the desired keywords and not get erroneous matches.

The keyword list approach shown in Figure 9-9 can work in any relational database because it is based on standard SQL. Although the text string approach facilitates AND/OR searching, it doesn't support queries that count by skill keyword.

Survey Questionnaire Data

HR departments often collect survey data from employees, especially when gathering peer and/or management review data. The department analyzes questionnaire responses to determine the average rating for a reviewed employee and within a department.

To handle questionnaire data in a dimensional model, a fact table with one row for each question on a respondent's survey is typically created, as illustrated in Figure 9-10. Two role-playing employee dimensions in the schema correspond to the responding employee and reviewed employee. The survey dimension has descriptors about the survey instrument. The question dimension provides the question and its categorization; presumably, the same question is asked on multiple surveys. The survey and question dimensions can be useful when searching for specific topics in a broad database of questionnaires. The response dimension contains the responses and perhaps categories of responses, such as favorable or hostile.

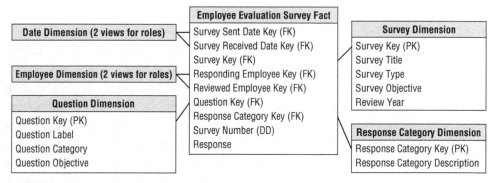

Figure 9-10: Survey schema.

Creating the simple schema in Figure 9-10 supports robust slicing and dicing of survey data. Variations of this schema design would be useful for analyzing all types of survey data, including customer satisfaction and product usage feedback.

Text Comments

Facts are typically thought of as continuously valued numeric measures; dimension attributes, on the other hand, are drawn from a discrete list of domain values. So how do you handle textual comments, such as a manager's remarks on a performance review or freeform feedback on a survey question, which seem to defy clean classification into the fact or dimension category? Although IT professionals may instinctively want to simply exclude them from a dimensional design, business users may demand they're retained to further describe the performance metrics.

After it's been confirmed the business is unwilling to relinquish the text comments, you should determine if the comments can be parsed into well-behaved dimension attributes. Although there are sometimes opportunities to categorize the text, such as a compliment versus complaint, the full text verbiage is typically also required.

Because freeform text takes on so many potential values, designers are sometimes tempted to store the text comment within the fact table. Although cognizant that fact tables are typically limited to foreign keys, degenerate dimensions, and numeric facts, they contend the text comment is just another degenerate dimension. Unfortunately, text comments don't qualify as degenerate dimensions.

Freeform text fields shouldn't be stored in the fact table because they just add bulky clutter to the table. Depending on the database platform, this relatively low value bulk may get dragged along on every operation involving the fact table's much more valuable performance metrics.

Rather than treating the comments as textual metrics, we recommend retaining them outside the fact table. The comments should either be captured in a separate comments dimensions (with a corresponding foreign key in the fact table) or as an attribute on a transaction-grained dimension table. In some situations, identical comments are observed multiple times. At a minimum, this typically occurs with the No Comment comment. If the cardinality of the comments is less than the number of transactions, the text should be captured in a comments dimension. Otherwise, if there's a unique comment for every event, it's treated as a transaction dimension attribute. In either case, regardless of whether the comments are handled in a comment or transaction dimension, the query performance when this sizeable dimension is joined to the fact table will be slow. However, by the time users are viewing comments, they've likely significantly filtered their query as they can realistically read only a limited number of comments. Meanwhile, the more common analyses focusing on the fact table's performance metrics won't be burdened by the extra weight of the textual comments on every fact table query.

Summary

In this chapter, we discussed several concepts in the context of HR data. First, we further elaborated on the advantages of embellishing an employee dimension table. In the world of HR, this single table is used to address a number of questions regarding the status and profile of the employee base at any point in time. We drafted a bus matrix representing multiple processes within the HR arena and highlighted a core headcount snapshot fact table, along with the potential advantages and disadvantages of vendor-designed solutions and data models. The handling of managerial rollups and multivalued dimension attributes was discussed. Finally, we provided a brief overview regarding the handling of survey or questionnaire data, along with text comments.

10 Financial Services

The financial services industry encompasses a wide variety of businesses, including credit card companies, brokerage firms, and mortgage providers. In this chapter, we'll primarily focus on the retail bank since most readers have some degree of personal familiarity with this type of financial institution. A full-service bank offers a breadth of products, including checking accounts, savings accounts, mortgage loans, personal loans, credit cards, and safe deposit boxes. This chapter begins with a very simplistic schema. We then explore several schema extensions, including the handling of the bank's broad portfolio of heterogeneous products that vary significantly by line of business.

We want to remind you that industry focused chapters like this one are not intended to provide full-scale industry solutions. Although various dimensional modeling techniques are discussed in the context of a given industry, the techniques are certainly applicable to other businesses. If you don't work in financial services, you still need to read this chapter. If you do work in financial services, remember that the schemas in this chapter should not be viewed as complete.

Chapter 10 discusses the following concepts:

- Bus matrix snippet for a bank
- Dimension triage to avoid the "too few dimensions" trap
- Household dimensions
- Bridge tables to associate multiple customers with an account, along with weighting factors
- Multiple mini-dimensions in a single fact table
- Dynamic value banding of facts for reporting
- Handling heterogeneous products across lines of business, each with unique metrics and/or dimension attributes, as supertype and subtype schemas
- Hot swappable dimensions

Banking Case Study and Bus Matrix

The bank's initial goal is to better analyze the bank's accounts. Business users want the ability to slice and dice individual accounts, as well as the residential household groupings to which they belong. One of the bank's major objectives is to market more effectively by offering additional products to households that already have one or more accounts with the bank. Figure 10-1 illustrates a portion of a bank's bus matrix.

	Date	Prospect	Customer	Account	Product	Household	Branch
New Business Solicitation	X	X			X		
Lead Tracking	X	X			X		X
Account Application Pipeline	X	X	X	X	X		X
Account Initiation	X	X	X	X	X	X	X
Account Transactions	X		X	X	X	X	X
Account Monthly Snapshot	X		X	X	X	X	X
Account Servicing Activities	X		X	X	X	X	X

Figure 10-1: Subset of bus matrix rows for a bank.

After conducting interviews with managers and analysts around the bank, the following set of requirements were developed:

- Business users want to see five years of historical monthly snapshot data on every account.
- Every account has a primary balance. The business wants to group different types of accounts in the same analyses and compare primary balances.
- Every type of account (known as products within the bank) has a set of custom dimension attributes and numeric facts that tend to be quite different from product to product.
- Every account is deemed to belong to a single household. There is a surprising amount of volatility in the account/household relationships due to changes in marital status and other life stage factors.
- In addition to the household identification, users are interested in demographic information both as it pertains to individual customers and households. In addition, the bank captures and stores behavior scores relating to the activity or characteristics of each account and household.

Dimension Triage to Avoid Too Few Dimensions

Based on the previous business requirements, the grain and dimensionality of the initial model begin to emerge. You can start with a fact table that records the primary balances of every account at the end of each month. Clearly, the grain of the fact table is one row for each account each month. Based on that grain declaration, you can initially envision a design with only two dimensions: month and account. These two foreign keys form the fact table primary key, as shown in Figure 10-2. A data-centric designer might argue that all the other description information, such as household, branch, and product characteristics should be embedded as descriptive attributes of the account dimension because each account has only one household, branch, and product associated with it.

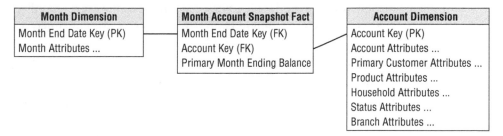

Figure 10-2: Balance snapshot with too few dimensions.

Although this schema accurately represents the many-to-one and many-to-many relationships in the snapshot data, it does not adequately reflect the natural business dimensions. Rather than collapsing everything into the huge account dimension table, additional analytic dimensions such as product and branch mirror the instinctive way users think about their business. These supplemental dimensions provide much smaller points of entry to the fact table. Thus, they address both the performance and usability objectives of a dimensional model. Finally, given a big bank may have millions of accounts, you should worry about type 2 slowly changing dimension effects potentially causing this huge dimension to mushroom into something unmanageable. The product and branch attributes are convenient groups of attributes to remove from the account dimension to cut down on the row growth caused by type 2 change tracking. In the section "Mini-Dimensions Revisited," the changing demographics and behavioral attributes will be squeezed out of the account dimension for the same reasons.

The product and branch dimensions are two separate dimensions as there is a many-to-many relationship between products and branches. They both change slowly, but on different rhythms. Most important, business users think of them as distinct dimensions of the banking business.

In general, most dimensional models end up with between five and 20 dimensions. If you are at or below the low end of this range, you should be suspicious that dimensions may have been inadvertently left out of the design. In this case, carefully consider whether any of the following kinds of dimensions are appropriate supplements to your initial dimensional model:

- Causal dimensions, such as promotion, contract, deal, store condition, or even weather. These dimensions, as discussed in Chapter 3: Retail Sales, provide additional insight into the cause of an event.
- Multiple date dimensions, especially when the fact table is an accumulating snapshot. Refer to Chapter 4: Inventory for sample fact tables with multiple date stamps.
- Degenerate dimensions that identify operational transaction control numbers, such as an order, an invoice, a bill of lading, or a ticket, as initially illustrated in Chapter 3.
- Role-playing dimensions, such as when a single transaction has several business entities associated with it, each represented by a separate dimension. In Chapter 6: Order Management, we described role playing to handle multiple dates.
- Status dimensions that identify the current status of a transaction or monthly snapshot within some larger context, such as an account status.
- An audit dimension, as discussed in Chapter 6, to track data lineage and quality.
- Junk dimensions of correlated indicators and flags, as described in Chapter 6.

These dimensions can typically be added gracefully to a design, even after the DW/BI system has gone into production because they do not change the grain of the fact table. The addition of these dimensions usually does not alter the existing dimension keys or measured facts in the fact table. All existing applications should continue to run without change.

NOTE Any descriptive attribute that is single-valued in the presence of the measurements in the fact table is a good candidate to be added to an existing dimension or to be its own dimension.

Based on further study of the bank's requirements, you can ultimately choose the following dimensions for the initial schema: month end date, branch, account, primary customer, product, account status, and household. As illustrated in Figure 10-3, at the intersection of these seven dimensions, you take a monthly snapshot and record the primary balance and any other metrics that make sense across all products, such as transaction count, interest paid, and fees charged. Remember account balances are just like inventory balances in that they are not additive across any measure of time. Instead, you must average the account balances by dividing the balance sum by the number of time periods.

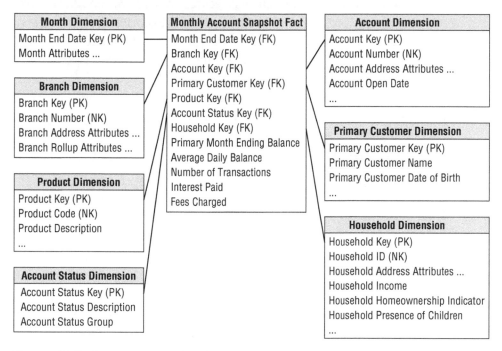

Figure 10-3: Supertype snapshot fact table for all accounts.

> **NOTE** In this chapter we use the basic object-oriented terms *supertype* and *subtype* to refer respectively to the single fact table covering all possible account types, as well as the multiple fact tables containing specific details of each individual account type. In past writings these have been called *core* and *custom* fact tables, but it is time to change to the more familiar and accepted terminology.

The product dimension consists of a simple hierarchy that describes all the bank's products, including the name of the product, type, and category. The need to construct a generic product categorization in the bank is the same need that causes grocery stores to construct a generic merchandise hierarchy. The main difference between the bank and grocery store examples is that the bank also develops a large number of subtype product attributes for each product type. We'll defer discussion regarding the handling of these subtype attributes until the "Supertype and Subtype Schemas for Heterogeneous Products" section at the end of the chapter.

The branch dimension is similar to the facility dimensions we discussed earlier in this book, such as the retail store or distribution center warehouse.

The account status dimension is a useful dimension to record the condition of the account at the end of each month. The status records whether the account is active or inactive, or whether a status change occurred during the month, such as a new account opening or account closure. Rather than whipsawing the large account dimension, or merely embedding a cryptic status code or abbreviation directly in the fact table, we treat status as a full-fledged dimension with descriptive status decodes, groupings, and status reason descriptions, as appropriate. In many ways, you could consider the account status dimension to be another example of a mini-dimension, as we introduced in Chapter 5: Procurement.

Household Dimension

Rather than focusing solely on the bank's accounts, business users also want the ability to analyze the bank's relationship with an entire economic unit, referred to as a household. They are interested in understanding the overall profile of a household, the magnitude of the existing relationship with the household, and what additional products should be sold to the household. They also want to capture key demographics regarding the household, such as household income, whether they own or rent their home, whether they are retirees, and whether they have children. These demographic attributes change over time; as you might suspect, the users want to track the changes. If the bank focuses on accounts for commercial entities, rather than consumers, similar requirements to identify and link corporate "households" are common.

From the bank's perspective, a household may be comprised of several accounts and individual account holders. For example, consider John and Mary Smith as a single household. John has a checking account, whereas Mary has a savings account. In addition, they have a joint checking account, credit card, and mortgage with the bank. All five of these accounts are considered to be a part of the same Smith household, despite the fact that minor inconsistencies may exist in the operational name and address information.

The process of relating individual accounts to households (or the commercial business equivalent) is not to be taken lightly. Householding requires the development of business rules and algorithms to assign accounts to households. There are specialized products and services to do the matching necessary to determine household assignments. It is very common for a large financial services organization to invest significant resources in specialized capabilities to support its householding needs.

The decision to treat account and household as separate dimensions is somewhat a matter of the designer's prerogative. Even though they are intuitively correlated, you decide to treat them separately because of the size of the account dimension and the volatility of the account constituents within a household dimension, as mentioned earlier. In a large bank, the account dimension is huge, with easily over 10 million rows that group into several million households. The household dimension provides a somewhat smaller point of entry into the fact table, without traversing a 10 million-row account dimension table. Also, given the changing nature of the relationship between accounts and households, you elect to use the fact table to capture the relationship, rather than merely including the household attributes on each account dimension row. In this way, you avoid using the type 2 slowly changing dimension technique with a 10-million row account dimension.

Multivalued Dimensions and Weighting Factors

As you just saw in the John and Mary Smith example, an account can have one, two, or more individual account holders, or customers, associated with it. Obviously, the customer cannot be included as an account attribute (beyond the designation of a primary customer/account holder); doing so violates the granularity of the dimension table because more than one individual can be associated with an account. Likewise, you cannot include a customer as an additional dimension in the fact table; doing so violates the granularity of the fact table (one row per account per month), again because more than one individual can be associated with any given account. This is another classic example of a multivalued dimension. To link an individual customer dimension to an account-grained fact table requires the use of an account-to-customer bridge table, as shown in Figure 10-4. At a minimum, the primary key of the bridge table consists of the surrogate account and customer keys. The time stamping of bridge table rows, as discussed in Chapter 7: Accounting, for time-variant relationships is also applicable in this scenario.

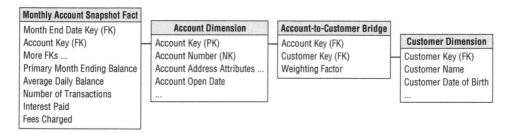

Figure 10-4: Account-to-customer bridge table with weighting factor.

If an account has two account holders, then the associated bridge table has two rows. You assign a numerical weighting factor to each account holder such that the sum of all the weighting factors is exactly 1.00. The weighting factors are used to allocate any of the numeric additive facts across individual account holders. In this way you can add up all numeric facts by individual holder, and the grand total will be the correct grand total amount. This kind of report is a *correctly weighted* report.

The weighting factors are simply a way to allocate the numeric additive facts across the account holders. Some would suggest changing the grain of the fact table to be account snapshot by account holder. In this case you would take the weighting factors and physically multiply them against the original numeric facts. This is rarely done for three reasons. First, the size of the fact table would be multiplied by the average number of account holders. Second, some fact tables have more than one multivalued dimension. The number of rows would get out of hand in this situation, and you would start to question the physical significance of an individual row. Finally, you may want to see the unallocated numbers, and it is hard to reconstruct these if the allocations have been combined physically with the numeric facts.

If you choose not to apply the weighting factors in a given query, you can still summarize the account snapshots by individual account holder, but in this case you get what is called an *impact report*. A question such as, "What is the total balance of all individuals with a specific demographic profile?" would be an example of an impact report. Business users understand impact analyses may result in overcounting because the facts are associated with both account holders.

In Figure 10-4, an SQL view could be defined combining the fact table and the account-to-customer bridge table so these two tables, when combined, would appear to BI tools as a standard fact table with a normal customer foreign key. Two views could be defined, one using the weighting factors and one not using the weighting factors.

> **NOTE** An open-ended, many-valued attribute can be associated with a dimension row by using a bridge table to associate the many-valued attributes with the dimension.

In some financial services companies, the individual customer is identified and associated with each transaction. For example, credit card companies often issue unique card numbers to each cardholder. John and Mary Smith may have a joint credit card account, but the numbers on their respective pieces of plastic are unique. In this case, there is no need for an account-to-customer bridge table because the atomic transaction facts are at the discrete customer grain; account and customer would both be foreign keys in this fact table. However, the bridge table would be required to analyze metrics that are naturally captured at the account level, such as the credit card billing data.

Mini-Dimensions Revisited

Similar to the discussion of the customer dimension in Chapter 8: Customer Relationship Management, there are a wide variety of attributes describing the bank's accounts, customers, and households, including monthly credit bureau attributes, external demographic data, and calculated scores to identify their behavior, retention, profitability, and delinquency characteristics. Financial services organizations are typically interested in understanding and responding to changes in these attributes over time.

As discussed earlier, it's unreasonable to rely on slowly changing dimension technique type 2 to track changes in the account dimension given the dimension row count and attribute volatility, such as the monthly update of credit bureau attributes. Instead, you can break off the browseable and changeable attributes into multiple mini-dimensions, such as credit bureau and demographics mini-dimensions, whose keys are included in the fact table, as illustrated in Figure 10-5. The type 4 mini-dimensions enable you to slice and dice the fact table, while readily tracking attribute changes over time, even though they may be updated at different frequencies. Although mini-dimensions are extremely powerful, be careful to avoid overusing the technique. Account-oriented financial services are a good environment for using mini-dimensions because the primary fact table is a very long-running periodic snapshot. Thus every month a fact table row is guaranteed to exist for every account, providing a home for all the associated foreign keys. You can always see the account together with all the mini-dimensions for any month.

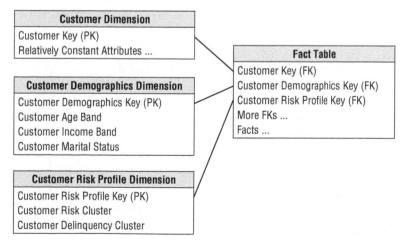

Figure 10-5: Multiple mini-dimensions associated with a fact table.

NOTE Mini-dimensions should consist of correlated clumps of attributes; each attribute shouldn't be its own mini-dimension or you end up with too many dimensions in the fact table.

As described in Chapter 4, one of the compromises associated with mini-dimensions is the need to band attribute values to maintain reasonable mini-dimension row counts. Rather than storing extremely discrete income amounts, such as $31,257.98, you store income ranges, such as $30,000 to $34,999 in the mini-dimension. Similarly, the profitability scores may range from 1 through 1200, which you band into fixed ranges such as less than or equal to 100, 101 to 150, and 151 to 200, in the mini-dimension.

Most organizations find these banded attribute values support their routine analytic requirements, however there are two situations in which banded values may be inadequate. First, data mining analysis often requires discrete values rather than fixed bands to be effective. Secondly, a limited number of power analysts may want to analyze the discrete values to determine if the bands are appropriate. In this case, you still maintain the banded value mini-dimension attributes to support consistent day-to-day analytic reporting but also store the key discrete numeric values as facts in the fact table. For example, if each account's profitability score were recalculated each month, you would assign the appropriate profitability range mini-dimension for that score each month. In addition, you would capture the discrete profitability score as a fact in the monthly account snapshot fact table. Finally, if needed, the current profitability range or score could be included in the account dimension where any changes are handled by deliberately overwriting the type 1 attribute. Each of these data elements should be uniquely labeled so that they are distinguishable. Designers must always carefully balance the incremental value of including such somewhat redundant facts and attributes versus the cost in terms of additional complexity for both the ETL processing and BI presentation.

Adding a Mini-Dimension to a Bridge Table

In the bank account example, the account-to-customer bridge table can get very large. If you have 20 million accounts and 25 million customers, the bridge table can grow to hundreds of millions of rows after a few years if both the account dimension and the customer dimension are slowly changing type 2 dimensions (where you track history by issuing new rows with new keys).

Now the experienced dimensional modeler asks, "What happens when my customer dimension turns out to be a rapidly changing monster dimension?" This could happen when rapidly changing demographics and status attributes are added to the customer dimension, forcing numerous type 2 additions to the customer dimension. Now the 25-million row customer dimension threatens to become several hundred million rows.

The standard response to a rapidly changing monster dimension is to split off the rapidly changing demographics and status attributes into a type 4 mini-dimension, often called a *demographics dimension*. This works great when this dimension attaches directly to the fact table along with a customer dimension because it stabilizes the large customer dimension and keeps it from growing every time a demographics or status attribute changes. But can you get this same advantage when the customer dimension is attached to a bridge table, as in the bank account example?

The solution is to add a foreign key reference in the bridge table to the demographics dimension, as shown in Figure 10-6.

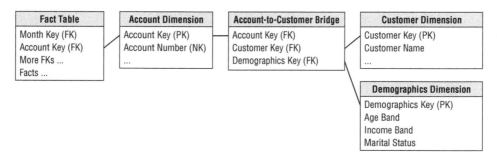

Figure 10-6: Account-to-customer bridge table with an added mini-dimension.

The way to visualize the bridge table is that it links every account to its associated customers and their demographics. The key for the bridge table now consists of the account key, customer key, and demographics key.

Depending on how frequently new demographics are assigned to each customer, the bridge table will perhaps grow significantly. In the above design because the grain of the root bank account fact table is month by account, the bridge table should be limited to changes recorded only at month ends. This takes some of the change tracking pressure off the bridge table.

Dynamic Value Banding of Facts

Suppose business users want the ability to perform *value band reporting* on a standard numeric fact, such as the account balance, but are not willing to live with the predefined bands in a dimension table. They may want to create a report based on the account balance snapshot, as shown in Figure 10-7.

Balance Range	Number of Accounts	Total of Balances
0–1000	456,783	$229,305,066
1001–2000	367,881	$552,189,381
2001–5000	117,754	$333,479,328
5001–10000	52,662	$397,229,466
10001 and up	8,437	$104,888,784

Figure 10-7: Report rows with dynamic value band groups.

Using the schema in Figure 10-3, it is difficult to create this report directly from the fact table. SQL has no generalization of the GROUP BY clause that clumps additive values into ranges. To further complicate matters, the ranges are of unequal size and have textual names, such as "10001 and up." Also, users typically need the flexibility to redefine the bands at query time with different boundaries or levels of precision.

The schema design shown in Figure 10-8 enables on-the-fly value band reporting. The band definition table can contain as many sets of different reporting bands as desired. The name of a particular group of bands is stored in the band group column. The band definition table is joined to the balance fact using a pair of less-than and greater-than joins. The report uses the band range name as the row header and sorts the report on the sort order attribute.

Monthly Account Snapshot Fact
Month End Date Key (FK)
Account Key (FK)
Product Key (FK)
More FKs ...
Primary Month Ending Balance

Band Definition Table
Band Group Key (PK)
Band Group Sort Order (PK)
Band Group Name
Band Range Name
Band Lower Value
Band Upper Value

≥
<

Figure 10-8: Dynamic value band reporting.

Controlling the performance of this query can be a challenge. A value band query is by definition very lightly constrained. The example report needed to scan the balances of more than 1 million accounts. Perhaps only the month dimension was constrained to the current month. Furthermore the funny joins to the value banding table are not the basis of a nice restricting constraint because they are grouping the 1 million balances. In this situation, you may need to place an index directly on the balance fact. The performance of a query that constrains or groups on the value of a fact-like balance will be improved enormously if the DBMS can efficiently sort and compress the individual fact. This approach was pioneered by the Sybase IQ columnar database product in the early 1990s and is now becoming a standard indexing option on several of the competing columnar DBMSs.

Supertype and Subtype Schemas for Heterogeneous Products

In many financial service businesses, a dilemma arises because of the heterogeneous nature of the products or services offered by the institution. As mentioned in the introduction, a typical retail bank offers a myriad of products, from checking accounts to credit cards, to the same customers. Although every account at the bank has a primary balance and interest amount associated with it, each product type has many special attributes and measured facts that are not shared by the other products. For instance, checking accounts have minimum balances, overdraft limits, service charges, and other measures relating to online banking; time deposits such as certificates of deposit have few attribute overlaps with checking, but have maturity dates, compounding frequencies, and current interest rate.

Business users typically require two different perspectives that are difficult to present in a single fact table. The first perspective is the global view, including the ability to slice and dice all accounts simultaneously, regardless of their product type. This global view is needed to plan appropriate customer relationship management cross-sell and up-sell strategies against the aggregate customer/household base spanning all possible products. In this situation, you need the single supertype fact table (refer to Figure 10-3) that crosses all the lines of business to provide insight into the complete account portfolio. Note, however, that the supertype fact table can present only a limited number of facts that make sense for virtually every line of business. You cannot accommodate incompatible facts in the supertype fact table because there may be several hundred of these facts when all the possible account types are considered. Similarly, the supertype product dimension must be restricted to the subset of common product attributes.

The second perspective is the line-of-business view that focuses on the in-depth details of one business, such as checking. There is a long list of special facts and attributes that make sense only for the checking business. These special facts cannot be included in the supertype fact table; if you did this for each line of business in a retail bank, you would end up with hundreds of special facts, most of which would have null values in any specific row. Likewise, if you attempt to include line-of-business attributes in the account or product dimension tables, these tables would have hundreds of special attributes, almost all of which would be empty for any given row. The resulting tables would resemble Swiss cheese, littered with data holes. The solution to this dilemma for the checking department in this example is to create a subtype schema for the checking line of business that is limited to just checking accounts, as shown in Figure 10-9.

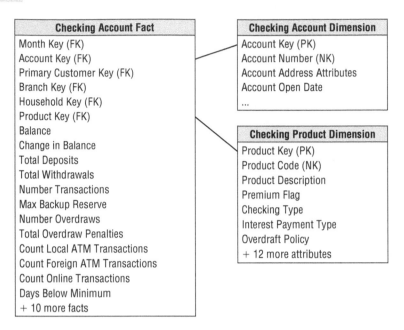

Figure 10-9: Line-of-business subtype schema for checking products.

Now both the subtype checking fact table and corresponding checking account dimension are widened to describe all the specific facts and attributes that make sense only for checking products. These subtype schemas must also contain the supertype facts and attributes to avoid joining tables from the supertype and subtype schemas for the complete set of facts and attributes. You can also build separate subtype fact and account tables for the other lines of business to support their in-depth analysis requirements. Although creating account-specific schemas sounds complex, only the DBA sees all the tables at once. From the business users' perspective, either it's a cross-product analysis that relies on the single supertype fact table and its attendant supertype account table, or the analysis focuses on a particular account type and only one of the subtype line of business schemas is utilized. In general, it makes less sense to combine data from more than one subtype schema, because by definition, the accounts' facts and attributes are disjointed (or nearly so).

The keys of the subtype account dimensions are the same keys used in the supertype account dimension, which contains all possible account keys. For example, if the bank offers a "$500 minimum balance with no per check charge" checking account, this account would be identified by the same surrogate key in both the supertype and subtype checking account dimensions. Each subtype account dimension is a shrunken conformed dimension with a subset of rows from the supertype account dimension table; each subtype account dimension contains attributes specific to a particular account type.

This supertype/subtype design technique applies to any business that offers widely varied products through multiple lines of business. If you work for a technology company that sells hardware, software, and services, you can imagine building supertype sales fact and product dimension tables to deliver the global customer perspective. The supertype tables would include all facts and dimension attributes that are common across lines of business. The supertype tables would then be supplemented with schemas that do a deep dive into subtype facts and attributes that vary by business. Again, a specific product would be assigned the same surrogate product key in both the supertype and subtype product dimensions.

> **NOTE** A family of supertype and subtype fact tables are needed when a business has heterogeneous products that have naturally different facts and descriptors, but a single customer base that demands an integrated view.

If the lines of business in your retail bank are physically separated so each has its own location, the subtype fact and dimension tables will likely not reside in the same space as the supertype fact and dimension tables. In this case, the data in the supertype fact table would be duplicated exactly once to implement all the subtype tables. Remember that the subtype tables provide a disjointed partitioning of the accounts, so there is no overlap between the subtype schemas.

Supertype and Subtype Products with Common Facts

The supertype and subtype product technique just discussed is appropriate for fact tables where a single logical row contains many product-specific facts. On the other hand, the metrics captured by some business processes, such as the bank's new account solicitations, may not vary by line of business. In this case, you do not need line-of-business fact tables; one supertype fact table suffices. However, you still can have a rich set of heterogeneous products with diverse attributes. In this case, you would generate the complete portfolio of subtype account dimension tables, and use them as appropriate, depending on the nature of the application. In a cross product analysis, the supertype account dimension table would be used because it can span any group of accounts. In a single account type analysis, you could optionally use the subtype account dimension table instead of the supertype dimension if you wanted to take advantage of the subtype attributes specific to that account type.

Hot Swappable Dimensions

A brokerage house may have many clients who track the stock market. All of them access the same fact table of daily high-low-close stock prices. But each client has a confidential set of attributes describing each stock. The brokerage house can support this multi-client situation by having a separate copy of the stock dimension for each client, which is joined to the single fact table at query time. We call these *hot swappable dimensions*. To implement hot swappable dimensions in a relational environment, referential integrity constraints between the fact table and the various stock dimension tables probably must be turned off to allow the switches to occur on an individual query basis.

Summary

We began this chapter by discussing the situation in which a fact table has too few dimensions and provided suggestions for ferreting out additional dimensions using a triage process. Approaches for handling the often complex relationship between accounts, customers, and households were described. We also discussed the use of multiple mini-dimensions in a single fact table, which is fairly common in financial services schemas.

We illustrated a technique for clustering numeric facts into arbitrary value bands for reporting purposes through the use of a separate band table. Finally, we provided recommendations for any organization that offers heterogeneous products to the same set of customers. In this case, we create a supertype fact table that contains performance metrics that are common across all lines of business. The companion dimension table contains rows for the complete account portfolio, but the attributes are limited to those that are applicable across all accounts. Multiple subtype schemas, one of each line of business, complement the supertype schema with account-specific facts and attributes.

11   Telecommunications

This chapter unfolds a bit differently than preceding chapters. We begin with a case study overview but we won't be designing a dimensional model from scratch this time. Instead, we'll step into a project midstream to conduct a design review, looking for opportunities to improve the initial draft schema. The bulk of this chapter focuses on identifying design flaws in dimensional models.

We'll use a billing vignette drawn from the telecommunications industry as the basis for the case study; it shares similar characteristics with the billing data generated by a utilities company. At the end of this chapter we'll describe the handling of geographic location information in the data warehouse.

Chapter 11 discusses the following concepts:

- Bus matrix snippet for telecommunications company
- Design review exercise
- Checklist of common design mistakes
- Recommended tactics when conducting design reviews
- Retrofitting existing data structures
- Abstract geographic location dimensions

Telecommunications Case Study and Bus Matrix

Given your extensive experience in dimensional modeling (10 chapters so far), you've recently been recruited to a new position as a dimensional modeler on the DW/BI team for a large wireless telecommunications company. On your first day, after a few hours of human resources paperwork and orientation, you're ready to get to work.

The DW/BI team is anxious for you to review its initial dimensional design. So far it seems the project is off to a good start. The business and IT sponsorship committee appreciates that the DW/BI program must be business-driven; as such, the committee was fully supportive of the business requirements gathering process. Based on the requirements initiative, the team drafted an initial data warehouse bus matrix, illustrated in Figure 11-1. The team identified several core business processes and a number of common dimensions. Of course, the complete enterprise matrix would have a much larger number of rows and columns, but you're comfortable that the key constituencies' major data requirements have been captured.

	Date	Product	Customer	Rate Plan	Sales Organization	Service Line #	Switch	Employee	Support Call Profile
Purchasing	X	X						X	
Internal Inventory	X	X							
Channel Inventory	X	X			X				
Service Activation	X	X	X	X	X	X			
Product Sales	X	X	X	X	X	X			
Promotion Participation	X	X	X	X	X	X		X	
Call Detail Traffic	X	X	X	X	X	X	X		
Customer Billing	X	X	X	X	X	X			
Customer Support Calls	X	X	X	X	X	X		X	X
Repair Work Orders	X	X	X			X		X	X

Figure 11-1: Sample bus matrix rows for telecommunications company.

The sponsorship committee decided to focus on the customer billing process for the initial DW/BI project. Business management determined better access to the metrics resulting from the billing process would have a significant impact on the business. Management wants the ability to see monthly usage and billing metrics (otherwise known as revenue) by customer, sales organization, and rate plan to perform sales channel and rate plan analyses. Fortunately, the IT team felt it was feasible to tackle this business process during the first warehouse iteration.

Some people in the IT organization thought it would be preferable to tackle individual call and message detail traffic, such as every call initiated or received by every phone. Although this level of highly granular data would provide interesting insights, it was determined by the joint sponsorship committee that the associated data presents more feasibility challenges while not delivering as much short-term business value.

Based on the sponsors' direction, the team looked more closely at the customer billing data. Each month, the operational billing system generates a bill for each phone number, also known as a service line. Because the wireless company has millions of service lines, this represents a significant amount of data. Each service line is associated with a single customer. However, a customer can have multiple wireless service lines, which appear as separate line items on the same bill; each service line has its own set of billing metrics, such as the number of minutes, number of text messages, amount of data, and monthly service charges. There is a single rate plan associated with each service line on a given bill, but this plan can change as customers' usage habits evolve. Finally, a sales organization and channel is associated with each service line to evaluate the ongoing billing revenue stream generated by each channel partner.

Working closely with representatives from the business and other DW/BI team members, the data modeler designed a fact table with the grain being one row per bill each month. The team proudly unrolls its draft dimensional modeling master-piece, as shown in Figure 11-2, and expectantly looks at you.

What do you think? Before moving on, please spend several minutes studying the design in Figure 11-2. Try to identify the design flaws and suggest improvements before reading ahead.

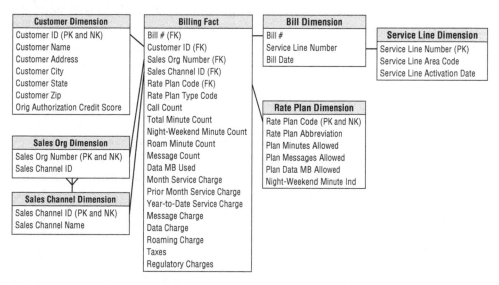

Figure 11-2: Draft schema prior to design review.

General Design Review Considerations

Before we discuss the specific issues and potential recommendations for the Figure 11-2 schema, we'll outline the design issues commonly encountered when conducting design reviews. Not to insinuate that the DW/BI team in this case study has stepped into all these traps, but it may be guilty of violating several. Again, the design review exercise will be a more effective learning tool if you take a moment to jot down your personal ideas regarding Figure 11-2 before proceeding.

Balance Business Requirements and Source Realities

Dimensional models should be designed based on a blended understanding of the business's needs, along with the operational source system's data realities. While requirements are collected from the business users, the underlying source data should be profiled. Models driven solely by requirements inevitably include data elements that can't be sourced. Meanwhile, models driven solely by source system data analysis inevitably omit data elements that are critical to the business's analytics.

Focus on Business Processes

As reinforced for 10 chapters, dimensional models should be designed to mirror an organization's primary business process events. Dimensional models should not be designed solely to deliver specific reports or answer specific questions. Of course, business users' analytic questions are critical input because they help identify which processes are priorities for the business. But dimensional models designed to produce a specific report or answer a specific question are unlikely to withstand the test of time, especially when the questions and report formats are slightly modified. Developing dimensional models that more fully describe the underlying business process are more resilient to change. Process-centric dimensional models also address the analytic needs from multiple business departments; the same is definitely not true when models are designed to answer a single department's specific need.

After the base processes have been built, it may be useful to design complementary schemas, such as summary aggregations, accumulating snapshots that look across a workflow of processes, consolidated fact tables that combine facts from multiple processes to a common granularity, or subset fact tables that provide access to a limited subset of fact data for security or data distribution purposes. Again, these are all secondary complements to the core process-centric dimensional models.

Granularity

The first question to always ask during a design review is, "What's the grain of the fact table?" Surprisingly, you often get inconsistent answers to this inquiry from a design team. Declaring a clear and concise definition of the grain of the fact table is critical to a productive modeling effort. The project team and business liaisons must share a common understanding of this grain declaration; without this agreement, the design effort will spin in circles.

Of course, if you've read this far, you're aware we strongly believe fact tables should be built at the lowest level of granularity possible for maximum flexibility and extensibility, especially given the unpredictable filtering and grouping required by business user queries. Users typically don't need to see a single row at a time, but you can't predict the somewhat arbitrary ways they'll want to screen and roll up the details. The definition of the lowest level of granularity possible depends on the business process being modeled. In this case, you want to implement the most granular data available for the selected billing process, not just the most granular data available in the enterprise.

Single Granularity for Facts

After the fact table granularity has been established, facts should be identified that are consistent with the grain declaration. To improve performance or reduce query complexity, aggregated facts such as year-to-date totals sometimes sneak into the fact row. These totals are dangerous because they are not perfectly additive. Although a year-to-date total reduces the complexity and run time of a few specific queries, having it in the fact table invites double counting the year-to-date column (or worse) when more than one date is included in the query results. It is important that once the grain of a fact table is chosen, all the additive facts are presented at a uniform grain.

You should prohibit text fields, including cryptic indicators and flags, from the fact table. They almost always take up more space in the fact table than a surrogate key. More important, business users generally want to query, constrain, and report against these text fields. You can provide quicker responses and more flexible access by handling these textual values in a dimension table, along with descriptive rollup attributes associated with the flags and indicators.

Dimension Granularity and Hierarchies

Each of the dimensions associated with a fact table should take on a single value with each row of fact table measurements. Likewise, each of the dimension attributes should take on one value for a given dimension row. If the attributes have a many-to-one relationship, this hierarchical relationship can be represented within a single dimension. You should generally look for opportunities to collapse or denormalize dimension hierarchies whenever possible.

Experienced data modelers often revert to the normalization techniques they've applied countless times in operational entity-relationship models. These modelers often need to be reminded that normalization is absolutely appropriate to support transaction processing and ensure referential integrity. But dimensional models support analytic processing. Normalization in the dimensional model negatively impacts the model's twin objectives of understandability and performance. Although normalization is not forbidden in the extract, transform, and load (ETL) system where data integrity must be ensured, it does place an additional burden on the dimension change handling subsystems.

Sometimes designers attempt to deal with dimension hierarchies within the fact table. For example, rather than having a single foreign key to the product dimension, they include separate foreign keys for the key elements in the product hierarchy, such as brand and category. Before you know it, a compact fact table turns into an unruly centipede fact table joining to dozens of dimension tables. If the fact table has more than 20 or so foreign keys, you should look for opportunities to combine or collapse dimensions.

Elsewhere, normalization appears with the snowflaking of hierarchical relationships into separate dimension tables linked to one another. We generally also discourage this practice. Although snowflaking may reduce the disk space consumed by dimension tables, the savings are usually insignificant when compared with the entire data warehouse environment and seldom offset the disadvantages in ease of use or query performance.

Throughout this book we have occasionally discussed outriggers as permissible snowflakes. Outriggers can play a useful role in dimensional designs, but keep in mind that the use of outriggers for a cluster of relatively low-cardinality should be the exception rather than the rule. Be careful to avoid abusing the outrigger technique by overusing them in schemas.

Finally, we sometimes review dimension tables that contain rows for both atomic and hierarchical rollups, such as rows for both products and brands in the same dimension table. These dimensions typically have a telltale "level" attribute to distinguish between its base and summary rows. This pattern was prevalent and generally accepted decades ago prior to aggregate navigation capabilities. However, we discourage its continued use given the strong likelihood of user confusion and the risk of overcounting if the level indicator in every dimension is not constrained in every query.

Date Dimension

Every fact table should have at least one foreign key to an explicit date dimension. Design teams sometimes join a generic date dimension to a fact table because they know it's the most common dimension but then can't articulate what the date refers to, presenting challenges for the ETL team and business users alike. We encourage a meaningful date dimension table with robust date rollup and filter attributes.

Fixed Time Series Buckets Instead of Date Dimension

Designers sometimes avoid a date dimension table altogether by representing a time series of monthly buckets of facts on a single fact table row. Legacy operational systems may contain metric sets that are repeated 12 times on a single record to represent month 1, month 2, and so on. There are several problems with this approach. First, the hard-coded identity of the time slots is inflexible. When you fill up all the buckets, you are left with unpleasant choices. You could alter the table to expand the row. Otherwise, you could shift everything over by one column, dropping the oldest data, but this wreaks havoc with existing query applications. The second problem with this approach is that all the attributes of the date are now the responsibility of the application, not the database. There is no date dimension in which to place calendar event descriptions for constraining. Finally, the fixed slot approach is inefficient if measurements are taken only in a particular time period, resulting in null columns in many rows. Instead, these recurring time buckets should be presented as separate rows in the fact table.

Degenerate Dimensions

Rather than treating operational transaction numbers such as the invoice or order number as degenerate dimensions, teams sometimes want to create a separate dimension table for the transaction number. In this case, attributes of the transaction number dimension include elements from the transaction header record, such as the transaction date and customer.

Remember, transaction numbers are best treated as degenerate dimensions. The transaction date and customer should be captured as foreign keys on the fact table, not as attributes in a transaction dimension. Be on the lookout for a dimension table that has as many (or nearly as many) rows as the fact table; this is a warning sign that there may be a degenerate dimension lurking within a dimension table.

Surrogate Keys

Instead of relying on operational keys or identifiers, we recommend the use of surrogate keys as the dimension tables' primary keys. The only permissible deviation from this guideline applies to the highly predictable and stable date dimension. If you are unclear about the reasons for pursuing this strategy, we suggest backtracking to Chapter 3: Retail Sales to refresh your memory.

Dimension Decodes and Descriptions

All identifiers and codes in the dimension tables should be accompanied by descriptive decodes. This practice often seems counterintuitive to experienced data modelers who have historically tried to reduce data redundancies by relying on look-up codes. In the dimensional model, dimension attributes should be populated with the values that business users want to see on BI reports and application pull-down menus. You need to dismiss the misperception that business users prefer to work with codes. To convince yourself, stroll down to their offices to see the decode listings filling their bulletin boards or lining their computer monitors. Most users do not memorize the codes outside of a few favorites. New hires are rendered helpless when assaulted with a lengthy list of meaningless codes.

The good news is that decodes can usually be sourced from operational systems with relatively minimal additional effort or overhead. Occasionally, the descriptions are not available from an operational system but need to be provided by business partners. In these cases, it is important to determine an ongoing maintenance strategy to maintain data quality.

Finally, project teams sometimes opt to embed labeling logic in the BI tool's semantic layer rather than supporting it via dimension table attributes. Although some BI tools provide the ability to decode within the query or reporting application, we recommend that decodes be stored as data elements instead. Applications should be data-driven to minimize the impact of decode additions and changes. Of course, decodes that reside in the database also ensure greater report labeling consistency because most organizations ultimately utilize multiple BI products.

Conformity Commitment

Last, but certainly not least, design teams must commit to using shared conformed dimensions across process-centric models. Everyone needs to take this pledge seriously. Conformed dimensions are absolutely critical to a robust data architecture that ensures consistency and integration. Without conformed dimensions, you inevitably perpetuate incompatible stovepipe views of performance across the organization. By the way, dimension tables should conform and be reused whether you drink the Kimball Kool-Aid or embrace a hub-and-spoke architectural alternative. Fortunately, operational master data management systems are facilitating the development and deployment of conformed dimensions.

Design Review Guidelines

Before diving into a review of the draft model in Figure 11-2, let's review some practical recommendations for conducting dimensional model design reviews. Proper advance preparation increases the likelihood of a successful review process. Here are some suggestions when setting up for a design review:

- **Invite the right players.** The modeling team obviously needs to participate, but you also want representatives from the BI development team to ensure that proposed changes enhance usability. Perhaps most important, it's critical that folks who are very knowledgeable about the business and their needs are sitting at the table. Although diverse perspectives should participate in a review, don't invite 25 people to the party.
- **Designate someone to facilitate the review.** Group dynamics, politics, and the design challenges will drive whether the facilitator should be a neutral resource or involved party. Regardless, their role is to keep the team on track toward a

common goal. Effective facilitators need the right mix of intelligence, enthusiasm, confidence, empathy, flexibility, assertiveness (and a sense of humor).

- **Agree on the review's scope.** Ancillary topics will inevitably arise during the review, but agreeing in advance on the scope makes it easier to stay focused on the task at hand.
- **Block time on everyone's calendar.** We typically conduct dimensional model reviews as a focused two day effort. The entire review team needs to be present for the full two days. Don't allow players to float in and out to accommodate other commitments. Design reviews require undivided attention; it's disruptive when participants leave intermittently.
- **Reserve the right space.** The same conference room should be blocked for the full two days. Optimally, the room should have a large white board; it's especially helpful if the white board drawings can be saved or printed. If a white board is unavailable, have flip charts on hand. Don't forget markers and tape; drinks and food also help.
- **Assign homework.** For example, ask everyone involved to make a list of their top five concerns, problem areas, or opportunities for improvement with the existing design. Encourage participants to use complete sentences when making their list so that it's meaningful to others. These lists should be sent to the facilitator in advance of the design review for consolidation. Soliciting advance input gets people engaged and helps avoid "group think" during the review.

After the team gathers to focus on the review, we recommend the following tactics:

- **Check attitudes at the door.** Although it's easier said than done, don't be defensive about prior design decisions. Embark on the review thinking change is possible; don't go in resigned to believing nothing can be done to improve the situation.
- **Ban technology unless needed for the review process.** Laptops and smartphones should also be checked at the door (at least figuratively). Allowing participants to check e-mail during the sessions is no different than having them leave to attend an alternative meeting.
- **Exhibit strong facilitation skills.** Review ground rules and ensure everyone is openly participating and communicating. The facilitator must keep the group on track and ban side conversations and discussions that are out of scope or spiral into the death zone.
- **Ensure a common understanding of the current model.** Don't presume everyone around the table already has a comprehensive perspective. It may be worthwhile to dedicate the first hour to walking through the current design and reviewing objectives before delving into potential improvements.

■ **Designate someone to act as scribe.** He should take copious notes about both the discussions and decisions being made.

■ **Start with the big picture.** Just as when you design from a blank slate, begin with the bus matrix. Focus on a single, high-priority business process, define its granularity and then move out to the corresponding dimensions. Follow this same "peeling back the layers of the onion" method with a design review, starting with the fact table and then tackling dimension-related issues. But don't defer the tough stuff to the afternoon of the second day.

■ **Remind everyone that business acceptance is critical.** Business acceptance is the ultimate measure of DW/BI success. The review should focus on improving the business users' experience.

■ **Sketch out sample rows with data values.** Viewing sample data during the review sessions helps ensure everyone has a common understanding of the recommended improvements.

■ **Close the meeting with a recap.** Don't let participants leave the room without clear expectations about their assignments and due dates, along with an established time for the next follow-up.

After the team completes the design review meeting, here are a few recommendations to wrap up the process:

■ **Assign responsibility for any remaining open issues.** Commit to wrestling these issues to the ground following the review, even though this can be challenging without an authoritative party involved.

■ **Don't let the team's hard work gather dust.** Evaluate the cost/benefit for the potential improvements; some changes will be more painless (or painful) than others. Action plans for implementing the improvements then need to be developed.

■ **Anticipate future reviews.** Plan to reevaluate models every 12 to 24 months. Try to view inevitable changes to the design as signs of success, rather than failure.

Draft Design Exercise Discussion

Now that you've reviewed the common dimensional modeling mistakes frequently encountered during design reviews, refer to the draft design in Figure 11-2. Several opportunities for improvement should immediately jump out at you.

The first thing to focus on is the grain of the fact table. The team stated the grain is one row for each bill each month. However, based on your understanding from the source system documentation and data profiling effort, the lowest level of billing data would be one row per service line on a bill. When you point this out, the team initially directs you to the bill dimension, which includes the service line number. However, when reminded that each service line has its own set of billing metrics, the team agrees the more appropriate grain declaration would be one row per service line per bill. The service line key is moved into the fact table as a foreign key to the service line dimension.

While discussing the granularity, the bill dimension is scrutinized, especially because the service line key was just moved into the fact table. As the draft model was originally drawn in Figure 11-2, every time a bill row is loaded into the fact table, a row also would be loaded into the bill dimension table. It doesn't take much to convince the team that something is wrong with this picture. Even with the modified granularity to include service line, you would still end up with nearly as many rows in both the fact and bill dimension tables because many customers are billed for one service line. Instead, the bill number should be treated as a degenerate dimension. At the same time, you move the bill date into the fact table and join it to a robust date dimension playing the role of bill date in this schema.

You've probably been bothered since first looking at the design by the double joins on the sales channel dimension table. The sales channel hierarchy has been unnecessarily snowflaked. You opt to collapse the hierarchy by including the sales channel identifiers (hopefully along with more meaningful descriptors) as additional attributes in the sales organization dimension table. In addition, you can eliminate the unneeded sales channel foreign key in the fact table.

The design inappropriately treats the rate plan type code as a textual fact. Textual facts are seldom a sound design choice. In this case study, the rate plan type code and its decode can be treated as rollup attributes in the rate plan dimension table.

The team spent some time discussing the relationship between the service line and the customer, sales organization, and rate plan dimensions. Because there is a single customer, sales organization, and rate plan associated with a service line number, the dimensions theoretically could be collapsed and modeled as service line attributes. However, collapsing the dimensions would result in a schema with just two dimensions: bill date and service line. The service line dimension already has millions of rows in it and is rapidly growing. In the end, you opt to treat the customer, sales organization, and rate plan as separate entities (or mini-dimensions) of the service line.

Surrogate keys are used inconsistently throughout the design. Many of the draft dimension tables use operational identifiers as primary keys. You encourage the team to implement surrogate keys for all the dimension primary keys and then reference them as fact table foreign keys.

The original design was riddled with operational codes and identifiers. Adding descriptive names makes the data more legible to the business users. If required by the business, the operational codes can continue to accompany the descriptors as dimension attributes.

Finally, you notice that there is a year-to-date metric stored in the fact table. Although the team felt this would enable users to report year-to-date figures more easily, in reality, year-to-date facts can be confusing and prone to error. You opt to remove the year-to-date fact. Instead, users can calculate year-to-date amounts on-the-fly by using a constraint on the year in the date dimension or leveraging the BI tool's capabilities.

After two exhausting days, the initial review of the design is complete. Of course, there's more ground to cover, including the handling of changes to the dimension attributes. In the meantime, everyone on the team agrees the revamped design, illustrated in Figure 11-3, is a vast improvement. You've earned your first week's pay.

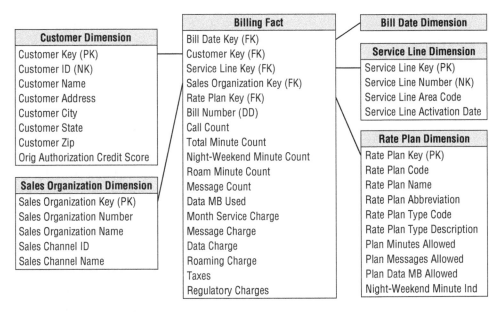

Figure 11-3: Draft schema following design review.

Remodeling Existing Data Structures

It's one thing to conduct a review and identify opportunities for improvement. However, implementing the changes might be easier said than done if the design has already been physically implemented.

For example, adding a new attribute to an existing dimension table feels like a minor enhancement. It is nearly pain-free if the business data stewards declare it to be a slowly changing dimension type 1 attribute. Likewise if the attribute is to be populated starting now with no attempt to backfill historically accurate values beyond a Not Available attribute value; note that while this tactic is relatively easy to implement, it presents analytic challenges and may be deemed unacceptable. But if the new attribute is a designated type 2 attribute with the requirement to capture historical changes, this seemingly simple enhancement just got much more complicated. In this scenario, rows need to be added to the dimension table to capture the historical changes in the attribute, along with the other dimension attribute changes. Some fact table rows then need to be recast so the appropriate dimension table row is associated with the fact table's event. This most robust approach consumes surprisingly more effort than you might initially imagine.

Much less surprising is the effort required to take an existing dimensional model and convert it into a structure that leverages newly created conformed dimensions. As discussed in Chapter 4: Inventory, at a minimum, the fact table's rows must be completely reprocessed to reference the conformed dimension keys. The task is obviously more challenging if there are granularity or other major issues.

In addition to thinking about the data-centric challenges of retrofitting existing data structures, there are also unwanted ripples in the BI reporting and analytic applications built on the existing data foundation. Using views to buffer the BI applications from the physical data structures provides some relief, but it's typically not adequate to avoid unpleasant whipsawing in the BI environment.

When considering enhancements to existing data structures, you must evaluate the costs of tackling the changes alongside the perceived benefits. In many cases, you'll determine improvements need to be made despite the pain. Similarly, you may determine the best approach is to decommission the current structures to put them out of their misery and tackle the subject area with a fresh slate. Finally, in some situations, the best approach is to simply ignore the suboptimal data structures because the costs compared to the potential benefits don't justify the remodeling and schema improvement effort. Sometimes, the best time to consider a remodeling effort is when other changes, such as a source system conversion or migration to a new BI tool standard, provide a catalyst.

Geographic Location Dimension

Let's shift gears and presume you work for a phone company with land lines tied to a specific physical location. The telecommunications and utilities industries have a very well-developed notion of location. Many of their dimensions contain a precise geographic location as part of the attribute set. The location may be resolved to a physical street, city, state, ZIP code, latitude, and longitude. Latitude and longitude geo-coding can be leveraged for geospatial analysis and map-centric visualization.

Some designers imagine a single master location table where address data is standardized and then the location dimension is attached as an outrigger to the service line telephone number, equipment inventory, network inventory (including poles and switch boxes), real estate inventory, service location, dispatch location, right of way, and customer entities. In this scenario, each row in the master location table is a specific point in space that rolls up to every conceivable geographic grouping.

Standardizing the attributes associated with points in space is valuable. However, this is a back room ETL task; you don't need to unveil the single resultant table containing all the addresses the organization interacts with to the business users. Geographic information is naturally handled as attributes within multiple dimensions, not as a standalone location dimension or outrigger. There is typically little overlap between the geographic locations embedded in various dimensions. You would pay a performance price for consolidating all the disparate addresses into a single dimension.

Operational systems often embrace data abstraction, but you should typically avoid generic abstract dimensions, such as a generalized location dimension in the DW/BI presentation area because they negatively impact the ease-of-use and query performance objectives. These structures are more acceptable behind the scenes in the ETL back room.

Summary

This chapter provided the opportunity to conduct a design review using an example case study. It provided recommendations for conducting effective design reviews, along with a laundry list of common design flaws to scout for when performing a review. We encourage you to use this laundry list to review your own draft schemas when searching for potential improvements.

12 Transportation

Voyages occur whenever a person or thing travels from one point to another, perhaps with stops in the middle. Obviously, voyages are a fundamental concept for organizations in the travel industry. Shippers and internal logistical functions also relate to the discussion, as well as package delivery services and car rental companies. Somewhat unexpected, many of this chapter's schemas are also applicable to telecommunications network route analyses; a phone network can be thought of as a map of possible voyages that a call makes between origin and destination phone numbers.

In this chapter we'll draw on an airline case study to explore voyages and routes because many readers are familiar (perhaps too familiar) with the subject matter. The case study lends itself to a discussion of multiple fact tables at different granularities. We'll also elaborate on dimension role playing and additional date and time dimension considerations. As usual, the intended audience for this chapter should not be limited to the industries previously listed.

Chapter 12 discusses the following concepts:

- Bus matrix snippet for an airline
- Fact tables at different levels of granularity
- Combining correlated role-playing dimensions
- Country-specific date dimensions
- Dates and times in multiple time zones
- Recap of localization issues

Airline Case Study and Bus Matrix

We'll begin by exploring a simplified bus matrix, and then dive into the fact tables associated with flight activity.

Figure 12-1 shows a snippet of an airline's bus matrix. This example includes an additional column to capture the degenerate dimension associated with most of the bus process events. Like most organizations, airlines are keenly interested in revenue. In this industry, the sale of a ticket represents unearned revenue; revenue is earned when a passenger takes a flight between origin and destination airports.

	Date	Time	Airport	Passenger	Booking Channel	Class of Service	Fare Basis	Aircraft	Communication Profile	Transaction ID #
Reservations	X	X	X	X	X	X	X	X		Conf #
Issued Tickets	X	X	X	X	X	X	X	X		Conf # Ticket #
Unearned Revenue & Availability	X	X	X			X		X		
Flight Activity	X	X	X	X	X	X	X	X		Conf # Ticket #
Frequent Flyer Account Credits	X		X	X	X	X	X			Conf # Ticket #
Customer Care Interactions	X	X	X	X					X	Case # Ticket #
Frequent Flyer Communications	X	X	X	X					X	
Maintenance Work Orders	X	X	X						X	Work Order #
Crew Scheduling	X	X	X			X			X	

Figure 12-1: Subset of bus matrix row for an airline.

The business and DW/BI team representatives decide the first deliverable should focus on flight activity. The marketing department wants to analyze what flights the company's frequent flyers take, what fare basis they pay, how often they upgrade, how they earn and redeem their frequent flyer miles, whether they respond to special fare promotions, how long their overnight stays are, and what proportion of these frequent flyers have gold, platinum, aluminum, or titanium status. The first project doesn't focus on reservation or ticketing activity data that didn't result in a passenger boarding a plane. The DW/BI team will contend with those other sources of data in subsequent phases.

Multiple Fact Table Granularities

When it comes to the grain as you work through the four-step design process, this case presents multiple potential levels of fact table granularity, each having different associated metrics.

At the most granular level, the airline captures data at the leg level. The leg represents an aircraft taking off at one airport and landing at another without any intermediate stops. Capacity planning and flight scheduling analysts are interested in this discrete level of information because they can look at the number of seats to calculate load factors by leg. Operational aircraft flight metrics are captured at the leg level, such as flight duration and the number of minutes late at departure and arrival. Perhaps there's even a dimension to easily identify on-time arrivals.

The next level of granularity corresponds to a segment. Segments refer to a single flight number (such as Delta flight number 40 or DL0040) flown by a single aircraft. Segments may have one or more legs associated with them; in most cases segments are composed of just one leg with a single take-off and landing. If you take a flight from San Francisco to Minneapolis with a stop in Denver but no aircraft or flight number change, you have flown one segment (SFO-MSP) but two legs (SFO-DEN and DEN-MSP). Conversely, if the flight flew nonstop from San Francisco to Minneapolis, you would have flown one segment as well as one leg. The segment represents the line item on an airline ticket coupon; passenger revenue and mileage credit is determined at the segment level. So although some airline departments focus on leg level operations, the marketing and revenue groups focus on segment-level metrics.

Next, you can analyze flight activity by trip. The trip provides an accurate picture of customer demand. In the prior example, assume the flights from San Francisco to Minneapolis required the flyer to change aircraft in Denver. In this case, the trip from San Francisco to Minneapolis would entail two segments corresponding to the two involved aircraft. In reality, the passenger just asked to go from San Francisco to Minneapolis; the fact that she needs to stop in Denver is merely a necessary evil. For this reason, sales and marketing analysts are also interested in trip level data.

Finally, the airline collects data for the itinerary, which is equivalent to the entire airline ticket or reservation confirmation number.

The DW/BI team and business representatives decide to begin at the segment-level grain. This represents the lowest level of data with meaningful revenue metrics. Alternatively, you could lean on the business for rules to allocate the segment-level metrics down to the leg, perhaps based on the mileage of each leg within the segment. The data warehouse inevitably will tackle the more granular leg level data for the capacity planners and flight schedulers at some future point. The conforming dimensions built during this first iteration will be leveraged at that time.

There will be one row in the fact table for each boarding pass collected from passengers. The dimensionality associated with this data is quite extensive, as illustrated in Figure 12-2. The schema extensively uses the role-playing technique. The multiple date, time, and airport dimensions link to views of a single underlying physical date, time, and airport dimension table, respectively, as we discussed originally in Chapter 6: Order Management.

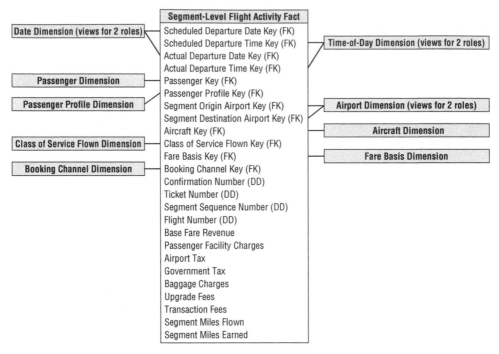

Figure 12-2: Initial segment flight activity schema.

The passenger dimension is a garden variety customer dimension with rich attributes captured about the most valuable frequent flyers. Interestingly, frequent flyers are motivated to help maintain this dimension accurately because they want to ensure they're receiving appropriate mileage credit. For a large airline, this dimension has tens to hundreds of millions of rows.

Marketing wants to analyze activity by the frequent flyer tier, which can change during the course of a year. In addition, you learned during the requirements process that the users are interested in slicing and dicing based on the flyers' home airports, whether they belong to the airline's airport club at the time of each flight, and their lifetime mileage tier. Given the change tracking requirements, coupled with the size of the passenger dimension, we opt to create a separate passenger profile mini-dimension, as we discussed in Chapter 5: Procurement, with one row for each unique combination of frequent flyer elite tier, home airport, club membership status, and lifetime mileage tier. Sample rows for this mini-dimension are illustrated in Figure 12-3. You considered treating these attributes as slowly changing type 2 attributes, especially because the attributes don't rapidly change. But given the number of passengers, you opt for a type 4 mini-dimension instead. As it turns out, marketing analysts often leverage this mini-dimension for their analysis and reporting without touching the millions of passenger dimension rows.

Passenger Profile Key	Frequent Flyer Tier	Home Airport	Club Membership Status	Lifetime Mileage Tier
1	Basic	ATL	Non-Member	Under 100,000 miles
2	Basic	ATL	Club Member	Under 100,000 miles
3	Basic	BOS	Non-Member	Under 100,000 miles
...	...	...	...	...
789	MidTier	ATL	Non-Member	100,000-499,999 miles
790	MidTier	ATL	Club Member	100,000-499,999 miles
791	MidTier	BOS	Non-Member	100,000-499,999 miles
...	...	...	...	...
2468	WarriorTier	ATL	Club Member	1,000,000-1,999,999 miles
2469	WarriorTier	ATL	Club Member	2,000,000-2,999,999 miles
2470	WarriorTier	BOS	Club Member	1,000,000-1,999,999 miles
...	...	...	...	...

Figure 12-3: Passenger mini-dimension sample rows.

The aircraft dimension contains information about each plane flown. The origin and destination airports associated with each flight are called out separately to simplify the user's view of the data and make access more efficient.

The class of service flown describes whether the passenger sat in economy, premium economy, business, or first class. The fare basis dimension describes the terms surrounding the fare. It would identify whether it's an unrestricted fare, a 21-day advance purchase fare with change and cancellation penalties, or a 10 percent off fare due to a special promotion.

The sales channel dimension identifies how the ticket was purchased, whether through a travel agency, directly from the airline's phone number, city ticket office, or website, or via another internet travel services provider. Although the sales channel relates to the entire ticket, each segment should inherit ticket-level dimensionality. In addition, several operational numbers are associated with the flight activity data, including the itinerary number, ticket number, flight number, and segment sequence number.

The facts captured at the segment level of granularity include the base fare revenue, passenger facility charges, airport and government taxes, other ancillary charges and fees, segment miles flown, and segment miles awarded (in those cases in which a minimum number of miles are awarded regardless of the flight distance).

Linking Segments into Trips

Despite the powerful dimensional framework you just designed, you cannot easily answer one of the most important questions about your frequent flyers, namely, "Where are they going?" The segment grain masks the true nature of the trip. If you fetch all the segments of a trip and sequence them by segment number, it is still nearly impossible to discern the trip start and endpoints. Most complete itineraries start and end at the same airport. If a lengthy stop were used as a criterion for a meaningful trip destination, it would require extensive and tricky processing at the BI reporting layer whenever you try to summarize trips.

The answer is to introduce two more airport role-playing dimensions, trip origin and trip destination, while keeping the grain at the flight segment level. These are determined during data extraction by looking on the ticket for any stop of more than four hours, which is the airline's official definition of a stopover. You need to exercise some caution when summarizing data by trip in this schema. Some of the dimensions, such as fare basis or class of service flown, don't apply at the trip level. On the other hand, it may be useful to see how many trips from San Francisco to Minneapolis included an unrestricted fare on a segment.

In addition to linking segments into trips on the segment flight activity schema, if the business users are constantly looking at information at the trip level, rather than by segment, you might create an aggregate fact table at the trip grain. Some of the earlier dimensions discussed, such as class of service and fare basis, obviously would not be applicable. The facts would include aggregated metrics like trip total base fare or trip total taxes, plus additional facts that would appear only in this complementary trip summary table, such as the number of segments in the trip. However, you would go to the trouble of creating this aggregate table only if there were obvious performance or usability issues when you use the segment-level table as the basis for rolling up the same reports. If a typical trip consists of three segments, you might barely see a three times performance improvement with such an aggregate table, meaning it may not be worth the bother.

Related Fact Tables

As discussed earlier, you would likely create a leg-grained flight activity fact table to satisfy the more operational needs surrounding the departure and arrival of each flight. Metrics at the leg level might include actual and blocked flight durations, departure and arrival delays, and departure and arrival fuel weights.

In addition to the flight activity, there will be fact tables to capture reservations and issued tickets. Given the focus on maximizing revenue, there might be a revenue and availability snapshot for each flight; it could provide snapshots for the final 90 days leading up to a flight departure with cumulative unearned revenue and remaining availability per class of service for each scheduled flight. The snapshot might include a dimension supporting the concept of "days prior to departure" to facilitate the comparison of similar flights at standard milestones, such as 60 days prior to scheduled departure.

Extensions to Other Industries

Using the airline case study to illustrate a voyage schema makes intuitive sense because most people have boarded a plane at one time or another. We'll briefly touch on several other variations on this theme.

Cargo Shipper

The schema for a cargo shipper looks quite similar to the airline schemas just developed. Suppose a transoceanic shipping company transports bulk goods in containers from foreign to domestic ports. The items in the containers are shipped from an original shipper to a final consignor. The trip can have multiple stops at intermediate ports. It is possible the containers may be off-loaded from one ship to another at a port. Likewise, it is possible one or more of the legs may be by truck rather than ship.

As illustrated in Figure 12-4, the grain of the fact table is the container on a specific bill-of-lading number on a particular leg of its trip. The ship mode dimension identifies the type of shipping company and specific vessel. The container dimension describes the size of the container and whether it requires electrical power or refrigeration. The commodity dimension describes the item in the container. Almost anything that can be shipped can be described by harmonized commodity codes, which are a kind of master conformed dimension used by agencies, including U.S. Customs. The consignor, foreign transporter, foreign consolidator, shipper, domestic consolidator, domestic transporter, and consignee are all roles played by a master business entity dimension that contains all the possible business parties associated with a voyage. The bill-of-lading number is a degenerate dimension. We assume the fees and tariffs are applicable to the individual leg of the voyage.

Travel Services

If you work for a travel services company, you can complement the flight activity schema with fact tables to track associated hotel stays and rental car usage. These schemas would share several common dimensions, such as the date and customer. For hotel stays, the grain of the fact table is the entire stay, as illustrated in Figure 12-5. The grain of a similar car rental fact table would be the entire rental episode. Of course, if constructing a fact table for a hotel chain rather than a travel services company, the schema would be much more robust because you'd know far more about the hotel property characteristics, the guest's use of services, and associated detailed charges.

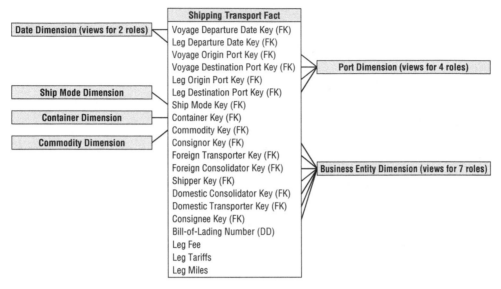

Figure 12-4: Shipper schema.

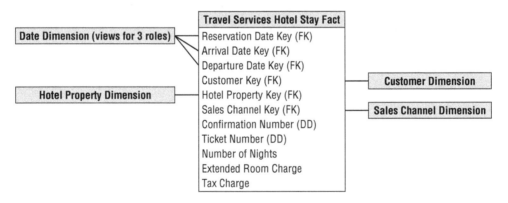

Figure 12-5: Travel services hotel stay schema.

Combining Correlated Dimensions

We stated previously that if a many-to-many relationship exists between two groups of dimension attributes, they should be modeled as separate dimensions with separate foreign keys in the fact table. Sometimes, however, you encounter situations where these dimensions can be combined into a single dimension rather than treating them as two separate dimensions with two separate foreign keys in the fact table.

Class of Service

The Figure 12-2 draft schema includes the class of service flown dimension. Following a design checkpoint with the business community, you learn the users also want to analyze the booking class purchased. In addition, the business users want to easily filter and report on activity based on whether an upgrade or downgrade occurred. Your initial reaction might be to include a second role-playing dimension and foreign key in the fact table to support both the purchased and flown class of service. In addition, you would need a third foreign key for the upgrade indicator; otherwise, the BI application would need to include logic to identify numerous scenarios as upgrades, including economy to premium economy, economy to business, economy to first, premium economy to business, and so on. In this situation, however, there are only four rows in the class dimension table to indicate first, business, premium economy, and economy classes. Likewise, the upgrade indicator dimension also would have just three rows in it, corresponding to upgrade, downgrade, or no class change. Because the row counts are so small, you can elect instead to combine the dimensions into a single class of service dimension, as illustrated in Figure 12-6.

Class of Service Key	Class Purchased	Class Flown	Purchased-Flown Group	Class Change Indicator
1	Economy	Economy	Economy-Economy	No Class Change
2	Economy	Prem Economy	Economy-Prem Economy	Upgrade
3	Economy	Business	Economy-Business	Upgrade
4	Economy	First	Economy-First	Upgrade
5	Prem Economy	Economy	Prem Economy-Economy	Downgrade
6	Prem Economy	Prem Economy	Prem Economy-Prem Economy	No Class Change
7	Prem Economy	Business	Prem Economy-Business	Upgrade
8	Prem Economy	First	Prem Economy-First	Upgrade
9	Business	Economy	Business-Economy	Downgrade
10	Business	Prem Economy	Business-Prem Economy	Downgrade
11	Business	Business	Business-Business	No Class Change
12	Business	First	Business-First	Upgrade
13	First	Economy	First-Economy	Downgrade
14	First	Prem Economy	First-Prem Economy	Downgrade
15	First	Business	First-Business	Downgrade
16	First	First	First-First	No Class Change

Figure 12-6: Combined class dimension sample rows.

The Cartesian product of the separate class dimensions results in a 16-row dimension table (4 class purchased rows times 4 class flown rows). You also have the opportunity in this combined dimension to describe the relationship between the purchased and flown classes, such as a class change indicator. Think of this combined class of service dimension as a type of junk dimension, introduced in Chapter 6. In this case study, the attributes are tightly correlated. Other airline fact tables, such as inventory availability or ticket purchases, would invariably reference a conformed class dimension table with just four rows.

NOTE In most cases, role-playing dimensions should be treated as separate logical dimensions created via views on a single physical table. In isolated situations, it may make sense to combine the separate dimensions into a single dimension, notably when the data volumes are extremely small or there is a need for additional attributes that depend on the combined underlying roles for context and meaning.

Origin and Destination

Likewise, consider the pros and cons of combining the origin and destination airport dimensions. In this situation the data volumes are more significant, so separate role-playing origin and destination dimensions seem more practical. However, the business users may need additional attributes that depend on the combination of origin and destination. In addition to accessing the characteristics of each airport, business users also want to analyze flight activity data by the distance between the city-pair airports, as well as the type of city pair (such as domestic or trans-Atlantic). Even the seemingly simple question regarding the total activity between San Francisco (SFO) and Denver (DEN), regardless of whether the flights originated in SFO or DEN, presents some challenges with separate origin and destination dimensions. SQL experts could surely answer the question programmatically with separate airport dimensions, but what about the less empowered? Even if experts can derive the correct answer, there's no standard label for the nondirectional city-pair route. Some reporting applications may label it SFO-DEN, whereas others might opt for DEN-SFO, San Fran-Denver, Den-SF, and so on. Rather than embedding inconsistent labels in BI reporting application code, the attribute values should be stored in a dimension table, so common standardized labels can be used throughout the organization. It would be a shame to go to the bother of creating a data warehouse and then allowing application code to implement inconsistent reporting labels. The business sponsors of the DW/BI system won't tolerate that for long.

To satisfy the need to access additional city-pair route attributes, you have two options. One is merely to add another dimension to the fact table for the city-pair route descriptors, including the directional route name, nondirectional route name, type, and distance, as shown in Figure 12-7. The other alternative is to combine the origin and destination airport attributes, plus the supplemental city-pair route attributes, into a single dimension. Theoretically, the combined dimension could have as many rows as the Cartesian product of all the origin and destination airports. Fortunately, in real life the number of rows is much smaller than this theoretical limit because airlines don't operate flights between every airport where they have a presence. However, with a couple dozen attributes about the origin airport, plus a couple dozen identical attributes about the destination airport, along with attributes about the route, you would probably be more tempted to treat them as separate dimensions.

City-Pair Route Key	Directional Route Name	Non-Directional Route Name	Route Distance in Miles	Route Distance Band	Dom-Intl Ind	Transocean Ind
1	BOS-JFK	BOS-JFK	191	Less than 200 miles	Domestic	Non-Oceanic
2	JFK-BOS	BOS-JFK	191	Less than 200 miles	Domestic	Non-Oceanic
3	BOS-LGW	BOS-LGW	3,267	3,000 to 3,500 miles	International	Transatlantic
4	LGW-BOS	BOS-LGW	3,267	3,000 to 3,500 miles	International	Transatlantic
5	BOS-NRT	BOS-NRT	6,737	More than 6,000 miles	International	Transpacific
6	NRT-BOS	BOS-NRT	6,737	More than 6,000 miles	International	Transpacific

Figure 12-7: City-pair route dimension sample rows.

Sometimes designers suggest using a bridge table containing the origin and destination airport keys to capture the route information. Although the origin and destination represent a many-to-many relationship, in this case, you can cleanly represent the relationship within the existing fact table rather than using a bridge.

More Date and Time Considerations

From the earliest chapters in this book we've discussed the importance of having a verbose date dimension, whether at the individual day, week, or month granularity, that contains descriptive attributes about the date and private labels for fiscal periods and work holidays. In this final section, we'll introduce several additional considerations for dealing with date and time dimensions.

Country-Specific Calendars as Outriggers

If the DW/BI system serves multinational needs, you must generalize the standard date dimension to handle multinational calendars in an open-ended number of countries. The primary date dimension contains generic calendar attributes about the date, regardless of the country. If your multinational business spans Gregorian, Hebrew, Islamic, and Chinese calendars, you would include four sets of days, months, and years in this primary dimension.

Country-specific date dimensions supplement the primary date table. The key to the supplemental dimension is the primary date key, along with the country code. The table would include country-specific date attributes, such as holiday or season names, as illustrated in Figure 12-8. This approach is similar to the handling of multiple fiscal accounting calendars, as described in Chapter 7: Accounting.

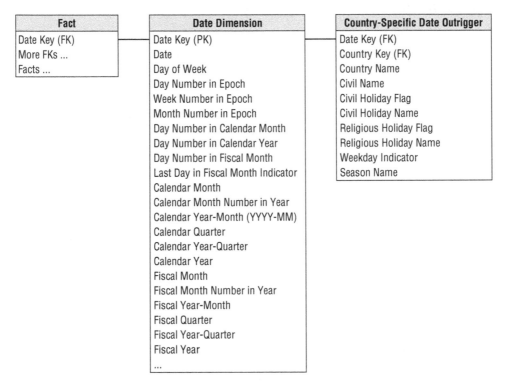

Figure 12-8: Country-specific calendar outrigger.

You can join this table to the main calendar dimension as an outrigger or directly to the fact table. If you provide an interface that requires the user to specify a country name, then the attributes of the country-specific supplement can be viewed as logically appended to the primary date table, allowing them to view the calendar through the eyes of a single country at a time. Country-specific calendars can be messy to build in their own right; things get even more complicated if you need to deal with local holidays that occur on different days in different parts of a country.

Date and Time in Multiple Time Zones

When operating in multiple countries or even just multiple time zones, you're faced with a quandary concerning transaction dates and times. Do you capture the date and time relative to local midnight in each time zone, or do you express the time period relative to a standard, such as the corporate headquarters date/time, Greenwich Mean Time (GMT), or Coordinated Universal Time (UTC), also known as Zulu time in the aviation world? To fully satisfy users' requirements, the correct answer is probably both. The standard time enables you to see the simultaneous nature of transactions across the business, whereas the local time enables you to understand transaction timing relative to the time of day.

Contrary to popular belief, there are more than 24 time zones (corresponding to the 24 hours of the day) in the world. For example, there is a single time zone in China despite its latitudinal span. Likewise, there is a single time zone in India, offset from UTC by 5.5 hours. In Australia, there are three time zones with its Central time zone offset by one-half hour. Meanwhile, Nepal and some other nations use one-quarter hour offset. The situation gets even more unpleasant when you account for switches to and from daylight saving time.

Given the complexities, it's unreasonable to think that merely providing a UTC offset in a fact table can support equivalized dates and times. Likewise, the offset can't reside in a time or airport dimension table because the offset depends on both location and date. The recommended approach for expressing dates and times in multiple time zones is to include separate date and time-of-day dimensions corresponding to the local and equivalized dates, as shown in Figure 12-9. The time-of-day dimensions, as discussed in Chapter 3: Retail Sales, support time period groupings such as shift numbers or rush period time block designations.

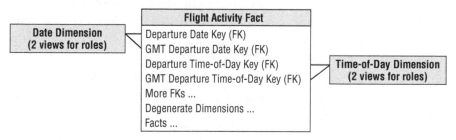

Figure 12-9: Local and equivalized date/time across time zones.

Localization Recap

We have discussed the challenges of international DW/BI system in several chapters of the book. In addition to the international time zones and calendars discussed in the previous two sections, we have also talked about multi-currency reporting in Chapter 6 and multi-language support in Chapter 8: Customer Relationship Management.

All these database-centric techniques fall under the general theme of *localization*. Localization in the larger sense also includes the translation of user interface text embedded in BI tools. BI tool vendors implement this form of localization with text databases containing all the text prompts and labels needed by the tool, which can then be configured for each local environment. Of course, this can become quite complicated because text translated from English to most European languages results in text strings that are longer than their English equivalents, which may force a redesign of the BI application. Also, Arabic text reads from right to left, and many Asian languages are completely different.

A serious international DW/BI system built to serve business users in many countries needs to be thoughtfully designed to account for a selected set of these localization issues. But perhaps it is worth thinking about how airport control towers and airplane pilots around the world deal with language incompatibilities when communicating critical messages about flight directions and altitudes. They all use one language (English) and unit of measure (feet).

Summary

In this chapter we turned our attention to airline trips or routes; we briefly touched on similar scenarios drawn from the shipping and travel services industries. We examined the situation in which we have multiple fact tables at multiple granularities with multiple grain-specific facts. We also discussed the possibility of combining dimensions into a single dimension table for cases in which the row count volumes are extremely small or when there are additional attributes that depend on the combined dimensions. Again, combining correlated dimensions should be viewed as the exception rather than the rule.

We wrapped up this chapter by discussing several date and time dimension techniques, including country-specific calendar outriggers and the handling of absolute and relative dates and times.

13

Education

We step into the world of an educational institution in this chapter, looking first at the applicant pipeline as an accumulating snapshot. When accumulating snapshot fact tables were introduced in Chapter 4: Inventory, a product movement pipeline illustrated the concept; order fulfillment workflows were captured in an accumulating snapshot in Chapter 6: Order Management. In this chapter, rather than watching products or orders move through various states, an accumulating snapshot is used to monitor prospective student applicants as they progress through admissions milestones.

The other primary concept discussed in this chapter is the factless fact table. We'll explore several case study illustrations drawn from higher education to further elaborate on these special fact tables and discuss the analysis of events that didn't occur.

Chapter 13 discusses the following concepts:

- Example bus matrix snippet for a university or college
- Applicant tracking and research grant proposals as accumulating snapshot fact tables
- Factless fact table for admission events, course registration facilities management, and student attendance
- Handling of nonexistent events

University Case Study and Bus Matrix

In this chapter you're working for a university, college, or other type of educational institution. Someone at a higher education client once remarked that running a university is akin to operating all the businesses needed to support a small village. Universities are simultaneously a real estate property management company (residential student housing), restaurant with multiple outlets (dining halls), retailer (bookstore), events management and ticketing agency (athletics and speaker events), police department (campus security), professional fundraiser (alumni development), consumer financial services company (financial aid), investment firm (endowment management), venture capitalist (research and development), job placement firm (career planning), construction company (buildings and facilities maintenance), and medical services provider (health clinic). In addition to these varied functions, higher education institutions are obviously also focused on attracting high caliber students and talented faculty to create a robust educational environment.

The bus matrix snippet in Figure 13-1 covers several core processes within an educational institution. Traditionally, there has been less focus on revenue and profit in higher education, but with ever-escalating costs and competition, universities and colleges cannot ignore these financial metrics. They want to attract and retain students who align with their academic and other institutional objectives. There's a strong interest in analyzing what students are "buying" in terms of courses each term and the associated academic outcomes. Colleges and universities want to understand many aspects of the student's experience, along with maintaining an ongoing relationship well beyond graduation.

Accumulating Snapshot Fact Tables

Chapter 4 used an accumulating snapshot fact table to track products identified by serial or lot numbers as they move through various inventory stages in a warehouse. Take a moment to recall the distinguishing characteristics of an accumulating snapshot fact table:

- A single row represents the complete history of a workflow or pipeline instance.
- Multiple dates represent the standard pipeline milestone events.
- The accumulating snapshot facts often included metrics corresponding to each milestone, plus status counts and elapsed durations.
- Each row is revisited and updated whenever the pipeline instance changes; both foreign keys and measured facts may be changed during the fact row updates.

Applicant Pipeline

Now envision these same accumulating snapshot characteristics as applied to the prospective student admissions pipeline. For those who work in other industries, there are obvious similarities to tracking job applicants through the hiring process or sales prospects as they are qualified and become customers.

	Date/Term	Applicant-Student-Alum	Employee (Faculty, Staff)	Course	Department	Facility	Account
Student Lifecycle Processes							
Admission Events	X	X	X				
Applicant Pipeline	X	X	X		X		
Financial Aid Awards	X	X	X		X		
Student Enrollment/Profile Snapshot	X	X	X		X	X	
Student Residential Housing	X	X			X	X	
Student Course Registration & Outcomes	X	X	X	X	X	X	
Student Course Instructor Evaluations	X	X	X	X	X	X	
Student Activities	X	X			X		
Career Placement Activities	X	X			X		
Advancement Contacts	X	X	X				
Advancement Pledges & Gifts	X	X	X				X
Financial Processes							
Budgeting	X		X		X		X
Endowment Tracking	X				X		X
GL Transactions	X				X		X
Payroll	X		X		X		X
Procurement	X		X		X		X
Employee Management Processes							
Employee Headcount Snapshot	X		X		X	X	
Employee Hiring & Separations	X		X		X		
Employee Benefits & Compensation	X		X		X		
Staff Performance Management	X		X		X		
Faculty Appointment Management	X		X		X		
Research Proposal Pipeline	X		X		X		
Research Expenditures	X		X		X		X
Faculty Publications	X		X		X		
Administrative Processes							
Facilities Utilization	X		X		X	X	
Energy Consumption & Waste Management	X				X	X	
Work Orders	X	X	X		X	X	X

Figure 13-1: Subset of bus matrix rows for educational institution.

In the case of applicant tracking, prospective students progress through a standard set of admissions hurdles or milestones. Perhaps you're interested in tracking activities around key dates, such as initial inquiry, campus visit, application submitted, application file completed, admissions decision notification, and enrolled or withdrawn. At any point in time, admissions and enrollment management analysts are interested in how many applicants are at each stage in the pipeline. The process is much like a funnel, where many inquiries enter the pipeline, but far less progress through to the final stage. Admission personnel also would like to analyze the applicant pool by a variety of characteristics.

The grain of the applicant pipeline accumulating snapshot is one row per prospective student; this granularity represents the lowest level of detail captured when the prospect enters the pipeline. As more information is collected while the prospective student progresses toward application, acceptance, and enrollment, you continue to revisit and update the fact table row, as illustrated in Figure 13-2.

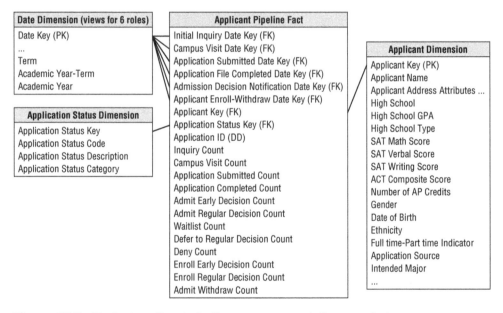

Figure 13-2: Student applicant pipeline as an accumulating snapshot.

Like earlier accumulating snapshots, there are multiple dates in the fact table corresponding to the standard milestone events. You want to analyze the prospect's progress by these dates to determine the pace of movement through the pipeline and spot bottlenecks. This is especially important if you see a significant lag involving a candidate whom you're interested in recruiting. Each of these dates is treated as a role-playing dimension, with a default surrogate key to handle the unknown dates for new and in-process rows.

The applicant dimension contains many interesting attributes about prospective students. Analysts are interested in slicing and dicing by applicant characteristics such as geography, incoming credentials (grade point average, college admissions test scores, advanced placement credits, and high school), gender, date of birth, ethnicity, preliminary major, application source, and a multitude of others. Analyzing these characteristics at various stages of the pipeline can help admissions personnel adjust their strategies to encourage more (or fewer) students to proceed to the next mile marker.

The facts in the applicant pipeline fact table include a variety of counts that are closely monitored by admissions personnel. If available, this table could include estimated probabilities that the prospect will apply and subsequently enroll if accepted to predict admission yields.

Alternative Applicant Pipeline Schemas

Accumulating snapshots are appropriate for short-lived processes that have a defined beginning and end, with standard intermediate milestones. This type of fact table enables you to see an updated status and ultimately final disposition of each applicant. However, because accumulating snapshot rows are updated, they do not preserve applicant counts and statuses at critical points in the admissions calendar, such as the early decision notification date. Given the close scrutiny of these numbers, analysts might also want to retain snapshots at several important cut-off dates. Alternatively, you could build an admission transaction fact table with one row per transaction per applicant for counting and period-to-period comparisons.

Research Grant Proposal Pipeline

The research proposal pipeline is another education-based example of an accumulating snapshot. Faculty and administration are interested in viewing the lifecycle of a grant proposal as it progresses through the pipeline from preliminary proposal to grant approval and award receipt. This would support analysis of the number of outstanding proposals in each stage of the pipeline by faculty, department, research topic area, or research funding source. Likewise, you could see success rates by various attributes. Having this information in a common repository would allow it to be leveraged by a broader university population.

Factless Fact Tables

So far we've largely designed fact tables with very similar structures. Each fact table typically has 5 to approximately 20 foreign key columns, followed by one to potentially several dozen numeric, continuously valued, preferably additive facts. The facts can be regarded as measurements taken at the intersection of the dimension key values. From this perspective, the facts are the justification for the fact table, and the key values are simply administrative structure to identify the facts.

There are, however, a number of business processes whose fact tables are similar to those we've been designing with one major distinction. There are no measured facts! We introduced factless fact tables while discussing promotion events in Chapter 3: Retail Sales, as well as in Chapter 6 to describe sales rep/customer assignments. There are numerous examples of factless events in higher education.

Admissions Events

You can envision a factless fact table to track each prospective student's attendance at an admission event, such as a high school visit, college fair, alumni interview or campus overnight, as illustrated in Figure 13-3.

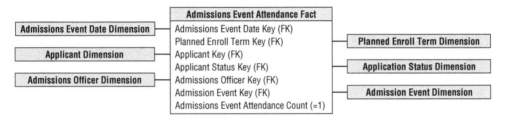

Figure 13-3: Admission event attendance as a factless fact table.

Course Registrations

Similarly, you can track student course registrations by term using a factless fact table. The grain would be one row for each registered course by student and term, as illustrated in Figure 13-4.

Term Dimension

In this fact table, the data is at the term level rather than at the more typical calendar day, week, or month granularity. The term dimension still should conform to the calendar date dimension. In other words, each date in the daily calendar dimension should identify the term (for example, Fall), term and academic year (for example, Fall 2013), and academic year (for example, 2013-2014). The column labels and values must be identical for the attributes common to both the calendar date and term dimensions.

Student Dimension and Change Tracking

The student dimension is an expanded version of the applicant dimension discussed in the first scenario. You still want to retain some information garnered from the application process (for example, geography, credentials, and intended major) but supplement it with on-campus information, such as part-time or full-time status, residence, athletic involvement indicator, declared major, and class level status (for example, sophomore).

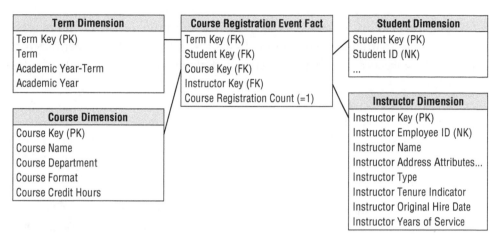

Figure 13-4: Course registration events as a factless fact table.

As discussed in Chapter 5: Procurement, you could imagine placing some of these attributes in a type 4 mini-dimension because factions throughout the university are interested in tracking changes to them, especially for declared major, class level, and graduation attainment. People in administration and academia are keenly interested in academic progress and retention rates by class, school, department, and major. Alternatively, if there's a strong demand to preserve the students' profiles at the time of course registration, plus filter and group by the students' current characteristics, you should consider handling the student information as a slowly changing dimension type 7 with dual student dimension keys in the fact table, as also described in Chapter 5. The surrogate student key would link to a dimension table with type 2 attributes; the student's durable identifier would link to a view of the complete student dimension containing only the current row for each student.

Artificial Count Metric

A fact table represents the robust set of many-to-many relationships among dimensions; it records the collision of dimensions at a point in time and space. This course registration fact table could be queried to answer a number of interesting questions regarding registration for the college's academic offerings, such as which students registered for which courses? How many declared engineering majors are taking an out-of-major finance course? How many students have registered for a given faculty member's courses during the last three years? How many students have registered for more than one course from a given faculty member? The only peculiarity in these examples is that you don't have a numeric fact tied to this registration data. As such, analyses of this data will be based largely on counts.

> **NOTE** Events are modeled as fact tables containing a series of keys, each representing a participating dimension in the event. Event tables sometimes have no variable measurement facts associated with them and hence are called factless fact tables.

The SQL for performing counts in this factless fact is asymmetric because of the absence of any facts. When counting the number of registrations for a faculty member, any key can be used as the argument to the COUNT function. For example:

```
select faculty, count(term_key)... group by faculty
```

This gives the simple count of the number of student registrations by faculty, subject to any constraints that may exist in the WHERE clause. An oddity of SQL is that you can count any key and still get the same answer because you are counting the number of keys that fly by the query, not their distinct values. You would need to use a COUNT DISTINCT if you want to count the unique instances of a key rather than the number of keys encountered.

The inevitable confusion surrounding the SQL statement, although not a serious semantic problem, causes some designers to create an artificial implied fact, perhaps called course registration count (as opposed to "dummy"), that is always populated by the value 1. Although this fact does not add any information to the fact table, it makes the SQL more readable, such as:

```
select faculty, sum(registration_count)... group by faculty
```

At this point the table is no longer strictly factless, but the "1" is nothing more than an artifact. The SQL will be a bit cleaner and more expressive with the registration count. Some BI query tools have an easier time constructing this query with a few simple user gestures. More important, if you build a summarized aggregate table above this fact table, you need a real column to roll up to meaningful aggregate registration counts. And finally, if deploying to an OLAP cube, you typically include an explicit count column (always equal to 1) for complex counts because the dimension join keys are not explicitly revealed in a cube.

If a measurable fact does surface during the design, it can be added to the schema, assuming it is consistent with the grain of student course registrations by term. For example, you could add tuition revenue, earned credit hours, and grade scores to this fact table, but then it's no longer a factless fact table.

Multiple Course Instructors

If courses are taught by a single instructor, you can associate an instructor key to the course registration events, as shown in Figure 13-4. However, if some courses are co-taught, then it is a dimension attribute that takes on multiple values for the fact table's declared grain. You have several options:

- Alter the grain of the fact table to be one row per instructor per course registration per student per term. Although this would address the multiple instructors associated with a course, it's an unnatural granularity that would be extremely prone to overstated registration count errors.
- Add a bridge table with an instructor group key in either the fact table or as an outrigger on the course dimension, as introduced in Chapter 8: Customer Relationship Management. There would be one row in this table for each instructor who teaches courses on his own. In addition, there would be two rows for each instructor team; these rows would associate the same group key with individual instructor keys. The concatenation of the group key and instructor key would uniquely identify each bridge table row. As described in Chapter 10: Financial Services, you could assign a weighting factor to each row in the bridge if the teaching workload allocation is clearly defined. This approach would be susceptible to the potential overstatement issues surrounding the bridge table usage described in Chapter 10.
- Concatenate the instructor names into a single, delimited attribute on the course dimension, as discussed in Chapter 9: Human Resources Management. This option enables users to easily label reports with a single dimension attribute, but it would not support analysis of registration events by instructor characteristics.
- If one of the instructors is identified as the primary instructor, then her instructor key could be handled as a single foreign key in the fact table, joined to a dimension where the attributes were prefaced with "primary" for differentiation.

Course Registration Periodic Snapshots

The grain of the fact table illustrated in Figure 13-4 is one row for each registered course by student and term. Some users at the college or university might be interested in periodic snapshots of the course registration events at key academic calendar dates, such as preregistration, start of the term, course drop/add deadline, and end of the term. In this case, the fact table's grain would be one row for each student's registered courses for a term per snapshot date.

Facility Utilization

The second type of factless fact table deals with coverage, which can be illustrated with a facilities management scenario. Universities invest a tremendous amount of capital in their physical plant and facilities. It would be helpful to understand which facilities were being used for what purpose during every hour of the day during each term. For example, which facilities were used most heavily? What was the average occupancy rate of the facilities as a function of time of day? Does utilization drop off significantly on Fridays when no one wants to attend (or teach) classes?

Again, the factless fact table comes to the rescue. In this case you'd insert one row in the fact table for each facility for standard hourly time blocks during each day of the week during a term regardless of whether the facility is being used. Figure 13-5 illustrates the schema.

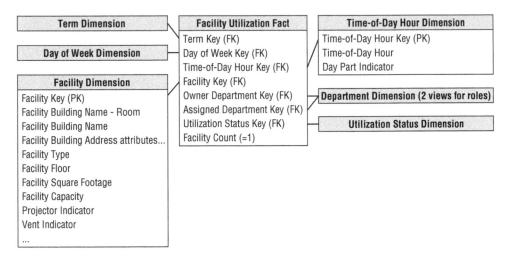

Figure 13-5: Facilities utilization as a coverage factless fact table.

The facility dimension would include all types of descriptive attributes about the facility, such as the building, facility type (for example, classroom, lab, or office), square footage, capacity, and amenities (for example, whiteboard or built-in projector). The utilization status dimension would include a text descriptor with values of Available or Utilized. Meanwhile, multiple organizations may be involved in facilities utilization. For example, one organization might own the facility during a time block, but the same or a different organization might be assigned as the facility user.

Student Attendance

You can visualize a similar schema to track student attendance in a course. In this case, the grain would be one row for each student who walks through the course's classroom door each day. This factless fact table would share a number of the same dimensions discussed with registration events. The primary difference would be the granularity is by calendar date in this schema rather than merely term. This dimensional model, illustrated in Figure 13-6, allows business users to answer questions concerning which courses were the most heavily attended. Which courses suffered the least attendance attrition over the term? Which students attended which courses? Which faculty member taught the most students?

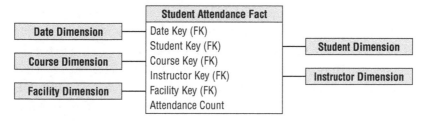

Figure 13-6: Student attendance fact table.

Explicit Rows for What Didn't Happen

Perhaps people are interested in monitoring students who were registered for a course but didn't show up. In this example you can envision adding explicit rows to the fact table for attendance events that didn't occur. The fact table would no longer be factless as there is an attendance metric equal to either 1 or 0.

Adding rows is viable in this scenario because the non-attendance events have the same exact dimensionality as the attendance events. Likewise, the fact table won't grow at an alarming rate, presuming (or perhaps hoping) the no-shows are a small percentage of the total students registered for a course. Although this approach is reasonable in this scenario, creating rows for events that didn't happen is ridiculous in many other situations, such as adding rows to a customer's sales transaction for promoted products that weren't purchased by the customer.

What Didn't Happen with Multidimensional OLAP

Multidimensional OLAP databases do an excellent job of helping users understand what didn't happen. When the cube is constructed, multidimensional databases handle the sparsity of the transaction data while minimizing the overhead burden of storing explicit zeroes. As such, at least for fact cubes that are not too sparse, the event and nonevent data is available for user analysis while reducing some of the complexities just discussed in the relational star schema world.

More Educational Analytic Opportunities

Many of the business processes described in earlier chapters, such as procurement and human resources, are obviously applicable to the university environment given the desire to better monitor and manage costs. Research grants and alumni contributions are key sources of revenue, in addition to the tuition revenue.

Research grant analysis is often a variation of financial analysis, as discussed in Chapter 7: Accounting, but at a lower level of detail, much like a subledger. The grain would include additional dimensions to further describe the research grant, such as the corporate or governmental funding source, research topic, grant duration, and faculty investigator. There is a strong need to better understand and manage the budgeted and actual spending associated with each research project. The objective is to optimize the spending so a surplus or deficit situation is avoided, and funds are deployed where they will be most productive. Likewise, understanding research spending rolled up by various dimensions is necessary to ensure proper institutional control of such monies.

Better understanding the university's alumni is much like better understanding a customer base, as described in Chapter 8. Obviously, there are many interesting characteristics that would be helpful in maintaining a relationship with your alumni, such as geographic, demographic, employment, interests, and behavioral information, in addition to the data you collected about them as students (for example, affiliations, residential housing, school, major, length of time to graduate, and honors designations). Improved access to a broad range of attributes about the alumni population would allow the institution to better target messages and allocate resources. In addition to alumni contributions, alumni relationships can be leveraged for potential recruiting, job placement, and research opportunities. To this end, a robust CRM operational system should track all the touch points with alumni to capture meaningful data for the DW/BI analytic platform.

Summary

In this chapter we focused on two primary concepts. First, we looked at the accumulating snapshot fact table to track application or research grant pipelines. Even though the accumulating snapshot is used much less frequently than the more common transaction and periodic snapshot fact tables, it is very useful for tracking the current status of a short-lived process with standard milestones. As we described, accumulating snapshots are often complemented with transactional or periodic snapshot tables.

Second, we explored several examples of factless fact tables. These fact tables capture the relationship between dimensions in the case of an event or coverage, but are unique in that no measurements are collected to serve as actual facts. We also discussed the handling of situations in which you want to track events that didn't occur.

14 Healthcare

The healthcare industry is undergoing tremendous change as it seeks to both improve patient outcomes, while simultaneously improving operational efficiencies. The challenges are plentiful as organizations attempt to integrate their clinical and administrative information. Healthcare data presents several interesting dimensional design patterns that we'll explore in this chapter.

Chapter 14 discusses the following concepts:

- Example bus matrix snippet for a healthcare organization
- Accumulating snapshot fact table to handle the claims billing and payment pipeline
- Dimension role playing for multiple dates and physicians
- Multivalued dimensions, such as patient diagnoses
- Supertype and subtype handling of healthcare charges
- Treatment of textual comments
- Measurement type dimension for sparse, heterogeneous measurements
- Handling of images with dimensional schemas
- Facility/equipment inventory utilization as transactions and periodic snapshots

Healthcare Case Study and Bus Matrix

In the face of unprecedented consumer focus and governmental policy regulations, coupled with internal pressures, healthcare organizations need to leverage information more effectively to impact both patient outcomes and operational efficiencies. Healthcare organizations typically wrestle with many disparate systems to collect their clinical, financial, and operational performance metrics. This information needs to be better integrated to deliver more effective patient care, while concurrently managing costs and risks. Healthcare analysts want to better understand which procedures deliver the best outcomes, while identifying opportunities to impact resource utilization, including labor, facilities, and associated equipment and supplies. Large healthcare consortiums with networks of physicians, clinics, hospitals, pharmacies, and laboratories are focused on these requirements, especially as both the federal government and private payers are encouraging providers to assume more responsibility for the quality and cost of their healthcare services. Figure 14-1 illustrates a sample snippet of a healthcare organization's bus matrix.

	Date	Patient	Physician	Employee	Facility	Diagnosis	Procedure	Payer
Clinical Events								
Patient Encounter Workflow	X	X	X	X	X	X		
Procedures	X	X	X	X	X	X	X	
Physician Orders	X	X	X		X	X		
Medications	X	X	X			X		
Lab Test Results	X	X	X	X	X	X	X	
Disease/Case Management Participation	X	X	X	X	X	X		
Patient Reported Outcomes	X	X	X		X	X	X	
Patient Satisfaction Surveys	X	X	X		X	X	X	
Billing/Revenue Events								
Inpatient Facility Charges	X	X	X		X	X	X	
Outpatient Professional Charges	X	X	X		X	X	X	
Claims Billing	X	X	X		X	X	X	X
Claims Payments	X	X	X		X	X	X	X
Collections and Write-Offs	X	X	X	X	X	X	X	X
Operational Events								
Bed Inventory Utilization	X	X	X	X	X			
Facilities Utilization	X	X	X	X	X			
Supply Procurement	X			X	X			
Supply Utilization	X	X	X	X	X	X	X	
Workforce Scheduling	X			X	X			

Figure 14-1: Subset of bus matrix row for a healthcare consortium.

Traditionally, healthcare insurance payers have leveraged claims information to better understand their risk, improve underwriting policies, and detect potential fraudulent activity. Payers have historically been more sophisticated than healthcare provider organizations in leveraging data analytically, perhaps in part because their prime data source, claims, was more reliably captured and structured than providers' data. However, claims data is both a benefit and curse for payers' analytic efforts because it historically hasn't provided the robust, granular clinical picture. Increasingly, healthcare payers are partnering with providers to leverage detailed patient information to support more predictive analysis. In many ways, the needs and objectives of the providers and payers are converging, especially with the push for shared-risk delivery models.

Every patient's episode of care with a healthcare organization generates mounds of information. Patient-centric transactional data falls into two prime categories: administrative and clinical. The claims billing data provides detail on a patient bill from a physician's office, clinic, hospital, or laboratory. The clinical medical record, on the other hand, is more comprehensive and includes not only the services result-ing in charges, but also the laboratory test results, prescriptions, physician's notes or orders, and sometimes outcomes.

The issues of conforming common dimensions remain exactly the same for healthcare as in other industries. Obviously, the most important conformed dimen-sion is the patient. In Chapter 8: Customer Relationship Management, we described the need for a 360-degree view of customers. It's easy to argue that a 360-degree view of patients is even more critical given the stakes; adoption of patient *electronic medical record (EMR)* and *electronic health record (EHR)* systems clearly focus on this objective.

Other dimensions that must be conformed include:

- Date
- Responsible party
- Employer
- Health plan
- Payer (primary and secondary)
- Physician
- Procedure
- Equipment
- Lab test
- Medication
- Diagnosis
- Facility (office, clinic, outpatient facility, and hospital)

In the healthcare arena, some of these dimensions are hard to conform, whereas others are easier than they look at first glance. The patient dimension has historically been challenging, at least in the United States, because of the lack of a reliable national identity number and/or consistent patient identifier across facilities and physicians. To further complicate matters, the *Health Insurance Portability and Accountability Act (HIPAA)* includes strict privacy and security requirements to protect the confidential nature of patient information. Operational process improvements, like electronic medical records, are ensuring more consistent master patient identification.

The diagnosis and treatment dimensions are considerably more structured and predictable than you might expect because the insurance industry and government have mandated their content. For example, diagnosis and disease classifications follow the *International Classification of Diseases (ICD)* standard for consistent reporting. Similarly, the *Healthcare Common Procedure Coding System (HCPCS)* is based on the American Medical Association's *Current Procedural Terminology (CPT)* to describe medical, surgical, and diagnostic services, along with supplies and devices. Dentists use the *Current Dental Terminology (CDT)* code set, which is updated and distributed by the American Dental Association.

Finally, beyond integrated patient-centric clinical and financial information, healthcare organizations also want to analyze operational information regarding the utilization of their workforce, facilities, and supplies. Much of the discussion from earlier chapters about human resources, inventory management, and procurement processes is also applicable to healthcare organizations.

Claims Billing and Payments

Imagine you work in the healthcare consortium's billing organization. You receive the primary charges from the physicians and facilities, prepare bills for the responsible payers, and track the progress of the claims payments received.

The dimensional model for the claims billing process must address a number of business objectives. You want to analyze the billed dollar amounts by every available dimension, including patient, physician, facility, diagnosis, procedure, and date. You want to see how these claims have been paid and what percentage of the claims have not been collected. You want to see how long it takes to get paid, and the current status of all unpaid claims.

As we discussed in Chapter 4: Inventory, whenever a source business process is considered for inclusion in the DW/BI system, there are three essential grain choices. Remember the fact table's granularity determines what constitutes a fact table row. In other words, what is the measurement event being recorded?

The transaction grain is the most fundamental. In the healthcare billing example, the transaction grain would include every billing transaction from the physicians and facilities, as well as every claim payment transaction received. We'll talk more about these fact tables in a moment.

The periodic snapshot is the grain of choice for long-running time series, such as bank accounts and insurance policies. However, the periodic snapshot doesn't do a good job of capturing the behavior of relatively short-lived processes, such as orders or medical claims billing.

The accumulating snapshot grain is chosen to analyze the claims billing and payment workflow. A single fact table row represents a single line on a medical claim. Furthermore, the row represents the accumulated history of the line item from the moment of creation to the current state. When anything about the line changes, the row is revisited and modified appropriately. From the point of view of the billing organization, let's assume the standard scenario of a claim includes:

- Treatment date
- Primary insurance billing date
- Secondary insurance billing date
- Responsible party billing date
- Last primary insurance payment date
- Last secondary insurance payment date
- Last responsible party payment date
- Zero balance date

These dates describe the normal claim workflow. An accumulating snapshot does not attempt to fully describe unusual situations. Business users undoubtedly need to see all the details of messy claim payment scenarios because multiple payments are sometimes received for a single line, or conversely, a single payment sometimes applies to multiple claims. Companion transaction schemas inevitably will be needed. In the meantime, the purpose of the accumulating snapshot grain is to place every claim into a standard framework so that the analytic objectives described earlier can be satisfied easily.

With a clear understanding that an individual fact table row represents the accumulated history of a line item on a claim bill, you can identify the dimensions by carefully listing everything known to be true in the context of this row. In this hypothetical scenario, you know the patient, responsible party, physician, physician organization, procedure, facility, diagnosis, primary insurance organization, secondary insurance organization, and master patient bill ID number, as shown in Figure 14-2.

The interesting facts accumulated over the claim line's history include the billed amount, primary insurance paid amount, secondary insurance paid amount, responsible party paid amount, total paid amount (calculated), amount sent to collections, amount written off, amount remaining to be paid (calculated), length of stay, number of days from billing to initial primary insurance, secondary insurance, and responsible party payments, and finally, number of days to zero balance.

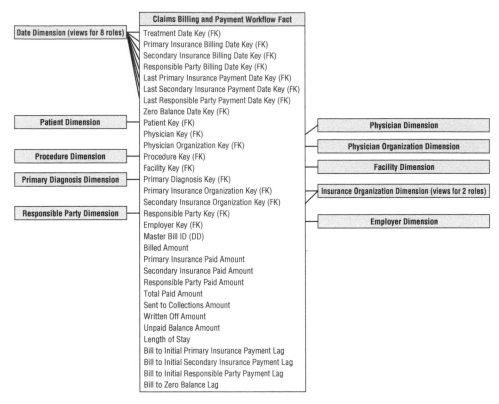

Figure 14-2: Accumulating snapshot fact table for medical claim billing and payment workflow.

A row is initially created in this fact table when the charge transactions are received from the physicians or facilities and the initial bills are generated. On a given bill, perhaps the primary insurance company is billed, but the secondary insurance and responsible party are not billed, pending a response from the primary insurance company. For a period of time after the row is first entered into the fact table, the last seven dates are not applicable. Because the surrogate date keys in the fact table must not be null, they will point to a date dimension row reserved for a To Be Determined date.

In the weeks after creation of the row, some payments are received. Bills are then sent to the secondary insurance company and responsible party. Each time these events take place, the same fact table row is revisited, and the appropriate keys and facts are destructively updated. This destructive updating poses some challenges for the database administrator. If most of the accumulating rows stabilize and stop changing within a given timeframe, a physical reorganization of the database at that time can recover disk storage and improve performance. If the fact table is partitioned on the treatment date key, the physical clustering or partitioning probably will be well preserved throughout these changes because the treatment date is not revisited and changed.

Date Dimension Role Playing

Accumulating snapshot fact tables always involve multiple date stamps, like the eight foreign keys pointing to the date dimension in Figure 14-2. The eight date foreign keys should not join to a single instance of the date dimension table. Instead, create eight views on the single underlying date dimension table, and join the fact table separately to these eight views, as if they were eight independent date dimension tables. The eight view definitions should cosmetically relabel the column names to be distinguishable, so BI tools accessing the views present understandable column names to the business users.

Although the role-playing behavior of the date dimension is a common characteristic of accumulating snapshot fact tables, other dimensions in Figure 14-2 play roles in similar ways, such as the payer dimension. In the section "Supertypes and Subtypes for Charges," the physician dimension will play multiple roles depending on whether the physician is the referring physician, attending physician, or working in a consulting or assisting capacity.

Multivalued Diagnoses

Normally the dimensions surrounding a fact table take on a single value in the context of the fact event. However, there are situations where multivaluedness is natural and unavoidable. The diagnosis dimension in healthcare fact tables is a good example. At the moment of a procedure or lab test, the patient has one or more diagnoses. Electronic medical record applications facilitate the physician's selection of multiple diagnoses well beyond the historical practice of providing the minimal coding needed for reimbursement; the result is a richer, more complete picture of the severity of the patient's medical condition. There is strong analytic incentive to retain the multivalued diagnoses, along with the other financial performance data, especially as organizations do more comparative utilization and cost benchmarking.

If there were always a maximum of three diagnoses, for instance, you might be tempted to create three diagnosis foreign keys in the fact table with corresponding dimensions, almost as if they were roles. However, diagnoses don't behave like independent roles. And unfortunately, there are often more than three diagnoses, especially for hospitalized elderly patients who may present 20 simultaneous diagnoses! Diagnoses don't fit into well-defined roles other than potentially the primary admitting and discharging diagnoses. Finally, a design with multiple diagnosis foreign keys would make for very inefficient BI applications because the query doesn't know which dimensional slot to constrain for a particular diagnosis.

The design shown in Figure 14-3 handles the open-ended nature of multiple diagnoses. The diagnosis foreign key in the fact table is replaced with a diagnosis group key. This diagnosis group key is connected by a many-to-many join to a diagnosis group bridge table, which contains a separate row for each individual diagnosis in a particular group.

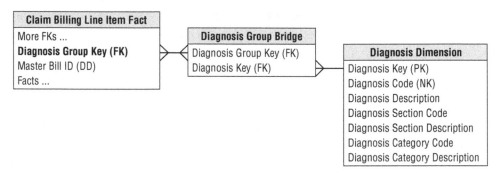

Figure 14-3: Bridge table to handle multivalued diagnoses.

If a patient has three diagnoses, he is assigned a diagnosis group with three corresponding rows in the bridge table. In Chapter 10: Financial Services, we described the use of a weighting factor on each bridge table row to allocate the fact table's metrics accordingly. However, in the case of multiple patient diagnoses, it's virtually impossible to weight their impact on a patient's treatment or bill, beyond the potential determination of a primary diagnosis. Without a realistic way of assigning weighting factors, the analysis of diagnosis codes must largely focus on impact questions like "What is the total billed amount for procedures involving the diagnosis of congestive heart failure?" Most healthcare analysts understand impact analysis may result in over counting as the same metrics are associated with multiple diagnoses.

NOTE Weighting factors in multivalued bridge tables provide an elegant way to prorate numeric facts to produce correctly weighted reports. However, these weighting factors are by no means required in a dimensional design. If there is no agreement or enthusiasm within the business community for the weighting factors, they should be left out. Also, in a schema with more than one multivalued dimension, it is not worth trying to decide how multiple weighting factors would interact.

If the many-to-many join in Figure 14-3 causes problems for a modeling tool that insists on proper foreign-key-to-primary-key relationships, the equivalent design of Figure 14-4 can be used. In this case an extra table whose primary key is a diagnosis group is inserted between the fact and bridge tables. There is likely no new information in this extra table, unless there were labels for a cluster of diagnoses, such as the Kimball Syndrome, but now both the fact table and bridge table have conventional many-to-one joins in all directions.

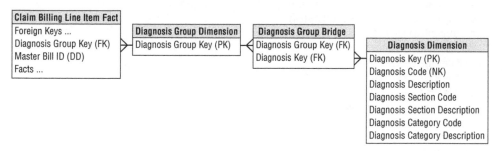

Figure 14-4: Diagnosis group dimension to create a primary key relationship.

If a unique diagnosis group is created for every patient encounter, the number of rows could become astronomical and many of the groups would be identical. Probably a better approach is to have a portfolio of diagnosis groups that are repeatedly used. Each set of diagnoses would be looked up in the master diagnosis group table during the ETL. If the existing group is found, it is used; if not found, a new diagnosis group is created. Chapter 19: ETL Subsystems and Techniques provides guidance for creating and administering bridge tables.

In an inpatient hospital stay scenario, the diagnosis group may be unique to each patient if it evolves over time during the patient's stay. In this case you would supplement the bridge table with two date stamps to capture begin and end dates. Although the twin date stamps complicate updates to the diagnosis group bridge table, they are useful for change tracking, as described more fully in Chapter 7: Accounting.

Supertypes and Subtypes for Charges

We've described a design for billed healthcare treatments to cover both inpatient and outpatient claims. In reality, healthcare charges resemble the supertype and subtype pattern described in Chapter 10. Facility charges for inpatient hospital stays differ from professional charges for outpatient treatments in clinics and doctor offices.

If you were focused exclusively on hospital stays, it would be reasonable to tweak the Figure 14-2 dimensional structure to incorporate more hospital-specific information. Figure 14-5 shows a revised set of dimensions specialized for hospital stays, with the new dimensions bolded.

Inpatient Hospital Claim Billing and Payment Workflow Fact
Treatment Date Key (FK)
Primary Insurance Billing Date Key (FK)
Secondary Insurance Billing Date Key (FK)
Responsible Party Billing Date Key (FK)
Last Primary Insurance Payment Date Key (FK)
Last Secondary Insurance Payment Date Key (FK)
Last Responsible Party Payment Date Key (FK)
Zero Balance Date Key (FK)
Patient Key (FK)
Admitting Physician Key (FK)
Admitting Physician Organization Key (FK)
Attending Physician Key (FK)
Attending Physician Organization Key (FK)
Procedure Key (FK)
Facility Key (FK)
Admitting Diagnosis Group Key (FK)
Discharge Diagnosis Group Key (FK)
Primary Insurance Organization Key (FK)
Secondary Insurance Organization Key (FK)
Responsible Party Key (FK)
Employer Key (FK)
Master Bill ID (DD)
Facts...

Figure 14-5: Accumulating snapshot for hospital stay charges.

Referring to Figure 14-5, you can see two roles for the physician: admitting physician and attending physician. The figure shows physician organizations for both roles because physicians may represent different organizations in a hospital setting. With more complex surgical events, such as a heart transplant operation, whole teams of specialists and assistants are assembled. In this case, you could include a key in the fact table for the primary responsible physician; the other physicians and medical staff would be linked to the fact row via a group key to a multivalued bridge table.

You also have two multivalued diagnosis dimensions on each fact table row. The admitting diagnosis group is determined at the beginning of the hospital stay and should be the same for every treatment row that is part of the same hospital stay. The discharge diagnosis group is not known until the patient is discharged.

Electronic Medical Records

Many healthcare organizations are moving from paper-based processes to electronic medical records. In the United States, federally mandated quality goals to support improved population health management may be achievable only with their adoption. Healthcare providers are aggressively implementing electronic health record systems; the movement is significantly impacting healthcare DW /BI initiatives.

Electronic medical records can present challenges for data warehouse environments because of their extreme variability and potentially extreme volumes. Patients' medical record data comes in many different forms, ranging from numeric data to freeform text comments entered by a healthcare professional to images and photographs. We'll further discuss unstructured data in Chapter 21: Big Data Analytics; electronic medical and/or health records may become a classic use case for big data. One thing is certain. The amount and variability of electronic data in the healthcare industry will continue to grow.

Measure Type Dimension for Sparse Facts

As designers, it is tempting to strive for a more standardized framework that could be extended to handle data variability. For example, you could potentially handle the variability of lab test results with a *measurement type dimension* describing what the fact row means, or in other words, what the generic fact represents. The unit of measure for a given numeric entry is found in the associated measurement type dimension row, along with any additivity restrictions, as shown in Figure 14-6.

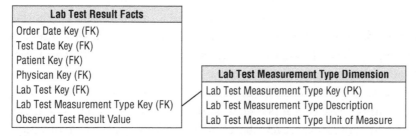

Figure 14-6: Lab test observations with measurement type dimension.

This approach is superbly flexible; you can add new measurement types simply by adding new rows in the measurement type dimension, not by altering the structure of the fact table. This approach also eliminates the nulls in the classic positional fact table design because a row exists only if the measurement exists. However, there are trade-offs. Using a measurement type dimension may generate lots of new fact table rows because the grain is "one row per measurement per event" rather than the more typical "one row per event." If a lab test results in 10 numeric measurements, there are now 10 rows in the fact table rather than a single row in the classic design. For extremely sparse situations, such as clinical laboratory or manufacturing test environments, this is a reasonable compromise. However, as the density of the facts grows, you end up spewing out too many fact rows. At this point you no longer have sparse facts and should return to the classic fact table design with fixed columns.

Moreover, this measurement type approach may complicate BI data access applications. In the relational star schema, combining two numbers that were captured as part of a single event is more difficult with this approach because now you must fetch two rows from the fact table. SQL likes to perform arithmetic functions within a row, not across rows. In addition, you must be careful not to mix incompatible amounts in a calculation because all the numeric measures reside in a single amount column. It's worth noting that multidimensional OLAP cubes are more tolerant of performing calculations across measurement types.

Freeform Text Comments

Freeform text comments, such as clinical notes, are sometimes associated with fact table events. Although text comments are not very analytically potent unless they're parsed into well-behaved dimension attributes, business users are often unwilling to part with them given the embedded nuggets of information.

Textual comments should not be stored in a fact table directly because they waste space and rarely participate in queries. Some designers think it's permissible to store textual fields in the fact table, as long as they're referred to as degenerate dimensions. Degenerate dimensions are most typically used for operational transaction control numbers and identifiers; it's not an acceptable approach or pattern for contending with bulky text fields. Storing freeform comments in the fact table adds clutter that may negatively impact the performance of analysts' more typical quantitative queries.

The unbounded text comments should either be stored in a separate comments dimension or treated as attributes in a transaction event dimension. A key consideration when evaluating these two approaches is the text field's cardinality. If there's nearly a unique comment for every fact table event, storing the textual field in a transaction dimension makes the most sense. However, in many cases, No Comment is associated with numerous fact rows. Because the number of unique text comments in this scenario is much smaller than the number of unique transactions, it would make more sense to store the textual data in a comments dimension with an associated foreign key in the fact table. In either case, queries involving both the text comments and fact metrics will perform relatively poorly given the need to resolve joins between two voluminous tables. Often business users want to drill into text comments for further investigation after highly selective fact table query filters have been applied.

Images

Sometimes the data captured in a patient's electronic medical record is an image, in addition to either quantitative numbers or qualitative notes. There are trade-offs between capturing a JPEG filename in the fact table to refer to an associated image versus embedding the image as a blob directly in the database. The advantage of using a JPEG filename is that other image creation, viewing, and editing programs can freely access the image. The disadvantage is that a separate database of graphic files must be maintained in synchrony with the fact table.

Facility/Equipment Inventory Utilization

In addition to financial and clinical data, healthcare organizations are also keenly interested in more operationally oriented metrics, such as utilization and availability of their assets, whether referring to patient beds or surgical operating theatres. In Chapter 4, we discussed product inventory data as transaction events as well as periodic snapshots. Facility or equipment inventories in a healthcare organization can be handled similarly.

For example, you can envision a bed utilization periodic snapshot with every bed's status at regularly recurring points in time, perhaps at midnight, the start of every shift, or even more frequently throughout the day. In addition to a snapshot date and potentially time-of-day, this factless fact table would include foreign keys to identify the patient, attending physician, and perhaps an assigned nurse on duty.

Conversely, you can imagine treating the bed inventory data as a transaction fact table with one row per movement into and out of a hospital bed. This may be a simplistic transaction fact table with transaction date and time dimension foreign keys, along with dimensions to describe the type of movement, such as filled or vacated. In the case of operating room utilization and availability, you can envision a lengthier list of statuses, such as pre-operation, post-operation, or downtime, along with time durations.

If the inventory changes are not terribly volatile, such as the beds in a rehabilitation or eldercare inpatient environment, you should consider a timespan fact table, as discussed in Chapter 8, with row effective and expiration dates and times to represent the various states of a bed over a period of time.

Dealing with Retroactive Changes

As DW/BI practitioners, we have well-developed techniques for accurately capturing the historical flow of data from our enterprise's source applications. Numeric measurements go into fact tables, which are surrounded with contemporary descriptions of what you know is true at the time of the measurements, packaged as dimension tables. The descriptions of patient, physician, facility, and payer evolve as slowly changing dimensions whenever these entities change their descriptions.

However, in the healthcare industry, especially with legacy operational systems, you often need to contend with late arriving data that should have been loaded into the data warehouse weeks or months ago. For example, you might receive data regarding patient procedures that occurred several weeks ago, or updates to patient profiles that were back-dated as effective several months ago. The more delayed the incoming records are, the more challenging the DW/BI system's ETL processing becomes. We'll discuss these late arriving fact and dimension scenarios in Chapter 19. Unfortunately, these patterns are common in healthcare DW/BI environments; in fact, they may be the dominant modes of processing rather than specialized techniques for outlier cases. Eventually, more effective source data capture systems should reduce the frequency of these late arriving data anomalies.

Summary

Healthcare provides a wealth of dimensional design examples. In this chapter, the enterprise data warehouse bus matrix illustrated the critical linkages between a healthcare organization's administrative and clinical data. We used an accumulating snapshot grain fact table with role-playing date dimensions for the healthcare claim billing and payment pipeline. We also saw role playing used for the physician and payer dimensions in other fact tables of this chapter.

Healthcare schemas are littered with multivalued dimensions, especially the diagnosis dimension. Complex surgical events might also use multivalued bridge tables to represent the teams of involved physicians and other staff members. The bridge tables used with healthcare data seldom contain weighting factors, as discussed in earlier chapters, because it is extremely difficult to establish weighting business rules, beyond the designation of a "primary" relationship.

We discussed medical records and test results, suggesting a measurement type dimension to organize sparse, heterogeneous measurements into a single, uniform framework. We also discussed the handling of text comments and linked images. Transaction and periodic snapshot fact tables were used to represent facility or equipment inventory utilization and availability. In closing, we touched upon retroactive fact and dimension changes that are often all too common with healthcare performance data.

15 Electronic Commerce

A web-intensive business's *clickstream* data records the gestures of every web visitor. In its most elemental form, the clickstream is every page event recorded by each of the company's web servers. The clickstream contains a number of new dimensions, such as page, session, and referrer, which are not found in other data sources. The clickstream is a torrent of data; it can be difficult and exasperating for DW/BI professionals. Does it connect to the rest of the DW/BI system? Can its dimensions and facts be conformed in the enterprise data warehouse bus architecture?

We start this chapter by describing the raw clickstream data source and designing its relevant dimensional models. We discuss the impact of Google Analytics, which can be thought of as an external data warehouse delivering information about your website. We then integrate clickstream data into a larger matrix of more conventional processes for a web retailer, and argue that the profitability of the web sales channel can be measured if you allocate the right costs back to the individual sales.

Chapter 15 discusses the following concepts:

- Clickstream data and its unique dimensionality
- Role of external services such as Google Analytics
- Integrating clickstream data with the other business processes on the bus matrix
- Assembling a complete view of profitability for a web enterprise

Clickstream Source Data

The clickstream is not just another data source that is extracted, cleaned, and dumped into the DW/BI environment. The clickstream is an evolving collection of data sources. There are a number of server log file formats for capturing clickstream data. These log file formats have optional data components that, if used, can be very helpful in identifying visitors, sessions, and the true meaning of behavior.

Because of the distributed nature of the web, clickstream data often is collected simultaneously by different physical servers, even when the visitor thinks they are interacting with a single website. Even if the log files collected by these separate servers are compatible, a very interesting problem arises in synchronizing the log files after the fact. Remember that a busy web server may be processing hundreds of page events per second. It is unlikely the clocks on separate servers will be in synchrony to one-hundredth of a second.

You also obtain clickstream data from different parties. Besides your own log files, you may get clickstream data from referring partners or from internet service providers (ISPs). Another important form of clickstream data is the search specification given to a search engine that then directs the visitor to the website.

Finally, if you are an ISP providing web access to directly connected customers, you have a unique perspective because you see every click of your captive customers that may allow more powerful and invasive analyses of the customer's sessions.

The most basic form of clickstream data from a normal website is stateless. That is, the log shows an isolated page retrieval event but does not provide a clear tie to other page events elsewhere in the log. Without some kind of contextual help, it is difficult or impossible to reliably identify a complete visitor session.

The other big frustration with basic clickstream data is the anonymity of the session. Unless visitors agree to reveal their identity in some way, you often cannot be sure who they are, or if you have ever seen them before. In certain situations, you may not distinguish the clicks of two visitors who are simultaneously browsing the website.

Clickstream Data Challenges

Clickstream data contains many ambiguities. Identifying visitor origins, visitor sessions, and visitor identities is something of an interpretive art. Browser caches and proxy servers make these identifications more challenging.

Identifying the Visitor Origin

If you are very lucky, your site is the default home page for the visitor's browser. Every time he opens his browser, your home page is the first thing he sees. This is pretty unlikely unless you are the webmaster for a portal site or an intranet home page, but many sites have buttons which, when clicked, prompt visitors to set their URL as the browser's home page. Unfortunately there is no easy way to determine from a log whether your site is set as a browser's home page.

A visitor may be directed to your site from a search at a portal such as Yahoo! or Google. Such referrals can come either from the portal's index, for which you may have paid a placement fee, or from a word or content search.

For some websites, the most common source of visitors is from a browser bookmark. For this to happen, the visitor must have previously bookmarked your site, and this can occur only after the site's interest and trust levels cross the visitor's bookmark threshold.

Finally, your site may be reached as a result of a clickthrough—a deliberate click on a text or graphical link from another site. This may be a paid-for referral via a banner ad, or a free referral from an individual or cooperating site. In the case of clickthroughs, the referring site will almost always be identifiable as a field in the web event record. Capturing this crucial clickstream data is important to verify the efficacy of marketing programs. It also provides crucial data for auditing invoices you may receive from clickthrough advertising charges.

Identifying the Session

Most web-centric analyses require every visitor session (visit) to have its own unique identity tag, similar to a supermarket receipt number. This is the session ID. Records for every individual visitor action in a session, whether they are derived from the clickstream or an application interaction, must contain this tag. But keep in mind the operational application, such as an order entry system generates this session ID, not the web server.

The basic protocol for the web, Hyper Text Transfer Protocol (HTTP) is stateless; that is, it lacks the concept of a session. There are no intrinsic login or logout actions built into the HTTP protocol, so session identity must be established in some other way. There are several ways to do this:

1. In many cases, the individual hits comprising a session can be consolidated by collating time-contiguous log entries from the same host (IP address). If the log contains a number of entries with the same host ID in a short period of time (for example, one hour), you can reasonably assume the entries are for the same session. This method breaks down for websites with large numbers of visitors because dynamically assigned IP addresses may be reused immediately by different visitors over a brief time period. Also, different IP addresses may be used within the same session for the same visitor. This approach also presents problems when dealing with browsers that are behind some firewalls. Notwithstanding these problems, many commercial log analysis products use this method of session tracking, and it requires no cookies or special web server features.

2. Another much more satisfactory method is to let the web browser place a session-level cookie into the visitor's web browser. This cookie will last as long as the browser is open and in general won't be available in subsequent

browser sessions. The cookie value can serve as a temporary session ID not only to the browser, but also to any application that requests the session cookie from the browser. But using a transient cookie has the disadvantage that you can't tell when the visitor returns to the site at a later time in a new session.

3. HTTP's secure sockets layer (SSL) offers an opportunity to track a visitor session because it may include a login action by the visitor and the exchange of encryption keys. The downside to using this method is that to track the session, the entire information exchange needs to be in high-overhead SSL, and the visitor may be put off by security advisories that can pop up using certain browsers. Also, each host must have its own unique security certificate.

4. If page generation is dynamic, you can try to maintain visitor state by placing a session ID in a hidden field of each page returned to the visitor. This session ID can be returned to the web server as a query string appended to a subsequent URL. This method of session tracking requires a great deal of control over the website's page generation methods to ensure the thread of a session ID is not broken. If the visitor clicks links that don't support this session ID ping-pong, a single session may appear to be multiple sessions. This approach also breaks down if multiple vendors supply content in a single session unless those vendors are closely collaborating.

5. Finally, the website may establish a persistent cookie in the visitor's machine that is not deleted by the browser when the session ends. Of course, it's possible the visitor will have his browser set to refuse cookies, or may manually clean out his cookie file, so there is no absolute guarantee that even a persistent cookie will survive. Although any given cookie can be read only by the website that caused it to be created, certain groups of websites can agree to store a common ID tag that would let these sites combine their separate notions of a visitor session into a "super session."

In summary, the most reliable method of session tracking from web server log records is obtained by setting a persistent cookie in the visitor's browser. Less reliable, but good results can be obtained by setting a session level and a nonpersistent cookie and by associating time-contiguous log entries from the same host. The latter method requires a robust algorithm in the log postprocessor to ensure satisfactory results and to decide when not to take the results seriously.

Identifying the Visitor

Identifying a specific visitor who logs into your site presents some of the most challenging problems facing a site designer, webmaster, or manager of the web analytics group.

- Web visitors want to be anonymous. They may have no reason to trust you, the internet, or their computer with personal identification or credit card information.
- If you request visitors' identity, they may not provide accurate information.
- You can't be sure which family member is visiting your site. If you obtain an identity by association, for instance from a persistent cookie left during a previous visit, the identification is only for the computer, not for the specific visitor. Any family member or company employee may have been using that particular computer at that moment in time.
- You can't assume an individual is always at the same computer. Server-provided cookies identify a computer, not an individual. If someone accesses the same website from an office computer, home computer, and mobile device, a different website cookie is probably put into each machine.

Clickstream Dimensional Models

Before designing clickstream dimensional models, let's consider all the dimensions that may have relevance in a clickstream environment. Any single dimensional model will not use all the dimensions at once, but it is nice to have a portfolio of dimensions waiting to be used. The list of dimensions for a web retailer could include:

- Date
- Time of day
- Part
- Vendor
- Status
- Carrier
- Facilities location
- Product
- Customer
- Media
- Promotion
- Internal organization
- Employee
- **Page**
- **Event**
- **Session**
- **Referral**

All the dimensions in the list, except for the last four shown in bold, are familiar dimensions, most of which we have already used in earlier chapters of this book. But the last four are the unique dimensions of the clickstream and warrant some careful attention.

Page Dimension

The *page dimension* describes the page context for a web page event, as illustrated in Figure 15-1. The grain of this dimension is the individual page. The definition of page must be flexible enough to handle the evolution of web pages from static page delivery to highly dynamic page delivery in which the exact page the customer sees is unique at that instant in time. We assume even in the case of the dynamic page that there is a well-defined function that characterizes the page, and we will use that to describe the page. We will not create a page row for every instance of a dynamic page because that would yield a dimension with an astronomical number of rows. These rows also would not differ in interesting ways. You want a row in this dimension for each interesting distinguishable type of page. Static pages probably get their own row, but dynamic pages would be grouped by similar function and type.

Page Dimension Attribute	Sample Data Values/Definitions
Page Key	Surrogate values (1..N)
Page Source	Static, Dynamic, Unknown, Corrupted, Inapplicable, ...
Page Function	Portal, Search, Product description, Corporate information, ...
Page Template	Sparse, Dense, ...
Item Type	Product SKU, Book ISBN number, Telco rate type, ...
Graphics Type	GIF, JPG, Progressive disclosure, Size pre-declared, ...
Animation Type	Similar to graphics type
Sound Type	Similar to graphics type
Page File Name	Optional application dependent name

Figure 15-1: Page dimension attributes and sample data values.

When the definition of a static page changes because it is altered by the webmaster, the page dimension row can either be type 1 overwritten or treated with an alternative slowly changing technique. This decision is a matter of policy for the data warehouse and depends on whether the old and new descriptions of the page differ materially, and whether the old definition should be kept for historical analysis purposes.

Website designers, data governance representatives from the business, and the DW/BI architects need to collaborate to assign descriptive codes and attributes to each page served by the web server, whether the page is dynamic or static. Ideally, the web page developers supply descriptive codes and attributes with each page they create and embed these codes and attributes into the optional fields of the web log files. This crucial step is at the foundation of the implementation of this page dimension.

Before leaving the page dimension, we want to point out that some internet companies track the more granular individual elements on each page of their web sites, including graphical elements and links. Each element generates its own row for each visitor for each page request. A single complex web page can generate hundreds of rows each time the page is served to a visitor. Obviously, this extreme granularity generates astronomical amounts of data, often exceeding 10 terabytes per day!

Similarly, gaming companies may generate a row for every gesture made by every online game player, which again can result in hundreds of millions of rows per day. In both cases, the most atomic fact table will have extra dimensions describing the graphical element, link, or game situation.

Event Dimension

The event dimension describes what happened on a particular page at a particular point in time. The main interesting events are Open Page, Refresh Page, Click Link, and Enter Data. You want to capture that information in this small event dimension, as illustrated in Figure 15-2.

Event Dimension Attribute	Sample Data Values/Definitions
Event Key	Surrogate values (1..N)
Event Type	Open page, Refresh page, Click link, Unknown, Inapplicable
Event Content	Application-dependent fields eventually driven by XML tags

Figure 15-2: Event dimension attributes and sample data values.

Session Dimension

The session dimension provides one or more levels of diagnosis for the visitor's session as a whole, as shown in Figure 15-3. For example, the local context of the session might be Requesting Product Information, but the overall session context might be Ordering a Product. The success status would diagnose whether the mission was completed. The local context may be decidable from just the identity of the current page, but the overall session context probably can be judged only by processing the visitor's complete session at data extract time. The customer status attribute is a convenient place to label the customer for periods of time, with labels that are not clear either from the page or immediate session. These statuses may be derived from auxiliary business processes in the DW/BI system, but by placing these labels deep within the clickstream, you can directly study the behavior of certain types of customers. Do not put these labels in the customer dimension because they may change over very short periods of time. If there are a large number of these statuses, consider creating a separate customer status mini-dimension rather than embedding this information in the session dimension.

Session Dimension Attribute	Sample Data Values/Definitions
Session Key	Surrogate values (1..N)
Session Type	Classified, Unclassified, Corrupted, Inapplicable
Local Context	Page-derived context like Requesting Product Information
Session Context	Trajectory-derived context like Ordering a Product
Action Sequence	Summary label for overall sequence of actions during session
Success Status	Identifies whether overall session mission was accomplished
Customer Status	New customer, High value customer, About to cancel, In default

Figure 15-3: Session dimension attributes and sample data values.

This dimension groups sessions for analysis, such as:

- How many customers consulted your product information before ordering?
- How many customers looked at your product information and never ordered?
- How many customers did not finish ordering? Where did they stop?

Referral Dimension

The referral dimension, illustrated in Figure 15-4, describes how the customer arrived at the current page. The web server logs usually provide this information. The URL of the previous page is identified, and in some cases additional information is present. If the referrer was a search engine, usually the search string is specified. It may not be worthwhile to put the raw search specification into your database because the search specifications are so complicated and idiosyncratic that an analyst may not be able to query them usefully. You can assume some kind of simplified and cleaned specification is placed in the specification attribute.

Referral Dimension Attribute	Sample Data Values/Definitions
Referral Key	Surrogate values (1..N)
Referral Type	Intra site, Remote site, Search engine, Corrupted, Inapplicable
Referring URL	www.organization-site.com/linkspage
Referring Site	www.organization-site.com
Referring Domain	www.organization-site.com
Search Type	Simple text match, Complex logical match
Specification	Actual spec used (useful if simple text, otherwise questionable)
Target	Meta tags, Body text, Title (where search found its match)

Figure 15-4: Referral dimension attributes and sample data values.

Clickstream Session Fact Table

Now that you have a portfolio of useful clickstream dimensions, you can design the primary clickstream dimensional models based on the web server log data. This business process can then be integrated into the family of other web retailing subject areas.

With an eye toward keeping the first fact table from growing astronomically, you should choose the grain to be one row for each completed customer session. This grain is significantly higher than the underlying web server logs which record each individual page event, including individual pages as well as each graphical element on each page. While we typically encourage designers to start with the most granular data available in the source system, this is a purposeful deviation from our standard practices. Perhaps you have a big site recording more than 100 million page fetches per day, and 1 billion micro page events (graphical elements), but you want to start with a more manageable number of rows to be loaded each day. We assume for the sake of argument that the 100 million page fetches boil down to 20 million complete visitor sessions. This could arise if an average visitor session touched 5 pages.

The dimensions that are appropriate for this first fact table are calendar date, time of day, customer, page, session, and referrer. Finally, you can add a set of measured facts for this session including session seconds, pages visited, orders placed, units ordered, and order dollars. The completed design is shown in Figure 15-5.

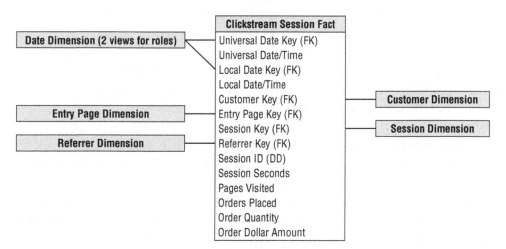

Figure 15-5: Clickstream fact table design for complete sessions.

There are a number of interesting aspects to this design. You may wonder why there are two connections from the calendar date dimension to the fact table and two date/time stamps. This is a case in which both the calendar date and the time of day must play two different roles. Because you are interested in measuring the precise times of sessions, you must meet two conflicting requirements. First, you want to make sure you can synchronize all session dates and times internationally across multiple time zones. Perhaps you have other date and time stamps from other web servers or nonweb systems elsewhere in the DW/BI environment. To achieve true synchronization of events across multiple servers and processes, you must record all session dates and times, uniformly, in a single time zone such as Greenwich Mean Time (GMT) or Coordinated Universal Time (UTC). You should interpret the session date and time combinations as the beginning of the session. Because you have the dwell time of the session as a numeric fact, you can tell when the session ended, if that is of interest.

The other requirement you meet with this design is to record the date and time of the session relative to the visitor's wall clock. The best way to represent this information is with a second calendar date foreign key and date/time stamp. Theoretically, you could represent the time zone of the customer in the customer dimension table, but constraints to determine the correct wall clock time would be horrendously complicated. The time difference between two cities (such as London and Sydney) can change by as much as two hours at different times of the year depending on when these cities go on and off daylight savings time. This is not the business of the BI reporting application to work out. It is the business of the database to store this information, so it can be constrained in a simple and direct way.

The two role-playing calendar date dimension tables are views on a single underlying table. The column names are massaged in the view definition, so they are slightly different when they show up in the user interface pick lists of BI tools. Note that the use of views makes the two instances of each table semantically independent.

We modeled the exact instant in time with a full date/time stamp rather than a time-of-day dimension. Unlike the calendar date dimension, a time-of-day dimension would contain few if any meaningful attributes. You don't have labels for each hour, minute, or second. Such a time-of-day dimension could be ridiculously large if its grain were the individual second or millisecond. Also, the use of an explicit date/time stamp allows direct arithmetic between different date/time stamps to calculate precise time gaps between sessions, even those crossing days. Calculating time gaps using a time-of-day dimension would be awkward.

The inclusion of the page dimension in Figure 15-5 may seem surprising given the grain of the design is the customer session. However, in a given session, a very interesting page is the entry page. The page dimension in this design is the page the session started with. In other words, how did the customer hop onto your bus just now? Coupled with the referrer dimension, you now have an interesting ability to analyze how and why the customer accessed your website. A more elaborate design would also add an exit page dimension.

You may be tempted to add the causal dimension to this design, but if the causal dimension focuses on individual products, it would be inappropriate to add it to this design. The symptom that the causal dimension does not mesh with this design is the multivalued nature of the causal factors for a given complete session. If you run ad campaigns or special deals for several products, how do you represent this multivalued situation if the customer's session involves several products? The right place for a product-oriented causal dimension will be in the more fine-grained table described in the next fact table example. Conversely, a more broadly focused market conditions dimension that describes conditions affecting all products would be appropriate for a session-grained fact table.

The session seconds fact is the total number of seconds the customer spent on the site during this session. There will be many cases in which you can't tell when the customer left. Perhaps the customer typed in a new URL. This won't be detected by conventional web server logs. (If the data is collected by an ISP who can see every click across sessions, this particular issue goes away.) Or perhaps the customer got up out of the chair and didn't return for 1 hour. Or perhaps the customer just closed the browser without making any more clicks. In all these cases, your extract software needs to assign a small and nominal number of seconds to this last session step, so the analysis is not unrealistically distorted.

We purposely designed this first clickstream fact table to focus on complete visitor sessions while keeping the size under control. The next schema drops down to the lowest practical granularity you can support in the data warehouse: the individual page event.

Clickstream Page Event Fact Table

The granularity of the second clickstream fact table is the individual page event in each customer session; the underlying micro events recording graphical elements such as JPGs and GIFs are discarded (unless you are Yahoo! or eBay as described previously). With simple static HTML pages, you can record only one interesting event per page view, namely the page view. As websites employ dynamically created XML-based pages, with the ability to establish an on-going dialogue through the page, the number and type of events will grow.

This fact table could become astronomical in size. You should resist the urge to aggregate the table up to a coarser granularity because that inevitably involves dropping dimensions. Actually, the first clickstream fact table represents just such an aggregation; although it is a worthwhile fact table, analysts cannot ask questions about visitor behavior or individual pages.

Having chosen the grain, you can choose the appropriate dimensions. The list of dimensions includes calendar date, time of day, customer, page, event, session, session ID, step (three roles), product, referrer, and promotion. The completed design is shown in Figure 15-6.

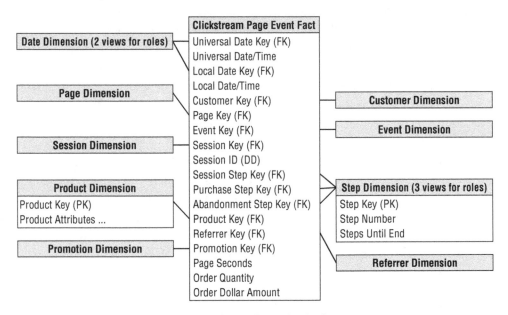

Figure 15-6: Clickstream fact table design for individual page use.

Figure 15-6 looks similar to the first design, except for the addition of the page, event, promotion, and step dimensions. This similarity between fact tables is typical of dimensional models. One of the charms of dimensional modeling is the "boring" similarity of the designs. But that is where they get their power. When the designs have a predictable structure, all the software up and down the DW/BI chain, from extraction, to database querying, to the BI tools, can exploit this similarity to great advantage.

The two roles played by the calendar date and date/time stamps have the same interpretation as in the first design. One role is the universal synchronized time, and the other role is the local wall clock time as measured by the customer. In this fact table, these dates and times refer to the individual page event.

The page dimension refers to the individual page. This is the main difference in grain between the two clickstream fact tables. In this fact table you can see all the pages accessed by the customers.

As described earlier, the session dimension describes the outcome of the session. A companion column, the session ID, is a degenerate dimension that does not have a join to a dimension table. This degenerate dimension is a typical dimensional modeling construct. The session ID is simply a unique identifier, with no semantic content, that serves to group together the page events of each customer session in an unambiguous way. You did not need a session ID degenerate dimension in the first fact table, but it is included as a "parent key" if you want to easily link to the individual page event fact table. We recommend the session dimension be at a higher level of granularity than the session ID; the session dimension is intended to describe classes and categories of sessions, not the characteristics of each individual session.

A product dimension is shown in this design under the assumption this website belongs to a web retailer. A financial services site probably would have a similar dimension. A consulting services site would have a service dimension. An auction site would have a subject or category dimension describing the nature of the items being auctioned. A news site would have a subject dimension, although with different content than an auction site.

You should accompany the product dimension with a promotion dimension so you can attach useful causal interpretations to the changes in demand observed for certain products.

For each page event, you should record the number of seconds that elapse before the next page event. Call this page seconds to contrast it with session seconds in the first fact table. This is a simple example of paying attention to conformed facts. If you call both of these measures simply "seconds," you risk having these seconds inappropriately added or combined. Because these seconds are not precisely equivalent, you should name them differently as a warning. In this particular case, you would expect the page seconds for a session in this second fact table to add up to the session seconds in the first fact table.

The final facts are units ordered and order dollars. These columns will be zero or null for many rows in this fact table if the specific page event is not the event that places the order. Nevertheless, it is highly attractive to provide these columns because they tie the all-important web revenue directly to behavior. If the units ordered and order dollars were only available through the production order entry system elsewhere in the DW/BI environment, it would be inefficient to perform the revenue-to-behavior analysis across multiple large tables. In many database management systems, these null facts are handled efficiently and may take up literally zero space in the fact table.

Step Dimension

Because the fact table grain is the individual page event, you can add the powerful step dimension described in Chapter 8: Customer Relationship Management. The step dimension, originally shown in Figure 8-11, provides the position of the specific page event within the overall session.

The step dimension becomes particularly powerful when it is attached to the fact table in various roles. Figure 15-6 shows three roles: overall session, purchase subsession, and abandonment subsession. A purchase subsession, by definition, ends in a successful purchase. An abandonment subsession is one that fails to complete a purchase transaction for some reason. Using these roles of the step dimension allows some very interesting queries. For example, if the purchase step dimension is constrained to step number 1, the query returns nothing but the starting page for successful purchase experiences. Conversely, if the abandonment step dimension is constrained to zero steps remaining, the query returns nothing but the last and presumably most unfulfilling pages visited in unsuccessful purchase sessions. Although the whole design shown in Figure 15-6 is aimed at product purchases, the step dimension technique can be used in the analysis of any sequential process.

Aggregate Clickstream Fact Tables

Both clickstream fact tables designed thus far are pretty large. There are many business questions that would be forced to summarize millions of rows from these tables. For example, if you want to track the total visits and revenue from major demographic groups of customers accessing your website on a month-by-month basis, you can certainly do that with either fact table. In the session-grained fact table, you would constrain the calendar date dimension to the appropriate time span (say January, February, and March of the current year). You would then create row headers from the demographics type attribute in the customer dimension and the month attribute in the calendar dimension (to separately label the three months in the output). Finally, you would sum the Order Dollars and count the number of sessions. This all works fine. But it is likely to be slow without help from an aggregate table. If this kind of query is frequent, the DBA will be encouraged to build an aggregate table, as shown in Figure 15-7.

You can build this table directly from your first fact table, whose grain is the individual session. To build this aggregate table, you group by month, demographic type, entry page, and session outcome. You count the number of sessions, and sum all the other additive facts. This results in a drastically smaller fact table, almost certainly less than 1% of the original session-grained fact table. This reduction in size translates directly to a corresponding increase in performance for most queries. In other words, you can expect queries directed to this aggregate table to run at least 100 times as fast.

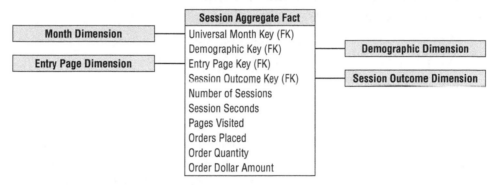

Figure 15-7: Aggregate clickstream fact table.

Although it may not have been obvious, we followed a careful discipline in building the aggregate table. This aggregate fact table is connected to a set of shrunken rollup dimensions directly related to the original dimensions in the more granular fact tables. The month dimension is a conformed subset of the calendar day dimension's attributes. The demographic dimension is a conformed subset of customer dimension attributes. You should assume the page and session tables are unchanged; a careful design of the aggregation logic could suggest a conformed shrinking of these tables as well.

Google Analytics

Google Analytics (GA) is a service provided by Google that is best described as an external data warehouse that provides many insights about how your website is used. To use GA, you modify each page of your website to include a GA tracking code (GATC) embedded in a Java code snippet located in the HTML `<head>` declaration of each page to be tracked. When a visitor accesses the page, information is sent to the Analytics service at Google, as long as the visitor has JavaScript enabled. Virtually all of the information described in this chapter can be collected through GA, with the exception of personally identifiable information (PII) which is forbidden by GA's terms of service. GA can be combined with Google's Adword service to track ad campaigns and conversions (sales). Reportedly, GA is used by more than 50% of the most popular web sites on the internet.

Data from GA can be viewed in a BI tool dashboard online directly from the underlying GA databases, or data can be delivered to you in a wide variety of standard and custom reports, making it possible to build your own local business process schema surrounding this data.

Interestingly, GA's detailed technical explanation of the data elements that can be collected through the service are described correctly as either dimensions or measures. Someone at Google has been reading our books…

Integrating Clickstream into Web Retailer's Bus Matrix

This section considers the business processes needed by a web-based computer retailer. The retailer's enterprise data warehouse bus matrix is illustrated in Figure 15-8. Note the matrix lists business process subject areas, not individual fact tables. Typically, each matrix row results in a suite of closely associated fact tables and/or OLAP cubes, which all represent a particular business process.

The Figure 15-8 matrix has a number of striking characteristics. There are a lot of check marks. Some of the dimensions, such as date/time, organization, and employee appear in almost every business process. The product and customer dimensions dominate the middle part of the matrix, where they are attached to business processes that describe customer-oriented activities. At the top of the matrix, suppliers and parts dominate the processes of acquiring the parts that make up products and building them to order for the customer. At the bottom of the matrix, you have classic infrastructure and cost driver business processes that are not directly tied to customer behavior.

The web visitor clickstream subject area sits squarely among the customer-oriented processes. It shares the date/time, product, customer, media, causal, and service policy dimensions with several other business processes nearby. In this sense it should be obvious that the web visitor clickstream data is well integrated into the fabric of the overall DW/BI system for this retailer. Applications tying the web visitor clickstream will be easy to integrate across all the processes sharing these conformed dimensions because separate queries to each fact table can be combined across individual rows of the report.

The web visitor clickstream business process contains the four special clickstream dimensions not found in the others. These dimensions do not pose a problem for applications. Instead, the ability of the web visitor clickstream data to bridge between the web world and the brick-and-mortar world is exactly the advantage you are looking for. You can constrain and group on attributes from the four web dimensions and explore the effect on the other business processes. For example, you can see what kinds of web experiences produce customers who purchase certain kinds of service policies and then invoke certain levels of service demands.

	Date and Time	Part	Vendor	Carrier	Facility	Product	Customer	Media	Promotion	Service Policy	Internal Organization	Employee	Clickstream (4 dims)
Supply Chain Management													
Supplier Purchase Orders	X	X	X		X						X	X	
Supplier Deliveries	X	X	X	X	X						X		
Part Inventories	X	X	X		X						X		
Product Assembly Bill of Materials	X	X	X		X	X					X	X	
Product Assembly to Order	X	X	X		X	X	X				X	X	
Customer Relationship Management													
Product Promotions	X					X	X	X	X		X		
Advertising	X					X		X	X		X		
Customer Communications	X					X	X				X	X	
Customer Inquiries	X				X	X	X			X	X	X	
Web Visitor Clickstream	**X**					**X**	**X**	**X**	**X**	**X**			**X**
Product Orders	X					X	X			X		X	
Service Policy Orders	X					X	X			X	X	X	
Product Shipments	X			X	X	X	X			X	X	X	
Customer Billing	X					X	X			X	X	X	
Customer Payments	X						X				X	X	
Product Returns	X				X	X	X			X	X	X	
Product Support	X					X	X	X		X	X	X	
Service Policy Responses	X					X	X	X		X	X	X	
Operations													
Employee Labor	X				X						X	X	
Human Resources	X				X						X	X	
Facilities Operations	X				X						X	X	
Web Site Operations	X				X						X	X	

Figure 15-8: Bus matrix for web retailer.

Finally, it should be pointed out that the matrix serves as a kind of communications vehicle for all the business teams and senior management to appreciate the need to conform dimensions and facts. A given column in the matrix is, in effect, an invitation list to the meeting for conforming the dimension!

Profitability Across Channels Including Web

After the DW/BI team successfully implements the initial clickstream fact tables and ties them to the sales transaction and customer communication business processes, the team may be ready to tackle the most challenging subject area of all: web profitability.

You can tackle web profitability as an extension of the sales transaction process. Fundamentally, you are allocating all the activity and infrastructure costs down to each sales transaction. You could, as an alternative, try to build web profitability on top of the clickstream, but this would involve an even more controversial allocation process in which you allocate costs down to each session. It would be hard to assign activity and infrastructure costs to a session that has no obvious product involvement and leads to no immediate sale.

A big benefit of extending the sales transaction fact table is that you get a view of profitability across all your sales channels, not just the web. In a way, this should be obvious because you know that you must sort out the costs and assign them to the various channels.

The grain of the profit and loss facts is each individual line item sold on a sales ticket to a customer at a point in time, whether it's a single sales ticket or single web purchasing session. This is the same as the grain of the sales transaction business process and includes all channels, assumed to be store sales, telesales, and web sales.

The dimensions of the profit and loss facts are also the same as the sales transaction fact table: date, time, customer, channel, product, promotion, and ticket number (degenerate). The big difference between the profitability and sales transaction fact tables is the breakdown of the costs, as illustrated in Figure 15-9.

Before discussing the allocation of costs, let us examine the format of the profit and loss facts. It is organized as a simple profit and loss (P&L) statement (refer to Figure 6-14). The first fact is familiar units sold. All the other facts are dollar values beginning with the value of the sale as if it were sold at the list or catalog price, referred to as gross revenue. Assuming sales often take place at lower prices, you would account for any difference with a manufacturer's allowance, marketing promotion that is a price reduction, or markdown done to move the inventory. When these effects are taken into account, you can calculate the net revenue, which is the true net price the customer pays times the number of units purchased.

The rest of the P&L consists of a series of subtractions, where you calculate progressively more far-reaching versions of profit. You can begin by subtracting the product manufacturing cost if you manufacture it, or equivalently, the product acquisition cost if it is acquired from a supplier. Then subtract the product storage cost. At this point, many enterprises call this partial result the gross profit. You can divide this gross profit by the gross revenue to get the gross margin ratio.

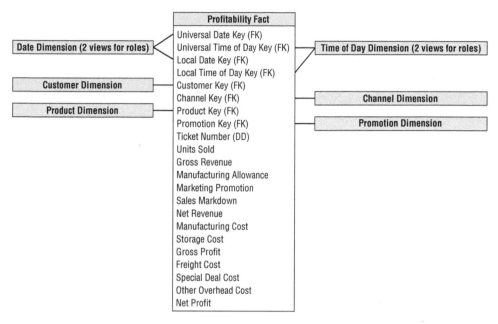

Figure 15-9: Profit and loss facts across sales channels, including web sales.

Obviously, the columns called net revenue and gross profit are calculated directly from the columns immediately preceding them in the fact table. But should you explicitly store these columns in the database? The answer depends on whether you provide access to this fact table through a view or whether users or BI applications directly access the physical fact table. The structure of the P&L is sufficiently complex that, as the data warehouse provider, you don't want to risk the important measures like net revenue and gross profit being computed incorrectly. If you provide all access through views, you can easily provide the computed columns without physically storing them. But if your users are allowed to access the underlying physical table, you should include net revenue, gross profit, and net profit as physical columns.

Below the gross profit you can continue subtracting various costs. Typically, the DW/BI team must separately source or estimate each of these costs. Remember the actual entries in any given fact table row are the fractions of these total costs allocated all the way down to the individual fact row grain. Often there is significant pressure on the DW/BI team to deliver the profitability business process. Or to put it another way, there is tremendous pressure to source all these costs. But how good are the costs in the various underlying data sets? Sometimes a cost is only available as a national average, computed for an entire year. Any allocation scheme is going to assign a kind of pro forma value that has no real texture to it. Other costs will be broken down a little more granularly, perhaps to calendar quarter and by geographic region (if relevant). Finally, some costs may be truly activity-based and vary in a highly dynamic, responsive, and realistic way over time.

Website system costs are an important cost driver in electronic commerce businesses. Although website costs are classic infrastructure costs, and are therefore difficult to allocate directly to the product and customer activity, this is a key step in developing a web-oriented P&L statement. Various allocation schemes are possible, including allocating the website costs to various product lines by the number of pages devoted to each product, allocating the costs by pages visited, or allocating the costs by actual web-based purchases.

The DW/BI team cannot be responsible for implementing activity-based costing (ABC) in a large organization. When the team is building a profitability dimensional model, the team gets the best cost data available at the moment and publishes the P&L. Perhaps some of the numbers are simple rule-of-thumb ratios. Others may be highly detailed activity-based costs. Over time, as the sources of cost improve, the DW/BI team incorporates these new sources and notifies the users that the business rules have improved.

Before leaving this design, it is worthwhile putting it in perspective. When a P&L structure is embedded in a rich dimensional framework, you have immense power. You can break down all the components of revenue, cost, and profit for every conceivable slice and dice provided by the dimensions. You can answer what is profitable, but also answer "why" because you can see all the components of the P&L, including:

- How profitable is each channel (web sales, telesales, and store sales)? Why?
- How profitable are your customer segments? Why?
- How profitable is each product line? Why?
- How profitable are your promotions? Why?
- When is your business most profitable? Why?

The symmetric dimensional approach enables you to combine constraints from many dimensions, allowing compound versions of the profitability analyses like:

- Who are the profitable customers in each channel? Why?
- Which promotions work well on the web but do not work well in other channels? Why?

Summary

The web retailer case study used in this chapter is illustrative of any business with a significant web presence. Besides tackling the clickstream subject area at multiple levels of granularity, the central challenge is effectively integrating the clickstream data into the rest of the business. We discussed ways to address the identification challenges associated with the web visitor, their origin, and session boundaries, along with the special dimensions unique to clickstream data, including the session, page, and step dimensions.

In the next chapter, we'll turn our attention to the primary business processes in an insurance company as we recap many of the dimensional modeling patterns presented throughout this book.

16 Insurance

We bring together concepts from nearly all the previous chapters to build a DW/BI system for a property and casualty insurance company in this final case study. If you are from the insurance industry and jumped directly to this chapter for a quick fix, please accept our apology, but this material depends heavily on ideas from the earlier chapters. You'll need to turn back to the beginning of the book to have this chapter make any sense.

As has been our standard procedure, this chapter launches with background information for a business case. While the requirements unfold, we'll draft the enterprise data warehouse bus matrix, much like we would in a real-life requirements analysis effort. We'll then design a series of dimensional models by overlaying the core techniques learned thus far.

Chapter 16 reviews the following concepts:

- Requirements-driven approach to dimensional design
- Value chain implications, along with an example bus matrix snippet for an insurance company
- Complementary transaction, periodic snapshot, and accumulating snapshot schemas
- Dimension role playing
- Handling of slowly changing dimension attributes
- Mini-dimensions for dealing with large, rapidly changing dimension attributes
- Multivalued dimension attributes
- Degenerate dimensions for operational control numbers
- Audit dimensions to track data lineage
- Heterogeneous supertypes and subtypes to handle products with varied attributes and facts
- Junk dimensions for miscellaneous indicators

- Conformed dimensions and facts
- Consolidated fact tables combining metrics from separate business processes
- Factless fact tables
- Common mistakes to avoid when designing dimensional models

Insurance Case Study

Imagine working for a large property and casualty insurer that offers automobile, homeowner, and personal property insurance. You conduct extensive interviews with business representatives and senior management from the claims, field operations, underwriting, finance, and marketing departments. Based on these interviews, you learn the industry is in a state of flux. Nontraditional players are leveraging alternative channels. Meanwhile, the industry is consolidating due to globalization, deregulation, and demutualization challenges. Markets are changing, along with customer needs. Numerous interviewees tell us information is becoming an even more important strategic asset. Regardless of the functional area, there is a strong desire to use information more effectively to identify opportunities more quickly and respond most appropriately.

The good news is that internal systems and processes already capture the bulk of the data required. Most insurance companies generate tons of nitty-gritty operational data. The bad news is the data is not integrated. Over the years, political and IT boundaries have encouraged the construction of tall barriers around isolated islands of data. There are multiple disparate sources for information about the company's products, customers, and distribution channels. In the legacy operational systems, the same policyholder may be identified several times in separate automobile, home, and personal property applications. Traditionally, this segmented approach to data was acceptable because the different lines of business functioned largely autonomously; there was little interest in sharing data for cross-selling and collaboration in the past. Now within our case study, business management is attempting to better leverage this enormous amount of inconsistent and somewhat redundant data.

Besides the inherent issues surrounding data integration, business users lack the ability to access data easily when needed. In an attempt to address this shortcoming, several groups within the case study company rallied their own resources and hired consultants to solve their individual short-term data needs. In many cases, the same data was extracted from the same source systems to be accessed by separate organizations without any strategic overall information delivery strategy.

It didn't take long to recognize the negative ramifications associated with separate analytic data repositories because performance results presented at executive meetings differed depending on the data source. Management understood this independent route was not viable as a long-term solution because of the lack of integration, large volumes of redundant data, and difficulty in interpreting and reconciling the results. Given the importance of information in this brave new insurance world, management was motivated to deal with the cost implications surrounding the development, support, and analytic inefficiencies of these supposed data warehouses that merely proliferated operational data islands.

Senior management chartered the chief information officer (CIO) with the responsibility and authority to break down the historical data silos to "achieve information nirvana." They charged the CIO with the fiduciary responsibility to manage and leverage the organization's information assets more effectively. The CIO developed an overall vision that wed an enterprise strategy for dealing with massive amounts of data with a response to the immediate need to become an information-rich organization. In the meantime, an enterprise DW/BI team was created to begin designing and implementing the vision.

Senior management has been preaching about a transformation to a more customer-centric focus, instead of the traditional product-centric approach, in an effort to gain competitive advantage. The CIO jumped on that bandwagon as a catalyst for change. The folks in the trenches have pledged intent to share data rather than squirreling it away for a single purpose. There is a strong desire for everyone to have a common understanding of the state of the business. They're clamoring to get rid of the isolated pockets of data while ensuring they have access to detail and summary data at both the enterprise and line-of-business levels.

Insurance Value Chain

The primary value chain of an insurance company is seemingly short and simple. The core processes are to issue policies, collect premium payments, and process claims. The organization is interested in better understanding the metrics spawned by each of these events. Users want to analyze detailed transactions relating to the formulation of policies, as well as transactions generated by claims processing. They want to measure performance over time by coverage, covered item, policyholder, and sales distribution channel characteristics. Although some users are interested in the enterprise perspective, others want to analyze the heterogeneous nature of the insurance company's individual lines of business.

Obviously, an insurance company is engaged in many other external processes, such as the investment of premium payments or compensation of contract agents, as well as a host of internally focused activities, such as human resources, finance, and purchasing. For now, we will focus on the core business related to policies and claims.

The insurance value chain begins with a variety of policy transactions. Based on your current understanding of the requirements and underlying data, you opt to handle all the transactions impacting a policy as a single business process (and fact table). If this perspective is too simplistic to accommodate the metrics, dimensionality, or analytics required, you should handle the transaction activities as separate fact tables, such as quoting, rating, and underwriting. As discussed in Chapter 5: Procurement, there are trade-offs between creating separate fact tables for each natural cluster of transaction types versus lumping the transactions into a single fact table.

There is also a need to better understand the premium revenue associated with each policy on a monthly basis. This will be key input into the overall profit picture. The insurance business is very transaction intensive, but the transactions themselves do not represent little pieces of revenue, as is the case with retail or manufacturing sales. You cannot merely add up policy transactions to determine the revenue amount. The picture is further complicated in insurance because customers pay in advance for services. This same advance-payment model applies to organizations offering magazine subscriptions or extended warranty contracts. Premium payments must be spread across multiple periods because the company earns the revenue over time as it provides insurance coverage. The complex relationship between policy transactions and revenue measurements often makes it impossible to answer revenue questions by crawling through the individual transactions. Not only is such crawling time-consuming, but also the logic required to interpret the effect of different transaction types on revenue can be horrendously complicated. The natural conflict between the detailed transaction view and the snapshot perspective almost always requires building both kinds of fact tables in the warehouse. In this case, the premium snapshot is not merely a summarization of the policy transactions; it is quite a separate thing that comes from a separate source.

Draft Bus Matrix

Based on the interview findings, along with an understanding of the key source systems, the team begins to draft an enterprise data warehouse bus matrix with the core policy-centric business processes as rows and core dimensions as columns. Two rows are defined in the matrix, one corresponding to the policy transactions and another for the monthly premium snapshot.

As illustrated in Figure 16-1, the core dimensions include date, policyholder, employee, coverage, covered item, and policy. When drafting the matrix, don't attempt to include all the dimensions. Instead, try to focus on the core common dimensions that are reused in more than one schema.

	Date	Policyholder	Covered Item	Coverage	Employee	Policy
Policy Transactions	X	X	X	X	X	X
Premium Snapshot	X Month	X	X	X	X Agent	X

Figure 16-1: Initial draft bus matrix.

Policy Transactions

Let's turn our attention to the first row of the matrix by focusing on the transactions for creating and altering a policy. Assume the policy represents a set of coverages sold to the policyholder. Coverages can be considered the insurance company's products. Homeowner coverages include fire, flood, theft, and personal liability; automobile coverages include comprehensive, collision damage, uninsured motorist, and personal liability. In a property and casualty insurance company, coverages apply to a specific covered item, such as a particular house or car. Both the coverage and covered item are carefully identified in the policy. A particular covered item usually has several coverages listed in the policy.

Agents sell policies to policyholders. Before the policy can be created, a pricing actuary determines the premium rate that will be charged given the specific coverages, covered items, and qualifications of the policyholder. An underwriter, who takes ultimate responsibility for doing business with the policyholder, makes the final approval.

The operational policy transaction system captures the following types of transactions:

- Create policy, alter policy, or cancel policy (with reason)
- Create coverage on covered item, alter coverage, or cancel coverage (with reason)
- Rate coverage or decline to rate coverage (with reason)
- Underwrite policy or decline to underwrite policy (with reason)

The grain of the policy transaction fact table should be one row for each individual policy transaction. Each atomic transaction should be embellished with as much context as possible to create a complete dimensional description of the transaction. The dimensions associated with the policy transaction business process include the transaction date, effective date, policyholder, employee, coverage, covered item, policy number, and policy transaction type. Now let's further discuss the dimensions in this schema while taking the opportunity to reinforce concepts from earlier chapters.

Dimension Role Playing

There are two dates associated with each policy transaction. The policy transaction date is the date when the transaction was entered into the operational system, whereas the policy transaction effective date is when the transaction legally takes effect. These two foreign keys in the fact table should be uniquely named. The two independent dimensions associated with these keys are implemented using a single physical date table. Multiple logically distinct tables are then presented to the user through views with unique column names, as described originally in Chapter 6: Order Management.

Slowly Changing Dimensions

Insurance companies typically are very interested in tracking changes to dimensions over time. You can apply the three basic techniques for handling slowly changing dimension (SCD) attributes to the policyholder dimension, as introduced in Chapter 5.

With the type 1 technique, you simply overwrite the dimension attribute's prior value. This is the simplest approach to dealing with attribute changes because the attributes always represent the most current descriptors. For example, perhaps the business agrees to handle changes to the policyholder's date of birth as a type 1 change based on the assumption that any changes to this attribute are intended as corrections. In this manner, all fact table history for this policyholder appears to have always been associated with the updated date of birth.

Because the policyholder's ZIP code is key input to the insurer's pricing and risk algorithms, users are very interested in tracking ZIP code changes, so the type 2 technique is used for this attribute. Type 2 is the most common SCD technique when there's a requirement for accurate change tracking over time. In this case, when the ZIP code changes, you create a new policyholder dimension row with a new surrogate key and updated geographic attributes. Do not go back and revisit the fact table. Historical fact table rows, prior to the ZIP code change, still reflect the old surrogate key. Going forward, you use the policyholder's new surrogate key, so new fact table rows join to the post-change dimension profile. Although this technique is extremely graceful and powerful, it places more burdens on ETL processing. Also, the number of rows in the dimension table grows with each type 2 SCD change. Given there might already be more than 1 million rows in your policyholder dimension table, you may opt to use a mini-dimension for tracking ZIP code changes, which we will review shortly.

Finally, let's assume each policyholder is classified as belonging to a particular segment. Perhaps nonresidential policyholders were historically categorized as either commercial or government entities. Going forward, the business users want more detailed classifications to differentiate between large multinational, middle market, and small business commercial customers, in addition to nonprofit organizations and governmental agencies. For a period of time, users want the ability to analyze results by either the historical or new segment classifications. In this case you could use a type 3 approach to track the change for a period of time by adding a column, labeled Historical for differentiation, to retain the old classifications. The new classification values would populate the segment attribute that has been a permanent fixture on the policyholder dimension. This approach, although not extremely common, allows you to see performance by either the current or historical segment maps. This is useful when there's been an en masse change, such as the customer classification realignment. Obviously, the type 3 technique becomes overly complex if you need to track more than one version of the historical map or before-and-after changes for multiple dimension attributes.

Mini-Dimensions for Large or Rapidly Changing Dimensions

As mentioned earlier, the policyholder dimension qualifies as a large dimension with more than 1 million rows. It is often important to accurately track content values for a subset of attributes. For example, you need an accurate description of some policyholder and covered item attributes at the time the policy was created, as well as at the time of any adjustment or claim. As discussed in Chapter 5, the practical way to track changing attributes in large dimensions is to split the closely monitored, more rapidly changing attributes into one or more type 4 mini-dimensions directly linked to the fact table with a separate surrogate key. The use of mini-dimensions has an impact on the efficiency of attribute browsing because users typically want to browse and constrain on these changeable attributes. If all possible combinations of the attribute values in the mini-dimension have been created, handling a mini-dimension change simply means placing a different key in the fact table row from a certain point in time forward. Nothing else needs to be changed or added to the database.

The covered item is the house, car, or other specific insured item. The covered item dimension contains one row for each actual covered item. The covered item dimension is usually somewhat larger than the policyholder dimension, so it's another good place to consider deploying a mini-dimension. You do not want to capture the variable descriptions of the physical covered objects as facts because most are textual and are not numeric or continuously valued. You should make every effort to put textual attributes into dimension tables because they are the target of textual constraints and the source of report labels.

Multivalued Dimension Attributes

We discussed multivalued dimension attributes when we associated multiple skills with an employee in Chapter 9: Human Resources Management. In Chapter 10: Financial Services, we associated multiple customers with an account, and then in Chapter 14: Healthcare, we modeled a patient's multiple diagnoses. In this case study, you'll look at another multivalued modeling situation: the relationship between commercial customers and their industry classifications.

Each commercial customer may be associated with one or more *Standard Industry Classification (SIC)* or *North American Industry Classification System (NAICS)* codes. A large, diversified commercial customer could be represented by a dozen or more classification codes. Much like you did with Chapter 14's diagnosis group, a bridge table ties together all the industry classification codes within a group. This industry classification bridge table joins directly to either the fact table or the customer dimension as an outrigger. It enables you to report fact table metrics by any industry classification. If the commercial customer's industry breakdown is proportionally identified, such as 50 percent agricultural services, 30 percent dairy products, and 20 percent oil and gas drilling, a weighting factor should be included on each bridge table row. To handle the case in which no valid industry code is associated with a given customer, you simply create a special bridge table row that represents Unknown.

Numeric Attributes as Facts or Dimensions

Let's move on to the coverage dimension. Large insurance companies have dozens or even hundreds of separate coverage products available to sell for a given type of covered item. The actual appraised value of a specific covered item, like someone's house, is a continuously valued numeric quantity that can even vary for a given item over time, so treat it as a legitimate fact. In the dimension table, you could store a more descriptive value range, such as $250,000 to $299,999 Appraised Value, for grouping and filtering. The basic coverage limit is likely to be more standardized and not continuously valued, like Replacement Value or Up to $250,000. In this case, it would also be treated as a dimension attribute.

Degenerate Dimension

The policy number will be handled as a degenerate dimension if you have extracted all the policy header information into other dimensions. You obviously want to avoid creating a policy transaction fact table with just a small number of keys while embedding all the descriptive details (including the policyholder, dates, and coverages) in an overloaded policy dimension. In some cases, there may be one or two attributes that still belong to the policy and not to another dimension. For example, if the underwriter establishes an overall risk grade for the policy based on the totality of the coverages and covered items, then this risk grade probably belongs in a policy dimension. Of course, then the policy number is no longer a degenerate dimension.

Low Cardinality Dimension Tables

The policy transaction type dimension is a small dimension for the transaction types listed earlier with reason descriptions. A transaction type dimension might contain less than 50 rows. Even though this table is both narrow in terms of the number of columns and shallow in terms of the number of rows, the attributes should still be handled in a dimension table; if the textual characteristics are used for query filtering or report labeling, then they belong in a dimension.

Audit Dimension

You have the option to associate ETL process metadata with transaction fact rows by including a key that links to an audit dimension row created by the extract process. As discussed in Chapter 6, each audit dimension row describes the data lineage of the fact row, including the time of the extract, source table, and extract software version.

Policy Transaction Fact Table

The policy transaction fact table in Figure 16-2 illustrates several characteristics of a classic transaction grain fact table. First, the fact table consists almost entirely of keys. Transaction schemas enable you to analyze behavior in extreme detail. As you descend to lower granularity with atomic data, the fact table naturally sprouts more dimensionality. In this case, the fact table has a single numeric fact; interpretation of the fact depends on the corresponding transaction type dimension. Because there are different kinds of transactions in the same fact table, in this scenario, you cannot label the fact more specifically.

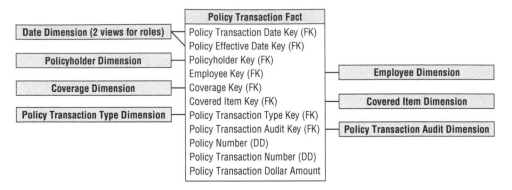

Figure 16-2: Policy transaction schema.

Heterogeneous Supertype and Subtype Products

Although there is strong support for an enterprise-wide perspective at our insurance company, the business users don't want to lose sight of their line-of-business specifics. Insurance companies typically are involved in multiple, very different lines of business. For example, the detailed parameters of homeowners' coverages differ significantly from automobile coverages. And these both differ substantially from personal property coverage, general liability coverage, and other types of insurance. Although all coverages can be coded into the generic structures used so far in this chapter, insurance companies want to track numerous specific attributes that make sense only for a particular coverage and covered item. You can generalize the initial schema developed in Figure 16-2 by using the supertype and subtype technique discussed in Chapter 10.

Figure 16-3 shows a schema to handle the specific attributes that describe automobiles and their coverages. For each line of business (or coverage type), subtype dimension tables for both the covered item and associated coverage are created. When a BI application needs the specific attributes of a single coverage type, it uses the appropriate subtype dimension tables.

Notice in this schema that you don't need separate line-of-business fact tables because the metrics don't vary by business, but you'd likely put a view on the supertype fact table to present only rows for a given subtype. The subtype dimension tables are introduced to handle the special line-of-business attributes. No new keys need to be generated; logically, all we are doing is extending existing dimension rows.

Complementary Policy Accumulating Snapshot

Finally, before leaving policy transactions, you should consider the use of an accumulating snapshot to capture the cumulative effect of the transactions. In this scenario, the grain of the fact table likely would be one row for each coverage and covered item on a policy. You can envision including policy-centric dates, such as quoted, rated, underwritten, effective, renewed, and expired. Likewise, multiple employee roles could be included on the fact table for the agent and underwriter. Many of the other dimensions discussed would be applicable to this schema, with the exception of the transaction type dimension. The accumulating snapshot likely would have an expanded fact set.

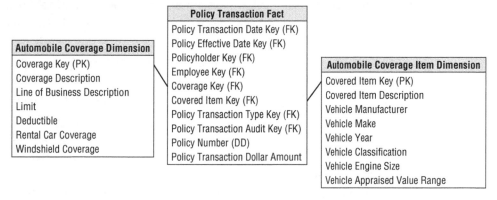

Figure 16-3: Policy transaction schema with subtype automobile dimension tables.

As discussed in Chapter 4: Inventory, an accumulating snapshot is effective for representing information about a pipeline process's key milestones. It captures the cumulative lifespan of a policy, covered items, and coverages; however, it does not store information about each and every transaction that occurred. Unusual transactional events or unexpected outliers from the standard pipeline would likely be masked with an accumulating perspective. On the other hand, an accumulating snapshot, sourced from the transactions, provides a clear picture of the durations or lag times between key process events.

Premium Periodic Snapshot

The policy transaction schema is useful for answering a wide range of questions. However, the blizzard of transactions makes it difficult to quickly determine the status or financial value of an in-force policy at a given point in time. Even if all the necessary detail lies in the transaction data, a snapshot perspective would require rolling the transactions forward from the beginning of history taking into account complicated business rules for when earned revenue is recognized. Not only is this nearly impractical on a single policy, but it is ridiculous to think about generating summary top line views of key performance metrics in this manner.

The answer to this dilemma is to create a separate fact table that operates as a companion to the policy transaction table. In this case, the business process is the monthly policy premium snapshot. The granularity of the fact table is one row per coverage and covered item on a policy each month.

Conformed Dimensions

Of course, when designing the premium periodic snapshot table, you should strive to reuse as many dimensions from the policy transaction table as possible. Hopefully, you have become a conformed dimension enthusiast by now. As described in Chapter 4, conformed dimensions used in separate fact tables either must be identical or must represent a shrunken subset of the attributes from the granular dimension.

The policyholder, covered item, and coverage dimensions would be identical. The daily date dimension would be replaced with a conformed month dimension table. You don't need to track all the employees who were involved in policy transactions on a monthly basis; it may be useful to retain the involved agent, especially because field operations are so focused on ongoing revenue performance analysis. The transaction type dimension would not be used because it does not apply at the periodic snapshot granularity. Instead, you introduce a status dimension so users can quickly discern the current state of a coverage or policy, such as new policies or cancellations this month and over time.

Conformed Facts

While we're on the topic of conformity, you also need to use conformed facts. If the same facts appear in multiple fact tables, such as facts common to this snapshot fact table as well as the consolidated fact table we'll discuss later in this chapter, then they must have consistent definitions and labels. If the facts are not identical, then they need to be given different names.

Pay-in-Advance Facts

Business management wants to know how much premium revenue was written (or sold) each month, as well as how much revenue was earned. Although a policyholder may contract and pay for coverages on covered items for a period of time, the revenue is not earned until the service is provided. In the case of the insurance company, the revenue from a policy is earned month by month as long as the policyholder doesn't cancel. The correct calculation of a metric like earned premium would mean fully replicating all the business rules of the operational revenue recognition system within the BI application. Typically, the rules for converting a transaction amount into its monthly revenue impact are complex, especially with mid-month coverage upgrades and downgrades. Fortunately, these metrics can be sourced from a separate operational system.

As illustrated in Figure 16-4, we include two premium revenue metrics in the periodic snapshot fact table to handle the different definitions of written versus earned premium. Simplistically, if an annual policy for a given coverage and covered item was written on January 1 for a cost of $600, then the written premium for January would be $600, but the earned premium is $50 ($600 divided by 12 months). In February, the written premium is zero and the earned premium is still $50. If the policy is canceled on March 31, the earned premium for March is $50, while the written premium is a negative $450. Obviously, at this point the earned revenue stream comes to a crashing halt.

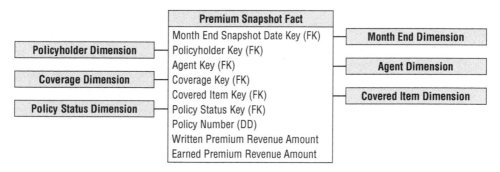

Figure 16-4: Periodic premium snapshot schema.

Pay-in-advance business scenarios typically require the combination of transaction and monthly snapshot fact tables to answer questions of transaction frequency and timing, as well as questions of earned income in a given month. You can almost never add enough facts to a snapshot schema to do away with the need for a transaction schema, or vice versa.

Heterogeneous Supertypes and Subtypes Revisited

We are again confronted with the need to look at the snapshot data with more specific line-of-business attributes, and grapple with snapshot facts that vary by line of business. Because the custom facts for each line are incompatible with each other, most of the fact row would be filled with nulls if you include all the line-of-business facts on every row. In this scenario, the answer is to separate the monthly snapshot fact table physically by line of business. You end up with the single supertype monthly snapshot schema and a series of subtype snapshots, one for each line of business or coverage type. Each of the subtype snapshot fact tables is a copy of a segment of the supertype fact table for just those coverage keys and covered item keys belonging to a particular line of business. We include the supertype facts as a convenience so analyses within a coverage type can use both the supertype and custom subtype facts without accessing two large fact tables.

Multivalued Dimensions Revisited

Automobile insurance provides another opportunity to discuss multivalued dimensions. Often multiple insured drivers are associated with a policy. You can construct a bridge table, as illustrated in Figure 16-5, to capture the relationship between the insured drivers and policy. In this case the insurance company can assign realistic weighting factors based on each driver's share of the total premium cost.

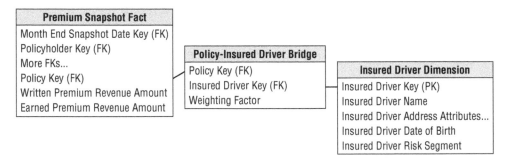

Figure 16-5: Bridge table for multiple drivers on a policy.

Because these relationships may change over time, you can add effective and expiration dates to the bridge table. Before you know it, you end up with a factless fact table to capture the evolving relationships between a policy, policy holder, covered item, and insured driver over time.

More Insurance Case Study Background

Unfortunately, the insurance business has a downside. We learn from the interviewees that there's more to life than collecting premium revenue payments. The main costs in this industry result from claim losses. After a policy is in effect, then a claim can be made against a specific coverage and covered item. A claimant, who may be the policyholder or a new party not previously known to the insurance company, makes the claim. When the insurance company opens a new claim, a reserve is usually established. The reserve is a preliminary estimate of the insurance company's eventual liability for the claim. As further information becomes known, this reserve can be adjusted.

Before the insurance company pays any claim, there is usually an investigative phase where the insurance company sends out an adjuster to examine the covered item and interview the claimant, policyholder, or other individuals involved. The investigative phase produces a stream of task transactions. In complex claims, various outside experts may be required to pass judgment on the claim and the extent of the damage.

In most cases, after the investigative phase, the insurance company issues a number of payments. Many of these payments go to third parties such as doctors, lawyers, or automotive body shop operators. Some payments may go directly to the claimant. It is important to clearly identify the employee responsible for every payment made against an open claim.

The insurance company may take possession of the covered item after replacing it for the policyholder or claimant. If the item has any remaining value, salvage payments received by the insurance company are a credit against the claim accounting.

Eventually, the payments are completed and the claim is closed. If nothing unusual happens, this is the end of the transaction stream generated by the claim. However, in some cases, further claim payments or claimant lawsuits may force a claim to be reopened. An important measure for an insurance company is how often and under what circumstances claims are reopened.

In addition to analyzing the detailed claims processing transactions, the insurance company also wants to understand what happens over the life of a claim. For example, the time lag between the claim open date and the first payment date is an important measure of claims processing efficiency.

Updated Insurance Bus Matrix

With a better understanding of the claims side of the business, the draft matrix from Figure 16-1 needs to be revisited. Based on the new requirements, you add another row to the matrix to accommodate claim transactions, as shown in Figure 16-6. Many of the dimensions identified earlier in the project will be reused; you add new columns to the matrix for the claim, claimant, and third-party payee.

	Date	Policyholder	Covered Item	Coverage	Employee	Policy	Claim	Claimant	3rd Party Payee
Policy Transactions	X	X	X	X	X	X			
Premium Snapshot	X Month	X	X	X	X Agent	X			
Claim Transactions	X	X	X	X	X	X	X	X	X

Figure 16-6: Updated insurance bus matrix.

Detailed Implementation Bus Matrix

DW/BI teams sometimes struggle with the level of detail captured in an enterprise data warehouse bus matrix. In the planning phase of an architected DW/BI project, it makes sense to stick with rather high-level business processes (or sources). Multiple fact tables at different levels of granularity may result from each of these business process rows. In the subsequent implementation phase, you can take a subset of the matrix to a lower level of detail by reflecting all the fact tables or OLAP cubes resulting from the process as separate matrix rows. At this point the matrix can be enhanced by adding columns to reflect the granularity and metrics associated with each fact table or cube. Figure 16-7 illustrates a more detailed implementation bus matrix.

Claim Transactions

The operational claim processing system generates a slew of transactions, including the following transaction task types:

- Open claim, reopen claim, close claim
- Set reserve, reset reserve, close reserve
- Set salvage estimate, receive salvage payment
- Adjuster inspection, adjuster interview
- Open lawsuit, close lawsuit
- Make payment, receive payment
- Subrogate claim

When updating the Figure 16-6 bus matrix, you determine that this schema uses a number of dimensions developed for the policy world. You again have two role-playing dates associated with the claim transactions. Unique column labels should distinguish the claim transaction and effective dates from those associated with policy transactions. The employee is the employee involved in the transactional task. As mentioned in the business case, this is particularly interesting for payment authorization transactions. The claim transaction type dimension would include the transaction types and groupings just listed.

As shown in Figure 16-8, there are several new dimensions in the claim transaction fact table. The claimant is the party making the claim, typically an individual. The third-party payee may be either an individual or commercial entity. Both the claimant and payee dimensions usually are dirty dimensions because of the difficulty of reliably identifying them across claims. Unscrupulous potential payees may go out of their way not to identify themselves in a way that would easily tie them to other claims in the insurance company's system.

Fact Table/OLAP Cube	Granularity	Facts	Date	Policyholder	Coverage	Covered Item	Employee	Policy	Claim	Claimant	3rd Party Payee
Policy Transactions											
Corporate Policy Transactions	1 row for every policy transaction	Policy Transaction Amount	Trxn Eff	X	X	X	X	X			
Auto Policy Transactions	1 row per auto policy transaction	Policy Transaction Amount	Trxn Eff	X	Auto	Auto	X	X			
Home Policy Transactions	1 row per home policy transaction	Policy Transaction Amount	Trxn Eff	X	Home	Home	X	X			
Policy Premium Snapshot											
Corporate Policy Premiums	1 row for every policy, covered item and coverage per month	Written Premium Revenue and Earned Premium Revenue Amounts	X	X	X	X	Agent	X			
Auto Policy Premiums	1 row per auto policy, covered item and coverage per month	Written Premium Revenue and Earned Premium Revenue Amounts	X	X	Auto	Auto	Agent	X			
Home Policy Premiums	1 row per home policy, covered item and coverage per month	Written Premium Revenue and Earned Premium Revenue Amounts	X	X	Home	Home	Agent	X			
Claim Events											
Claim Transactions	1 row for every claim task transaction	Claim Transaction Amount	Trxn Eff	X	X	X	X	X	X	X	X
Claim Workflow	1 row per claim	Original Reserve, Estimate, Current Reserve, Claim Paid, Salvage Collected, and Subro Collected Amounts; Loss to Open, Open to Estimate, Open to 1st Payment, Open to Subro, and Open to Closed Lags; # of Transactions	X	X	X	X	Agent	X	X	X	
Accident Involvements	1 row per loss party and affiliation on an auto claim	Accident Involvement Count	X	X	Auto	Auto		X	Auto	X	

Figure 16-7: Detailed implementation bus matrix.

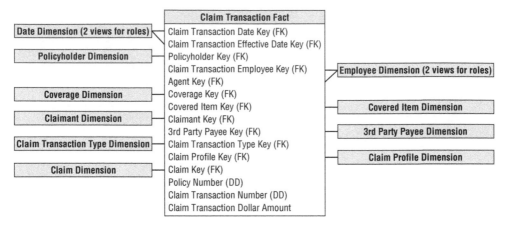

Figure 16-8: Claim transaction schema.

Transaction Versus Profile Junk Dimensions

Beyond the reused dimensions from the policy-centric schemas and the new claim-centric dimensions just listed, there are a large number of indicators and descriptions related to a claim. Designers are sometimes tempted to dump all these descriptive attributes into a claim dimension. This approach makes sense for high-cardinality descriptors, such as the specific address where the loss occurred or a narrative describing the event. However, in general, you should avoid creating dimensions with the same number of rows as the fact table.

As we described in Chapter 6, low-cardinality codified data, like the method used to report the loss or an indicator denoting whether the claim resulted from a catastrophic event, are better handled in a junk dimension. In this case, the junk dimension would more appropriately be referred to as the claim profile dimension with one row per unique combination of profile attributes. Grouping or filtering on the profile attributes would yield faster query responses than if they were alternatively handled as claim dimension attributes.

Claim Accumulating Snapshot

Even with a robust transaction schema, there is a whole class of urgent business questions that can't be answered using only transaction detail. It is difficult to derive claim-to-date performance measures by traversing through every detailed claim task transaction from the beginning of the claim's history and appropriately applying the transactions.

On a periodic basis, perhaps at the close of each day, you can roll forward all the transactions to update an accumulating claim snapshot incrementally. The granularity is one row per claim; the row is created once when the claim is opened and then is updated throughout the life of a claim until it is finally closed.

Many of the dimensions are reusable, conformed dimensions, as illustrated in Figure 16-9. You should include more dates in this fact table to track the key claim milestones and deliver time lags. These lags may be the raw difference between two dates, or they may be calculated in a more sophisticated way by accounting for only workdays in the calculations. A status dimension is added to quickly identify all open, closed, or reopened claims, for example. Transaction-specific dimensions such as employee, payee, and claim transaction type are suppressed, whereas the list of additive, numeric measures has been expanded.

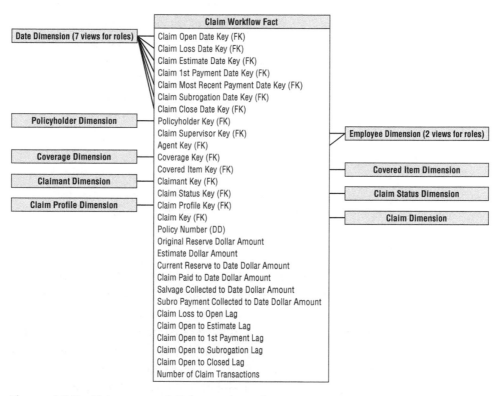

Figure 16-9: Claim accumulating snapshot schema.

Accumulating Snapshot for Complex Workflows

Accumulating snapshot fact tables are typically appropriate for predictable workflows with well-established milestones. They usually have five to 10 key milestone dates representing the pipeline's start, completion, and key events in between. However, sometimes workflows are less predictable. They still have a definite start and end date, but the milestones in between are numerous and less stable. Some occurrences may skip over some intermediate milestones, but there's no reliable pattern.

In this situation, the first task is to identify the key dates that link to role-playing date dimensions. These dates represent the most important milestones. The start and end dates for the process would certainly qualify; in addition, you should consider other commonly occurring critical milestones. These dates (and their associated dimensions) will be used extensively for BI application filtering.

However, if the number of additional milestones is both voluminous and unpredictable, they can't all be handled as additional date foreign keys in the fact table. Typically, business users are more interested in the lags between these milestones, rather than filtering or grouping on the dates themselves. If there were a total of 20 potential milestone events, there would be 190 potential lag durations: event A-to-B, A-to-C, ... (19 possible lags from event A), B-to-C, ... (18 possible lags from event B), and so on. Instead of physically storing 190 lag metrics, you can get away with just storing 19 of them and then calculate the others. Because every pipeline occurrence starts by passing through milestone A, which is the workflow begin date, you could store all 19 lags from the anchor event A and then calculate the other variations. For example, if you want to know the lag from B-to-C, take the A-to-C lag value and subtract the A-to-B lag. If there happens to be a null for one of the lags involved in a calculation, then the result also needs to be null because one of the events never occurred. But such a null result is handled gracefully if you are counting or averaging that lag across a number of claim rows.

Timespan Accumulating Snapshot

An accumulating snapshot does a great job presenting a workflow's current state, but it obliterates the intermediate states. For example, a claim can move in and out of various states such as opened, denied, closed, disputed, opened again, and closed again. The claim transaction fact table will have separate rows for each of these events, but as discussed earlier, it doesn't accumulate metrics across transactions; trying to re-create the evolution of a workflow from these transactional events would be a nightmare. Meanwhile, a classic accumulating snapshot doesn't allow you to re-create the claim workflow at any arbitrary date in the past.

Alternatively, you could add effective and expiration dates to the accumulating snapshot. In this scenario, instead of destructively updating each row as changes occur, you add a new row that preserves the state of a claim for a span of time.

Similar to a type 2 slowly changing dimension, the fact row includes the following additional columns:

- Snapshot start date
- Snapshot end date (updated when a new row for a given claim is added)
- Snapshot current flag (updated when a new row is added)

Most users are only interested in the current view provided by a classic accumulating snapshot; you can meet their needs by defining a view that filters the historical snapshot rows based on the current flag. The minority of users and reports who need to look at the pipeline as of any arbitrary date in the past can do so by filtering on the snapshot start and end dates.

The timespan accumulating snapshot fact table is more complicated to maintain than a standard accumulating snapshot, but the logic is similar. Where the classic accumulating snapshot updates a row, the timespan snapshot updates the administrative columns on the row formerly known as current, and inserts a new row.

Periodic Instead of Accumulating Snapshot

In cases where a claim is not so short-lived, such as with long-term disability or bodily injury claims that have a multiyear life span, you may represent the snapshot as a periodic snapshot rather than an accumulating snapshot. The grain of the periodic snapshot would be one row for every active claim at a regular snapshot interval, such as monthly. The facts would represent numeric, additive facts that occurred during the period such as amount claimed, amount paid, and change in reserve.

Policy/Claim Consolidated Periodic Snapshot

With the fact tables designed thus far, you can deliver a robust perspective of the policy and claim transactions, in addition to snapshots from both processes. However, the business users are also interested in profit metrics. Although premium revenue and claim loss financial metrics could be derived by separately querying two fact tables and then combining the results set, you opt to go the next step in the spirit of ease of use and performance for this common drill-across requirement.

You can construct another fact table that brings together the premium revenue and claim loss metrics, as shown in Figure 16-10. This table has a reduced set of dimensions corresponding to the lowest level of granularity common to both processes. As discussed in Chapter 7: Accounting, this is a consolidated fact table because it combines data from multiple business processes. It is best to develop consolidated fact tables after the base metrics have been delivered in separate atomic dimensional models.

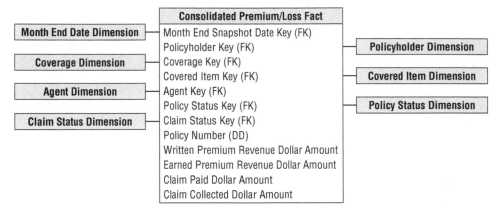

Figure 16-10: Policy/claim consolidated fact table.

Factless Accident Events

We earlier described factless fact tables as the collision of keys at a point in space and time. In the case of an automobile insurer, you can record literal collisions using a factless fact table. In this situation, the fact table registers the many-to-many correlations between the loss parties and loss items, or put in laymen's terms, all the correlations between the people and vehicles involved in an accident.

Two new dimensions appear in the factless fact table shown in Figure 16-11. The loss party captures the individuals involved in the accident, whereas the loss party role identifies them as passengers, witnesses, legal representation, or some other capacity. As we did in Chapter 3: Retail Sales, we include a fact that is always valued at 1 to facilitate counting and aggregation. This factless fact table can represent complex accidents involving many individuals and vehicles because the number of involved parties with various roles is open-ended. When there is more than one claimant or loss party associated with an accident, you can optionally treat these dimensions as multivalued dimensions using claimant group and loss party group bridge tables. This has the advantage that the grain of the fact table is preserved as one record per accident claim. Either schema variation could answer questions such as, "How many bodily injury claims did you handle where ABC Legal Partners represented the claimant and EZ-Dent-B-Gone body shop performed the repair?"

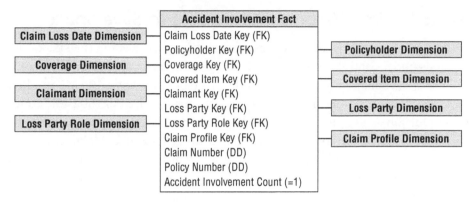

Figure 16-11: Factless fact table for accident involvements.

Common Dimensional Modeling Mistakes to Avoid

As we close this final chapter on dimensional modeling techniques, we thought it would be helpful to establish boundaries beyond which designers should *not* go. Thus far in this book, we've presented concepts by positively stating dimensional modeling best practices. Now rather than reiterating the to-dos, we focus on not-to-dos by elaborating on dimensional modeling techniques that should be avoided. We've listed the not-to-dos in reverse order of importance; be aware, however, that even the less important mistakes can seriously compromise your DW/BI system.

Mistake 10: Place Text Attributes in a Fact Table

The process of creating a dimensional model is always a kind of triage. The numeric measurements delivered from an operational business process source belong in the fact table. The descriptive textual attributes comprising the context of the measurements go in dimension tables. In nearly every case, if an attribute is used for constraining and grouping, it belongs in a dimension table. Finally, you should make a field-by-field decision about the leftover codes and pseudo-numeric items, placing them in the fact table if they are more like measurements and used in calculations or in a dimension table if they are more like descriptions used for filtering and labeling. Don't lose your nerve and leave true text, especially comment fields, in the fact table. You need to get these text attributes off the main runway of the data warehouse and into dimension tables.

Mistake 9: Limit Verbose Descriptors to Save Space

You might think you are being a conservative designer by keeping the size of the dimensions under control. However, in virtually every data warehouse, the dimension tables are geometrically smaller than the fact tables. Having a 100 MB product dimension table is insignificant if the fact table is one hundred or thousand times as large! Our job as designers of easy-to-use dimensional models is to supply as much verbose descriptive context in each dimension as possible. Make sure every code is augmented with readable descriptive text. Remember the textual attributes in the dimension tables provide the browsing, constraining, or filtering parameters in BI applications, as well as the content for the row and column headers in reports.

Mistake 8: Split Hierarchies into Multiple Dimensions

A hierarchy is a cascaded series of many-to-one relationships. For example, many products roll up to a single brand; many brands roll up to a single category. If a dimension is expressed at the lowest level of granularity, such as product, then all the higher levels of the hierarchy can be expressed as unique values in the product row. Business users understand hierarchies. Your job is to present the hierarchies in the most natural and efficient manner in the eyes of the users, not in the eyes of a data modeler who has focused his entire career on designing third normal form entity-relationship models for transaction processing systems.

A fixed depth hierarchy belongs together in a single physical flat dimension table, unless data volumes or velocity of change dictate otherwise. Resist the urge to snowflake a hierarchy by generating a set of progressively smaller subdimension tables. Finally, if more than one rollup exists simultaneously for a dimension, in most cases it's perfectly reasonable to include multiple hierarchies in the same dimension as long as the dimension has been defined at the lowest possible grain (and the hierarchies are uniquely labeled).

Mistake 7: Ignore the Need to Track Dimension Changes

Contrary to popular belief, business users often want to understand the impact of changes on at least a subset of the dimension tables' attributes. It is unlikely users will settle for dimension tables with attributes that always reflect the current state of the world. Three basic techniques track slowly moving attribute changes; don't rely on type 1 exclusively. Likewise, if a group of attributes changes rapidly, you can split a dimension to capture the more volatile attributes in a mini-dimension.

Mistake 6: Solve All Performance Problems with More Hardware

Aggregates, or derived summary tables, are a cost-effective way to improve query performance. Most BI tool vendors have explicit support for the use of aggregates. Adding expensive hardware should be done as part of a balanced program that includes building aggregates, partitioning, creating indices, choosing query-efficient DBMS software, increasing real memory size, increasing CPU speed, and adding parallelism at the hardware level.

Mistake 5: Use Operational Keys to Join Dimensions and Facts

Novice designers are sometimes too literal minded when designing the dimension tables' primary keys that connect to the fact tables' foreign keys. It is counterproductive to declare a suite of dimension attributes as the dimension table key and then use them all as the basis of the physical join to the fact table. This includes the unfortunate practice of declaring the dimension key to be the operational key, along with an effective date. All types of ugly problems will eventually arise. The dimension's operational or intelligent key should be replaced with a simple integer surrogate key that is sequentially numbered from 1 to N, where N is the total number of rows in the dimension table. The date dimension is the sole exception to this rule.

Mistake 4: Neglect to Declare and Comply with the Fact Grain

All dimensional designs should begin by articulating the business process that generates the numeric performance measurements. Second, the exact granularity of that data must be specified. Building fact tables at the most atomic, granular level will gracefully resist the ad hoc attack. Third, surround these measurements with dimensions that are true to that grain. Staying true to the grain is a crucial step in the design of a dimensional model. A subtle but serious design error is to add helpful facts to a fact table, such as rows that describe totals for an extended timespan or a large geographic area. Although these extra facts are well known at the time of the individual measurement and would seem to make some BI applications simpler, they cause havoc because all the automatic summations across dimensions overcount these higher-level facts, producing incorrect results. Each different measurement grain demands its own fact table.

Mistake 3: Use a Report to Design the Dimensional Model

A dimensional model has nothing to do with an intended report! Rather, it is a model of a measurement process. Numeric measurements form the basis of fact tables. The dimensions appropriate for a given fact table are the context that describes the circumstances of the measurements. A dimensional model is based solidly on the physics of a measurement process and is quite independent of how a user chooses to define a report. A project team once confessed it had built several hundred fact tables to deliver order management data to its business users. It turned out each fact table had been constructed to address a specific report request; the same data was extracted many, many times to populate all these slightly different fact tables. Not surprising, the team was struggling to update the databases within the nightly batch window. Rather than designing a quagmire of report-centric schemas, the team should have focused on the measurement processes. The users' requirements could have been handled with a well-designed schema for the atomic data along with a handful (not hundreds) of performance-enhancing aggregations.

Mistake 2: Expect Users to Query Normalized Atomic Data

The lowest level data is always the most dimensional and should be the foundation of a dimensional design. Data that has been aggregated in any way has been deprived of some of its dimensions. You can't build a dimensional model with aggregated data and expect users and their BI tools to seamlessly drill down to third normal form (3NF) data for the atomic details. Normalized models may be helpful for preparing the data in the ETL kitchen, but they should never be used for presenting the data to business users.

Mistake 1: Fail to Conform Facts and Dimensions

This final not-to-do should be presented as two separate mistakes because they are both so dangerous to a successful DW/BI design, but we've run out of mistake numbers to assign, so they're lumped into one.

It would be a shame to get this far and then build isolated data repository stovepipes. We refer to this as snatching defeat from the jaws of victory. If you have a numeric measured fact, such as revenue, in two or more databases sourced from different underlying systems, then you need to take special care to ensure the technical definitions of these facts exactly match. If the definitions do not exactly match, then they shouldn't both be referred to as revenue. This is conforming the facts.

Finally, the single most important design technique in the dimensional modeling arsenal is conforming dimensions. If two or more fact tables are associated with the same dimension, you must be fanatical about making these dimensions identical or carefully chosen subsets of each other. When you conform dimensions across fact tables, you can drill across separate data sources because the constraints and row headers mean the same thing and match at the data level. Conformed dimensions are the secret sauce needed for building distributed DW/BI environments, adding unexpected new data sources to an existing warehouse, and making multiple incompatible technologies function together harmoniously. Conformed dimensions also allow teams to be more agile because they're not re-creating the wheel repeatedly; this translates into a faster delivery of value to the business community.

Summary

In this final case study we designed a series of insurance dimensional models representing the culmination of many important concepts developed throughout this book. Hopefully, you now feel comfortable and confident using the vocabulary and tools of a dimensional modeler.

With dimensional modeling mastered, in the next chapter we discuss all the other activities that occur during the life of a successful DW/BI project. Before you go forth to be dimensional, it's useful to have this holistic perspective and understanding, even if your job focus is limited to modeling.

17 Kimball DW/BI Lifecycle Overview

The gears shift rather dramatically in this chapter. Rather than focusing on Kimball dimensional modeling techniques, we turn your attention to everything else that occurs during the course of a data warehouse/business intelligence design and implementation project. In this chapter, we'll cover the life of a DW/BI project from inception through ongoing maintenance, identifying best practices at each step, as well as potential vulnerabilities. More comprehensive coverage of the Kimball Lifecycle is available in *The Data Warehouse Lifecycle Toolkit*, *Second Edition* by Ralph Kimball, Margy Ross, Warren Thornthwaite, Joy Mundy, and Bob Becker (Wiley, 2008). This chapter is a crash course drawn from the complete text, which weighs in at a hefty 600+ pages.

You may perceive this chapter's content is only applicable to DW/BI project managers, but we feel differently. Implementing a DW/BI system requires tightly integrated activities. We believe everyone on the project team, including the analysts, architects, designers, and developers, needs a high-level understanding of the complete Lifecycle.

This chapter provides an overview of the entire Kimball Lifecycle approach; specific recommendations regarding dimensional modeling and ETL tasks are deferred until subsequent chapters. We will dive into the collaborative modeling workshop process in Chapter 18: Dimensional Modeling Process and Tasks, then make a similar plunge into ETL activities in Chapter 20: ETL System Design and Development Process and Tasks.

Chapter 17 covers the following concepts:

- Kimball Lifecycle orientation
- DW/BI program/project planning and ongoing management
- Tactics for collecting business requirements, including prioritization
- Process for developing the technical architecture and selecting products

- Physical design considerations, including aggregation and indexing
- BI application design and development activities
- Recommendations for deployment, ongoing maintenance, and future growth

Lifecycle Roadmap

When driving to a place we've never been to before, most of us rely on a roadmap, albeit displayed via a GPS. Similarly, a roadmap is extremely useful if we're about to embark on the unfamiliar journey of data warehousing and business intelligence. The authors of *The Data Warehouse Lifecycle Toolkit* drew on decades of experience to develop the Kimball Lifecycle approach. When we first introduced the Lifecycle in 1998, we referred to it as the Business Dimensional Lifecycle, a name that reinforced our key tenets for data warehouse success: Focus on the business's needs, present dimensionally structured data to users, and tackle manageable, iterative projects. In the 1990s, we were one of the few organizations emphasizing these core principles, so the moniker differentiated our methods from others. We are still very firmly wed to these principles, which have since become generally-accepted industry best practices, but we renamed our approach to be the Kimball Lifecycle because that's how most people refer to it.

The overall Kimball Lifecycle approach is encapsulated in Figure 17-1. The diagram illustrates task sequence, dependency, and concurrency. It serves as a roadmap to help teams do the right thing at the right time. The diagram does not reflect an absolute timeline; although the boxes are equally wide, there's a vast difference in the time and effort required for each major activity.

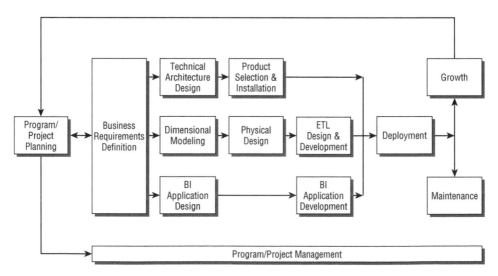

Figure 17-1: Kimball Lifecycle diagram.

NOTE   Given the recent industry focus on agile methodologies, we want to remind readers about the discussion of the topic in Chapter 1: Data Warehousing, Business Intelligence, and Dimensional Modeling Primer. The Kimball Lifecycle approach and agile methodologies share some common doctrines: Focus on business value, collaborate with the business, and develop incrementally. However, we also feel strongly that DW/BI system design and development needs to be built on a solid data architecture and governance foundation, driven by the bus architecture. We also believe most situations warrant the bundling of multiple agile "deliverables" into a more full-function release before being broadly deployed to the general business community.

Roadmap Mile Markers

Before diving into specifics, take a moment to orient yourself to the roadmap. The Lifecycle begins with program/project planning, as you would expect. This module assesses the organization's readiness for a DW/BI initiative, establishes the preliminary scope and justification, obtains resources, and launches the program/project. Ongoing project management serves as a foundation to keep the remaining activities on track.

The second major task in Figure 17-1 focuses on business requirements definition. There's a two-way arrow between program/project planning and the business requirements definition due to the interplay between these activities. Aligning the DW/BI initiative with business requirements is absolutely crucial. Best-of-breed technologies won't salvage a DW/BI environment that fails to focus on the business. Business users and their requirements have an impact on almost every design and implementation decision made during the course of a DW/BI project. In Figure 17-1's roadmap, this is reflected by the three parallel tracks that follow.

The top track of Figure 17-1 deals with technology. Technical architecture design establishes the overall framework to support the integration of multiple technologies. Using the capabilities identified in the architecture design as a shopping list, you then evaluate and select specific products. Notice that product selection is not the first box on the roadmap. One of the most frequent mistakes made by novice teams is to select products without a clear understanding of what they're trying to accomplish. This is akin to grabbing a hammer whether you need to pound a nail or tighten a screw.

The middle track emanating from business requirements definition focuses on data. It begins by translating the requirements into a dimensional model, as we've been practicing. The dimensional model is then transformed into a physical structure. The focus is on performance tuning strategies, such as aggregation, indexing, and partitioning, during the physical design. Last but not least, the ETL system is designed and developed. As mentioned earlier, the equally sized boxes don't represent equally sized efforts; this becomes obvious with the workload differential between the physical design and the demanding ETL-centric activities.

The final set of tasks spawned by the business requirements is the design and development of the BI applications. The DW/BI project isn't done when you deliver data. BI applications, in the form of parameter-driven templates and analyses, will satisfy a large percentage of the business users' analytic needs.

The technology, data, and BI application tracks, along with a healthy dose of education and support, converge for a well-orchestrated deployment. From there, on-going maintenance is needed to ensure the DW/BI system remains healthy. Finally, you handle future growth by initiating subsequent projects, each returning to the beginning of the Lifecycle all over again.

Now that you have a high-level understanding of the overall roadmap, we'll describe each of the boxes in Figure 17-1 in more detail.

Lifecycle Launch Activities

The following sections outline best practices, and pitfalls to avoid, as you launch a DW/BI project.

Program/Project Planning and Management

Not surprisingly, the DW/BI initiative begins with a series of program and project planning activities.

Assessing Readiness

Before moving ahead with a DW/BI effort, it is prudent to take a moment to assess the organization's readiness to proceed. Based on our cumulative experience from hundreds of client engagements, three factors differentiate projects that were predominantly smooth sailing versus those that entailed a constant struggle. These factors are leading indicators of DW/BI success; we'll describe the characteristics in rank order of importance.

The most critical readiness factor is to have a strong executive business sponsor. Business sponsors should have a clear vision for the DW/BI system's potential impact on the organization. Optimally, business sponsors have a track record of success with other internal initiatives. They should be politically astute leaders who can convince their peers to support the effort. It's a much riskier scenario if the chief information officer (CIO) is the designated sponsor; we much prefer visible commitment from a business partner-in-crime instead.

The second readiness factor is having a strong, compelling business motivation for tackling the DW/BI initiative. This factor often goes hand in hand with sponsorship. The DW/BI project needs to solve critical business problems to garner the resources required for a successful launch and healthy lifespan. Compelling motivation typically creates a sense of urgency, whether the motivation is from external sources, such as competitive factors, or internal sources, such as the inability to analyze cross-organization performance following acquisitions.

The third factor when assessing readiness is feasibility. There are several aspects of feasibility, including technical and resource feasibility, but data feasibility is the most crucial. Are you collecting real data in real operational source systems to support the business requirements? Data feasibility is a major concern because there is no short-term fix if you're not already collecting reasonably clean source data at the right granularity.

Scoping and Justification

When you're comfortable with the organization's readiness, it's time to put boundaries around an initial project. Scoping requires the joint input of the IT organization and business management. The scope of a DW/BI project should be both meaningful to the business organization and manageable for the IT organization. You should initially tackle projects that focus on data from a single business process; save the more challenging, cross-process projects for a later phase. Remember to avoid the *Law of Too* when scoping—too brief of a timeline for a project with too many source systems and too many users in too many locations with too diverse analytic requirements.

Justification requires an estimation of the benefits and costs associated with the DW/BI initiative. Hopefully, the anticipated benefits grossly outweigh the costs. IT usually is responsible for deriving the expenses. DW/BI systems tend to expand rapidly, so be sure the estimates allow room for short-term growth. Unlike operational system development where resource requirements tail off after production, ongoing DW/BI support needs will not decline appreciably over time.

The business community should have prime responsibility for determining the anticipated financial benefits. DW/BI environments typically are justified based on increased revenue or profit opportunities rather than merely focusing on expense reduction. Delivering "a single version of the truth" or "flexible access to information" isn't sufficient financial justification. You need to peel back the layers to determine the quantifiable impact of improved decision making made possible by these sound bites. If you are struggling with justification, this is likely a symptom that the initiative is focused on the wrong business sponsor or problem.

Staffing

DW/BI projects require the integration of a cross-functional team with resources from both the business and IT communities. It is common for the same person to fill multiple roles on the team; the assignment of named resources to roles depends on the project's magnitude and scope, as well as the individual's availability, capacity, and experience.

From the business side of the house, we'll need representatives to fill the following roles:

- **Business sponsor.** The sponsor is the DW/BI system's ultimate client, as well as its strongest advocate. Sponsorship sometimes takes the form of an executive steering committee, especially for cross-enterprise initiatives.
- **Business driver.** In a large organization, the sponsor may be too far removed or inaccessible to the project team. In this case, the sponsor sometimes delegates less strategic DW/BI responsibilities to a middle manager in the organization. This driver should possess the same characteristics as the sponsor.
- **Business lead.** The business project lead is a well-respected person who is highly involved in the project, communicating with the project manager on a daily basis. Sometimes the business driver fills this role.
- **Business users.** Optimally, the business users are the enthusiastic fans of the DW/BI environment. You need to involve them early and often, beginning with the project scope and business requirements. From there, you must find creative ways to maintain their interest and involvement throughout the project. Remember, business user involvement is critical to DW/BI acceptance. Without business users, the DW/BI system is a technical exercise in futility.

Several positions are staffed from either the business or IT organizations. These straddlers can be technical resources who understand the business or business resources who understand technology:

- **Business analyst.** This person is responsible for determining the business needs and translating them into architectural, data, and BI application requirements.
- **Data steward.** This subject matter expert is often the current go-to resource for ad hoc analysis. They understand what the data means, how it is used, and where data inconsistencies are lurking. Given the need for organizational consensus around core dimensional data, this can be a politically challenging role, as we described in Chapter 4: Inventory.
- **BI application designer/developer.** BI application resources are responsible for designing and developing the starter set of analytic templates, as well as providing ongoing BI application support.

The following roles are typically staffed from the IT organization:

- **Project manager.** The project manager is a critical position. This person should be comfortable with and respected by business executives, as well as technical resources. The project manager's communication and project management skills must be stellar.
- **Technical architect.** The architect is responsible for the overall technical architecture. This person develops the plan that ties together the required technical functionality and helps evaluate products on the basis of the overall architecture.
- **Data architect/modeler.** This resource likely comes from a transactional data background with heavy emphasis on normalization. This person should embrace dimensional modeling concepts and be empathetic to the requirements of the business rather than focused strictly on saving space or reducing the ETL workload.
- **Database administrator.** Like the data modeler, the database administrator must be willing to set aside some traditional database administration truisms, such as having only one index on a relational table.
- **Metadata coordinator.** This person helps establish the metadata repository strategy and ensures that the appropriate metadata is collected, managed, and disseminated.
- **ETL architect/designer.** This role is responsible for designing the ETL environment and processes.
- **ETL developer.** Based on direction from the ETL architect/designer, the developer builds and automates the processes, likely using an ETL tool.

We want to point out again that this is a list of roles, not people. Especially in smaller shops, talented individuals will fill many of these roles simultaneously.

Developing and Maintaining the Plan

The DW/BI project plan identifies all the necessary Lifecycle tasks. A detailed task list is available on the Kimball Group website at www.kimballgroup.com; check out the Tools & Utilities tab under *The Data Warehouse Lifecycle Toolkit, Second Edition* book title.

Any good project manager knows key team members should develop estimates of the effort required for their tasks; the project manager can't dictate the amount of time allowed and expect conformance. The project plan should identify acceptance checkpoints with business representatives after every major roadmap milestone and deliverable to ensure the project remains on track.

DW/BI projects demand broad communication. Although project managers typically excel at intra-team communications, they should also establish a communication strategy describing the frequency, forum, and key messaging for other constituencies, including the business sponsors, business community, and other IT colleagues.

Finally, DW/BI projects are vulnerable to scope creep largely due to a strong need to satisfy business users' requirements. You have several options when confronted with changes: Increase the scope (by adding time, resources, or budget), play the zero-sum game (by retaining the original scope by giving up something in exchange), or say "no" (without actually saying "no" by handling the change as an enhancement request). The most important thing about scope decisions is that they shouldn't be made in an IT vacuum. The right answer depends on the situation. Now is the time to leverage the partnership with the business to arrive at an answer that everyone can live with.

Business Requirements Definition

Collaborating with business users to understand their requirements and ensure their buy-in is absolutely essential to successful data warehousing and business intelligence. This section focuses on back-to-basics techniques for gathering business requirements.

Requirements Preplanning

Before sitting down with business representatives to collect their requirements, we suggest the following to ensure productive sessions:

Choose the Forum

Business user requirements sessions are typically interwoven with source system expert data discovery sessions. This dual-pronged approach gives you insight into the needs of the business with the realities of the data. However, you don't ask business representatives about the granularity or dimensionality of their critical data. You need to talk to them about what they do, why they do it, how they make decisions, and how they hope to make decisions in the future. Like organizational therapy, you're trying to detect the issues and opportunities.

There are two primary techniques for gathering requirements: interviews or facilitated sessions. Both have their advantages and disadvantages. Interviews encourage individual participation and are also easier to schedule. Facilitated sessions may reduce the elapsed time to gather requirements but require more time commitment from each participant.

Based on our experience, surveys are not a reasonable tool for gathering requirements because they are flat and two-dimensional. The self-selected respondents answer only the questions we've thought to ask in advance; there's no option to probe more deeply. In addition, survey instruments do not help forge the bond between business users and the DW/BI initiative that we strive for.

We generally use a hybrid approach with interviews to gather the details and then facilitation to bring the group to consensus. Although we'll describe this hybrid approach in more detail, much of the discussion applies to pure facilitation as well. The requirements gathering forum choice depends on the team's skills, the organization's culture, and what the business users have already been subjected to. One size definitely does not fit all.

Identify and Prepare the Requirements Team

Regardless of the approach, you need to identify and prepare the involved project team members. If you're doing interviews, you need to identify a lead interviewer whose primary responsibility is to ask great open-ended questions. Meanwhile, the interview scribe takes copious notes. Although a tape recorder may provide more complete coverage of each interview, we don't use one because it changes the meeting dynamics. Our preference is to have a second person in the room with another brain and a set of eyes and ears rather than relying on technology. We often invite one or two additional project members (depending on the number of interviewees) as observers, so they can hear the users' input directly.

Before sitting down with business users, you need to make sure you're approaching the sessions with the right mindset. Don't presume you already know it all; you will definitely learn more about the business during the sessions. On the other hand, you should do some homework by researching available sources, such as the annual report, website, and internal organization chart.

Because the key to getting the right answers is asking the right questions, we recommend drafting questionnaires. The questionnaire should not be viewed as a script; it is a tool to organize your thoughts and serve as a fallback device in case your mind goes blank during the session. The questionnaire will be updated throughout the interview process as the team becomes better versed in the business's subject matter.

Select, Schedule, and Prepare Business Representatives

If this is your first foray into DW/BI, or an effort to develop a cohesive strategy for dealing with existing data stovepipes, you should talk to business people representing a reasonable horizontal spectrum of the organization. This coverage is critical to formulating the enterprise data warehouse bus matrix blueprint. You need to understand the common data and vocabulary across core business functions to build an extensible environment.

Within the target user community, you should cover the organization vertically. DW/BI project teams naturally gravitate toward the business's power analysts. Although their insight is valuable, you can't ignore senior executives and middle management. Otherwise, you are vulnerable to being overly focused on the tactical here-and-now and lose sight of the group's strategic direction.

Scheduling the business representatives can be the most onerous requirements task; be especially nice to the department's administrative assistants. We prefer to meet with executives individually. Meeting with a homogeneous group of two to three people is appropriate for those lower on the organization chart. Allow 1 hour for individual meetings and 1½ hours for small groups. The scheduler needs to allow ½ hour between meetings for debriefing and other necessities. Interviewing is extremely taxing due to the focus required. Consequently, don't schedule more than three to four sessions in a day.

When it comes to preparing the interviewees, the business sponsor should communicate with them, stressing their commitment to the effort and the importance of everyone's participation. The interviewees should be asked to bring copies of their key reports and analyses to the session. This communication disseminates a consistent message about the project, plus conveys the business's ownership of the initiative. Occasionally interviewees will be reluctant to bring the business's "crown jewel" reports to the meeting, especially with an outside consultant. However, almost always we have found these people will enthusiastically race back to their offices at the end of the interview to bring back those same reports.

Collecting Business Requirements

It's time to sit down face-to-face to gather the business's requirements. The process usually flows from an introduction through structured questioning to a final wrap-up.

Launch

Responsibility for introducing the session should be established prior to gathering in a conference room. The designated kickoff person should script the primary talking points for the first few minutes when the tone of the interview meeting is set. The introduction should convey a crisp, business-centric message and not ramble with hardware, software, and other technical jargon.

Interview Flow

The objective of an interview is to get business users to talk about what they do and why they do it. A simple, nonthreatening place to begin is to ask about job responsibilities and organizational fit. This is a lob-ball that interviewees can easily respond to. From there, you typically ask about their key performance metrics. Determining how they track progress and success translates directly into the dimensional model; they're telling you about their key business processes and facts without you asking those questions directly.

If you meet with a person who has more hands-on data experience, you should probe to better understand the business's dimensionality. Questions like "How do you distinguish between products (or agents, providers, or facilities)?" or "How do you naturally categorize products?" help identify key dimension attributes and hierarchies.

If the interviewee is more analytic, ask about the types of analysis currently generated. Understanding the nature of these analyses and whether they are ad hoc or standardized provides input into the BI tool requirements, as well as the BI application design process. Hopefully, the interviewee brought along copies of key spreadsheets and reports. Rather than stashing them in a folder, it is helpful to understand how the interviewee uses the analysis today, as well as opportunities for improvement. Contrary to the advice of some industry pundits, you cannot design an extensible analytic environment merely by getting users to agree on their top five reports. The users' questions are bound to change; consequently, you must resist the temptation to narrow your design focus to a supposed top five.

If you meet with business executives, don't dive into these tactical details. Instead, ask them about their vision for better leveraging information throughout the organization. Perhaps the project team is envisioning a totally ad hoc environment, whereas business management is more interested in the delivery of standardized analyses. You need to ensure the DW/BI deliverable matches the business demand and expectations.

Ask each interviewee about the impact of improved access to information. You likely already received preliminary project funding, but it never hurts to capture more potential, quantifiable benefits.

Wrap-Up

As the interview is coming to a conclusion, ask each interviewee about their success criteria for the project. Of course, each criterion should be measurable. "Easy to use" and "fast" mean something different to everyone, so the interviewees need to articulate specifics, such as their expectations regarding the amount of training required to run predefined BI reports.

At this point, always make a broad disclaimer. The interviewees must understand that just because you discussed a capability in the meeting doesn't guarantee it'll be included in the first phase of the project. Thank interviewees for their brilliant insights, and let them know what's happening next and what their involvement will be.

Conducting Data-Centric Interviews

While we're focused on understanding the business's requirements, it is helpful to intersperse sessions with the source system data gurus or subject matter experts to evaluate the feasibility of supporting the business needs. These data-focused interviews are quite different from the ones just described. The goal is to ascertain whether the necessary core data exists before momentum builds behind the requirements. In these data-centric interviews, you may go so far as to ask for some initial data profiling results, such as domain values and counts of a few critical data fields, to be provided subsequently, just to ensure you are not standing on quicksand. A more complete data audit will occur during the dimensional modeling process. Try to learn enough at this point to manage the organization's expectations appropriately.

Documenting Requirements

Immediately following the interview, the interview team should debrief. You must ensure everyone is on the same page about what was learned. It is also helpful if everyone reviews their notes shortly after the session to fill in gaps while the interview is still fresh. Abbreviations and partial sentences in the notes become incomprehensible after a few days! Likewise, examine the reports gathered to gain further insight into the dimensionality that must be supported in the data warehouse.

At this point, it is time to document what you've heard. Although documentation is everyone's least favorite activity, it is critical for both user validation and project team reference materials. There are two potential levels of documentation resulting from the requirements process. The first is to write up each individual interview; this activity is time-consuming because the write-up should not be merely a stream-of-consciousness transcript but should make sense to someone who wasn't in the interview. The more critical documentation is a consolidated findings document. This document is organized around key business processes. Because you tackle DW/BI projects on a process-by-process basis, it is appropriate to structure the business's requirements into the same buckets that will, in turn, become implementation efforts.

When writing up the findings document, you should begin with an executive summary, followed by a project overview covering the process used and participants involved. The bulk of the document centers on the business processes; for each process, describe why business users want to analyze the process's performance metrics, what capabilities they want, their current limitations, and potential benefits or impact. Commentary about the feasibility of tackling each process is also important.

As described in Chapter 4 and illustrated in Figure 4-11, the processes are sometimes unveiled in an opportunity/stakeholder matrix to convey the impact across the organization. In this case, the rows of the opportunity matrix identify business processes, just like a bus matrix. However, in the opportunity matrix, the columns identify the organizational groups or functions. Surprisingly, this matrix is usually quite dense because many groups want access to the same core performance metrics.

Prioritizing Requirements

The consolidated findings document serves as the basis for presentations back to senior management and other requirements participants. Inevitably you uncovered more than can be tackled in a single iteration, so you need to prioritize. As discussed with project scope, don't make this decision in a vacuum; you need to leverage (or foster) your partnership with the business community to establish appropriate priorities.

The requirements wrap-up presentation is positioned as a findings review and prioritization meeting. Participants include senior business representatives (who optimally participated in the interviews), as well as the DW/BI manager and other senior IT management. The session begins with an overview of each identified business process. You want everyone in the room to have a common understanding of the opportunities. Also review the opportunity/stakeholder matrix, as well as a simplified bus matrix.

After the findings have been presented, it is time to prioritize using the prioritization grid, illustrated in Figure 17-2. The grid's vertical axis refers to the potential impact or value to the business. The horizontal axis conveys feasibility. Each of the finding's business process themes is placed on the grid based on the representatives' composite agreement regarding impact and feasibility. It's visually obvious where you should begin; projects that warrant immediate attention are located in the upper-right corner because they're high-impact projects, as well as highly feasible. Projects in the lower-left cell should be avoided like the plague; they're missions impossible that do little for the business. Likewise, projects in the lower-right cell don't justify short-term attention, although project teams sometimes gravitate here because these projects are doable but not very crucial. Finally, projects in the upper-left cell represent meaningful opportunities. These projects have large potential business payback but are currently infeasible. While the DW/BI project team focuses on projects in the shaded upper-right corner, other IT teams should address the current feasibility limitations of those in the upper left.

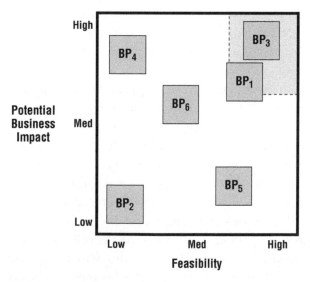

Figure 17-2: Prioritization grid based on business impact and feasibility.

Lifecycle Technology Track

On the Kimball Lifecycle roadmap in Figure 17-1, the business requirements definition is followed immediately by three concurrent tracks focused on technology, data, and BI applications, respectively. In the next several sections we'll zero in on the technology track.

Technical Architecture Design

Much like a blueprint for a new home, the technical architecture is the blueprint for the DW/BI environment's technical services and infrastructure. As the enterprise data warehouse bus architecture introduced in Chapter 4 supports data integration, the architecture plan is an organizing framework to support the integration of technologies and applications.

Like housing blueprints, the technical architecture consists of a series of models that unveil greater detail regarding each major component. In both situations, the architecture enables you to catch problems on paper (such as having the dishwasher too far from the sink) and minimize mid-project surprises. It supports the coordination of parallel efforts while speeding development through the reuse of modular components. The architecture identifies immediately required components versus those that will be incorporated at a later date (such as the deck and screened porch). Most important, the architecture serves as a communication tool. Home construction blueprints enable the architect, general contractor, subcontractors, and homeowner to communicate from a common document. Likewise, the DW/BI technical architecture supports communication regarding a consistent set of technical requirements within the team, upward to management, and outward to vendors.

In Chapter 1, we discussed several major components of the architecture, including ETL and BI services. In this section, we focus on the process of creating the architecture design.

DW/BI teams typically approach the architecture design process from opposite ends of the spectrum. Some teams simply don't understand the benefits of an architecture and feel that the topic and tasks are too nebulous. They're so focused on delivery that the architecture feels like a distraction and impediment to progress, so they opt to bypass architecture design. Instead, they piece together the technical components required for the first iteration with chewing gum and bailing wire, but the integration and interfaces get taxed as more data, more users, or more functionality are added. Eventually, these teams often end up rebuilding because the non-architected structure couldn't withstand the stresses. At the other extreme, some teams want to invest two years designing the architecture while forgetting that the primary purpose of a DW/BI environment is to solve business problems, not address any plausible (and not so plausible) technical challenge.

Neither end of the spectrum is healthy; the most appropriate response lies somewhere in the middle. We've identified the following eight-step process to help navigate these architectural design waters. Every DW/BI system has a technical architecture; the question is whether it is planned and explicit or merely implicit.

Establish an Architecture Task Force

It is useful to create a small task force of two to three people focused on architecture design. Typically, it is the technical architect, along with the ETL architect/designer and BI application architect/designer who ensure both back room and front room representation.

Collect Architecture-Related Requirements

As illustrated in Figure 17-1, defining the technical architecture is not the first box in the Lifecycle diagram. The architecture is created to support business needs; it's not meant to be an excuse to purchase the latest, greatest products. Consequently, key input into the design process should come from the business requirements definition. However, you should listen to the business's requirements with a slightly different filter to drive the architecture design. The primary focus is uncovering the architectural implications associated with the business's needs. Listen closely for timing, availability, and performance requirements.

You should also conduct additional interviews within the IT organization. These are technology-focused sessions to understand current standards, planned technical directions, and nonnegotiable boundaries. In addition, you should uncover lessons learned from prior information delivery projects, as well as the organization's willingness to accommodate operational change on behalf of the DW/BI initiative, such as identifying updated transactions in the source system.

Document Architecture Requirements

After leveraging the business requirements process and conducting supplemental IT interviews, you need to document your findings. We recommend using a simplistic tabular format, just listing each business requirement impacting the architecture, along with a laundry list of architectural implications. For example, if there is a need to deliver global sales performance data on a nightly basis, the technical implications might include 24/7 worldwide availability, data mirroring for loads, robust metadata to support global access, adequate network bandwidth, and sufficient ETL horsepower to handle the complex integration of operational data.

Create the Architecture Model

After the architecture requirements have been documented, you should begin formulating models to support the identified needs. At this point, the architecture team often sequesters itself in a conference room for several days of heavy thinking.

The architecture requirements are grouped into major components, such as ETL, BI, metadata, and infrastructure. From there the team drafts and refines the high-level architectural model. This drawing is similar to the front elevation page on housing blueprints. It illustrates what the architecture will look like from the street, but it can be dangerously simplistic because significant details are embedded in the pages that follow.

Determine Architecture Implementation Phases

Like the homeowner's dream house, you likely can't implement all aspects of the technical architecture at once. Some are nonnegotiable mandatory capabilities, whereas others are nice-to-haves. Again, refer back to the business requirements to establish architecture priorities because you must minimally provide the architectural elements needed to deliver the initial project.

Design and Specify the Subsystems

A large percentage of the needed functionality will likely be met by the major tool vendor's standard offerings, but there are always a few subsystems that may not be found in off-the-shelf products. You must define these subsystems in enough detail, so either someone can build it for you or you can evaluate products against your needs.

Create the Architecture Plan

The technical architecture needs to be documented, including the planned implementation phases, for those who were not sequestered in the conference room. The technical architecture plan document should include adequate detail so skilled professionals can proceed with construction of the framework, much like carpenters frame a house based on the blueprint. However, it doesn't typically reference specific products, except those already in-house.

Review and Finalize the Technical Architecture

Eventually we come full circle with the architecture design process. The architecture task force needs to communicate the architecture plan at varying levels of detail to the project team, IT colleagues, and business leads. Following the review, documentation should be updated and put to use immediately in the product selection process.

Product Selection and Installation

In many ways the architecture plan is similar to a shopping list for selecting products that fit into the plan's framework. The following six tasks associated with DW/BI product selection are quite similar to any technology selection.

Understand the Corporate Purchasing Process

The first step before selecting new products is to understand the internal hardware and software purchase processes.

Develop a Product Evaluation Matrix

Using the architecture plan as a starting point, a spreadsheet-based evaluation matrix should be developed that identifies the evaluation criteria, along with weighting factors to indicate importance; the more specific the criteria, the better. If the criteria are too vague or generic, every vendor will say they can satisfy your needs.

Conduct Market Research

To become informed buyers when selecting products, you should do market research to better understand the players and their offerings. A request for proposal (RFP) is a classic product evaluation tool. Although some organizations have no choice about their use, you should avoid this technique, if possible. Constructing the RFP and evaluating responses are tremendously time-consuming for the team. Meanwhile, vendors are motivated to respond to the questions in the most positive light, so the response evaluation is often more of a beauty contest. In the end, the value of the expenditure may not warrant the effort.

Evaluate a Short List of Options

Despite the plethora of products available in the market, usually only a small number of vendors can meet both functionality and technical requirements. By comparing preliminary scores from the evaluation matrix, you can focus on a narrow list of vendors and disqualify the rest. After dealing with a limited number of vendors, you can begin the detailed evaluations. Business representatives should be involved in this process if you're evaluating BI tools. As evaluators, you should drive the process rather than allow the vendors to do the driving, sharing relevant information from the architecture plan, so the sessions focus on your needs rather than on product bells and whistles. Be sure to talk with vendor references, both those formally provided and those elicited from your informal network.

If Necessary, Conduct a Prototype

After performing the detailed evaluations, sometimes a clear winner bubbles to the top, often based on the team's prior experience or relationships. In other cases, the leader emerges due to existing corporate commitments such as site licenses or legacy hardware purchases. In either situation, when a sole candidate emerges as the winner, you can bypass the prototype step (and the associated investment in both time and money). If no vendor is the apparent winner, you should conduct a prototype with no more than two products. Again, take charge of the process by developing a limited yet realistic business case study.

Select Product, Install on Trial, and Negotiate

It is time to select a product. Rather than immediately signing on the dotted line, preserve your negotiating power by making a private, not public, commitment to a single vendor. Instead of informing the vendor that you're completely sold, embark on a trial period where you have the opportunity to put the product to real use in your environment. It takes significant energy to install a product, get trained, and begin using it, so you should walk down this path only with the vendor you fully intend to buy from; a trial should not be pursued as another tire-kicking exercise. As the trial draws to a close, you have the opportunity to negotiate a purchase that's beneficial to all parties involved.

Lifecycle Data Track

In the Figure 17-1 Kimball Lifecycle diagram, the middle track following the business requirements definition focuses on data. We turn your attention in that direction throughout the next several sections.

Dimensional Modeling

Given this book's focus for the first 16 chapters, we won't spend any time discussing dimensional modeling techniques here. The next chapter provides detailed recommendations about the participants, process, and deliverables surrounding our iterative workshop approach for designing dimensional models in collaboration with business users. It's required reading for anyone involved in the modeling activity.

Physical Design

The dimensional models developed and documented via a preliminary source-to-target mapping need to be translated into a physical database. With dimensional modeling, the logical and physical designs bear a close resemblance; you don't want the database administrator to convert your lovely dimensional schema into a normalized structure during the physical design process.

Physical database implementation details vary widely by platform and project. In addition, hardware, software, and tools are evolving rapidly, so the following physical design activities and considerations merely scratch the surface.

Develop Naming and Database Standards

Table and column names are key elements of the users' experience, both for navigating the data model and viewing BI applications, so they should be meaningful to the business. You must also establish standards surrounding key declarations and the permissibility of nulls.

Develop Physical Database Model

This model should be initially built in the development server where it will be used by the ETL development team. There are several additional sets of tables that need to be designed and deployed as part of the DW/BI system, including staging tables to support the ETL system, auditing tables for ETL processing and data quality, and structures to support secure access to a subset of the data warehouse.

Develop Initial Index Plan

In addition to understanding how the relational database's query optimizer and indexes work, the database administrator also needs to be keenly aware that DW/BI requirements differ significantly from OLTP requirements. Because dimension tables have a single column primary key, you'll have a unique index on that key. If bitmapped indexes are available, you typically add single column bitmapped indexes to dimension attributes used commonly for filtering and grouping, especially those attributes that will be jointly constrained; otherwise, you should evaluate the usefulness of B-tree indexes on these attributes. Similarly, the first fact table index will typically be a B-tree or clustered index on the primary key; placing the date foreign key in the index's leading position speeds both data loads and queries because the date is frequently constrained. If the DBMS supports high-cardinality bitmapped indexes, these can be a good choice for individual foreign keys in the fact tables because they are more agnostic than clustered indexes when the user constrains dimensions in unexpected ways. The determination of other fact table indexes depends on the index options and optimization strategies within the platform. Although OLAP database engines also use indexes and have a query optimizer, unlike the relational world, the database administrator has little control in these environments.

Design Aggregations, Including OLAP Database

Contrary to popular belief, adding more hardware isn't necessarily the best weapon in the performance-tuning arsenal; leveraging aggregate tables is a far more cost-effective alternative. Whether using OLAP technology or relational aggregation tables, aggregates need to be designed in the DW/BI environment, as we'll further explore in Chapter 19: ETL Subsystems and Techniques, and Chapter 20. When performance metrics are aggregated, you either eliminate dimensions or associate the metrics with a shrunken rollup dimension that conforms to the atomic base dimension. Because you can't possibly build, store, and administer every theoretical aggregation, two primary factors need to be evaluated. First, think about the business users' access patterns derived from the requirements findings, as well as from input gained by monitoring actual usage patterns. Second, assess the data's statistical distribution to identify aggregation points that deliver bang for the buck.

Finalize Physical Storage Details

This includes the nuts-and-bolts storage structures of blocks, files, disks, partitions, and table spaces or databases. Large fact tables are typically partitioned by activity date, with data segmented by month into separate partitions while appearing to users as a single table. Partitioning by date delivers data loading, maintenance, and query performance advantages.

The aggregation, indexing and other performance tuning strategies will evolve as actual usage patterns are better understood, so be prepared for the inevitable ongoing modifications. However, you must deliver appropriately indexed and aggregated data with the initial rollout to ensure the DW/BI environment delivers reasonable query performance from the start.

ETL Design and Development

The Lifecycle's data track wraps up with the design and development of the ETL system. Chapter 19 describes the factors, presented as 34 subsystems, which must be considered during the design. Chapter 20 then provides more granular guidance about the ETL system design and development process and associated tasks. Stay tuned for more details regarding ETL.

Lifecycle BI Applications Track

The final set of parallel activities following the business requirements definition in Figure 17-1 is the BI application track where you design and develop the applications that address a portion of the users' analytic requirements. As a BI application developer once said, "Remember, this is the fun part!" You're finally using the investment in technology and data to help business users make better decisions.

Although some may feel that the data warehouse should be a completely ad hoc, self-service query environment, delivering parameter-driven BI applications will satisfy a large percentage of the business community's needs. For many business users, "ad hoc" implies the ability to change the parameters on a report to create their personalized version. There's no sense making every user start from scratch. Constructing a set of BI applications establishes a consistent analytic framework for the organization, rather than allowing each spreadsheet to tell a slightly different story. BI applications also serve to capture the analytic expertise of the organization, from monitoring performance to identifying exceptions, determining causal factors, and modeling alternative responses; this encapsulation provides a jump start for the less analytically inclined.

BI Application Specification

Following the business requirements definition, you need to review the findings and collected sample reports to identify a starter set of approximately 10 to 15 BI reports and analytic applications. You want to narrow the initial focus to the most critical capabilities to manage expectations and ensure on-time delivery. Business community input will be critical to this prioritization process. Although 15 applications may not sound like much, numerous analyses can be created from a single template merely by changing variables.

Before you start designing the initial applications, it's helpful to establish standards, such as common pull-down menus and consistent output look and feel. Using these standards, you specify each application template and capture sufficient information about the layout, input variables, calculations, and breaks, so both the application developer and business representatives share a common understanding.

During the BI application specification activity, you should also consider the applications' organization. You need to identify structured navigational paths to access the applications, reflecting the way users think about their business. Leveraging customizable information portals or dashboards are the dominant strategies for disseminating access.

BI Application Development

When you move into the development phase for the BI applications, you again need to focus on standards; naming conventions, calculations, libraries, and coding standards should be established to minimize future rework. The application development activity can begin when the database design is complete, the BI tools and metadata are installed, and a subset of historical data has been loaded. The BI application template specifications should be revisited to account for the inevitable changes to the model since the specifications were completed.

Each BI tool has product-specific tricks that can cause it to jump through hoops backward. Rather than trying to learn the techniques via trial and error, we suggest investing in appropriate tool-specific education or supplemental resources for the development team.

While the BI applications are being developed, several ancillary benefits result. BI application developers, armed with a robust access tool, will quickly find needling problems in the data haystack despite the quality assurance performed by the ETL application. This is one reason we prefer to start the BI application development activity prior to the supposed completion of the ETL system. The developers also will be the first to realistically test query response times. Now is the time to review the preliminary performance-tuning strategies.

The BI application quality assurance activities cannot be completed until the data is stabilized. You must ensure there is adequate time in the schedule beyond the final ETL cutoff to allow for an orderly wrap-up of the BI application development tasks.

Lifecycle Wrap-up Activities

The following sections provide recommendations to ensure your project comes to an orderly conclusion, while ensuring you're poised for future expansion.

Deployment

The technology, data, and BI application tracks converge at deployment. Unfortunately, this convergence does not happen naturally but requires substantial preplanning. Perhaps more important, successful deployment demands the courage and willpower to honestly assess the project's preparedness to deploy. Deployment is similar to serving a large holiday meal to friends and relatives. It can be difficult to predict exactly how long it will take to cook the meal's main entrée. Of course, if the entrée is not done, the cook is forced to slow down the side dishes to compensate for the lag before calling everyone to the table.

In the case of DW/BI deployment, the data is the main entrée. "Cooking" the data in the ETL kitchen is the most unpredictable task. Unfortunately, even if the data isn't fully cooked, you often still proceed with the DW/BI deployment because you told the warehouse guests they'd be served on a specific date and time. Because you're unwilling to slow down the pace of deployment, you march into their offices with undercooked data. No wonder users sometimes refrain from coming back for a second helping.

Although testing has undoubtedly occurred during the DW/BI development tasks, you need to perform end-to-end system testing, including data quality assurance, operations processing, performance, and usability testing. In addition to critically assessing the readiness of the DW/BI deliverables, you also need to package it with education and support for deployment. Because the user community must adopt the DW/BI system for it to be deemed successful, education is critical. The DW/BI support strategy depends on a combination of management's expectations and the realities of the deliverables. Support is often organized into a tiered structure. The first tier is website and self-service support; the second tier is provided by the power users residing in the business area; centralized support from the DW/BI team provides the final line of defense.

Maintenance and Growth

You made it through deployment, so now you're ready to kick back and relax. Not so quickly! Your job is far from complete after you deploy. You need to continue to manage the existing environment by investing resources in the following areas:

- **Support.** User support is immediately crucial following the deployment to ensure the business community gets hooked. You can't sit back in your cubicle and assume that no news from the business community is good news. If you're not hearing from them, chances are no one is using the DW/BI system. Relocate (at least temporarily) to the business community so the users have easy access to support resources. If problems with the data or BI applications are uncovered, be honest with the business to build credibility while taking immediate action to correct the problems. If the DW/BI deliverable is not of high quality, the unanticipated support demands for data reconciliation and application rework can be overwhelming.

- **Education.** You must provide a continuing education program for the DW/BI system. The curriculum should include formal refresher and advanced courses, as well as repeat introductory courses. More informal education can be offered to the developers and power users to encourage the interchange of ideas.

- **Technical support.** The DW/BI system needs to be treated as a production environment with service level agreements. Of course, technical support should proactively monitor performance and system capacity trends. You don't want to rely on the business community to tell you that performance has degraded.

- **Program support.** The DW/BI program lives on beyond the implementation of a single phase. You must closely monitor and then market your success. Communication with the varied DW/BI constituencies must continue. You must also ensure that existing implementations continue to address the needs of the business. Ongoing checkpoint reviews are a key tool to assess and identify opportunities for improvement.

If you've done your job correctly, inevitably there will be demand for growth, either for new users, new data, new BI applications, or major enhancements to existing deliverables. Unlike traditional systems development initiatives, DW/BI change should be viewed as a sign of success, not failure. As we advised earlier when discussing project scoping, the DW/BI team should not make decisions about these growth options in a vacuum; the business needs to be involved in the prioritization process. This is a good time to leverage the prioritization grid illustrated in Figure 17-2. If you haven't done so already, an executive business sponsorship committee should be established to set DW/BI priorities that align with the organization's overall objectives. After new priorities have been identified, then you go back to the beginning of the Lifecycle and do it all again, leveraging and building on the technical, data, and BI application foundations that have already been established, while turning your attention to the new requirements.

Common Pitfalls to Avoid

Although we can provide positive recommendations about data warehousing and business intelligence, some readers better relate to a listing of common pitfalls. Here is our favorite top 10 list of common errors to avoid while building a DW/BI system. These are all quite lethal errors—one alone may be sufficient to bring down the initiative:

- **Pitfall 10**: Become overly enamored with technology and data rather than focusing on the business's requirements and goals.
- **Pitfall 9**: Fail to embrace or recruit an influential, accessible, and reasonable senior management visionary as the business sponsor of the DW/BI effort.
- **Pitfall 8**: Tackle a galactic multiyear project rather than pursuing more manageable, although still compelling, iterative development efforts.
- **Pitfall 7**: Allocate energy to construct a normalized data structure, yet run out of budget before building a viable presentation area based on dimensional models.
- **Pitfall 6**: Pay more attention to back room operational performance and ease-of-development than to front room query performance and ease of use.
- **Pitfall 5**: Make the supposedly queryable data in the presentation area overly complex. Database designers who prefer a more complex presentation should spend a year supporting business users; they'd develop a much better appreciation for the need to seek simpler solutions.
- **Pitfall 4**: Populate dimensional models on a standalone basis without regard to a data architecture that ties them together using shared, conformed dimensions.
- **Pitfall 3**: Load only summarized data into the presentation area's dimensional structures.
- **Pitfall 2**: Presume the business, its requirements and analytics, and the underlying data and the supporting technology are static.
- **Pitfall 1**: Neglect to acknowledge that DW/BI success is tied directly to business acceptance. If the users haven't accepted the DW/BI system as a foundation for improved decision making, your efforts have been exercises in futility.

Summary

This chapter provided a high-speed tour of the Kimball Lifecycle approach for DW/BI projects. We touched on the key processes and best practices. Although each project is a bit different from the next, they all require attention to the major tasks discussed to ensure a successful initiative.

The next chapter provides much more detailed coverage of the Kimball Lifecycle's collaborative workshop approach for iteratively designing dimensional models with business representatives. Chapters 19 and 20 delve into ETL system design considerations and recommended development processes.

18

Dimensional Modeling Process and Tasks

We've described countless dimensional modeling patterns in Chapters 1 through 16 of this book. Now it's time to turn your attention to the tasks and tactics of the dimensional modeling process.

This chapter, condensed from content in *The Data Warehouse Lifecycle Toolkit, Second Edition* (Wiley, 2008), begins with a practical discussion of preliminary preparation activities, such as identifying the participants (including business representatives) and arranging logistics. The modeling team develops an initial high-level model diagram, followed by iterative detailed model development, review, and validation. Throughout the process, you are reconfirming your understanding of the business's requirements.

Chapter 18 reviews the following concepts:

- Overview of the dimensional modeling process
- Tactical recommendations for the modeling tasks
- Key modeling deliverables

Modeling Process Overview

Before launching into the dimensional modeling design effort, you must involve the right players. Most notably, we strongly encourage the participation of business representatives during the modeling sessions. Their involvement and collaboration strongly increases the likelihood that the resultant model addresses the business's needs. Likewise, the organization's business data stewards should participate, especially when you're discussing the data they're responsible for governing.

Creating a dimensional model is a highly iterative and dynamic process. After a few preparation steps, the design effort begins with an initial graphical model derived from the bus matrix, identifying the scope of the design and clarifying the grain of the proposed fact tables and associated dimensions.

After completing the high-level model, the design team dives into the dimension tables with attribute definitions, domain values, sources, relationships, data quality concerns, and transformations. After the dimensions are identified, the fact tables are modeled. The last phase of the process involves reviewing and validating the model with interested parties, especially business representatives. The primary goals are to create a model that meets the business requirements, verify that data is available to populate the model, and provide the ETL team with a solid starting source-to-target mapping.

Dimensional models unfold through a series of design sessions with each pass resulting in a more detailed and robust design that's been repeatedly tested against the business needs. The process is complete when the model clearly meets the business's requirements. A typical design requires three to four weeks for a single business process dimensional model, but the time required can vary depending on the team's experience, the availability of detailed business requirements, the involvement of business representatives or data stewards authorized to drive to organizational consensus, the complexity of the source data, and the ability to leverage existing conformed dimensions.

Figure 18-1 shows the dimensional modeling process flow. The key inputs to the dimensional modeling process are the preliminary bus matrix and detailed business requirements. The key deliverables of the modeling process are the high-level dimensional model, detailed dimension and fact table designs, and issues log.

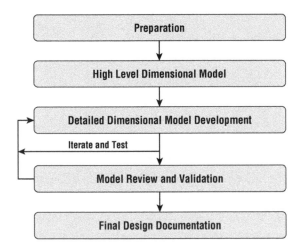

Figure 18-1: Dimensional modeling process flow diagram.

Although the graphic portrays a linear progression, the process is quite iterative. You will make multiple passes through the dimensional model starting at a high level and drilling into each table and column, filling in the gaps, adding more detail, and changing the design based on new information.

If an outside expert is engaged to help guide the dimensional modeling effort, insist they facilitate the process with the team rather than disappearing for a few weeks and returning with a completed design. This ensures the entire team understands the design and associated trade-offs. It also provides a learning opportunity, so the team can carry the model forward and independently tackle the next model.

Get Organized

Before beginning to model, you must appropriately prepare for the dimensional modeling process. In addition to involving the right resources, there are also basic logistical considerations to ensure a productive design effort.

Identify Participants, Especially Business Representatives

The best dimensional models result from a collaborative team effort. No single individual is likely to have the detailed knowledge of the business requirements and the idiosyncrasies of the source systems to effectively create the model themselves. Although the data modeler facilitates the process and has primary responsibility for the deliverables, we believe it's critically important to get subject matter experts from the business involved to actively collaborate; their insights are invaluable, especially because they are often the individuals who have historically figured out how to get data out of the source systems and turned it into valuable analytic information. Although involving more people in the design activities increases the risk of slowing down the process, the improved richness and completeness of the design justifies the additional overhead.

It's always helpful to have someone with keen knowledge of the source system realities involved. You might also include some physical DBA and ETL team representatives so they can learn from the insights uncovered during the modeling effort and resist the temptations to apply third normal form (3NF) concepts or defer complexities to the BI applications in an effort to streamline the ETL processing. Remember the goal is to trade off ETL processing complexity for simplicity and predictability at the BI presentation layer.

Before jumping into the modeling process, you should take time to consider the ongoing stewardship of the DW/BI environment. If the organization has an active data governance and stewardship initiative, it is time to tap into that function. If there is no preexisting stewardship program, it's time to initiate it. An enterprise DW/BI effort committed to dimensional modeling must also be committed to a conformed dimension strategy to ensure consistency across business processes. An active data stewardship program helps the organization achieve its conformed dimension strategy. Agreeing on conformed dimensions in a large enterprise can be a challenge; the difficulty is usually less a technical issue and more an organizational communication and consensus building challenge.

Different groups across the enterprise are often committed to their own proprietary business rules and definitions. Data stewards must work closely with the interested groups to develop common business rules and definitions, and then cajole the organization into embracing the common rules and definitions to develop enterprise consensus. Over the years, some have criticized the concept of conformed dimensions as being "too hard." Yes, it's difficult to get people in different corners of the business to agree on common attribute names, definitions, and values, but that's the crux of unified, integrated data. If everyone demands their own labels and business rules, then there's no chance of delivering the single version of the truth promised by DW/BI systems. And finally, one of the reasons the Kimball approach is sometimes criticized as being hard from people who are looking for quick solutions is because we have spelled out the detailed steps for actually getting the job done. In Chapter 19: ETL Subsystems and Techniques, these down-in-the-weeds details are discussed in the coverage of ETL subsystems 17 and 18.

Review the Business Requirements

Before the modeling begins, the team must familiarize itself with the business requirements. The first step is to carefully review the requirements documentation, as we described in Chapter 17: Kimball DW/BI Lifecycle Overview. It's the modeling team's responsibility to translate the business requirements into a flexible dimensional model that can support a broad range of analysis, not just specific reports. Some designers are tempted to skip the requirements review and move directly into the design, but the resulting models are typically driven exclusively by the source data without considering the added value required by the business community. Having appropriate business representation on the modeling team helps further avoid this data-driven approach.

Leverage a Modeling Tool

Before jumping into the modeling activities, it's helpful to have a few tools in place. Using a spreadsheet as the initial documentation tool is effective because it enables you to quickly and easily make changes as you iterate through the modeling process.

After the model begins to firm up in the later stages of the process, you can convert to whatever modeling tool is used in your organization. Most modeling tools are dimensionally aware with functions to support the creation of a dimensional model. When the detailed design is complete, the modeling tools can help the DBA forward engineer the model into the database, including creating the tables, indexes, partitions, views, and other physical elements of the database.

Leverage a Data Profiling Tool

Throughout the modeling process, the teams needs to develop an ever-increasing understanding of the source data's structure, content, relationships, and derivation rules. You need to verify the data exists in a usable state, or at least its flaws can be managed, and understand what it takes to convert it into the dimensional model. *Data profiling* uses query capabilities to explore the actual content and relationships in the source system rather than relying on perhaps incomplete or outdated documentation. Data profiling can be as simple as writing some SQL statements or as sophisticated as a special purpose tool. The major ETL vendors include data profiling capabilities in their products.

Leverage or Establish Naming Conventions

The issue of naming conventions inevitably arises during the creation of the dimensional model. The data model's labels must be descriptive and consistent from a business perspective. Table and column names become key elements of the BI application's interface. A column name such as "Description" may be perfectly clear in the context of a data model but communicates nothing in the context of a report.

Part of the process of designing a dimensional model is agreeing on common definitions and common labels. Naming is complex because different business groups have different meanings for the same name and different names with the same meaning. People are reluctant to give up the familiar and adopt a new vocabulary. Spending time on naming conventions is one of those tiresome tasks that seem to have little payback but is worth it in the long run.

Large organizations often have an IT function that owns responsibility for naming conventions. A common approach is to use a naming standard with three parts: prime word, qualifiers (if appropriate), and class word. Leverage the work of this IT function, understanding that sometimes existing naming conventions need to be extended to support more business-friendly table and column names. If the organization doesn't already have a set of naming conventions, you must establish them during the dimensional modeling.

Coordinate Calendars and Facilities

Last, but not least, you need to schedule the design sessions on participants' calendars. Rather than trying to reserve full days, it's more realistic to schedule morning and afternoon sessions that are two to three hours in duration for three or four days each week. This approach recognizes that the team members have other responsibilities and allows them to try to keep up in the hours before, after, and between design sessions. The design team can leverage the unscheduled time to research the source data and confirm requirements, as well as allow time for the data modeler to update the design documentation prior to each session.

As we mentioned earlier, the modeling process typically takes three to four weeks for a single business process, such as sales orders, or a couple of tightly related business processes such as healthcare facility and professional claim transactions in a set of distinct but closely aligned fact tables. There are a multitude of factors impacting the magnitude of the effort. Ultimately, the availability of previously existing core dimensions allows the modeling effort to focus almost exclusively on the fact table's performance metrics, which significantly reduces the time required.

Finally, you must reserve appropriate facilities. It is best to set aside a dedicated conference room for the duration of the design effort—no easy task in most organizations where meeting room facilities are always in short supply. Although we're dreaming, big floor-to-ceiling whiteboards on all four walls would be nice, too! In addition to a meeting facility, the team needs some basic supplies, such as self-stick flip chart paper. A laptop projector is often useful during the design sessions and is absolutely required for the design reviews.

Design the Dimensional Model

As outlined in Chapter 3: Retail Sales, there are four key decisions made during the design of a dimensional model:

- Identify the business process.
- Declare the grain of the business process.
- Identify the dimensions.
- Identify the facts.

The first step of identifying the business process is typically determined at the conclusion of the requirements gathering. The prioritization activity described in Chapter 17 establishes which bus matrix row (and hence business process) will be modeled. With that grounding, the team can proceed with the design tasks.

The modeling effort typically works through the following sequence of tasks and deliverables, as illustrated in Figure 18-1:

- High-level model defining the model's scope and granularity
- Detailed design with table-by-table attributes and metrics
- Review and validation with IT and business representatives
- Finalization of the design documentation

As with any data modeling effort, dimensional modeling is an iterative process. You will work back and forth between business requirements and source details to further refine the model, changing the model as you learn more.

This section describes each of these major tasks. Depending on the design team's experience and exposure to dimensional modeling concepts, you might begin with basic dimensional modeling education before kicking off the effort to ensure everyone is on the same page regarding standard dimensional vocabulary and best practices.

Reach Consensus on High-Level Bubble Chart

The initial task in the design session is to create a high-level dimensional model diagram for the target business process. Creating the first draft is relatively straightforward because you start with the bus matrix. Although an experienced designer could develop the initial high-level dimensional model and present it to the team for review, we recommend against this approach because it does not allow the entire team to participate in the process.

The high-level diagram graphically represents the business process's dimension and fact tables. Shown in Figure 18-2, we often refer to this diagram as the *bubble chart* for obvious reasons. This entity-level graphical model clearly identifies the grain of the fact table and its associated dimensions to a non-technical audience.

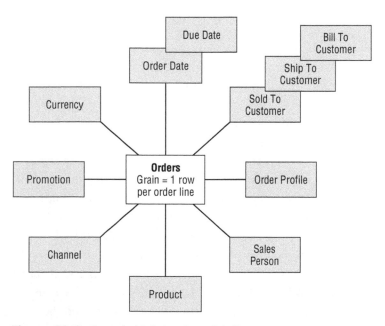

Figure 18-2: Sample high-level model diagram.

Declaring the grain requires the modeling team to consider what is needed to meet the business requirements and what is possible based on the data collected by the source system. The bubble chart must be rooted in the realities of available physical data sources. A single row of the bus matrix may result in multiple bubble charts, each corresponding to a unique fact table with unique granularity.

Most of the major dimensions will fall out naturally after you determine the grain. One of the powerful effects of a clear fact table grain declaration is you can precisely visualize the associated dimensionality. Choosing the dimensions may also cause you to rethink the grain declaration. If a proposed dimension doesn't match the grain of the fact table, either the dimension must be left out, the grain of the fact table changed, or a multivalued design solution needs to be considered.

Figure 18-2's graphical representation serves several purposes. It facilitates discussion within the design team before the team dives into the detailed design, ensuring everyone is on the same page before becoming inundated with minutiae. It's also a helpful introduction when the team communicates with interested stake-holders about the project, its scope, and data contents.

To aid in understanding, it is helpful to retain consistency across the high-level model diagrams for a given business process. Although each fact table is documented on a separate page, arranging the associated dimensions in a similar sequence across the bubble charts is useful.

Develop the Detailed Dimensional Model

After completing the high-level bubble chart designs, it's time to focus on the details. The team should meet on a very regular basis to define the detailed dimensional model, table by table, column by column. The business representatives should remain engaged during these interactive sessions; you need their feedback on attributes, filters, groupings, labels, and metrics.

It's most effective to start with the dimension tables and then work on the fact tables. We suggest launching the detailed design process with a couple of straight-forward dimensions; the date dimension is always a favorite starting point. This enables the modeling team to achieve early success, develop an understanding of the modeling process, and learn to work together as a team.

The detailed modeling identifies the interesting and useful attributes within each dimension and appropriate metrics for each fact table. You also want to capture the sources, definitions, and preliminary business rules that specify how these attributes and metrics are populated. Ongoing analyses of the source system and systematic data profiling during the design sessions helps the team better understand the realities of the underlying source data.

Identify Dimensions and their Attributes

During the detailed design sessions, key conformed dimensions are defined. Because the DW/BI system is an enterprise resource, these definitions must be acceptable across the enterprise. The data stewards and business analysts are key resources to achieve organizational consensus on table and attribute naming, descriptions, and definitions. The design team can take the lead in driving the process and leveraging naming conventions, if available. But it is ultimately a business task to agree on standard business definitions and names; the column names must make sense to the business users. This can take some time, but it is an investment that will deliver huge returns for the users' understanding and willingness to accept the dimensional model. Don't be surprised if the governance steering committee must get involved to resolve conformed dimension definition and naming issues.

At this point, the modeling team often also wrestles with the potential inclusion of junk dimensions or mini-dimensions in a dimensional model. It may not be apparent that these more performance-centric patterns are warranted until the team is deeply immersed in the design.

Identify the Facts

Declaring the grain crystallizes the discussion about the fact table's metrics because the facts must all be true to the grain. The data profiling effort identifies the counts and amounts generated by the measurement event's source system. However, fact tables are not limited to just these base facts. There may be additional metrics the business wants to analyze that are derived from the base facts.

Identify Slowly Changing Dimension Techniques

After the dimension and fact tables from the high-level model diagram have been initially drafted, you then circle back to the dimension tables. For each dimension table attribute, you define how source system data changes will be reflected in the dimension table. Again, input from the business data stewards is critical to establishing appropriate rules. It's also helpful to ask the source system experts if they can determine whether a data element change is due to a source data correction.

Document the Detailed Table Designs

The key deliverables of the detailed modeling phase are the design worksheets, as shown in Figure 18-3; a digital template is available on our website at www.kimballgroup.com under the Tools and Utilities Tab for *The Data Warehouse Lifecycle Toolkit, Second Edition*. The worksheets capture details for communication to interested stakeholders including other analytical business users, BI application developers, and most important, the ETL developers who will be tasked with populating the design.

Table Name	**DimOrderProfile**
Table Type	Dimension
Display Name	OrderProfile
Description	Order Profile is the "junk" dimension for miscellaneous information about order transactions
Used in schemas	Orders
Size	12 rows

Target							Source			
Column Name	Description	Datatype	Size	Example Values	SCD Type	Source System	Source Table	Source Field Name	Source Datatype	ETL Rules
OrderProfileKey	Surrogate primary key	smallint		1, 2, 3...		Derived				Surrogate key
OrderMethod	Method used to place order (phone, fax, internet)	varchar	8	Phone, Fax, Internet	1	OEI	OrderHeader	Ord_Meth	int	1=Phone, 2=Fax, 3=Internet
OrderSource	Source of the order (reseller, direct sales)	varchar	12	Reseller, Direct Sales	1	OEI	OrderHeader	Ord_Src	char	R=Reseller, D=Direct Sales
CommissionInd	Indicates whether order is commissionable or not	varchar	14	Commission, Non-Commission	1	OEI	OrderHeader	Comm_Code	int	0=Non-Commission, 1=Commission

Figure 18-3: Sample detailed dimensional design worksheet.

Each dimension and fact table should be documented in a separate worksheet. At a minimum, the supporting information required includes the attribute/fact name, description, sample values, and a slowly changing dimension type indicator for every dimension attribute. In addition, the detailed fact table design should identify each foreign key relationship, appropriate degenerate dimensions, and rules for each fact to indicate whether it's additive, semi-additive, or non-additive.

The dimensional design worksheet is the first step toward creating the source-to-target mapping document. The physical design team will further flesh out the mapping with physical table and column names, data types, and key declarations.

Track Model Issues

Any issues, definitions, transformation rules, and data quality challenges discovered during the design process should be captured in an issues tracking log. Someone should be assigned the task of capturing and tracking issues during the sessions; the project manager, if they're participating in the design sessions, often handles this responsibility because they're typically adept at keeping the list updated and encouraging progress on resolving open issues. The facilitator should reserve adequate time at the end of every session to review and validate new issue entries and their assignments. Between design sessions, the design team is typically busy profiling data, seeking clarification and agreement on common definitions, and meeting with source system experts to resolve outstanding issues.

Maintain Updated Bus Matrix

During the detailed modeling process, there are often new discoveries about the business process being modeled. Frequently, these findings result in the introduction of new fact tables to support the business process, new dimensions, or the splitting or combining of dimensions. You must keep the bus matrix updated throughout the design process because it is a key communication and planning tool. As discussed in Chapter 16: Insurance, the detailed bus matrix often captures additional information about each fact table's granularity and metrics.

Review and Validate the Model

Once the design team is confident about the model, the process moves into the review and validation phase to get feedback from other interested parties, including:

- IT resources, such as DW/BI team members not involved in the modeling effort, source system experts, and DBAs
- Analytical or power business users not involved in the modeling effort
- Broader business user community

IT Reviews

Typically, the first review of the detailed dimensional model is with peers in the IT organization. This audience is often composed of reviewers who are intimately familiar with the target business process because they wrote or manage the system that runs it. They are also at least partly familiar with the target data model because you've already been pestering them with source data questions.

IT reviews can be challenging because the participants often lack an understanding of dimensional modeling. In fact, most of them probably fancy themselves as proficient 3NF modelers. Their tendency will be to apply transaction processing-oriented modeling rules to the dimensional model. Rather than spending the bulk of your time debating the merits of different modeling disciplines, it is best to proactively provide some dimensional modeling education as part of the review process.

When everyone has the basic concepts down, you should begin with a review of the bus matrix. This gives everyone a sense of the project scope and overall data architecture, demonstrates the role of conformed dimensions, and shows the relative business process priorities. Next, illustrate how the selected row on the matrix translates directly into the high-level dimensional model diagram. This gives everyone the entity-level map of the model and serves as the guide for the rest of the discussion.

Most of the review session should be spent going through the dimension and fact table worksheet details. It is also a good idea to review any remaining open issues for each table as you work through the model.

Changes to the model will likely result from this meeting. Remember to assign the task of capturing the issues and recommendations to someone on the team.

Core User Review

In many projects, this review is not required because the core business users are members of the modeling team and are already intimately knowledgeable about the dimensional model. Otherwise, this review meeting is similar in scope and structure to the IT review meeting. The core business users are more technical than typical business users and can handle details about the model. In smaller organizations, we often combine the IT review and core user review into one session.

Broader Business User Review

This session is as much education as it is design review. You want to educate people without overwhelming them, while at the same time illustrating how the dimensional model supports their business requirements. You should start with the bus matrix as the enterprise DW/BI data roadmap, review the high-level model bubble charts, and finally, review the critical dimensions, such as customer and product. Sometimes the bubble charts are supplemented with diagrams similar to Figure 18-4 to illustrate the hierarchical drill paths within a dimension.

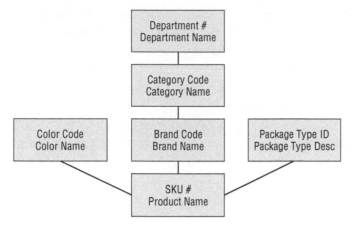

Figure 18-4: Illustration of hierarchical attribute relationships for business users.

Be sure to allocate time during this education/review to illustrate how the model can be used to answer a broad range of questions about the business process. We often pull some examples from the requirements document and walk through how they would be answered.

Finalize the Design Documentation

After the model is in its final form, the design documentation should be compiled from the design team's working papers. This document typically includes:

- Brief description of the project
- High-level data model diagram
- Detailed dimensional design worksheet for each fact and dimension table
- Open issues

Summary

Dimensional modeling is an iterative design process requiring the cooperative effort of people with a diverse set of skills, including business representatives. The design effort begins with an initial graphical model pulled from the bus matrix and presented at the entity level. The detailed modeling process drills down into the definitions, sources, relationships, data quality problems, and required transformations for each table. The primary goals are to create a model that meets the business requirements, verify the data is available to populate the model, and provide the ETL team with a clear direction.

The task of determining column and table names is interwoven into the design process. The organization as a whole must agree on the names, definitions, and derivations of every column and table in the dimensional model. This is more of a political process than a technical one, which requires the full attention of the most diplomatic team member. The resulting column names exposed through the BI tool must make sense to the business community.

The detailed modeling effort is followed by several reviews. The end result is a dimensional model that has been successfully tested against both the business needs and data realities.

19

ETL Subsystems and Techniques

The extract, transformation, and load (ETL) system consumes a disproportionate share of the time and effort required to build a DW/BI environment. Developing the ETL system is challenging because so many outside constraints put pressure on its design: the business requirements, source data realities, budget, processing windows, and skill sets of the available staff. Yet it can be hard to appreciate just why the ETL system is so complex and resource-intensive. Everyone understands the three letters: You get the data out of its original source location (E), you do something to it (T), and then you load it (L) into a final set of tables for the business users to query.

When asked about the best way to design and build the ETL system, many designers say, "Well, that depends." It depends on the source; it depends on limitations of the data; it depends on the scripting languages and ETL tools available; it depends on the staff's skills; and it depends on the BI tools. But the "it depends" response is dangerous because it becomes an excuse to take an unstructured approach to developing an ETL system, which in the worse-case scenario results in an undifferentiated spaghetti-mess of tables, modules, processes, scripts, triggers, alerts, and job schedules. This "creative" design approach should not be tolerated. With the wisdom of hindsight from thousands of successful data warehouses, a set of ETL best practices have emerged. There is no reason to tolerate an unstructured approach.

Careful consideration of these best practices has revealed 34 subsystems are required in almost every dimensional data warehouse back room. No wonder the ETL system takes such a large percentage of the DW/BI development resources!

This chapter is drawn from *The Data Warehouse Lifecycle Toolkit*, *Second Edition* (Wiley, 2008). Throughout the chapter we've sprinkled pointers to resources on the Kimball Group's website for more in-depth coverage of several ETL techniques.

Chapter 19 reviews the following concepts:

- Requirements and constraints to be considered before designing the ETL system
- Three subsystems focused on extracting data from source systems

- Five subsystems to deal with value-added cleaning and conforming, including dimensional structures to monitor quality errors
- Thirteen subsystems to deliver data into now-familiar dimensional structures, such as a subsystem to implement slowly changing dimension techniques
- Thirteen subsystems to help manage the production ETL environment

Round Up the Requirements

Establishing the architecture of an ETL system begins with one of the toughest challenges: rounding up the requirements. By this we mean gathering and understanding all the known requirements, realities, and constraints affecting the ETL system. The list of requirements can be pretty overwhelming, but it's essential to lay them on the table before launching into the development of the ETL system.

The ETL system requirements are mostly constraints you must live with and adapt your system to. Within the framework of these requirements, there are opportunities to make your own decisions, exercise judgment, and leverage creativity, but the requirements dictate the core elements that the ETL system must deliver. The following ten sections describe the major requirements areas that impact the design and development of the ETL system.

Before launching the ETL design and development effort, you should provide a short response for each of the following ten requirements. We have provided a sample checklist (as a note) for each to get you started. The point of this exercise is to ensure you visit each of these topics because any one of them can be a show-stopper at some point in the project.

Business Needs

From an ETL designer's view, the business needs are the DW/BI system users' information requirements. We use the term *business needs* somewhat narrowly here to mean the information content that business users need to make informed business decisions. Because the business needs directly drive the choice of data sources and their subsequent transformation in the ETL system, the ETL team must understand and carefully examine the business needs.

NOTE You should maintain a list of the key performance indicators (KPIs) uncovered during the business requirements definition that the project intends to support, as well as the drill-down and drill-across targets required when a business user needs to investigate "why?" a KPI changed.

Compliance

Changing legal and reporting requirements have forced many organizations to seriously tighten their reporting and provide proof that the reported numbers are accurate, complete, and have not been tampered with. Of course, DW/BI systems in regulated businesses, such as telecommunications, have complied with regulatory reporting requirements for years. But certainly the whole tenor of financial reporting has become much more rigorous for everyone.

NOTE In consultation with your legal department or chief compliance officer (if you have one!) and the BI delivery team, you should list all data and final reports subject to compliance restrictions. List those data inputs and data transformation steps for which you must maintain the "chain of custody" showing and proving that final reports were derived from the original data delivered from your data sources. List the data that you must provide proof of security for the copies under your control, both offline and online. List those data copies you must archive, and list the expected usable lifetime of those archives. Good luck with all this. This is why you are paid so well....

Data Quality

Three powerful forces have converged to put data quality concerns near the top of the list for executives. First, the long-term cultural trend that says, "If only I could see the data, then I could manage my business better" continues to grow; today's knowledge workers believe instinctively that data is a crucial requirement for them to function in their jobs. Second, most organizations understand their data sources are profoundly distributed, typically around the world, and that effectively integrating a myriad of disparate data sources is required. And third, the sharply increased demands for compliance mean careless handling of data will not be overlooked or excused.

NOTE You should list those data elements whose quality is known to be unacceptable, and list whether an agreement has been reached with the source systems to correct the data before extraction. List those data elements discovered during data profiling, which will be continuously monitored and flagged as part of the ETL process.

Security

Security awareness has increased significantly in the last few years across IT but often remains an afterthought and an unwelcome burden to most DW/BI teams. The basic rhythms of the data warehouse are at odds with the security mentality; the data warehouse seeks to publish data widely to decision makers, whereas the security interests assume data should be restricted to those with a need to know. Additionally, security must be extended to physical backups. If the media can easily be removed from the backup vault, then security has been compromised as effectively as if the online passwords were compromised.

During the requirements roundup, the DW/BI team should seek clear guidance from senior management as to what aspects of the DW/BI system carry extra security sensitivity. If these issues have never been examined, it is likely the question will be tossed back to the team. That is the moment when an experienced security manager should be invited to join the design team. Compliance requirements are likely to overlap security requirements; it may be wise to combine these two topics during the requirements roundup.

> **NOTE**   You should expand the compliance checklist to encompass known security and privacy requirements.

Data Integration

Data integration is a huge topic for IT because, ultimately, it aims to make all systems seamlessly work together. The "360 degree view of the enterprise" is a familiar name for data integration. In many cases, serious data integration must take place among the organization's primary transaction systems before data arrives at the data warehouse's back door. But rarely is that data integration complete, unless the organization has a comprehensive and centralized master data management (MDM) system, and even then it's likely other important operational systems exist outside the primary MDM system.

Data integration usually takes the form of conforming dimensions and conforming facts in the data warehouse. Conforming dimensions means establishing common dimensional attributes across separated databases, so drill-across reports can be generated using these attributes. Conforming facts means making agreements on common business metrics such as key performance indicators (KPIs) across separated databases so these numbers can be compared mathematically by calculating differences and ratios.

> **NOTE** You should use the bus matrix of business processes to generate a priority list for conforming dimensions (columns of the bus matrix). Annotate each row of the bus matrix with whether there is a clear executive demand for the business process to participate in the integration process, and whether the ETL team responsible for that business process has agreed.

Data Latency

Data latency describes how quickly source system data must be delivered to the business users via the DW/BI system. Obviously, data latency requirements have a huge effect on the ETL architecture. Clever processing algorithms, parallelization, and potent hardware can speed up traditional batch-oriented data flows. But at some point, if the data latency requirement is sufficiently urgent, the ETL system's architecture must convert from batch to microbatch or streaming-oriented. This switch isn't a gradual or evolutionary change; it's a major paradigm shift in which almost every step of the data delivery pipeline must be re-implemented.

> **NOTE** You should list all legitimate and well-vetted business demands for data that must be provided on a daily basis, on a many times per day basis, within a few seconds, or instantaneously. Annotate each demand with whether the business community understands the data quality trade-offs associated with their particular choice. Near the end of Chapter 20: ETL System Design and Development Process and Tasks, we discuss data quality compromises caused by low latency requirements.

Archiving and Lineage

Archiving and lineage requirements were hinted at in the previous compliance and security sections. Even without the legal requirements for saving data, every data warehouse needs various copies of old data, either for comparisons with new data to generate change capture records or reprocessing. We recommend staging the data (writing it to disk) after each major activity of the ETL pipeline: after it's been extracted, cleaned and conformed, and delivered.

So when does staging turn into archiving where the data is kept indefinitely on some form of permanent media? Our simple answer is a conservative answer. All staged data should be archived unless a conscious decision is made that specific data sets will never be recovered in the future. It's almost always less problematic to read the data from permanent media than it is to reprocess the data through the ETL system at a later time. And, of course, it may be impossible to reprocess the data according to the old processing algorithms if enough time has passed or the original extraction cannot be re-created.

And while we are at it, each staged/archived data set should have accompanying metadata describing the origins and processing steps that produced the data. Again, the tracking of this lineage is explicitly required by certain compliance requirements but should be part of every archiving situation.

NOTE   You should list the data sources and intermediate data steps that will be archived, together with retention policies, and compliance, security, and privacy constraints.

BI Delivery Interfaces

The final step for the ETL system is the handoff to the BI applications. We take a strong and disciplined position on this handoff. We believe the ETL team, working closely with the modeling team, must take responsibility for the content and structure of the data that makes the BI applications simple and fast. This attitude is more than a vague motherhood statement. We believe it's irresponsible to hand off data to the BI application in such a way as to increase the complexity of the application, slow down the query or report creation, or make the data seem unnecessarily complex to the business users. The most elementary and serious error is to hand across a full-blown, normalized physical model and walk away from the job. This is why we go to such lengths to build dimensional structures that comprise the final handoff.

The ETL team and data modelers need to closely work with the BI application developers to determine the exact requirements for the data handoff. Each BI tool has certain sensitivities that should be avoided and certain features that can be exploited if the physical data is in the right format. The same considerations apply to data prepared for OLAP cubes.

NOTE   You should list all fact and dimension tables that will be directly exposed to your BI tools. This should come directly from the dimensional model specification. List all OLAP cubes and special database structures required by BI tools. List all known indexes and aggregations you have agreed to build to support BI performance.

Available Skills

Some ETL system design decisions must be made on the basis of available resources to build and manage the system. You shouldn't build a system that depends on critical C++ processing modules if those programming skills aren't in-house or can't be reasonably acquired. Likewise, you may be much more confident in building the ETL system around a major vendor's ETL tool if you already have those skills in-house and know how to manage such a project.

Consider the big decision of whether to hand code the ETL system or use a vendor's ETL package. Technical issues and license costs aside, don't go off in a direction that your employees and managers find unfamiliar without seriously considering the decision's long-term implications.

NOTE You should inventory your department's operating system, ETL tool, scripting language, programming language, SQL, DBMS, and OLAP skills so you understand how exposed you are to a shortage or loss of these skills. List those skills required to support your current systems and your likely future systems.

Legacy Licenses

Finally, in many cases, major design decisions will be made implicitly by senior management's insistence that you use existing legacy licenses. In many cases, this requirement is one you can live with because the environmental advantages are clear to everyone. But in a few cases, the use of a legacy license for ETL development is a mistake. This is a difficult position to be in, and if you feel strongly enough, you may need to bet your job. If you must approach senior management and challenge the use of an existing legacy license, be well prepared in making the case, and be willing to accept the final decision or possibly seek employment elsewhere.

NOTE You should list your legacy operating system, ETL tool, scripting language, programming language, SQL, DBMS, and OLAP licenses and whether their exclusive use is mandated or merely recommended.

The 34 Subsystems of ETL

With an understanding of the existing requirements, realities, and constraints, you're ready to learn about the 34 critical subsystems that form the architecture for every ETL system. This chapter describes all 34 subsystems with equal emphasis. The next chapter then describes the practical steps of implementing those subsystems needed for each particular situation. Although we have adopted the industry vernacular, ETL, to describe these steps, the process really has four major components:

■ **Extracting**. Gathering raw data from the source systems and usually writing it to disk in the ETL environment before any significant restructuring of the data takes place. Subsystems 1 through 3 support the extracting process.

■ **Cleaning and conforming**. Sending source data through a series of processing steps in the ETL system to improve the quality of the data received from the source, and merging data from two or more sources to create and enforce conformed dimensions and conformed metrics. Subsystems 4 through 8 describe the architecture required to support the cleaning and conforming processes.

■ **Delivering**. Physically structuring and loading the data into the presentation server's target dimensional models. Subsystems 9 through 21 provide the capabilities for delivering the data to the presentation server.

■ **Managing**. Managing the related systems and processes of the ETL environment in a coherent manner. Subsystems 22 through 34 describe the components needed to support the ongoing management of the ETL system.

Extracting: Getting Data into the Data Warehouse

To no surprise, the initial subsystems of the ETL architecture address the issues of understanding your source data, extracting the data, and transferring it to the data warehouse environment where the ETL system can operate on it independent of the operational systems. Although the remaining subsystems focus on the transforming, loading, and system management within the ETL environment, the initial subsystems interface to the source systems for access to the required data.

Subsystem 1: Data Profiling

Data profiling is the technical analysis of data to describe its content, consistency, and structure. In some sense, any time you perform a `SELECT DISTINCT` investigative query on a database field, you are doing data profiling. There are a variety of tools specifically designed to do powerful profiling. It probably pays to invest in a tool rather than roll your own because the tools enable many data relationships to be easily explored with simple user interface gestures. You can be much more productive in the data profiling stages of a project using a tool rather than hand coding all the data content questions.

Data profiling plays two distinct roles: strategic and tactical. As soon as a candidate data source is identified, a light profiling assessment should be made to determine its suitability for inclusion in the data warehouse and provide an early go/no go decision. Ideally, this strategic assessment should occur immediately after identifying a candidate data source during the business requirements analysis. Early disqualification of a data source is a responsible step that can earn you respect from the rest of the team, even if it is bad news. A late revelation that the data source doesn't support the mission can knock the DW/BI initiative off its tracks (and be a potentially fatal career outcome for you), especially if this revelation occurs months into a project.

After the basic strategic decision is made to include a data source in the project, a lengthy tactical data profiling effort should occur to squeeze out as many problems as possible. Usually, this task begins during the data modeling process and extends into the ETL system design process. Sometimes, the ETL team is expected to include a source with content that hasn't been thoroughly evaluated. Systems may support the needs of the production processes, yet present ETL challenges, because fields that aren't central to production processing may be unreliable and incomplete for analysis purposes. Issues that show up in this subsystem result in detailed specifications that are either 1) sent back to the originator of the data source as requests for improvement or 2) form requirements for the data quality processing described in subsystems 4 through 8.

The profiling step provides the ETL team with guidance as to how much data cleaning machinery to invoke and protects them from missing major project milestones due to the unexpected diversion of building systems to deal with dirty data. Do the data profiling upfront! Use the data profiling results to set the business sponsors' expectations regarding realistic development schedules, limitations in the source data, and the need to invest in better source data capture practices.

Subsystem 2: Change Data Capture System

During the data warehouse's initial historic load, capturing source data content changes is not important because you load all data from a point in time forward. However, many data warehouse tables are so large that they cannot be refreshed during every ETL cycle. You must have a capability to transfer only the relevant changes to the source data since the last update. Isolating the latest source data is called change data capture (CDC). The idea behind CDC is simple enough: Just transfer the data that has changed since the last load. But building a good CDC system is not as easy as it sounds. The key goals for the change data capture subsystem are:

- Isolate the changed source data to allow selective processing rather than a complete refresh.
- Capture all changes (deletions, edits, and insertions) made to the source data, including changes made through nonstandard interfaces.
- Tag changed data with reason codes to distinguish error corrections from true updates.

- Support compliance tracking with additional metadata.
- Perform the CDC step as early as possible, preferably before a bulk data transfer to the data warehouse.

Capturing data changes is far from a trivial task. You must carefully evaluate your strategy for each data source. Determining the appropriate strategy to identify changed data may take some detective work. The data profiling tasks described earlier can help the ETL team make this determination. There are several ways to capture source data changes, each effective in the appropriate situation, including:

Audit Columns

In some cases, the source system includes audit columns that store the date and time a record was added or modified. These columns are usually populated via database triggers that are fired off automatically as records are inserted or updated. Sometimes, for performance reasons, the columns are populated by the source application instead of database triggers. When these fields are loaded by any means other than database triggers, pay special attention to their integrity, analyzing and testing each column to ensure that it's a reliable source to indicate change. If you uncover any NULL values, you must find an alternative approach for detecting change. The most common situation that prevents the ETL system from using audit columns is when the fields are populated by the source application, but the DBA team allows back-end scripts to modify data. If this occurs in your environment, you face a high risk of missing changed data during the incremental loads. Finally, you need to understand what happens when a record is deleted from the source because querying the audit column may not capture this event.

Timed Extracts

With a timed extract, you typically select all rows where the create or modified date fields equal SYSDATE-1, meaning all of yesterday's records. Sounds perfect, right? Wrong. Loading records based purely on time is a common mistake made by inexperienced ETL developers. This process is horribly unreliable. Time-based data selection loads duplicate rows when it is restarted from mid-process failures. This means manual intervention and data cleanup is required if the process fails for any reason. Meanwhile, if the nightly load process fails to run and skips a day, there's a risk that the missed data will never make it into the data warehouse.

Full Diff Compare

A full *diff compare* keeps a full snapshot of yesterday's data, and compares it, record by record, against today's data to find what changed. The good news is this technique is thorough: You are guaranteed to find every change. The obvious bad news is that, in many cases, this technique is very resource-intensive. If a full diff compare is required, try to do the comparison on the source machine, so you don't have to transfer the entire table or database into the ETL environment. Of course, the source support folks may have an opinion about this. Also, investigate using cyclic redundancy checksum (CRC) algorithms to quickly tell if a complex record has changed without examining each individual field.

Database Log Scraping

Log scraping effectively takes a snapshot of the database redo log at a scheduled point in time (usually midnight) and scours it for transactions affecting the tables of interest for the ETL load. Sniffing involves a polling of the redo log, capturing transactions on-the-fly. Scraping the log for transactions is probably the messiest of all techniques. It's not uncommon for transaction logs to get full and prevent new transactions from processing. When this happens in a production transaction environment, the knee-jerk reaction from the responsible DBA may be to empty the log so that business operations can resume, but when a log is emptied, all transactions within them are lost. If you've exhausted all other techniques and find log scraping is your last resort for finding new or changed records, persuade the DBA to create a special log to meet your specific needs.

Message Queue Monitoring

In a message-based transaction system, the queue is monitored for all transactions against the tables of interest. The contents of the stream are similar to what you get with log sniffing. One benefit of this process is relatively low overhead, assuming the message queue is already in place. However, there may be no replay feature on the message queue. If the connection to the message queue is lost, you lose data.

Subsystem 3: Extract System

Obviously, extracting data from the source systems is a fundamental component of the ETL architecture. If you are extremely lucky, all the source data will be in a single system that can be readily extracted using an ETL tool. In the more common situation, each source might be in a different system, environment, and/or DBMS.

The ETL system might be expected to extract data from a wide variety of systems involving many different types of data and inherent challenges. Organizations needing to extract data from mainframe environments often run into issues involving COBOL copybooks, EBCDIC to ASCII conversions, packed decimals, redefines, OCCURS fields, and multiple and variable record types. Other organizations might need to extract from sources in relational DBMS, flat files, XML sources, web logs, or a complex ERP system. Each presents a variety of possible challenges. Some sources, especially older legacy systems, may require the use of different procedural languages than the ETL tool can support or the team is experienced with. In this situation, request that the owner of the source system extract the data into a flat file format.

> **NOTE** Although XML-formatted data has many advantages because it is self-describing, you may not want it for large, frequent data transfers. The payload portion of a typical XML formatted file can be less than 10 percent of the total file. The exception to this recommendation could be where the XML payload is a complex deeply hierarchical XML structure, such as an industry standard data exchange. In these cases, the DW/BI team must decide whether to "shred" the XML into a large number of destination tables or persist the XML structure within the data warehouse. Recent advances in RDBMS vendors' support for XML via XPath have made this latter option feasible.

There are two primary methods for getting data from a source system: as a file or a stream. If the source is an aging mainframe system, it is often easier to extract into files and then move those files to the ETL server.

> **NOTE** If the source data is unstructured, semistructured, or even hyperstructured "big data," then rather than loading such data as an un-interpretable RDBMS "blob," it is often more effective to create a MapReduce/Hadoop extract step that behaves as an ETL fact extractor from the source data, directly delivering loadable RDBMS data.

If you use an ETL tool and the source data is in a database (not necessarily an RDBMS), you may set up the extract as a stream where the data flows out of the source system, through the transformation engine, and into the staging database as a single process. By contrast, an extract to file approach consists of three or four discrete steps: Extract to the file, move the file to the ETL server, transform the file contents, and load the transformed data into the staging database.

> **NOTE** Although the stream extract is more appealing, extracts to file have some advantages. They are easy to restart at various points. As long as you save the extract file, you can rerun the load without impacting the source system. You can easily encrypt and compress the data before transferring across the network. Finally, it is easy to verify that all data has moved correctly by comparing file row counts before and after the transfer. Generally, we recommend a data transfer utility such as FTP to move the extracted file.

Data compression is important if large amounts of data need to be transferred over a significant distance or through a public network. In this case, the communications link is often the bottleneck. If too much time is spent transmitting the data, compression can reduce the transmission time by 30 to 50 percent or more, depending on the nature of the original data file.

Data encryption is important if data is transferred through a public network, or even internally in some situations. If this is the case, it is best to send everything through an encrypted link and not worry about what needs to be secure and what doesn't. Remember to compress before encrypting because encrypted files do not compress very well.

Cleaning and Conforming Data

Cleaning and conforming data are critical ETL system tasks. These are the steps where the ETL system adds value to the data. The other activities, extracting and delivering data, are obviously necessary, but they simply move and load the data. The cleaning and conforming subsystems actually change data and enhance its value to the organization. In addition, these subsystems can be architected to create metadata used to diagnosis what's wrong with the source systems. Such diagnoses can eventually lead to business process reengineering initiatives to address the root causes of dirty data and improve data quality over time.

Improving Data Quality Culture and Processes

It is tempting to blame the original data source for any and all errors that appear downstream. If only the data entry clerks were more careful! We are only slightly more forgiving of keyboard-challenged salespeople who enter customer and product information into their order forms. Perhaps you can fix data quality problem by imposing constraints on the data entry user interfaces. This approach provides a hint about how to think about fixing data quality because a technical solution often avoids the real problem. Suppose Social Security number fields for customers were often blank or filled with garbage on an input screen. Someone comes up with brilliant idea to require input in the 999-99-9999 format, and to cleverly disallow nonsensical entries such as all 9s. What happens? The data entry clerks are forced to supply valid Social Security numbers to progress to the next screen, so when they don't have the customer's number, they type in an artificial number that passes the roadblock.

Michael Hammer, in his revolutionary book *Reengineering the Corporation* (Collins, revised 2003), struck the heart of the data quality problem with a brilliant observation. Paraphrasing Hammer: "Seemingly small data quality issues are, in reality, important indications of broken business processes." Not only does this insight correctly focus your attention on the source of data quality problems, but it also shows you the way to the solution.

Technical attempts to address data quality will not prevail unless they are part of an overall quality culture that must come from the top of an organization. The famous Japanese car manufacturing quality attitude permeates every level of those organizations, and quality is embraced enthusiastically by all levels, from the CEO to the assembly line worker. To cast this in a data context, imagine a company such as a large drugstore chain, where a team of buyers contracts with thousands of suppliers to provide the inventory. The buyers have assistants, whose job it is to enter the detailed descriptions of everything purchased by the buyers. These descriptions contain dozens of attributes. But the problem is the assistants have a deadly job and are judged on how many items they enter per hour. The assistants have almost no awareness of who uses their data. Occasionally, the assistants are scolded for obvious errors. But more insidiously, the data given to the assistants is itself incomplete and unreliable. For example, there are no formal standards for toxicity ratings, so there is significant variation over time and over product categories for this attribute. How does the drugstore improve data quality? Here is a nine-step template, not only for the drugstore, but for any organization addressing data quality:

- Declare a high-level commitment to a data quality culture.
- Drive process reengineering at the executive level.
- Spend money to improve the data entry environment.
- Spend money to improve application integration.
- Spend money to change how processes work.
- Promote end-to-end team awareness.
- Promote interdepartmental cooperation.
- Publicly celebrate data quality excellence.
- Continuously measure and improve data quality.

At the drugstore, money needs to be spent to improve the data entry system, so it provides the content and choices needed by the buyers' assistants. The company's executives need to assure the buyers' assistants that their work is important and affects many decision makers in a positive way. Diligent efforts by the assistants should be publicly praised and rewarded. And end-to-end team awareness and appreciation of the business value derived from quality data is the final goal.

Subsystem 4: Data Cleansing System

The ETL data cleansing process is often expected to fix dirty data, yet at the same time the data warehouse is expected to provide an accurate picture of the data as it was captured by the organization's production systems. Striking the proper balance between these conflicting goals is essential.

One of our goals in describing the cleansing system is to offer a comprehensive architecture for cleansing data, capturing data quality events, as well as measuring and ultimately controlling data quality in the data warehouse. Some organizations may find this architecture challenging to implement, but we are convinced it is important for the ETL team to make a serious effort to incorporate as many of these capabilities as possible. If you are new to ETL and find this a daunting challenge, you might well wonder, "What's the minimum I should focus on?" The answer is to start by undertaking the best possible data profiling analysis. The results of that effort can help you understand the risks of moving forward with potentially dirty or unreliable data and help you determine how sophisticated your data cleansing system needs to be.

The purpose of the cleansing subsystems is to marshal technology to support data quality. Goals for the subsystem should include:

- Early diagnosis and triage of data quality issues
- Requirements for source systems and integration efforts to supply better data
- Provide specific descriptions of data errors expected to be encountered in ETL
- Framework for capturing all data quality errors and precisely measuring data quality metrics over time
- Attachment of quality confidence metrics to final data

Quality Screens

The heart of the ETL architecture is a set of quality screens that act as diagnostic filters in the data flow pipelines. Each quality screen is a test. If the test against the data is successful, nothing happens and the screen has no side effects. But if the test fails, then it must drop an error event row into the error event schema and choose to either halt the process, send the offending data into suspension, or merely tag the data.

Although all quality screens are architecturally similar, it is convenient to divide them into three types, in ascending order of scope. Jack Olson, in his seminal book *Data Quality: The Accuracy Dimension* (Morgan Kaufmann, 2002), classified data quality screens into three categories: column screens, structure screens, and business rule screens.

Column screens test the data within a single column. These are usually simple, somewhat obvious tests, such as testing whether a column contains unexpected null values, if a value falls outside of a prescribed range, or if a value fails to adhere to a required format.

Structure screens test the relationship of data across columns. Two or more attributes may be tested to verify they implement a hierarchy, such as a series of many-to-one relationships. Structure screens also test foreign key/primary key relationships between columns in two tables, and also include testing whole blocks of columns to verify they implement valid postal addresses.

Business rule screens implement more complex tests that do not fit the simpler column or structure screen categories. For example, a customer profile may be tested for a complex time-dependent business rule, such as requiring a lifetime platinum frequent flyer to have been a member for at least five years and have flown more than 2 million miles. Business rule screens also include aggregate threshold data quality checks, such as checking to see if a statistically improbable number of MRI examinations have been ordered for minor diagnoses like a sprained elbow. In this case, the screen throws an error only after a threshold of such MRI exams is reached.

Responding to Quality Events

We have already remarked that each quality screen has to decide what happens when an error is thrown. The choices are: 1) halting the process; 2) sending the offending record(s) to a suspense file for later processing; and 3) merely tagging the data and passing it through to the next step in the pipeline. The third choice is by far the best choice, whenever possible. Halting the process is obviously a pain because it requires manual intervention to diagnose the problem, restart or resume the job, or abort completely. Sending records to a suspense file is often a poor solution because it is not clear when or if these records will be fixed and re-introduced to the pipeline. Until the records are restored to the data flow, the overall integrity of the database is questionable because records are missing. We recommend not using the suspense file for minor data transgressions. The third option of tagging the data with the error condition often works well. Bad fact table data can be tagged with the audit dimension, as described in subsystem 6. Bad dimension data can also be tagged using an audit dimension, or in the case of missing or garbage data can be tagged with unique error values in the attribute itself.

Subsystem 5: Error Event Schema

The error event schema is a centralized dimensional schema whose purpose is to record every error event thrown by a quality screen anywhere in the ETL pipeline. Although we focus on data warehouse ETL processing, this approach can be used in generic data integration (DI) applications where data is being transferred between legacy applications. The error event schema is shown in Figure 19-1.

The main table is the error event fact table. Its grain is every error thrown (produced) by a quality screen anywhere in the ETL system. Remember the grain of a fact table is the physical description of why a fact table row exists. Thus every quality screen error produces exactly one row in this table, and every row in the table corresponds to an observed error.

The dimensions of the error event fact table include the calendar date of the error, the batch job in which the error occurred, and the screen that produced the error. The calendar date is not a minute and second time stamp of the error, but rather provides a way to constrain and summarize error events by the usual attributes of the calendar, such as weekday or last day of a fiscal period. The error date/time fact is a full relational date/time stamp that specifies precisely when the error occurred. This format is useful for calculating the time interval between error events because you can take the difference between two date/time stamps to get the number of seconds separating events.

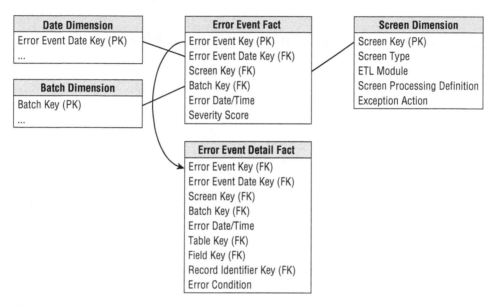

Figure 19-1: Error event schema.

The batch dimension can be generalized to be a processing step in cases in which data is streamed, rather than batched. The screen dimension identifies precisely what the screen criterion is and where the code for the screen resides. It also defines what to do when the screen throws an error. (For example, halt the process, send the record to a suspense file, or tag the data.)

The error event fact table also has a single column primary key, shown as the error event key. This surrogate key, like dimension table primary keys, is a simple integer assigned sequentially as rows are added to the fact table. This key column is necessary in those situations in which an enormous burst of error rows is added to the error event fact table all at once. Hopefully this won't happen to you.

The error event schema includes a second error event detail fact table at a lower grain. Each row in this table identifies an individual field in a specific record that participated in an error. Thus a complex structure or business rule error that triggers a single error event row in the higher level error event fact table may generate many rows in this error event detail fact table. The two tables are tied together by the error event key, which is a foreign key in this lower grain table. The error event detail table identifies the table, record, field, and precise error condition. Thus a complete description of complex multi-field, multi-record errors is preserved by these tables.

The error event detail table could also contain a precise date/time stamp to provide a full description of aggregate threshold error events where many records generate an error condition over a period of time. You should now appreciate that each quality screen has the responsibility for populating these tables at the time of an error.

Subsystem 6: Audit Dimension Assembler

The audit dimension is a special dimension that is assembled in the back room by the ETL system for each fact table, as we discussed in Chapter 6: Order Management. The audit dimension in Figure 19-2 contains the metadata context at the moment when a specific fact table row is created. You might say we have elevated metadata to real data! To visualize how audit dimension rows are created, imagine this shipments fact table is updated once per day from a batch file. Suppose today you have a perfect run with no errors flagged. In this case, you would generate only one audit dimension row, and it would be attached to every fact row loaded today. All the categories, scores, and version numbers would be the same.

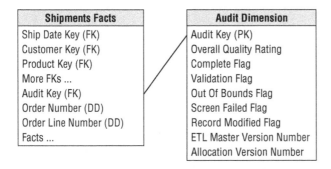

Figure 19-2: Sample audit dimension attached to a fact table.

Now let's relax the strong assumption of a perfect run. If you had some fact rows whose discount dollars triggered an out-of-bounds error, then one more audit dimension row would be needed to flag this condition.

Subsystem 7: Deduplication System

Often dimensions are derived from several sources. This is a common situation for organizations that have many customer-facing source systems that create and manage separate customer master tables. Customer information may need to be merged from several lines of business and outside sources. Sometimes, the data can be matched through identical values in some key column. However, even when a definitive match occurs, other columns in the data might contradict one another, requiring a decision on which data should survive.

Unfortunately, there is seldom a universal column that makes the merge operation easy. Sometimes, the only clues available are the similarity of several columns. The different sets of data being integrated and the existing dimension table data may need to be evaluated on different fields to attempt a match. Sometimes, a match may be based on fuzzy criteria, such as names and addresses that may nearly match except for minor spelling differences.

Survivorship is the process of combining a set of matched records into a unified image that combines the highest quality columns from the matched records into a conformed row. Survivorship involves establishing clear business rules that define the priority sequence for column values from all possible source systems to enable the creation of a single row with the best-survived attributes. If the dimensional design is fed from multiple systems, you must maintain separate columns with back references, such as natural keys, to all participating source systems used to construct the row.

There are a variety of data integration and data standardization tools to consider if you have difficult deduplicating, matching, and survivorship data issues. These tools are quite mature and in widespread use.

Subsystem 8: Conforming System

Conforming consists of all the steps required to align the content of some or all the columns in a dimension with columns in similar or identical dimensions in other parts of the data warehouse. For instance, in a large organization you may have fact tables capturing invoices and customer service calls that both utilize the customer dimension. It is highly likely the source systems for invoices and customer service have separate customer databases. It is likely there will be little guaranteed consistency between the two sources of customer information. The data from these two customer sources needs to be conformed to make some or all the columns describing customer share the same domains.

> **NOTE** The process of creating conformed dimensions aligns with an agile approach. For two dimensions to be conformed, they must share at least one common attribute with the same name and same contents. You can start with a single conformed attribute such as Customer Category and systematically add this column in a nondisruptive way to customer dimensions in each of the customer-facing processes. As you augment each customer-facing process, you expand the list of processes that are integrated and can participate in drill-across queries. You can also incrementally grow the list of conformed attributes, such as city, state, and country. All this can be staged to align with a more agile implementation approach.

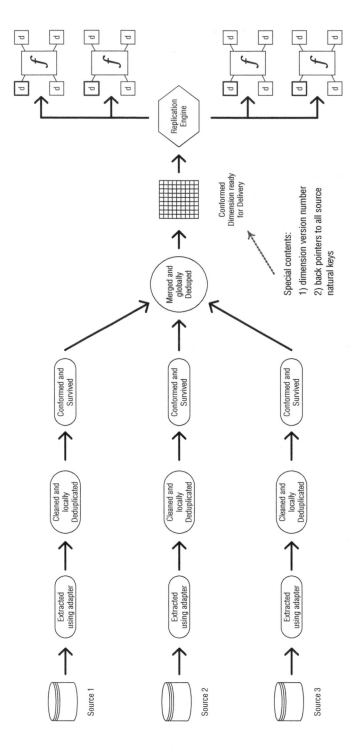

Figure 19-3: Deduplicating and survivorship processing for conformed dimension process.

The conforming subsystem is responsible for creating and maintaining the conformed dimensions and conformed facts described in Chapter 4: Inventory. To accomplish this, incoming data from multiple systems needs to be combined and integrated, so it is structurally identical, deduplicated, filtered of invalid data, and standardized in terms of content rows in a conformed image. A large part of the conforming process is the deduplicating, matching, and survivorship processes previously described. The conforming process flow combining the deduplicating and survivorship processing is shown in Figure 19-3.

The process of defining and delivering conformed dimensions and facts is described later in subsystems 17 (dimension manager) and 18 (fact provider).

Delivering: Prepare for Presentation

The primary mission of the ETL system is the handoff of the dimension and fact tables in the delivery step. For this reason, the delivery subsystems are the most pivotal subsystems in the ETL architecture. Although there is considerable variation in source data structures and cleaning and conforming logic, the delivery processing techniques for preparing the dimensional table structures are more defined and disciplined. Use of these techniques is critical to building a successful dimensional data warehouse that is reliable, scalable, and maintainable.

Many of these subsystems focus on dimension table processing. Dimension tables are the heart of the data warehouse. They provide the context for the fact tables and hence for all the measurements. Although dimension tables are usually smaller than the fact tables, they are critical to the success of the DW/BI system as they provide the entry points into the fact tables. The delivering process begins with the cleaned and conformed data resulting from the subsystems just described. For many dimensions, the basic load plan is relatively simple: You perform basic transformations to the data to build dimension rows for loading into the target presentation table. This typically includes surrogate key assignment, code lookups to provide appropriate descriptions, splitting or combining columns to present the appropriate data values, or joining underlying third normal form table structures into denormalized flat dimensions.

Preparing fact tables is certainly important because fact tables hold the key measurements of the business that the users want to see. Fact tables can be large and time-consuming to load. However, preparing fact tables for presentation is typically more straightforward.

Subsystem 9: Slowly Changing Dimension Manager

One of the more important elements of the ETL architecture is the capability to implement slowly changing dimension (SCD) logic. The ETL system must determine how to handle an attribute value that has changed from the value already stored in the data warehouse. If the revised description is determined to be a legitimate and reliable update to previous information, the appropriate SCD technique must be applied.

As described in Chapter 5: Procurement, when the data warehouse receives notification that an existing row in a dimension has changed, there are three basic responses: type 1 overwrite, type 2 add a new row, and type 3 add a new column. The SCD manager should systematically handle the time variance in the dimensions using these three techniques, as well as the other SCD techniques. In addition, the SCD manager should maintain appropriate housekeeping columns for type 2 changes. Figure 19-4 shows the overall processing flow for handling surrogate key management for processing SCDs.

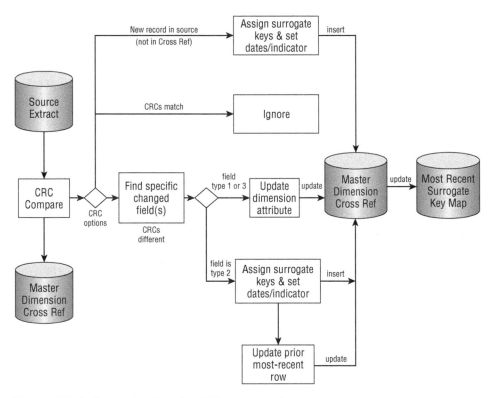

Figure 19-4: Processing flow for SCD surrogate key management.

The change data capture process described in subsystem 2 obviously plays an important role in presenting the changed data to the SCD process. Assuming the change data capture process has effectively delivered appropriate changes, the SCD process can take the appropriate actions.

Type 1: Overwrite

The type 1 technique is a simple overwrite of one or more attributes in an existing dimension row. You take the revised data from the change data capture system and overwrite the dimension table contents. Type 1 is appropriate when correcting data or when there is no business need to keep the history of previous values. For instance, you may receive a corrected customer address. In this case, overwriting is the right choice. Note that if the dimension table includes type 2 change tracking, you should overwrite the affected column in all existing rows for that particular customer. Type 1 updates must be propagated forward from the earliest permanently stored staging tables to all affected staging tables, so if any of them are used to re-create the final load tables, the effect of the overwrite is preserved.

Some ETL tools contain UPDATE else INSERT functionality. This functionality may be convenient for the developer but can be a performance killer. For maximum performance, existing row UPDATEs should be segregated from new row INSERTs. If type 1 updates cause performance problems, consider disabling database logging or use of the DBMS bulk loader.

Type 1 updates invalidate any aggregates built upon the changed column, so the dimension manager (subsystem 17) must notify the affected fact providers (subsystem 18) to drop and rebuild the affected aggregates.

Type 2: Add New Row

The type 2 SCD is the standard technique for accurately tracking changes in dimensions and associating them correctly with fact rows. Supporting type 2 changes requires a strong change data capture system to detect changes as soon as they occur. For type 2 updates, copy the previous version of the dimension row and create a new dimension row with a new surrogate key. If there is not a previous version of the dimension row, create a new one from scratch. Then update this row with the columns that have changed and add any other columns that are needed. This is the main workhorse technique for handling dimension attribute changes that need to be tracked over time.

The type 2 ETL process must also update the most recent surrogate key map table, assuming the ETL tool doesn't automatically handle this. These little two-column tables are of immense importance when loading fact table data. Subsystem 14, the surrogate key pipeline, supports this process.

Refer to Figure 19-4 to see the lookup and key assignment logic for handling a changed dimension row during the extract process. In this example, the change data capture process (subsystem 2) uses a CRC compare to determine which rows have changed in the source data since the last update. If you are lucky, you already know which dimension records have changed and can omit this CRC compare step. After you identify rows that have changes in type 2 attributes, you can generate a new surrogate key from the key sequence and update the surrogate key map table.

When a new type 2 row is created, you need at least a pair of time stamps, as well as an optional change description attribute. The pair of time stamps defines a span of time from the beginning effective time to the ending effective time when the complete set of dimension attributes is valid. A more sophisticated treatment of a type 2 SCD row involves adding five ETL housekeeping columns. Referring to Figure 19-4, this also requires the type 2 ETL process to find the prior effective row and make appropriate updates to these housekeeping columns:

- Change Date (change date as foreign key to date dimension outrigger)
- Row Effective Date/Time (exact date/time stamp of change)
- Row End Date/Time (exact date/time stamp of next change, defaults to 12/31/9999 for most current dimension row)
- Reason for Change column (optional attribute)
- Current Flag (current/expired)

NOTE   It is possible that back-end scripts are run within the transaction database to modify data without updating the respective metadata fields such as the last_modified_date. Using these fields for the dimension time stamps can cause inconsistent results in the data warehouse. Always use the system or as-of date to derive the type 2 effective time stamps.

The type 2 process does not change history as the type 1 process does; thus type 2 changes don't require rebuilding affected aggregate tables as long as the change was made "today" and not backward in time.

NOTE   *Kimball Design Tip #80* (available at www.kimballgroup.com under the Tools and Utilities tab for this book title) provides in-depth guidance on adding a row change reason code attribute to dimension tables.

Type 3: Add New Attribute

The type 3 technique is designed to support attribute "soft" changes that allow a user to refer either to the old value of the attribute or the new value. For example, if a sales team is assigned to a newly named sales region, there may be a need to track the old region assignment, as well as the new one. The type 3 technique requires the ETL system to alter the dimension table to add a new column to the schema, if this situation was not anticipated. Of course, the DBA assigned to work with the ETL team will in all likelihood be responsible for this change. You then need to push the existing column values into the newly created column and populate the original column with the new values provided to the ETL system. Figure 19-5 shows how a type 3 SCD is implemented.

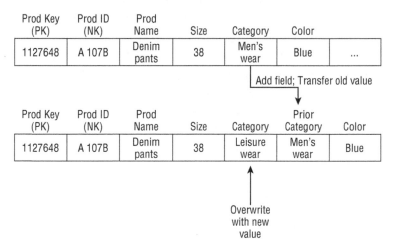

Figure 19-5: Type 3 SCD process.

Similar to the type 1 process, type 3 change updates invalidate any aggregates built upon the changed column; the dimension manager must notify the affected fact providers, so they drop and rebuild the affected aggregates.

Type 4: Add Mini-Dimension

The type 4 technique is used when a group of attributes in a dimension change sufficiently rapidly so that they are split off to a mini-dimension. This situation is sometimes called a rapidly changing monster dimension. Like type 3, this situation calls for a schema change, hopefully done at design time. The mini-dimension requires its own unique primary key, and both the primary key of the main dimension and the primary key of the mini-dimension must appear in the fact table. Figure 19-6 shows how a type 4 SCD is implemented.

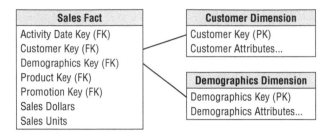

Figure 19-6: Type 4 SCD process.

Type 5: Add Mini-Dimension and Type 1 Outrigger

The type 5 technique builds on the type 4 mini-dimension by also embedding a type 1 reference to the mini-dimension in the primary dimension. This allows accessing the current values in the mini-dimension directly from the base dimension without linking through a fact table. The ETL team must add the type 1 key reference in the base dimension and must overwrite this key reference in all copies of the base dimension whenever the current status of the mini-dimension changes over time. Figure 19-7 shows how a type 5 SCD is implemented.

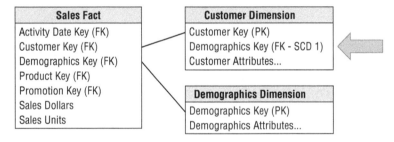

Figure 19-7: Type 5 SCD process.

Type 6: Add Type 1 Attributes to Type 2 Dimension

The type 6 technique has an embedded attribute that is an alternate value of a normal type 2 attribute in the base dimension. Usually such an attribute is simply a type 3 alternative reality, but in this case the attribute is systematically overwritten whenever the attribute is updated. Figure 19-8 shows how a type 6 SCD is implemented.

Type 7: Dual Type 1 and Type 2 Dimensions

The type 7 technique is a normal type 2 dimension paired with a specially constructed fact table that has both a normal foreign key to the dimension for type 2 historical processing, and also a foreign durable key (FDK in Figure 19-9) that is used alternatively for type 1 current processing, connected to the durable key in the dimension table labeled PDK. The dimension table also contains a current row indicator that indicates whether the particular row is the one to be used for current SCD 1 perspective. The ETL team must augment a normally constructed fact table with this constant value foreign durable key. Figure 19-9 shows how a type 7 SCD is implemented.

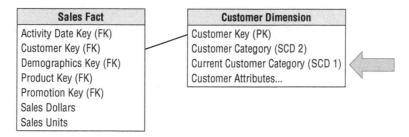

Figure 19-8: Type 6 SCD process.

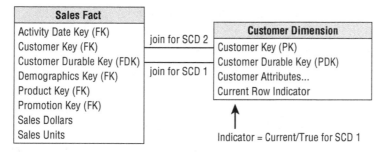

Figure 19-9: Type 7 SCD process.

Subsystem 10: Surrogate Key Generator

As you recall from Chapter 3: Retail Sales, we strongly recommend the use of surrogate keys for all dimension tables. This implies you need a robust mechanism for producing surrogate keys in the ETL system. The surrogate key generator should independently generate surrogate keys for every dimension; it should be independent of database instance and able to serve distributed clients. The goal of the surrogate key generator is to generate a meaningless key, typically an integer, to serve as the primary key for a dimension row.

Although it may be tempting to create surrogate keys via database triggers, this technique may create performance bottlenecks. If the DBMS is used to assign surrogate keys, it is preferable for the ETL process to directly call the database sequence generator. For improved efficiency, consider having the ETL tool generate and maintain the surrogate keys. Avoid the temptation of concatenating the operational key of the source system and a date/time stamp. Although this approach seems simple, it is fraught with problems and ultimately will not scale.

Subsystem 11: Hierarchy Manager

It is normal for a dimension to have multiple, simultaneous, embedded hierarchical structures. These multiple hierarchies simply coexist in the same dimension as dimension attributes. All that is necessary is that every attribute be single valued in the presence of the dimension's primary key. Hierarchies are either fixed or ragged. A fixed depth hierarchy has a consistent number of levels and is simply modeled and populated as separate dimension attributes for each of the levels. Slightly ragged hierarchies like postal addresses are most often modeled as a fixed hierarchy. Profoundly ragged hierarchies are typically found with organization structures that are unbalanced and of indeterminate depth. The data model and ETL solution required to support these needs require the use of a bridge table containing the organization map.

Snowflakes or normalized data structures are not recommended for the presentation level. However, the use of a normalized design may be appropriate in the ETL staging area to assist in the maintenance of the ETL data flow for populating and maintaining the hierarchy attributes. The ETL system is responsible for enforcing the business rules to assure the hierarchy is populated appropriately in the dimension table.

Subsystem 12: Special Dimensions Manager

The special dimensions manager is a catch-all subsystem: a placeholder in the ETL architecture for supporting an organization's specific dimensional design characteristics. Some organizations' ETL systems require all the capabilities discussed here, whereas others will be concerned with few of these design techniques:

Date/Time Dimensions

The date and time dimensions are unique in that they are completely specified at the beginning of the data warehouse project, and they don't have a conventional source. This is okay! Typically, these dimensions are built in an afternoon with a spreadsheet. But in a global enterprise environment, even this dimension can be challenging when taking into account multiple financial reporting periods or multiple cultural calendars.

Junk Dimensions

Junk dimensions are made up from text and miscellaneous flags left over in the fact table after you remove all the critical attributes. There are two approaches for creating junk dimensions in the ETL system. If the theoretical number of rows in the dimension is fixed and known, the junk dimension can be created in advance. In other cases, it may be necessary to create newly observed junk dimension rows on-the-fly while processing fact row input. As illustrated in Figure 19-10, this process requires assembling the junk dimension attributes and comparing them to the existing junk dimension rows to see if the row already exists. If not, a new dimension row must be assembled, a surrogate key created, and the row loaded into the junk dimension on-the-fly during the fact table load process.

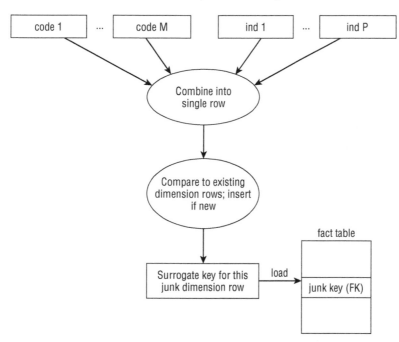

Figure 19-10: Architecture for building junk dimension rows.

> **NOTE** *Kimball Design Tip #113* (available at www.kimballgroup.com under the Tools and Utilities tab for this book title) provides more in-depth guidance on building and maintaining junk dimension tables.

Mini-Dimensions

As we just discussed in subsystem 9, mini-dimensions are a technique used to track dimension attribute changes in a large dimension when the type 2 technique is infeasible, such as a customer dimension. From an ETL perspective, creation of the mini-dimension is similar to the junk dimension process previously described. Again, there are two alternatives: building all valid combinations in advance or recognizing and creating new combinations on-the-fly. Although junk dimensions are usually built from the fact table input, mini-dimensions are built from dimension table inputs. The ETL system is responsible for maintaining a multicolumn surrogate key lookup table to identify the base dimension member and appropriate mini-dimension row to support the surrogate pipeline process described in Subsystem 14, Surrogate Key Pipeline. Keep in mind that very large, complex customer dimensions often require several mini-dimensions.

> **NOTE** *Kimball Design Tip #127* (available at www.kimballgroup.com under the Tools and Utilities tab for this book title) provides more in-depth guidance on building and maintaining mini-dimension tables.

Shrunken Subset Dimensions

Shrunken dimensions are conformed dimensions that are a subset of rows and/or columns of one of your base dimensions. The ETL data flow should build conformed shrunken dimensions from the base dimension, rather than independently, to assure conformance. The primary key for the shrunken dimension, however, must be independently generated; if you attempt to use a key from an "example" base dimension row, you will get into trouble if this key is retired or superseded.

> **NOTE** *Kimball Design Tip #137* (available at www.kimballgroup.com under the Tools and Utilities tab for this book title) provides more in-depth guidance on building shrunken dimension tables.

Small Static Dimensions

A few dimensions are created entirely by the ETL system without a real outside source. These are usually small lookup dimensions where an operational code is translated into words. In these cases, there is no real ETL processing. The lookup dimension is simply created directly by the ETL team as a relational table in its final form.

User Maintained Dimensions

Often the warehouse requires that totally new "master" dimension tables be created. These dimensions have no formal system of record; rather they are custom descriptions, groupings, and hierarchies created by the business for reporting and analysis purposes. The ETL team often ends up with stewardship responsibility for these dimensions, but this is typically not successful because the ETL team is not aware of changes that occur to these custom groupings, so the dimensions fall into disrepair and become ineffective. The best-case scenario is to have the appropriate business user department agree to own the maintenance of these attributes. The DW/BI team needs to provide a user interface for this maintenance. Typically, this takes the form of a simple application built using the company's standard visual programming tool. The ETL system should add default attribute values for new rows, which the user owner needs to update. If these rows are loaded into the warehouse before they are changed, they still appear in reports with whatever default description is supplied.

NOTE   The ETL process should create a unique default dimension attribute description that shows someone hasn't yet done their data stewardship job. We favor a label that concatenates the phrase Not Yet Assigned with the surrogate key value: "Not Yet Assigned 157." That way, multiple unassigned values do not inadvertently get lumped together in reports and aggregate tables. This also helps identify the row for later correction.

Subsystem 13: Fact Table Builders

Fact tables hold the measurements of an organization. Dimensional models are deliberately built around these numerical measurements. The fact table builder subsystem focuses on the ETL architectural requirements to effectively build the three primary types of fact tables: transaction, periodic snapshot, and accumulating snapshot. An important requirement for loading fact tables is maintaining referential integrity with the associated dimension tables. The surrogate key pipeline (subsystem 14) is designed to help support this need.

Transaction Fact Table Loader

The transaction grain represents a measurement event defined at a particular instant. A line item on an invoice is an example of a transaction event. A scanner event at a cash register is another. In these cases, the time stamp in the fact table is very simple. It's either a single daily grain foreign key or a pair consisting of a daily grain foreign key together with a date/time stamp, depending on what the source system provides and the analyses require. The facts in this transaction table must be true to the grain and should describe only what took place in that instant.

Transaction grain fact tables are the largest and most detailed of the three types of fact tables. The transaction fact table loader receives data from the changed data capture system and loads it with the proper dimensional foreign keys. The pure addition of the most current records is the easiest case: simply bulk loading new rows into the fact table. In most cases, the target fact table should be partitioned by time to ease the administration and speed the performance of the table. An audit key, sequential ID, or date/time stamp column should be included to allow backup or restart of the load job.

The addition of late arriving data is more difficult, requiring additional processing capabilities described in subsystem 16. In the event it is necessary to update existing rows, this process should be handled in two phases. The first step is to insert the corrected rows without overwriting or deleting the original rows, and then delete the old rows in a second step. Using a sequentially assigned single surrogate key for the fact table makes it possible to perform the two steps of insertion followed by deletion.

Periodic Snapshot Fact Table Loader

The periodic snapshot grain represents a regular repeating measurement or set of measurements, like a bank account monthly statement. This fact table also has a single date column, representing the overall period. The facts in this periodic snapshot table must be true to the grain and should describe only measures appropriate to the timespan defined by the period. Periodic snapshots are a common fact table type and are frequently used for account balances, monthly financial reporting, and inventory balances. The periodicity of a periodic snapshot is typically daily, weekly, or monthly.

Periodic snapshots have similar loading characteristics to those of transaction grain fact tables. The same processing applies for inserts and updates. Assuming data is promptly delivered to the ETL system, all records for each periodic load can cluster in the most recent time partition. Traditionally, periodic snapshots have been loaded en masse at the end of the appropriate period.

For example, a credit card company might load a monthly account snapshot table with the balances in effect at the end of the month. More frequently, organizations will populate a hot rolling periodic snapshot. In addition to the rows loaded at the end of every month, there are special rows loaded with the most current balances in effect as of the previous day. As the month progresses, the current month rows are continually updated with the most current information and continue in this manner rolling through the month. Note that the hot rolling snapshot can sometimes be difficult to implement if the business rules for calculating the balances at the period end are complex. Often these complex calculations are dependent on other periodic processing outside the data warehouse, and there is not enough information available to the ETL system to perform these complex calculations on a more frequent basis.

Accumulating Snapshot Fact Table Loader

The accumulating snapshot grain represents the current evolving status of a process that has a finite beginning and end. Usually, these processes are of short duration and therefore don't lend themselves to the periodic snapshot. Order processing is the classic example of an accumulating snapshot. The order is placed, shipped, and paid for within one reporting period. The transaction grain provides too much detail separated into individual fact table rows, and the periodic snapshot just is the wrong way to report this data.

The design and administration of the accumulating snapshot is quite different from the first two fact table types. All accumulating snapshot fact tables have a set of dates which describe the typical process workflow. For instance, an order might have an order date, actual ship date, delivery date, final payment date, and return date. In this example, these five dates appear as five separate date-valued foreign surrogate keys. When the order row is first created, the first of these dates is well defined, but perhaps none of the others have yet happened. This same fact row is subsequently revisited as the order winds its way through the order pipeline. Each time something happens, the accumulating snapshot fact row is destructively modified. The date foreign keys are overwritten, and various facts are updated. Often the first date remains inviolate because it describes when the row was created, but all the other dates may well be overwritten, sometimes more than once.

Many RDBMSs utilize variable row lengths. Repeated updates to accumulating snapshot fact rows may cause the rows to grow due to these variable row lengths, affecting the residency of disk blocks. It may be worthwhile to occasionally drop and reload rows after the update activity to improve performance.

An accumulating snapshot fact table is an effective way to represent finite processes with well-defined beginnings and endings. However, the accumulating snapshot by definition is the most recent view. Often it makes sense to utilize all three fact table types to meet various needs. Periodic history can be captured with periodic extracts, and all the infinite details involved in the process can be captured in an associated transaction grain fact table. The presence of many situations that violate standard scenarios or involve repeated looping though the process would prohibit the use of an accumulating snapshot.

Subsystem 14: Surrogate Key Pipeline

Every ETL system must include a step for replacing the operational natural keys in the incoming fact table row with the appropriate dimension surrogate keys. Referential integrity (RI) means that for each foreign key in the fact table, an entry exists in the corresponding dimension table. If there's a row in a sales fact table for product surrogate key 323442, you need to have a row in the product dimension table with the same key, or you won't know what you've sold. You have a sale for what appears to be a nonexistent product. Even worse, without the product key in the dimension, a business user can easily construct a query that will omit this sale without even realizing it.

The key lookup process should result in a match for every incoming natural key or a default value. In the event there is an unresolved referential integrity failure during the lookup process, you need to feed these failures back to the responsible ETL process for resolution, as shown in Figure 19-11. Likewise, the ETL process needs to resolve any key collisions that might be encountered during the key lookup process.

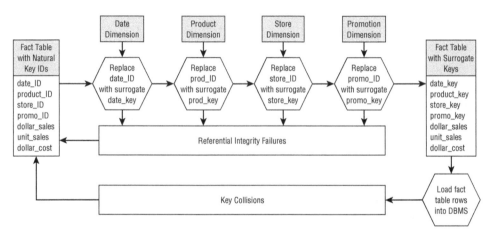

Figure 19-11: Replacing fact record's operational natural keys with dimension surrogate keys.

After the fact table data has been processed and just before loading into the presentation layer, a surrogate key lookup needs to occur to substitute the operational natural keys in the fact table record with the proper current surrogate key. To preserve referential integrity, always complete the updating of the dimension tables first. In that way, the dimension tables are always the legitimate source of primary keys you must replace in the fact table (refer to Figure 19-11).

The most direct approach is to use the actual dimension table as the source for the most current value of the surrogate key corresponding to each natural key. Each time you need the current surrogate key, look up all the rows in the dimension with the natural key equal to the desired value, and then select the surrogate key that aligns with the historical context of the fact row using the current row indicator or begin and end effect dates. Current hardware environments offer nearly unlimited addressable memory, making this approach practical.

During processing, each natural key in the incoming fact record is replaced with the correct current surrogate key. Don't keep the natural key in the fact row—the fact table needs to contain only the surrogate key. Do not write the input data to disk until all fact rows have passed all the processing steps. If possible, all required dimension tables should be pinned in memory, so they can be randomly accessed as each incoming record presents its natural keys.

As illustrated at the bottom of Figure 19-11, the surrogate key pipeline needs to handle key collisions in the event you attempt to load a duplicate row. This is an example of a data quality problem appropriate for a traditional structure data quality screen, as discussed in subsystem 4. In the event a key collision is recognized, the surrogate key pipeline process needs to choose to halt the process, send the offending data into suspension, or apply appropriate business rules to determine if it is possible to correct the problem, load the row, and write an explanatory row into the error event schema.

Note a slightly different process is needed to perform surrogate key lookups if you need to reload history or if you have a lot of late arriving fact rows because you don't want to map the most current value to a historical event. In this case, you need to create logic to find the surrogate key that applied at the time the fact record was generated. This means finding the surrogate key where the fact transaction date is between the key's effective start date and end date.

When the fact table natural keys have been replaced with surrogate keys, the fact row is ready to load. The keys in the fact table row have been chosen to be proper foreign keys, and the fact table is guaranteed to have referential integrity with respect to the dimension tables.

Subsystem 15: Multivalued Dimension Bridge Table Builder

Sometimes a fact table must support a dimension that takes on multiple values at the lowest granularity of the fact table, as described in Chapter 8: Customer Relationship Management. If the grain of the fact table cannot be changed to directly support this dimension, then the multivalued dimension must be linked to the fact table via a bridge table. Bridge tables are common in the healthcare industry, in sales commission environments, and for supporting variable depth hierarchies, as discussed in subsystem 11.

The challenge for the ETL team is building and maintaining the bridge table. As multivalued relationships to the fact row are encountered, the ETL system has the choice of either making each set of observations a unique group or reusing groups when an identical set of observations occurs. Unfortunately, there is no simple answer for the right choice. In the event the multivalued dimension has type 2 attributes, the bridge table must also be time varying, such as a patient's time variant set of diagnoses.

One of the bridge table constructs presented in Chapter 10: Financial Services was the inclusion of a weighting factor to support properly weighted reporting from the bridge table. In many cases, the weighting factor is a familiar allocation factor, but in other cases, the identification of the appropriate weighting factor can be problematic because there may be no rational basis for assigning the weighting factor.

NOTE *Kimball Design Tip #142* (available at www.kimballgroup.com under the Tools and Utilities tab for this book title) provides more in-depth guidance on building and maintaining bridge tables.

Subsystem 16: Late Arriving Data Handler

Data warehouses are usually built around the ideal assumption that measured activity (fact records) arrive in the data warehouse at the same time as the context of the activity (dimension records). When you have both the fact records and the correct contemporary dimension rows, you have the luxury of first maintaining the dimension keys and then using these up-to-date keys in the accompanying fact rows. However, for a variety of reasons, the ETL system may need to process late arriving fact or dimension data.

In some environments, there may need to be special modifications to the standard processing procedures to deal with late arriving facts, namely fact records that come into the warehouse very much delayed. This is a messy situation because you have to search back in history to decide which dimension keys were in effect when the activity occurred. In addition, you may need to adjust any semi-additive balances in subsequent fact rows. In a heavily compliant environment, it is also necessary to interface with the compliance subsystem because you are about to change history.

Late arriving dimensions occur when the activity measurement (fact record) arrives at the data warehouse without its full context. In other words, the statuses of the dimensions attached to the activity measurement are ambiguous or unknown for some period of time. If you are living in the conventional batch update cycle of one or more days' latency, you can usually just wait for the dimensions to be reported. For example, the identification of the new customer may come in a separate feed delayed by several hours; you may just be able to wait until the dependency is resolved.

But in many situations, especially real-time environments, this delay is not acceptable. You cannot suspend the rows and wait for the dimension updates to occur; the business requirements demand that you make the fact row visible before knowing the dimensional context. The ETL system needs additional capabilities to support this requirement. Using customer as the problem dimension, the ETL system needs to support two situations. The first is to support late arriving type 2 dimension updates. In this situation, you need to add the revised customer row to the dimension with a new surrogate key and then go in and destructively modify any subsequent fact rows' foreign key to the customer table. The effective dates for the affected dimension rows also need to be reset. In addition, you need to scan forward in the dimension to see if there have been any subsequent type 2 rows for this customer and change this column in any affected rows.

The second situation occurs when you receive a fact row with what appears to be a valid customer natural key, but you have not yet loaded this customer in the customer dimension. It would be possible to load this row pointing to a default row in the dimension table. This approach has the same unpleasant side effect discussed earlier of requiring destructive updates to the fact rows' foreign keys when the dimension updates are finally processed. Alternatively, if you believe the customer is a valid, but not yet processed customer, you should assign a new customer surrogate key with a set of dummy attribute values in a new customer dimension row. You then return to this dummy dimension row at a later time and make type 1 overwrite changes to its attributes when you get complete information on the new customer. At least this step avoids destructively changing any fact table keys.

There is no way to avoid a brief provisional period in which the dimensions are "not quite right." But these maintenance steps can minimize the impact of the unavoidable updates to the keys and other columns.

Subsystem 17: Dimension Manager System

The dimension manager is a centralized authority who prepares and publishes conformed dimensions to the data warehouse community. A conformed dimension is by necessity a centrally managed resource: Each conformed dimension must have a single, consistent source. It is the dimension manager's responsibility to administer and publish the conformed dimension(s) for which he has responsibility. There may be multiple dimension managers in an organization, each responsible for a dimension. The dimension manager's responsibilities include the following ETL processing:

- Implement the common descriptive labels agreed to by the data stewards and stakeholders during the dimension design.
- Add new rows to the conformed dimension for new source data, generating new surrogate keys.
- Add new rows for type 2 changes to existing dimension entries, generating new surrogate keys.

- Modify rows in place for type 1 changes and type 3 changes, without changing the surrogate keys.
- Update the version number of the dimension if any type 1 or type 3 changes are made.
- Replicate the revised dimension simultaneously to all fact table providers.

It is easier to manage conformed dimensions in a single tablespace DBMS on a single machine because there is only one copy of the dimension table. However, managing conformed dimensions becomes more difficult in multiple tablespace, multiple DMBS, or multimachine distributed environments. In these situations, the dimension manager must carefully manage the simultaneous release of new versions of the dimension to every fact provider. Each conformed dimension should have a version number column in each row that is overwritten in every row whenever the dimension manager releases the dimension. This version number should be utilized to support any drill-across queries to assure that the same release of the dimension is being utilized.

Subsystem 18: Fact Provider System

The fact provider is responsible for receiving conformed dimensions from the dimension managers. The fact provider owns the administration of one or more fact tables and is responsible for their creation, maintenance, and use. If fact tables are used in any drill-across applications, then by definition the fact provider must be using conformed dimensions provided by the dimension manager. The fact provider's responsibilities are more complex and include:

- Receive or download replicated dimension from the dimension manager.
- In an environment in which the dimension cannot simply be replicated but must be locally updated, the fact provider must process dimension records marked as new and current to update current key maps in the surrogate key pipeline and also process any dimension records marked as new but postdated.
- Add all new rows to fact tables after replacing their natural keys with correct surrogate keys.
- Modify rows in all fact tables for error correction, accumulating snapshots, and late arriving dimension changes.
- Remove aggregates that have become invalidated.
- Recalculate affected aggregates. If the new release of a dimension does not change the version number, aggregates have to be extended to handle only newly loaded fact data. If the version number of the dimension has changed, the entire historical aggregate may have to be recalculated.

- Quality ensure all base and aggregate fact tables. Be satisfied the aggregate tables are correctly calculated.
- Bring updated fact and dimension tables online.
- Inform users that the database has been updated. Tell them if major changes have been made, including dimension version changes, postdated records being added, and changes to historical aggregates.

Subsystem 19: Aggregate Builder

Aggregates are the single most dramatic way to affect performance in a large data warehouse environment. Aggregations are like indexes; they are specific data structures created to improve performance. Aggregates can have a significant impact on performance. The ETL system needs to effectively build and use aggregates without causing significant distraction or consuming extraordinary resources and processing cycles.

You should avoid architectures in which aggregate navigation is built into the proprietary query tool. From an ETL viewpoint, the aggregation builder needs to populate and maintain aggregate fact table rows and shrunken dimension tables where needed by aggregate fact tables. The fastest update strategy is incremental, but a major change to a dimension attribute may require dropping and rebuilding the aggregate. In some environments, it may be faster to dump data out of the DBMS and build aggregates with a sort utility rather than building the aggregates inside the DBMS. Additive numeric facts can be aggregated easily at extract time by calculating break rows in one of the sort packages. Aggregates must always be consistent with the atomic base data. The fact provider (subsystem 18) is responsible for taking aggregates off-line when they are not consistent with the base data.

User feedback on the queries that run slowly is critical input to designing aggregations. Although you can depend on informal feedback to some extent, a log of frequently attempted slow-running queries should be captured. You should also try to identify the nonexistent slow-running queries that never made it into the log because they never run to completion, or aren't even attempted due to known performance challenges.

Subsystem 20: OLAP Cube Builder

OLAP servers present dimensional data in an intuitive way, enabling a range of analytic users to slice and dice data. OLAP is a sibling of dimensional star schemas in the relational database, with intelligence about relationships and calculations defined on the server that enable faster query performance and more interesting analytics from a broad range of query tools. Don't think of an OLAP server as a competitor to a relational data warehouse, but rather an extension. Let the relational database do what it does best: Provide storage and management.

The relational dimensional schema should be viewed as the foundation for OLAP cubes if you elect to include them in your architecture. The process of feeding data from the dimensional schema is an integral part of the ETL system; the relational schemas are the best and preferred source for OLAP cubes. Because many OLAP systems do not directly address referential integrity or data cleaning, the preferred architecture is to load OLAP cubes after the completion of conventional ETL processes. Note that some OLAP tools are more sensitive to hierarchies than relational schemas. It is important to strongly enforce the integrity of hierarchies within dimensions before loading an OLAP cube. Type 2 SCDs fit an OLAP system well because a new surrogate key is just treated as a new member. Type 1 SCDs that restate history do not fit OLAP well. Overwrites to an attribute value can cause all the cubes using that dimension to be reprocessed in the background, become corrupted, or be dropped. Read this last sentence again.

Subsystem 21: Data Propagation Manager

The data propagation manager is responsible for the ETL processes required to present conformed, integrated enterprise data from the data warehouse presentation server to other environments for special purposes. Many organizations need to extract data from the presentation layer to share with business partners, customers, and/or vendors for strategic purposes. Similarly, some organizations are required to submit data to various government organizations for reimbursement purposes, such as healthcare organizations that participate in the Medicare program. Many organizations have acquired package analytic applications. Typically, these applications cannot be pointed directly against the existing data warehouse tables, so data needs to be extracted from the presentation layer and loaded into proprietary data structures required by the analytic applications. Finally, most data mining tools do not run directly against the presentation server. They need data extracted from the data warehouse and fed to the data mining tool in a specific format.

All the situations previously described require extraction from the DW/BI presentation server, possibly some light transformation, and loading into a target format—in other words ETL. Data propagation should be considered a part of the ETL system; ETL tools should be leveraged to provide this capability. What is different in this situation is that the requirements of the target are not negotiable; you *must* provide the data as specified by the target.

Managing the ETL Environment

A DW/BI environment can have a great dimensional model, well-deployed BI applications, and strong management sponsorship. But it cannot be a success until it can be relied upon as a dependable source for business decision making. One of the goals for the DW/BI system is to build a reputation for providing timely, consistent, and reliable data to empower the business. To achieve this goal, the ETL system must constantly work toward fulfilling three criteria:

- **Reliability**. The ETL processes must consistently run. They must run to completion to provide data on a timely basis that is trustworthy at any level of detail.
- **Availability**. The data warehouse must meet its service level agreements (SLAs). The warehouse should be up and available as promised.
- **Manageability**. A successful data warehouse is never done. It constantly grows and changes along with the business. The ETL processes need to gracefully evolve as well.

The ETL management subsystems are the key components of the architecture to help achieve the goals of reliability, availability, and manageability. Operating and maintaining a data warehouse in a professional manner is not much different than any other systems operations: Follow standard best practices, plan for disaster, and practice. Most of the requisite management subsystems that follow might be familiar to you.

Subsystem 22: Job Scheduler

Every enterprise data warehouse should have a robust ETL scheduler. The entire ETL process should be managed, to the extent possible, through a single metadata-driven job control environment. Major ETL tool vendors package scheduling capabilities into their environments. If you elect not to use the scheduler included with the ETL tool, or do not use an ETL tool, you need to utilize existing production scheduling or perhaps manually code the ETL jobs to execute.

Scheduling is much more than just launching jobs on a schedule. The scheduler needs to be aware of and control the relationships and dependencies between ETL jobs. It needs to recognize when a file or table is ready to be processed. If the organization is processing in real time, you need a scheduler that supports your selected real-time architecture. The job control process must also capture metadata regarding the progress and statistics of the ETL process during its execution. Finally, the scheduler should support a fully automated process, including notifying the problem escalation system in the event of any situation that requires resolution.

The infrastructure to manage this can be as basic (and labor-intensive) as a set of SQL stored procedures, or as sophisticated as an integrated tool designed to manage and orchestrate multiplatform data extract and loading processes. If you use an ETL tool, it should provide this capability. In any case, you need to set up an environment for creating, managing, and monitoring the ETL job stream.

The job control services needed include:

- **Job definition.** The first step in creating an operations process is to have some way to define a series of steps as a job and to specify some relationship among jobs. This is where the execution flow of the ETL process is written. In many cases, if the load of a given table fails, it can impact your ability to load tables that depend on it. For example, if the customer table is not properly updated, loading sales facts for new customers that did not make it into the customer table is risky. In some databases, it is impossible.

- **Job scheduling.** At a minimum, the environment needs to provide standard capabilities, such as time- and event-based scheduling. ETL processes are often based on some upstream system event, such as the successful completion of the general ledger close or the successful application of sales adjustments to yesterday's sales figures. This includes the ability to monitor database flags, check for the existence of files, and compare creation dates.

- **Metadata capture.** No self-respecting systems person would tolerate a black box scheduling system. The folks responsible for running the loads will demand a workflow monitoring system (subsystem 27) to understand what is going on. The job scheduler needs to capture information about what step the load is on, what time it started, and how long it took. In a handcrafted ETL system, this can be accomplished by having each step write to a log file. The ETL tool should capture this data every time an ETL process executes.

- **Logging.** This means collecting information about the entire ETL process, not just what is happening at the moment. Log information supports the recovery and restarting of a process in case of errors during the job execution. Logging to text files is the minimum acceptable level. We prefer a system that logs to a database because the structure makes it easier to create graphs and reports. It also makes it possible to create time series studies to help analyze and optimize the load process.

- **Notification.** After the ETL process has been developed and deployed, it should execute in a hands-off manner. It should run without human intervention, without fail. If a problem does occur, the control system needs to interface to the problem escalation system (subsystem 30).

NOTE Somebody needs to know if anything unforeseen happened during the load, especially if a response is critical to continuing the process.

Subsystem 23: Backup System

The data warehouse is subject to the same risks as any other computer system. Disk drives will fail, power supplies will go out, and sprinkler systems will accidentally turn on. In addition to these risks, the warehouse also has a need to keep more data for longer periods of time than operational systems. Although typically not managed by the ETL team, the backup and recovery process is often designed as part of the ETL system. Its goal is to allow the data warehouse to get back to work after a failure. This includes backing up the intermediate staging data necessary to restart failed ETL jobs. The archive and retrieval process is designed to enable user access to older data that has been moved out of the main warehouse onto a less costly, usually lower-performing media.

Backup

Even if you have a fully redundant system with a universal power supply, fully RAIDed disks, and parallel processors with failover, some system crisis will eventually visit. Even with perfect hardware, someone can always drop the wrong table (or database). At the risk of stating the obvious, it is better to prepare for this than to handle it on-the-fly. A full scale backup system needs to provide the following capabilities:

- **High performance.** The backup needs to fit into the allotted timeframe. This may include online backups that don't impact performance significantly, including real-time partitions.
- **Simple administration.** The administration interface should provide tools that easily allow you to identify objects to back up (including tables, tablespaces, and redo logs), create schedules, and maintain backup verification and logs for subsequent restore.
- **Automated, lights-out operations.** The backup facility must provide storage management services, automated scheduling, media and device handling, reporting, and notification.

The backup for the warehouse is usually a physical backup. This is an image of the database at a certain point in time, including indexes and physical layout information.

Archive and Retrieval

Deciding what to move out of the warehouse is a cost-benefit issue. It costs money to keep the data around—it takes up disk space and slows the load and query times. On the other hand, the business users just might need this data to do some critical historical analyses. Likewise an auditor may request archived data as part of a compliance procedure. The solution is not to throw the data away but to put it some place that costs less but is still accessible. Archiving is the data security blanket for the warehouse.

As of this writing, the cost of online disk storage is dropping so rapidly that it makes sense to plan many of archiving tasks to simply write to disk. Especially if disk storage is handled by a separate IT resource, the requirement to "migrate and refresh" is replaced by "refresh." You need to make sure that you can interpret the data at various points in the future.

How long it takes the data to get stale depends on the industry, the business, and the particular data in question. In some cases, it is fairly obvious when older data has little value. For example, in an industry with rapid evolution of new products and competitors, history doesn't necessarily help you understand today or predict tomorrow.

After a determination has been made to archive certain data, the issue becomes "what are the long-term implications of archiving data?" Obviously, you need to leverage existing mechanisms to physically move the data from its current media to another media and ensure it can be recovered, along with an audit trail that accounts for the accesses and alterations to the data. But what does it mean to "keep" old data? Given increasing audit and compliance concerns, you may face archival requirements to preserve this data for five, 10, or perhaps even 50 years. What media should you utilize? Will you be able to read that media in future years? Ultimately, you may find yourself implementing a library system capable of archiving and regularly refreshing the data, and then migrating it to more current structures and media.

Finally, if you are archiving data from a system that is no longer going to be used, you may need to "sunset" the data by extracting it from the system and writing it in a vanilla format that is independent of the original application. You might need to do this if the license to use the application will terminate.

Subsystem 24: Recovery and Restart System

After the ETL system is in production, failures can occur for countless reasons beyond the control of the ETL process. Common causes of ETL production failures include:

- Network failure
- Database failure
- Disk failure
- Memory failure
- Data quality failure
- Unannounced system upgrade

To protect yourself from these failures, you need a solid backup system (subsystem 23) and a companion recovery and restart system. You must plan for unrecoverable errors during the load because they will happen. The system should anticipate this and provide crash recovery, stop, and restart capability. First, look for appropriate tools and design processes to minimize the impact of a crash. For example, a load process should commit relatively small sets of records at a time and keep track of what has been committed. The size of the set should be adjustable because the transaction size has performance implications on different DBMSs.

The recovery and restart system is used, of course, for either resuming a job that has halted or for backing out the whole job and restarting it. This system is significantly dependent on the capabilities of the backup system. When a failure occurs, the initial knee-jerk reaction is to attempt to salvage whatever has processed and restart the process from that point. This requires an ETL tool with solid and reliable checkpoint functionality, so it can perfectly determine what has processed and what has not to restart the job at exactly the right point. In many cases, it may be best to back out any rows that have been loaded as part of the process and restart from the beginning.

We often recommend designing fact tables with a single column primary surrogate key. This surrogate key is a simple integer that is assigned in sequence as rows are created to be added to the fact table. With the fact table surrogate key, you can easily resume a load that is halted or back out all the rows in the load by constraining on a range of surrogate keys.

NOTE Fact table surrogate keys have a number of uses in the ETL back room. First, as previously described, they can be used as the basis for backing out or resuming an interrupted load. Second, they provide immediate and unambiguous identification of a single fact row without needing to constrain multiple dimensions to fetch a unique row. Third, updates to fact table rows can be replaced by inserts plus deletes because the fact table surrogate key is now the actual key for the fact table. Thus, a row containing updated columns can be inserted into the fact table without overwriting the row it is to replace. When all such insertions are complete, then the underlying old rows can be deleted in a single step. Fourth, the fact table surrogate key is an ideal parent key to be used in a parent/child design. The fact table surrogate key appears as a foreign key in the child, along with the parent's dimension foreign keys.

The longer an ETL process runs, the more you must be aware of vulnerabilities due to failure. Designing a modular ETL system made up of efficient processes that are resilient against crashes and unexpected terminations can reduce the risk of a failure resulting in a massive recovery effort. Careful consideration of when to physically stage data by writing it to disk, along with carefully crafted points of recovery and load date/time stamps or sequential fact table surrogate keys enable you to specify appropriate restart logic.

Subsystem 25: Version Control System

The version control system is a "snapshotting" capability for archiving and recovering all the logic and metadata of the ETL pipeline. It controls check-out and check-in processing for all ETL modules and jobs. It should support source comparisons to reveal differences between versions. This system provides a librarian function for saving and restoring the complete ETL context of a single version. In certain highly compliant environments, it will be equally important to archive the complete ETL system context alongside the relevant archived and backup data. Note that master version numbers need to be assigned for the overall ETL system, just like software release version numbers.

> **NOTE** You have a master version number for each part of the ETL system as well as one for the system as a whole, don't you? And you can restore yesterday's complete ETL metadata context if it turns out there is a big mistake in the current release? Thank you for reassuring us.

Subsystem 26: Version Migration System

After the ETL team gets past the difficult process of designing and developing the ETL process and completes the creation of the jobs required to load the data warehouse, the jobs must be bundled and migrated to the next environment—from development to test and on to production—according to the lifecycle adopted by the organization. The version migration system needs to interface to the version control system to control the process and back out a migration if needed. It should provide a single interface for setting connection information for the entire version.

Most organizations isolate the development, testing, and production environments. You need to be able to migrate a complete version of the ETL pipeline from development, into test, and finally into production. Ideally, the test system is identically configured to its corresponding production system. Everything done to the production system should have been designed in development and the deployment script tested on the test environment. Every back room operation should go through rigorous scripting and testing, whether deploying a new schema, adding a column, changing indexes, changing the aggregate design, modifying a database parameter, backing up, or restoring. Centrally managed front room operations such as deploying new BI tools, deploying new corporate reports, and changing security plans should be equally rigorously tested and scripted if the BI tools allow it.

Subsystem 27: Workflow Monitor

Successful data warehouses are consistently and reliably available, as agreed to with the business community. To achieve this goal, the ETL system must be constantly monitored to ensure the ETL processes are operating efficiently and the warehouse is being loaded on a consistently timely basis. The job scheduler (subsystem 22) should capture performance data every time an ETL process is initiated. This data is part of the process metadata captured in the ETL system. The workflow monitor leverages the metadata captured by the job scheduler to provide a dashboard and reporting system taking many aspects of the ETL system into consideration. You'll want to monitor job status for all job runs initiated by the job scheduler including pending, running, completed and suspended jobs, and capture the historical data to support trending performance over time. Key performance measures include the number of records processed, summaries of errors, and actions taken. Most ETL tools capture the metrics for measuring ETL performance. Be sure to trigger alerts whenever an ETL job takes significantly more or less time to complete than indicated by the historical record.

In combination with the job scheduler, the workflow monitor should also track performance and capture measurements of the performance of infrastructure components including CPU usage, memory allocation and contention, disk utilization and contention, buffer pool usage, database performance, and server utilization and contention. Much of this information is process metadata about the ETL system and should be considered as part of the overall metadata strategy (subsystem 34).

The workflow monitor has a more significant strategic role than you might suspect. It is the starting point for the analysis of performance problems across the ETL pipeline. ETL performance bottlenecks can occur in many places, and a good workflow monitor shows where the bottlenecks are occurring. Chapter 20, discusses many ways to improve performance in the ETL pipeline, but this list is more or less ordered starting with the most important bottlenecks:

- Poorly indexed queries against a source system or intermediate table
- SQL syntax causing wrong optimizer choice
- Insufficient random access memory (RAM) causing thrashing
- Sorting in the RDBMS
- Slow transformation steps
- Excessive I/O
- Unnecessary writes followed by reads
- Dropping and rebuilding aggregates from scratch rather than incrementally
- Filtering (change data capture) applied too late in the pipeline
- Untapped opportunities for parallelizing and pipelining

- Unnecessary transaction logging especially if doing updates
- Network traffic and file transfer overhead

Subsystem 28: Sorting System

Certain common ETL processes call for data to be sorted in a particular order, such as aggregating and joining flat file sources. Because sorting is such a fundamental ETL processing capability, it is called out as a separate subsystem to ensure it receives proper attention as a component of the ETL architecture. There are a variety of technologies available to provide sorting capabilities. An ETL tool can undoubtedly provide a sort function, the DBMS can provide sorting via the SQL SORT clause, and there are a number of sort utilities available.

Sorting simple delimited text files with a dedicated sort package is awesomely fast. These packages typically allow a single read operation to produce up to eight different sorted outputs. Sorting can produce aggregates where each break row of a given sort is a row for the aggregate table, and sorting plus counting is often a good way to diagnose data quality issues.

The key is to choose the most efficient sort resource to support the requirements within your infrastructure. The easy answer for most organizations is to simply utilize the ETL tool's sort function. However, in some situations it may be more efficient to use a dedicated sort package; although ETL and DBMS vendors claim to have made up much of the performance differences.

Subsystem 29: Lineage and Dependency Analyzer

Two increasingly important elements being requested of the ETL system are the ability to track both the lineage and dependencies of data in the DW/BI system:

- **Lineage.** Beginning with a specific data element in an intermediate table or BI report, identify the source of that data element, other upstream intermediate tables containing that data element and its sources, and all transformations that data element and its sources have undergone.
- **Dependency.** Beginning with a specific data element in a source table or an intermediate table, identify all downstream intermediate tables and final BI reports containing that data element or its derivations and all transformations applied to that data element and its derivations.

Lineage analysis is often an important component in a highly compliant environment where you must explain the complete processing flow that changed any data result. This means the ETL system must display the ultimate physical sources and all subsequent transformations of any selected data element, chosen either from the middle of the ETL pipeline or on a final delivered report. Dependency analysis is important when assessing changes to a source system and the downstream impacts on the data warehouse and ETL system. This implies the ability to display all affected downstream data elements and final report fields affected by a potential change in any selected data element, chosen either in the middle of the ETL pipeline or an original source (dependency).

Subsystem 30: Problem Escalation System

Typically, the ETL team develops the ETL processes and the quality assurance team tests them thoroughly before they are turned over to the group responsible for day-to-day systems operations. To make this work, the ETL architecture needs to include a proactively designed problem escalation system similar to what is in place for other production systems.

After the ETL processes have been developed and tested, the first level of operational support for the ETL system should be a group dedicated to monitoring production applications. The ETL development team becomes involved only if the operational support team cannot resolve a production problem.

Ideally, you have developed ETL processes, wrapped them into an automated scheduler, and have robust workflow monitoring capabilities peering into the ETL processes as they execute. The execution of the ETL system should be a hands-off operation. It should run like clockwork without human intervention and without fail. If a problem does occur, the ETL process should automatically notify the problem escalation system of any situation that needs attention or resolution. This automatic feed may take the form of simple error logs, operator notification messages, supervisor notification messages, and system developer messages. The ETL system may notify an individual or a group depending on the severity of the situation or the processes involved. ETL tools can support a variety of messaging capabilities including e-mail alerts, operator messages, and notifications to mobile devices.

Each notification event should be written to a database used to understand the types of problems that arise, their status, and resolution. This data forms part of the process metadata captured by the ETL system (subsystem 34). You need to ensure that organizational procedures are in place for proper escalation, so every problem is resolved appropriately.

In general, the support structure for the ETL system should follow a fairly standard support structure. First, level support is typically a help desk that is the first point of contact when a user notices an error. The help desk is responsible for resolution whenever feasible. If the help desk cannot resolve the issue, the second level support is notified. This is typically a systems administrator or DBA on the production control technical staff capable of supporting general infrastructure failures. The ETL manager is the third level support and should be knowledgeable to support most issues that arise in the ETL production process. Finally, when all else fails, the ETL developer should be called in to analyze the situation and assist with resolution.

Subsystem 31: Parallelizing/Pipelining System

The goal of the ETL system, in addition to providing high quality data, is to load the data warehouse within the allocated processing window. In large organizations with huge data volumes and a large portfolio of dimensions and facts, loading the data within these constraints can be a challenge. The paralleling/pipelining system provides capabilities to enable the ETL system to deliver within these time constraints. The goal of this system is to take advantage of multiple processors or grid computing resources commonly available. It is highly desirable, and in many cases necessary, that parallelizing and pipelining be automatically invoked for every ETL process unless specific conditions preclude it from processing in such a manner, such as waiting on a condition in the middle of the process.

Parallelizing is a powerful performance technique at every stage of the ETL pipeline. For example, the extraction process can be parallelized by logically partitioning on ranges of an attribute. Verify that the source DBMS handles parallelism correctly and doesn't spawn conflicting processes. If possible, choose an ETL tool that handles parallelizing of intermediate transformation processes automatically. In some tools it is necessary to hand create parallel processes. This is fine until you add additional processors, and the ETL system then can't take advantage of the greater parallelization opportunities unless you modify the ETL modules by hand to increase the number of parallel flows.

Subsystem 32: Security System

Security is an important consideration for the ETL system. A serious security breach is much more likely to come from within the organization than from someone hacking in from the outside. Although we don't like to think it, the folks on the ETL team present as much a potential threat as any group inside the organization. We recommend administering role-based security on all data and metadata in the ETL system. To support compliance requirements, you may need to prove that a version of an ETL module hasn't been changed or show who made changes to a module. You should enforce comprehensive authorized access to all ETL data and metadata by individual and role. In addition, you'll want to maintain a historical record of all accesses to ETL data and metadata by individual and role. Another issue to be careful of is the bulk data movement process. If you move data across the network, even if it is within the company firewall, it pays to be careful. Make sure to use data encryption or a file transfer utility that uses a secure transfer protocol.

Another back room security issue to consider is administrator access to the production warehouse server and software. We've seen situations where no one on the team had security privileges; in other cases, everyone had access to everything. Obviously, many members of the team should have privileged access to the development environment, but the production warehouse should be strictly controlled. On the other hand, someone from the DW/BI team needs to be able to reset the warehouse machine if something goes wrong. Finally, the backup media should be guarded. The backup media should have as much security surrounding them as the online systems.

Subsystem 33: Compliance Manager

In highly compliant environments, supporting compliance requirements is a significant new requirement for the ETL team. Compliance in the data warehouse involves "maintaining the chain of custody" of the data. In the same way a police department must carefully maintain the chain of custody of evidence to argue that the evidence has not been changed or tampered with, the data warehouse must also carefully guard the compliance-sensitive data entrusted to it from the moment it arrives. Furthermore, the data warehouse must always show the exact condition and content of such data at any point in time that it may have been under the control of the data warehouse. The data warehouse must also track who had authorized access to the data. Finally, when the suspicious auditor looks over your shoulder, you need to link back to an archived and time-stamped version of the data as it was originally received, which you have stored remotely with a trusted third party. If the data warehouse is prepared to meet all these compliance requirements, then the stress of being audited by a hostile government agency or lawyer armed with a subpoena should be greatly reduced.

The compliance requirements may mean you cannot actually change any data, for any reason. If data must be altered, then a new version of the altered records must be inserted into the database. Each row in each table therefore must have begin and end time stamps that accurately represents the span of time when the record was the "current truth." The big impact of these compliance requirements on the data warehouse can be expressed in simple dimensional modeling terms. Type 1 and type 3 changes are dead. In other words, all changes become inserts. No more deletes or overwrites.

Figure 19-12 shows how a fact table can be augmented so that overwrite changes are converted into a fact table equivalent of a type 2 change. The original fact table consisted of the lower seven columns starting with activity date and ending with net dollars. The original fact table allowed overwrites. For example, perhaps there is a business rule that updates the discount and net dollar amounts after the row is originally created. In the original version of the table, history is lost when the overwrite change takes place, and the chain of custody is broken.

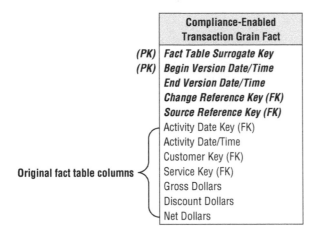

Figure 19-12: Compliance-enabled transaction fact table.

To convert the fact table to be compliance-enabled, five columns are added, as shown in bold. A fact table surrogate key is created for each original unmodified fact table row. This surrogate key, like a dimension table surrogate key, is just a unique integer that is assigned as each original fact table row is created. The begin version date/time stamp is the exact time of creation of the fact table row. Initially, the end version date/time is set to a fictitious date/time in the future. The change reference is set to "original," and the source reference is set to the operational source.

When an overwrite change is needed, a new row is added to the fact table with the same fact table surrogate key, and the appropriate regular columns changed, such as discount dollars and net dollars. The begin version date/time column is set to the exact date/time when the change in the database takes place. The end version date/time is set to a fictitious date/time in the future. The end version date/time of the original fact row is now set to the exact date/time when the change in the database takes place. The change reference now provides an explanation for the change, and the source reference provides the source of the revised columns.

Referring to the design in Figure 19-12, a specific moment in time can be selected and the fact table constrained to show exactly what the rows contained at that moment. The alterations to a given row can be examined by constraining to a specific fact table surrogate key and sorting by begin version date/time.

The compliance machinery is a significant addition to a normal fact table (refer to Figure 19-12). If the compliance-enabled table is actually used for only demonstrating compliance, then a normal version of the fact table with just the original columns can remain as the main operational table, with the compliance-enabled table existing only in the background. The compliance-enabled table doesn't need to be indexed for performance because it will not be used in a conventional BI environment.

For heaven's sake, don't assume that all data is now subject to draconian compliance restrictions. It is essential you receive firm guidelines from the chief compliance officer before taking any drastic steps.

The foundation of a compliance system is the interaction of several of the subsystems already described married to a few key technologies and capabilities:

- **Lineage analysis.** Show where a final piece of data came from to prove the original source data plus the transformations including stored procedures and manual changes. This requires full documentation of all the transforms and the technical ability to rerun the transforms against the original data.
- **Dependency analysis.** Show where an original source data element was ever used.
- **Version control.** It may be necessary to rerun the source data through the ETL system in effect at the time, requiring the exact version of the ETL system for any given data source.
- **Backup and restore.** Of course, the requested data may have been archived years ago and need to be restored for audit purposes. Hopefully, you archived the proper version of the ETL system alongside the data, so both the data and the system can be restored. It may be necessary to prove the archived data hasn't been altered. During the archival process, the data can be hash-coded and the hash and data separated. Have the hash codes archived separately by a trusted third party. Then, when demanded, restore the original data, hash code it again, and then compare to the hash codes retrieved from the trusted third party to prove the authenticity of the data.
- **Security.** Show who has accessed or modified the data and transforms. Be prepared to show roles and privileges for users. Guarantee the security log can't be altered by using a write once media.
- **Audit dimension.** The audit dimension ties runtime metadata context directly with the data to capture quality events at the time of the load.

Subsystem 34: Metadata Repository Manager

The ETL system is responsible for the use and creation of much of the metadata involved in the DW/BI environment. Part of the overall metadata strategy should be to specifically capture ETL metadata, including the process metadata, technical metadata, and business metadata. Develop a balanced strategy between doing nothing and doing too much. Make sure there's time in the ETL development tasks to capture and manage metadata. And finally, make sure someone on the DW/BI team is assigned the role of metadata manager and owns the responsibility for creating and implementing the metadata strategy.

Summary

In this chapter we have introduced the key building blocks of the ETL system. As you may now better appreciate, building an ETL system is unusually challenging; the ETL system must address a number of demanding requirements. This chapter identified and reviewed the 34 subsystems of ETL and gathered these subsystems into four key areas that represent the ETL process: extracting, cleaning and conforming, delivering, and managing. Careful consideration of all the elements of the ETL architecture is the key to success. You must understand the full breadth of requirements and then set an appropriate and effective architecture in place. ETL is more than simply extract, transform, and load; it's a host of complex and important tasks. In the next chapter we will describe the processes and tasks for building the ETL system.

20 ETL System Design and Development Process and Tasks

Developing the extract, transformation, and load (ETL) system is the hidden part of the iceberg for most DW/BI projects. So many challenges are buried in the data sources and systems that developing the ETL application invariably takes more time than expected. This chapter is structured as a 10-step plan for creating the data warehouse's ETL system. The concepts and approach described in this chapter, based on content from *The Data Warehouse Lifecycle Toolkit*, *Second Edition* (Wiley, 2008), apply to systems based on an ETL tool, as well as hand-coded systems.

Chapter 20 discusses the following concepts:

- ETL system planning and design consideration
- Recommendations for one-time historic data loads
- Development tasks for incremental load processing
- Real-time data warehousing considerations

ETL Process Overview

This chapter follows the flow of planning and implementing the ETL system. We implicitly discuss the 34 ETL subsystems presented in Chapter 19: ETL Subsystems and Techniques, broadly categorized as extracting data, cleaning and conforming, delivering for presentation, and managing the ETL environment.

Before beginning the ETL system design for a dimensional model, you should have completed the logical design, drafted your high-level architecture plan, and drafted the source-to-target mapping for all data elements.

The ETL system design process is critical. Gather all the relevant information, including the processing burden the extracts will be allowed to place on the operational source systems, and test some key alternatives. Does it make sense to host the transformation process on the source system, target system, or its own platform? What tools are available on each, and how effective are they?

Develop the ETL Plan

ETL development starts out with the high-level plan, which is independent of any specific technology or approach. However, it's a good idea to decide on an ETL tool before doing any detailed planning; this can avoid redesign and rework later in the process.

Step 1: Draw the High-Level Plan

We start the design process with a very simple schematic of the known pieces of the plan: sources and targets, as shown in Figure 20-1. This schematic is for a fictitious utility company's data warehouse, which is primarily sourced from a 30-year-old COBOL system. If most or all the data comes from a modern relational transaction processing system, the boxes often represent a logical grouping of tables in the transaction system model.

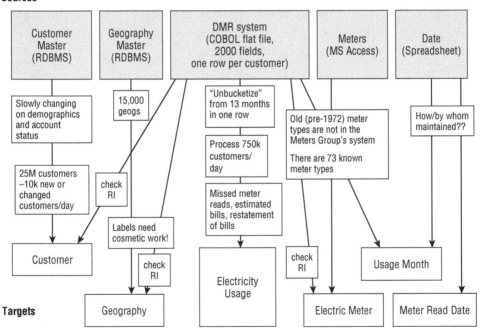

Figure 20-1: Example high-level data staging plan schematic.

As you develop the detailed ETL system specification, the high-level view requires additional details. Figure 20-1 deliberately highlights contemporary questions and unresolved issues; this plan should be frequently updated and released. You might sometimes keep two versions of the diagram: a simple one for communicating with people outside the team and a detailed version for internal DW/BI team documentation.

Step 2: Choose an ETL Tool

There are a multitude of ETL tools available in the data warehouse marketplace. Most of the major database vendors offer an ETL tool, usually at additional licensing cost. There are also excellent ETL tools available from third-party vendors.

ETL tools read data from a range of sources, including flat files, ODBC, OLE DB, and native database drivers for most relational databases. The tools contain functionality for defining transformations on that data, including lookups and other kinds of joins. They can write data into a variety of target formats. And they all contain some functionality for managing the overall logic flow in the ETL system.

If the source systems are relational, the transformation requirements are straightforward, and good developers are on staff, the value of an ETL tool may not be immediately obvious. However, there are several reasons that using an ETL tool is an industry standard best practice:

- Self-documentation that comes from using a graphical tool. A hand-coded system is usually an impenetrable mess of staging tables, SQL scripts, stored procedures, and operating system scripts.
- Metadata foundation for all steps of the ETL process.
- Version control for multi-developer environments and for backing out and restoring consistent versions.
- Advanced transformation logic, such as fuzzy matching algorithms, integrated access to name and address deduplication routines, and data mining algorithms.
- Improved system performance at a lower level of expertise. Relatively few SQL developers are truly expert on how to use the relational database to manipulate extremely large data volumes with excellent performance.
- Sophisticated processing capabilities, including automatically parallelizing tasks, and automatic fail-over when a processing resource becomes unavailable.
- One-step conversion of virtualized data transformation modules into their physical equivalents.

Don't expect to recoup the investment in an ETL tool on the first phase of the DW/BI project. The learning curve is steep enough that developers sometimes feel the project could have been implemented faster by coding. The big advantages come with future phases, and particularly with future modifications to existing systems.

Step 3: Develop Default Strategies

With an overall idea of what needs to happen and what the ETL tool's infrastructure requires, you should develop a set of default strategies for the common activities in the ETL system. These activities include:

- **Extract from each major source system.** At this point in the design process, you can determine the default method for extracting data from each source system. Will you normally push from the source system to a flat file, extract in a stream, use a tool to read the database logs, or another method? This decision can be modified on a table-by-table basis. If using SQL to access source system data, make sure the native data extractors are used rather than ODBC, if that's an option.

- **Archive extracted and staged data.** Extracted or staged data, before it's been transformed, should be archived for at least a month. Some organizations permanently archive extracted and staged data.

- **Police data quality for dimensions and particularly facts.** Data quality must be monitored during the ETL process rather than waiting for business users to find data problems. Chapter 19 describes a comprehensive architecture for measuring and responding to data quality issues in ETL subsystems 4 through 8.

- **Manage changes to dimension attributes.** In Chapter 19, we described the logic required to manage dimension attribute changes in ETL subsystem 9.

- **Ensure the data warehouse and ETL system meet the system availability requirements.** The first step to meeting availability requirements is to document them. You should document when each data source becomes available and block out high-level job sequencing.

- **Design the data auditing subsystem.** Each row in the data warehouse tables should be tagged with auditing information that describes how the data entered the system.

- **Organize the ETL staging area.** Most ETL systems stage the data at least once or twice during the ETL process. By staging, we mean the data will be written to disk for a later ETL step and for system recovery and archiving.

Step 4: Drill Down by Target Table

After overall strategies for common ETL tasks have been developed, you should start drilling into the detailed transformations needed to populate each target table in the data warehouse. As you're finalizing the source-to-target mappings, you also perform more data profiling to thoroughly understand the necessary data transformations for each table and column.

Ensure Clean Hierarchies

It's particularly important to investigate whether hierarchical relationships in the dimension data are perfectly clean. Consider a product dimension that includes a hierarchical rollup from product stock keeping unit (SKU) to product category.

In our experience, the most reliable hierarchies are well managed in the source system. The best source systems normalize the hierarchical levels into multiple tables, with foreign key constraints between the levels. In this case, you can be confident the hierarchies are clean. If the source system is not normalized—especially if the source for the hierarchies is an Excel spreadsheet on a business user's desktop—then you must either clean it up or acknowledge that it is not a hierarchy.

Develop Detailed Table Schematics

Figure 20-2 illustrates the level of detail that's useful for the table-specific drilldown; it's for one of the tables in the utility company example previously illustrated.

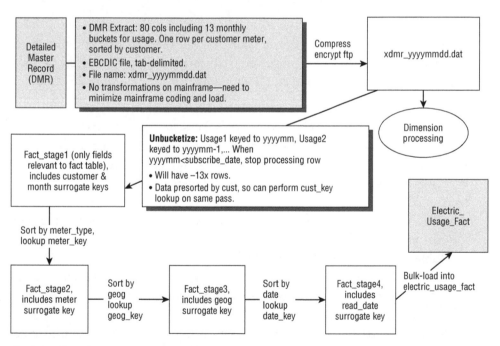

Figure 20-2: Example draft detailed load schematic for the fact table.

All the dimension tables must be processed before the key lookup steps for the fact table. The dimension tables are usually independent from each other, but sometimes they also have processing dependencies. It's important to clarify these dependencies, as they become fixed points around which the job control flows.

Develop the ETL Specification Document

We've walked through some general strategies for high-level planning and the physical design of the ETL system. Now it's time to pull everything together and develop a detailed specification for the entire ETL system.

All the documents developed so far—the source-to-target mappings, data profiling reports, physical design decisions—should be rolled into the first sections of the ETL specification. Then document all the decisions discussed in this chapter, including:

- Default strategy for extracting from each major source system
- Archiving strategy
- Data quality tracking and metadata
- Default strategy for managing changes to dimension attributes
- System availability requirements and strategy
- Design of the data auditing subsystem
- Locations of staging areas

The next section of the ETL specification describes the historic and incremental load strategies for each table. A good specification includes between two and 10 pages of detail for each table, and documents the following information and decisions:

- Table design (column names, data types, keys, and constraints)
- Historic data load parameters (number of months) and volumes (row counts)
- Incremental data volumes, measured as new and updated rows per load cycle
- Handling of late arriving data for facts and dimensions
- Load frequency
- Handling of slowly changing dimension (SCD) changes for each dimension attribute
- Table partitioning, such as monthly
- Overview of data sources, including a discussion of any unusual source characteristics, such as an unusually brief access window
- Detailed source-to-target mapping
- Source data profiling, including at least the minimum and maximum values for each numeric column, count of distinct values in each column, and incidence of NULLs
- Extract strategy for the source data (for example, source system APIs, direct query from database, or dump to flat files)
- Dependencies, including which other tables must be loaded before this table is processed
- Document the transformation logic. It's easiest to write this section as pseudo code or a diagram, rather than trying to craft complete sentences.

- Preconditions to avoid error conditions. For example, the ETL system must check for file or database space before proceeding.
- Cleanup steps, such as deleting working files
- An estimate of whether this portion of the ETL system will be easy, medium, or difficult to implement

NOTE Although most people would agree that all the items described in the ETL system specification document are necessary, it's a lot of work to pull this document together, and even more work to keep it current as changes occur. Realistically, if you pull together the "one-pager" high-level flow diagram, data model and source-to-target maps, and a five-page description of what you plan to do, you'll get a better start than most teams.

Develop a Sandbox Source System

During the ETL development process, the source system data needs to be investigated at great depth. If the source system is heavily loaded, and there isn't some kind of reporting instance for operational queries, the DBAs may be willing to set up a static snapshot of the database for the ETL development team. Early in the development process, it's convenient to poke around sandbox versions of the source systems without worrying about launching a kind of killer query.

It's easy to build a sandbox source system that simply copies the original; build a sandbox with a subset of data only if the data volumes are extremely large. On the plus side, this sandbox could become the basis of training materials and tutorials after the system is deployed into production.

Develop One-Time Historic Load Processing

After the ETL specification has been created, you typically focus on developing the ETL process for the one-time load of historic data. Occasionally, the same ETL code can perform both the initial historic load and ongoing incremental loads, but more often you build separate ETL processes for the historic and ongoing loads. The historic and incremental load processes have a lot in common, and depending on the ETL tool, significant functionality can be reused from one to the other.

Step 5: Populate Dimension Tables with Historic Data

In general, you start building the ETL system with the simplest dimension tables. After these dimension tables have been successfully built, you tackle the historic loads for dimensions with one or more columns managed as SCD type 2.

Populate Type 1 Dimension Tables

The easiest type of table to populate is a dimension table for which all attributes are managed as type 1 overwrites. With a type 1–only dimension, you extract the current value for each dimension attribute from the source system.

Dimension Transformations

Even the simplest dimension table may require substantial data cleanup and will certainly require surrogate key assignment.

Simple Data Transformations

The most common, and easiest, form of data transformation is data type conversion. All ETL tools have rich functions for data type conversion. This task can be tedious, but it is seldom onerous. We strongly recommend replacing NULL values with default values within dimension tables; as we have discussed previously, NULLs can cause problems when they are directly queried.

Combine from Separate Sources

Often dimensions are derived from several sources. Customer information may need to be merged from several lines of business and from outside sources. There is seldom a universal key pre-embedded in the various sources that makes this merge operation easy.

Most consolidation and deduplicating tools and processes work best if names and addresses are first parsed into their component pieces. Then you can use a set of passes with fuzzy logic that account for misspellings, typos, and alternative spellings such as I.B.M., IBM, and International Business Machines. In most organizations, there is a large one-time project to consolidate existing customers. This is a tremendously valuable role for master data management systems.

Decode Production Codes

A common merging task in data preparation is looking up text equivalents for production codes. In some cases, the text equivalents are sourced informally from a nonproduction source such as a spreadsheet. The code lookups are usually stored in a table in the staging database. Make sure the ETL system includes logic for creating a default decoded text equivalent for the case in which the production code is missing from the lookup table.

Validate Many-to-One and One-to-One Relationships

The most important dimensions probably have one or more rollup paths, such as products rolling up to product model, subcategory, and category, as illustrated in Figure 20-3. These hierarchical rollups need to be perfectly clean.

Product Dimension
Product Key (PK)
Product SKU
Product Name
Product Description
Product Model
Product Model Description
Subcategory Description
Category Description
Category Manager

Figure 20-3: Product dimension table with a hierarchical relationship.

Many-to-one relationships between attributes, such as a product to product model, can be verified by sorting on the "many" attribute and verifying that each value has a unique value on the "one" attribute. For example, this query returns the products that have more than one product model:

```
SELECT Product_SKU,
count[*] as Row_Count,
count(distinct Product_Model) as Model_Count
FROM StagingDatabase.Product
GROUP BY Product_SKU
HAVING count(distinct Product_Model) > 1 ;
```

Database administrators sometimes want to validate many-to-one relationships by loading data into a normalized snowflake version of the dimension table in the staging database, as illustrated in Figure 20-4. Note that the normalized version requires individual keys at each of the hierarchy levels. This is not a problem if the source system supplies the keys, but if you normalize the dimension in the ETL environment, you need to create them.

The snowflake structure has some value in the staging area: It prevents you from loading data that violates the many-to-one relationship. However, in general, the relationships should be pre-verified as just described, so that you never attempt to load bad data into the dimension table. After the data is pre-verified, it's not tremendously important whether you make the database engine reconfirm the relationship at the moment you load the table.

If the source system for a dimensional hierarchy is a normalized database, it's usually unnecessary to repeat the normalized structure in the ETL staging area. However, if the hierarchical information comes from an informal source such as a spreadsheet managed by the marketing department, you may benefit from normalizing the hierarchy in the ETL system.

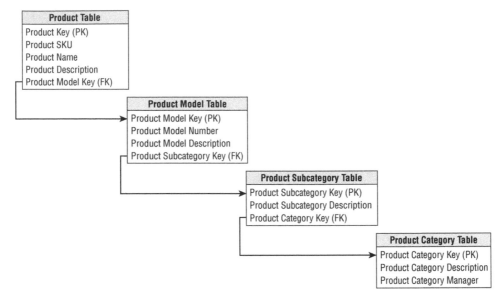

Figure 20-4: Snowflaked hierarchical relationship in the product dimension.

Dimension Surrogate Key Assignment

After you are confident you have dimension tables with one row for each true unique dimension member, the surrogate keys can be assigned. You maintain a table in the ETL staging database that matches production keys to surrogate keys; you can use this key map later during fact table processing.

Surrogate keys are typically assigned as integers, increasing by one for each new key. If the staging area is in an RDBMS, surrogate key assignment is elegantly accomplished by creating a sequence. Although syntax varies among the relational engines, the process is first to create a sequence and then to populate the key map table.

Here's the syntax for the one-time creation of the sequence:

```
create sequence dim1_seq cache=1000; — choose appropriate cache level
```

And then here's the syntax to populate the key map table:

```
insert into dim1_key_map (production_key_id, dim1_key)
select production_key_id, dim1_seq.NEXT
from dim1_extract_table;
```

Dimension Table Loading

After the dimension data is properly prepared, the load process into the target tables is fairly straightforward. Even though the first dimension table is usually small, use the database's bulk or fast-loading utility or interface. You should use fast-loading techniques for most table inserts. Some databases have extended the SQL syntax to include a `BULK INSERT` statement. Others have published an API to load data into the table from a stream.

The bulk load utilities and APIs come with a range of parameters and transformation capabilities including the following:

- **Turn off logging**. Transaction logging adds significant overhead and is not valuable when loading data warehouse tables. The ETL system should be designed with one or more recoverability points where you can restart processing should something go wrong.
- **Bulk load in fast mode**. However, most of the database engines' bulk load utilities or APIs require several stringent conditions on the target table to bulk load in fast mode. If these conditions are not met, the load should not fail; it simply will not use the "fast" path.
- **Presort the file**. Sorting the file in the order of the primary index significantly speeds up indexing.
- **Transform with caution**. In some cases, the loader supports data conversions, calculations, and string and date/time manipulation. Use these features carefully and test performance. In some cases, these transformations cause the loader to switch out of high-speed mode into a line-by-line evaluation of the load file. We recommend using the ETL tool to perform most transformations.
- **Truncate table before full refresh**. The `TRUNCATE TABLE` statement is the most efficient way to delete all the rows in the table. It's commonly used to clean out a table from the staging database at the beginning of the day's ETL processing.

Load Type 2 Dimension Table History

Recall from Chapter 5: Procurement, that dimension attribute changes are typically managed as type 1 (overwrite) or type 2 (track history by adding new rows to the dimension table). Most dimension tables contain a mixture of type 1 and type 2 attributes. More advanced SCD techniques are described in Chapter 5.

During the historic load, you need to re-create history for dimension attributes that are managed as type 2. If business users have identified an attribute as important for tracking history, they want that history going back in time, not just from the date the data warehouse is implemented. It's usually difficult to re-create dimension attribute history, and sometimes it's completely impossible.

This process is not well suited for standard SQL processing. It's better to use a database cursor construct or, even better, a procedural language such as Visual Basic, C, or Java to perform this work. Most ETL tools enable script processing on the data as it flows through the ETL system.

When you've completely reconstructed history, make a final pass through the data to set the row end date column. It's important to ensure there are no gaps in the series. We prefer to set the row end date for the older version of the dimension member to the day before the row effective date for the new row if these row dates have a granularity of a full day. If the effective and end dates are actually precise date/time stamps accurate to the minute or second, then the end date/time must be set to exactly the begin date/time of the next row so that no gap exists between rows.

Populate Date and Other Static Dimensions

Every data warehouse database should have a date dimension, usually at the granularity of one row for each day. The date dimension should span the history of the data, starting with the oldest fact transaction in the data warehouse. It's easy to set up the date dimension for the historic data because you know the date range of the historic fact data being loaded. Most projects build the date dimension by hand, typically in a spreadsheet.

A handful of other dimensions will be created in a similar way. For example, you may create a budget scenario dimension that holds the values Actual and Budget. Business data governance representatives should sign off on all constructed dimension tables.

Step 6: Perform the Fact Table Historic Load

The one-time historic fact table load differs fairly significantly from the ongoing incremental processing. The biggest worry during the historic load is the sheer volume of data, sometimes thousands of times bigger than the daily incremental load. On the other hand, you have the luxury of loading into a table that's not in production. If it takes several days to load the historic data, that's usually tolerable.

Historic Fact Table Extracts

As you identify records that fall within the basic parameters of the extract, make sure these records are useful for the data warehouse. Many transaction systems keep operational information in the source system that may not be interesting from a business point of view.

It's also a good idea to accumulate audit statistics during this step. As the extract creates the results set, it is often possible to capture various subtotals, totals, and row counts.

Audit Statistics

During the planning phase for the ETL system, you identified various measures of data quality. These are usually calculations, such as counts and sums, that you compare between the data warehouse and source systems to cross-check the integrity of the data. These numbers should tie backward to operational reports and forward to the results of the load process in the warehouse. The tie back to the operational system is important because it is what establishes the credibility of the warehouse.

> **NOTE**   There are scenarios in which it's difficult or impossible for the warehouse to tie back to the source system perfectly. In many cases, the data warehouse extract includes business rules that have not been applied to the source systems. Even more vexing are errors in the source system! Also, differences in timing make it even more difficult to cross-check the data. If it's not possible to tie the data back exactly, you need to explain the differences.

Fact Table Transformations

In most projects, the fact data is relatively clean. The ETL system developer spends a lot of time improving the dimension table content, but the facts usually require a fairly modest transformation. This makes sense because in most cases the facts come from transaction systems used to operate the organization.

The most common transformations to fact data include transformation of null values, pivoting or unpivoting the data, and precomputing derived calculations. All fact rows then enter the surrogate key pipeline to exchange the natural keys for the dimension surrogate keys managed in the ETL system.

Null Fact Values

All major database engines explicitly support a null value. In many source systems, however, the null value is represented by a special value of what should be a legitimate fact. Perhaps the special value of –1 is understood to represent null. For most fact table metrics, the "–1" in this scenario should be replaced with a true NULL. A null value for a numeric measure is reasonable and common in the fact table. Nulls do the "right thing" in calculations of sums and averages across fact table rows. It's only in the dimension tables that you should strive to replace null values with specially crafted default values. Finally, you should not allow any null values in the fact table columns that reference the dimension table keys. These foreign key columns should always be defined as NOT NULL.

Improve Fact Table Content

As we have stressed, all the facts in the final fact table row must be expressed in the same grain. This means there must be no facts representing totals for the year in a daily fact table or totals for some geography larger than the fact table's grain. If the extract includes an interleaving of facts at different grains, the transformation process must eliminate these aggregations, or move them into the appropriate aggregate tables.

The fact row may contain derived facts; although, in many cases it is more efficient to calculate derived facts in a view or an online analytical processing (OLAP) cube rather than in the physical table. For instance, a fact row that contains revenues and costs may want a fact representing net profit. It is very important that the net profit value be correctly calculated every time a user accesses it. If the data warehouse forces all users to access the data through a view, it would be fine to calculate the net profit in that view. If users are allowed to see the physical table, or if they often filter on net profit and thus you'd want to index it, precomputing it and storing it physically is preferable.

Similarly, if some facts need to be simultaneously presented with multiple units of measure, the same logic applies. If business users access the data through a view or OLAP database, then the various versions of the facts can efficiently be calculated at access time.

Pipeline the Dimension Surrogate Key Lookup

It is important that referential integrity (RI) is maintained between the fact table and dimension tables; you must never have a fact row that references a dimension member that doesn't exist. Therefore, you should not have a null value for any foreign key in the fact table nor should any fact row violate referential integrity to any dimension.

The surrogate key pipeline is the final operation before you load data into the target fact table. All other data cleaning, transformation, and processing should be complete. The incoming fact data should look just like the target fact table in the dimensional model, except it still contains the natural keys from the source system rather than the warehouse's surrogate keys. The surrogate key pipeline is the process that exchanges the natural keys for the surrogate keys and handles any referential integrity errors.

Dimension table processing must complete before the fact data enters the surrogate key pipeline. Any new dimension members or type 2 changes to existing dimension members must have already been processed, so their keys are available to the surrogate key pipeline.

First let's discuss the referential integrity problem. It's a simple matter to confirm that each natural key in the historic fact data is represented in the dimension tables. This is a manual step. The historic load is paused at this point, so you can investigate and fix any referential integrity problems before proceeding. The dimension table is either fixed, or the fact table extract is redesigned to filter out spurious rows, as appropriate.

Now that you're confident there will be no referential integrity violations, you can design the historic surrogate key pipeline, as shown in Figure 19-11 in the previous chapter. In this scenario, you need to include BETWEEN logic on any dimension with type 2 changes to locate the dimension row that was in effect when the historical fact measurement occurred.

There are several approaches for designing the historic load's surrogate key pipeline for best performance; the design depends on the features available in your ETL tool, the data volumes you're processing, and your dimensional design. In theory, you could define a query that joins the fact staging table and each dimension table on the natural keys, returning the facts and surrogate keys from each dimension table. If the historic data volumes are not huge, this can actually work quite well, assuming you staged the fact data in the relational database and indexed the dimension tables to support this big query. This approach has several benefits:

- It leverages the power of the relational database.
- It performs the surrogate key lookups on all dimensions in parallel.
- It simplifies the problem of picking up the correct dimension key for type 2 dimensions. The join to type 2 dimensions must include a clause specifying that the transaction date falls between the row effective date and row end date for that image of the dimension member in the table.

No one would be eager to try this approach if the historic fact data volumes were large in the hundreds of gigabytes to terabyte range. The complex join to the type 2 dimension tables create the greatest demands on the system. Many dimensional designs include a fairly large number of (usually small) dimension tables that are fully type 1, and a smaller number of dimensions containing type 2 attributes. You could use this relational technique to perform the surrogate key lookups for all the type 1 dimensions in one pass and then separately handle the type 2 dimensions. You should ensure the effective date and end date columns are properly indexed.

An alternative to the database join technique described is to use the ETL tool's lookup operator.

When all the fact source keys have been replaced with surrogate keys, the fact row is ready to load. The keys in the fact table row have been chosen to be proper foreign keys to the respective dimension tables, and the fact table is guaranteed to have referential integrity with respect to the dimension tables.

Assign Audit Dimension Key

Fact tables often include an audit key on each fact row. The audit key points to an audit dimension that describes the characteristics of the load, including relatively static environment variables and measures of data quality. The audit dimension can be quite small. An initial design of the audit dimension might have just two environment variables (master ETL version number and profit allocation logic number), and only one quality indicator whose values are Quality Checks Passed and Quality Problems Encountered. Over time, these variables and diagnostic indicators can be made more detailed and more sophisticated. The audit dimension key is added to the fact table either immediately after or immediately before the surrogate key pipeline.

Fact Table Loading

The main concern when loading the fact table is load performance. Some database technologies support fast loading with a specified batch size. Look at the documentation for the fast-loading technology to see how to set this parameter. You can experiment to find the ideal batch size for the size of the rows and the server's memory configuration. Most people don't bother to get so precise and simply choose a number like 10,000 or 100,000 or 1 million.

Aside from using the bulk loader and a reasonable batch size (if appropriate for the database engine), the best way to improve the performance of the historic load is to load into a partitioned table, ideally loading multiple partitions in parallel. The steps to loading into a partitioned table include:

1. Disable foreign key (referential integrity) constraints between the fact table and each dimension table before loading data.
2. Drop or disable indexes on the fact table.
3. Load the data using fast-loading techniques.
4. Create or enable fact table indexes.
5. If necessary, perform steps to stitch together the table's partitions.
6. Confirm each dimension table has a unique index on the surrogate key column.
7. Enable foreign key constraints between the fact table and dimension tables.

Develop Incremental ETL Processing

One of the biggest challenges with the incremental ETL process is identifying new, changed, and deleted rows. After you have a stream of inserts, modifications, and deletions, the ETL system can apply transformations following virtually identical business rules as for the historic data loads.

The historic load for dimensions and facts consisted largely or entirely of inserts. In incremental processing, you primarily perform inserts, but updates for dimensions and some kinds of fact tables are inevitable. Updates and deletes are expensive operations in the data warehouse environment, so we'll describe techniques to improve the performance of these tasks.

Step 7: Dimension Table Incremental Processing

As you might expect, the incremental ETL system development begins with the dimension tables. Dimension incremental processing is very similar to the historic processing previously described.

Dimension Table Extracts

In many cases, there is a customer master file or product master file that can serve as the single source for a dimension. In other cases, the raw source data is a mixture of dimensional and fact data.

Often it's easiest to pull the current snapshots of the dimension tables in their entirety and let the transformation step determine what has changed and how to handle it. If the dimension tables are large, you may need to use the fact table technique described in the section "Step 8: Fact Table Incremental Processing" for identifying the changed record set. It can take a long time to look up each entry in a large dimension table, even if it hasn't changed from the existing entry.

If possible, construct the extract to pull only rows that have changed. This is particularly easy and valuable if the source system maintains an indicator of the type of change.

Identify New and Changed Dimension Rows

The DW/BI team may not be successful in pushing the responsibility for identifying new, updated, and deleted rows to the source system owners. In this case, the ETL process needs to perform an expensive comparison operation to identify new and changed rows.

When the incoming data is clean, it's easy to find new dimension rows. The raw data has an operational natural key, which must be matched to the same column in the current dimension row. Remember, the natural key in the dimension table is an ordinary dimensional attribute and is not the dimension's surrogate primary key.

You can find new dimension members by performing a lookup from the incoming stream to the master dimension, comparing on the natural key. Any rows that fail the lookup are new dimension members and should be inserted into the dimension table.

If the dimension contains any type 2 attributes, set the row effective date column to the date the dimension member appeared in the system; this is usually yesterday if you are processing nightly. Set the row end date column to the default value for current rows. This should be the largest date, very far in the future, supported by the system. You should avoid using a null value in this second date column because relational databases may generate an error or return the special value Unknown if you attempt to compare a specific value to a NULL.

The next step is to determine if the incoming dimension row has changed. The simplest technique is to compare column by column between the incoming data and the current corresponding member stored in the master dimension table.

If the dimension is large, with more than a million rows, the simple technique of column-wise comparison may be too slow, especially if there are many columns in the dimension table. A popular alternative method is to use a hash or checksum function to speed the comparison process. You can add two new housekeeping columns to the dimension table: hash type1 and hash type2. You should place a hash of a concatenation of the type 1 attributes in the hash type1 column and similarly for hash type2. Hashing algorithms convert a very long string into a much shorter string that is close to unique. The hashes are computed and stored in the dimension table. Then compute hashes on the incoming rowset in exactly the same way, and compare them to the stored values. The comparison on a single, relatively short string column is far more efficient than the pair-wise comparison on dozens of separate columns. Alternatively, the relational database engine may have syntax such as EXCEPT that enables a high-performance query to find the changed rows.

As a general rule, you do not delete dimension rows that have been deleted in the source system because these dimension members probably still have fact table data associated with them in the data warehouse.

Process Changes to Dimension Attributes

The ETL application contains business rules to determine how to handle an attribute value that has changed from the value already stored in the data warehouse. If the revised description is determined to be a legitimate and reliable update to previous information, then the techniques of slowly changing dimensions must be used.

The first step in preparing a dimension row is to decide if you already have that row. If all the incoming dimensional information matches the corresponding row in the dimension table, no further action is required. If the dimensional information has changed, then you can apply changes to the dimension, such as type 1 or type 2.

> **NOTE** You may recall from Chapter 5 that there are three primary methods for tracking changes in attribute values, as well as a set of advanced hybrid techniques. Type 3 requires a change in the structure of the dimension table, creating a new set of columns to hold the "previous" versus "current" versions of the attributes. This type of structural change is seldom automated in the ETL system; it's more likely to be handled as a one-time change in the data model.

The lookup and key assignment logic for handling a changed dimension record during the extract process is shown in Figure 20-5. In this case, the logic flow does not assume the incoming data stream is limited only to new or changed rows.

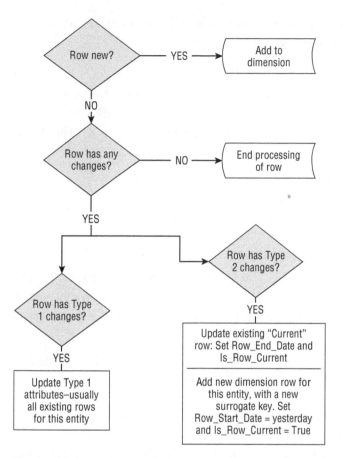

Figure 20-5: Logic flow for handling dimension updates.

Step 8: Fact Table Incremental Processing

Most data warehouse databases are too large to entirely replace the fact tables in a single load window. Instead, new and updated fact rows are incrementally processed.

NOTE It is much more efficient to incrementally load only the records that have been added or updated since the previous load. This is especially true in a journal-style system where history is never changed and only adjustments in the current period are allowed.

The ETL process for fact table incremental processing differs from the historic load. The historic ETL process doesn't need to be fully automated; you can stop the process to examine the data and prepare for the next step. The incremental processing, by contrast, must be fully automated.

Fact Table Extract and Data Quality Checkpoint

As soon as the new and changed fact rows are extracted from the source system, a copy of the untransformed data should be written to the staging area. At the same time, measures of data quality on the raw extracted data are computed. The staged data serves three purposes:

- Archive for auditability
- Provide a starting point after data quality verification
- Provide a starting point for restarting the process

Fact Table Transformations and Surrogate Key Pipeline

The surrogate key pipeline for the incremental fact data is similar to that for the historic data. The key difference is that the error handling for referential integrity violations must be automated. There are several methods for handling referential integrity violations:

- **Halt the load**. This is seldom a useful solution; although, it's often the default in many ETL tools.
- **Throw away error rows**. There are situations in which a missing dimension value is a signal that the data is irrelevant to the business requirements underlying the data warehouse.
- **Write error rows to a file or table for later analysis**. Design a mechanism for moving corrected rows into a suspense file. This approach is not a good choice for a financial system, where it is vital that all rows be loaded.
- **Fix error rows by creating a dummy dimension row and returning its surrogate key to the pipeline**. The most attractive error handling for referential integrity violations in the incremental surrogate key pipeline is to create a dummy dimension row on-the-fly for the unknown natural key. The natural key is the only piece of information that you may have about the dimension member; all the other attributes must be set to default values. This dummy dimension row will be corrected with type 1 updates when the detailed information about that dimension member becomes available.
- **Fix error rows by mapping to a single unknown member in each dimension**. This approach is not recommended. The problem is that all error rows are mapped to the same dimension member, for any unknown natural key values in the fact table extract.

For most systems, you perform the surrogate key lookups against a query, view, or physical table that subsets the dimension table. The dimension table rows are filtered, so the lookup works against only the current version of each dimension member.

Late Arriving Facts and the Surrogate Key Pipeline

In most data warehouses, the incremental load process begins soon after midnight and processes all the transactions that occurred the previous day. However, there are scenarios in which some facts arrive late. This is most likely to happen when the data sources are distributed across multiple machines or even worldwide, and connectivity or latency problems prevent timely data collection.

If all the dimensions are managed completely as type 1 overwrites, late arriving facts present no special challenges. But most systems have a mixture of type 1 and type 2 attributes. The late arriving facts must be associated with the version of the dimension member that was in effect when the fact occurred. That requires a lookup in the dimension table using the row begin and end effective dates.

Incremental Fact Table Load

In the historic fact load, it's important that data loads use fast-load techniques. In most data warehouses, these fast-load techniques may not be available for the incremental load. The fast-load technologies often require stringent conditions on the target table (for example, empty or unindexed). For the incremental load, it's usually faster to use non-fast-load techniques than to fully populate or index the table. For small to medium systems, insert performance is usually adequate.

If your fact table is very large, you should already have partitioned the fact table for manageability reasons. If incremental data is always loading into an empty partition, you should use fast-load techniques. With daily loads, you would create 365 new fact table partitions each year. This is probably too many partitions for a fact table with long history, so consider implementing a process to consolidate daily partitions into weekly or monthly partitions.

Load Snapshot Fact Tables

The largest fact tables are usually transactional. Transaction fact tables are typically loaded only through inserts. Periodic snapshot fact tables are usually loaded at month end. Data for the current month is sometimes updated each day for current-month-to-date. In this scenario, monthly partitioning of the fact table makes it easy to reload the current month with excellent performance.

Accumulating snapshot fact tables monitor relatively short-lived processes, such as filling an order. The accumulating snapshot fact table is characterized by many updates for each fact row over the life of the process. This table is expensive to maintain; although accumulating snapshots are almost always much smaller than the other two types of fact tables.

Speed Up the Load Cycle

Processing only data that has been changed is one way to speed up the ETL cycle. This section lists several additional techniques.

More Frequent Loading

Although it is a huge leap to move from a monthly or weekly process to a nightly one, it is an effective way to shorten the load window. Every nightly process involves 1/30 the data volume of a monthly one. Most data warehouses are on a nightly load cycle.

If nightly processing is too expensive, consider performing some preprocessing on the data throughout the day. During the day, data is moved into a staging database or operational data store where data cleansing tasks are performed. After midnight, you can consolidate multiple changes to dimension members, perform final data quality checks, assign surrogate keys, and move the data into the data warehouse.

Parallel Processing

Another way to shorten the load time is to parallelize the ETL process. This can happen in two ways: multiple steps running in parallel and a single step running in parallel.

- **Multiple load steps.** The ETL job stream is divided into several independent jobs submitted together. You need to think carefully about what goes into each job; the primary goal is to create independent jobs.
- **Parallel execution.** The database itself can also identify certain tasks it can execute in parallel. For example, creating an index can typically be parallelized across as many processors as are available on the machine.

NOTE There are good ways and bad ways to break processing into parallel steps. One simple way to parallelize is to extract all source data together, then load and transform the dimensions, and then simultaneously check referential integrity between the fact table and all dimensions. Unfortunately, this approach is likely to be no faster—and possibly much slower—than the even simpler sequential approach because each step launches parallel processes that compete for the same system resources such as network bandwidth, I/O, and memory. To structure parallel jobs well, you need to account not just for logically sequential steps but also for system resources.

Parallel Structures

You can set up a three-way mirror or clustered configuration on two servers to maintain a continuous load data warehouse, with one server managing the loads and the second handling the queries. The maintenance window is reduced to a few minutes daily to swap the disks attached to each server. This is a great way to provide high system availability.

Depending on the requirements and available budget, there are several similar techniques you can implement for tables, partitions, and databases. For example, you can load into an offline partition or table, and swap it into active duty with minimum downtime. Other systems have two versions of the data warehouse database, one for loading and one for querying. These are less effective, but less expensive, versions of the functionality provided by clustered servers.

Step 9: Aggregate Table and OLAP Loads

An aggregate table is logically easy to build. It's simply the results of a really big aggregate query stored as a table. The problem with building aggregate tables from a query on the fact table, of course, occurs when the fact table is just too big to process within the load window.

If the aggregate table includes an aggregation along the date dimension, perhaps to monthly grain, the aggregate maintenance process is more complex. The current month of data must be updated, or dropped and re-created, to incorporate the current day's data.

A similar problem occurs if the aggregate table is defined on a dimension attribute that is overwritten as a type 1. Any type 1 change in a dimension attribute affects all fact table aggregates and OLAP cubes that are defined on that attribute. An ETL process must "back out" the facts from the old aggregate level and move them to the new one.

It is extremely important that the aggregate management system keep aggregations in sync with the underlying fact data. You do not want to create a system that returns a different result set if the query is directed to the underlying detail facts or to a precomputed aggregation.

Step 10: ETL System Operation and Automation

The ideal ETL operation runs the regular load processes in a lights-out manner, without human intervention. Although this is a difficult outcome to attain, it is possible to get close.

Schedule Jobs

Scheduling jobs is usually straightforward. The ETL tool should contain functionality to schedule a job to kick off at a certain time. Most ETL tools also contain functionality to conditionally execute a second task if the first task successfully completed. It's common to set up an ETL job stream to launch at a certain time, and then query a database or filesystem to see if an event has occurred.

You can also write a script to perform this kind of job control. Every ETL tool has a way to invoke a job from the operating system command line. Many organizations are very comfortable using scripting languages, such as Perl, to manage their job schedules.

Automatically Handle Predictable Exceptions and Errors

Although it's easy enough to launch jobs, it's a harder task to make sure they run to completion, gracefully handling data errors and exceptions. Comprehensive error handling is something that needs to be built into the ETL jobs from the outset.

Gracefully Handle Unpredictable Errors

Some errors are predictable, such as receiving an early arriving fact or a NULL value in a column that's supposed to be populated. For these errors, you can generally design your ETL system to fix the data and continue processing. Other errors are completely unforeseen and range from receiving data that's garbled to experiencing a power outage during processing.

We look for ETL tool features and system design practices to help recover from the unexpected. We generally recommend outfitting fact tables with a single column surrogate key that is assigned sequentially to new records that are being loaded. If a large load job unexpectedly halts, the fact table surrogate key allows the load to resume from a reliable point, or back out the load by constraining on a contiguous range of the surrogate keys.

Real-Time Implications

Real-time processing is an increasingly common requirement in data warehousing. There is a strong possibility that your DW/BI system will have a real-time requirement. Some business users expect the data warehouse to be continuously updated throughout the day and grow impatient with stale data. Building a real-time DW/BI system requires gathering a very precise understanding of the true business requirements for real-time data and identifying an appropriate ETL architecture, incorporating a variety of technologies married with a solid platform.

Real-Time Triage

Asking business users if they want "real-time" delivery of data is a frustrating exercise for the DW/BI team. Faced with no constraints, most users will say, "That sounds good; go for it!" This kind of response is almost worthless.

To avoid this situation, we recommend dividing the real-time design challenge into three categories, called instantaneous, intra-day, and daily. We use these terms when we talk to business users about their needs and then design our data delivery pipelines differently for each option. Figure 20-6 summarizes the issues that arise as data is delivered faster.

Daily	Intra-Day	Instantaneous
Batch processing ETL	Micro-batch ETL	Streaming EII/ETL
Wait for file ready	Probe with queries or subscribe to message bus	Drive user presentation from source application
Conventional file table time partition	Daily hot fact table time partition	Separate from fact table
Reconciled	Provisional	Provisional
Complete transaction set	Individual transactions	Transaction fragments
Column screens	Column screens	Column screens
Structure screens	Structure screens	--
Business rule screens	--	--
Final results	Results updated, corrected nightly	Results updated, possibly repudiated nightly

Figure 20-6: Data quality trade-offs with low latency delivery.

Instantaneous means the data visible on the screen represents the true state of the source transaction system at every instant. When the source system status changes, the screen instantly and synchronously responds. An instantaneous real-time system is usually implemented as an enterprise information integration (EII) solution, where the source system itself is responsible for supporting the update of remote users' screens and servicing query requests. Obviously, such a system must limit the complexity of the query requests because all the processing is done on the source system. EII solutions typically involve no caching of data in the ETL pipeline because EII solutions by definition have no delays between the source systems and the users' screens. Some situations are plausible candidates for an instantaneous real-time solution. Inventory status tracking may be a good example, where the decision maker has the right to commit available inventory to a customer in real time.

Intra-day means the data visible on the screen is updated many times per day but is not guaranteed to be the absolute current truth. Most of us are familiar with stock market quote data that is current to within 15 minutes but is not instantaneous.

The technology for delivering frequent real-time data (as well as the slower daily data) is distinctly different from instantaneous real-time delivery. Frequently delivered data is usually processed as micro-batches in a conventional ETL architecture. This means the data undergoes the full gamut of change data capture, extract, staging to file storage in the ETL back room of the data warehouse, cleaning and error checking, conforming to enterprise data standards, assigning of surrogate keys, and possibly a host of other transformations to make the data ready to load into the presentation server. Almost all these steps must be omitted or drastically reduced in an EII solution. The big difference between intra-day and daily delivered data is in the first two steps: change data capture and extract. To capture data many times per day from the source system, the data warehouse usually must tap into a high bandwidth communications channel, such as message queue traffic between legacy applications, an accumulating transaction log file, or low level database triggers coming from the transaction system every time something happens.

Daily means the data visible on the screen is valid as of a batch file download or reconciliation from the source system at the end of the previous working day. There is a lot to recommend daily data. Quite often processes are run on the source system at the end of the working day that correct the raw data. When this reconciliation becomes available, that signals the ETL system to perform a reliable and stable download of the data. If you have this situation, you should explain to the business users what compromises they will experience if they demand instantaneous or intra-day updated data. Daily updated data usually involves reading a batch file prepared by the source system or performing an extract query when a source system readiness flag is set. This, of course, is the simplest extract scenario because you wait for the source system to be ready and available.

Real-Time Architecture Trade-Offs

Responding to real-time requirements means you need to change the DW/BI architecture to get data to the business users' screens faster. The architectural choices involve trade-offs that affect data quality and administration.

You can assume the overall goals for ETL system owners are not changed or compromised by moving to real-time delivery. You can remain just as committed to data quality, integration, security, compliance, backup, recovery, and archiving as you were before starting to design a real-time system. If you agree with this statement, then read the following very carefully! The following sections discuss the typical trade-offs that occur as you implement a more real-time architecture:

Replace Batch Files

Consider replacing a batch file extract with reading from a message queue or transaction log file. A batch file delivered from the source system may represent a clean and consistent view of the source data. The batch file may contain only those records resulting from completed transactions. Foreign keys in the batch files are probably resolved, such as when the file contains an order from a new customer whose complete identity may be delivered with the batch file. Message queue and log file data, on the other hand, is raw instantaneous data that may not be subject to any corrective process or business rule enforcement in the source system. In the worst case, this raw data may 1) be incorrect or incomplete because additional transactions may arrive later; 2) contain unresolved foreign keys that the DW/BI system has not yet processed; and 3) require a parallel batch-oriented ETL data flow to correct or even replace the hot real-time data each 24 hours. And if the source system subsequently applies complex business rules to the input transactions first seen in the message queues or the log files, then you really don't want to recapitulate these business rules in the ETL system!

Limit Data Quality Screens

Consider restricting data quality screening only to column screens and simple decode lookups. As the time to process data moving through the ETL pipeline is reduced, it may be necessary to eliminate more costly data quality screening, especially structure screens and business rule screens. Remember that column screens involve single field tests and/or simple lookups to replace or expand known values. Even in the most aggressive real-time applications, most column screens should survive. But structure screens and business rule screens by definition require multiple fields, multiple records, and possibly multiple tables. You may not have time to pass an address block of fields to an address analyzer. You may not check referential integrity between tables. You may not be able to perform a remote credit check through a web service. All this may require informing the users of the provisional and potentially unreliable state of the raw real-time data and may require that you implement a parallel, batch-oriented ETL pipeline that overwrites the real-time data periodically with properly checked data.

Post Facts with Dimensions

You should allow early arriving facts to be posted with old copies of dimensions. In the real-time world, it is common to receive transaction events before the context (such as the identity of the customer) of those transactions is updated. In other words, the facts arrive before the dimensions. If the real-time system cannot wait for the dimensions to be resolved, then old copies of the dimensions must be used if they are available, or generic empty versions of the dimensions must be used otherwise. If and when revised versions of the dimensions are received, the data warehouse may decide to post those into the hot partition or delay updating the dimension until a batch process takes over, possibly at the end of the day. In any case, the users need to understand there may be an ephemeral window of time where the dimensions don't exactly describe the facts.

Eliminate Data Staging

Some real-time architectures, especially EII systems, stream data directly from the production source system to the users' screens without writing the data to permanent storage in the ETL pipeline. If this kind of system is part of the DW/BI team's responsibility, then the team should have a serious talk with senior management about whether backup, recovery, archiving, and compliance responsibilities can be met, or whether those responsibilities are now the sole concern of the production source system.

Real-Time Partitions in the Presentation Server

To support real-time requirements, the data warehouse must seamlessly extend its existing historical time series right up to the current instant. If the customer has placed an order in the last hour, you need to see this order in the context of the entire customer relationship. Furthermore, you need to track the hourly status of this most current order as it changes during the day. Even though the gap between the production transaction processing systems and the DW/BI system has shrunk in most cases to 24 hours, the insatiable needs of your business users require the data warehouse to fill this gap with real-time data.

One design solution for responding to this crunch is building a real-time partition as an extension of the conventional, static data warehouse. To achieve real-time reporting, a special partition is built that is physically and administratively separated from the conventional data warehouse tables. Ideally, the real-time partition is a true database partition where the fact table in question is partitioned by activity date.

In either case, the real-time partition ideally should meet the following tough set of requirements:

- Contain all the activity that has occurred since the last update of the static data warehouse.
- Link as seamlessly as possible to the grain and content of the static data warehouse fact tables, ideally as a true physical partition of the fact table.
- Be indexed so lightly that incoming data can continuously be "dribbled in." Ideally, the real-time partition is completely unindexed; however, this may not be possible in certain RDBMSs where indexes have been built that are not logically aligned with the partitioning scheme.
- Support highly responsive queries even in the absence of indexes by pinning the real-time partition in memory.

The real-time partition can be used effectively with both transaction and periodic snapshot fact tables. We have not found this approach needed with accumulating snapshot fact tables.

Transaction Real-Time Partition

If the static data warehouse fact table has a transaction grain, it contains exactly one row for each individual transaction in the source system from the beginning of "recorded history." The real-time partition has exactly the same dimensional structure as its underlying static fact table. It contains only the transactions that have occurred since midnight when you last loaded the regular fact tables. The real-time partition may be completely unindexed, both because you need to maintain a continuously open window for loading and because there is no time series because only today's data is kept in this table.

In a relatively large retail environment experiencing 10 million transactions per day, the static fact table would be pretty big. Assuming each transaction grain row is 40 bytes wide (seven dimensions plus three facts, all packed into 4-byte columns), you accumulate 400 MB of data each day. Over a year, this would amount to approximately 150 GB of raw data. Such a fact table would be heavily indexed and supported by aggregates. But the daily real-time slice of 400 MB should be pinned in memory. The real-time partition can remain biased toward very fast-loading performance but at the same time provide speedy query performance.

Periodic Snapshot Real-Time Partition

If the static data warehouse fact table has a periodic grain (say, monthly), then the real-time partition can be viewed as the current hot rolling month. Suppose you are a big retail bank with 15 million accounts. The static fact table has the grain of account by month. A 36-month time series would result in 540 million fact table rows. Again, this table would be extensively indexed and supported by aggregates to provide query good performance. The real-time partition, on the other hand, is just an image of the current developing month, updated continuously as the month progresses. Semi-additive balances and fully additive facts are adjusted as frequently as they are reported. In a retail bank, the supertype fact table spanning all account types is likely to be quite narrow, with perhaps four dimensions and four facts, resulting in a real-time partition of 480 MB. The real-time partition again can be pinned in memory.

On the last day of the month, the periodic real-time partition can, with luck, just be merged onto the less volatile fact table as the most current month, and the process can start again with an empty real-time partition.

Summary

The previous chapter introduced 34 subsystems that are possible within a comprehensive ETL implementation. In this chapter, we provided detailed practical advice for actually building and deploying the ETL system. Perhaps the most interesting perspective is to separate the initial historical loads from the ongoing incremental loads. These processes are quite different.

In general we recommend using a commercial ETL tool as opposed to maintaining a library of scripts, even though the ETL tools can be expensive and have a significant learning curve. ETL systems, more than any other part of the DW/BI edifice, are legacy systems that need to be maintainable and scalable over long periods of time and over changes of personnel.

We concluded this chapter with some design perspectives for real-time (low latency) delivery of data. Not only are the real-time architectures different from conventional batch processing, but data quality is compromised as the latency is progressively lowered. Business users need to be thoughtful participants in this design trade-off.

21

Big Data Analytics

In this chapter, we introduce big data in all its glory and show how it expands the mission of the DW/BI system. We conclude with a comprehensive list of big data best practices.

Chapter 21 discusses the following concepts:

- Comparison of two architectural approaches for tackling big data analytics
- Management, architecture, modeling, and governance best practices for dealing with big data

Big Data Overview

What is *big data*? Its bigness is actually not the most interesting characteristic. Big data is structured, semistructured, unstructured, and raw data in many different formats, in some cases looking totally different than the clean scalar numbers and text you have stored in your data warehouses for the last 30 years. Much big data cannot be analyzed with anything that looks like SQL. But most important, big data is a paradigm shift in how you think about data assets, where you collect them, how you analyze them, and how you monetize the insights from the analysis.

The big data movement has gathered momentum as a large number of use cases have been recognized that fall into the category of big data analytics. These use cases include:

- Search ranking
- Ad tracking
- Location and proximity tracking
- Causal factor discovery
- Social CRM
- Document similarity testing

- Genomics analysis
- Cohort group discovery
- In-flight aircraft status
- Smart utility meters
- Building sensors
- Satellite image comparison
- CAT scan comparison
- Financial account fraud detection and intervention
- Computer system hacking detection and intervention
- Online game gesture tracking
- Big science data analysis
- Generic name-value pair analysis
- Loan risk analysis and insurance policy underwriting
- Customer churn analysis

Given the breadth of potential use cases, this chapter focuses on the architectural approaches for tackling big data, along with our recommended best practices, but not specific dimensional designs for each use case.

Conventional RDBMSs and SQL simply cannot store or analyze this wide range of use cases. To fully address big data, a candidate system would have to be capable of the following:

1. Scaling to easily support petabytes (thousands of terabytes) of data.
2. Being distributed across thousands of processors, potentially geographically dispersed and potentially heterogeneous.
3. Storing the data in the original captured formats while supporting query and analysis applications without converting or moving the data.
4. Subsecond response time for highly constrained standard SQL queries.
5. Embedding arbitrarily complex user-defined functions (UDFs) within processing requests.
6. Implementing UDFs in a wide variety of industry-standard procedural languages.
7. Assembling extensive libraries of reusable UDFs crossing most or all the use cases.
8. Executing UDFs as relation scans over petabyte-sized data sets in a few minutes.
9. Supporting a wide variety of data types growing to include images, waveforms, arbitrarily hierarchical data structures, and collections of name-value pairs.
10. Loading data to be ready for analysis, at very high rates, at least gigabytes per second.

11. Integrating data from multiple sources during the load process at very high rates (GB/sec).

12. Loading data into the database before declaring or discovering its structure.

13. Executing certain streaming analytic queries in real time on incoming load data.

14. Updating data in place at full load speeds.

15. Joining a billion-row dimension table to a trillion-row fact table without preclustering the dimension table with the fact table.

16. Scheduling and executing complex multi-hundred node workflows.

17. Being configured without being subject to a single point of failure.

18. Having failover and process continuation when processing nodes fail.

19. Supporting extreme, mixed workloads including thousands of geographically dispersed online users and programs executing a variety of requests ranging from ad hoc queries to strategic analysis, while loading data in batch and streaming fashion.

In response to these challenges, two architectures have emerged: extended RDBMSs and MapReduce/Hadoop.

Extended RDBMS Architecture

Existing RDBMS vendors are extending the classic relational data types to include some of the new data types required by big data, as shown by the arrows in the Figure 21-1.

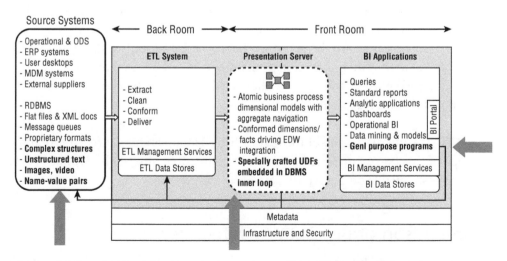

Figure 21-1: Relational DBMS architecture showing big data extensions.

Existing RDBMSs must open their doors to loading and processing a much broader range of data types including complex structures such as vectors, matrices, and custom *hyperstructured data*. At the other end of the spectrum, the RDBMSs need to load and process unstructured and semistructured text, as well as images, video, and collections of name-value pairs, sometimes called *data bags*.

But it is not sufficient for RDBMSs to merely host the new data types as *blobs* to be delivered at some later time to a BI application that can interpret the data, although this alternative has always been possible. To really own big data, RDBMSs must allow the new data types to be processed within the DBMS inner loop by means of specially crafted user-defined functions (UDFs) written by business user analysts.

Finally, a valuable use case is to process the data twice through the RDBMS, where in the first pass the RDBMS is used as a *fact extractor* on the original data, and then in the second pass, these results are automatically fed back to the RDBMS input as conventional relational rows, columns, and data types.

MapReduce/Hadoop Architecture

The alternative architecture, MapReduce/Hadoop, is an open source top-level Apache project with many components. MapReduce is a processing framework originally developed by Google in the early 2000s for performing web page searches across thousands of physically separated machines. The MapReduce approach is extremely general. Complete MapReduce systems can be implemented in a variety of languages; the most significant implementation is in Java. MapReduce is actually a UDF execution framework, where the "F" can be extraordinarily complex. The most significant implementation of MapReduce is Apache Hadoop, known simply as Hadoop. The Hadoop project has thousands of contributors and a whole industry of diverse applications. Hadoop runs natively on its own *Hadoop distributed file system* (*HDFS*) and can also read and write to Amazon S3 and others. Conventional database vendors are also implementing interfaces to allow Hadoop jobs to be run over massively distributed instances of their databases.

> **NOTE**   A full discussion of the MapReduce/Hadoop architecture is beyond the scope of this book. Interested readers are invited to study the in depth big data resources available on our website at www.kimballgroup.com.

Comparison of Big Data Architectures

The two big data architecture approaches have separate long-term advantages and are likely to coexist far into the future. At the time of this writing, the characteristics of the two architectures are summarized in the Figure 21-2.

Extended Relational DBMS	MapReduce/Hadoop
Proprietary, mostly	Open source
Expensive	Less expensive
Data must be structured	Data does not require structuring
Great for speedy indexed lookups	Great for massive full data scans
Deep support for relational semantics	Indirect support for relational semantics, e.g., Hive
Indirect support for complex data structures	Deep support for complex data structures
Indirect support for iteration, complex branching	Deep support for iteration, complex branching
Deep support for transaction processing	Little or no support for transaction processing

Figure 21-2: Comparison of relational DBMS and MapReduce/Hadoop architectures.

Recommended Best Practices for Big Data

Although the big data marketplace is anything but mature, the industry now has a decade of accumulated experience. In that time, a number of best practices specific to big data have emerged. This section attempts to capture these best practices, steering a middle ground between high-level motherhood admonitions versus down-in-the-weeds technical minutiae specific to a single tool.

Having said that, one should recognize that the industry has a well-tested set of best practices developed over the last 30 years for relationally-based data warehouses that surely are relevant to big data. We list them briefly. They are to:

- Drive the choice of data sources feeding the data warehouse from business needs.
- Focus incessantly on user interface simplicity and performance.
- Think dimensionally: Divide the world into dimensions and facts.
- Integrate separate data sources with conformed dimensions.
- Track time variance with slowly changing dimensions (SCDs).
- Anchor all dimensions with durable surrogate keys.

In the remainder of this section, we divide big data best practices into four categories: management, architecture, data modeling, and governance.

Management Best Practices for Big Data

The following best practices apply to the overall management of a big data environment.

Structure Big Data Environments Around Analytics

Consider structuring big data environments around analytics and not ad hoc querying or standard reporting. Every step in the data pathway from original source to analyst's screen must support complex analytic routines implemented as user-defined functions (UDFs) or via a metadata-driven development environment that can be programmed for each type of analysis. This includes loaders, cleansers, integrators, user interfaces, and finally BI tools, as further discussed in the architectural best practices section.

Delay Building Legacy Environments

It's not a good idea to attempt building a legacy big data environment at this time. The big data environment is changing too rapidly to consider building a long-lasting legacy foundation. Rather, plan for disruptive changes coming from every direction: new data types, competitive challenges, programming approaches, hardware, networking technology, and services offered by literally hundreds of new big data providers. For the foreseeable future, maintain a balance among several implementation approaches including Hadoop, traditional grid computing, pushdown optimization in an RDBMS, on-premise computing, cloud computing, and even the mainframe. None of these approaches will be the single winner in the long run. Platform as a service (PaaS) providers offer an attractive option that can help assemble a compatible set of tools.

Think of Hadoop as a flexible, general purpose environment for many forms of ETL processing, where the goal is to add sufficient structure and context to big data so that it can be loaded into an RDBMS. The same data in Hadoop can be accessed and transformed with Hive, Pig, HBase, and MapReduce code written in a variety of languages, even simultaneously.

This demands flexibility. Assume you will reprogram and rehost all your big data applications within two years. Choose approaches that can be reprogrammed and rehosted. Consider using a metadata-driven codeless development environment to increase productivity and help insulate from underlying technology changes.

Build From Sandbox Results

Consider embracing sandbox silos and building a practice of productionizing sandbox results. Allow data scientists to construct their data experiments and prototypes using their preferred languages and programming environments. Then, after proof of concept, systematically reprogram these implementations with an IT turnover team. Here are a couple of examples to illustrate this recommendation:

The production environment for custom analytic programming might be MatLab within PostgreSQL or SAS within a Teradata RDBMS, but the data scientists might be building their proofs of concept in a wide variety of their own preferred languages and architectures. The key insight here: IT must be uncharacteristically tolerant of the range of technologies the data scientists use and be prepared in many cases to re-implement the data scientists' work in a standard set of technologies that can be supported over the long haul. The sandbox development environment might be custom R code directly accessing Hadoop, but controlled by a metadata-driven driven ETL tool. Then when the data scientist is ready to hand over the proof of concept, much of the logic could immediately be redeployed under the ETL tool to run in a grid computing environment that is scalable, highly available, and secure.

Try Simple Applications First

You can put your toe in the water with a simple big data application, such as backup and archiving. While starting with a big data program, and searching for valuable business use cases with limited risk and when assembling the requisite big data skills, consider using Hadoop as a low-cost, flexible backup and archiving technology. Hadoop can store and retrieve data in the full range of formats from totally unstructured to highly structured specialized formats. This approach may also enable you address the *sunsetting* challenge where original applications may not be available in the distant future (perhaps because of licensing restrictions); you can dump data from those applications into your documented format.

Architecture Best Practices for Big Data

The following best practices affect the overall structure and organization of your big data environment.

Plan a Data Highway

You should plan for a logical *data highway* with multiple caches of increasing latency. Physically implement only those caches appropriate for your environment. The data highway can have as many as five caches of increasing data latency, each with its distinct analytic advantages and trade-offs, as shown in Figure 21-3.

Figure 21-3: Big data caches of increasing latency and data quality.

Here are potential examples of the five data caches:

- **Raw source applications:** Credit card fraud detection, immediate complex event processing (CEP) including network stability and cyber attack detection.
- **Real time applications:** Web page ad selection, personalized price promotions, on-line games monitoring.
- **Business activity applications:** Low-latency KPI dashboards pushed to users, trouble ticket tracking, process completion tracking, "fused" CEP reporting, customer service portals and dashboards, and mobile sales apps.

- ■ **Top line applications:** Tactical reporting, promotion tracking, midcourse corrections based on social media buzz. *Top line* refers to the common practice by senior managers of seeing a quick top line review of what has happened in the enterprise over the past 24 hours.

- ■ **Data warehouse and long time series applications:** All forms of reporting, ad hoc querying, historical analysis, master data management, large scale temporal dynamics, and Markov chain analysis.

Each cache that exists in a given environment is physical and distinct from the other caches. Data moves from the raw source down this highway through ETL processes. There may be multiple paths from the raw source to intermediate caches. For instance, data could go to the real-time cache to drive a zero latency-style user interface, but at the same time be extracted directly into a daily top line cache that would look like a classic operational data store (ODS). Then the data from this ODS could feed the data warehouse. Data also flows in the reverse direction along the highway. We'll discuss implementing backflows later in this section.

Much of the data along this highway must remain in nonrelational formats ranging from unstructured text to complex multistructured data, such as images, arrays, graphs, links, matrices, and sets of name-value pairs.

Build a Fact Extractor from Big Data

It's a good idea to use big data analytics as a fact extractor to move data to the next cache. For example, the analysis of unstructured text tweets can produce a whole set of numerical, trendable sentiment measures including share of voice, audience engagement, conversation reach, active advocates, advocate influence, advocacy impact, resolution rate, resolution time, satisfaction score, topic trends, sentiment ratio, and idea impact.

Build Comprehensive Ecosystems

You can use big data integration to build comprehensive ecosystems that integrate conventional structured RDBMS data, documents, e-mails, and in-house, business-oriented social networking. One of the potent messages from big data is the ability to integrate disparate data sources of different modalities. You get streams of data from new data producing channels such as social networks, mobile devices, and automated alert processes. Imagine a big financial institution handling millions of accounts, tens of millions of associated paper documents, and thousands of professionals both within the organization and in the field as partners or customers. Now set up a secure social network of all the trusted parties to communicate as business is conducted. Much of this communication is significant and should be saved in a queryable way. You could capture all this information in Hadoop, dimensionalize it (as you see in the following modeling best practices), use it in the course of business, and then back it up and archive it.

Plan for Data Quality

You can plan for data quality to be better further along the data highway. This is the classic trade-off of latency versus quality. Analysts and business users must accept the reality that very low latency (that is, immediate) data is unavoidably dirty because there are limits to how much cleansing and diagnosing can be done in very short time intervals. Tests and corrections on individual field contents can be performed at the fastest data transfer rates. Tests and corrections on structural relationships among fields and across data sources are necessarily slower. Tests and corrections involving complex business rules range from being instantaneous (such as a set of dates being in a certain order) to taking arbitrarily long times (such as waiting to see if a threshold of unusual events has been exceeded). And finally, slower ETL processes, such as those feeding the daily top line cache, often are built on fundamentally more complete data, for example where incomplete transaction sets and repudiated transactions have been eliminated. In this case, the instantaneous data feeds simply do not have the correct information.

Add Value to Data as Soon as Possible

You should apply filtering, cleansing, pruning, conforming, matching, joining, and diagnosing at the earliest touch points possible. This is a corollary of the previous best practice. Each step on the data highway provides more time to add value to the data. Filtering, cleansing, and pruning the data reduces the amount transferred to the next cache and eliminates irrelevant or corrupted data. To be fair, there is a school of thought that applies cleansing logic only at analysis run time because cleansing might delete "interesting outliers." Conforming takes the active step of placing highly administered enterprise attributes into major entities such as customer, product, and date. The existence of these conformed attributes allows high value joins to be made across separate application domains. A shorter name for this step is "integration!" Diagnosing allows many interesting attributes to be added to data, including special confidence tags and textual identifiers representing behavior clusters identified by a data mining professional.

Implement Backflow to Earlier Caches

You should implement backflows, especially from the data warehouse, to earlier caches on the data highway. The highly administered dimensions in the data warehouse, such as customer, product, and date, should be connected back to data in earlier caches. Ideally, all that is needed are unique durable keys for these entities in all the caches. The corollary here is that Job One in each ETL step from one cache to the next is to replace idiosyncratic proprietary keys with the unique durable keys so that analysis in each cache can take advantage of the rich upstream content with a simple join on the unique durable key. Can this ETL step be performed even when transferring raw source data into the real time cache in less than a second? Maybe....

Dimension data is not the only data to be transferred back down the highway toward the source. Derived data from fact tables, such as historical summaries and complex data mining findings, can be packaged as simple indicators or grand totals and then transferred to earlier caches on the data highway.

Implement Streaming Data

You should implement streaming data analytics in selected data flows. An interesting angle on low latency data is the need to begin serious analysis on the data as it streams in, but possibly far before the data transfer process terminates. There is significant interest in streaming analysis systems, which allow SQL-like queries to process the data as it flows into the system. In some use cases, when the results of a streaming query surpass a threshold, the analysis can be halted without running the job to the bitter end. An academic effort, known as continuous query language (CQL), has made impressive progress in defining the requirements for streaming data processing including clever semantics for dynamically moving time windows on the streaming data. Look for CQL language extensions and streaming data query capabilities in the load programs for both RDBMSs and HDFS deployed data sets. An ideal implementation would allow streaming data analysis to take place while the data is loaded at gigabytes per second.

Avoid Boundary Crashes

You should implement far limits on scalability to avoid a *boundary crash*. In the early days of computer programming, when machines had pathetically small hard drives and real memories, boundary crashes were common and were the bane of applications development. When the application ran out of disk space or real memory, the developer resorted to elaborate measures, usually requiring significant programming that added nothing to the application's primary function. Boundary crashes for normal database applications have more or less been eliminated, but big data raises this issue again. Hadoop is an architecture that dramatically reduces programming scalability concerns because you can, for the most part, indefinitely add commodity hardware. Of course, even commodity hardware must be provisioned, plugged in, and have high bandwidth network connections. The lesson is to plan far ahead for scaling out to huge volumes and throughputs.

Move Prototypes to a Private Cloud

Consider performing big data prototyping on a public cloud and then moving to a private cloud. The advantage of a public cloud is it can be provisioned and scaled up instantly. In those cases in which the sensitivity of the data allows quick in-and-out prototyping, this can be effective. Just remember not to leave a huge data set online with the public cloud provider over the weekend when the programmers have gone home!

However, keep in mind that in some cases in which you are trying to exploit data locality with rack-aware MapReduce processes, you may not use a public cloud service because it may not provide the data storage control needed.

Strive for Performance Improvements

Search for and expect tenfold to hundredfold performance improvements over time, recognizing the paradigm shift for analysis at high speeds. The openness of the big data marketplace has encouraged hundreds of special purpose tightly coded solutions for specific kinds of analysis. This is a giant blessing and a curse. When free from being controlled by a big vendor's RDBMS optimizer and inner loop, smart developers can implement spot solutions that are truly 100 times as fast as standard techniques. For instance, some impressive progress has been made on the infamous "big join" problem in which a billion-row dimension is joined to a trillion-row fact table. The challenge is these individual spot solutions may not be part of a unified single architecture.

One very current big data theme is visualization of data sets. "Flying around" a petabyte of data requires spectacular performance! Visualization of big data is an exciting new area of development that enables both analysis and discovery of unexpected features and data profiling.

Another exciting application that imposes huge performance demands is "semantic zooming without pre-aggregations," in which the analyst descends from a highly aggregated level to progressively more detailed levels in unstructured or semistructured data, analogous to zooming in on a map.

The important lesson behind this best practice is that revolutionary advances in your power to consume and analyze big data can result from 10x to 100x performance gains, and you have to be prepared to add these developments to your suite of tools.

Monitor Compute Resources

You should separate big data analytic workloads from the conventional data warehouse to preserve service level agreements. If your big data is hosted in Hadoop, it probably doesn't compete for resources with your conventional RDBMS-based data warehouse. However, be cautious if your big data analytics run on the data warehouse machine because big data requirements change rapidly and inevitably in the direction of requiring more compute resources.

Exploit In-Database Analytics

Remember to exploit the unique capabilities of in-database analytics. The major RDBMS players all significantly invest in in-database analytics. After you pay the price of loading data into relational tables, SQL can be combined with analytic extensions in extremely powerful ways. In particular, PostgreSQL, an open source database, has extensible syntax for adding powerful user defined functions in the inner loop.

Data Modeling Best Practices for Big Data

The following best practices affect the logical and physical structures of the data.

Think Dimensionally

By thinking dimensionally, we mean dividing the world into dimensions and facts. Business users find the concept of dimensions to be natural and obvious. No matter what the format of the data, the basic associated entities such as customer, product, service, location, or time can always be found. In the following best practice you see how, with a little discipline, dimensions can be used to integrate data sources. But before getting to the integration finish line, you must identify the dimensions in each data source and attach them to every low-level atomic data observation. This process of dimensionalization is a good application for big data analytics. For example, a single Twitter tweet "Wow! That is awesome!" may not seem to contain anything worth dimensionalizing, but with some analysis you often can get customer (or citizen or patient), location, product (or service or contract or event), marketplace condition, provider, weather, cohort group (or demographic cluster), session, triggering prior event, final outcome, and the list goes on. Some form of automated dimensionalizing is required to stay ahead of the high-velocity streams of data. As we point out in a subsequent best practice, incoming data should be fully dimensionalized at the earliest extraction step in as close to real time as possible.

Integrate Separate Data Sources with Conformed Dimensions

Conformed dimensions are the glue that holds together separate data sources and enable them to be combined in a single analysis. Conformed dimensions are perhaps the most powerful best practice from the conventional DW/BI world that should be inherited by big data.

The basic idea behind conformed dimensions is the presence of one or more enterprise attributes (fields) in the versions of dimensions associated with separate data sources. For instance, every customer-facing process in an enterprise will have some variation of a customer dimension. These variations of the customer dimension may have different keys, different field definitions, and even different granularity. But even in the worst cases of incompatible data, one or more enterprise attributes can be defined that can be embedded in all the customer dimension variations. For instance, a customer demographic category is a plausible choice. Such a descriptor could be attached to nearly every customer dimension, even those at higher levels of aggregation. After this has been done, analyses on this customer demographic category can cross every participating data source with a simple sort-merge process after separate queries are run against the different data sources. Best of all, the step of introducing the enterprise attributes into the separate databases can be done in an incremental, agile, and nondisruptive way as described in Chapter 8: Customer Relationship Management and Chapter 19: ETL Subsystems and Techniques. All existing analysis applications will continue to run as the conformed dimension content is rolled out.

Anchor Dimensions with Durable Surrogate Keys

If there is one lesson we have learned in the data warehouse world, it is not to anchor major entities such as customer, product, and time with the natural keys defined by a specific application. These natural keys turn out to be a snare and a delusion in the real world. They are incompatible across applications and are poorly administered, and they are administered by someone else who may not have the interests of the data warehouse at heart. The first step in every data source is to augment the natural key coming from a source with an enterprisewide durable surrogate key. Durable means there is no business rule that can change the key. The durable key belongs to the DW/BI system, not to the data source. Surrogate means the keys themselves are simple integers either assigned in sequence or generated by a robust hashing algorithm that guarantees uniqueness. An isolated surrogate key has no applications content. It is just an identifier.

The big data world is filled with obvious dimensions that must possess durable surrogate keys. Earlier in this chapter when we proposed pushing data backward down the data highway, we relied on the presence of the durable surrogate keys to make this process work. We also stated that Job One on every data extraction from a raw source was to embed the durable surrogate keys in the appropriate dimensions.

Expect to Integrate Structured and Unstructured Data

Big data considerably broadens the integration challenge. Much big data will never end up in a relational database; rather it will stay in Hadoop or a grid. But after you are armed with conformed dimensions and durable surrogate keys, all forms of data can be combined in single analyses. For example, a medical study can select a group of patients with certain demographic and health status attributes and then combine their conventional DW/BI data with image data (photographs, X-rays, EKGs, and so on), free form text data (physician's notes), social media sentiments (opinions of treatment), and cohort group linkages (patients with similar situations), and doctors with similar patients.

Use Slowly Changing Dimensions

You should track time variance with slowly changing dimensions (SCDs). Tracking time variance of dimensions is an old and venerable best practice from the data warehouse world. Chapter 5: Procurement makes a powerful case for using SCD techniques for handling time variance. This is just as important in the big data world as it is in the conventional data warehouse world.

Declare Data Structure at Analysis Time

You must get used to not declaring data structures until analysis time. One of the charms of big data is putting off declaring data structures at the time of loading into Hadoop or a data grid. This brings many advantages. The data structures may not be understood at load time. The data may have such variable content that a single data structure either makes no sense or forces you to modify the data to fit into a structure. If you can load data into Hadoop, for instance, without declaring its structure, you can avoid a resource intensive step. And finally, different analysts may legitimately see the same data in different ways. Of course, there is a penalty in some cases because data without a declared structure may be difficult or impossible to index for rapid access, as in an RDBMS. However, most big data analysis algorithms process entire data sets without expecting precise filtering of subsets of the data.

This best practice conflicts with traditional RDBMS methodologies, which puts a lot of emphasis on modeling the data carefully before loading. But this does not lead to a deadly conflict. For data destined for an RDBMS, the transfer from a Hadoop or data grid environment and from a name-value pair structure into RDBMS named columns can be thought of as a valuable ETL step.

Load Data as Simple Name-Value Pairs

Consider building technology around name-value pair data sources. Big data sources are filled with surprises. In many cases, you open the fire hose and discover unexpected or undocumented data content, which you must nevertheless load at gigabytes per second. The escape from this problem is to load this data as simple name-value pairs. For example, if an applicant were to disclose her financial assets, as illustrated with Figures 8-7 and 8-8, she might declare something unexpected such as "rare postage stamp = $10,000." In a name-value pair data set, this would be loaded gracefully, even though you had never seen "rare postage stamp" and didn't know what to do with it at load time. Of course, this practice meshes nicely with the previous practice of deferring the declaration of data structures until past load time.

Many MapReduce programming frameworks require data to be presented as name-value pairs, which makes sense given the complete possible generality of big data.

Rapidly Prototype Using Data Virtualization

Consider using data virtualization to allow rapid prototyping and schema altera-tions. Data virtualization is a powerful technique for declaring different logical data structures on underlying physical data. Standard view definitions in SQL are a good example of data virtualization. In theory, data virtualization can present a data source in any format the analyst needs. But data virtualization trades off the cost of computing at run time with the cost of ETL to build physical tables before run time. Data virtualization is a powerful way to prototype data structures and make rapid alterations or provide distinct alternatives. The best data virtualization strategy is to expect to materialize the virtual schemas when they have been tested and vetted and the analysts want the performance improvements of actual physical tables.

Data Governance Best Practices for Big Data

The following best practices apply to managing big data as a valuable enterprise asset.

There is No Such Thing as Big Data Governance

Now that we have your attention, the point is that data governance must be a comprehensive approach for the entire data ecosystem, not a spot solution for big data in isolation. Data governance for big data should be an extension of the approach used to govern all the enterprise data. At a minimum, data governance embraces privacy, security, compliance, data quality, metadata management, master data management, and the business glossary that exposes definitions and context to the business community.

Dimensionalize the Data before Applying Governance

Here is an interesting challenge big data introduces: You must apply data governance principles even when you don't know what to expect from the content of the data. You may receive data arriving at gigabytes per minute, often as name-value pairs with unexpected content. The best chance at classifying data in ways that are important to your data governance responsibilities is to dimensionalize it as fully as possible at the earliest stage in the data pipeline. Parse it, match it, and apply identity resolution on-the-fly. We made this same point when arguing for the benefits of data integration, but here we advocate against even using the data before this dimensionalizing step.

Privacy is the Most Important Governance Perspective

If you analyze data sets that include identifying information about individuals or organizations, privacy is the most important governance perspective. Although every aspect of data governance looms as critically important, in these cases, privacy carries the most responsibility and business risk. Egregious episodes of compromising the privacy of individuals or groups can damage your reputation, diminish marketplace trust, expose you to civil lawsuits, and get you in trouble with the law. At the least, for most forms of analysis, personal details must be masked, and data aggregated enough to not allow identification of individuals. At the time of this writing, special attention must be paid when storing sensitive data in Hadoop because after data is written to Hadoop, Hadoop doesn't manage updates very well. Data should either be masked or encrypted on write (persistent data masking) or data should be masked on read (dynamic data masking).

Don't Choose Big Data over Governance

Don't put off data governance completely in the rush to use big data. Even for exploratory big data prototype projects, maintain a checklist of issues to consider when going forward. You don't want an ineffective bureaucracy, but maybe you can strive to deliver an agile bureaucracy!

Summary

Big data brings a host of changes and opportunities to IT, and it is easy to think that a whole new set of rules must be created. But with the benefit of big data experience, many best practices have emerged. Many of these practices are recognizable extensions from the DW/BI world, and admittedly quite a few are new and novel ways of thinking about data and the mission of IT. But the recognition that the mission has expanded is welcome and is in some ways overdue. The current explosion of data-collecting channels, new data types, and new analytic opportunities mean the list of best practices will continue to grow in interesting ways.

Index